Rhino 6.0 for Jewelry

Dana Buscaglia

ISBN: 978-0-5785-3425-1 (sc)
ISBN: 978-1-4834-7061-0 (e)

Dana Buscaglia
520 East 72nd Street, New York, NY 10021
917-439-1221
Dana Buscaglia

Lulu Publishing Services rev. date: 08/12/2019

INTRODUCTION

The chapters in this book were conceived as step-by-step tutorials to be used for Rhinoceros™ courses for jewelry students and professionals.

This book is divided into two sections:
- **The creation of 2-dimensional drawings and layouts**
  - Basic creation and editing of 2-dimensional objects, such as lines and curves and the creation of technical drawings and layouts.
- **The modeling of 3-dimensional objects**
  - Using knowledge covered in the first part of the book to create 3-dimensional jewelry objects.

- Go through this book from the beginning and, slowly and thoughtfully, take yourself through the step-by-step chapters. Repeat a chapter if you feel that you had a struggle getting through it. The extra time spent will pay off! Stay calm and understand that everyone goes through this stage!
- Avail yourself of the Help Menu in Rhino. The reader is urged to take advantage of this resource. If you are in a command described in a tutorial that you may not fully understand, press "F1" and you will be taken to the Help menu *for that command.*
- Take Rhino courses. You will always learn something more in each course.
- Avail yourself of the Rhino Training Manual, Level 1 is also available for download on the Rhino website - www.rhino3d.com.
- There are many Rhino tutorials on the Internet. If you do a search, you will find free videos on sites like YouTube. Also, check out the Rhino website,
- Understand that most of the learning starts at home, working on your own computer. Don't feel that you have to keep taking courses to continue learning. The hard work is done by you alone, applying commands to your own needs and doing your own problem solving. Repetition is important. It how you become comfortable in the Rhino workspace and how you get used to drawing and modeling certain shapes.
- Start using Rhino in your own work. The sooner you do that, the faster you will learn.

Table of Contents

CREATING & EDITING 2-DIMENSIONAL OBJECTS

Introduction to the Rhino Workspace
Opening Rhino   1
The Rhino Workspace   3
    The Rhino Screen   3
    Viewports   4
    Menu Bar   4
    Command Line   5
    Command History Window   5
    Toolbars   6
    Toolbar Flyouts   6
    Tooltips   6
    Toolbar Groups & Default Rhino Workspace   7
    Adding Tabbed Toolbars to the Workspace   9
    Adding a Floating Toolbar to the Workspace   9
    Panels   10
    If No Panels are Showing in the Workspace   11
    Status Bar   12
    Rhino Help   13
Your Workspace - Settings for Document Properties & a Document Template   14
    Document Properties   14
    Saving Your Document Properties Settings as a Template   15
Rhino Options: Basic Settings   16
Exporting and Importing Rhino Options   19
Downloading Supporting Files from the Rhino for Jewelry website   21
Downloading Rhino Training Files - Rhino's basic manual and files   23

The Basics
Viewport Navigation for 2D Drawings   25
    Specific Zoom Commands   26
    Moving ("Panning") the View   27
    Getting Back into Top View   28
Selecting and De-Selecting Objects   29
    Simple Cursor Selecting and De--Selecting   29
    The Selection Menu   30
Join Command   31

Basic Objects
Anatomy of a Line and a Polyline   33
Anatomy of a Circle   38

Modeling Aids
Ortho and Grid Snap modes   41
Object Snap ("Osnap")   43
Analysis Commands - Measuring Length, Distance, Radius, Diameter, Angle   46
Applying Dimensions   49

Creating and Editing Drawings - More Basics
Move and Copy Commands   62
Trim Command   68
From a Polyline to a Butterfly - Distance & Angle Constraints - Point Editing   73
Technical Drawing: Stone & Prong Layout - Drawing with Circles - Layers   83
Intro to Some More Basic Shapes   105
Rotate 2D Command   117
Technical Drawing: Simple Pearl Ring   122
Draw Order Commands - Controlling Display of Overlapping Objects   137
Printing Technical Drawings   139
Freeform Curves   149
Picture Plane Command - Placing and Tracing a Design Image   157
Creating Designs with the Leaf Tracing   169
1D and 2D Scaling   184

Arc Commands   199
Technical Drawing: Necklace Layout   203
Arraying Around a Square   216
Cluster Around an Oval Center Stone - Array Along Curve Command   219
Arraying Along a Freeform Curve   227

CREATING & EDITING 3-DIMENSIONAL OBJECTS

Introduction to working in 3D Space

Introduction to 3D Space - Viewports - Navigation - Display Modes   237
Working in Different Viewports   247
The Set View Toolbar - Changing from One Viewport to Another   250
Introduction to Simple Solid Objects - Solid Volume   254
Extrusions, Polysurfaces, and Surfaces - Differences and Characteristics   266
Point Editing Basic Solid Objects   271
Mirror and Polar Array Commands in 3D Space   276

Creating and Editing 3D Models

Ring from Basic Solid Objects   283
Sculpting Simple Rings - Control Point Editing a Torus   289
Applying Dimensions to 3D Objects   303
Display - the 2-D Draw Command   308
Display - Rhino Rendering - Raytrace, Raytrace w Neon, Rendered Viewport Modes   311
Display - the Layout Command   328
Zebra Surface Analysis - Evaluating Surface Smoothness & Tangency   350
Extruded Jewelry Shapes - Extruding Curves and Surfaces   352
Briolette - Step Cut - Using Lines & Surfaces to Create Faceted Objects   364
Briolette - Brilliant Cut   369
Revolved Ring Band - Revolve with History   372
Revolve Command - Round Cabochon in Bezel Setting   380
Rail Revolve & Sweep 1 Rail commands - Oval Cabochon in Bezel Setting   385
Rail Revolve - Puffed Heart   389
Sweep 1 Rail Command - Simple Ring with History   400
Sweep 2 Rails Command - Band Ring to Specifications   405
Naked Edges   414

More Complex Projects

Bombe Ring - Surface from a Network of Curves   416
Bombe Ring Hollowed Out - Surface Offset & Boolean Difference   427
8 x 10mm Oval Signet Ring   435
Hollowing Out the Signet Ring   466
Signet Rings - Different Shapes   479
Signet Ring - Rounded Top   495
Twisted Wire Look - Band Ring - Flow Along Curve   502
1mm Stone Maquette - with stone seat and stone hole cutters   518
Eternity Band - Prong Set Wirework 1ct Band   525
Flat Tapered Ring with Enamel and Flush Set Stones - Unroll, Flow Along Surface   547
Additional Enamel Strategies   576
Model of a Flower - Cage Edit   588
Ring Band with Wavy Pave Design   605

More Rhino Options

Rhino Options: Command Shortcuts - Creating Aliases and Hotkeys   633
Using Command Shortcuts   637

Index

641

Biography of Author

646

- **Double-click** on the Rhino icon that is placed on your desktop when you install the program.

Fig. 1

The Rhino Splash Screen

- The Rhino Splash Screen will open, giving you some options and information.

- **Recent** tab:
  - This shows title and thumbnails of the Rhino files most recently opened.
  - You have the option of clicking on one of these to open it.

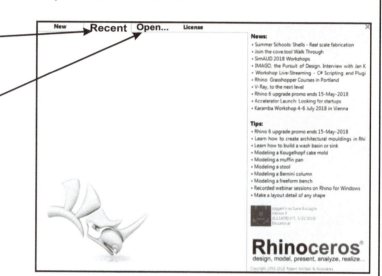

- **Open** tab:
  - This is a browse button for finding a file that was already saved on your computer.

- **New** tab:
  - Shows a list of templates with different settings for scale and unit measurement.

  - Notice that the cursor is rolling over the last template on the list, **Small Objects - Millimeters.**
    - A description of the template's characteristics appears in the yellow box to the right.
      - **Measurement units**: millimeters
      - **Absolute tolerance**: .001mm
        - Absolute tolerance is the smallest distance recognized by the settings of this template.

  - Click on this template to choose it as it's small scale and millimeter unit measurement is good for small objects.

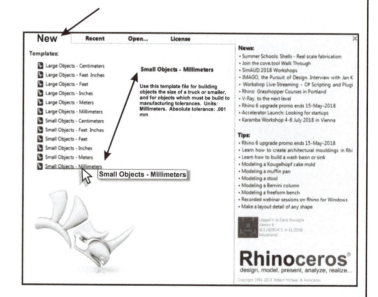

Fig. 2

- Notice that Rhino is opening behind the Splash Screen. ***Don't worry if you have not yet clicked on your choice of file or template.***

- As long as you <u>**keep your cursor inside the Splash Screen**</u>, the Splash Screen will not go away.

- When you click on the Template or File that you want to open, ***the Rhino screen will update to your selection*** and the Splash Screen will go away.

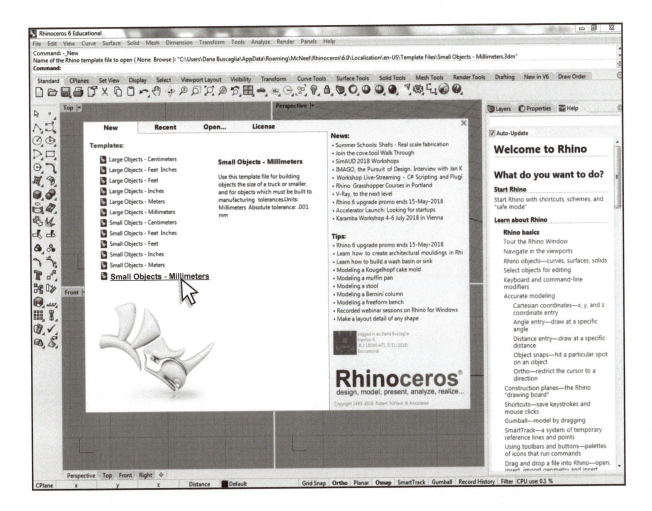

Fig. 3

The Rhino Workspace
A brief tour

The Rhino Screen

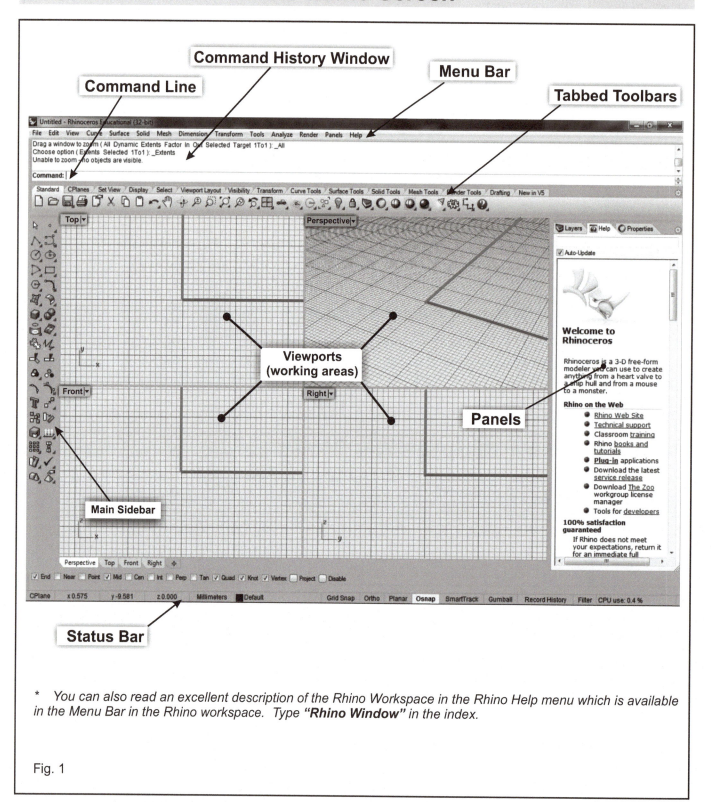

Command Line

Command History Window

Menu Bar

Tabbed Toolbars

Viewports (working areas)

Panels

Main Sidebar

Status Bar

*   You can also read an excellent description of the Rhino Workspace in the Rhino Help menu which is available in the Menu Bar in the Rhino workspace. Type **"Rhino Window"** in the index.

Fig. 1

Viewports

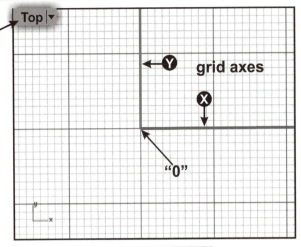

- **Viewports** are the working areas of Rhino.

- **Double-click** on a viewport title to maximize the viewport. **Double-click** again to minimize the viewport and show more than one viewport at a time.

- The **Grid** units are specified in the title of the chosen template.
  - In this template, each grid intersection represents 1mm.
  - The **Grid** rests on the **Construction Plane.**
    - The **Construction Plane** is an imaginary surface upon which objects are created by default.
  - The grid has X and Y axes. Where these two axes meet is called, in terms of absolute coordinates, **"0,0"**, or just **"0"**. **This organizes the workspace.**

grid axes

"0"

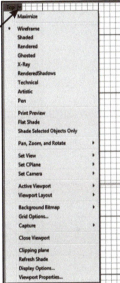

- Click on the little arrow on the right side of the viewport title.

  - A context menu will drop down with many options and settings that will be covered in later chapters.

Fig. 2

Menu Bar

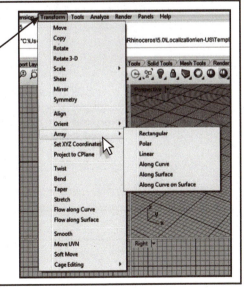

- Just about every Rhino tool and command can be found in the drop-down menus in the menu bar at the top of the workspace.

Fig. 3

Command Line
Guides you through the commands with step-by-step prompts.

- This is how the **Command Line**, or **Command Prompt**, looks when there is no command active.

- In this example, the **Circle** command is has been activated. The **Command Line** is "prompting" for the location of the **Center of the circle.**

- Within the parentheses are **links** that give you options to tailor the command to your needs.

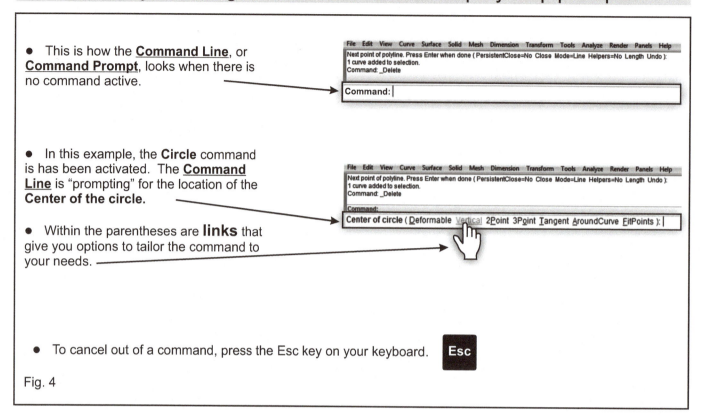

- To cancel out of a command, press the Esc key on your keyboard. **Esc**

Fig. 4

Command History Window

- The **Command History Window** displays the commands that immediately preceded the current command.

- It is also a source of information, depending on the command.

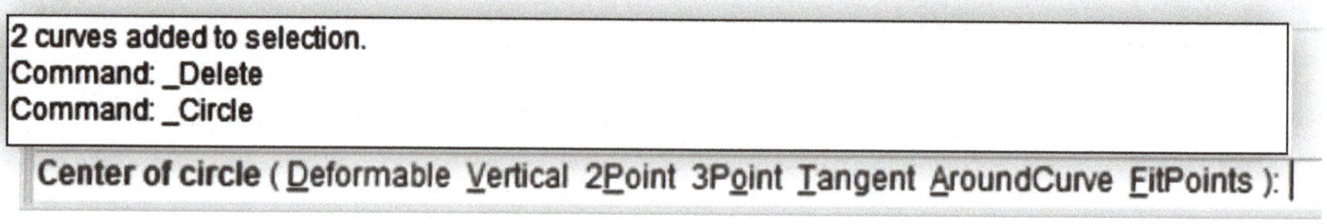

```
2 curves added to selection.
Command: _Delete
Command: _Circle
```
```
Center of circle ( Deformable  Vertical  2Point  3Point  Tangent  AroundCurve  FitPoints ): |
```

Fig. 5

Toolbars

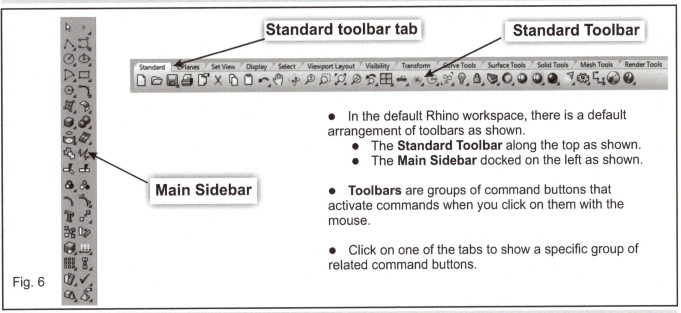

Standard toolbar tab

Standard Toolbar

Main Sidebar

- In the default Rhino workspace, there is a default arrangement of toolbars as shown.
  - The **Standard Toolbar** along the top as shown.
  - The **Main Sidebar** docked on the left as shown.

- **Toolbars** are groups of command buttons that activate commands when you click on them with the mouse.

- Click on one of the tabs to show a specific group of related command buttons.

Fig. 6

Toolbar Flyouts

- A little black triangle at the lower right corner of a button means if you **right-click on this button** (or hold **down the left mouse button**), another toolbar will appear - a **"toolbar flyout"**.

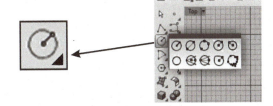

- Click the dark band on the top of the toolbar and drag the toolbar out further into the viewport.
- It's appearance will change and it will remain on the workspace as a **"floating toolbar"** until you choose to close it by clicking in the upper right corner.

Fig. 7

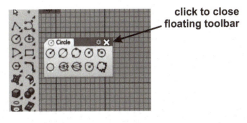

click to close floating toolbar

Tooltips

- If you hover the cursor over a single button, a little text box will appear - **a "Tooltip"**.

- Tooltips describe the commands enabled by the button.

- In this example, notice that there are two lines to the tooltip, indicating functionality for **both left and right mouse buttons.**
  - The little symbols indicate the left and right mouse buttons.

Fig. 8

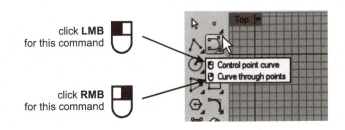

click **LMB** for this command

click **RMB** for this command

Toolbar Groups & the Default Rhino Workspace

- The default Rhino window features the **Standard Toolbar Group**.
  - Individual toolbars are accessible by clicking on the various tabs shown.
  - Click on the **Standard** tab to display the command buttons of the **Standard Toolbar.**

- Included in this Rhino default workspace is the **Main Sidebar** which is docked on the left whenever the Standard Toolbar is displayed on top.

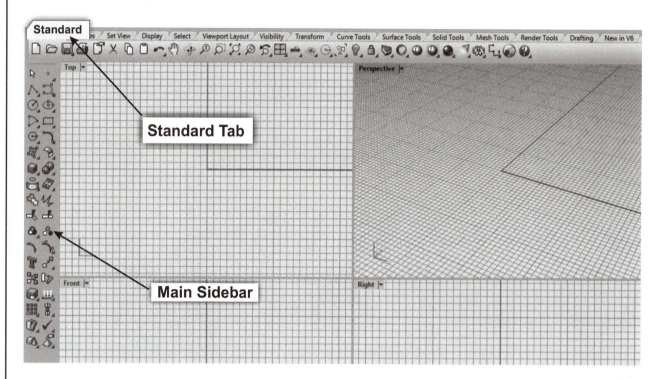

Standard Tab

Main Sidebar

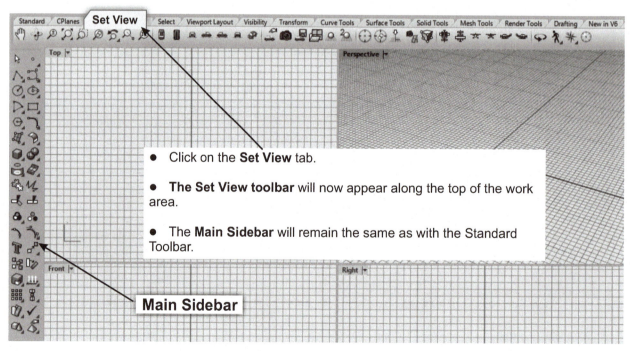

- Click on the **Set View** tab.

- **The Set View toolbar** will now appear along the top of the work area.

- The **Main Sidebar** will remain the same as with the Standard Toolbar.

Main Sidebar

Fig. 9

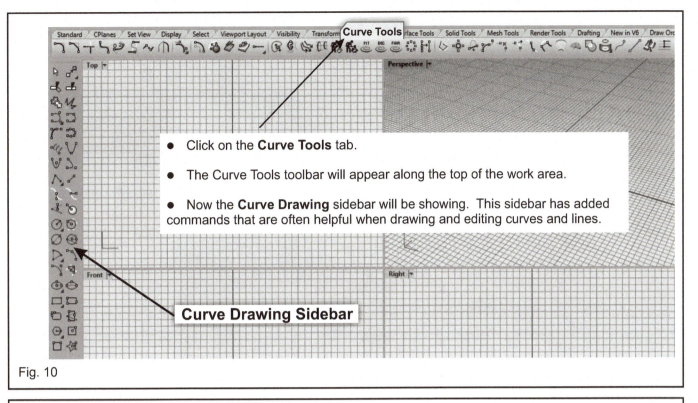

Standard
CPlanes
Set View
Display
Select
Viewport Layout
Visibility
Transform
Curve Tools
Solid Tools
Mesh Tools
Render Tools
Drafting
New in V6
Top
Perspective
Front
Right
● Click on the **Curve Tools** tab.
● The Curve Tools toolbar will appear along the top of the work area.
● Now the **Curve Drawing** sidebar will be showing. This sidebar has added commands that are often helpful when drawing and editing curves and lines.
Curve Drawing Sidebar

Fig. 10

● Click on these tabs and you will see sidebars that compliment them, usually pertaining to further relevant editing and transformation commands.

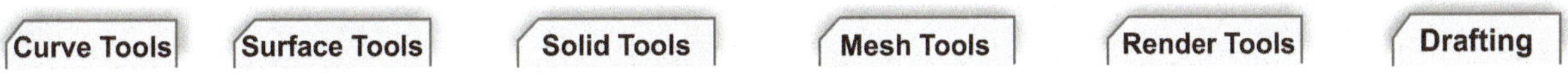

Curve Tools
Surface Tools
Solid Tools
Mesh Tools
Render Tools
Drafting

Fig. 11

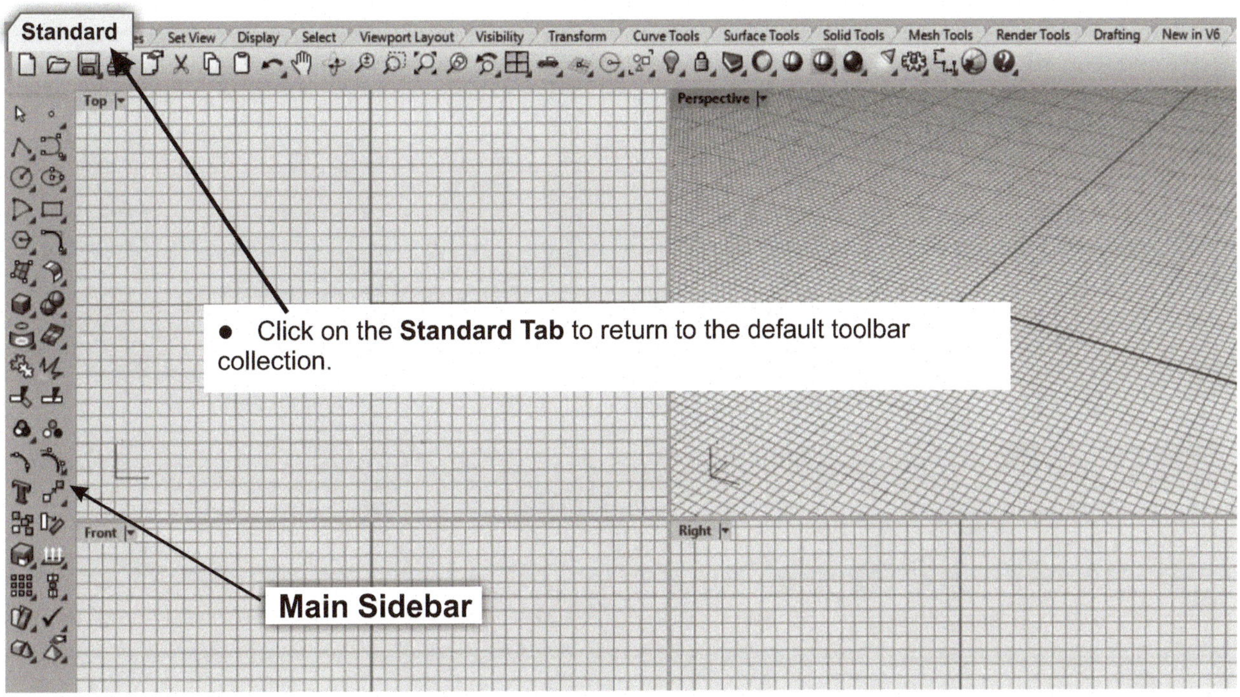

Standard
Set View
Display
Select
Viewport Layout
Visibility
Transform
Curve Tools
Surface Tools
Solid Tools
Mesh Tools
Render Tools
Drafting
New in V6
Top
Perspective
Front
Right
● Click on the **Standard Tab** to return to the default toolbar collection.
Main Sidebar

Fig. 12

Adding Tabbed Toolbars to the Workspace

- **Right-click** on any tab. ❶

- Click on the **Show or Hide Tabs** option in the drop-down menu. ❷

- Click on the **Analyze** tab option in the sub menu that appears from the **Show or Hide Tabs** option. ❸

- The **Analyze Tabbed Toolbar** will now be added to the toolbar collection.

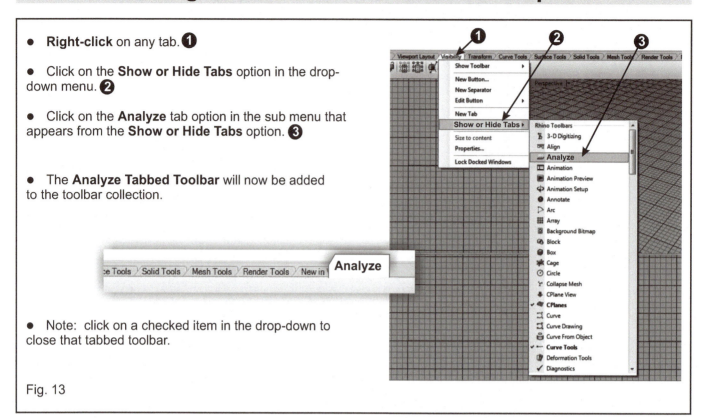

- Note: click on a checked item in the drop-down to close that tabbed toolbar.

Fig. 13

Adding a Floating Toolbar to the Workspace

- **Right-click** on any Tab. ❶

- Click on the **Show Toolbar** option in the drop-down menu. ❷

- Click on the **Analyze** toolbar option in the sub menu that appears from the **Show Toolbar** option as shown. ❸

- The **Analyze** toolbar will appear as a **Floating Toolbar** that can be closed out by clicking on the **X** on the top right.

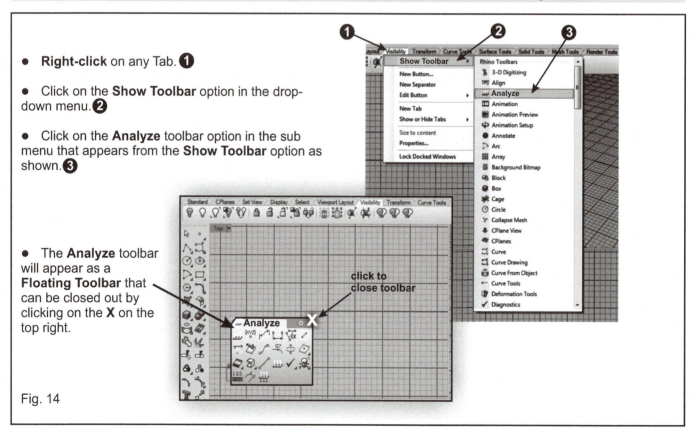

click to close toolbar

Fig. 14

Panels

- Many Rhino settings and controls are contained in the **Panels** that dock on the right of the workspace.

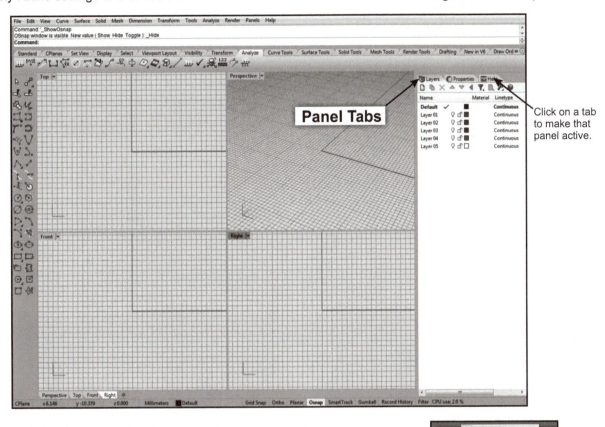

Panel Tabs

Click on a tab to make that panel active.

- **Right-click** on one of the tabs **❶** to get a drop-down list. Click on one of the categories, **❷** and it's tab will become accessible.

tab to newly added panel

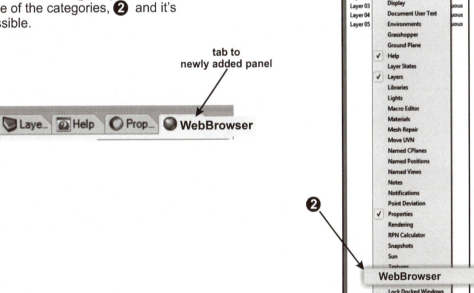

Fig. 15

If No Panels are Showing in the Workspace

- The **Panels** drop-down ❶ in the **Menu Bar** at the top of the workspace offers most of the available categories that can be included in the panels grouping.
- Click on the **Layers** category as shown. ❷

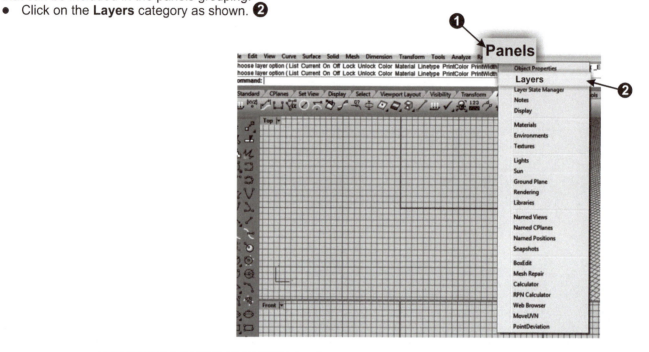

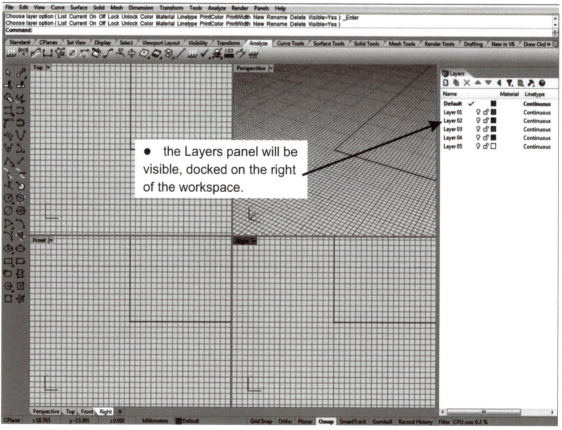

- the Layers panel will be visible, docked on the right of the workspace.

Fig. 16

- To add more panels, **right-click** on any panel tab to get the drop-down list of other categories.

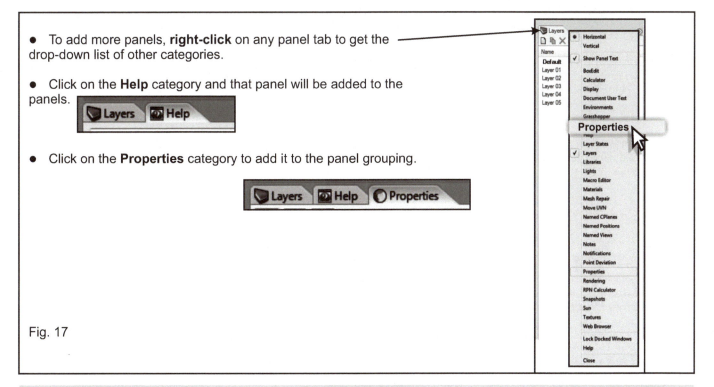

- Click on the **Help** category and that panel will be added to the panels.

- Click on the **Properties** category to add it to the panel grouping.

Fig. 17

Status Bar

- The **Status Bar** is at the bottom of the workspace. It has two general functions:
  - A source of information and status.
  - Toggles for Modeling Aids

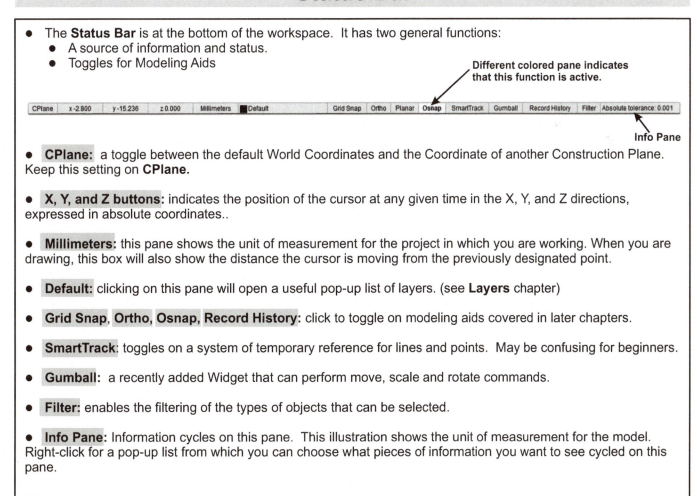

- **CPlane:** a toggle between the default World Coordinates and the Coordinate of another Construction Plane. Keep this setting on **CPlane.**

- **X, Y, and Z buttons:** indicates the position of the cursor at any given time in the X, Y, and Z directions, expressed in absolute coordinates..

- **Millimeters:** this pane shows the unit of measurement for the project in which you are working. When you are drawing, this box will also show the distance the cursor is moving from the previously designated point.

- **Default:** clicking on this pane will open a useful pop-up list of layers. (see **Layers** chapter)

- **Grid Snap, Ortho, Osnap, Record History:** click to toggle on modeling aids covered in later chapters.

- **SmartTrack**: toggles on a system of temporary reference for lines and points. May be confusing for beginners.

- **Gumball:** a recently added Widget that can perform move, scale and rotate commands.

- **Filter:** enables the filtering of the types of objects that can be selected.

- **Info Pane:** Information cycles on this pane. This illustration shows the unit of measurement for the model. Right-click for a pop-up list from which you can choose what pieces of information you want to see cycled on this pane.

Fig. 18

Rhino Help

- Click on **Help** in the **Menu Bar** to see many helpful links. Help Topics will bring you to the Rhino Help window. The **F1 key** will also open this window.

F1

- If you are in a command and press **F1**, *Rhino Help will open up to explain the same command that is active in your workspace.*

click on
Help tab

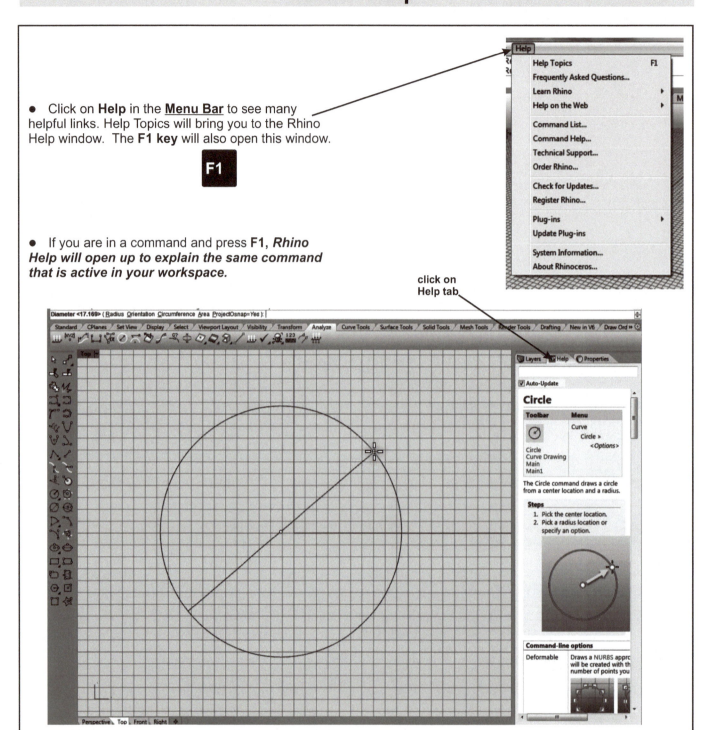

- Click on the **Help** tab to activate the **Help Panel.**

- Click on a command and the panel will display the help chapter that describes the command in which you are working.

- This illustration shows the Circle command in progress with the help panel displaying information about the Circle command.

Fig. 19

Document Properties

- Click on the **Tools** category in the **Menu Bar** at the top of the workspace. ❶
  - Click on **Options** in the drop-down menu. ❷

- The **Rhino Options** box will open.

- Click to highlight the **Units** category. ❸
  - Millimeters ❹ are the unit of measurement for this Rhino file.
  - This is the unit of measurement in the **small objects - Millimeters** startup template file that you originally opened in Rhino.
  - Notice that **Absolute Tolerance** ❺ is set to .001mm as this is another setting in the template that you opened.

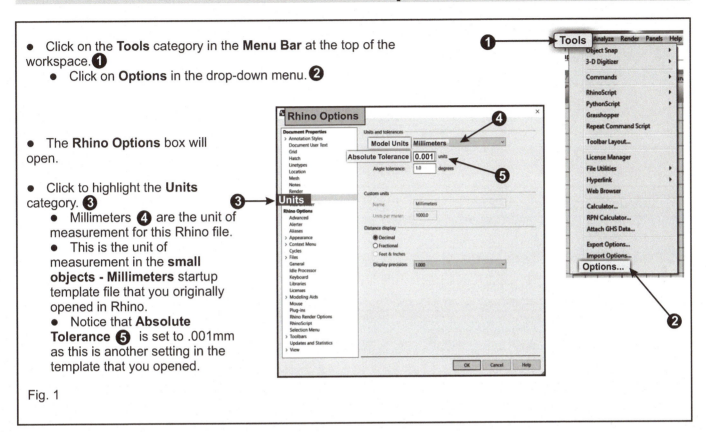

Fig. 1

- Click to display the **Grid** category.
  - The **Minor Grid Lines** setting is set at **1mm.**
    - Minor grid lines will show every millimeter.
  - Change the **Major Grid Lines** setting to **every 5 grid lines.**
    - The darker thicker grid lines will show at every **5mm minor grid lines**.

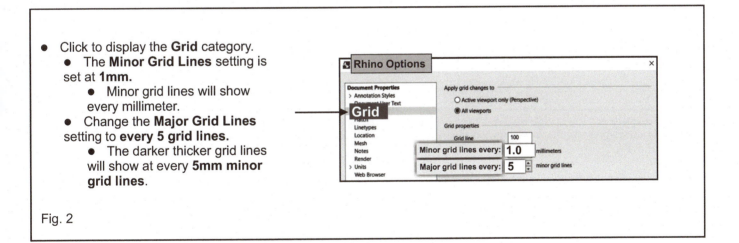

Fig. 2

Saving your document properties settings as a template

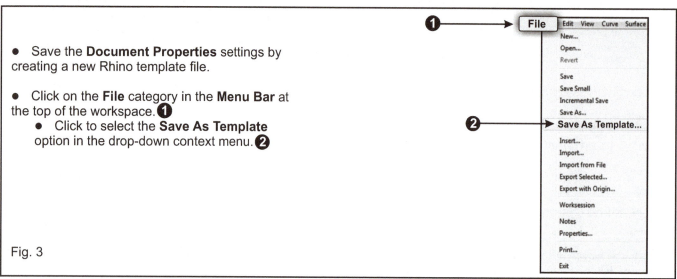

- Save the **Document Properties** settings by creating a new Rhino template file.

- Click on the **File** category in the **Menu Bar** at the top of the workspace. ❶
  - Click to select the **Save As Template** option in the drop-down context menu. ❷

Fig. 3

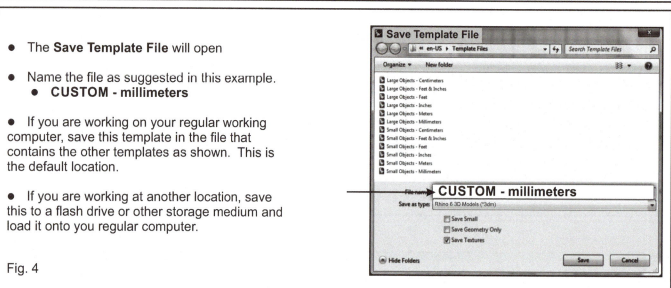

- The **Save Template File** will open

- Name the file as suggested in this example.
  - **CUSTOM - millimeters**

- If you are working on your regular working computer, save this template in the file that contains the other templates as shown. This is the default location.

- If you are working at another location, save this to a flash drive or other storage medium and load it onto you regular computer.

Fig. 4

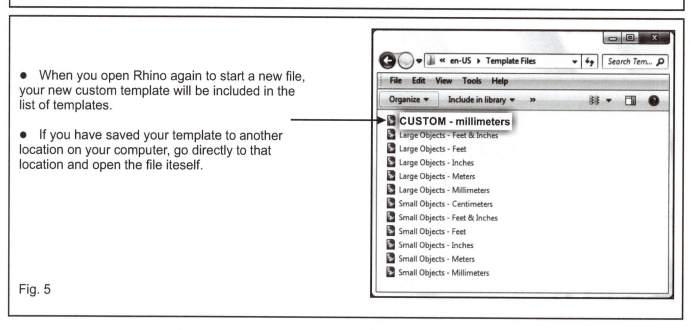

- When you open Rhino again to start a new file, your new custom template will be included in the list of templates.

- If you have saved your template to another location on your computer, go directly to that location and open the file iteself.

Fig. 5

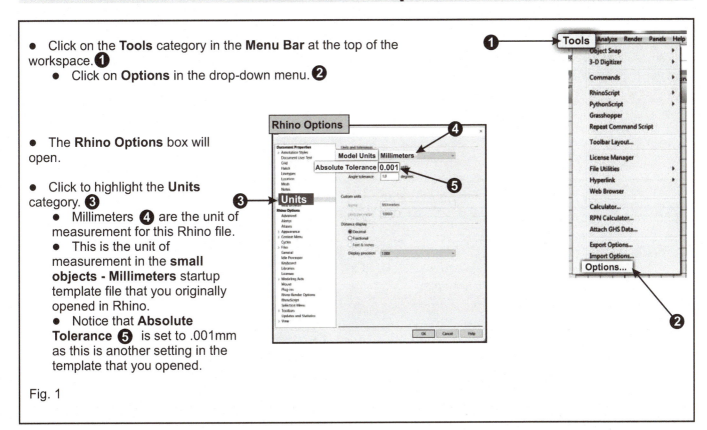

Fig. 5

Rhino Options: Basic Settings
Settings that will remain each time Rhino is opened

- Click on the **Tools** heading in the **Menu Bar** at the top of the workspace. ❶

- Click on **Options** at the bottom of the **Tools Drop-down.** ❷

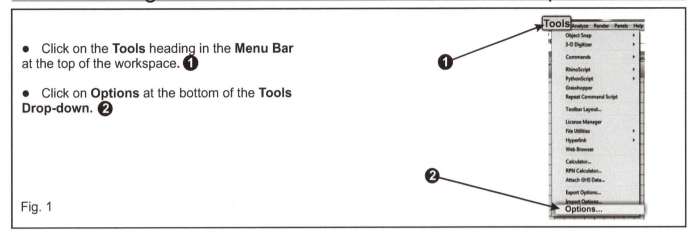

Fig. 1

- Under the large heading, **Rhino Options,**❶ Click on the **Mouse** category. ❷
    - The settings in Rhino Options will be retained every time you open Rhino.

- Click to **uncheck** the following two options: ❸
    - Allow selecting objects with points on.
    - Turn on control points when selecting a curve, light or annotation.
        - These two options can be very confusing if left activated.

click to UNCHECK these options ❸

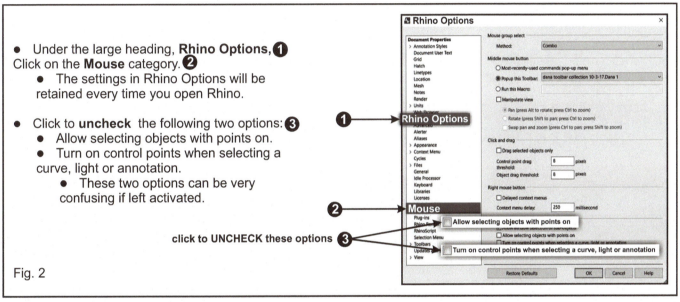

Fig. 2

- Click to open the **View** category. ❶

- Open the **Display Modes** category. ❷

- Open the **Wireframe** mode category. ❸

- Under the Wireframe mode category, click on the **Objects** category.❹

    - Change the **Edge Thickness** to **3.** ❺
        - This pertains to the edge of Rhino surfaces which are used in 3D modeling.
- Use these settings for these display modes:
    - **Shaded**
    - **Ghosted**

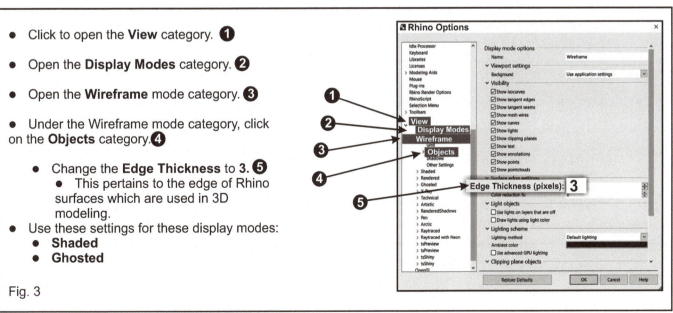

Fig. 3

16

- Click to open the **Objects** category. ❶

- **Control point size** catagory:
  - Change the **Point Size** to **4**.

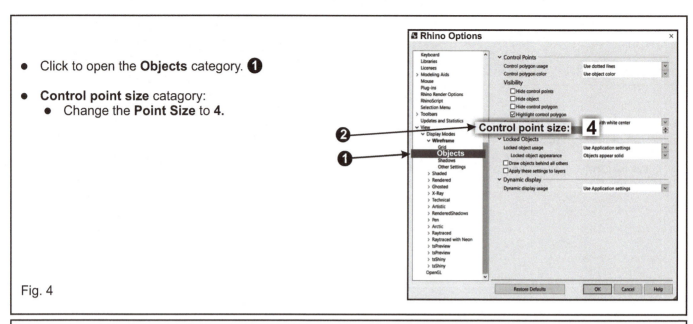

Fig. 4

- Click to open the **Objects** category. ❶

- Under the Objects category, click to select the **Points** category. ❷
  - Change the **Point Size** to **4**. ❸

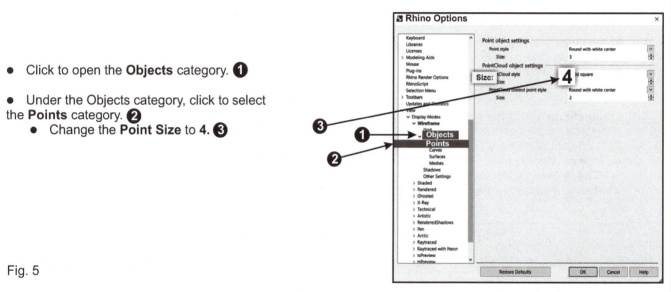

Fig. 5

- Click on the **curves** category. ❶

  - Change the **Curve width** to **3 pixels**. ❷

- Click on the **OK button** ❸ to exit the Rhino Options box.
  - You must click on the **OK button** to retain the options you have just set.
  - *If you just "X out" of the box, the settings will not be retained.*

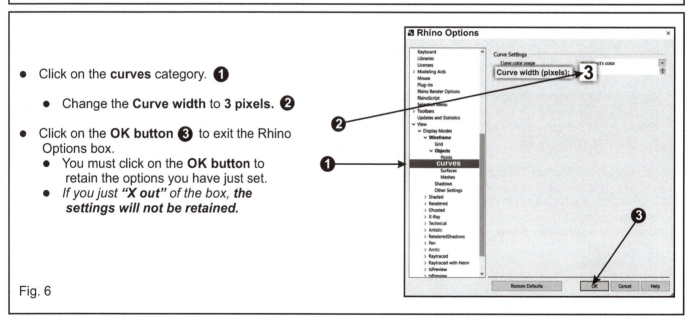

Fig. 6

- **RIGHT-CLICK** on the **History** button ❶ at the bottom of the workspace.
    - Select the options ❷ shown in the context menu.
    - This will change the default setting that has History enabled all of the time.

- Note: Keeping History on all of the time can lead to complications as you don't always want to use it.

Fig. 7

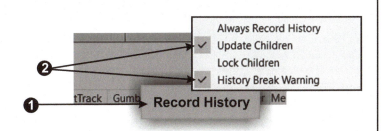

Exporting & Importing Rhino Options
Loading your Rhino Options into another Computer

Exporting Rhino Options

- Click on the **Tools** heading in the **Menu Bar.** ❶

- Click on **Export Options** at the bottom of the **Tools Drop-down.** ❷

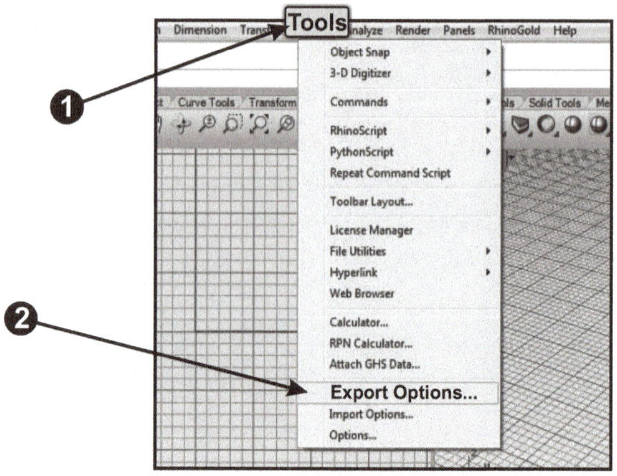

- Save your Rhino options to a designated location in your computer when the **Save As** box opens. ❸

- Click the **Save button** to save your Rhino Options file and exit.

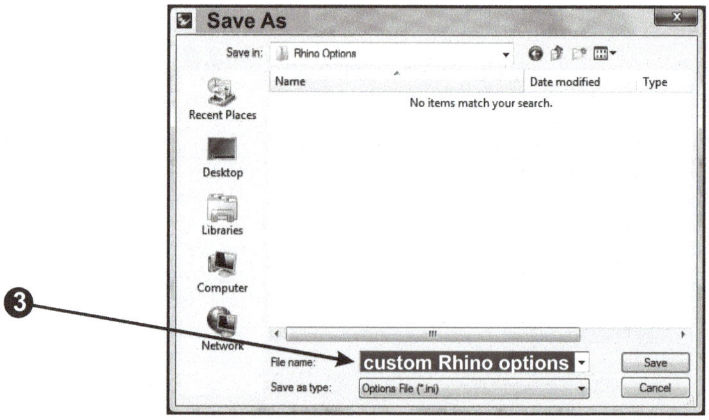

Fig. 1

Importing Rhino Options

- Click on the **Tools** heading in the **Menu Bar.** ❶

- Click on **Import Options** at the bottom of the **Tools Drop-down.** ❷

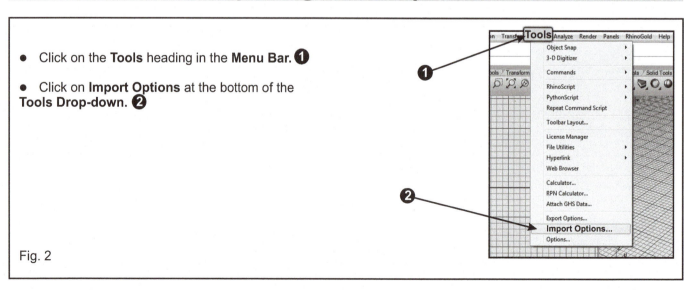

Fig. 2

- The **Import Options** dialog box will open.

- Click on the **browse button** ❶ to navigate to the **custom Rhino options** file that you saved from another computer onto a flash drive or some other storage media. ❷

- Navigate to your **custom Rhino options** file and click on the **Open button.** ❸

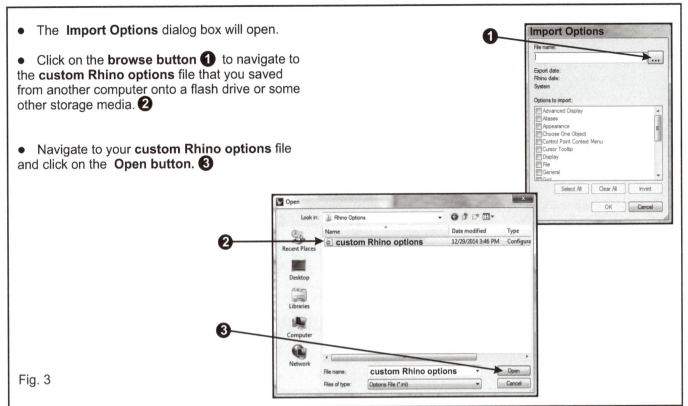

Fig. 3

- The **custom Rhino options** file will now be showing in the **file name** line at the top of the **Import Options** box. ❶

- Click on the **Select All button** so that all of the categories of options will be checked for importing into the Rhino workspace. ❷

- You can drag the bottom edge of the box down to see that all options have been checked.

- Click on the **OK button** to exit out of the box. ❸

- The options will be imported into the Rhino workspace.

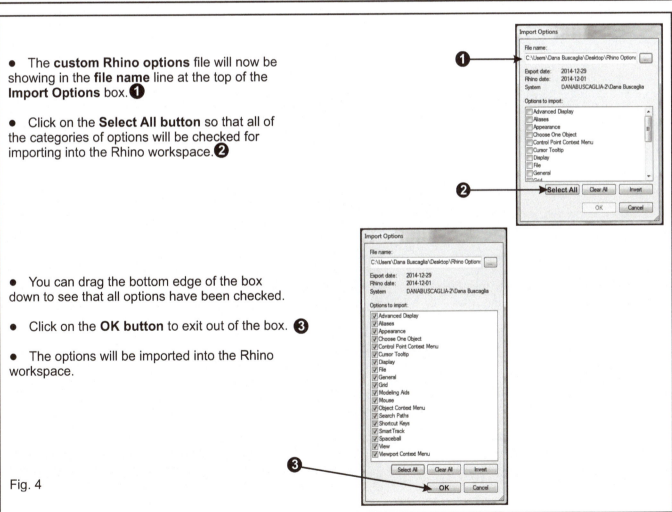

Fig. 4

Downloading Supporting Files from the rhinoforjewelry website
Saving the supporting files to a file on your computer.

- Type this URL address to access the opening page of the website: **www.rhinoforjewelry.com**

- In the Navigation Menu on the left, click on the **support files for textbook** link. ❶

Fig. 1

- You will arrive at a page with the following links:
  - **Files for the textbook**
  - **Textures and Environment maps used in the textbook**

- Click on the **Files for Textbook** link. ❷

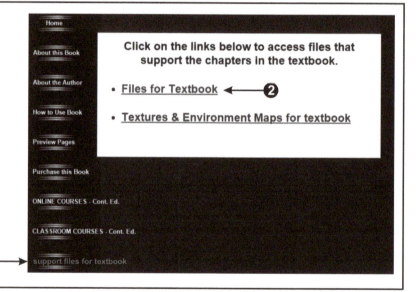

Fig. 2

- A new window will open up, showing a list of the files that support the chapters in the textbook.
  - If you click on any of these files, a Rhino file will open (after a moment).
    - Save each file to a designated folder on your computer.

- The last link is a ZIP file that contains all of the above files.
  - If you have WINZIP on your computer, you can upzip this file and save all the files to a designated folder on your computer.

Note: files may be different from the illustration shown.

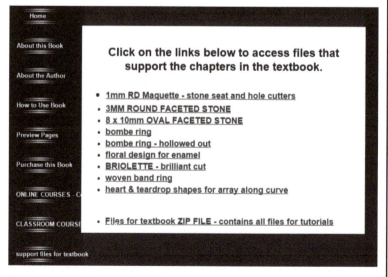

Fig. 3

● Navigate back to the page with the main list as shown.

● Click on the **Textures & Environment Maps for textbook** link.

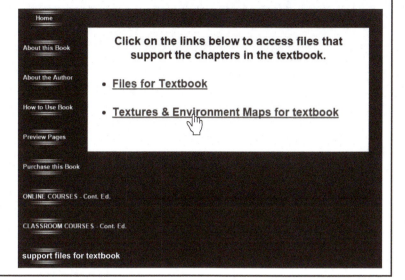

Fig. 4

● You will now see Textures and Environment maps for Diamonds, Polished Silver, Polished Gold, and texture bitmaps that will be used to generate textured surfaces in the 3D section of the textbook.

    ● When the jpeg image opens, right-click on the image and choose **"save as"** or **"save image as"** in the context drop-down menu.

● As before, open and save these files to a designated folder in your computer.

● Note the ZIP file below that will save you time if you have WINZIP on your computer.

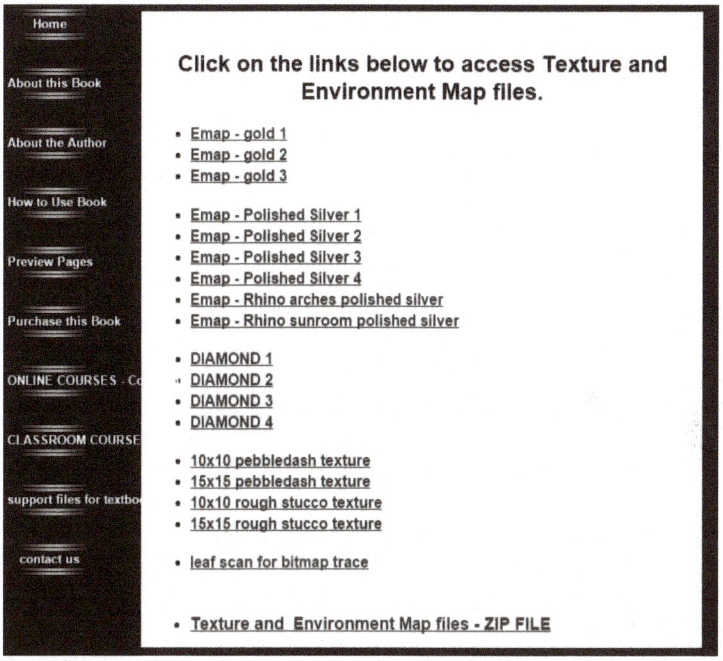

Fig. 5

● These files will be imported into Rhino files in the course of this book.

● It is easier if you have these files saved to your computer because the Import command in Rhno will not be successful at importing them directly from the Internet.

Downloading Rhino Training Files
Downloading Rhino's Basic Manual and Accompanying files

- Use your browser to access the Rhino website.

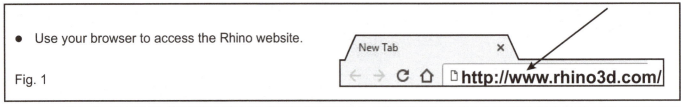

Fig. 1

- Click on the **download** link ❶

Fig. 2

- The **Downloads** page will open.

- Under the **Documentation** heading, ❷ click on the link for <u>**Level 1 - Training Guide and Models.**</u> ❸

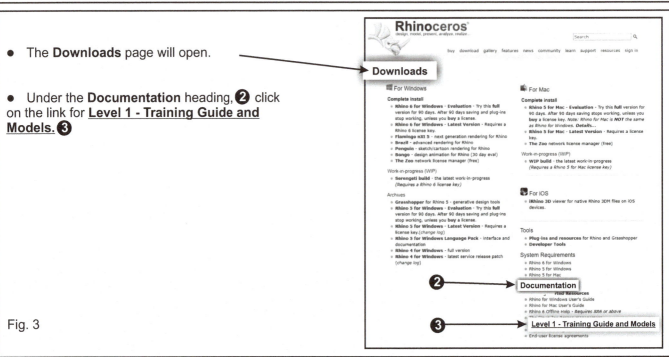

Fig. 3

- You will be prompted to enter your email address.

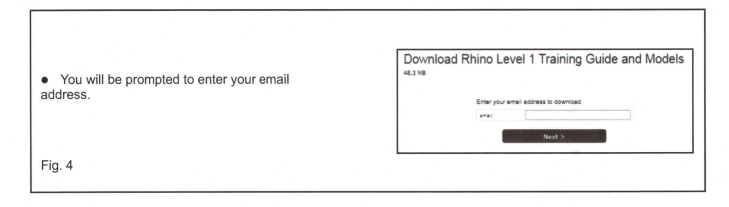

Fig. 4

- You will be prompted to download Rhino in English or to select another language.

Download Rhino Level 1 Training Guide and Models

Rhino 6 Rhino5Level1Training | 48.3 MB

Download English Now

- or -

Select Another Language

Fig. 5

- Choose the **Save** option and save to a location on your computer.

- The Training Manual Level I and accompanying files will be saved as a Winzip file.

Fig. 6

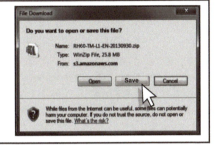

- When you open the downloaded Winzip file, you will see a folder ❶ containing the training models and a Training Manual in PDF format. ❷

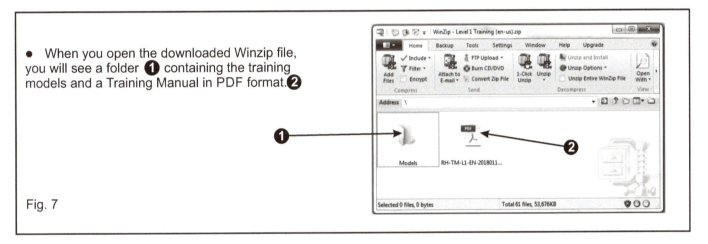

❶   ❷

Fig. 7

- Open the folder to see the training models.

Fig. 8

Viewport Navigation for 2D Drawings
Panning and Zooming in 2D Drawings

Zooming the View - using the Mouse Wheel

- Open the file from the Rhino I Training Files called **Filletex.3dm**
  - See previous chapter on **Downloading Rhino Training Files.**

scroll wheel

- **Rotate the mouse's scroll wheel downward** to zoom out. ❶

  - **Rotate the scroll wheel upward** and the view zooms in again. ❷

Fig. 1

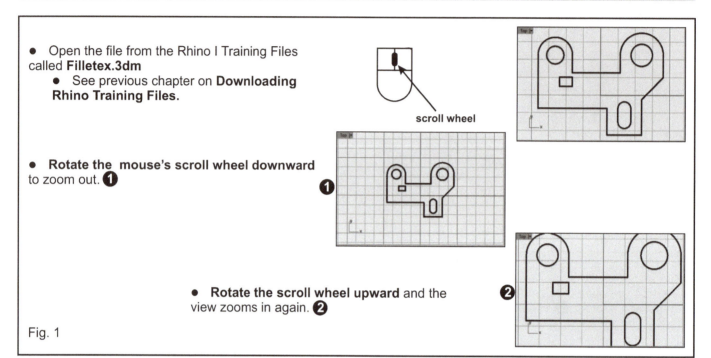

Zooming the View - a Smoother Method

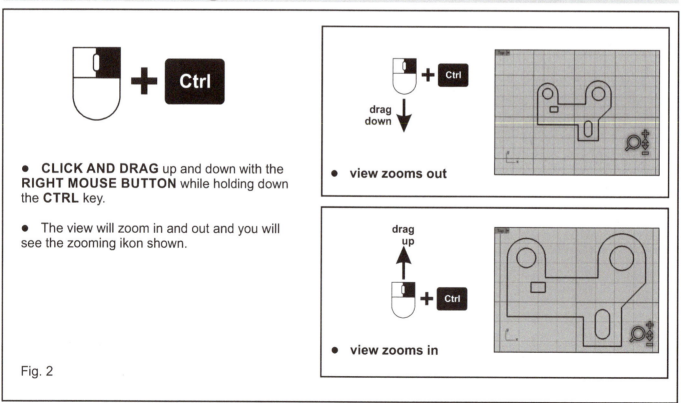

Ctrl

- **CLICK AND DRAG** up and down with the **RIGHT MOUSE BUTTON** while holding down the **CTRL** key.

- The view will zoom in and out and you will see the zooming ikon shown.

drag down

+ **Ctrl**

- **view zooms out**

drag up

+ **Ctrl**

- **view zooms in**

Fig. 2

25

Specific Zoom Commands

- **Standard tabbed toolbar.**

- Select the small oblong line shown and click on the **Zoom Selected** command in the Standard Toolbar.

Zoom Selected
command

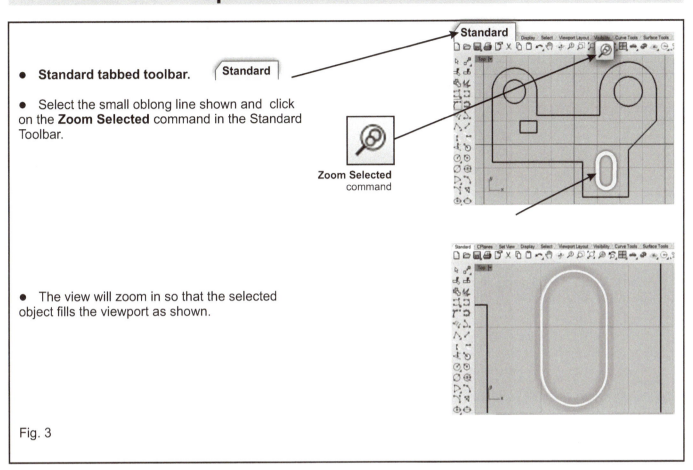

- The view will zoom in so that the selected object fills the viewport as shown.

Fig. 3

- **LEFT-CLICK** on the **Zoom Extents** command.

Zoom Extents
command

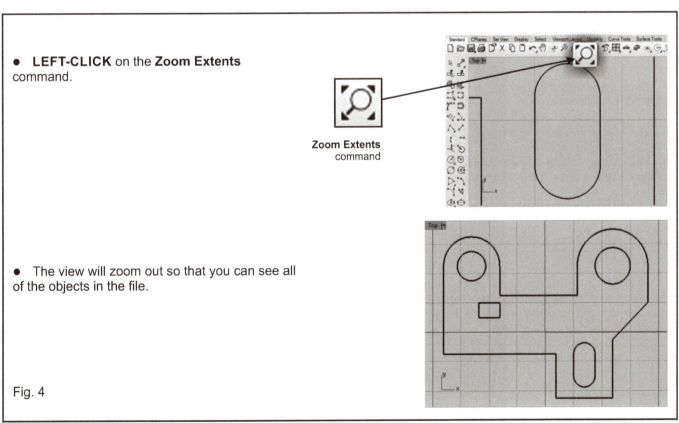

- The view will zoom out so that you can see all of the objects in the file.

Fig. 4

- **Left-click** on the **Zoom Window** command.
  - **Drag a window to zoom** prompt:
    - Drag a window ❶ ❷ to delineate a specific area that you want to zoom in on.

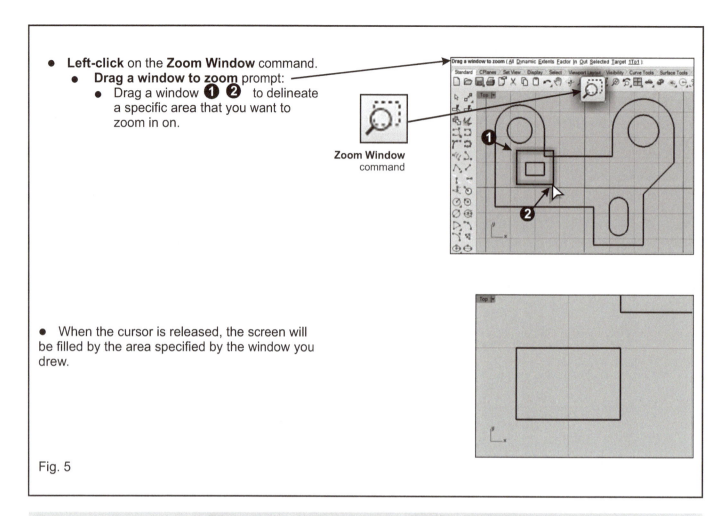

Zoom Window
command

- When the cursor is released, the screen will be filled by the area specified by the window you drew.

Fig. 5

Moving ("Panning") the View

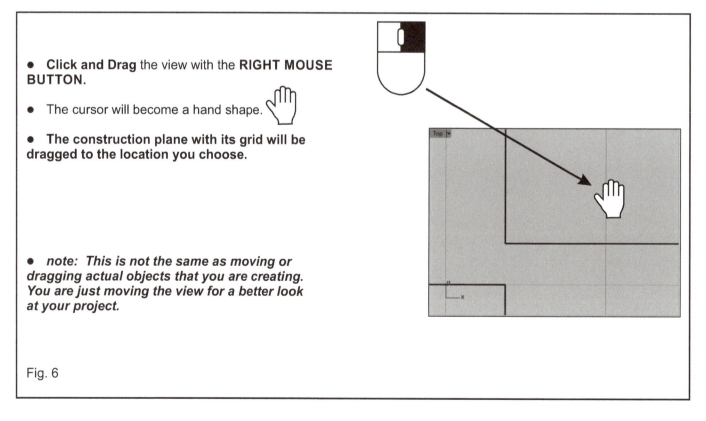

- **Click and Drag** the view with the **RIGHT MOUSE BUTTON.**

- The cursor will become a hand shape.

- **The construction plane with its grid will be dragged to the location you choose.**

- *note: This is not the same as moving or dragging actual objects that you are creating. You are just moving the view for a better look at your project.*

Fig. 6

Getting Back Into Top View
When you accidentally tip the view into 3D space

- Ways that you can accidentally tip the view into 3D space.
  - Panning with both shift and ctrl keys held down.
  - Clicking on the Perspective button in the Set View commands.

- In this illustration, clicking and dragging has resulted in a tipped, or rotated view.
  - **The hand cursor has been replaced by a rotate cursor when you try to Pan the view and the view will rotate and spin, rather than panning.**

Fig. 7

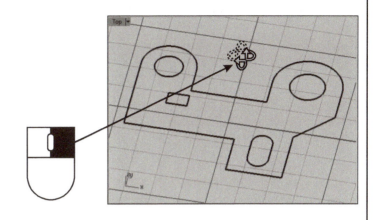

- *The Grid seems to be made of diagonal lines, instead of a horizontal and vertical configuration.*

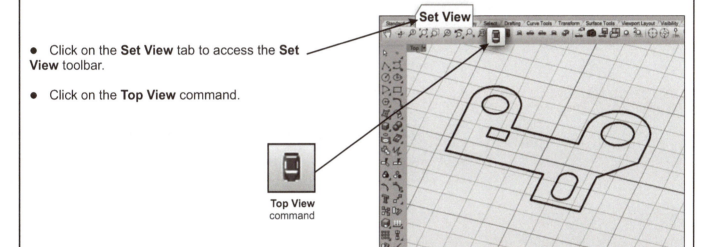

- Click on the **Set View** tab to access the **Set View** toolbar.

- Click on the **Top View** command.

Top View command

- The Top View has been restored.

- Notice how the grid looks squared up again because you are now looking straight down on it.

- **When you Pan, you will see the Hand Cursor once again.**

- This is called a *Plan, or Parallel, View.*

Fig. 8

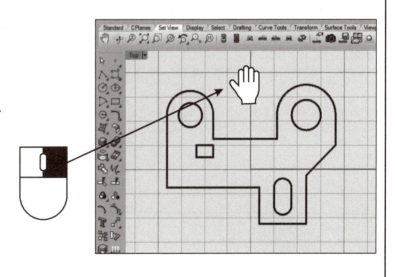

Selecting and De-Selecting Objects
Clicking to Select and Using Selection Windows

Simple cursor selecting and de-selecting

- Open the file from the Rhino I Training Files called **Filletex.3dm.**
  - See the previous chapter on **Downloading Rhino Training Files.**

- **Left-click** to select the circle shown.
- The circle will turn yellow, indicating that it has been selected.

- Click away from the selected object to immediately de-select it.
- The circle is now its original black color.

Fig. 1

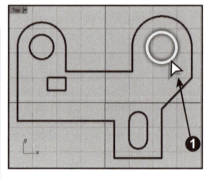
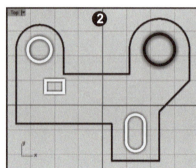

- Hold the **Shift** key down and click to multi-select each of the 4 objects shown. **1**

- Hold the **Ctrl** key down and select one of the selected objects to de-select it. **2**

Fig. 2

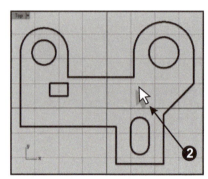
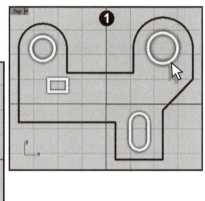

- Click and Drag (**1** & **2**), to create a window that intersects with two of the curves that make up the drawing as shown.
  - This **"Crossing Window"** will have a dashed outline.

- The two curves that were touched by the selection window (**"Crossing Window"**) will be selected.

- Click away to de-select.

Fig. 3

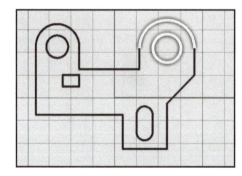
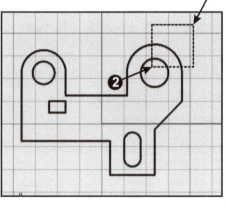

- Click and drag (**1** & **2**), to create a window that encloses the circle and square shown.

- Only the objects that were **totally enclosed** by the **Enclosing Window** will be selected.

- Click away to de-select

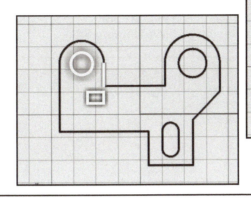

Fig. 4

The Selection Menu

- If you click to select an object at the point where it is very near to another object or objects, **1** Rhino will open a **Selection Menu.**

- The purpose of this menu is to ascertain which object you wanted to select.
  - When the **Selection Menu** appears, if you press **Enter,** the highlighted name at the top of the list will be selected **2** and the list will disappear.

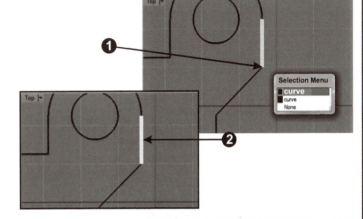

- Click on the intersections of the two lines again to get the **Selection Menu** back.

- This time, roll the cursor over the list in the **Selection Menu** and notice how it's line or other object turns pink. **3**
  - If you click on that item on the list, it's object will turn yellow **4** because you will be choosing it for selection and the Selection Menu will disappear.

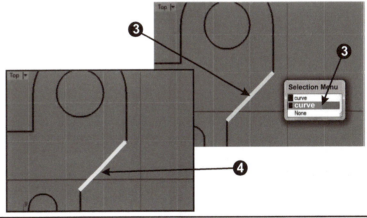

Fig. 5

- To avoid having to deal with the **Selection Menu** which is a nuisance because it holds up your workflow:
  - When you select an object, select it at a location where it is not near to other objects, if possible.
  - The cursor in this illustration is located where it can select the line and you will not have to deal with a **Selection Menu.**

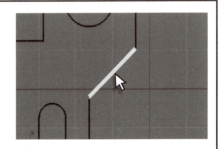

Fig. 6

Join Command
Joining curves together end to end to create a Polyline.

- Open the file from the Rhino I Training Files called **Filletex.3dm.**
  - See the previous chapter on **Downloading Rhino Training Files.**

- If you select one or more of the lines of the shape that surrounds the smaller elements inside this drawing, you will see that each one selects as a single line.

- Click away to de-select.

Fig. 1

- Click on the **Join** command.
  - **Select object to join. Curves, surfaces and polysurfaces must be open** prompt:
    - Select the line shown. ❶

Join
command

- **Select curve to join. Press Enter when done** prompt:
  - Select another line ❷ that is touching the previously selected curve.

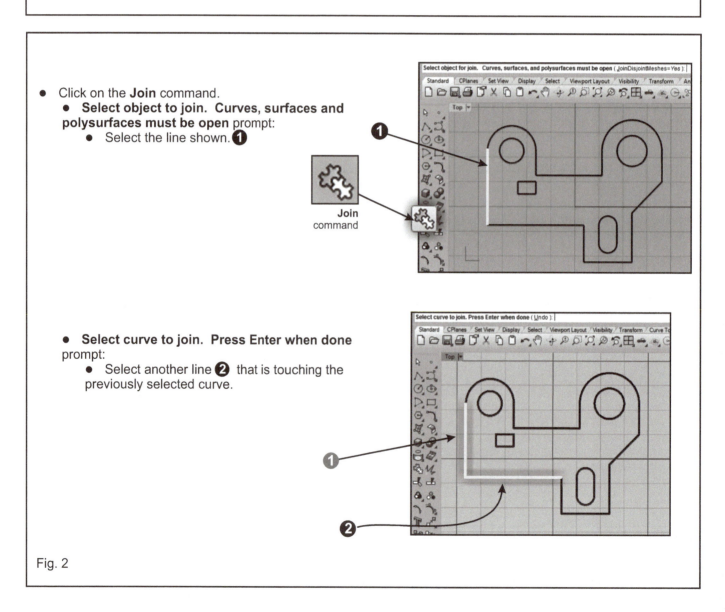

Fig. 2

- Continue to select curves as the **Command Line** prompts.

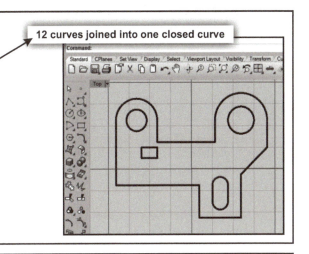

12 curves joined into one closed curve

- If you select the last line in the frame drawing, the curves will all de-select because no more lines can be added to a **Closed Curve.**

- Notice that the History Line is informing you that you have joined 12 curves into 1 closed curve.

Fig. 3

- If you press **Enter** before selecting all of the lines of the frame, the **Join** command will be finished and you will have created an **open curve.**

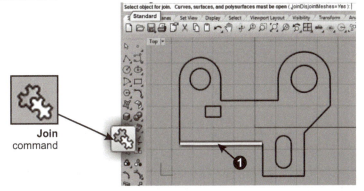

selected lines show an open curve

this line was not selected

Fig. 4

- **Standard tabbed toolbar.**　　Standard

- Click on the **Join** command.
  - **Select object to join. Curve, Surfaces and polysurfaces must be open** prompt:
    - Click to select one of the lines as shown. ❶

Join command

- **Select object to join. Press Enter when done** prompt:
  - Click to select another line or curve that is not touching the first curve. ❷

- The **Rhinoceros 5.0 Join** box will appear, warning that the ends of the two selected curves are not touching.
- Click the **No button** ❸ as it is not a good idea for Rhino to try to join these curves together as the result is usually not what you want.

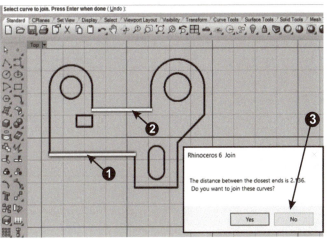

Fig. 5

Anatomy of a Line & a Polyline
Basic Rhino Line Commands

Line Command

- **Curve Tools tabbed toolbar.**
  - The curve tools group of command buttons will display on both **Curve Tools Toolbar** and the **Curve Drawing Sidebar.**

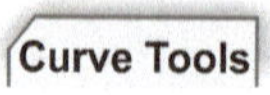

  Curve Tools

- Click on the **Top viewport title** to make sure that you are working in the **Top Viewport.**

- **LEFT-CLICK** on the **Line** command.

  Line command

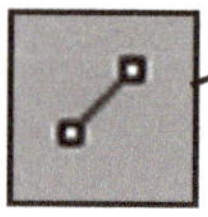

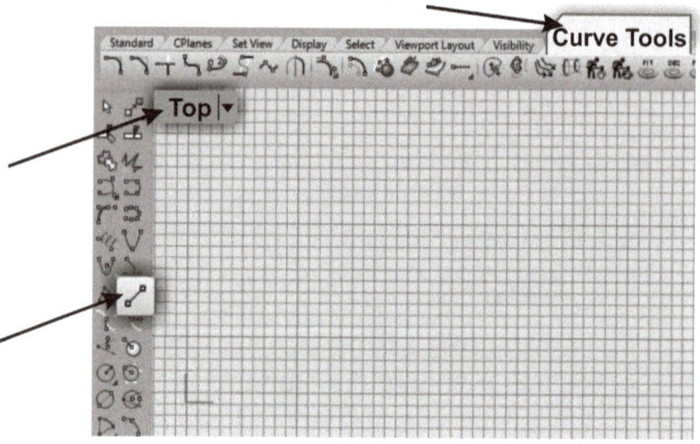

Fig. 1

- **Start of Line** prompt:
  - **LEFT-CLICK** on a location on the construction plane as shown. ❶
  - This will set the location of the start of your line.

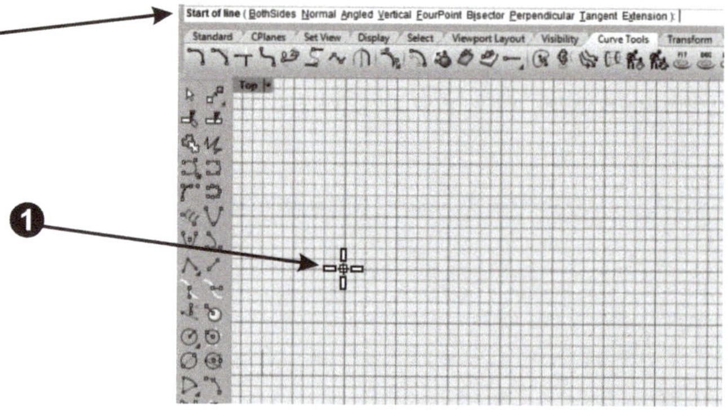

Fig. 2

- **End of Line** prompt:
  - Draw the cursor across the construction plane to arrive at the location that you want to choose for the end of the line
  - A "rubber band" preview line will follow the cursor.
  - **LEFT-CLICK** to set the location of the end of the line. ❷

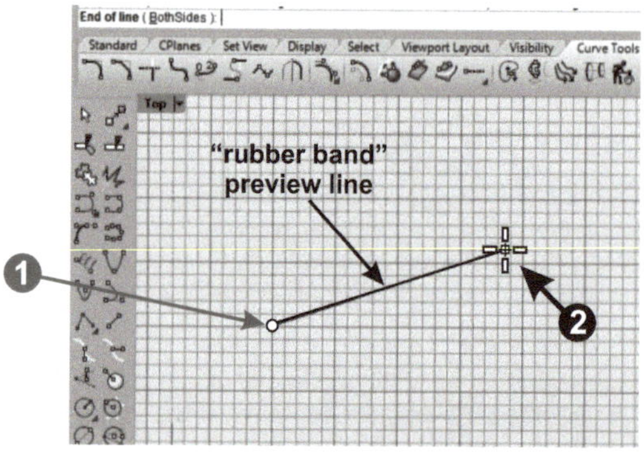

  "rubber band" preview line

Fig. 3

- The new line has been created and the Line command is finished.

- Notice that the **Command Line** is now prompting for the next command.

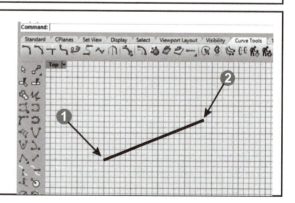

Fig. 4

Line with Specified Length of 15mm

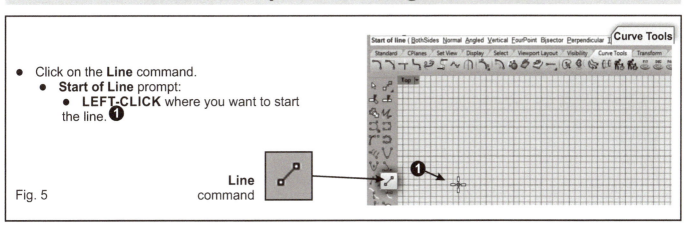

- Click on the **Line** command.
  - **Start of Line** prompt:
    - **LEFT-CLICK** where you want to start the line. ❶

Line command

Fig. 5

- **End of Line** prompt:
  - Type the number **"15"** in the **Command Line**.
  - Press the **"Enter"** key.

  - Note: after specifying a number in Rhino, ***you always need to press "Enter"*** to tell Rhino that this is the number you want.

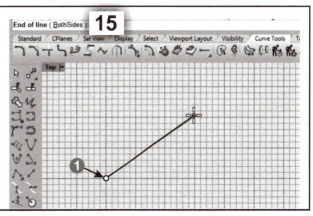

Fig. 6

- **End of Line** prompt continues:
  - The line is now constrained to a length of 15mm.
  - If drag the cursor out past the end of the preview, you will see a **white constraint line.** ❷
  - **LEFT-CLICK** to set a location for the end of the line.

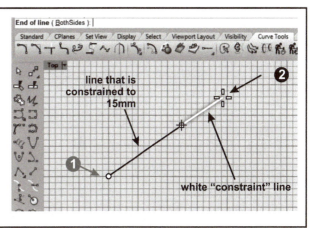

line that is constrained to 15mm

white "constraint" line

Fig. 7

- A 15mm line has been created.

- Notice that the **Command Line** is now prompting for the next command.

- The **Aligned dimension** added here is described in the chapter on **Applying Dimensions.**

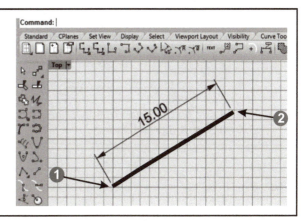

15.00

Fig. 8

Polyline Command
A Polyline is a line with more than one segment.

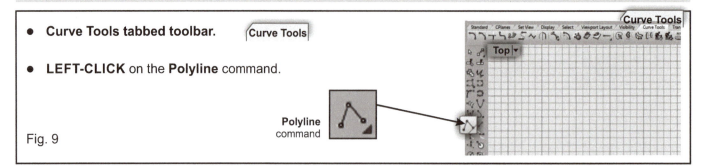

- **Curve Tools tabbed toolbar.** |Curve Tools|

- **LEFT-CLICK** on the **Polyline** command.

Polyline
command

Fig. 9

- **Start of Polyline** prompt:
  - **LEFT-CLICK** on the location for the start of the polyline. **1**

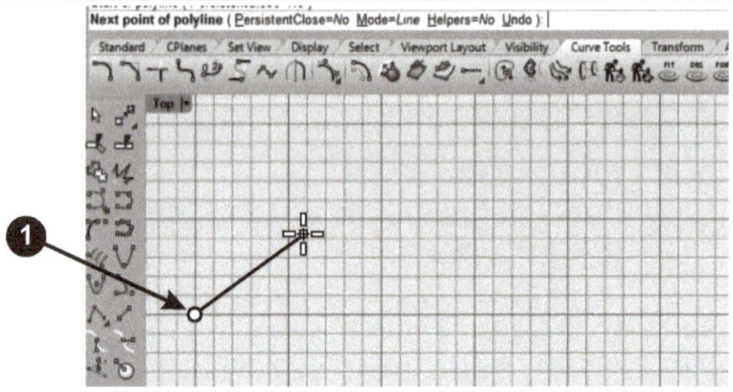

Fig. 10

- **Next Point of polyline** prompt:
  - **LEFT-CLICK** on a location for the end of the first line segment. **2**

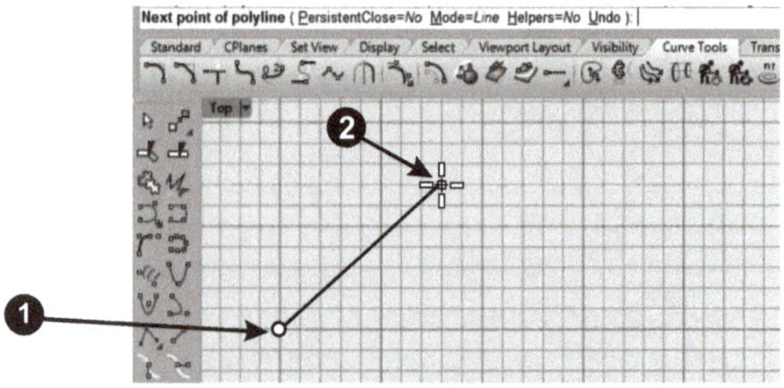

Fig. 11

- **Next point of polyline. Press Enter when done** prompt:
  - Click on another location. **3**

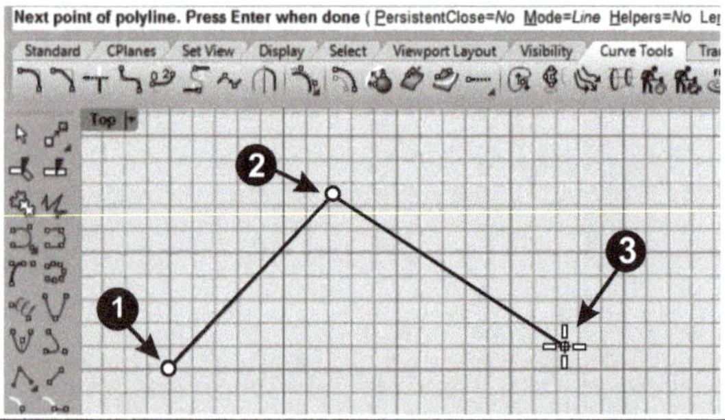

Fig. 12

- **Next point of polyline. Press Enter when done** prompt:
  - Click on a couple more locations as shown. **4** **5**
  - Click on the **Undo** option in the **Command Line** as shown.

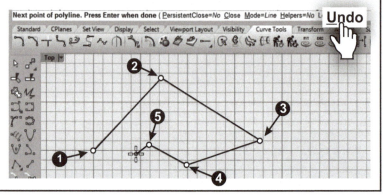

Fig. 13

- The most recent location **5** has been removed. If you continue to click on **Undo,** the locations will disappear in order.
- Click on the **Close** option in the **Command Line** as shown.

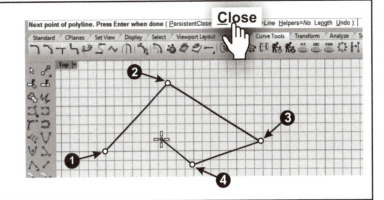

Fig. 14

- A new line segment has been created that joins the first line segment. **1**

- This is now a **closed polyline**.

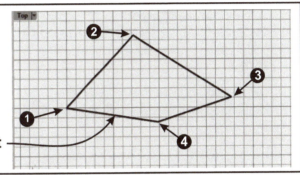

new line segment

Fig. 15

Length & Angle Constraints

- **LEFT-CLICK** on the **Polyline** command on the Main Sidebar.
  - **Start of polyline** prompt:
    - Click to select a location for the start of the polyline. **1**

Polyline command

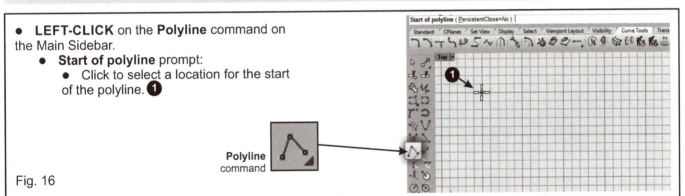

Fig. 16

- **Next point of polyline** prompt:
  - Type **"10"** in the **Command Line.**
  - Press **"Enter"** to tell Rhino that this is the number you want.

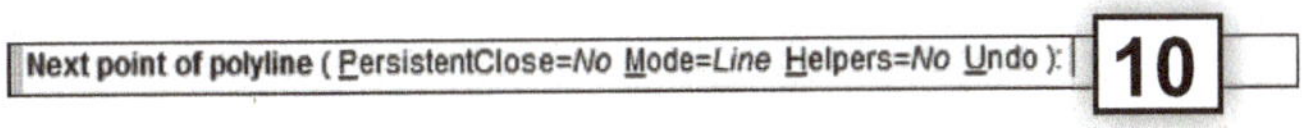

Next point of polyline (PersistentClose=*No* Mode=*Line* Helpers=*No* Undo): **10**

Fig. 17

- Your line will be constrained to a length of 10mm.

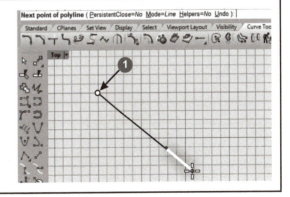

Fig. 18

- Now type **"<45"** in the <u>**Command Line**</u> and press **Enter.**
  - The **"<"** symbol is the upper case on the Comma key on your keyboard.

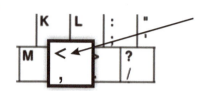

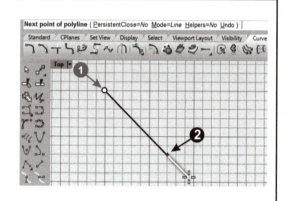

Fig. 19

- Now the line will not only be constrained to a length of 10mm but will also be constrained to a 45° angle.

- Draw the cursor around so that the line's angle is as shown and click to set location. ❷

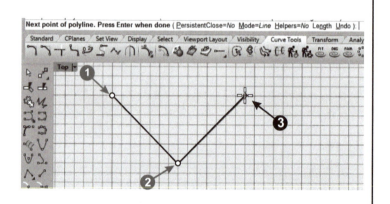

Fig. 20

- Type **"10"** again and press **"Enter".**
- Type **"<45"** again and press **"Enter".**
- Move the cursor around to choose the angle shown .
- Click to set the location of the end of the line segment as before. ❸

Fig. 21

- **Next point of polyline. Press Enter when done** prompt:
  - Press **"Enter"** to end the command.
  - The result is an **Open Polyline.**

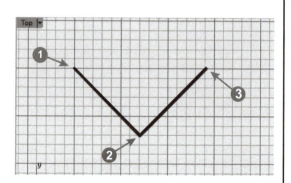

Fig. 22

Anatomy of a Circle
Basic Rhino Line Commands

Circle: Center, Radius command

- **Curve Tools tabbed toolbar**.

- **LEFT-CLICK** on the **Circle: Center, Radius** command.

Curve Tools

Circle: Center, Radius
command

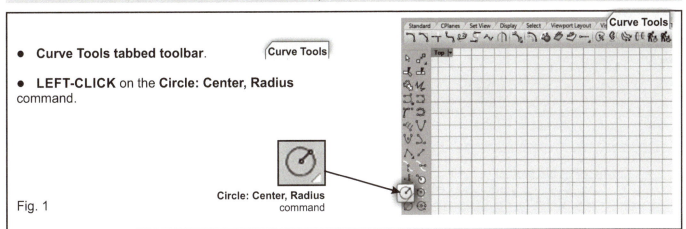

Fig. 1

- **Center of circle** prompt:
  - Left-click to set the desired location of the center of the circle. ❶

Fig. 2

- **Radius** prompt:
  - Draw the cursor out and notice that the preview of the circle follows it.
  - **LEFT-CLICK** to set the radius of the circle. ❷

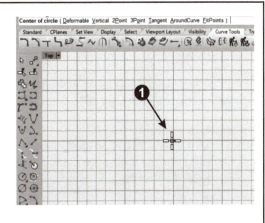

- The command is ended.

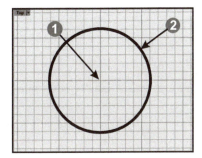

Fig. 3

Creating a Circle with a Specified Radius or Diameter

- **Curve Tools tabbed toolbar**.

Curve Tools

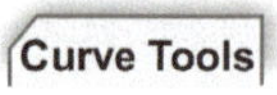

- **LEFT-CLICK** on the **Circle: Center, Radius** command.

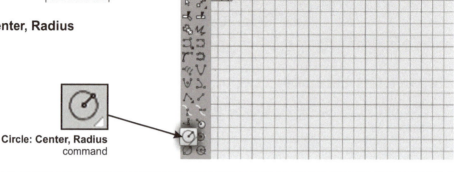

Circle: Center, Radius
command

Curve Tools

Fig. 4

- **Center of circle** prompt:
  - Type **"0"** in the **Command Line.**
  - Press **"Enter"**.

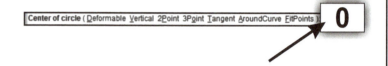

Center of circle (Deformable Vertical 2Point 3Point Tangent AroundCurve FitPoints)
0

Fig. 5

- The circle is now centered around the exact center of the grid, at the meeting of the X and Y axes.
  - In absolute coordinates this is "0,0". Rhino lets you just type **"0"**.
- **Radius** prompt:
  - **LEFT-CLICK** on the **Diameter** option within the parentheses in the **Command Line** as shown.

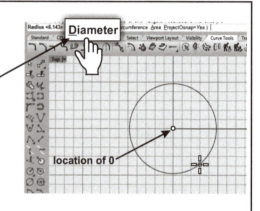

Diameter
location of 0

Fig. 6

- **Diameter** prompt:
  - You are now being prompted for the **Diameter**, not the Radius because you changed the option in the Command Line.
  - Type **"15"** in the **Command Line** and press **"Enter".**

15

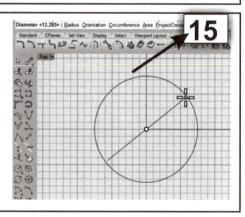

Fig. 7

- You have created a circle around "0" with a diameter of 15mm.

Ø15.00

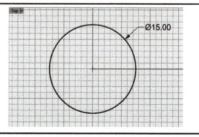

Fig. 8

Circle: Diameter command
A circle command defined by the diameter.

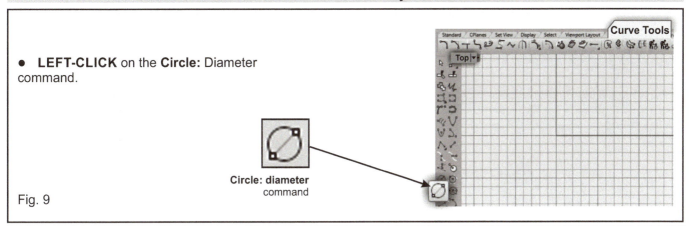

- **LEFT-CLICK** on the **Circle:** Diameter command.

Circle: diameter
command

Fig. 9

- **Start of diameter** prompt:
  - Type a **"0"** in the **Command Line** and press **"Enter"**.

Fig. 10

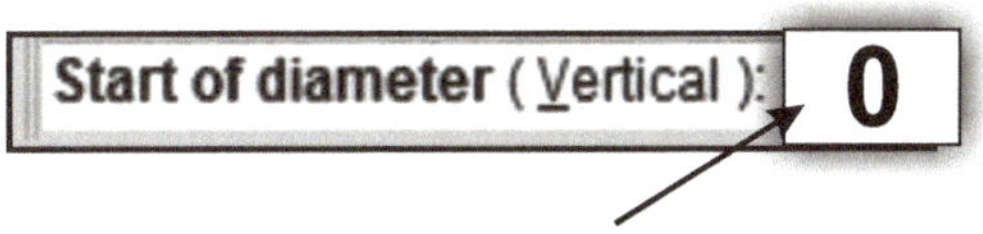

Start of diameter (Vertical): **0**

- The start of the circle passes exactly through "0" ❶

- **End of diameter** prompt:
  - When you pull out the cursor, notice that the space between it and the start point is defined by the **Diameter** or the circle, not the Radius!
  - Type **"15"** in the **Command Line** and press **"Enter"**.

Fig. 11

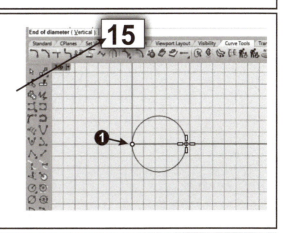

- **End of diameter** prompt continues:
  - The diameter of the circle is constrained to 15mm.
  - **LEFT-CLICK** on the location that places the circle the way you want it to be.

Fig. 12

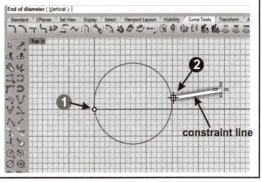

constraint line

- A 15mm diameter circle has been created by defining the start and end points of its diameter as well as the exact measurement of the diameter.

Fig. 13

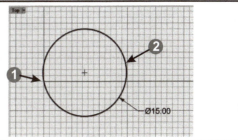

Ø15.00

Ortho and Grid Snap Modes
Constraining the Movement of the Cursor

Ortho Mode

- On the Status Bar at the bottom of the workspace, click on the **Ortho** button to turn on **Ortho mode.**

Fig. 1

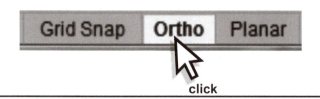

click

- **Curve Tools tabbed toolbar.**   Curve Tools

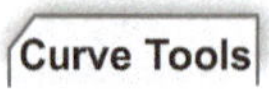

- Click on the **Polyline** command and start to click on locations for your line segments.

- You can only create lines that are either perfectly horizontal or perfectly vertical.

- **Ortho** is constraining the placement of the lines to 90° directions.

Polyline
command

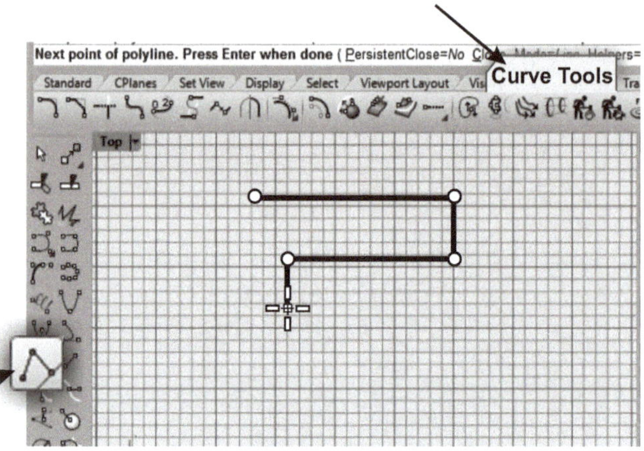

Fig. 2

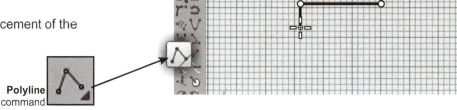

- Click on the **Ortho** button again to *toggle off Ortho mode.*

Fig. 3

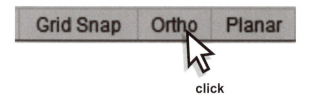

click

- Click to place some more line segments and you will see that you are not longer constrained by **Ortho.**

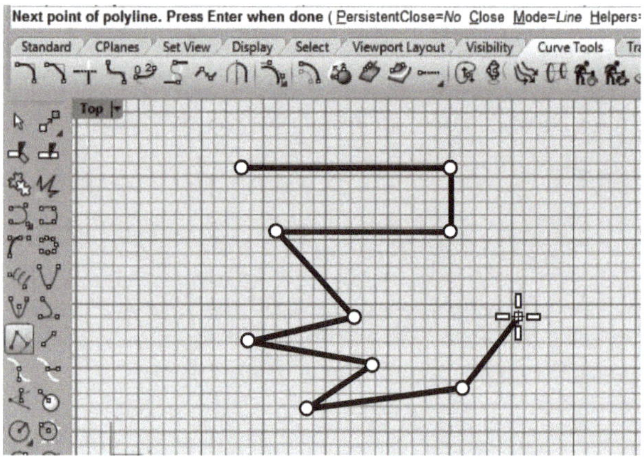

- Other ways to *Toggle Ortho on and off.*

  - *Tapping the F8 key.* **F8**

  - *Holding down and releasing the Shift key to temporarily toggle ortho on or off.*

Shift

Fig. 4

Grid Snap Mode

- On the Status Bar at the bottom of the workspace, click on the **Grid Snap** button to turn on **Grid Snap mode.**

Fig. 5

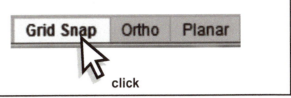
click

- Click on the **Polyline** command.
  - **Start of polyline** prompt:
    - When you start clicking on locations for your line segments, notice that *you can only click on GRID INTERSECTIONS.*

Fig. 6

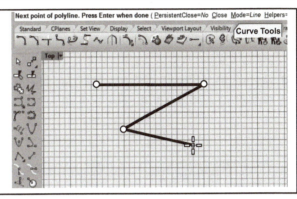

- **LEFT-CLICK** on the **Grid Snap** button again to toggle off **Grid Snap** mode.
  - Notice that the appearance of the **Grid Snap** button reverts to its original gray color.

Fig. 7

click

- Click on some more locations.

- Notice that now that the last 4 clicks are in locations that were not constrained to grid intersections because *Grid Snap was toggled off.*

Fig. 8

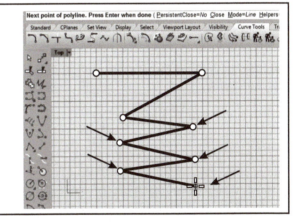

- **Grid Snap** makes certain tasks very easy.

- The polylines in the illustration were all made with easy accuracy in **Grid Snap** mode.

Fig. 9

Object Snap "OSNAP"
Accurate Placement of Objects in Relation to Each Other

- **There is no modeling aid in Rhino that is more important than Object Snap.**

- **Object Snap is crucial for the accuracy of drawings and models.**

- Save this file as **osnap & analysis.3dm.** We will use this file again in the next exercise for measuring lines, distances and angles.

- The **Object Snap** pane will appear when you click on the **Osnap button** in the **Status Bar** as shown.

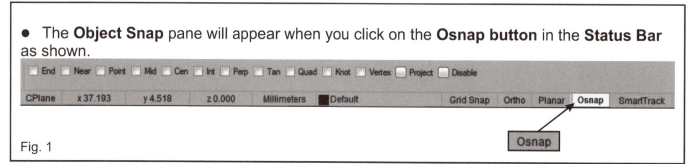

Fig. 1

- **Curve Tools tabbed toolbar.**

- Toggle on **Grid Snap** at the bottom of the workspace.

- Use the **Circle: center, radius** and the **Polyline** commands to create the simple circles and squares shown.
  - **Circles: 10mm diameter**
  - **Squares: 10mm sides**
  - **placement: All objects are 5mm apart.**

- **Grid Snap** makes these objects easy to create.

- Toggle off **Grid Snap** when you are done creating the circles and squares.

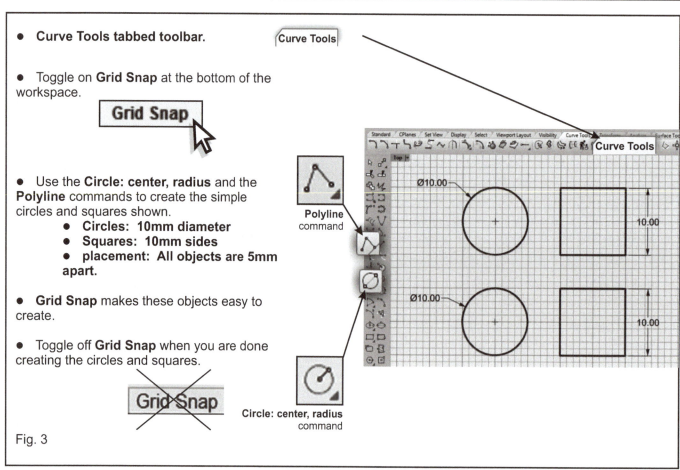

Fig. 3

43

- **LEFT-CLICK** on the box or text of **End Osnap** (**Endpoint Object Snap**) to toggle it on. A little check mark will appear in the box as shown.

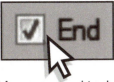

- Use the **Line** command to draw a line from the corners of the two boxes as shown.

- As the cursor is drawn over the corners of the squares, the cursor will be pulled to them (will "snap" to them) - the corners are *End Points* of lines that make up the squares.
    - Click for the locations of the start and end of the line **when you see the little tool-tip that says "End".** ❶ & ❷

- The Line's placement will accurately start and end exactly on the end points that the cursor snapped to.

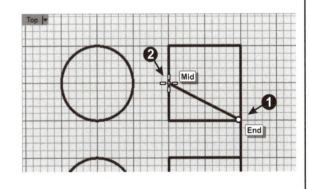

Line
command

Fig. 4

- Now, click on the box or text of **Mid Osnap (Midpoint Object Snap)** to toggle it on.

- Use the **Line** command to draw a line that connects an **end point** and a **mid point** as shown. ❶ & ❷

Fig. 5

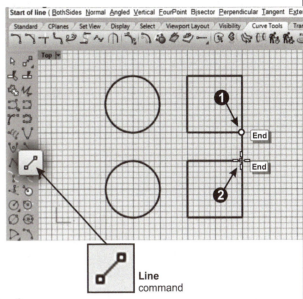

- Click on **Cen osnap (Center Object Snap)** to toggle it on.

- Use the **Line** command to draw a line from the center of the lower circle to the center of the lower square as shown.

- *NOTE: Center Snap requires you to guide the cursor over the line that defines the circle or square.*

- *Click to set start and end of line ONLY when you see the little* Cen *box which is telling you that you are snapping to the center of the object.*

Fig. 6

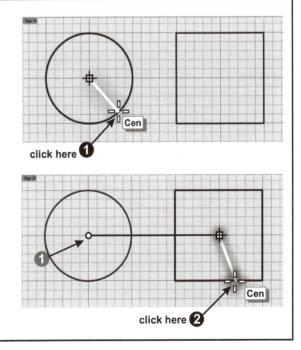

click here ❶

click here ❷

- Click again on the enabled object snaps to *toggle them off.*

- Then toggle on both **Int osnap (Intersection Object Snap)** and **Tan osnap (Tangent Object Snap)**.

- Create a **Line** that starts at the intersection shown ❶ and ends at the tangent point on the circle shown. ❷

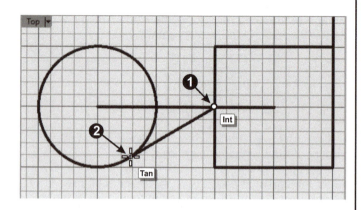

Fig. 7

- **RIGHT-CLICK** on the **Quad osnap (Quadrant Object Snap)**.

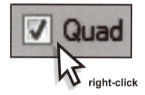

right-click

- **Quad Osnap** will be turned on and the other object snaps will be disabled because you right-clicked on one of them.

- Create a **Polyline** that connects all 4 **Quad** points of the top circle as shown.

- The **Quad** points of a circle, oval, arc or wavy curve are the locations that are at the furthest extant of the X and Y grid directions.

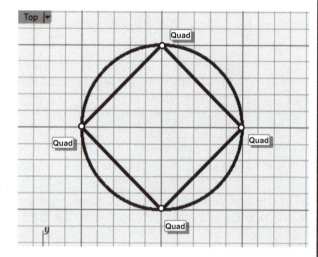

Fig. 8

- Toggle on the **Near Osnap (Near to Object Snap)** and **Perp Osnap (Perpendicular Object Snap)**.

 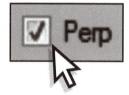

- Create a **Line** that starts somewhere on the curve of the top circle as shown. ❶
  - **Near Osnap** simply means that the cursor snaps to an object but the exact location is not set until you click to set it.

- The end of the line will snap to a point that creates a line that is perfectly perpendicular to it's ending location. ❷

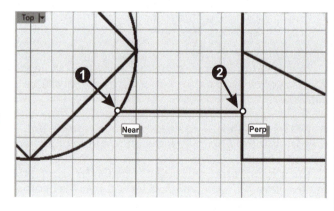

Fig. 9

Measuring the Length of a Line

- Open your Rhino file, **osnap & analysis.3dm** from the previous **Object Snap** chapter.

- Access the **Analyze tabbed toolbar.** [Analyze]
  - Ref: **"Adding Tabbed Toolbars to the Workspace"** in the **The Rhino Workspace** chapter.

- **LEFT-CLICK** on the **Length** command.

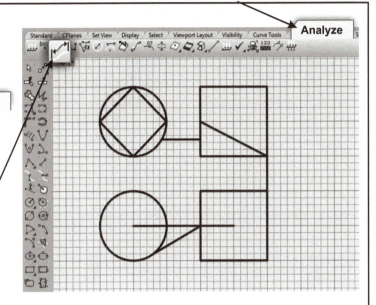

Length
command

Fig. 1

- **Select curves to measure** prompt:
  - Select the diagonal line in the upper right square as shown.
  - Press **Enter.**

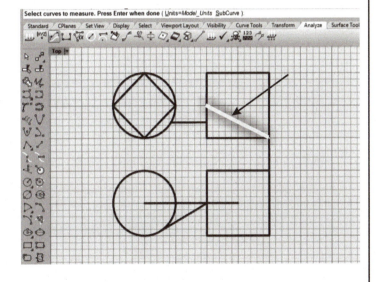

Fig. 2

- The History window will report the exact length of the line you just selected.

- *Note: If the History line only displays one line of text, drag the lower edge of the Command Line downward until three lines or more of text are visible in the History Line.*

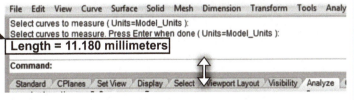

Length = 11.180 millimeters

click and drag for more
lines to show in the History window

Fig. 3

Measuring the Distance Between Two Points

- To measure the **Distance between two locations**, **LEFT-CLICK** on the **Distance** command in the **Analyze tabbed toolbar**.

  - **First point for distance** prompt:
    - Use **End Osnap** to snap to the lower corner of the lower square and click to set location. **❶**

Fig. 4

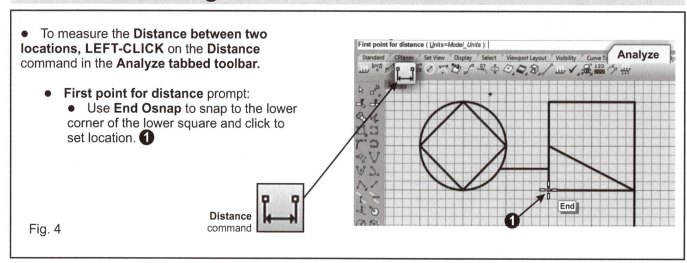

Distance
command

- **Second point for distance** prompt:
  - Click on the upper right corner of the same square and click to set location. **❷**

Fig. 5

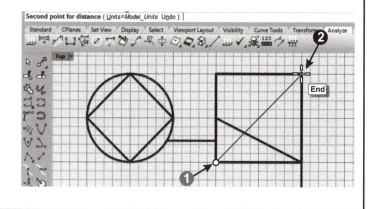

- The History line will show you the distance measurement (in addition to a lot of extra information!)

Fig. 6

| CPlane angles and deltas: | xy = 45.000 elevation = 0.000 | dx = 10.000 dy = 10.000 dz = 0.000 |
| World angles and deltas: | xy = 45.000 elevation = 0.000 | dx = 10.000 dy = 10.000 dz = 0.000 |

Distance = 14.142 millimeters

Command:

Measuring an Angle

- To measure the **Angle formed by two lines**, **LEFT-CLICK** on the **Angle** command in the **Analyze tabbed toolbar**.
  - **Start of first line** prompt:
    - Snap to the end point of the diagonal line and click to set location. **❶**

Fig. 7

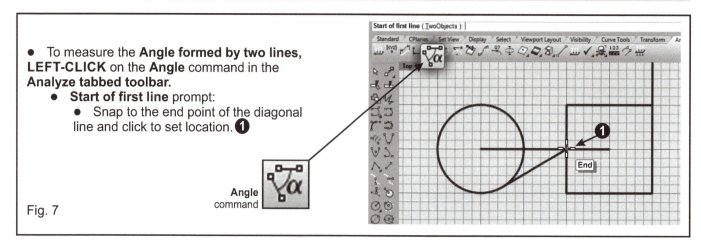

Angle
command

- **End of first line** prompt:
  - Snap to the other **end** of the diagonal line and click to set location. ❷

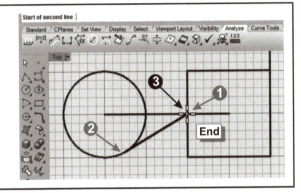

Fig. 8

- **Start of second line** prompt:
  - Click on the **end** of the start of the horizontal line. ❸
  - *This is the same location as the start of the first line.*

Fig. 9

- **End of second line** prompt:
  - Snap to the **end** of the second line and click to set location. ❹
  - The History line will report the measurement of the angle.

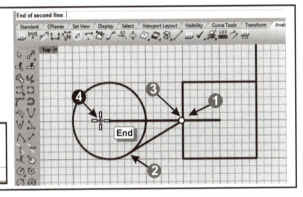

| Start of second line: |
| End of second line: |
| **Angle = 30** |
| Command: |

Fig. 10

Measuring Diameter & Radius

- Select one of the circles and **LEFT-CLICK** on the **Measure Diameter** command.

- The History line will display both the Radius and the Diameter of the selected circle.

Radius = 5.000
Diameter = 10.000

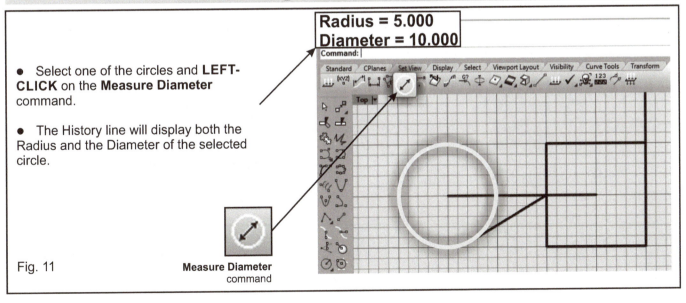

Fig. 11

Measure Diameter
command

Applying Dimensions
Applying Dimensions and Adjusting Dimension Settings

- Open your previously saved file, **osnap & analysis.3dm.**

- Click on the **Drafting tabbed toolbar.**

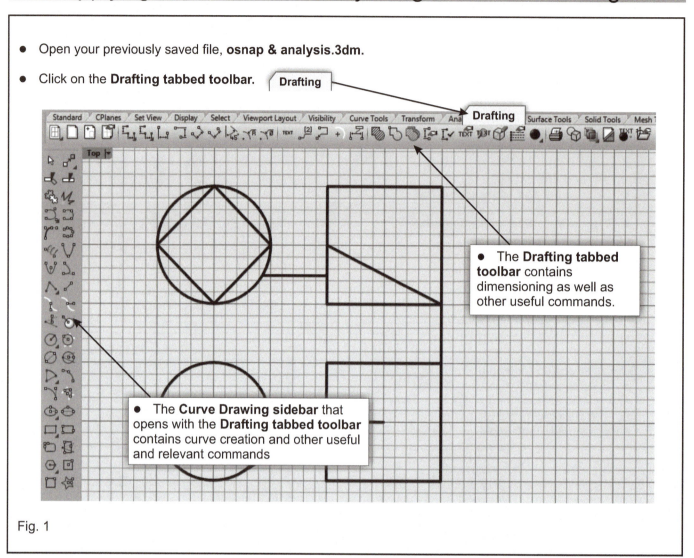

- The **Drafting tabbed toolbar** contains dimensioning as well as other useful commands.

- The **Curve Drawing sidebar** that opens with the **Drafting tabbed toolbar** contains curve creation and other useful and relevant commands

Fig. 1

Horizontal and Vertical Dimensioning

- Make sure that **End Osnap** is enabled.

✓ End

- Click on the **Linear Dimension** command as shown.

Linear Dimension command

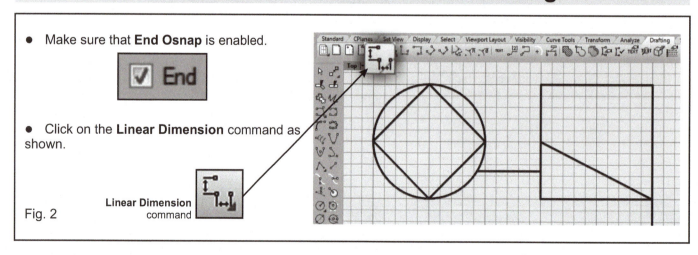

Fig. 2

49

- **First dimension point** prompt:
  - Snap to the one of the corners - **End Osnap** will work here because of the two lines that make up the corner. ❶

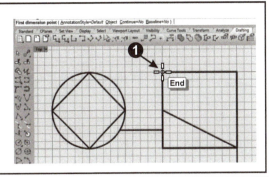

Fig. 3

- **Second dimension point** prompt:
  - Snap to the other **End** of the line that you want to dimension and click to set location. ❷

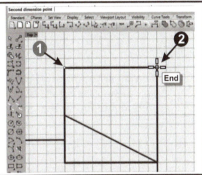

Fig. 4

- **Dimension location** prompt:
  - Pull the cursor outward and click to set the location of the extension lines and text. ❸

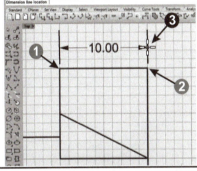

Fig. 5

- Click on the same command again to get a vertical dimension, using **End Osnap** to click on the locations ❶ and ❷ . Click on location ❸ for placement of text and extension lines.

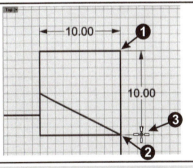

Fig. 6

Diagonal Dimensioning - Aligned Dimension command

- Click on the **Aligned Dimension** command.
  - **First dimension point** prompt:
    - Snap to an **End** of the diagonal line. ❶

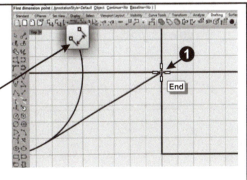

Aligned Dimension command

Fig. 7

- **Second dimension point** prompt:
  - Snap to the other end of the diagonal line as shown and click to set location. ❷

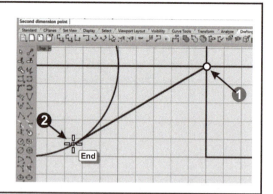

Fig. 8

- **Dimension location** prompt:
  - Draw the cursor outward and click to set final location for text and extension lines. ❸

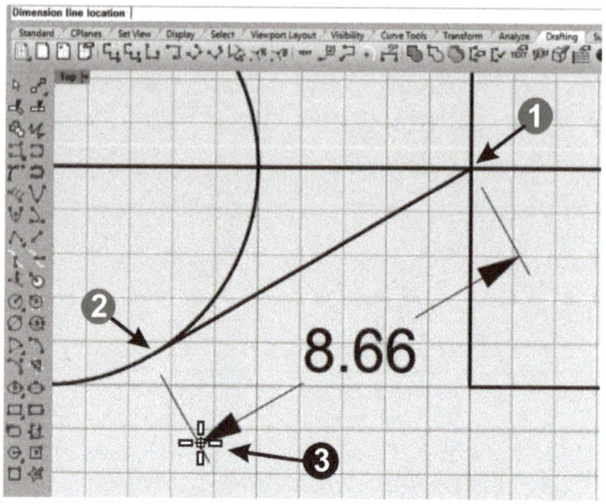

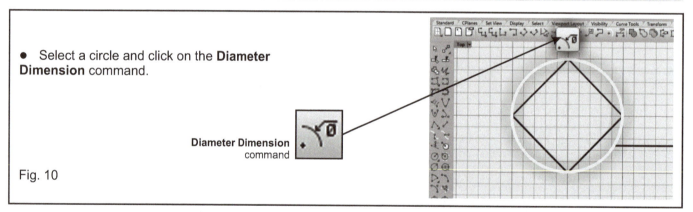

Fig. 9

Diameter & Radius Dimensioning

- Select a circle and click on the **Diameter Dimension** command.

Diameter Dimension command

Fig. 10

- **Diameter location** prompt:
  - Draw the cursor out and click to set desired location of the dimension text and extension line.

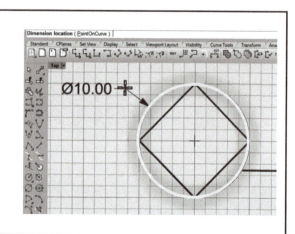

Fig. 11

- Click on the **Radial Dimension** command to get a dimension for the **Radius** of the circle.

Radial Dimension
command

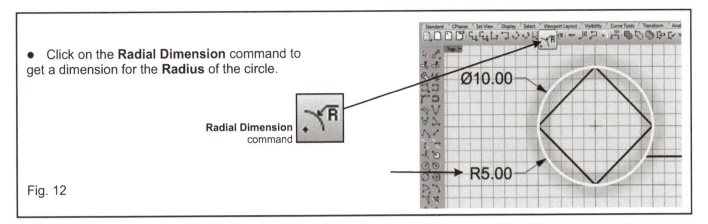

Fig. 12

Angle Dimensioning

- Click to select the **Angle Dimension** command.
  - **Select arc or first line** prompt:
    - Click to select the line shown. ❶

Angle Dimension
command

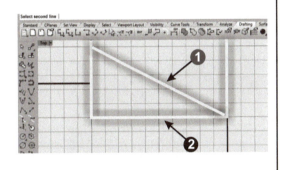

Fig. 13

- **Select second line** prompt:
  - Click on the line shown. ❷
    - The rest of the square polyline will also select because all of the segments are joined together.

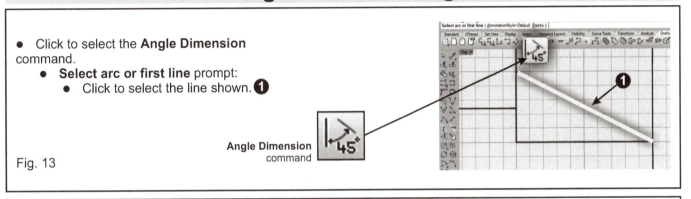

Fig. 14

- **Dimension location** prompt:
  - Pull the cursor outward and click on the desired location. ❸

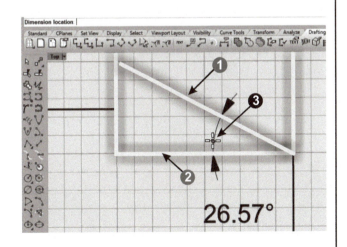

Fig. 15

- Click to open the **Tools** drop-down on the **Menu Bar** at the top of the workspace. **1**

- Click on the **Options** category at the bottom of the drop-down.**2**

- The **Rhino Options** box will open.

- Click to open the **Annotation Styles** category. **1**
  - Click to **uncheck** the **"enable layout space scaling"** option.
  - This a better setting with layouts, which will be covered later in this book.

- Click to open up the **Annotation** category.
  - A single **default** style will be listed. **3**

- The **default** style window will show the different categories of default settings.

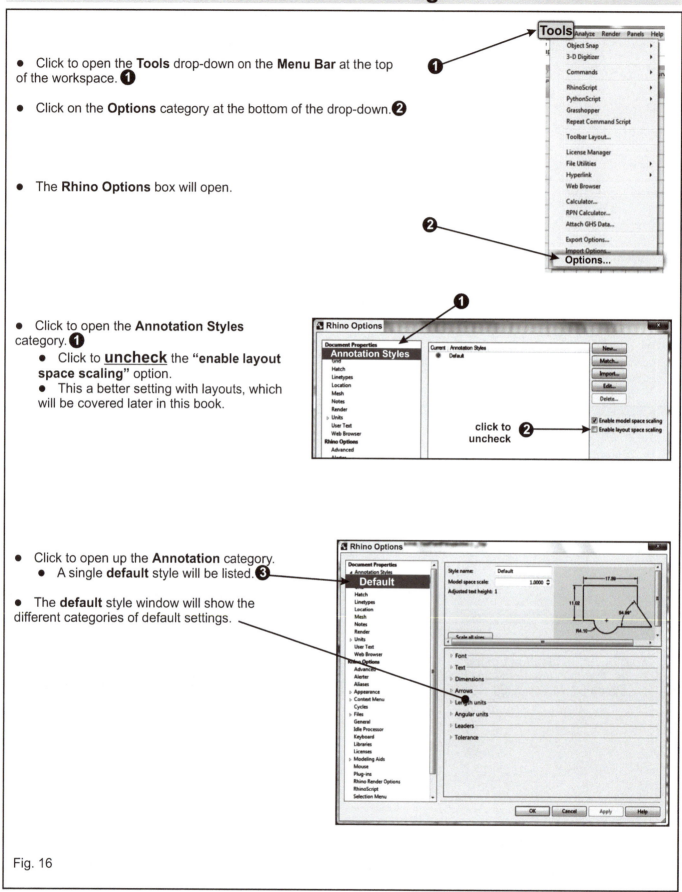

Fig. 16

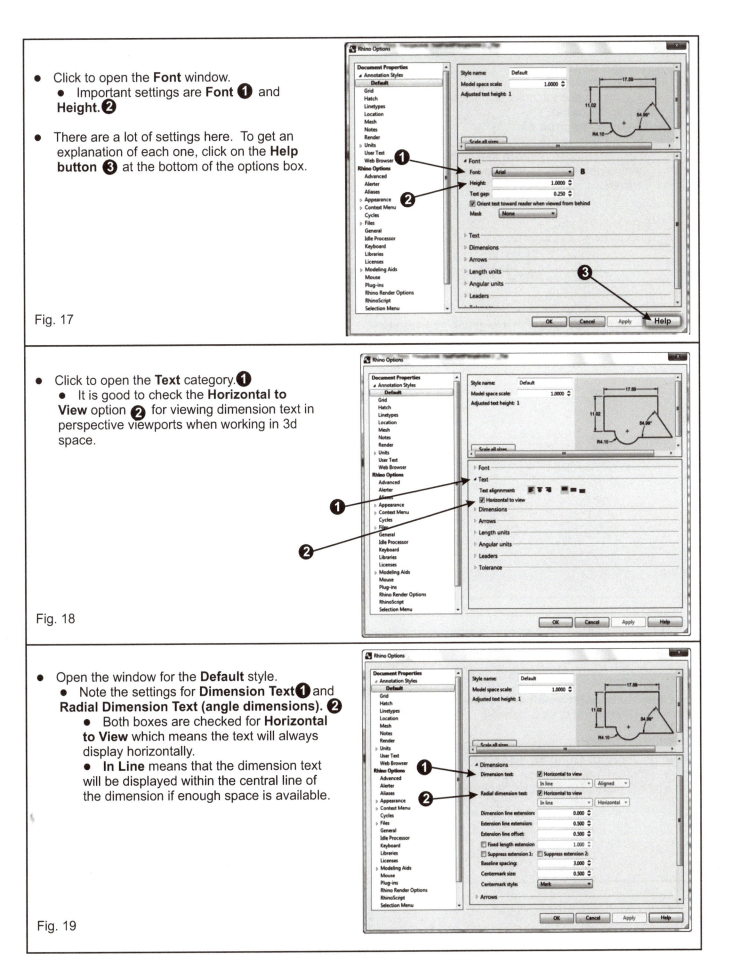

- Click to open the **Font** window.
  - Important settings are **Font ❶** and **Height.❷**

- There are a lot of settings here. To get an explanation of each one, click on the **Help button ❸** at the bottom of the options box.

Fig. 17

- Click to open the **Text** category.**❶**
  - It is good to check the **Horizontal to View** option **❷** for viewing dimension text in perspective viewports when working in 3d space.

Fig. 18

- Open the window for the **Default** style.
  - Note the settings for **Dimension Text❶** and **Radial Dimension Text (angle dimensions). ❷**
    - Both boxes are checked for **Horizontal to View** which means the text will always display horizontally.
    - **In Line** means that the dimension text will be displayed within the central line of the dimension if enough space is available.

Fig. 19

- The **Length Units** category.
  - **Units - formats** ❶
    - Designates the units and decimal or fractional format.
  - **Linear Resolution** ❷
    - Designates the amount of precision in the measurements - note that in this setting, the measurement is accurate to .01mm.

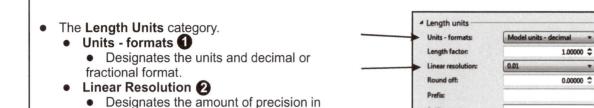

Fig. 20

Adding a New Dimension Style

- Create a horizontal line with a length of **184.15mm**.

- A new dimension style will be needed so that dimensioning this line will express a value in inches instead of millimeters.

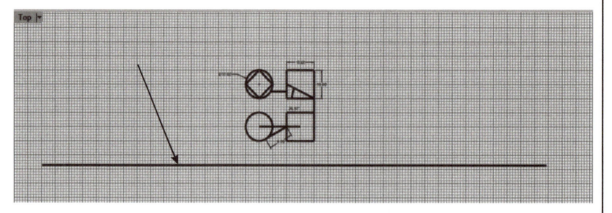

Fig. 21

- Access the **Rhino Options** box again.

- Open the **Annotation Styles** category ❶ to show the **Default** annotation style. ❷

- The **Default** will be the only dimension style shown in the **Annotation Styles** list. ❷
  - You will now add a new dimension style that will read inches instead of millimeters.

- Click on the **New** button. ❸

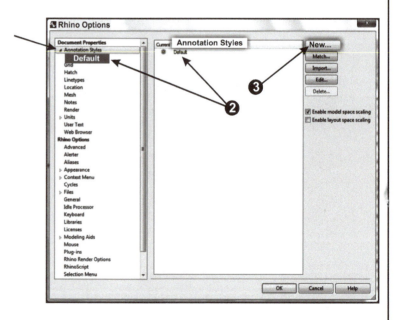

Fig. 22

55

- The **New Annotation Style** box will open.

- Create a name for the new annotation style. **1**

- Select the **(built in) Template Inch Fractional 2** annotation style which is one of Rhino's templates.

- Click on the **OK button. 3**

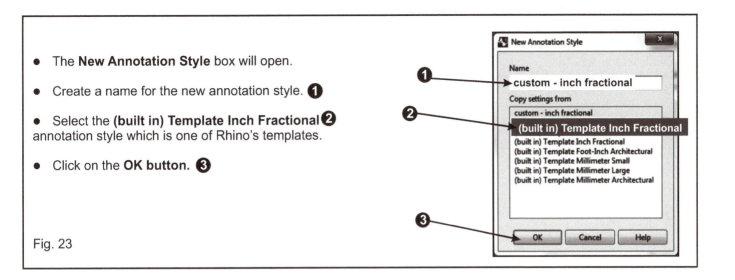

Fig. 23

- The new style template **1** will be added to the Annotation Styles list.

- Click on the radio button to make the **Template Inch Fractional** annotation style current. **2**

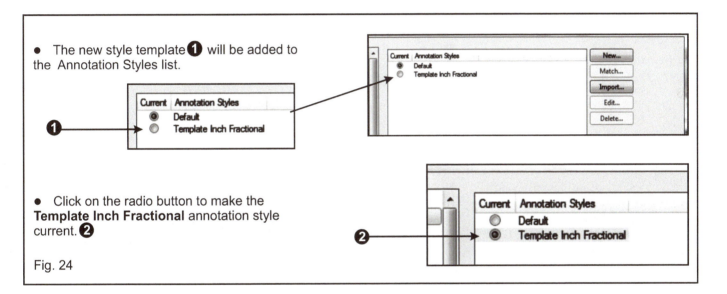

Fig. 24

- After you have made the new annotation style current, click on the **Edit button.**

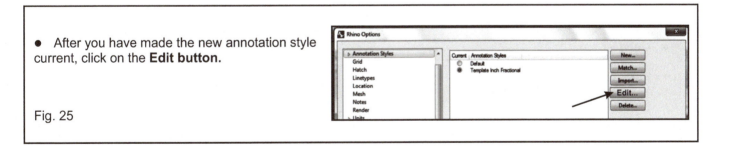

Fig. 25

- **Font** height: **.5mm**

Fig. 26

- **Dimensions ❶**
  - **Dimension text: ❷**
    - **In Line ❸**

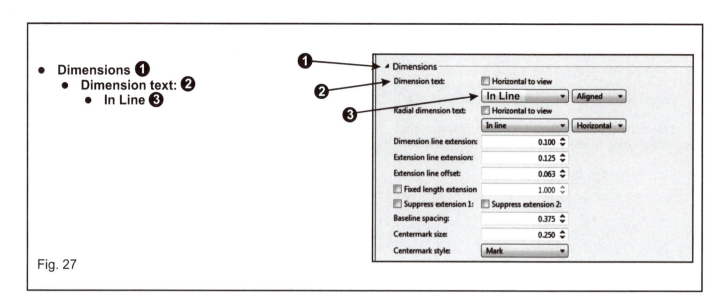

Fig. 27

- **Arrows: ❶**
  - **Arrowheads:**
    - **Arrow ❷**
  - **Arrow Size:**
    - **.5 ❸**

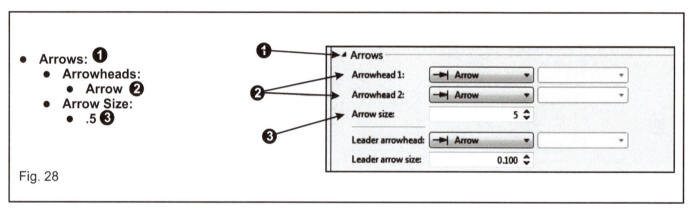

Fig. 28

- **Length Units ❶**
  - **Units - Formats: ❷**
    - **Inches - Fractional**
  - **Linear Resolution: ❸**
    - **1/16**
  - **Fraction Stacking Format: ❹**
    - **No stack**

- Click on the **OK button** at the bottom of the Rhino Options box to apply the settings.

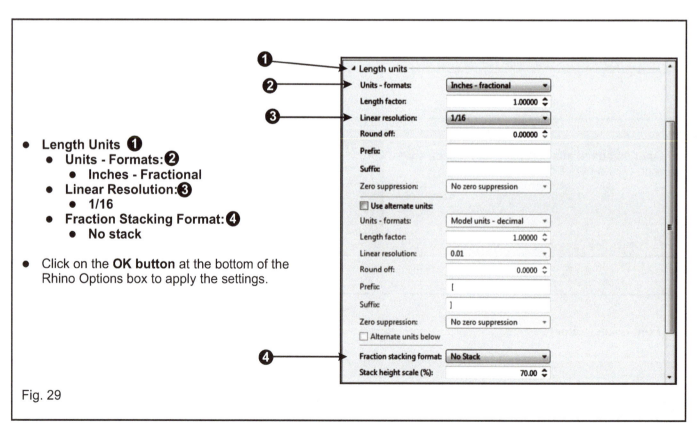

Fig. 29

- Apply the **Linear Dimension** command to the new line.
  - The dimension properties will reflect the settings for the new annotation style.

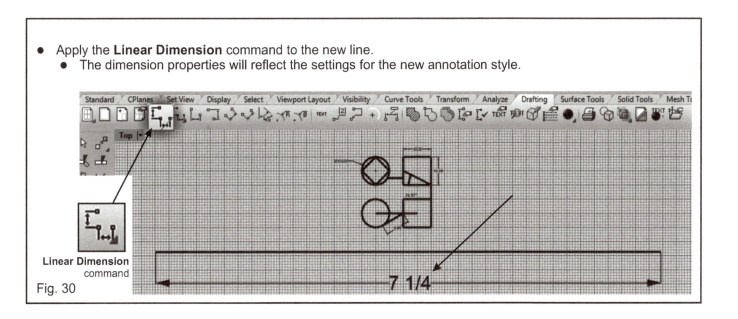

Linear Dimension
command

Fig. 30

Changing the Style of a Dimension

- If your dimension still shows the number 184.13, you have created the dimension in the **Default** style, which displays in millimeters.

- The style for this dimension needs to be changed.

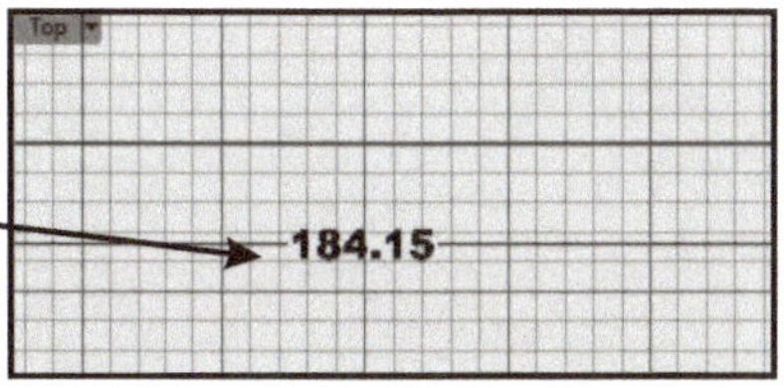

Fig. 31

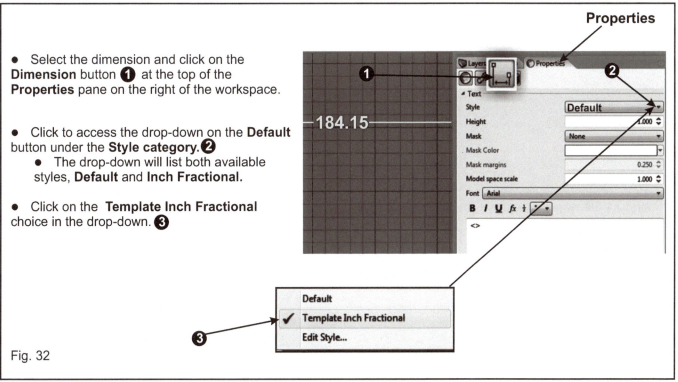

Properties

- Select the dimension and click on the **Dimension** button ❶ at the top of the **Properties** pane on the right of the workspace.

- Click to access the drop-down on the **Default** button under the **Style category.** ❷
  - The drop-down will list both available styles, **Default** and **Inch Fractional.**

- Click on the **Template Inch Fractional** choice in the drop-down. ❸

Fig. 32

- The dimension settings will show that the selected dimension has been changed to the **Template Inch Fractional** style.

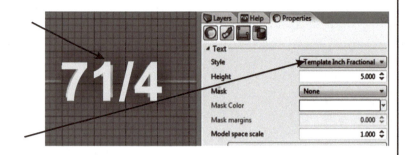

Fig. 33

Control Point Editing a Dimension

- Select the diagonal **Aligned Dimension** and press the **F10 Hotkey** to turn on that dimension's control points.
  - The **F10** key is a convenient shortcut for turning on control points.

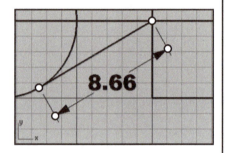

- The 5 control points of the dimension will appear.

- Select the three control points shown.

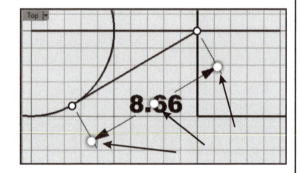

- Drag the control points and click to set a new location for the text and extension lines.

- Click away to de-select.

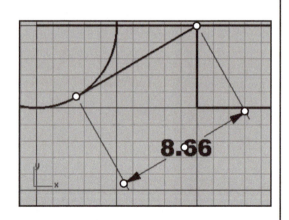

Fig. 34

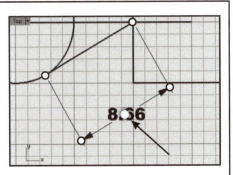

- Select the single point over the text.

- Drag the text and click to set new location.

- Press the **Esc** key a couple of times to turn off control points.

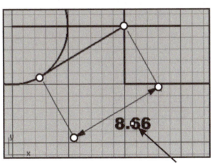

Fig. 35

- Dimensioning small distances can result in the dimension text being offset to the top or side.

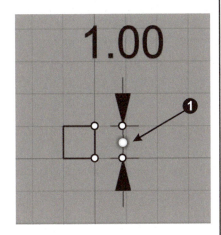

- Select the dimension and press the **F10 hotkey** to turn on its control points.

F10

- Select the middle of three control points ❶ between the dimension arrows.

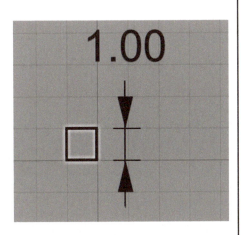

Fig. 36

- When you **Drag** the selected control point, the text will jump to a position under the cursor. ❷

- You can move the dimension text to a location of your choosing.

- Press the **Esc key** a couple of times to de-select and turn off control points.

Fig. 37

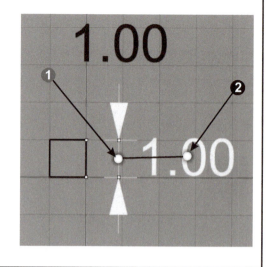

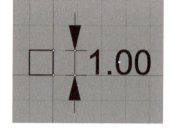

Editing a Dimension Text

- **Double-click** on the dimension text ❶ and the **Edit Linear Dimension** text box will open. ❷

- The two symbols **<>** represent the existing text. ❸

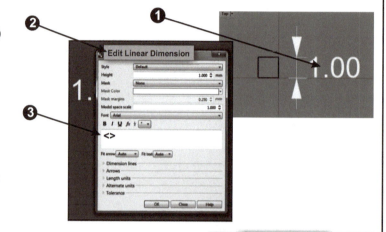

- Select the two symbols and type in **1mm.** ❸ This will replace the existing text with the text that you have just typed in.

- Notice other options to change the text format and size, including arrow size and other dimension characteristics.

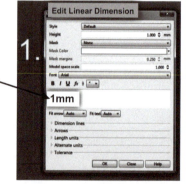

- Click the OK button to close the box.

- The dimension text has been edited.

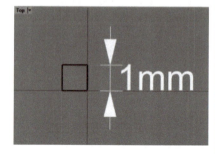

Fig. 38

Move & Copy Commands
Click & Drag, Move, Copy

Simple Move with "Click & Drag"

- **Curve Tools tabbed toolbar.**   Curve Tools

- Create a circle with a diameter of 8mm, using one of the **Circle** commands.

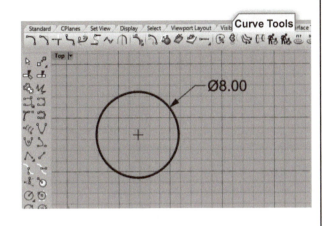

Fig. 1

- **LEFT-CLICK** on the circle and start dragging it in the desired direction.

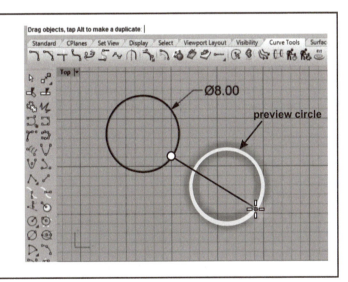

Fig. 2

- Release the cursor, when you have dragged the object to the desired location.

- The circle has been moved to a new location.

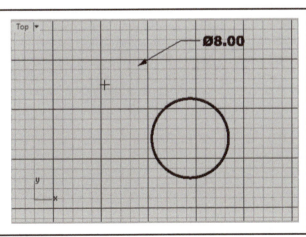

Fig. 3

Move Command

- Click on the **Move** command in the **Curve Tools** tabbed toolbar.

  - **Select objects to move**.
    - Click on the circle to select it.
    - Press **Enter**.

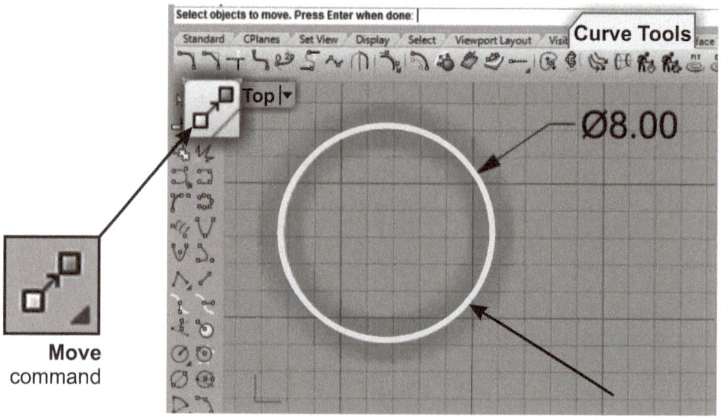

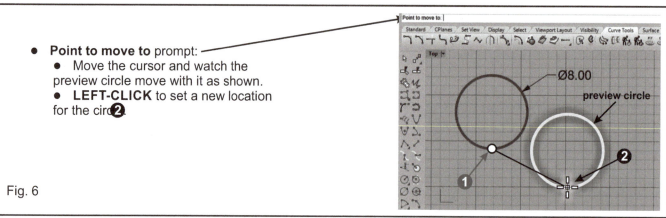

Move command

Fig. 4

- **Point to move from** prompt:
  - Snap to the bottom **Quad** point of the circle and **left-click.** ❶

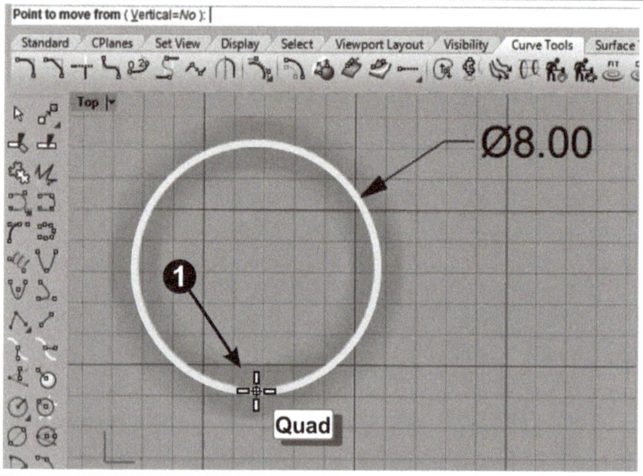

Fig. 5

- **Point to move to** prompt:
  - Move the cursor and watch the preview circle move with it as shown.
  - **LEFT-CLICK** to set a new location for the circle. ❷

Fig. 6

- The circle has been moved to a new location.

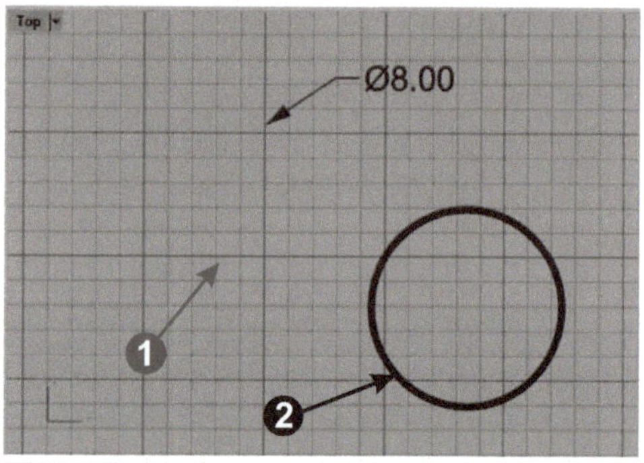

Fig. 7

Moving a Specified Distance

- **Curve Tools tabbed toolbar.** [Curve Tools]

- Select the circle and click on the **Move** command.

- *Note: pre-selection saves time by eliminating the step in a command in which you are prompted to make a selection and press Enter.*

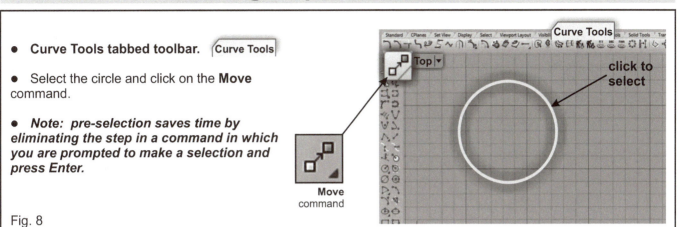

Move command

click to select

Fig. 8

- **Point to move from** prompt:
  - Use **Center Osnap** to snap to the center of the circle and click when you see the **Cen** tooltip as shown. ❶

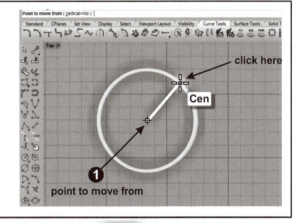

click here

Cen

point to move from

Fig. 9

- **Point to move to** prompt:
  - Type **"10"** in the **Command Line** and press **Enter.** ❷
    - The distance of the move will be constrained to 10mm.
  - Click to set the new location for the circle. ❸

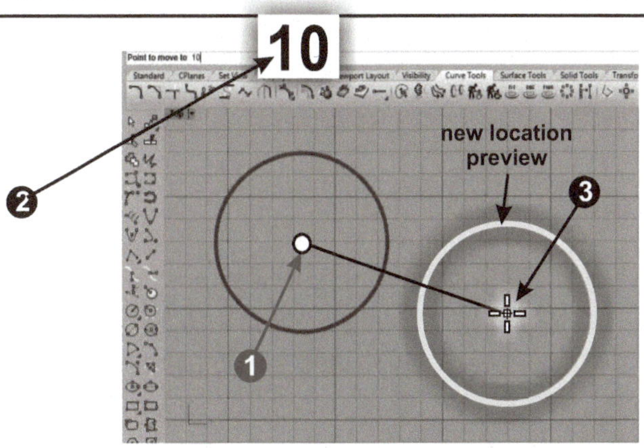

new location preview

Fig. 10

- The circle has been moved **10mm**.

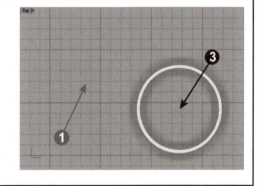

Fig. 11

Moving to a Specified Location

- Use the **Polyline** command to create a line with 3 segments, similar to the one shown.

- Specified lengths and angles are not needed for this exercise.

Polyline
command

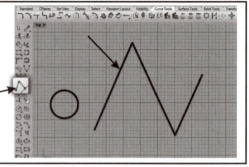

Fig. 12

- Turn on **Center osnap** and **End osnap**.

- Select the circle ❶ and click on the **Move** command.

Move
command

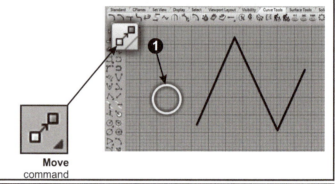

Fig. 13

- **Point to move from** prompt:
  - Use **Center osnap** to snap to the center of the circle and **left-click.** ❷

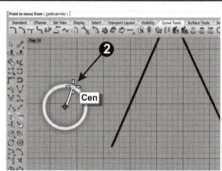

Fig. 14

- **Point to move to** prompt:
  - Use **End osnap** to snap to the end point of the nearby polyline as shown.
  - **Left-click** to set the new location for the circle. ❸

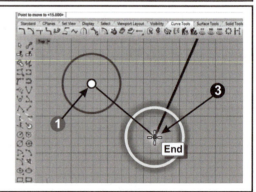

Fig. 15

- The circle is now perfectly centered on the end of the polyline.

- *If the circle is still selected when the command is over, click on the grid anywhere to de-select.*

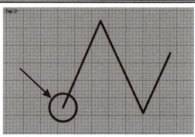

Fig. 16

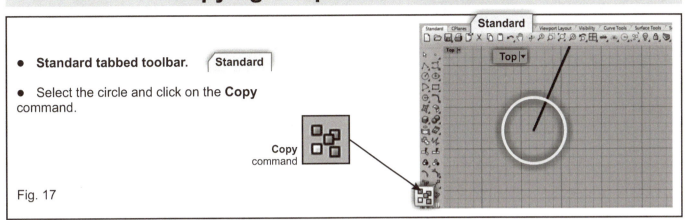

- **Standard tabbed toolbar.** ⎡Standard⎤

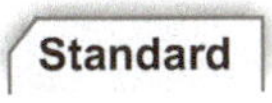

- Select the circle and click on the **Copy** command.

Copy
command

Fig. 17

- **Point to copy from** prompt:
  - Use **End osnap** to snap to the end of the polyline and click to set this location.❶

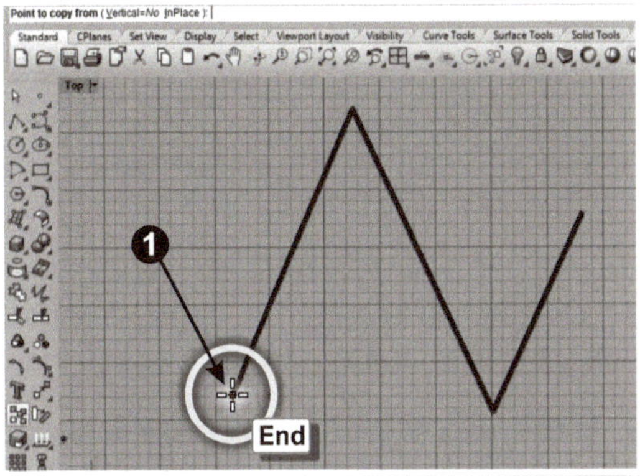

Fig. 18

- **Point to copy to** prompt:
  - Use **End osnap** to snap to the next end point as shown.
  - Click to set this location for the first copy. ❷

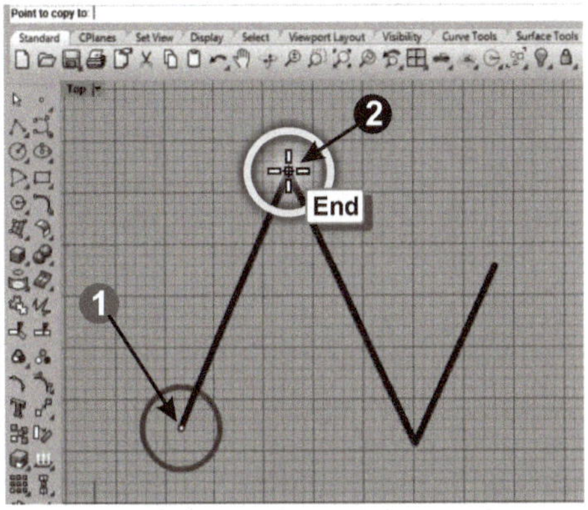

Fig. 19

- Snap to the other end points and click to make copies at desired locations. ❸ & ❹

- Press **Enter** when you have finished making the desired copies.

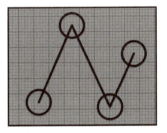

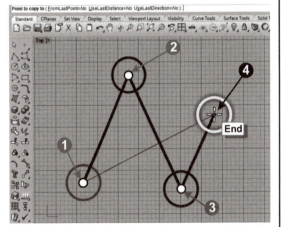

Fig. 20

- Select the circle you want to copy.

- Start to **click and drag** with the **left mouse button.**

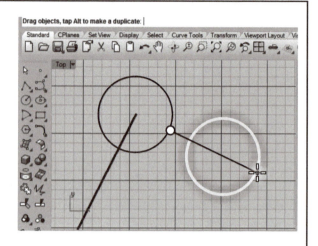

Fig. 21

- After you have started to drag the circle, **softly tap the Alt key on your keyboard once.**

- A little Plus sign will appear next to the cursor.
  - When you see this plus sign, you will know that you are making a copy!

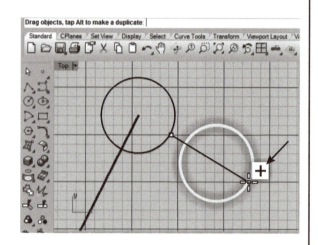

Fig. 22

- Click where you want to place the copy.

- If your circle copy is still selected, **left click** somewhere on the grid and the circle will de-select.

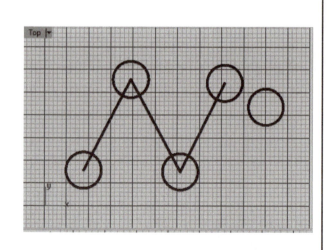

Fig. 23

Trim Command
Cutting away unwanted lines and curves for more design definition.

- **Standard tabbed toolbar.** ⎡ Standard ⎤

- Click to turn on **Grid Snap.** **Grid Snap**

Fig. 1

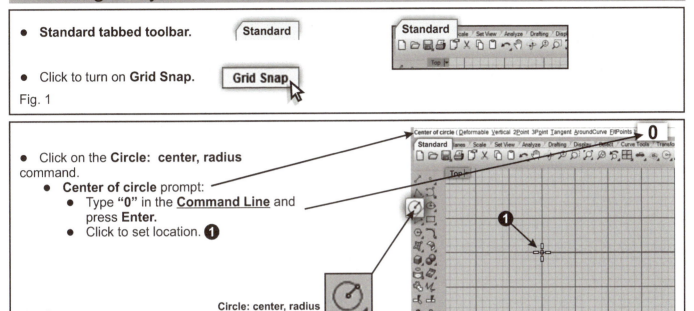

- Click on the **Circle: center, radius** command.
  - **Center of circle** prompt:
    - Type **"0"** in the **Command Line** and press **Enter.**
    - Click to set location. ❶

Circle: center, radius
command

Fig. 2

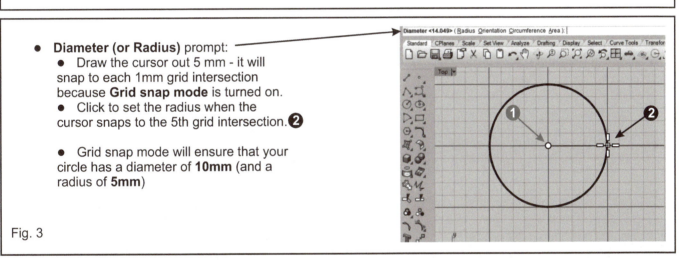

- **Diameter (or Radius)** prompt:
  - Draw the cursor out 5 mm - it will snap to each 1mm grid intersection because **Grid snap mode** is turned on.
  - Click to set the radius when the cursor snaps to the 5th grid intersection.❷

  - Grid snap mode will ensure that your circle has a diameter of **10mm** (and a radius of **5mm**)

Fig. 3

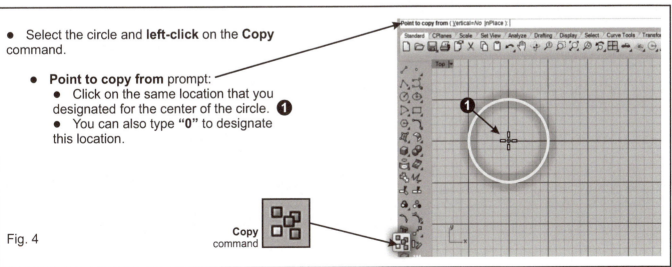

- Select the circle and **left-click** on the **Copy** command.

  - **Point to copy from** prompt:
    - Click on the same location that you designated for the center of the circle. ❶
    - You can also type **"0"** to designate this location.

Copy
command

Fig. 4

- **Point to copy to** prompt:
  - Draw the cursor out and click to set the location of the copy on the **next heavy grid line** as shown.
    - Grid Snap mode will ensure that this copy is exactly 5mm away from the original circle.
  - Click to set location. ❷
  - Press **Enter** to end the command.

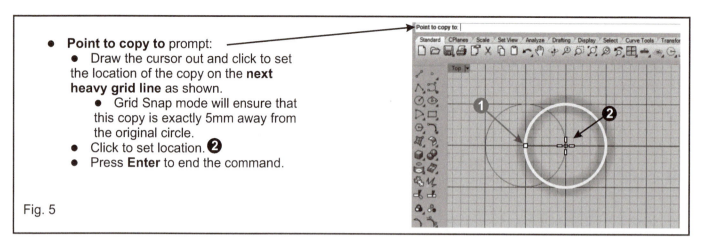

Fig. 5

- **Left-click** on the **Trim** command.
  - **Select cutting objects. Press Enter when done** prompt:
    - Select the circle shown.
    - Press **Enter.**

left-click for
Trim
command

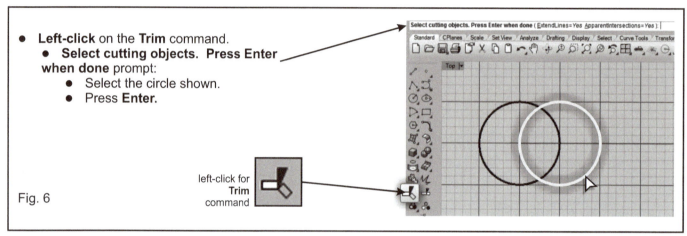

Fig. 6

- **Select object to trim** prompt:
  - Click on the part of the circle outside the cutting object as shown. ❶

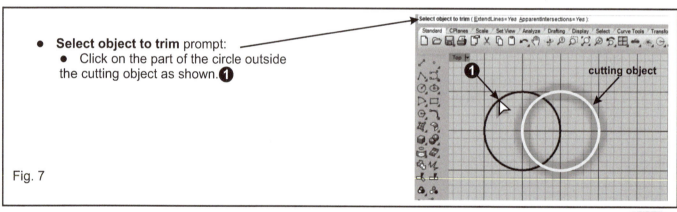

Fig. 7

- The part of the circle that you selected to trim has been trimmed away to the boundary of the cutting object.
  - Click on the **Undo** option in the **Command Line** as shown.

- The Trim has been undone and the trimmed circle has been restored.

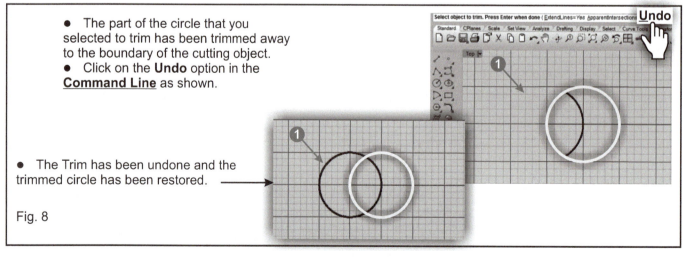

Fig. 8

- **Select object to trim. Press Enter when done** prompt:
    - This time click on the part of the circle that is running through the inside of the designated cutting object as shown.

    - The segment on the inside of the cutting object has been trimmed away.
    - Press **Enter** to end the command.

Fig. 9

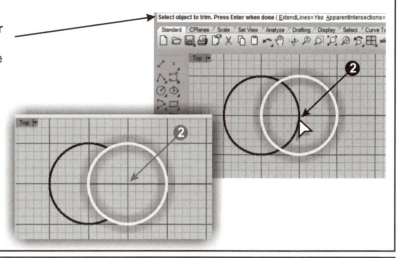

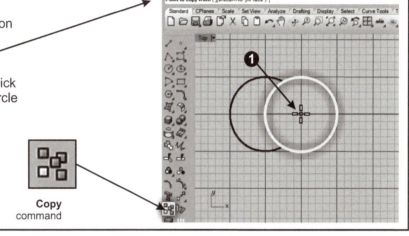

- Select the circle as shown and **left-click** on the **Copy** command.

    - **Point to copy from** prompt:
        - **Grid Snap** will make is easy to click in the exact center of the selected circle as shown. **①**

Fig. 10

Copy
command

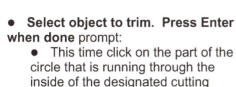

- Drag the cursor 5mm to the right and click to make the first copy.**②**
    - **Grid Snap** will make it easy to make a copy to the right, exactly 5mm away.

Fig. 11

- Make some more copies as shown, continuing to use **Grid Snap** for easy accuracy in placing a **copy every 5mm**.
- Press **Enter** to end the command.

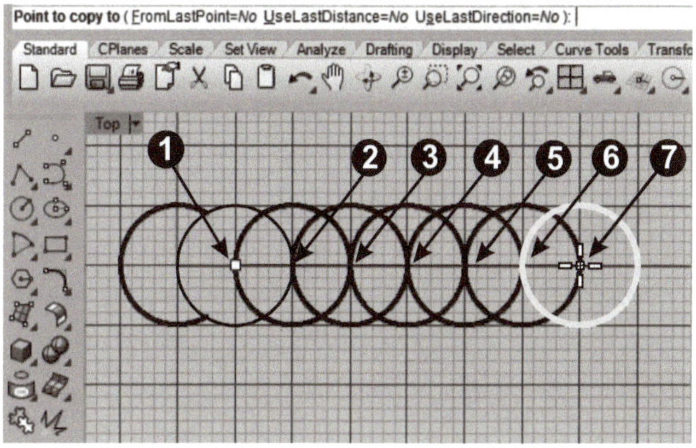

Fig. 12

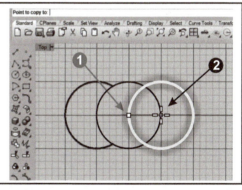

- Pre-select all of the circles as shown.

- **Left-click** on the **Trim** command.

  - **Select object to trim. Press Enter to clear selection and start over** prompt:
    - Select the circle segment as shown. ❶

Fig. 13

left-click for
Trim
command

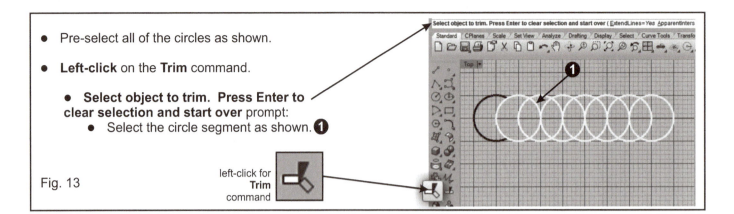

- The segment that you selected will be trimmed away. ❶
- Click on the lower segment as shown. ❷

- *Remember: if you make a mistake when you are in this command, click on the **Undo** option in the **Command Line** to go back to the previous trimming step.*

  - *You can click **Undo** as many times as you want to go back as many steps as you need.*

Fig. 14

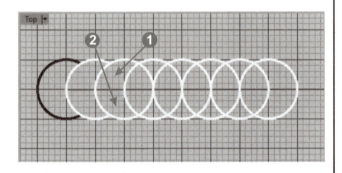

- Another segment has been trimmed away.

Fig. 15

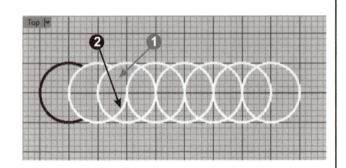

- Keep trimming away until you create the design shown.
- Press **Enter** to end the command.
- Click away to de-select all objects.

Fig. 16

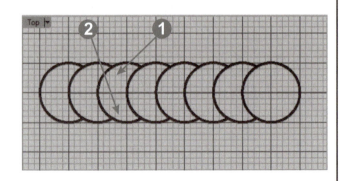

- See if you can create these simple designs, using the Circle, Polyline (or Line), and Trim commands. Grid snap will be useful.

- Create some designs of your own.

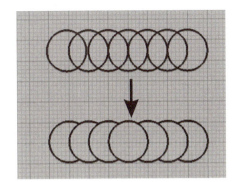

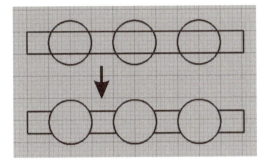

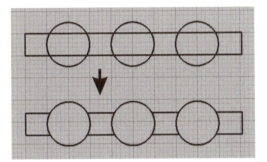

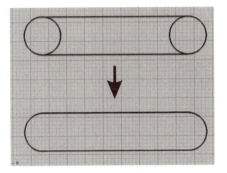

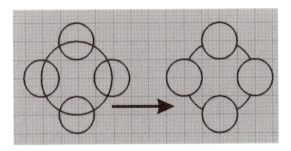

- *Try turning off grid snap and doing some more freeform designs, copying a single circle to create a more organic or freeform concept.*

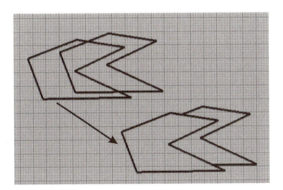

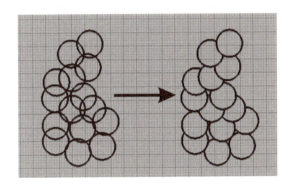

Fig. 17

From a Polyline to a Butterfly
Distance and Angle Constraints
Rebuild and Point Editing

Save this file as **polyline for butterfly.3dm** as it will be used again in a future chapter.

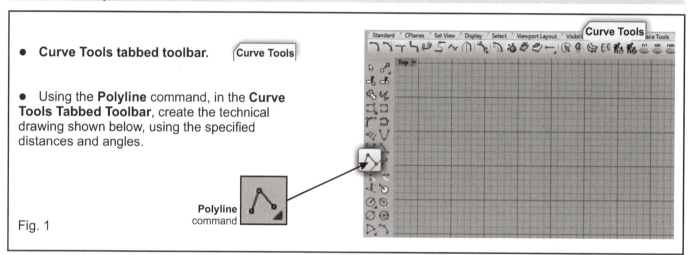

- **Curve Tools tabbed toolbar.** [Curve Tools]

- Using the **Polyline** command, in the **Curve Tools Tabbed Toolbar**, create the technical drawing shown below, using the specified distances and angles.

Polyline command

Fig. 1

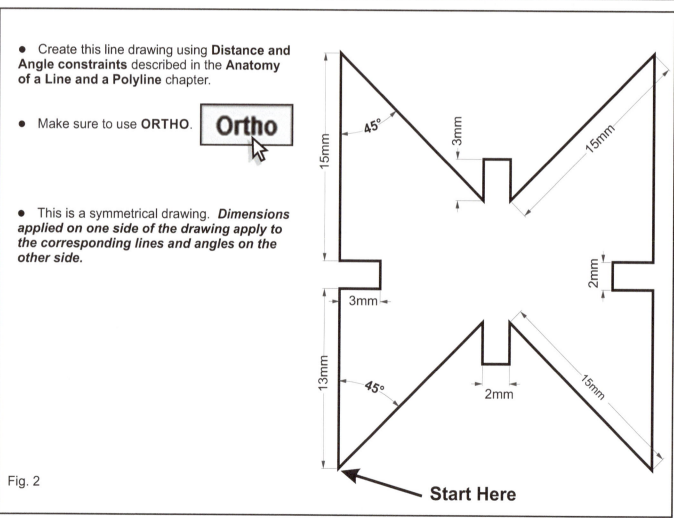

- Create this line drawing using **Distance and Angle constraints** described in the **Anatomy of a Line and a Polyline** chapter.

- Make sure to use ORTHO. **Ortho**

- This is a symmetrical drawing. *Dimensions applied on one side of the drawing apply to the corresponding lines and angles on the other side.*

45°   3mm   15mm

15mm

2mm

3mm

13mm   45°   2mm   15mm

Fig. 2

Start Here

- When you are creating the last line segment, draw the cursor over the starting point of the first line.

- You will snap to this starting point and you will see a little cursor tip that says **"Point"**, *even if you don't have Point osnap enabled at the bottom of the workspace.*

- Click on this point and your polyline will be automatically fully closed - it will be a **Closed Polyline.**

Fig. 3

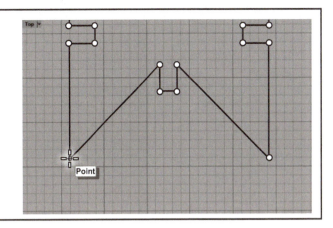

- **What if** you unintentionally end the **Polyline** command before you are finished with the drawing?

Fig. 4

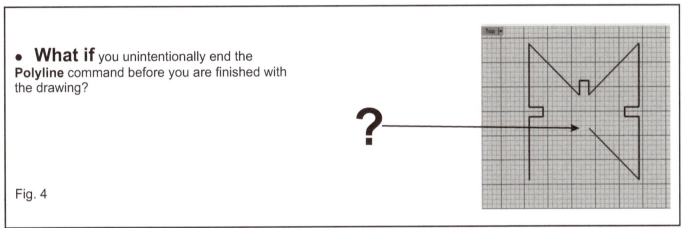

- **Left-click** on the **Continue control point curve** command.

left-click for the
Continue control pont curve
command

Fig. 5

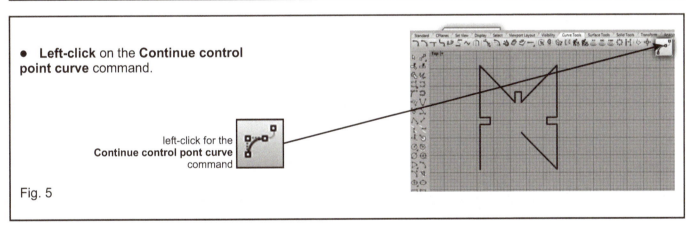

- **Select curve near end to continue** prompt:
    - Click on the line near the end from which you wish to continue as shown.

Fig. 6

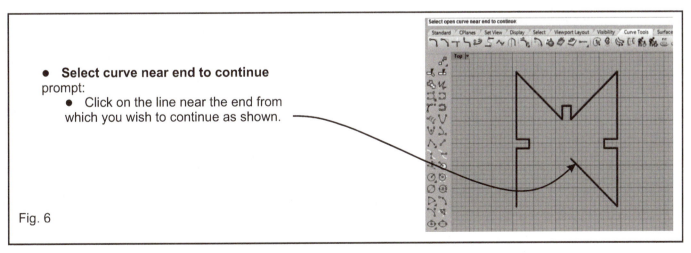

- **Next point. Press Enter when done**
prompt:
  - Type **"3"** in the **<u>Command Line</u>** and press **Enter.**

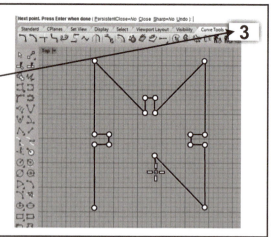

Fig. 7

- With **Ortho** enabled, click to place the next point.

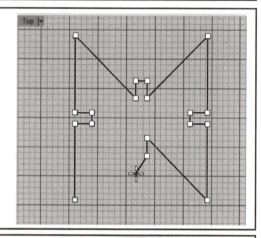

Fig. 8

- Continue with the drawing, clicking on the **Close** option in the **<u>Command Line</u>** when you are ready to create the last line segment.

- *Clicking on the **Close** option is another way of ensuring that you will be creating a **closed polyline**.*

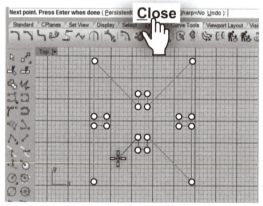

Fig. 9

- The resulting closed polyline.

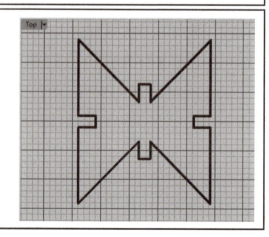

Fig. 10

Rebuilding the Polyline
Rebuilding to Create a Single Graceful Curve from a Polyline

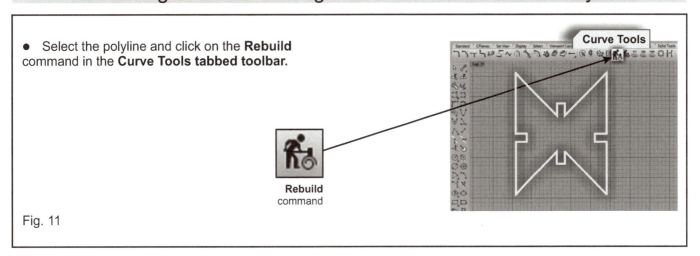

- Select the polyline and click on the **Rebuild** command in the **Curve Tools tabbed toolbar.**

Rebuild
command

Fig. 11

- The **Rebuild Curve** dialog box will appear.

- Click on the **Preview** button and a **black Preview line** will appear showing how the line will be transformed if you use the suggested point count of 10.

- See the detailed description for the **Rebuild** dialog box below.

Fig. 12

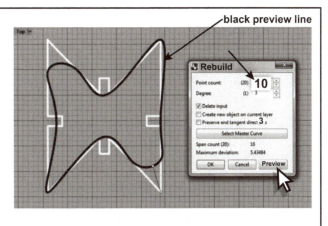

black preview line

The **Rebuild Curve** dialog box explained

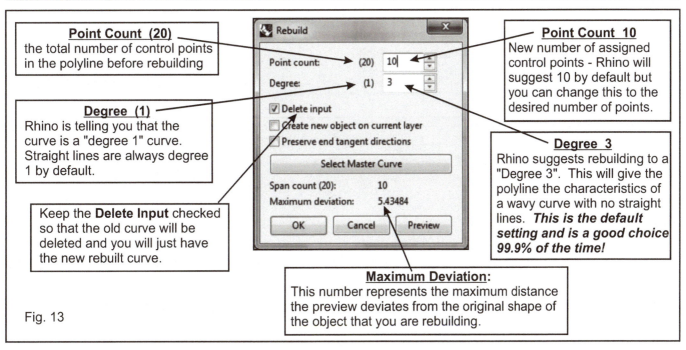

Point Count (20)
the total number of control points in the polyline before rebuilding

Degree (1)
Rhino is telling you that the curve is a "degree 1" curve. Straight lines are always degree 1 by default.

Keep the **Delete Input** checked so that the old curve will be deleted and you will just have the new rebuilt curve.

Point Count 10
New number of assigned control points - Rhino will suggest 10 by default but you can change this to the desired number of points.

Degree 3
Rhino suggests rebuilding to a "Degree 3". This will give the polyline the characteristics of a wavy curve with no straight lines. *This is the default setting and is a good choice 99.9% of the time!*

Maximum Deviation:
This number represents the maximum distance the preview deviates from the original shape of the object that you are rebuilding.

Fig. 13

- Change the number of points to **30** and click on the **Preview Button** again to update.

- Increasing the number of control points has given you much more detail and the resulting rebuilt curve will follow the general shape of the original polyline much more closely.

- **PROBLEM:** The preview line shows a shape that is <u>not symmetrical</u>!

- Click on the **Cancel** button to abort the command.

Fig. 14

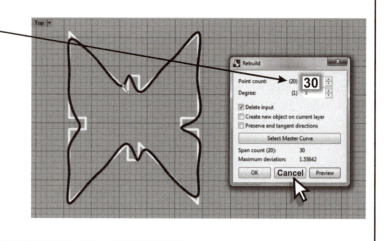

- *It is necessary to alter the geometry of the polyline so that it can be rebuilt into a symmetrical shape.*

- Select the polyline and click on the **Adjust closed curve seam** command as shown.

Adjust closed curve seam
command

Fig. 15

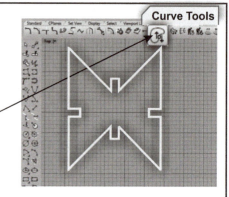

- **Drag seam point to adjust. Press Enter when done** prompt:
    - Notice that at one angle, a point and an arrow will appear. This is the **"Curve Seam"**.
        - *Note: your curve seam may be at a different location - that does not matter.*
    - It is necessary to move this curve seam so that it is in a more central location on the polyline.

Fig. 16

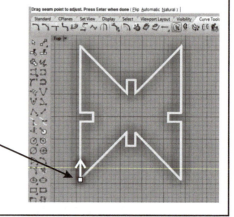

- Click to enable **Mid osnap.**

- Click and drag the point and arrow along the polyline as shown.
- While you are dragging, a little **OnCrv** tip will appear.

Fig. 17

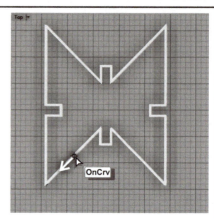

- Draw the cursor along the polyline until it snaps to the **Midpoint** of the line shown.
- **Left-click** to set this new *central location* for the curve seam.

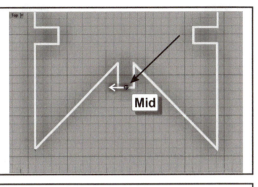

Fig. 18

- After you have **left-clicked,** you will see the new location of the curve seam.

- The **curve seam** is now placed on the exact midpoint of the short horizontal line shown.

- Press **Enter** to end the command.

- **Save the file at this point as: polyline for butterfly.3dm. We will be using this polyline again for chapters further along in the book.**

Fig. 19

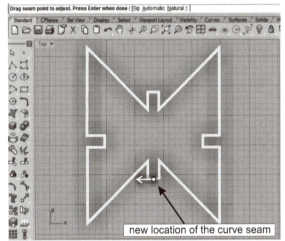

new location of the curve seam

- Select the polyline and click on the **Rebuild** command once again.

- Click on the **Preview** button in the **Rebuild Curve** dialog box.
    - **Notice that now the preview is symmetrical!**
    - Make sure that you assign the point count as **30.**
    - Click on the **OK** button in the **Rebuild Curve** dialog box.

Fig. 20

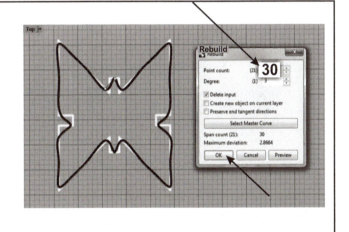

- The rebuilt curve is now symmetrical.

- Pre-select the polyline.

- Press the **Esc** key to turn control points off.

left-click for
Points On
command

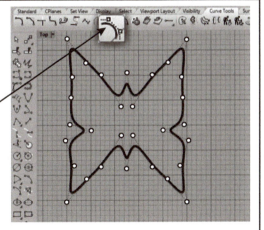

Fig. 21

- Window select the 2 control points shown.
  - For a selection window, click and drag from **1** to **2**, making sure that the window includes just the two points indicated.

- Press the **Delete** key on your keyboard to delete these points.

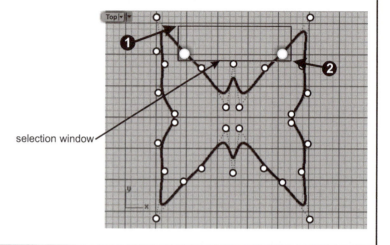

Fig. 22

- The shape of the wings has been simplified.

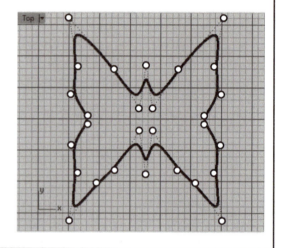

Fig. 23

- Start to click and drag control points to create the final butterfly shape.

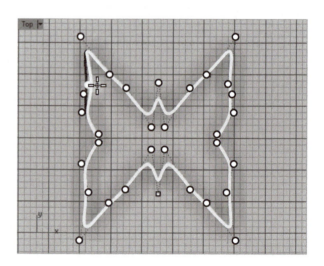

Fig. 24

- Making sure to use **ORTHO**, create 2 horizontal straight lines on the head and lower body of the butterfly as shown.

- You are going to add some control points to the head and lower body to allow for more design definition in these areas.

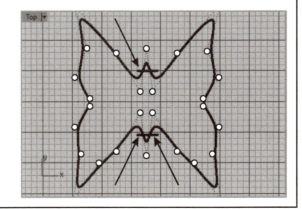

Fig. 25

- Enable **Intersection osnap**.

- Click on the **Insert Knot** command in the **Point Edit** toolbar flyout.

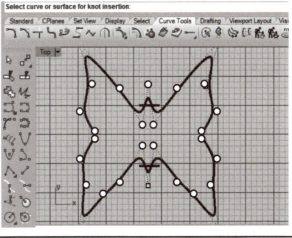

accesses the **Point Edit** toolbar flyout

Insert Knot command

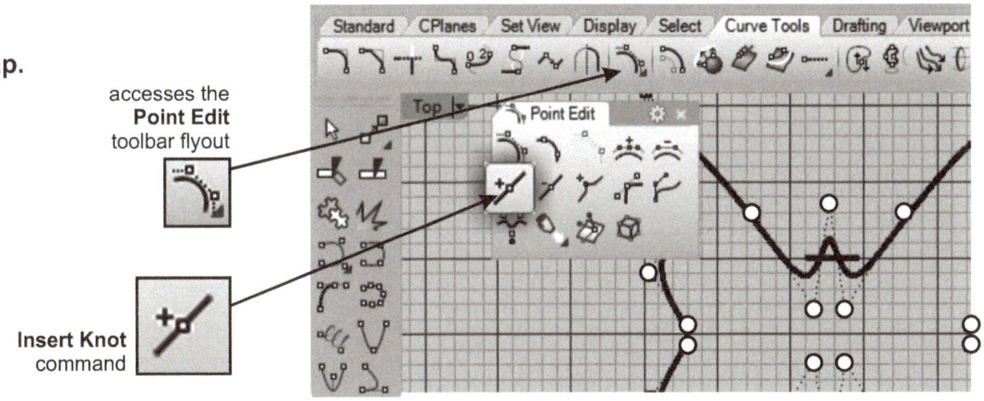

Fig. 26

- **Select curve or surface for knot insertion** prompt:
  - Select the butterfly curve.
    - note: The butterfly curve will not turn yellow when selected but that is OK for this command.

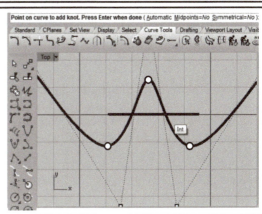

Fig. 27

- **Point on curve to add knot. Press Enter when done** prompt:
  - **Zoom** in and **Pan** up to the head of the butterfly.
  - Snap to the intersection shown and click to add a control point. ❶

Fig. 28

● Click on the intersection on the other side as shown to add another control point. **2**

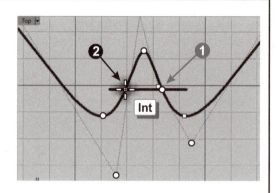

Fig. 29

● Pan to the bottom of the design to add 2 more control points as shown - **3** & **4**

● Press **Enter** to end the command.

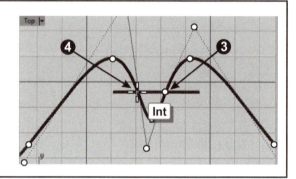

Fig. 30

● At the top and the bottom of the body of the butterfly, 2 control points have been added at each location.

● The two horizontal reference lines added in Fig. 25 can be deleted or hidden by selecting them and pressing the **Delete key**.

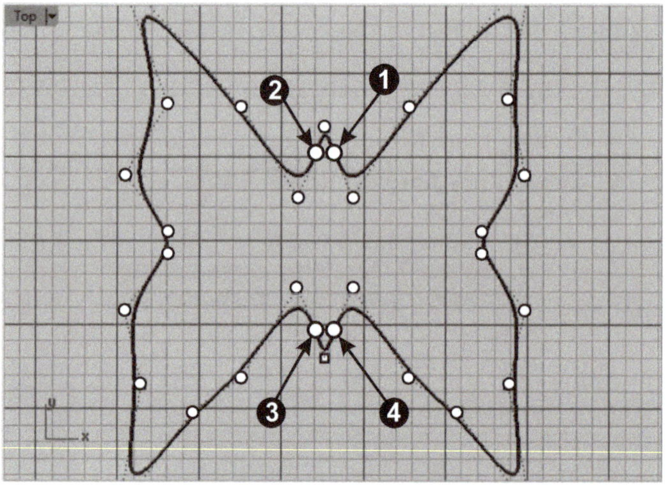

Fig. 31

● Point edit with your newly added control points and notice how much more flexibility you have to form the head and body of the butterfly.

● Save this file as **butterfly design.3dm** because you want the original **polyline for butterfly.3dm** file for a future chapter.

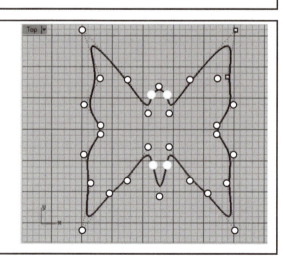

Fig. 32

Some Ways to Create a Butterfly Shape in this Exercise

● Total symmetry is not important for this exercise but will be covered later in the **Scale 1-D** and **Scale 2-D** commands which are very useful for point editing with symmetry.

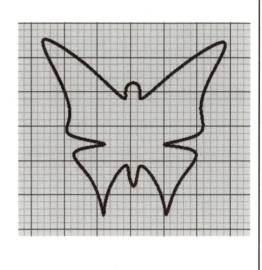

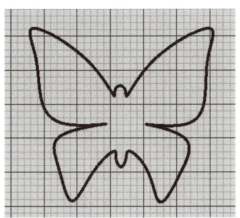

Fig. 33

● Many points on the right of the line were deleted to create this side view of a butterfly.

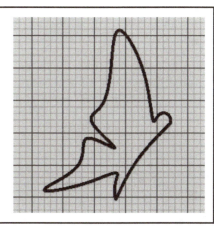

Fig. 34

● Deleting control points can create simplified shapes.

● Using the **Copy** and the **Trim** commands can open up many creative opportunities.

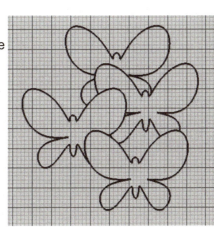

Fig. 35

Stone & Prong Layout
Creating with circles. Working with Layers.

Drawing the Stones

- Open Rhino and save the file as **stones & prongs.3dm**.

- **Curve Tools tabbed toolbar.**   Curve Tools

- Use the **Circle: center, radius** command to create a **10mm diameter** circle around "**0**" as shown.

Fig. 1

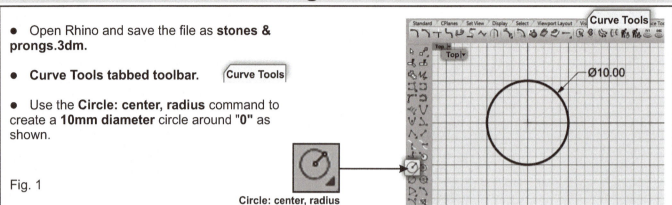

Circle: center, radius
command

- Make sure that **Quad osnap** is enabled.

  ☑ Quad

- Click on the **Circle: diameter** command:
  - **Start of diameter** prompt:
    - Snap to the **Quad** point on the right side of the 10mm circle as shown.
    - Click to set location. **❶**

Fig. 2

Circle: diameter
command

- **End of diameter** prompt:
  - Type a "**6**" in the **Command Line**.
  - Press **Enter**.

Fig. 3

- Draw the cursor out to the right, using **ORTHO** to keep the diameter perfectly horizontal.

  - Click to set location of the end of the diameter. **❷**

- A new 6mm diameter circle will be created in contact with the 10mm circle.

Fig. 4

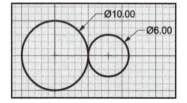

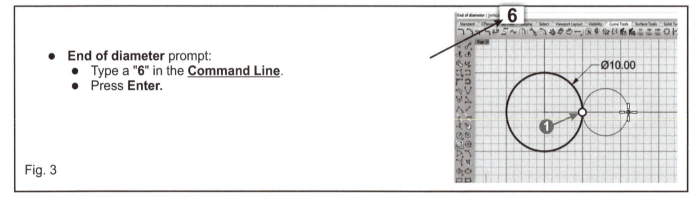

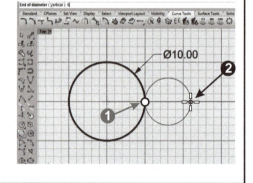

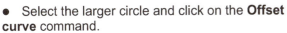

- Select the larger circle and click on the **Offset curve** command.
  - **Side to offset** prompt:
    - Draw the cursor into the inside of the circle to determine on which side of the line the offset will be created.

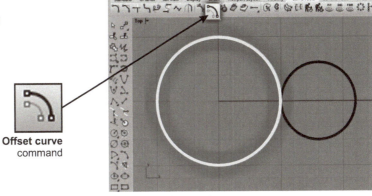

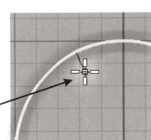

Offset curve
command

- Notice that a ***preview of the offset distance*** is now attached to the cursor, previewing the default 1mm offset distance (or the distance when the command was last used) which you will change.

  - *Note: Make sure that the cursor is on the inside of the circle as this will decide what side of the curve the offset will be created.*

Fig. 5

Side to offset (<u>D</u>istance=*1* <u>C</u>orner=*Sharp* <u>T</u>hroughPoint T<u>o</u>lerance=*0.001* <u>B</u>othSides <u>I</u>nCPlane=*Yes* C<u>a</u>p=*None*): **.5**

- **Side to offset** prompt:
  - Type **".5"** in the **Command Line** to set the offset distance.
  - Press **Enter.**
    - The offset distance preview will reflect the new designated offset distance of .5mm.

  - Click to set location.

Fig. 6

- The large circle now has a smaller circle inside it at an offset distance of .5mm.

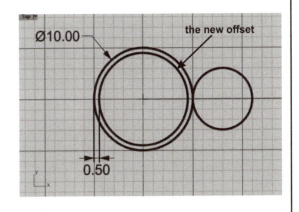

Ø10.00

the new offset

0.50

Fig. 7

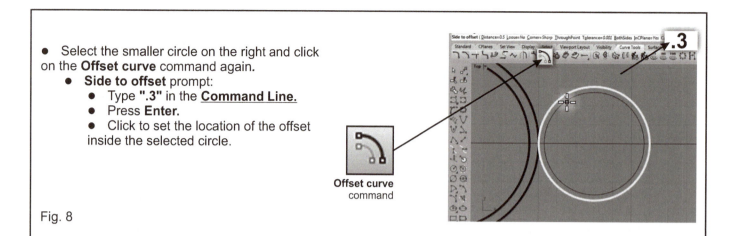

- Select the smaller circle on the right and click on the **Offset curve** command again.
  - **Side to offset** prompt:
    - Type **".3"** in the **Command Line.**
    - Press **Enter.**
    - Click to set the location of the offset inside the selected circle.

Offset curve
command

Fig. 8

- Both circles now have offsets that will guide the placement of prongs.
  - The offset for the larger circle is .5mm.
  - The offset for the smaller circle is .3mm.

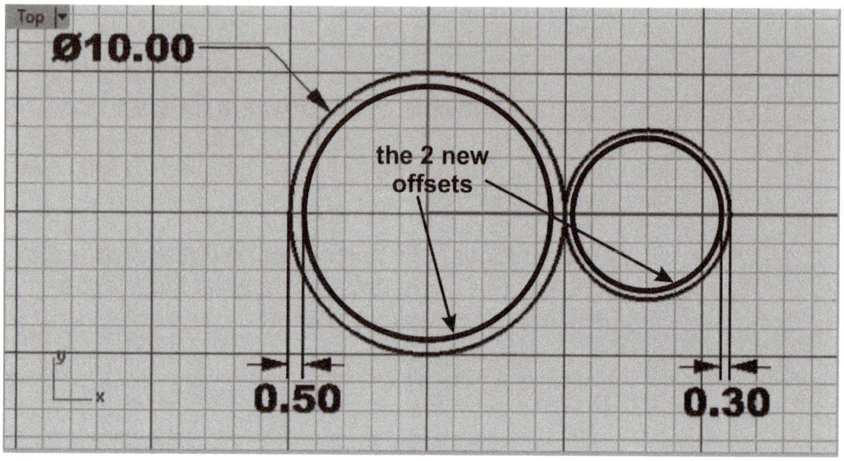

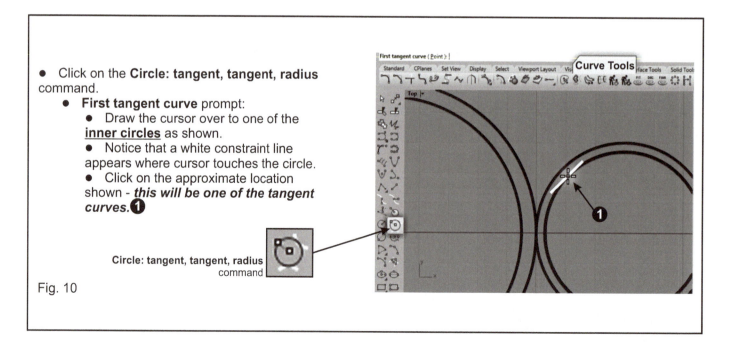

Ø10.00

the 2 new offsets

0.50

0.30

Fig. 9

Drawing the Shared Prong
Circle: Tangent, Tangent, Radius Command

- Click on the **Circle: tangent, tangent, radius** command.
  - **First tangent curve** prompt:
    - Draw the cursor over to one of the **inner circles** as shown.
    - Notice that a white constraint line appears where cursor touches the circle.
    - Click on the approximate location shown - *this will be one of the tangent curves.*❶

Circle: tangent, tangent, radius
command

Fig. 10

- **<u>Second tangent curve or radius</u>** prompt:
  - Draw the cursor over to the **<u>inner circle</u>** on the other side and notice the white constraint line where the cursor touches the inner circle.
  - Click to set location. ❷

- **<u>Radius</u>** prompt:
  - Type "**.75**" and press **Enter.**

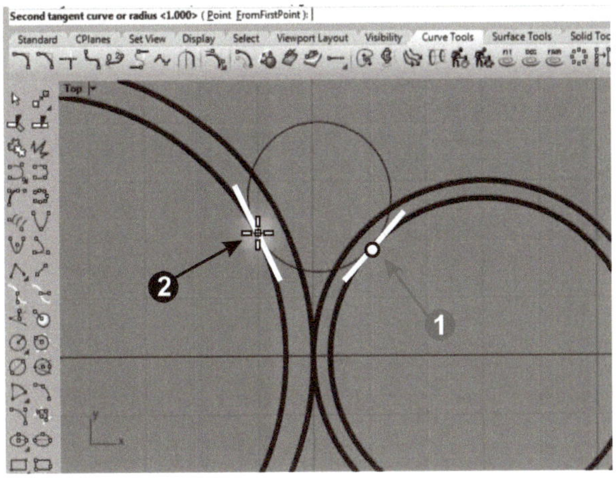

Fig. 11

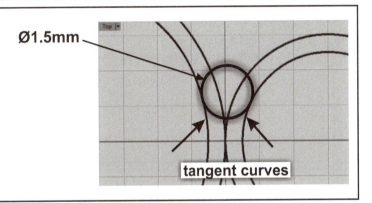

- The resulting prong will be tangent to both assigned tangent curves.

- The prong will have a diameter of 1.5mm because the assigned radius was .75mm

Fig. 12

Ø1.5mm

tangent curves

Drawing the Other Prongs

- Click to activate **Quad osnap.**

  ☑ Quad

- Click on the **Circle: diameter** command.
  - **Start of diameter** prompt:
    - Snap to the upper quad point of the **<u>inner</u>** large circle as shown.
    - Click to set location. ❶

Fig. 13

Circle: diameter command

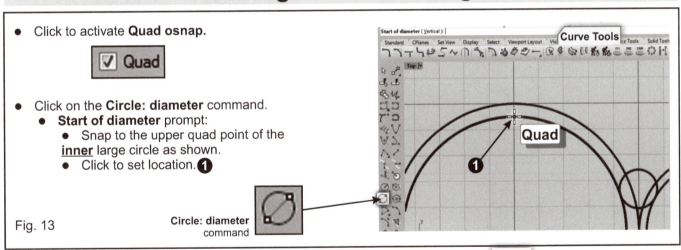

Quad

- **End of diameter** prompt:
  - Type "**1.5**" in the **<u>Command Line.</u>** ❷
  - Press **Enter.**
  - Using **ORTHO**, draw the cursor upward and click to set location. ❸

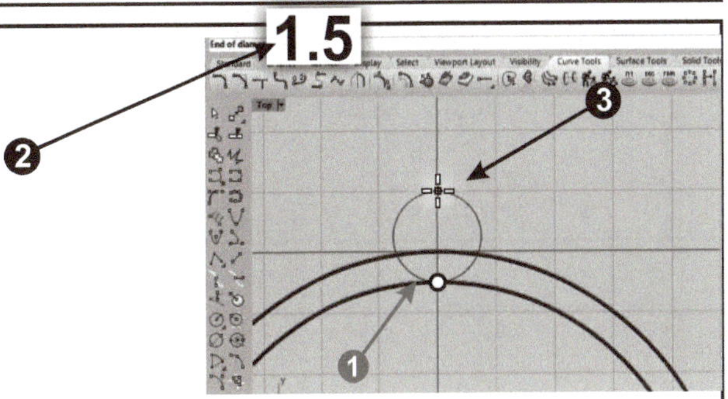

Fig. 14

1.5

- Select the outer smaller curve as shown and click on the **Offset Curve** command.
  - **Side to offset** prompt:
    - Type "**.5**" in the **Command Line**.
    - Press **Enter**.
    - Click to set location on the inside of the circle being offset.

Fig. 15

Offset curve
command

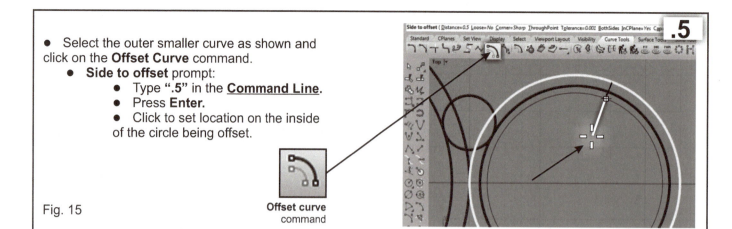

- A new offset has been created on the inside of the small circle for the purpose of providing an offset distance for the last prong.

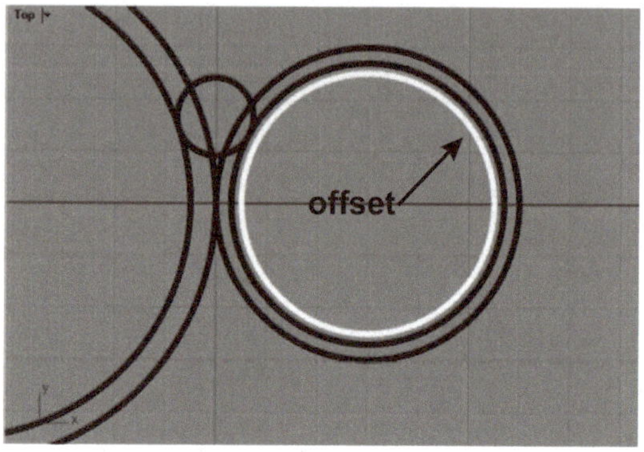

Fig. 16

offset

- Click on the **Circle: diameter** command once again.
  - **Start of diameter** prompt:
    - Snap to the **Quad** of the inner circle shown and click to set location. ❶
    - Type "**1.5**" in the **Command Line** and press **Enter**.

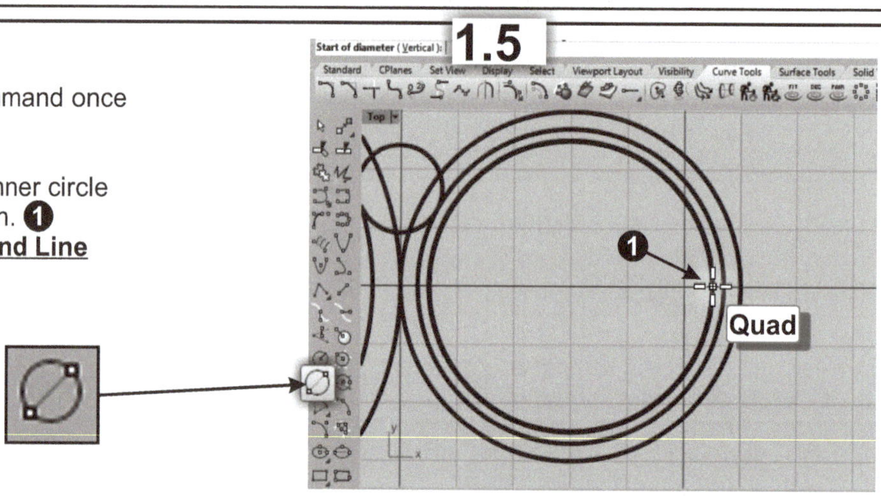

Circle: diameter
command

Fig. 17

1.5

Quad

❶

- The diameter is constrained to 1.5mm.
  - Use **ORTHO** to make sure that the cursor is being drawn out in a perfectly horizontal direction so that the prong will be evenly placed along the X axis.
- Click to set location. ❷

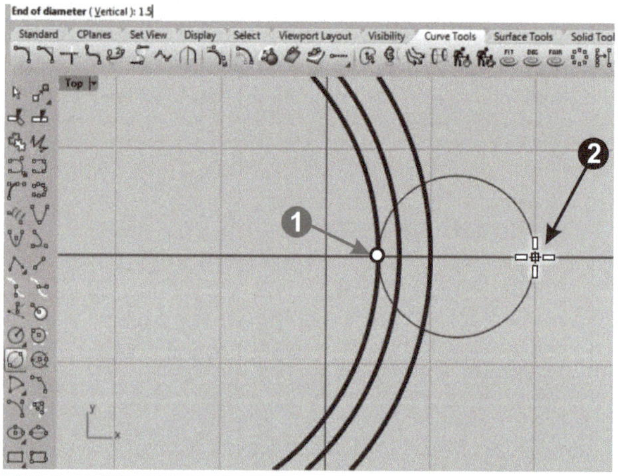

Fig. 18

❶

❷

87

- The 3 prongs have been created.

- All are **1.5mm in diameter.**

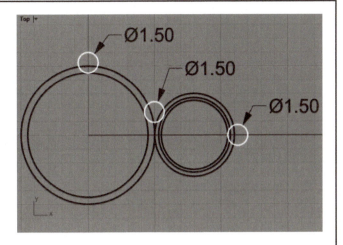

Fig. 19

Drawing a Stone within a Square Frame

- Navigate your view to a clear area above the 3-stone drawing just created.

- Click on **Grid Snap.**

- Click on the **Circle: center, radius** command.
  - **Center of circle** prompt:
    - Click on the intersection of the Y axis (green color) and a major (darker) grid line as shown. ❶

Circle: center, radius
command

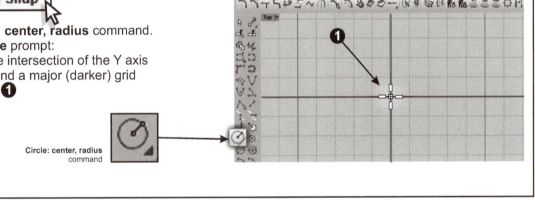

Fig. 20

- **Diameter** prompt:
  - Type a **"10"** in the **Command Line.**
  - Press **Enter.**
  - Click to set location.

- Make sure that your **Diameter** option was enabled in the **Command Line.** If your **Radius** option was enabled, you needed to type a **"5"** because you would be designating the radius, not the diameter of the 10mm circle!

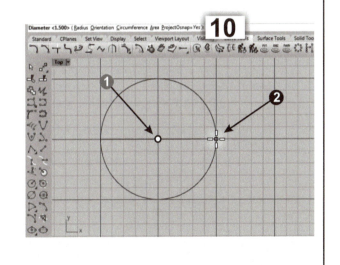

Fig. 21

88

- Use the **Polyline** command to draw an accurate 10mm x 10mm square to enclose the circle as shown, ***drawing the polyline segments along the heavy grid lines.***

- Grid snap will make this an easy and accurate task.

Grid Snap

Fig. 22

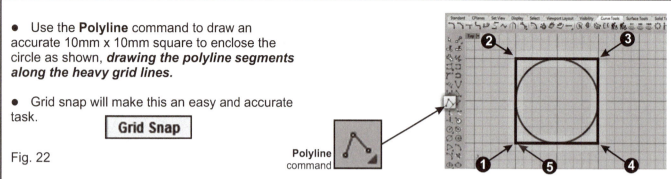

Polyline
command

- **Offset** the circle to create an inner circle.
  - **Offset distance: .5mm**
  - **Diameter of new offset circle: 9m**

- **Clicl to toggle off Grid Snap.**

Grid Snap

Fig. 23

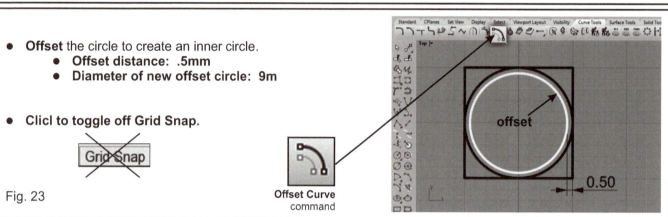

Offset Curve
command

offset

0.50

Drawing the Corner Prong
Circle: Tangent to 3 Curves Command

- Click on the **Circle: tangent to 3 curves** command in the **Circle** toolbar flyout.
  - **First tangent curve** prompt:
    - Draw the cursor over the curve shown.
    - A point and a white constraint line will appear when the cursor snaps to the line.
    - Click to assign this line as the first tangent curve. **1**

accesses the
Circle
toolbar flyout

Fig. 24

Circle: tangent to 3 curves
command

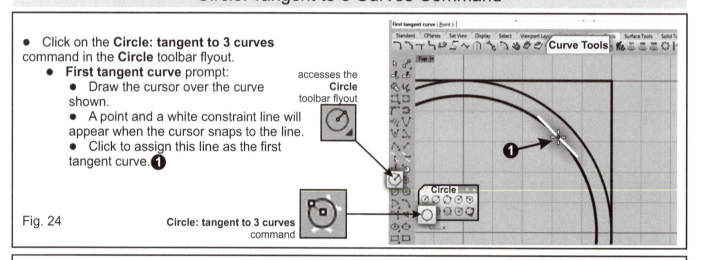

- **Second tangent curve or radius** prompt:
  - Draw the cursor over to the line shown.
  - A point and white constraint line will appear again.
  - Click to assign this line as the second tangent curve. **2**

Fig. 25

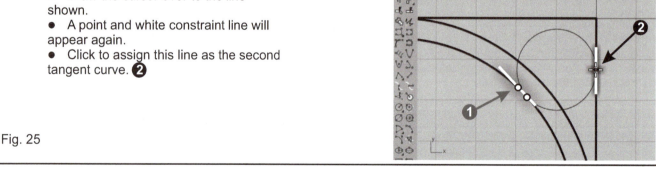

89

- **Third tangent curve. Press Enter to draw circle from first two points** prompt:
  - Draw the cursor across the line shown.
  - Click to set location when you see the point and white constraint line. ❸

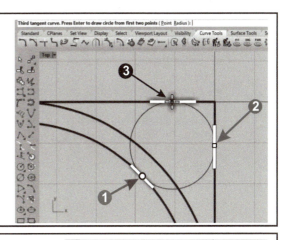

Fig. 26

- The circle is accurately touching all 3 tangent curves.

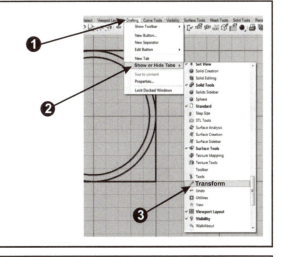

Fig. 27

Symmetrical Completion of the Stone & Prong Layout
Mirror Command

- **Transform tabbed toolbar.**

- If the tab for this toolbar is not showing among the other tabs, follow these steps to access it:

> **accessing the Transform tabbed toolbar**
>
> - **Right-click** on any tab. ❶
> - Click on the **Show or Hide Tabs** option in the drop down menu. ❷
> - Click on the **Transform** option in the second drop-down menu. ❸

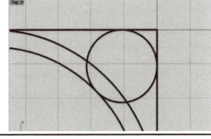

Fig. 28

- Click to enable **Grid Snap.** | **Grid Snap**

- Select the Prong circle and left-click on the **Mirror** command in the **Transform Tabbed Toolbar.**

  - **Start of mirror plane** prompt:
    - Snap to a grid location along the **Y Axis which runs through the center of the drawing.**
    - Click to set location. ❶

left click for **Mirror** command

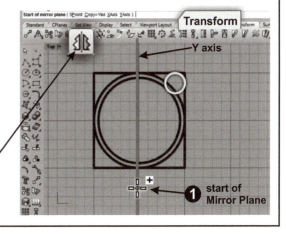

Fig. 29

- **End of mirror plane** prompt:
  - Draw the cursor straight up **along the Y axis.**
  - Snap to a grid intersection on the Y axis.
  - Click as shown to assign location of the end of the mirror plane.❷

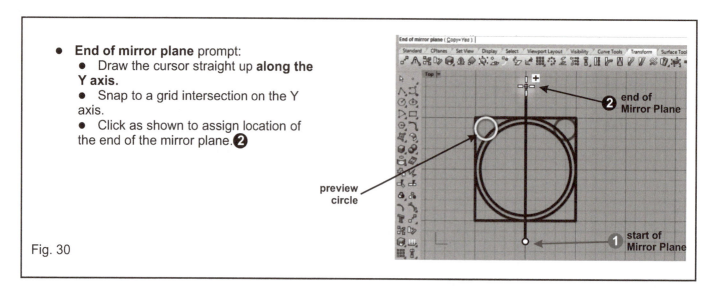

Fig. 30

- Click to enable **Center Osnap.** ☑ Cen

Select the two prongs shown and left-click on the **Mirror** command again.

- **Start of mirror plane** prompt:
  - Snap to the center of the circles as shown.❶
  - Click to set location.

- **End of mirror plane** prompt:
  - Using **ORTHO,** draw the cursor out ⬚ Ortho horizontally.
  - Click to set the **End of the mirror plane**. ❷

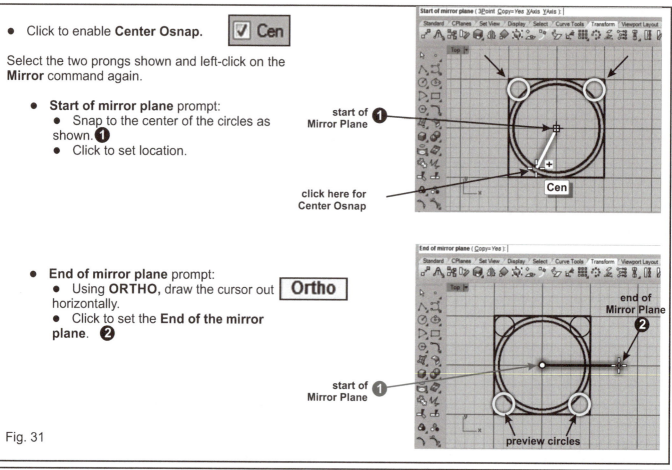

Fig. 31

- The **Mirror Planes** were both set so that they ran through the exact center of the drawing.

- All 4 prongs are now in place for a symmetrical drawing.

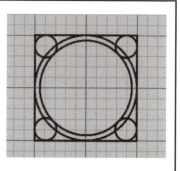

Fig. 32

- Navigate to the other drawing.

- Select the 2 prongs shown and click on the **Mirror** command.

    - **Start of mirror plane** prompt:
        - Type **"0"** in the **Command Line.**
        - Press **Enter.**

- The **Start of the Mirror Plane** will be located exactly at **"0", where the X and Y axes cross.** ❶

    - **End of mirror plane** prompt:
        - Using **Ortho**, draw the cursor out to the right. **Ortho**

        - Click to set the **End of Mirror Plane.** ❷

start of Mirror Plane "0"

left-click for **Mirror** command

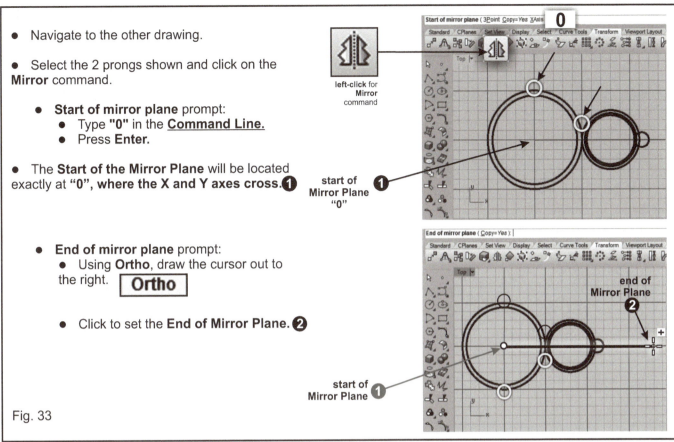

Fig. 33

- Select the 3 prongs and the outer small circle shown and click on the **Mirror** command.

    - **Start of mirror plane** prompt:
        - Type **"0"** in the **Command Line.**
        - Press **Enter.** ❶

start of Mirror Plane "0"

    - **End of mirror plane** prompt:
        - Using **ORTHO**, draw the cursor straight upward.
        - Click to set the **End of the Mirror Plane.** ❷

start of Mirror Plane ❶

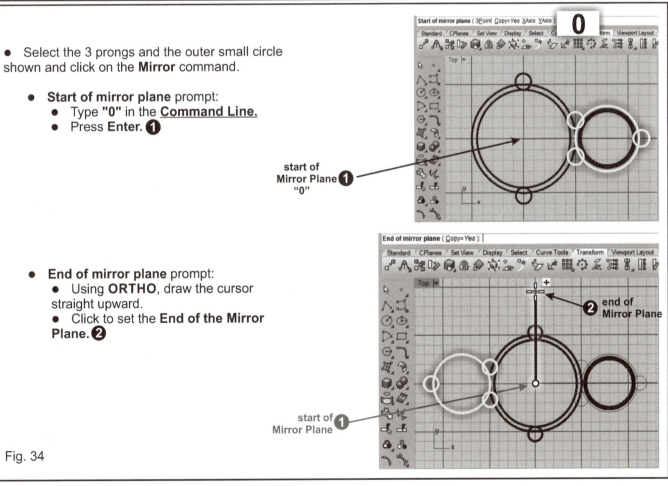

Fig. 34

92

- A symmetrical drawing has been created as both mirror planes ran through the center of the drawing.

- *note: Some of the inner circles were not mirrored over because they are no longer needed for the final drawing.*

- Notice that all of your lines are the same color. That is because they have all been created on the same **"Layer"**.

Fig. 35

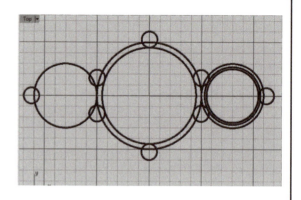

Organizing Your Work by Assigning Layers to Objects
Applying Layers to Stone & Prong Layout

- **Standard tabbed toolbar.** 〈 **Standard** 〉

- The **Tabbed Panels** are docked on the right of your workspace.

- Click on the **Layers tab** if another panel is showing its window. This will bring the Layers panel to the front as shown.

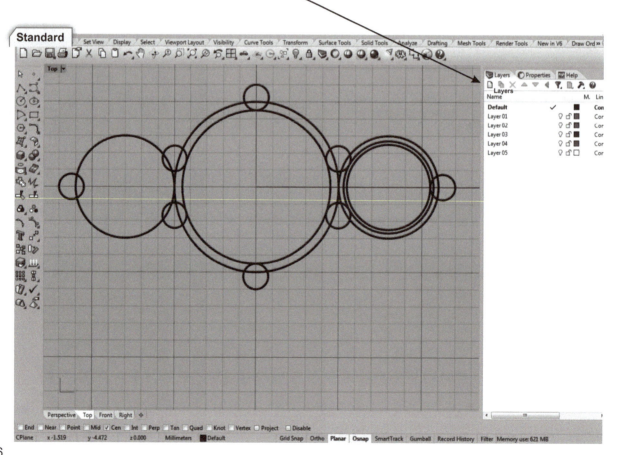

Fig. 36

If there is no Layers Tabbed Panel Showing
Opening the Layers Tabbed Panel

- In this illustration, the Layers Panel is not included in the group of docked Panels on the right of the workspace.

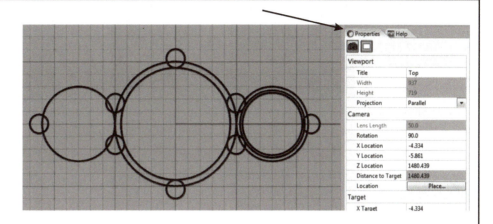

Fig. 37

- **Right-click** on one of the **tabs** in the panel as shown. ❶

- A drop-down context menu will appear listing the various panels that are available for docking.

- Click on the **Layers** line as shown. ❷

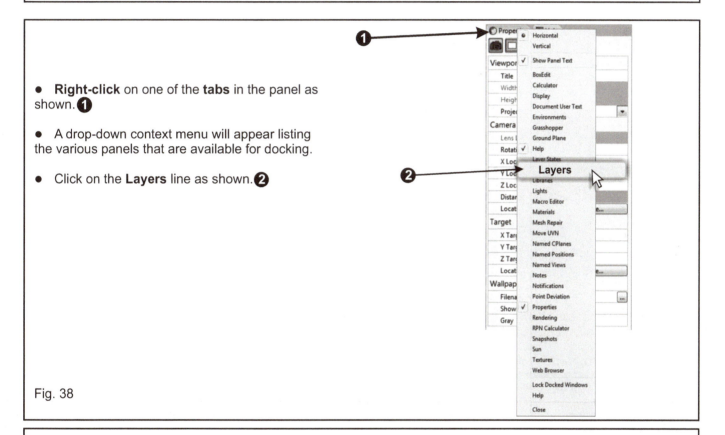

Fig. 38

- The **Layers** tab will now be added to the group as shown.

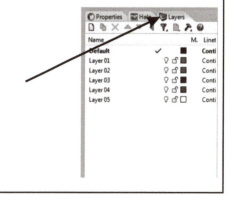

Fig. 39

If No Panels are Showing in the Workspace

- The **Panels** drop-down ❶ in the **Menu Bar** at the top of the workspace offers most of the available categories that can be included in the panels grouping.
- Click on the **Layers** category as shown. ❷

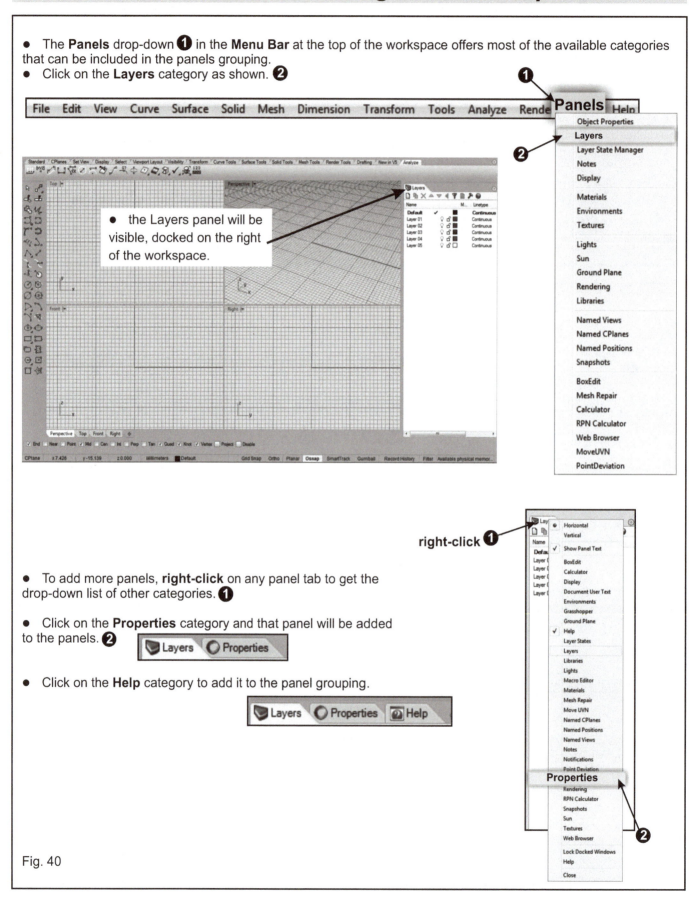

- To add more panels, **right-click** on any panel tab to get the drop-down list of other categories. ❶

- Click on the **Properties** category and that panel will be added to the panels. ❷

- Click on the **Help** category to add it to the panel grouping.

Fig. 40

● If the panel already contains more than one tab and you can not see the layers window, click on the **Layers** tab and the Layers window will be displayed.

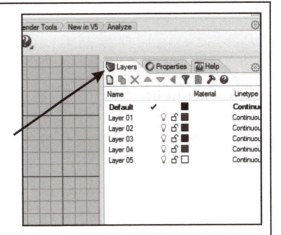

Fig. 41

The Layers Panel

● The list of layers that you see here is the default configuration.

● To read the full names of the tabs and layers, pull the panel ❶ and column headings ❷ out to widen it's visibility.

pull out layers panel ❶

pull out individual column headings
❷

● Click to place a check mark in the **Default** layer as shown. ❸
  ● This indicates that this is the **"Current"** layer. Anything that you draw will be on the **Current** layer

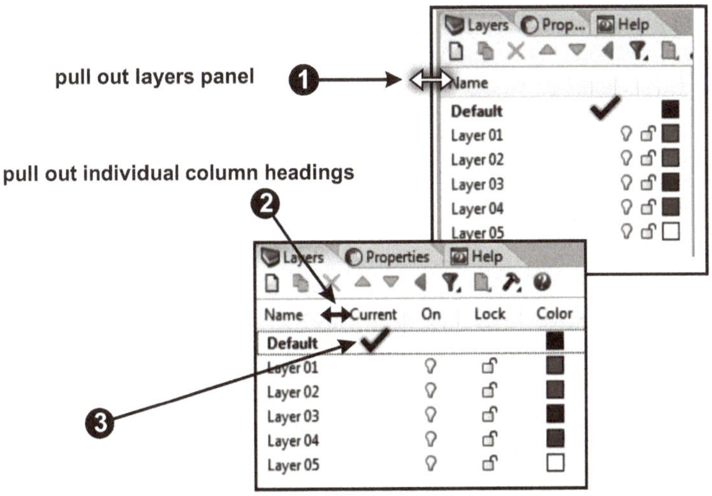

❸

Fig. 42

● **Right-click** on the word **"Default** in the column with the word **"Name"** at its head. ❶

● A drop-down context menu will appear.

● Slide the cursor down to **"Rename Layer"** and **left-click** to select that option. ❷

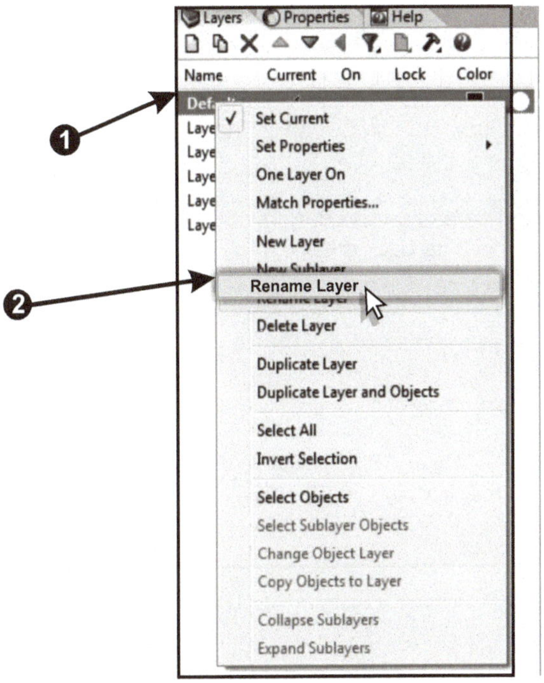

❶

❷

Set Current
Set Properties
One Layer On
Match Properties...

New Layer
New Sublayer
Rename Layer
Delete Layer

Duplicate Layer
Duplicate Layer and Objects

Select All
Invert Selection

Select Objects
Select Sublayer Objects
Change Object Layer
Copy Objects to Layer

Collapse Sublayers
Expand Sublayers

Fig. 43

- Rename the **default** layer **STONES**, as shown.

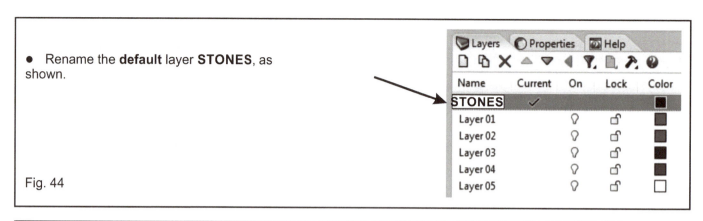

Fig. 44

- Rename the next 3 layers as shown, using the same procedure.

- Notice that some layer names are in upper case and some are in lower case.
  - This is a suggested way to organize the layers for quick and easy identification and selection.

Fig. 45

- Click on the little color box on the **PRONGS** layer line as shown.

- The **Select Layer Color** dialog box will open.

- Click on the **Dark Green** color in the list on the left as shown.
  - You may have to scroll up to see the basic colors at the top of the list that you see here.

- Click the OK button at the bottom of the dialog box.

- The assigned color for the **PRONGS** layer will now be dark green.

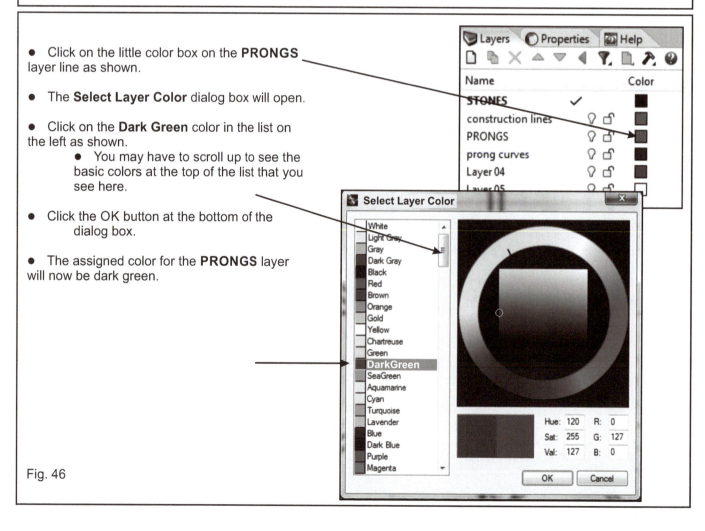

Fig. 46

97

- Assign colors for all the layers:
  - **STONES:** Black (already black)
  - **construction lines: Red**
  - **PRONGS:** Dark Green
  - **prong curves:** Brown

- This color coding is a useful way to quickly and easily identify and select objects as you work.

Fig. 47

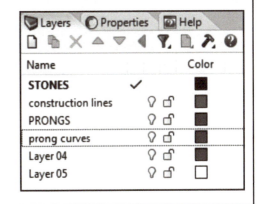

- Select all of the prong circles for both drawings as shown.

- **Right-click** on the **PRONGS** line as shown.

Fig. 48

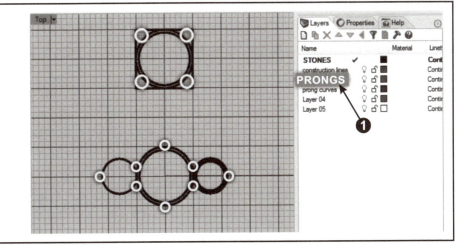

- A context drop-down menu will appear.

- Run the cursor down the list and click on the line that says **Change Object Layer.** ❷

Fig. 49

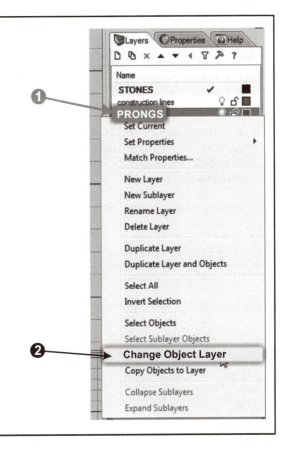

98

- Click away to de-select the prongs and notice that they are now green because they are now all on the **PRONGS** layer.

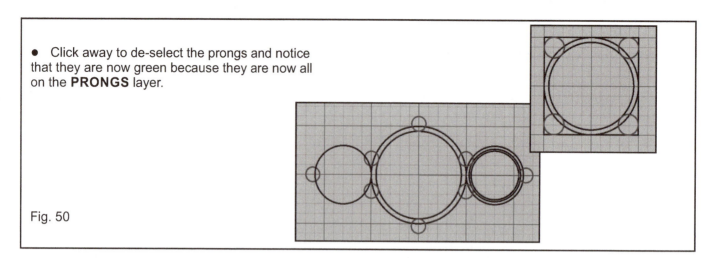

Fig. 50

Changing Layers using the
Alternative Status Bar Method

- Select the 4 inner circles as shown.

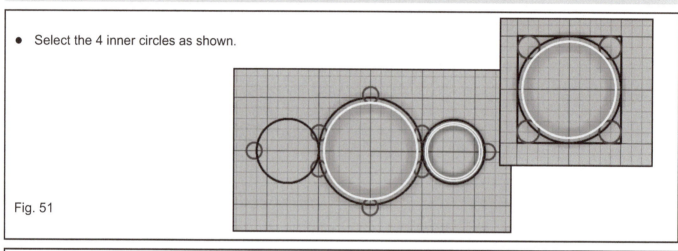

Fig. 51

- Click on the **Layer** button in the **Status Bar** at the bottom of the workspace. ❶

    - *[The button says **STONES** because that is the active layer at present. If an object from another layer is presently selected, the button will read the name of the layer of the selected object.]*

- A context pop-up menu will appear.

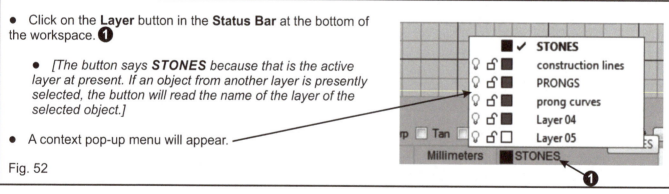

Fig. 52

Click on the **prong curves** line. ❷

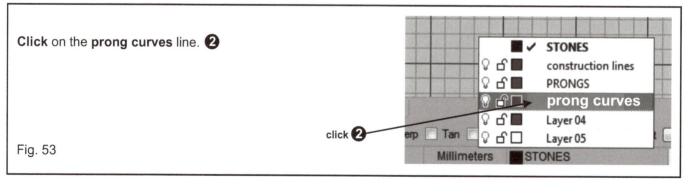

click ❷

Fig. 53

99

- Click away to de-select the inner circles.

- All of the inner circles are on the **prong curves layer** - note their **brown coloration.**

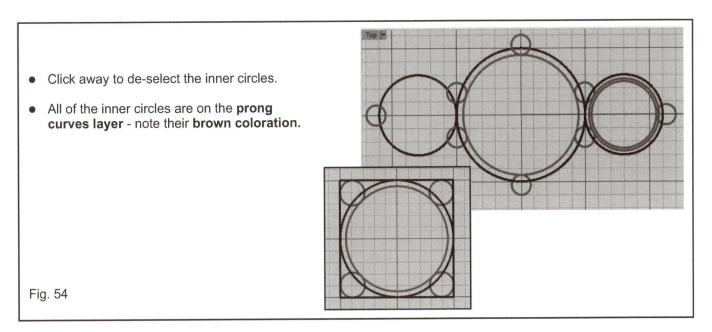

Fig. 54

- Select the square around the square setting and change it to the **construction lines** layer.

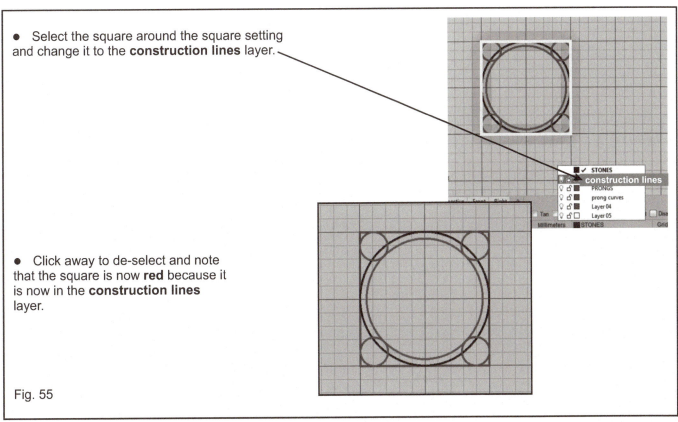

- Click away to de-select and note that the square is now **red** because it is now in the **construction lines** layer.

Fig. 55

Adjusting the Layers Panel
Deleting and Adding Layers

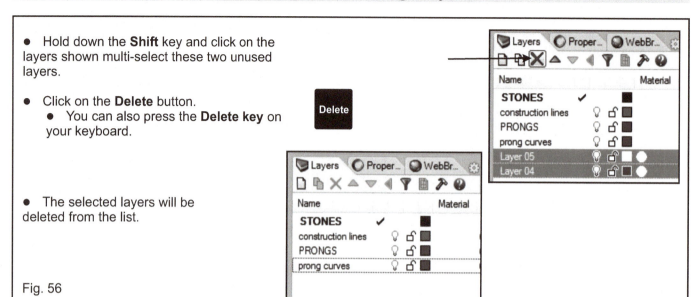

- Hold down the **Shift** key and click on the layers shown multi-select these two unused layers.

- Click on the **Delete** button.
  - You can also press the **Delete key** on your keyboard.

Delete

- The selected layers will be deleted from the list.

Fig. 56

- Select the **prong curves** layer and click on the **Delete button** or **Delete Key** as in the previous step.

- The **Objects on Layer** warning box will appear because the selected layer has objects on it.

- Click on the **No button** to save the objects on the layer from being deleted.

Fig. 57

Objects on Layer

Layer "prong curves" has 4 objects.
Are you sure you want to delete the objects and the layer?

To delete, click Yes.
To cancel, click No.

Yes   No

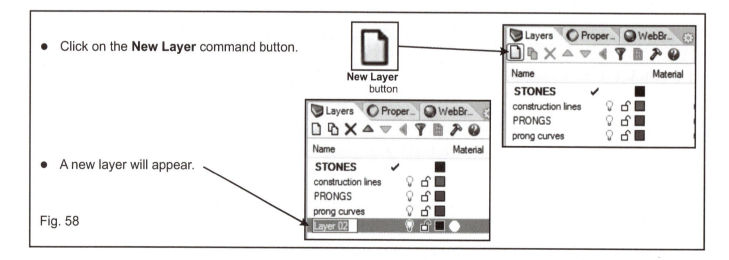

- Click on the **New Layer** command button.

New Layer
button

- A new layer will appear.

Fig. 58

Moving Layers Up and Down in the Layers Panel List

- Select the new layer ❶ and click on the **Move Up** button. ❷

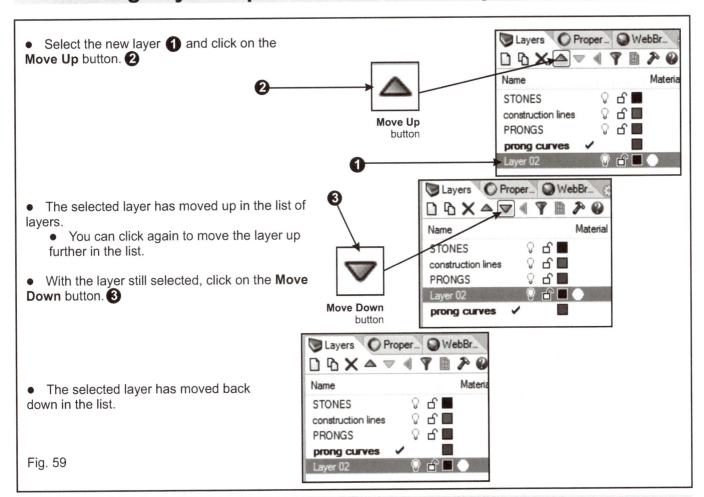

Move Up button

- The selected layer has moved up in the list of layers.
  - You can click again to move the layer up further in the list.

- With the layer still selected, click on the **Move Down** button. ❸

Move Down button

- The selected layer has moved back down in the list.

Fig. 59

Trimming For More Design Definition
Trim command

- On the **prong curves** line, click on the little lock ikon as shown.

- The little lock will turn blue and will look like a closed padlock.

- The **prong curves** layer has been **"locked"**.
  - You will be able to see the prong curves but you will not be able to select them.

- *Note: if you click on the LOCK ikon again, the layer will be unlocked and you will be able to select the prong curves again.*

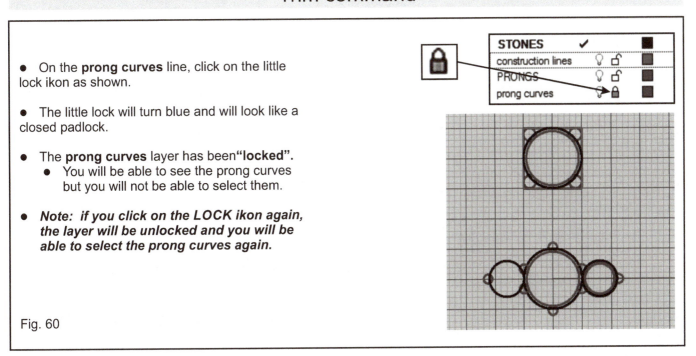

Fig. 60

- **Curve Tools tabbed toolbar.** [Curve Tools]

- Left-click on the **Trim** command.

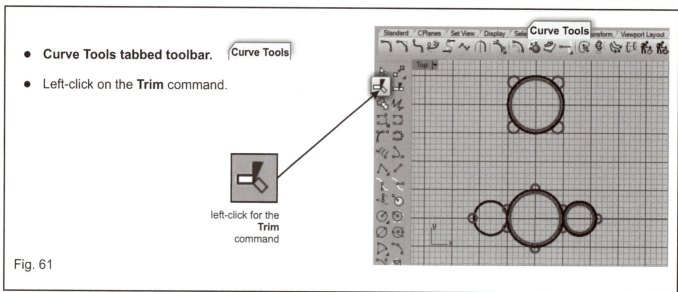

left-click for the
Trim
command

Fig. 61

- **Select cutting objects** prompt:

Select cutting objects (ExtendLines=*Yes* ApparentIntersections=*No*):

- Click to access the **Layers pop-up menu** in the **Status Bar** as shown. **1**

- **Right-click** on the PRONGS layer. **2**

right-click **2**

- Click on the **Select Objects** option in the context menu as shown. **3**

- All of the objects on the **PRONGS** layer will now be selected.

- Press **Enter** to tell Rhino that you have finished selecting the **cutting objects**.

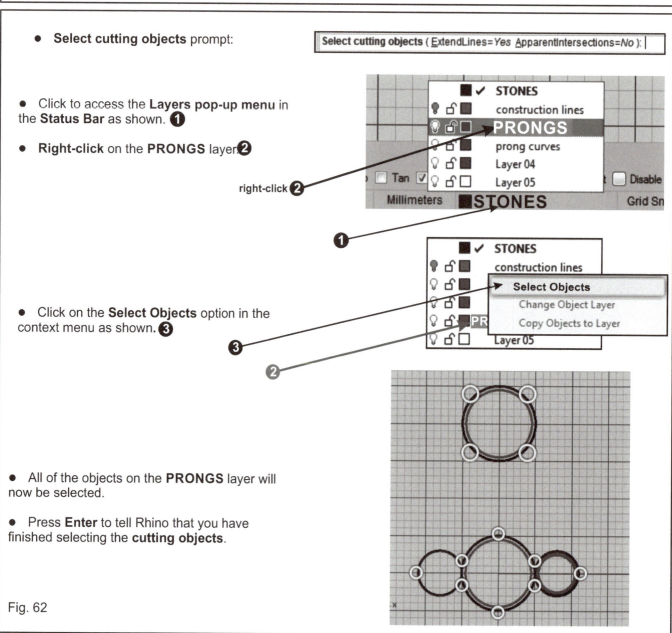

Fig. 62

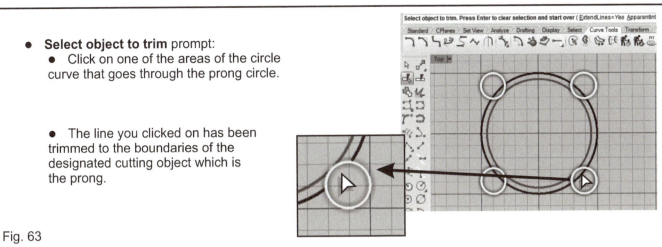

- **Select object to trim** prompt:
  - Click on one of the areas of the circle curve that goes through the prong circle.

  - The line you clicked on has been trimmed to the boundaries of the designated cutting object which is the prong.

Fig. 63

- Continue to trim out all of the prongs in the same way.

- Press **Enter** when you are finished trimming and the command will be ended.

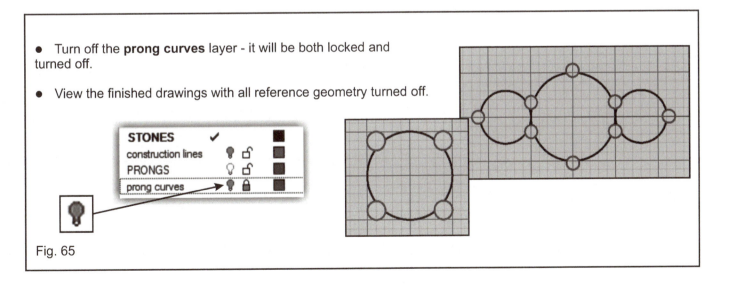

Fig. 64

- Turn off the **prong curves** layer - it will be both locked and turned off.

- View the finished drawings with all reference geometry turned off.

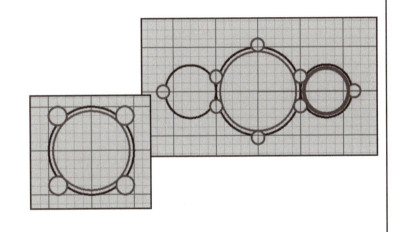

Fig. 65

Intro to Some More Basic 2-D Shapes
Ellipse, Rectangle, Polygon, Star

Ellipse: From Center - Freehand

- Open Rhino and save the file as **Basic Shapes.3dm**

- **Curve Tools tabbed toolbar.** `Curve Tools`

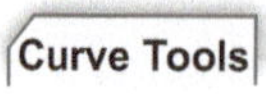

- Click on the **Ellipse: from center** command.

  - **Ellipse center** prompt:
    - Click on a location for the center of the ellipse. ❶

Fig. 1

Ellipse: from center command

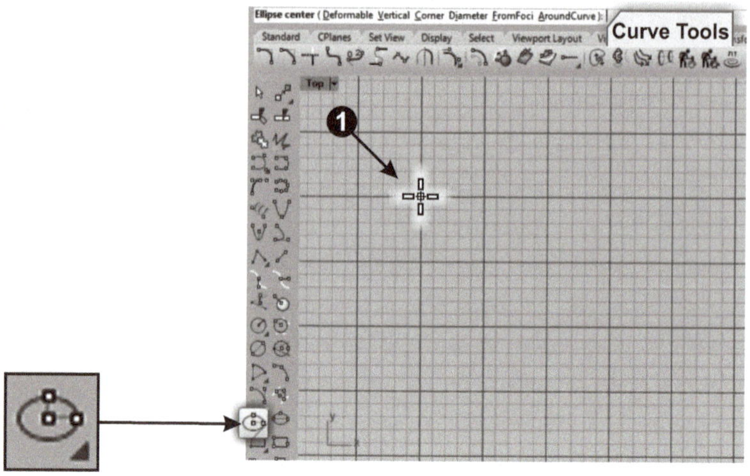

- **End of first axis** prompt:
  - Using **Ortho,** draw the cursor out as shown.
  - Click on the desired location for the end of the first axis as shown.❷

Fig. 2

- **End of second axis** prompt:
  - Draw the cursor upward until you arrive at the desired ellipse shape.
  - Click to set the location of the second axis. ❸

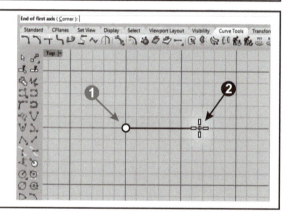

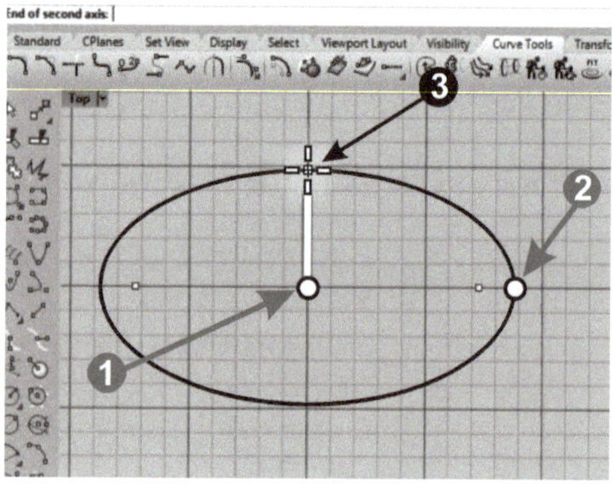

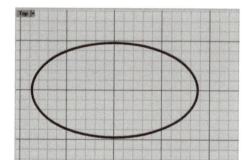

- The completed ellipse.

Fig. 3

Ellipse: Diameter - with Specified Dimensions

- **Curve Tools tabbed toolbar.**   Curve Tools

- Click on the **Ellipse: diameter** command.

    - **Start of first axis** prompt:
        - Click to set desired location. ❶

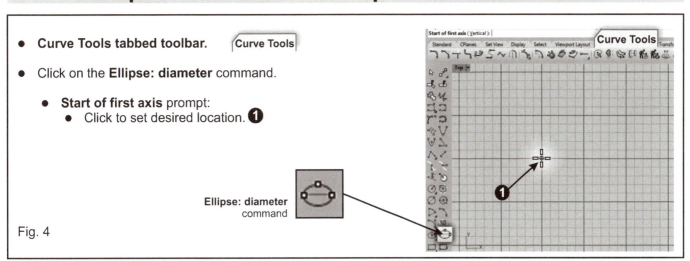

Ellipse: diameter
command

Fig. 4

- **End of first axis** prompt:
    - Type **"10"** in the **Command Line.**
    - Press **Enter.**   Fig. 5

End of first axis: **10**

- The length of the first axis is constrained to **10mm**.

- Click to set the desired location of the end of the first axis.
    - Notice that the cross hairs symbol that marks the actual end of the first axis. ❷

Fig. 6

- **End of second axis** prompt:
    - Type **"3"** in the **Command Line**.
    - Press **Enter.**   Fig. 7

End of second axis: **3**

- **End of second axis** prompt:
    - Click to set location. ❸

- Dimensions have been added using the **Aligned Dimension** command ***with control points turned on.***

- **Quad Osnap** was used to place the dimensions.

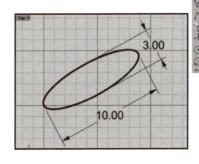

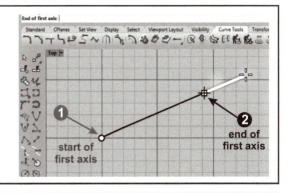

Aligned Dimension
command

Fig. 8

Rectangle: Corner to Corner - with Specified Dimensions

- **Curve Tools tabbed toolbar.** [Curve Tools]

- Click on the **Rectangle: corner to corner** command.

  - **First corner of rectangle** prompt:
    - Click to set the location of the first corner or the rectangle. **❶**

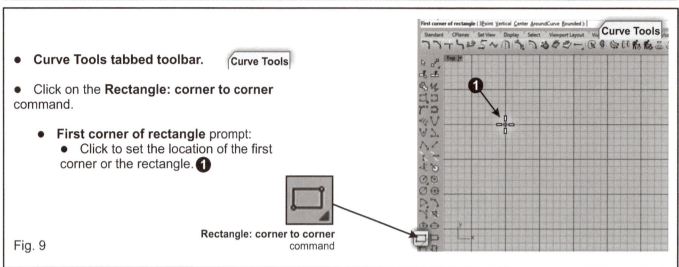

Rectangle: corner to corner
command

Fig. 9

- **Other corner or length** prompt:
  - Type **"15"** in the **Command Line.**
  - Press **Enter.**

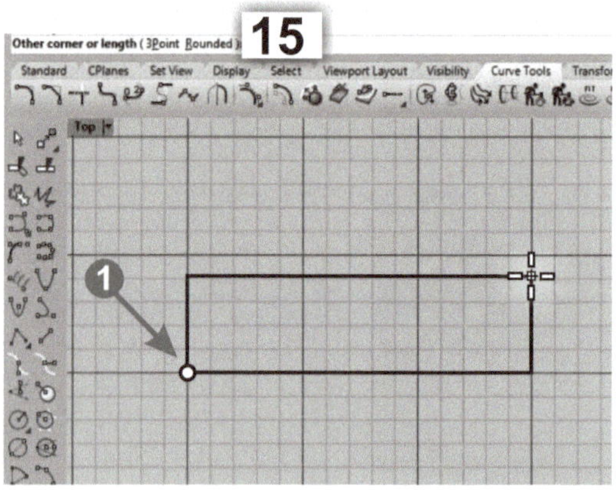

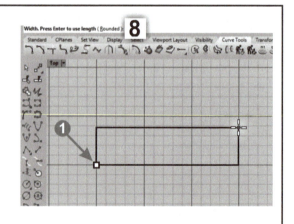

Fig. 10

- The horizontal length of the rectangle will be **15mm**.

- **Width. Press Enter to use length** prompt:
  - Type **"8"** in the **Command Line.**
  - Press **Enter.**

- **Note:** If you had pressed **Enter,** instead of specifying a number, the width of the rectangle would **automatically be the same as the height**, creating a **square**, instead of a rectangle.

Fig. 11

- The finished rectangle.

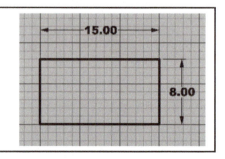

Fig. 12

Rectangle: Center, Corner

- **Curve Tools tabbed toolbar.**   Curve Tools

- Click on the **Rectangle: corner to corner** command.

  - **First corner of rectangle** prompt:
    - Click on the <u>**Center**</u> option in the <u>**Command Line.**</u>

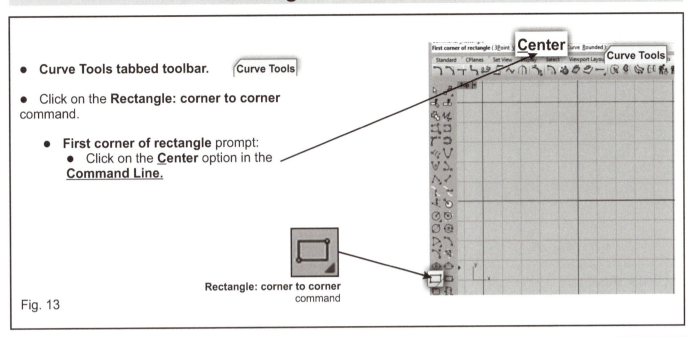

Rectangle: corner to corner command

Fig. 13

- **Center of rectangle** prompt:
  - Then, type **"0"** in the <u>**Command Line.**</u>
  - Press **Enter.**

- **Other corner or length** prompt:
  - Type **"20".**
  - Press **Enter.**

Center of rectangle (<u>R</u>ounded): **0**

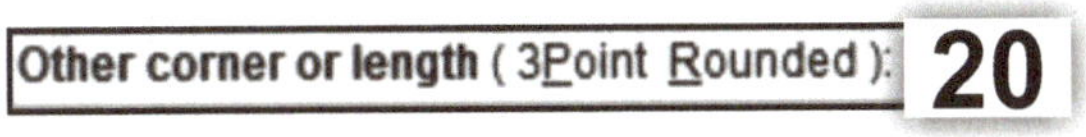

Other corner or length (3<u>P</u>oint <u>R</u>ounded): **20**

Fig. 14

- The rectangle is centered on **0.**

- The **horizontal length** along the **X axis** is constrained to **20mm.**

  - **Width. Press Enter to use length** prompt:
    - Type **"5".**
    - Press **Enter.**

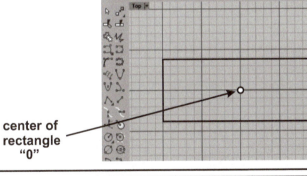

center of rectangle "0"

Fig. 15

- The finished rectangle.

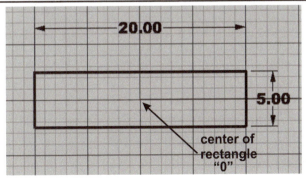

center of rectangle "0"

Fig. 16

Rectangle - Rounded Arc Corners

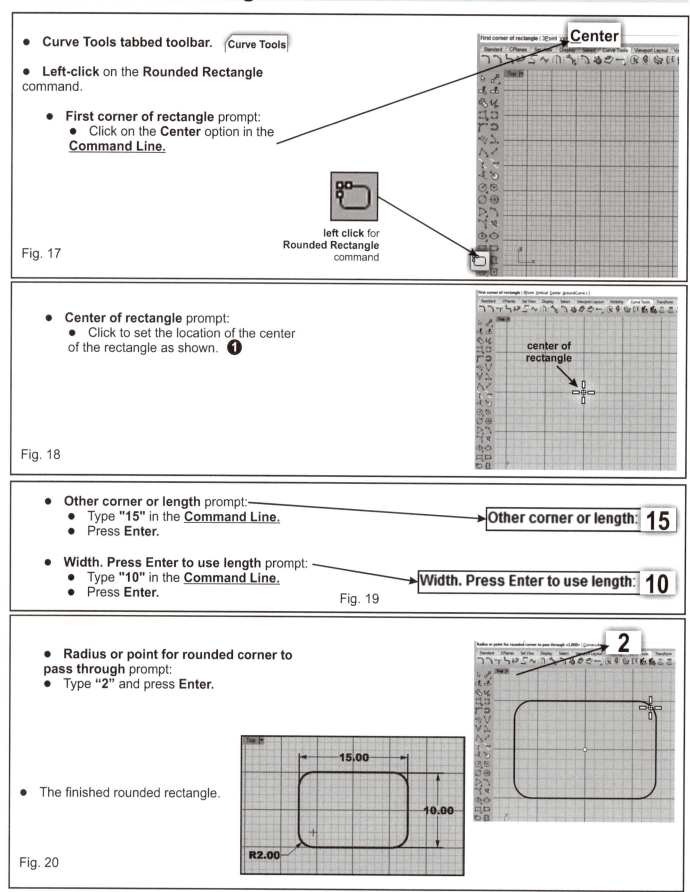

- ● **Curve Tools tabbed toolbar.** [Curve Tools]

- ● **Left-click** on the **Rounded Rectangle** command.

    - ● **First corner of rectangle** prompt:
        - ● Click on the **Center** option in the **Command Line.**

Center

left click for **Rounded Rectangle** command

Fig. 17

- ● **Center of rectangle** prompt:
    - ● Click to set the location of the center of the rectangle as shown. ❶

center of rectangle

Fig. 18

- ● **Other corner or length** prompt:
    - ● Type **"15"** in the **Command Line.**
    - ● Press **Enter.**

Other corner or length: **15**

- ● **Width. Press Enter to use length** prompt:
    - ● Type **"10"** in the **Command Line.**
    - ● Press **Enter.**

Width. Press Enter to use length: **10**

Fig. 19

- ● **Radius or point for rounded corner to pass through** prompt:
- ● Type **"2"** and press **Enter.**

2

- ● The finished rounded rectangle.

15.00

10.00

R2.00

Fig. 20

- **Curve Tools** tabbed toolbar.

- **Right-click** on the same button for the **Rounded Rectangle: conic corners** command.

    - **First corner of rectangle** prompt:
        - Click on the desired location for the first corner of the rectangle. **❶**

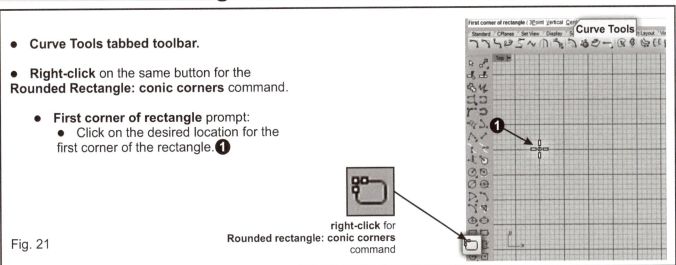

right-click for
Rounded rectangle: conic corners
command

Fig. 21

- **Other corner or length** prompt:
    - Type **"15"** in the **Command Line**.
    - Press **Enter**.

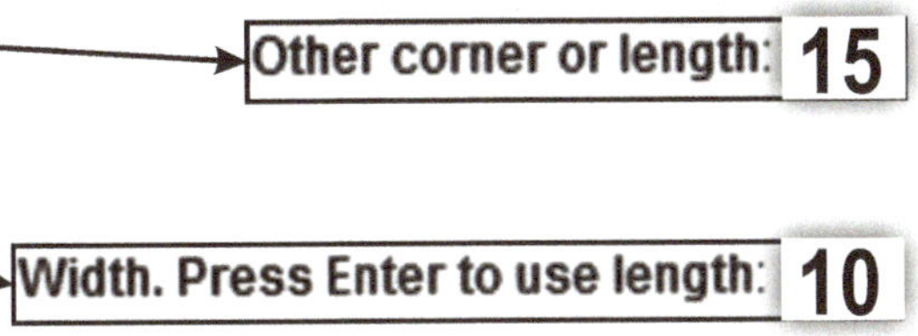

Other corner or length: **15**

- **Width. Press Enter to use length** prompt:
    - Type **"10"** in the **Command Line**.
    - Press **Enter**.

Fig. 22

Width. Press Enter to use length: **10**

- **Rho or point for conic corner to pass through** prompt:
    - Draw the cursor in and click when you have the desired rectangle. **❷**

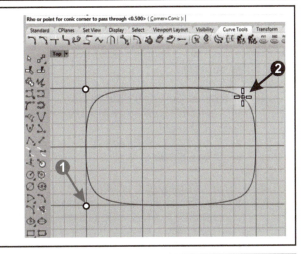

Fig. 23

- Note the difference between the finished **Conic rectangle** and the finished rectangle with **Arc corners**.

- Control points are turned on to see the difference in geometry.

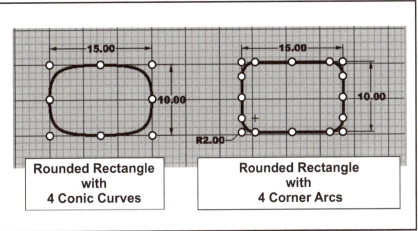

Rounded Rectangle
with
4 Conic Curves

Rounded Rectangle
with
4 Corner Arcs

Fig. 24

Polygon: center radius

- Click on the **Polygon: center, radius** command.
  - Make sure that the **Mode=**_Inscribed_ option in the **Command Line** is enabled.
  - **Center of inscribed polygon** prompt:
    - Click on a location for the center of the polygon. ❶

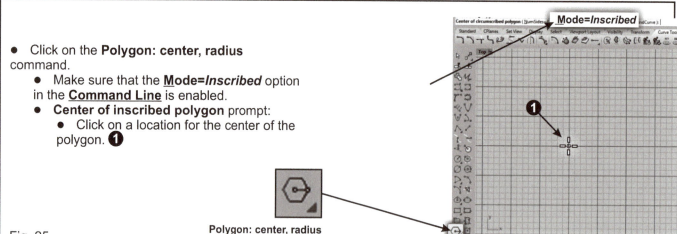

Polygon: center, radius
command

Fig. 25

- **Corner of polygon** prompt:
  - Click on the **(NumSides=5)** option in the **Command Line**.

- **Number of sides** prompt:
  - Type **"6"** in the **Command Line**
  - Press **Enter.**

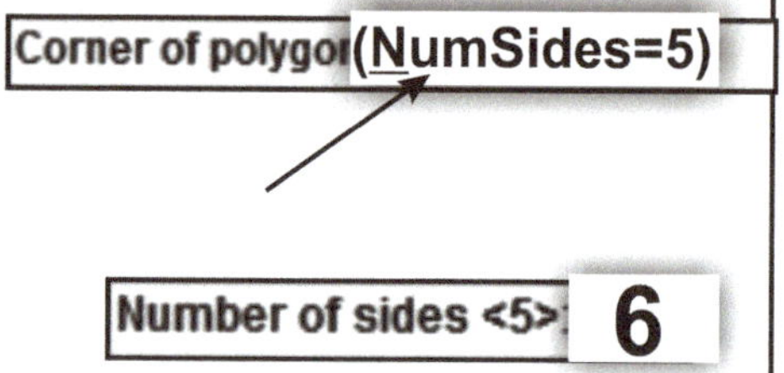

Fig. 26

Corner of polygon (**N**umSides=5)

Number of sides <5> **6**

- Notice that the cursor is pulling the polygon out by **one of its corners**.

  - **Corner of polygon** prompt:
    - Use **Ortho** when pulling the polygon up to keep it straight.
    - Type **"7"** to set the radius of the polygon.
    - Press **Enter**.

  - **Corner of polygon** prompt:
    - Notice the white constraint line that is constraining the radius of the polygon to **7mm**. ❷
    - Click to finish the polygon command.

Fig. 27

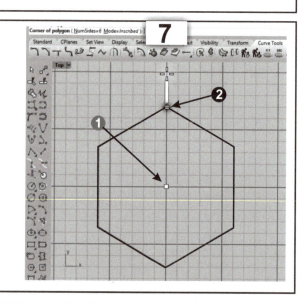

- The finished **6-sided polygon**.

- Note that the **"7"** that you entered fixed the distance between the **Center** of the polygon and **one of its corners** as shown by the dimension.
  - The dimension was placed with the use of **Center osnap** and **End osnap.**

Fig. 28

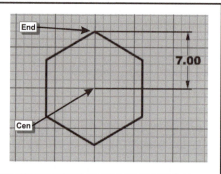

Circumscribed Polygon: center, radius

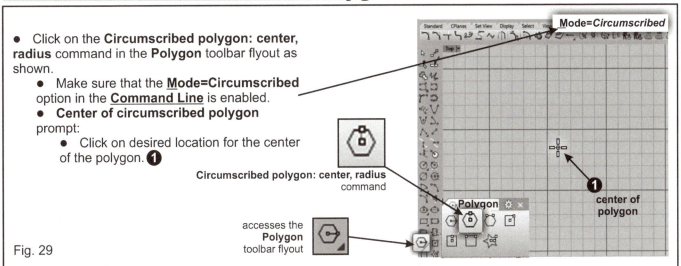

- Click on the **Circumscribed polygon: center, radius** command in the **Polygon** toolbar flyout as shown.
  - Make sure that the **Mode=Circumscribed** option in the **Command Line** is enabled.
  - **Center of circumscribed polygon** prompt:
    - Click on desired location for the center of the polygon. ❶

Circumscribed polygon: center, radius
command

accesses the
Polygon
toolbar flyout

center of
polygon

Fig. 29

- **Midpoint of polygon edge** prompt:
  - Click on the number of sides option in the **Command Line.**

- **Number of sides** prompt:
  - Type **"8"** in the **Command Line.**
  - Press **Enter.**

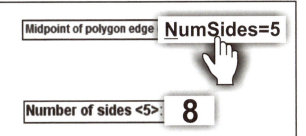

Fig. 30

- Notice that the cursor is pulling the polygon out by the **midpoint of one of its edges.**

- **Midpoint of polygon edge** prompt:
  - Notice the 8 sides of the polygon as you draw the cursor up.

  - Type **"10"** in the **Command Line** to set the radius of the polygon.
  - Press **Enter.**

  - Draw the cursor straight up using **Ortho.**
  - Click to set location. ❷

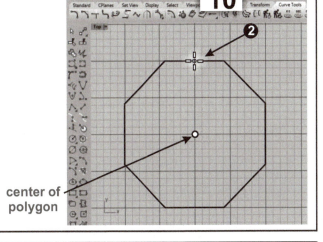

center of
polygon

Fig. 31

- The finished polygon.

- The radius dimension measures the distance between the **Center** of the polygon and the **Midpoint of the Edge.**

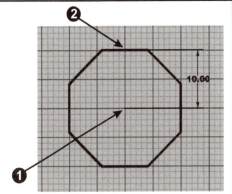

Fig. 32

- Click on the **Polygon: edge** command in the **Polygon** toolbar flyout.

  - **Start of edge** prompt:
    - Click on desired location. **❶**

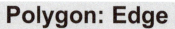
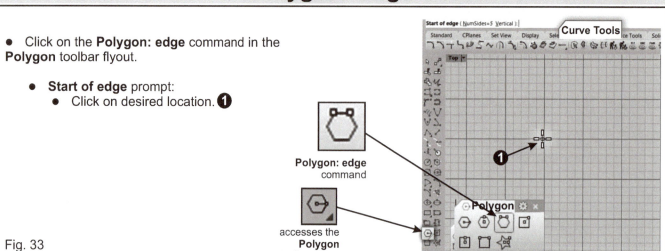

Polygon: edge
command

accesses the
Polygon
toolbar flyout

Fig. 33

- **End of edge** prompt:
  - Click on the **NumSides=8** option in the **Command Line.**

- **Number of sides** prompt:
  - Type **"6"** in the **Command Line.**
  - Press **Enter.**

Fig. 34

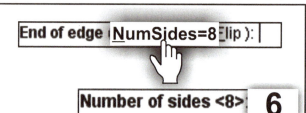

- The polygon now has **6 sides.**

- Click on the **Flip** option in the **Command Line.**

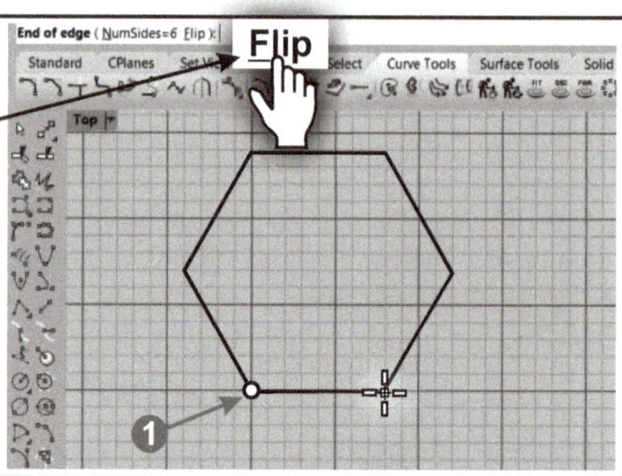

Fig. 35

- The orientation of the polygon has been "flipped" so it is now pointed downward.

- **End of edge** prompt:
  - Type **"5"** in the **Command Line.**
  - Press **Enter.**

- **End of edge** prompt:
  - The length of the edge is now **constrained to the designated 5mm.**
  - Click to set the location of the end of edge. **❷**

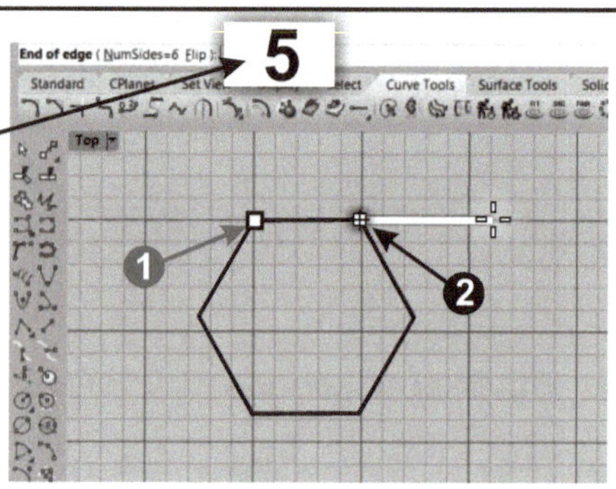

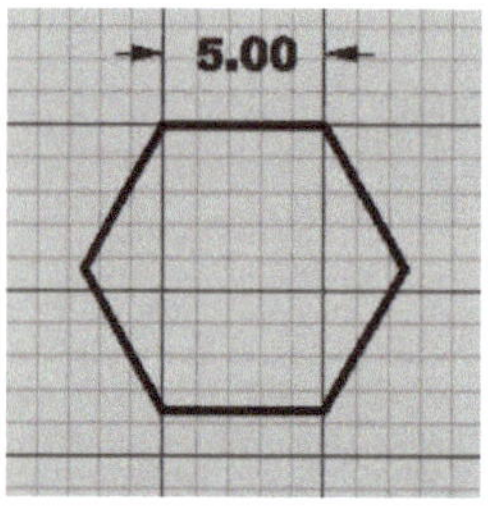

5.00

- The finished polygon with **5mm edges.**

Fig. 36

- **Curve Tools tabbed toolbar.**   Curve Tools

- Click on the **Polygon: star** command.

  - **Center of star** prompt:
    - Click on the location for the center of your star.❶

Polygon: star
command

Fig. 37

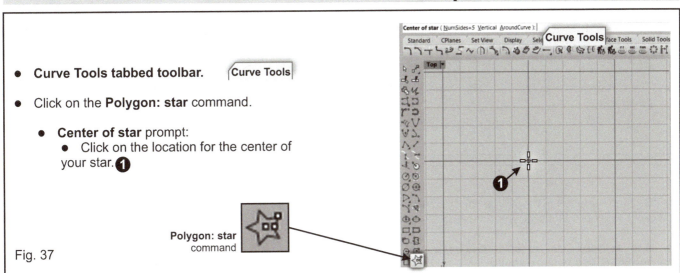

- **Corner of star** prompt:
  - The star will probably have the default number of 5 "sides" as you can see from the options line in the **Command Line**. Keep this default number of sides.
  - To set the **radius of the star,** type **"5"** in the **Command Line.**
  - Press **Enter.**

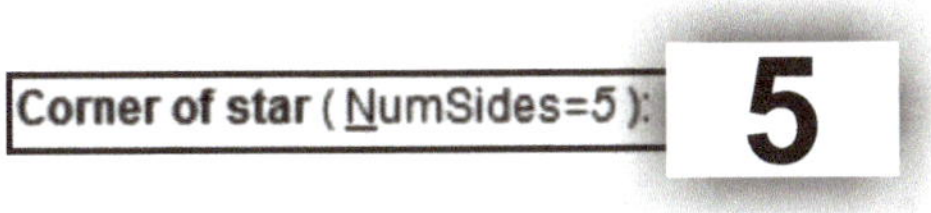

Corner of star (NumSides=5): **5**

Fig. 38

- The distance between the Center of the star ❶ and the point has been set to **5mm.** ❷

- Click to set location.
- In this illustration, **Ortho** has been used to keep the star in line with the grid.

click

Fig. 39

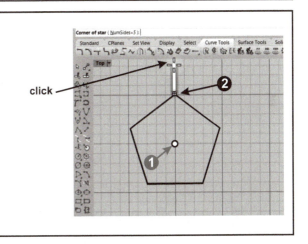

- Move the cursor inward toward the center of the star and see a preview of the star taking shape.

  - **Second star radius. Press Enter for automatic** prompt:
    - You can click anywhere to get your desired star shape but, in this exercise, **press Enter** for the default star shape.

Fig. 40

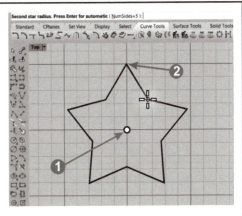

- The star will take a default, or **"automatic"** shape.

- This is the shape of the most commonly designed star that you see everywhere.

- The Dimension was created using **Center** and **End osnaps**.

Fig. 41

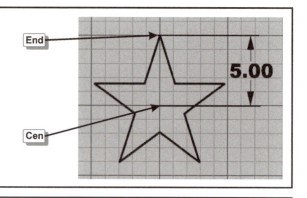

- See the variations you can get by specifying different numbers of sides when creating the star.

- Both of these stars were made using the **"automatic"** option used above.

Fig. 42

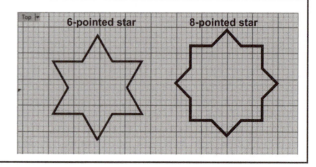

Star with Specified Radii

- **Curve Tools tabbed toolbar.** Curve Tools

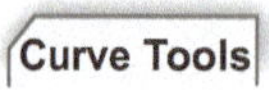

- For reference, create two circles with the same center point. Note the diameter dimensions of **5mm and 15mm.**

- Click on the **Polygon: star** command.

Fig. 43

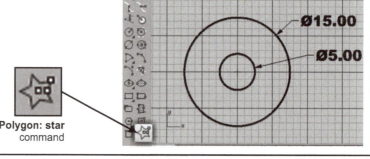

Polygon: star
command

- **Center of star** prompt:
  - Use **Center osnap** to snap to the center of the inner star.
  - Click to set location for the center of the star. ❶

Fig. 44

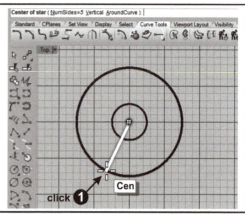

- **Corner of star** prompt:

  - Click on the **NumSides=5** option in the **Command Line.**
  - **Number of sides** prompt:
    - Type **"15"** and press **Enter.**

Fig. 45

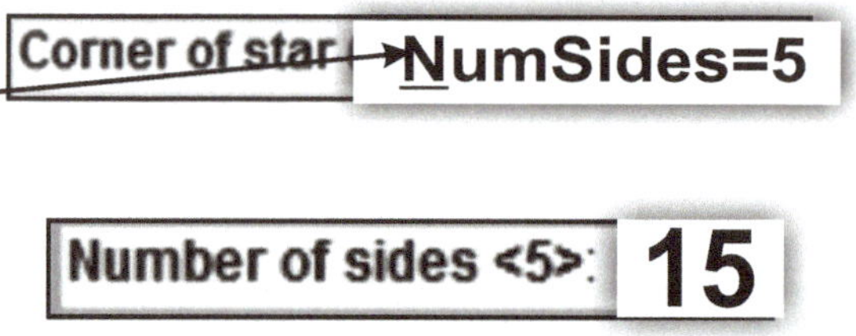

Corner of star → NumSides=5

Number of sides <5>: 15

- **Corner of star** prompt:
  - Draw the cursor up to the **quad** of the larger outer circle .
  - Click to set location. ❷

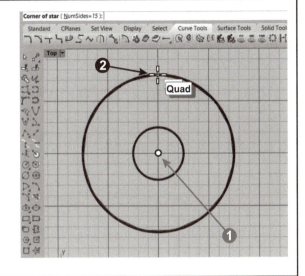

Fig. 46

- **Second star radius** prompt:
  - Draw the cursor down and snap to the upper quad point of the small inner circle.
  - Click to set location. ❸

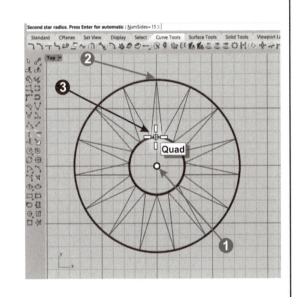

Fig. 47

- Hide or Delete the circles.

- You don't have to have circles to snap to. This exercise used circles to illustrate how the star is constructed, specifying inner and outer radii.

- This star has 15 "sides".

- Save this file as **basic shapes.3dm.**

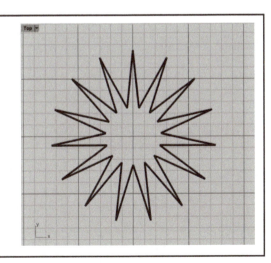

Fig. 48

116

Rotate 2-D Command
Using the rotate command for 2-D drawings.

Basic 2-D Rotate: Freehand Rotating by Eye

- Open the **Basic Shapes.3dm** file created in the *Intro to Some More Basic 2D Shapes* Chapter..

- **Standard tabbed toolbar.** | Standard |

- Your file will not look like this one as many of the basic shapes were arbitrarily placed when creating this file.

Fig. 1

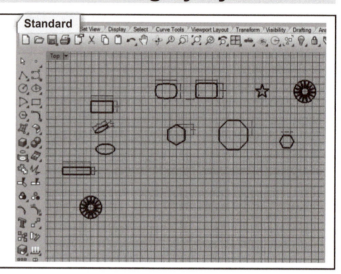

- Zoom in on the 5-pointed star.

- **Select the star** and press the **F10 Hotkey** to turn on the star's control points. **F10**

- **Left-click** on the **Rotate 2-D** command.

  - **Select objects to rotate** prompt:
    - Select the outer control points of the star as shown.
    - Press **Enter.**

left-click for the **Rotate 2-D** commaned

Fig. 2

- **Center of rotation** prompt:
  - Use **Cen osnap** to snap to the center of the star.
  - Click to set location. ❶

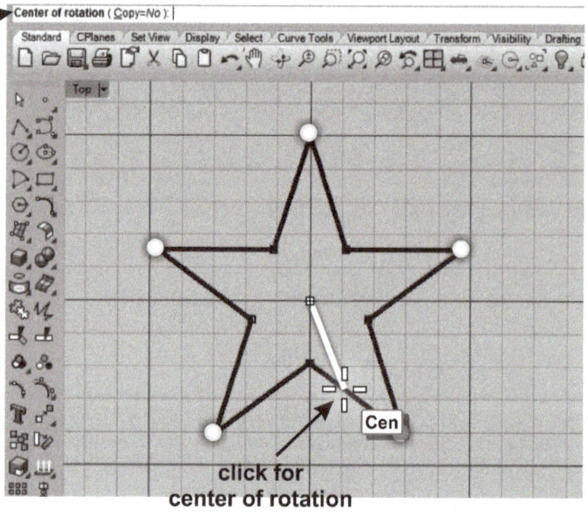

Fig. 3

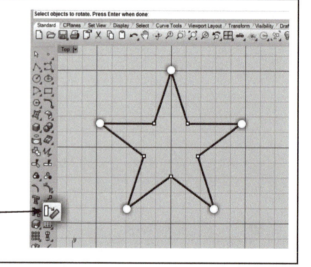

click for center of rotation

- **Angle or first reference point** prompt:
  - As you draw the cursor out, you will see a **black preview line** that represents the radius of the rotation. You will also see a white circle that represents the **arc of rotation.**
  - Click to set a first reference point as shown. This is done at random in this illustration. ❶

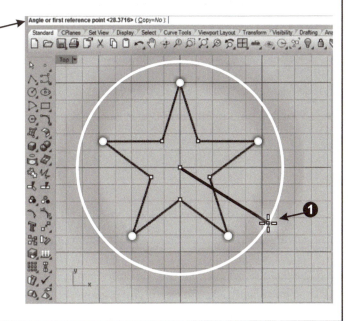

Fig. 4

- **Second reference point** prompt:
  - Notice that the white circle has changed to a black circle.
  - As you draw the cursor around, the angle of rotation is previewed.
  - Also, notice the preview of the new star shape and the thin lines showing its original shape.
  - Click to set the **Second reference point.** ❸

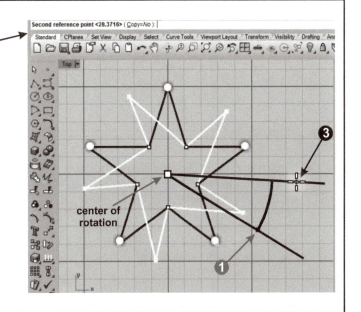

Fig. 5

- The finished revolve.

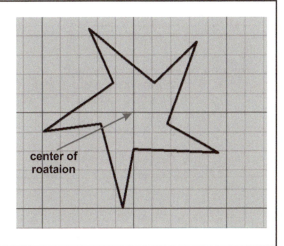

Fig. 6

- **Zoom** in on the tilted ellipse as shown.

- Select both the Ellipse and it's dimensions.

- **Left-click** on the **Rotate 2-D** command.

left-click for the
Rotate 2-D
commaned

Fig. 7

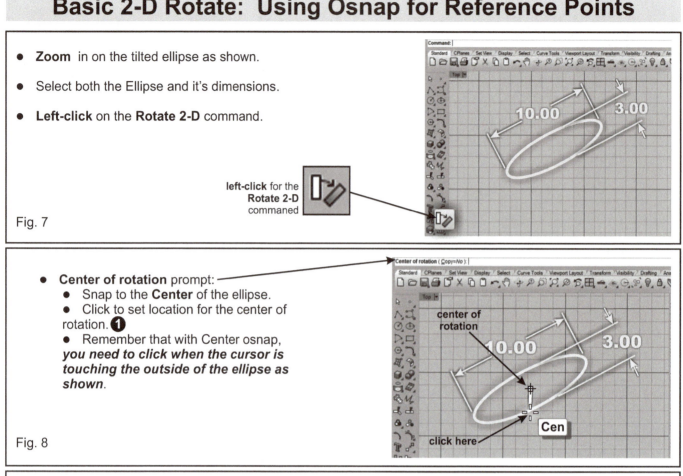

- **Center of rotation** prompt:
  - Snap to the **Center** of the ellipse.
  - Click to set location for the center of rotation. **1**
  - Remember that with Center osnap, *you need to click when the cursor is touching the outside of the ellipse as shown*.

Fig. 8

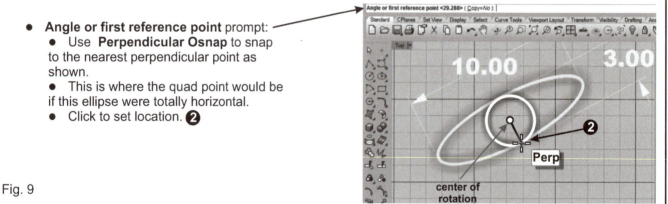

- **Angle or first reference point** prompt:
  - Use **Perpendicular Osnap** to snap to the nearest perpendicular point as shown.
  - This is where the quad point would be if this ellipse were totally horizontal.
  - Click to set location. **2**

Fig. 9

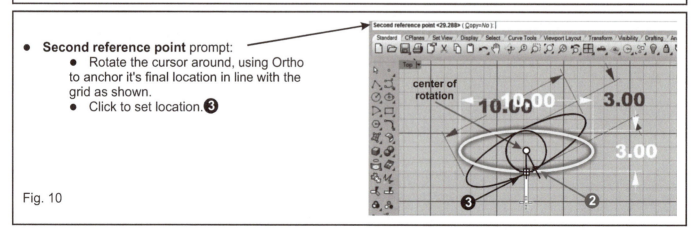

- **Second reference point** prompt:
  - Rotate the cursor around, using Ortho to anchor it's final location in line with the grid as shown.
  - Click to set location. **3**

Fig. 10

- The finished revolve.

- The ellipse is perfectly horizontal.

- Notice that the orientation of the dimension extension lines and text have been updated in their new position.

Fig. 10

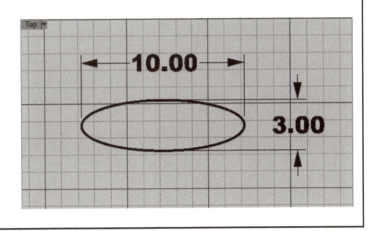

Basic 2-D Rotate: Using Specified Rotation Angles

- When specifying an angle of rotation, note that when you are rotating clockwise, you need to put a "minus" sign in front of the number of the angle when you are typing it.
  - Example: **-45**

Fig. 11

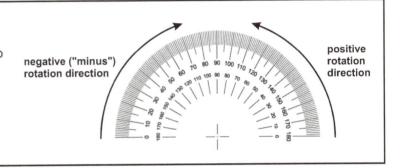

- Zoom in on the **15 x 8 Rectangle.**

- Click the **Copy=No** option in the **Command Line**. The option will be toggled to **Copy=Yes.**

  - **Center of rotation** prompt:
    - Use **Center osnap** to snap to the center of the rectangle.
    - Click to set location

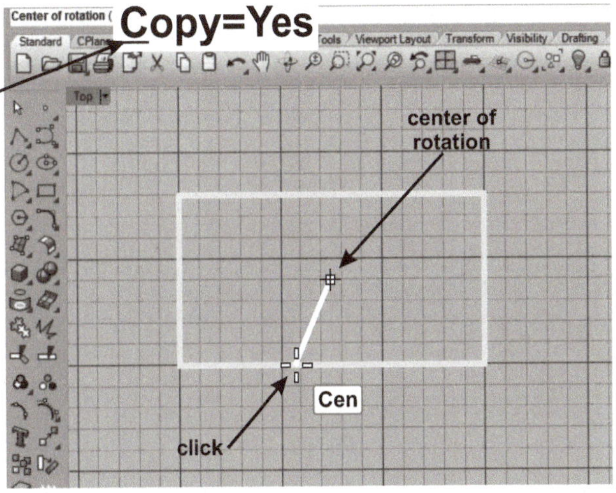

Fig. 12

- **Angle or first reference point** prompt:
  - Type **"45"** in the **Command Line.**
  - Press **Enter.**

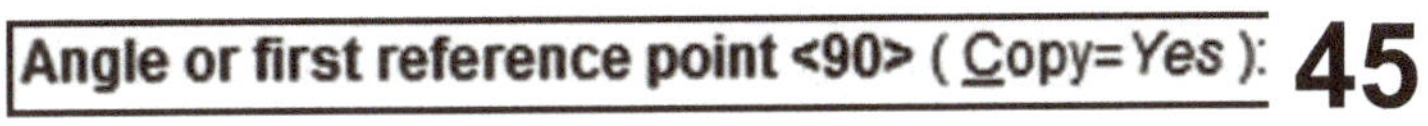

Angle or first reference point <90> (Copy=Yes): **45**

Fig. 13

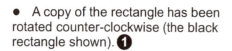

- A copy of the rectangle has been rotated counter-clockwise (the black rectangle shown). ❶

- **Angle or first reference point** prompt:
  - Now, type a "**-45**" (note the "minus" sign before the number).
  - Press **Enter.**

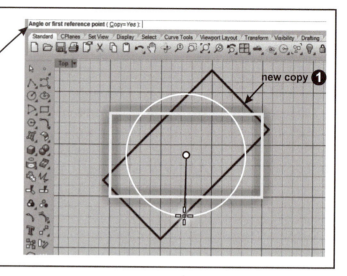

Fig. 14

- A new rectangle has been created, rotated in the other direction as shown. ❷

- You can make as many copies as you wish. You can also switch to freehand placement at any time within the command.

- Press **Enter** to end the command.

- The completed rotation has created 2 copies.

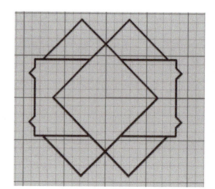

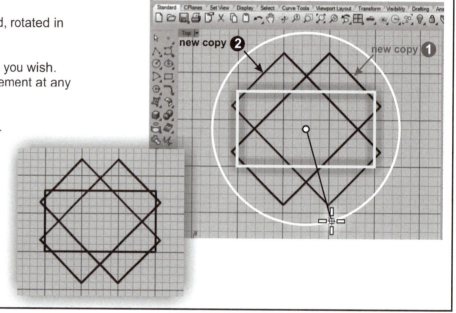

Fig. 15

- Use the Trim command to try some design concepts.

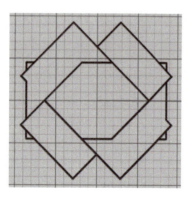

Fig. 16

Technical Drawing - Simple Pearl Ring
Drawing with Circles

- Open Rhino and save the file as **pearl ring technical drawing.3dm.**

- As with all technical drawings, you will be working in the **Top Viewport.**
  - Maximize the top viewport for optimal visibility.
  - Note: In this book, the top viewport is not maximized due to page space considerations.

Drawing the Front View of the Ring Shank

- Create the layers shown.

- Click to place the check mark on the **TECH LINES** layer line.

- The check mark means that this layer is "Current". *Anything you create now will be on this layer.*

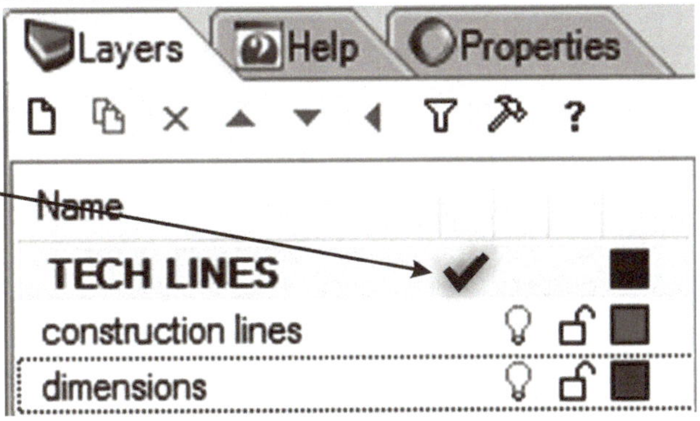

Fig. 1

- **Curve Tools tabbed toolbar.** Curve Tools

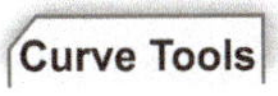

- Use the **Circle: center, radius** command to create a circle.
  - **Center of circle: 0**
  - **Circle Diameter: 17.35mm**

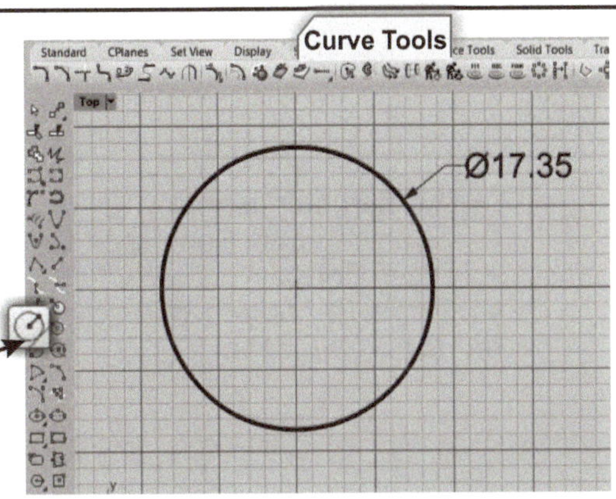

Fig. 2

- Select the circle and click on the **Offset curve** command.
  - **Side to offset** prompt:
    - Type **"2"** in the **Command Line.**
    - Press **Enter.**
    - This will assign a thickness of 2mm to the ring band in this Front view elevation.

Offset Curve
command

Fig. 3

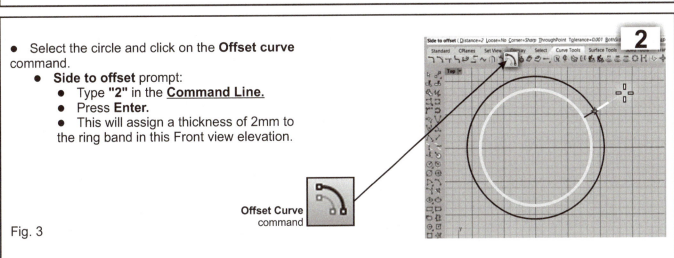

- The new offset has been completed to show the 2mm thickness of the shank as seen from the front.

Fig. 4

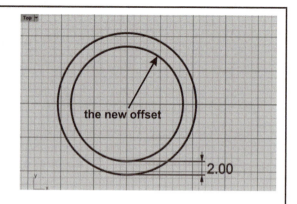

the new offset

2.00

Adding the Pearls to the Front View of the Shank

- Click on the **Circle: diameter** command in the **Circle** toolbar flyout.

  - **Start of diameter** prompt:
    - Snap to the upper **Quad** point of the outer circle as shown.
    - Click to set location. ❶

Circle: diameter
command

Fig. 5

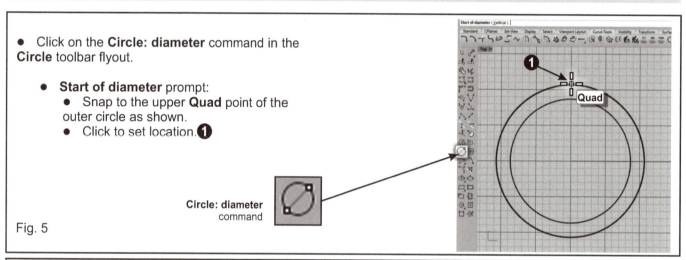

Quad

❶

- **End of diameter** prompt:
  - Type **"5"** in the **Command Line.**
  - Press **Enter.**
  - *This will assign a **5mm diameter** to the center pearl on the top of the band.*

Fig. 6

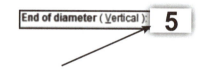

End of diameter (Vertical): 5

- **End of diameter** prompt:
  - Use **Ortho** and draw the cursor straight up for a vertical diameter.
  - The diameter of the pearl is constrained to 5mm.
  - Click to set location. ❷

- A 5mm pearl has been drawn on the top of the ring band.

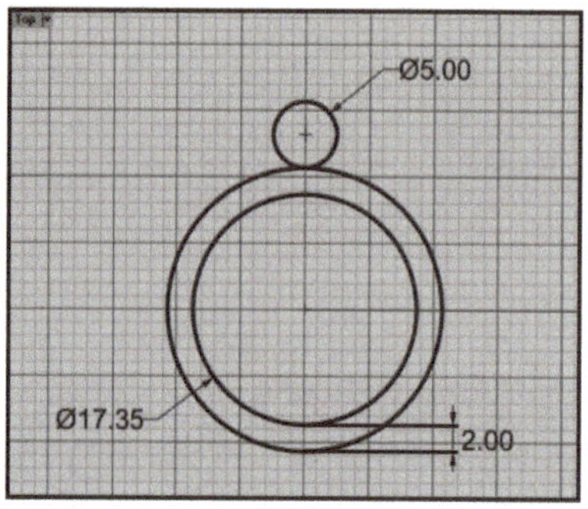

Fig. 7

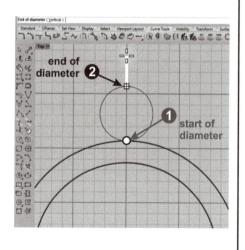

end of diameter ❷

start of diameter ❶

Ø5.00

Ø17.35

2.00

- Click on the **Circle: tangent, tangent, radius** command.

  - **First tangent curve** prompt:
    - Move the cursor until it snaps to the circle as shown. (see the white constraint line.)
    - Click to set location. **1**

Circle: tangent, tangent, radius command

Fig. 8

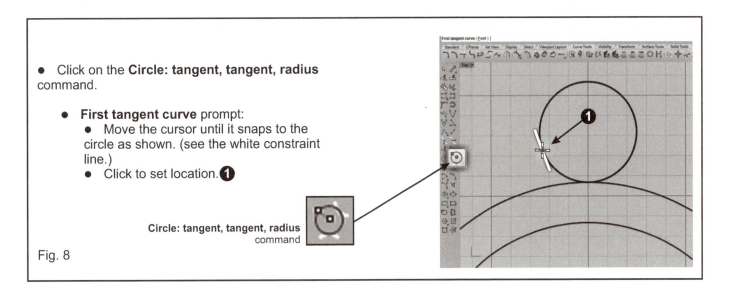

- **Second tangent curve or radius** prompt:
  - Draw the cursor down until it snaps to the large circle as shown. (See the white constraint line.)
  - Click to set location. **2**
- **Radius** prompt:
  - Type "**2**" and press **Enter. 3**

Fig. 9

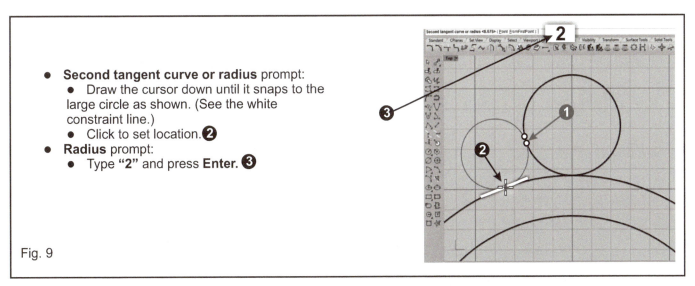

- The new circle will be constrained to a **4mm diameter.**
- The new circle is tangent to both the large pearl and the ring band.

- Use the same technique to add a **3mm** pearl as shown.

Fig. 10

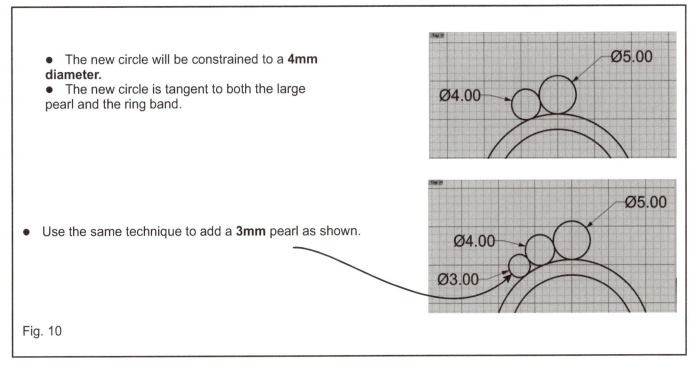

- Click on the line for the **construction lines** layer just below the check mark above.

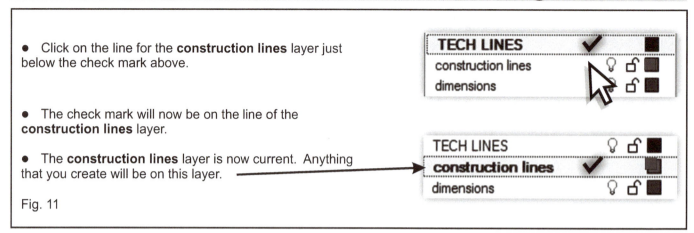

- The check mark will now be on the line of the **construction lines** layer.

- The **construction lines** layer is now current. Anything that you create will be on this layer. ⟶

Fig. 11

- Click to turn on **Grid Snap**. | Grid Snap |

- Click on the **Line: from midpoint** command in the **Lines** toolbar flyout.

  - **Middle of line** prompt:
    - Click on the intersection of the **green Y axis** and **one of the heavy grid lines** as shown. ❶

accesses the **Lines** toolbar lfyout

Line: from midpoint command

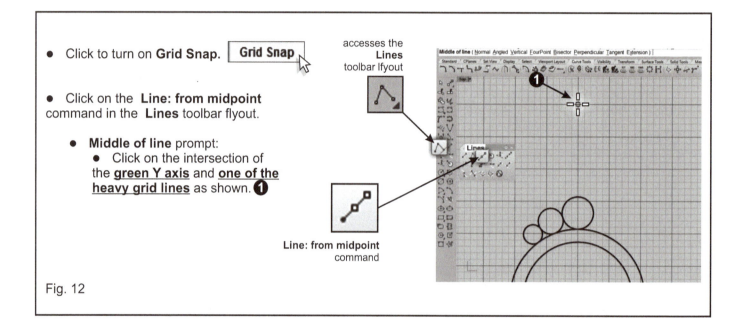

Fig. 12

- Draw the cursor out and notice that the line generates from the midpoint ❶ as shown. *Use **Ortho** as extra insurance that this line will be perfectly horizontal.*

- **End of line** prompt:
  - Click to set location. ❷
  - *Notice that the length of the line is quite a bit wider than the outside diameter of the ring band below.*

- Click to **Disable Grid Snap.**   Grid Snap

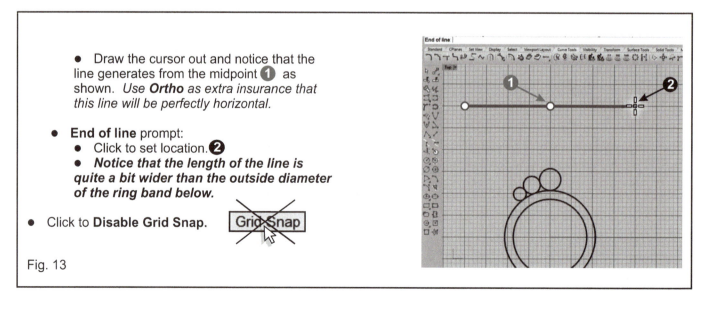

Fig. 13

- Click on the **Line** command.

    - **Start of line** prompt:
        - Snap to the **Quad** on the left of the outer circle as shown.
        - Click to set location. ❶

Line
command

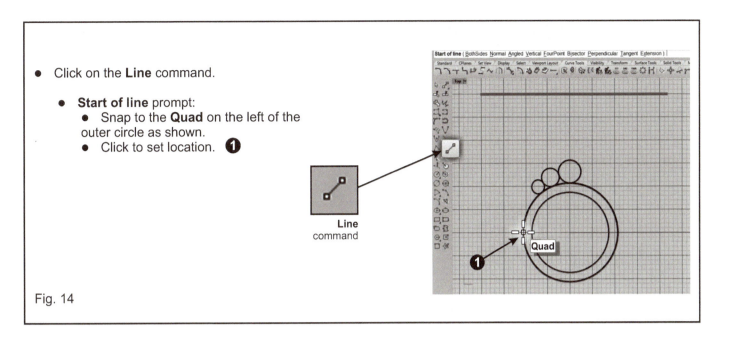

Fig. 14

- **End of line** prompt:

    - Draw the cursor up, using **ORTHO** for accuracy.

    - Click to set location when the line is high enough to cross the horizontal line as shown. ❷

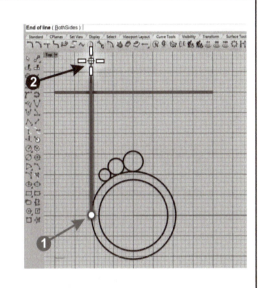

Fig. 15

- **Transform tabbed toolbar.** ⟨Transform⟩

- Select the perpendicular line and the two outer circles as shown.

- Click on the **Mirror** command.

Mirror
command

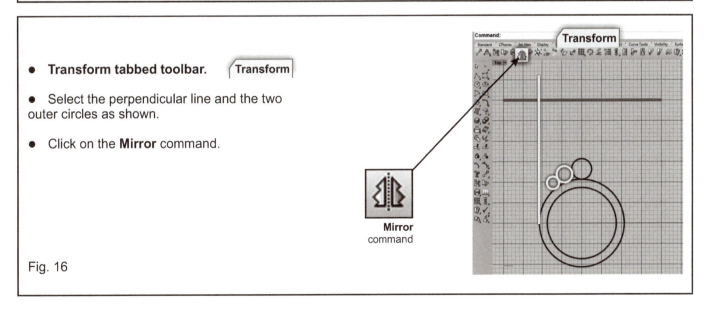

Fig. 16

- **Start of mirror plane** prompt:
  - Type **"0"**.
  - Press **Enter**.

Start of mirror plane (3Point Copy=Yes XAxis YAxis) 0

Fig. 17

- **End of mirror plane** prompt:
  - Using **Ortho** draw the cursor straight up.
    - A preview image of a mirrored copy will appear as shown.
  - Click to set the **End of the mirror plane.**

- **The selected objects are now mirrored over to the other side of the ring.**

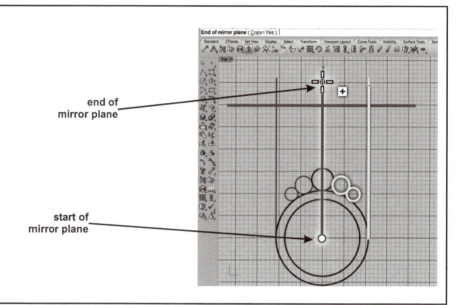

end of mirror plane

start of mirror plane

Fig. 18

- Create a center line for the ring.
  - Start of line: **"0"** **1**
  - End of line: perpendicular to first point. **2** **Use ORTHO!**

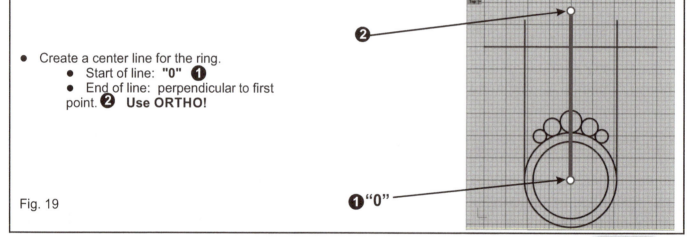

2

1 "0"

Fig. 19

- **Curve tools tabbed toolbar.** Curve Tools

- Select the horizontal construction line as shown.

- Click on the **Offset Curve** command.

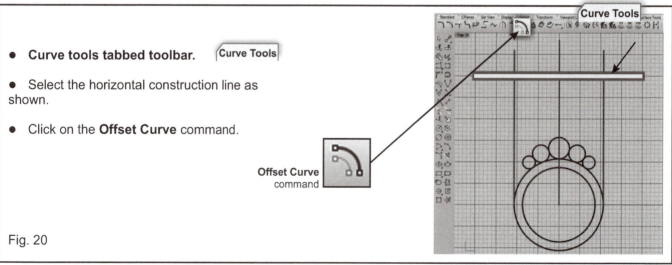

Curve Tools

Offset Curve command

Fig. 20

- **Side to offset** prompt:
  - Click to toggle on the **BothSides** option in the **Command Line.**

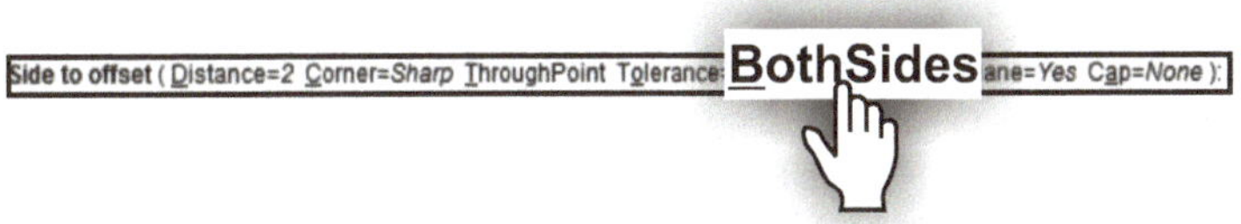

Side to offset (Distance=2 Corner=Sharp ThroughPoint Tolerance
BothSides
ane=Yes Cap=None):

- **Side to offset** prompt:
  - Type **"1.5** in the **Command Line.**
  - Press **Enter.**

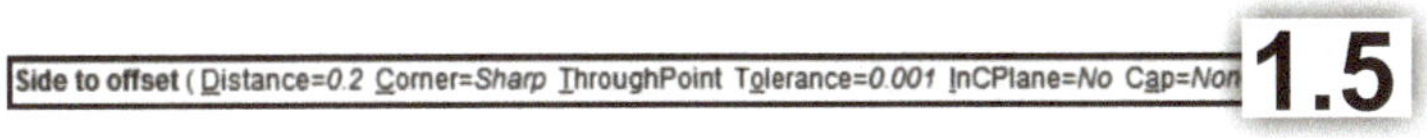

Side to offset (Distance=0.2 Corner=Sharp ThroughPoint Tolerance=0.001 InCPlane=No Cap=Non
1.5

Fig. 21

- *Notice the preview:*
  - *The offset will be on* ***both sides*** *of the assigned line.*
  - *The distance is constrained to* ***1.5mm*** *offset for each side.*
    - Click to set location.

Side to offset (Distance=1.5 Loose=No Corner=Sharp ThroughPoint Tolerance=0.001 InCPlane=Yes Cap=None)

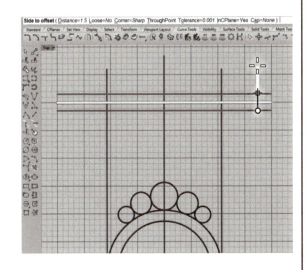

Fig. 22

- Two offsets have been created that are parallel to the middle, original, line.

- In the Top View, the thickness of the ring shank will be **3mm.**

1.50
3.00
1.50

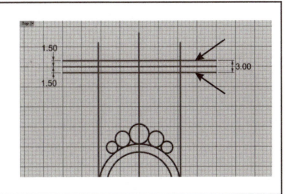

Fig. 23

- Click to put the check mark on the **TECH LINES** layer.
  - **TECH LINES** layer is now current.

TECH LINES
construction lines
dimensions

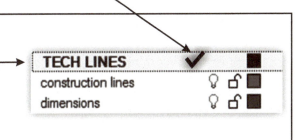

Fig. 24

- Click on the **Rectangle: corner to corner** command.

  - **First corner of rectangle** prompt:
    - Snap to the **intersection** of the two construction lines shown.
    - Click to set location. ❶

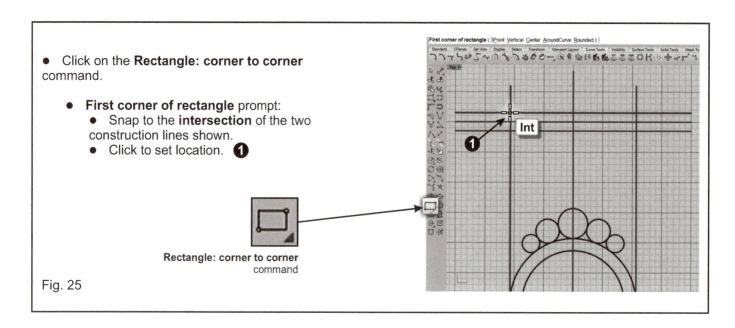

Rectangle: corner to corner
command

Fig. 25

- **Other corner or length** command:
  - Draw the cursor diagonally over so that it snaps to the **intersection** shown.
  - Click to set location. ❷

- *Don't worry if you can't see the preview line of the rectangle. The red construction lines may be hiding it.*

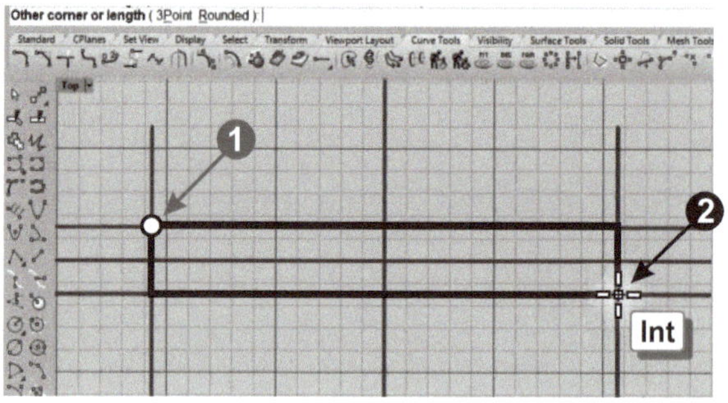

Fig. 26

- If you turn off the **construction lines** layer, you can see the rectangle you have just created.

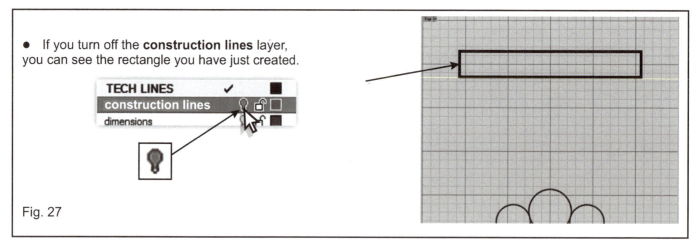

Fig. 27

- Click to make the **construction lines** layer current and it will *automatically turn on again and become visible.*

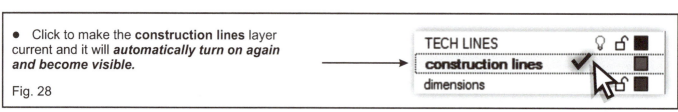

Fig. 28

- Click on the **Line** command.

  - **Start of line** prompt:
    - Click on the **quad** of the inner circle as shown. ❶

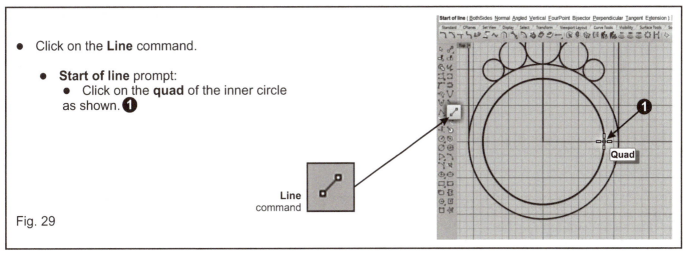

Line command

Fig. 29

- **End of line** prompt:
  - Using **ORTHO,** draw the cursor up and click to set a perpendicular line that crosses the 3 horizontal lines as shown.
  - Click to set the end of the line. ❷

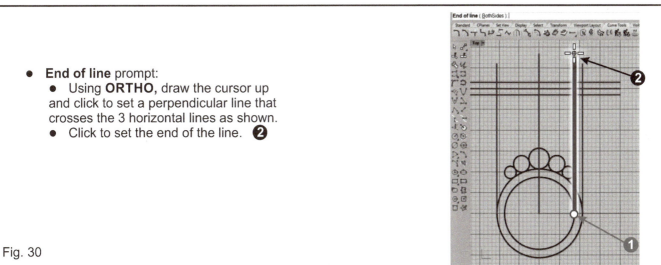

Fig. 30

- Click to put the check mark on the **TECH LINES** layer.
  - **TECH LINES** layer is now current.

Fig. 31

TECH LINES	✔	■
construction lines	♀ 🔓	■
dimensions	♀ 🔓	■

- Click on the **Ellipse: diameter** command:

  - **Start of first axis** prompt:
    - Snap to the **intersection** shown.
    - Click to set location. ❶

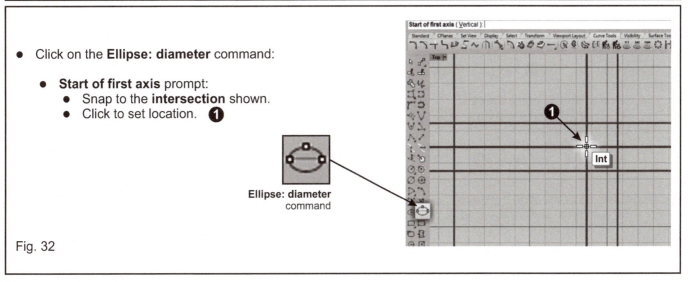

Ellipse: diameter command

Fig. 32

- **End of first axis** prompt:
  - Draw the cursor over and snap to the **intersection** shown.
  - Click to set location. ❷

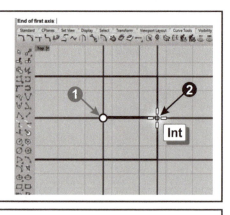

Fig. 33

- **End of second axis** prompt:
  - Draw the cursor up and snap to the **Intersection to the right.**
  - The **end of the second axis** will be placed in line with the intersection as shown.
  - Click to set location. ❸

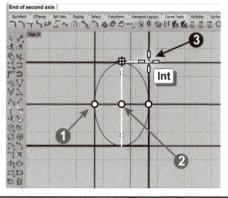

Fig. 34

- Click on the light bulb to turn off the **construction lines** layer.

Fig. 35

- The ellipse that you have just made is a cross-section of the ring band.

  - ***The cross-section is oval, not round, because the 2mm width of the shank in the front view is different the 3mm width in the top view.***

Fig. 36

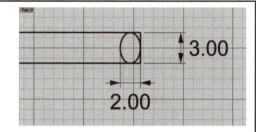

- **Transform tabbed toolbar.** ⌐Transform⌐

- Select the new oval ❶ and click on the **Mirror command.**
  - **Start of Mirror plane** prompt:
    - Type "0" and press **Enter.** ❷
  - **End of Mirror plane:**
    - Using **Ortho,** draw the cursor and click to set mirror plane. ❸

- *A new ellipse has been mirrored over from the other side of the ring.*

Fig. 37

Mirror command

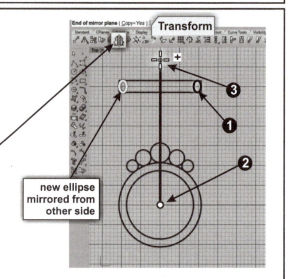

new ellipse mirrored from other side

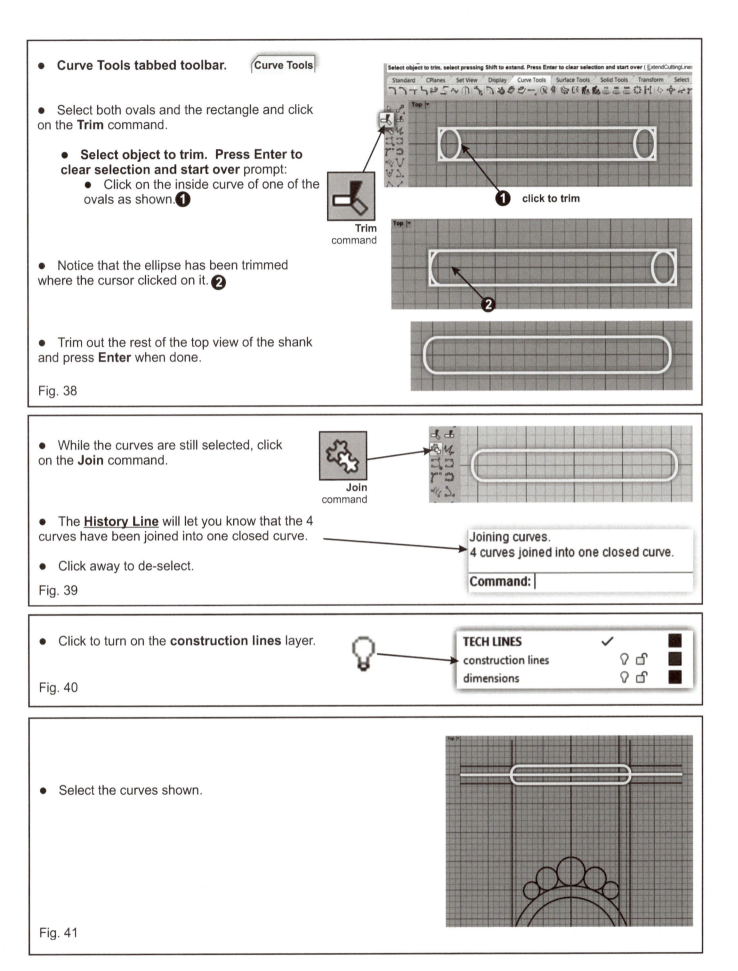

- **Curve Tools tabbed toolbar.**   Curve Tools

- Select both ovals and the rectangle and click on the **Trim** command.

    - **Select object to trim. Press Enter to clear selection and start over** prompt:
        - Click on the inside curve of one of the ovals as shown.❶

Trim command

❶ click to trim

- Notice that the ellipse has been trimmed where the cursor clicked on it. ❷

❷

- Trim out the rest of the top view of the shank and press **Enter** when done.

Fig. 38

- While the curves are still selected, click on the **Join** command.

Join command

- The **History Line** will let you know that the 4 curves have been joined into one closed curve.

Joining curves.
4 curves joined into one closed curve.

Command:

- Click away to de-select.

Fig. 39

- Click to turn on the **construction lines** layer.

TECH LINES   ✓   ■
construction lines   ♀ ⌂   ■
dimensions   ♀ ⌂   ■

Fig. 40

- Select the curves shown.

Fig. 41

- **Transform tabbed toolbar.** [Transform]

- Left-click on the **Rotate 2D** command in the **Transform tabbed toolbar.**

  - **Center of rotation** prompt:
    - Type **"0"** in the **Command Line**
    - Press **Enter. ❶**

left-click for the
Rotate 2-D
command

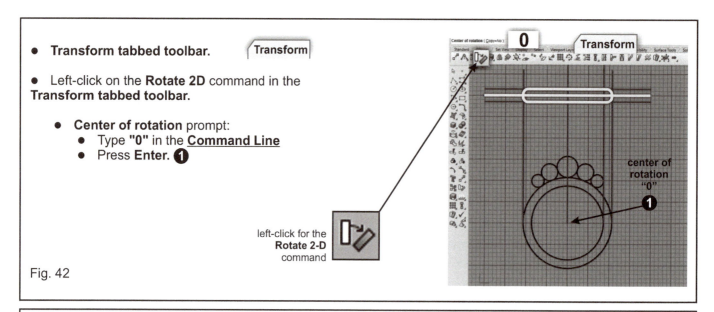

center of
rotation
"0"

Fig. 42

- **Angle or first reference point** prompt:
  - Click on the **Copy=No** option in the command line to toggle it to **Copy=Yes. ❷**
  - Using **ORTHO**, draw the cursor straight up as shown.
  - Click to set location. ❸

- **Second reference point** prompt:
  - Draw the cursor around to the side shown and, using **Ortho**, click to set the location of the copy that you are making ❹
  - Press **Enter** to end the command.

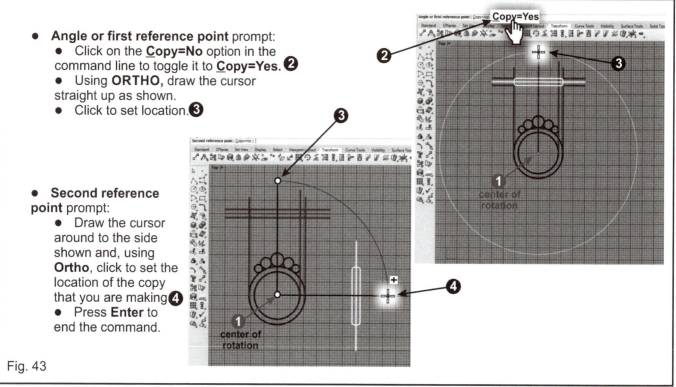

center of
rotation

Fig. 43

- Click away to de-select if necessary.

  - *You have rotated to create a copy of the top view of the ring to create a side view for this basic ring shank.*

    - For better visibility for the **TECH LINES**, refer to the next chapter, **Draw Order Commands**.

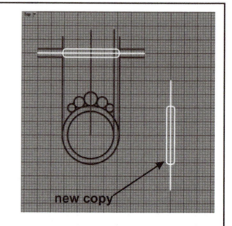

new copy

Fig. 44

Adding the Pearls to the Top and Side Views of the Band

- Make sure that **Center** and **Perpendicular osnaps** are enabled.

- Select the large pearl circle and click on the **Copy** command.
  - **Point to copy from** prompt:
    - Snap to the **Center** of the selected pearl as shown.
    - Click to set location. ❶

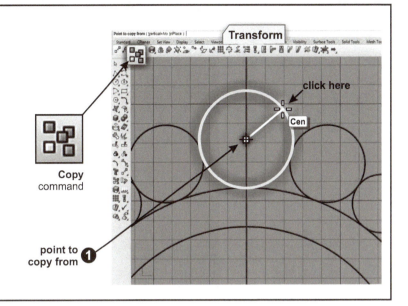

Fig. 45

- **Point to copy to** prompt:
  - Draw the cursor up and snap to the **Perpendicular** point on the horizontal center line of the Top View as shown.
  - Click to set location. ❷

- The new copy is exactly vertical to the original circle.

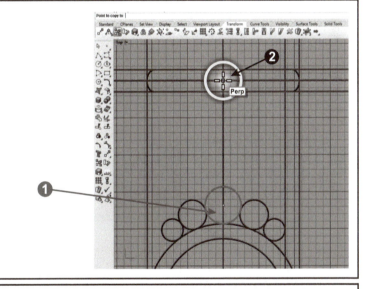

Fig. 46

- **Point to copy to** prompt:
  - For the next copy, draw the cursor over to the right and snap to the **Perpendicular** point on the vertical center line of the Side View.
  - Click to set location. ❸
  - Press **Enter** to end the command.

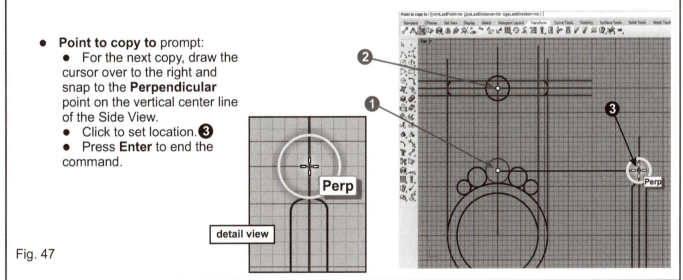

Fig. 47

134

- Select the next pearl down and click on the **Copy** command.

  - **Point to copy from** prompt:
    - Like before, snap to the **Center** of the circle.
    - Click to set location. ❶

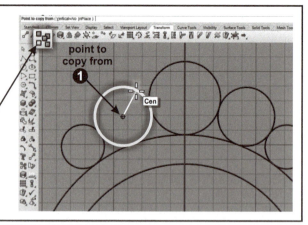

Fig. 48

Copy command

- **Point to copy to** prompt:
  - Draw the cursor up and snap to the point on the center line of the Top View that is exactly **Perpendicular** to the point to copy from. ❷
  - Click to set location.

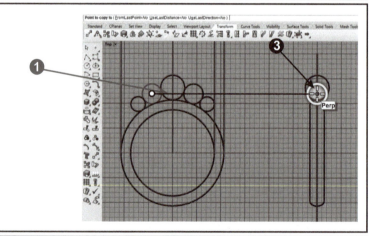

Fig. 49

- **Point to copy to** prompt:
  - Like before, draw the cursor over to the right and snap to the point that is **Perpendicular** to the point copied from.
  - Click to set location. ❸
  - Press **Enter** to end the command.

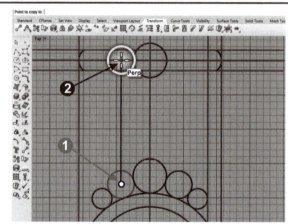

Fig. 50

- Two of the pearls have been placed on the top and side views.

Fig. 51

- Use the same technique to set the copies of the smallest pearl on the Top and Side views.

- Zoom in close to place the small pearl on the perpendicular point on the side view!

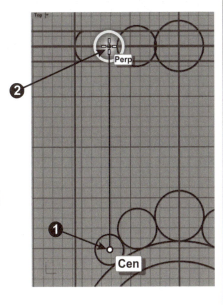

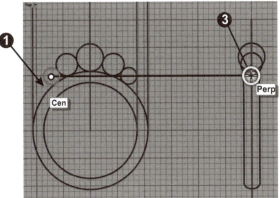

Fig. 52

- **Mirror** the side pearls in the top elevation over to the other side of the ring.
  - **Start of mirror plane: "0"** ❶
  - Using **Ortho,** draw the cursor up and click on the Y Axis to set the direction of the mirror plane. ❷

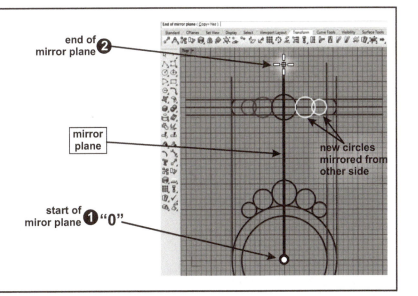

Fig. 53

- Use the **Trim** command to trim out the pearls for final design definition as shown.

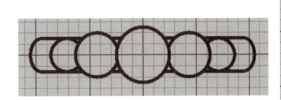

- Save the file as **pearl ring technical drawing.3dm.**
- This drawing will be used in the next chapter on printing technical drawings.

Fig. 54

Draw Order Commands
Controlling Display of Overlapping Objects

Controlling Display of Overlapping Lines

- Create the layers shown.

- **TECH LINES** layer current.

Fig. 1

TECH LINES	✓	■
ref geo	♀ 🔓	☐

- Create some parallel (or non-parallel) lines. No particular length required for this exercise.

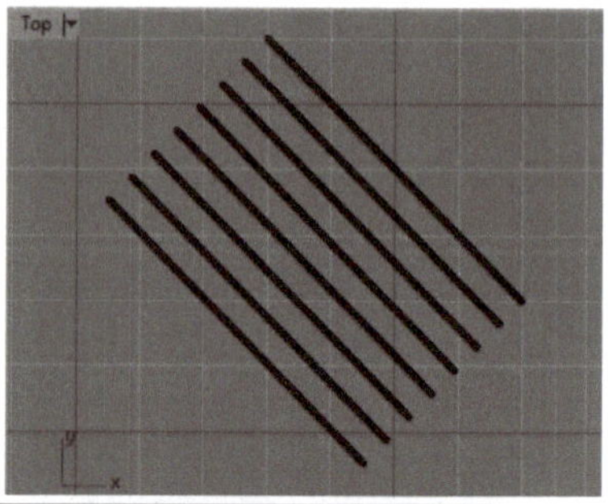

ref geo	✓	■

- Create some lines that overlap the lines you just created as shown.

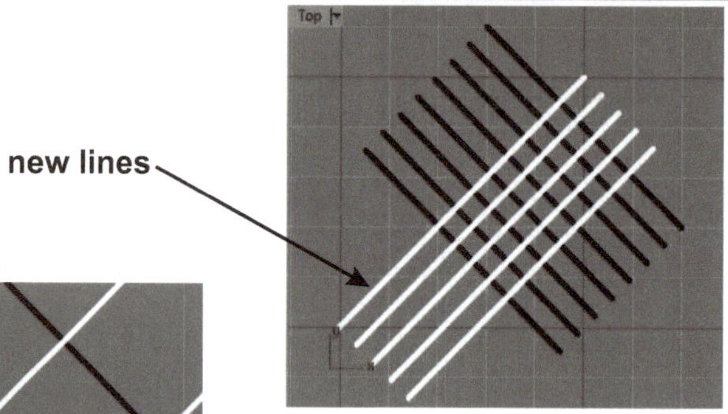

new lines

- Notice that the new lines overlap the previous ones, giving the appearance that they are "in front" of the original lines.

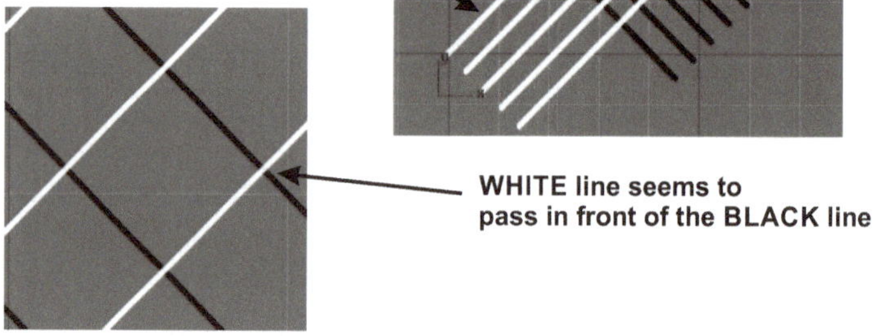

WHITE line seems to pass in front of the BLACK line

Fig. 2

- **RIGHT-CLICK** on any tab. ❶

- Click on the **Show Toolbar** option in the drop-down menu. ❷

- Click on the **Draw Order** toolbar option in the drop-down that lists toolbars. ❸

- The **Draw Order** toolbar will appear as a *floating toolbar*.

- *note: you can also add this as a tabbed toolbar if you want.*

Fig. 3

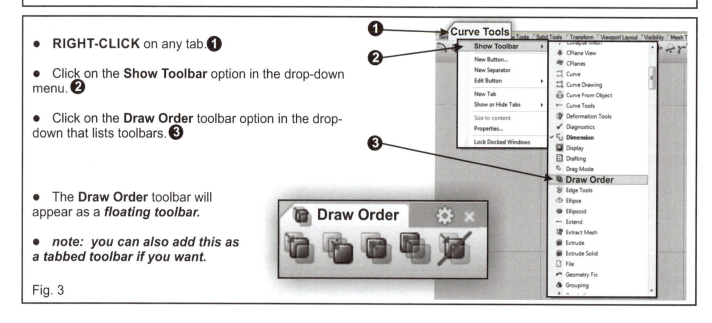

- Select all of the original dark lines that you created first.

- Click on the **Display order: bring to front** button in the **Draw Order** toolbar.

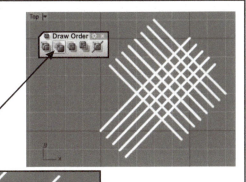

Display order: bring to front
command

- When you click away to de-select, notice that now the darker original lines seem to be in front of the white lines.

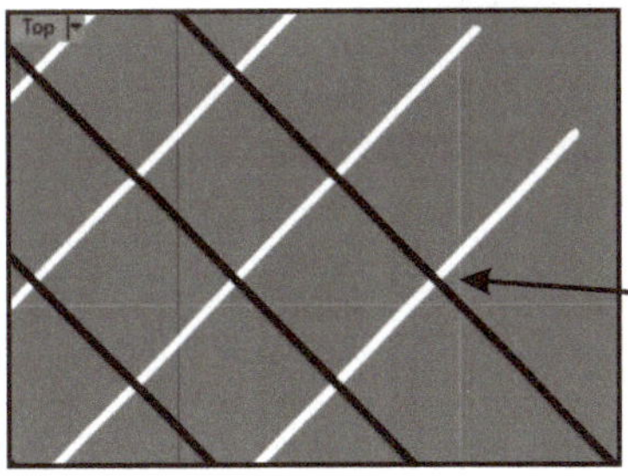

dark line now seems to overlap the light color

Fig. 4

- **Important note: This is about the change of display only. No objects get actually moved in this command!**

- The selected object has been created in the **Simple Pearl Ring Technical Drawing** with the use of construction lines that are a warmer color than the selected object which is black. Also, they were created first, before the selected object.

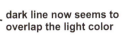

- Click away to de-select and notice that this object is almost completely hidden from view by the overlapping construction lines.

Fig. 5

- Select all of the overlapping construction lines and click on the **Display order: send to back** command

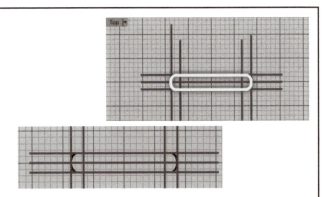

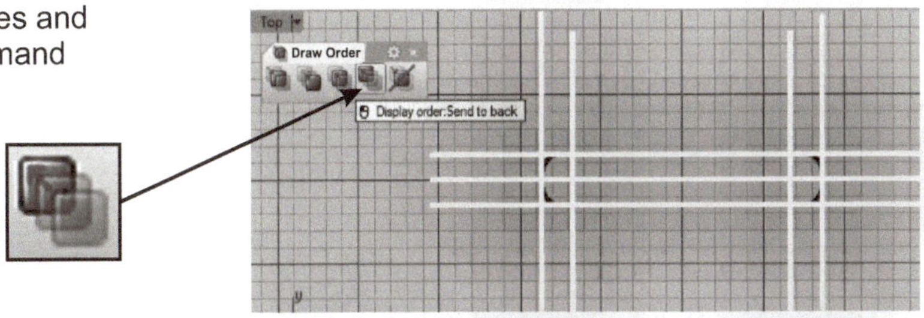

Display order: send to back
command

- Click away to de-select and notice that now the darker object seems to be in front of the construction lines.

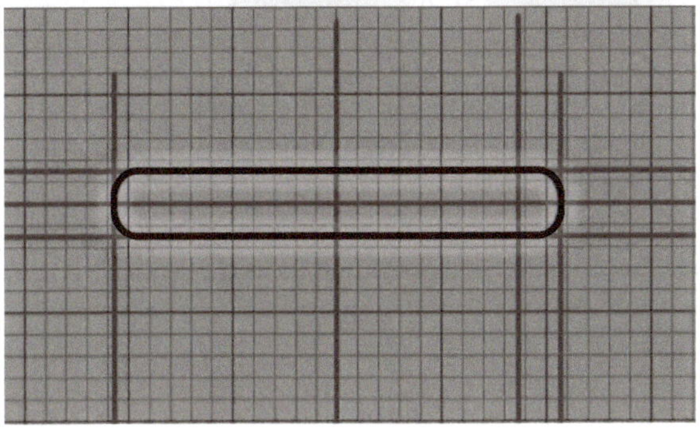

Fig. 6

Printing

- Open your Rhino file: **pearl ring technical drawing.3dm.**

- **Top** viewport.
  - Rhino will print in the active viewport so make sure that the **Top Viewport** is active by clicking anywhere in it.

- The **construction lines** layer is turned off.

Fig. 1

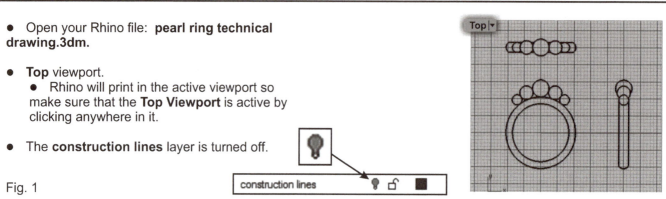

- Select the **construction lines** layer. **1**

- Click on the **New Layer** button. **2**

New Layer button

- A new layer will appear under the selected **construction lines** layer.
  - Name this new layer **display construction lines. 3**
  - Assign the color **red.**

Fig. 2

- **display construction lines** layer current.

- Use **grid snap** and **quad osnap** to create the 7 lines shown.

  - These lines will become dotted or center lines when we assign their linetypes later in this exercise.

Fig. 3

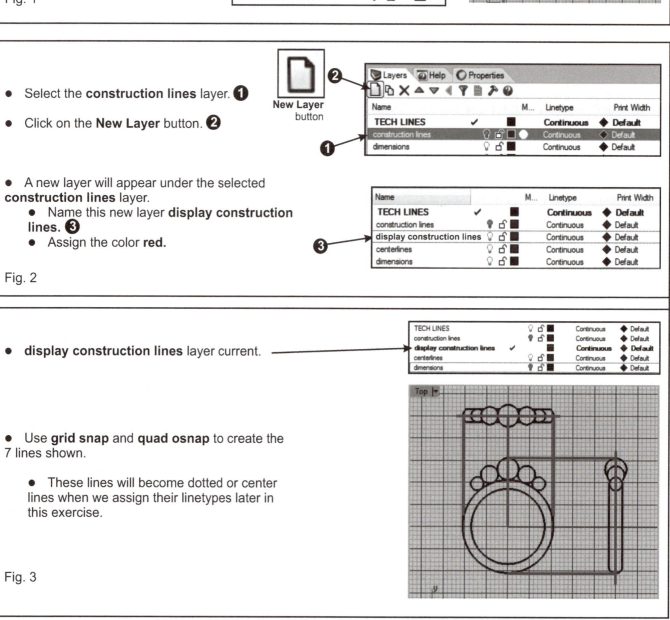

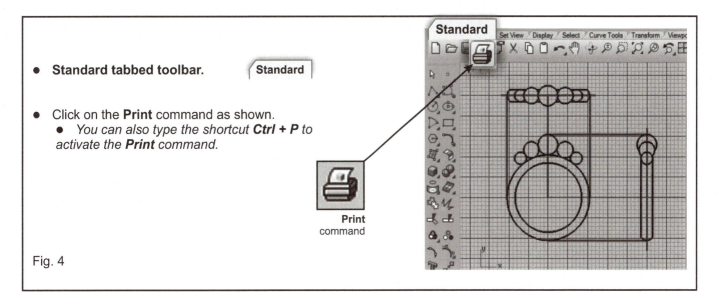

- **Standard tabbed toolbar.** `Standard`

- Click on the **Print** command as shown.
  - *You can also type the shortcut **Ctrl + P** to activate the **Print** command.*

Print
command

Fig. 4

- The **Print Setup** box will open.

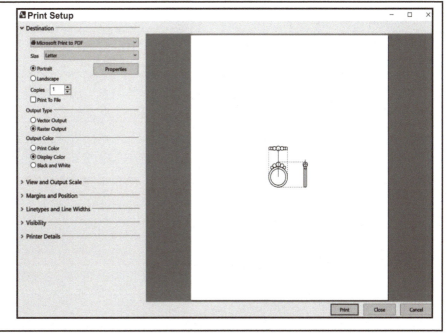

Fig. 5

- **Destination:** ❶
  - Your designated printer will be the default destination.
  - Click on the **Properties** button for familiar settings associated with your printer. ❷
- **Output Type:** ❸
  - This should be set at **Vector Output** because you are printing lines and don't need pixels until you get into rendered images in 3D modeling.
- **Output Color:** ❹
  - The default **Print Color** is the color of the layers you used.
  - Display color refers to colors assigned by you for printing.

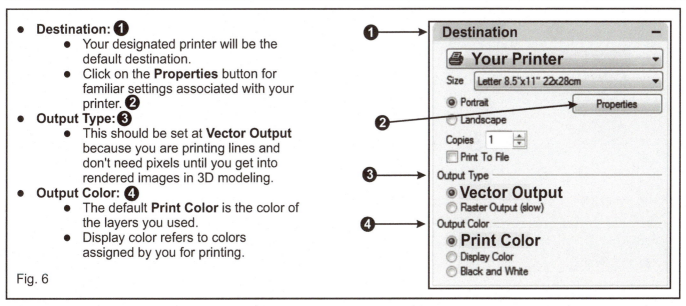

Fig. 6

- **View and Output Scale** category:
  - Select the **Extents** option.

- Notice that the default scale setting is **Scale to Fit.**
  - Click on the little triangle to open up a drop-down list of scale settings. ❶

Fig. 7

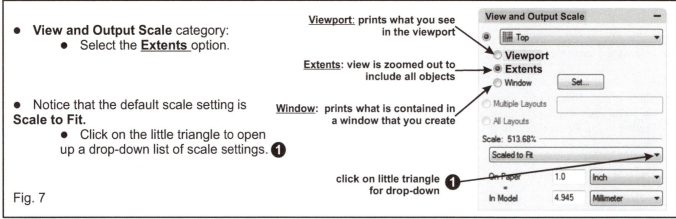

Viewport: prints what you see in the viewport

Extents: view is zoomed out to include all objects

Window: prints what is contained in a window that you create

click on little triangle for drop-down ❶

- A drop-down list will appear, showing different Scale settings.

- Scroll up to the top of the drop-down list and click on the **1:1** setting. ❷
  - Your printed image will be *scaled to the exact size of the drawing.*

Fig. 8

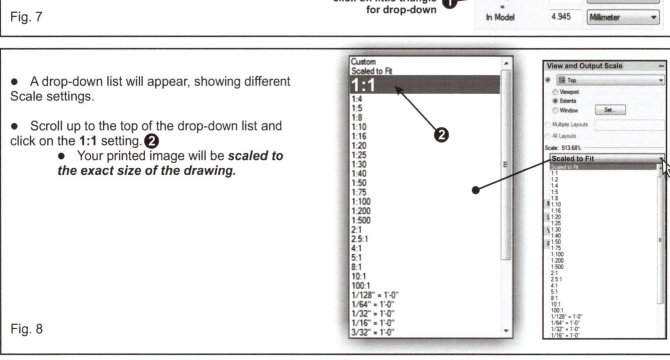

- Close the previous categories by clicking in their upper right corners.

- Open the **Margins and Position** category as shown. ❶
  - Notice that the **Centered** option is selected. ❷
  - The drawing is centered on the print preview as shown.

Fig. 9

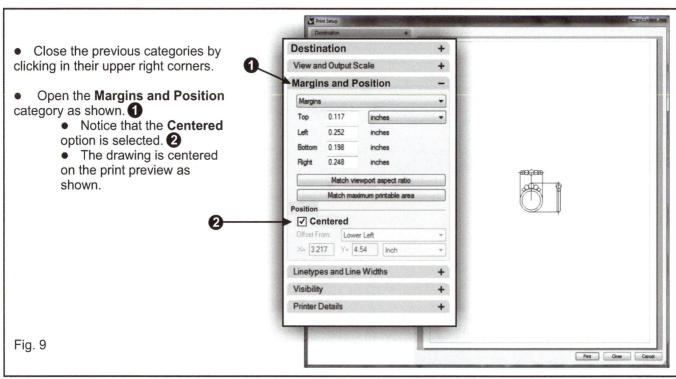

- Open the **Linetypes and Line Widths** category. ❶
  - The default line width is a hairline. ❷
  - The default line type is a continuous line until more specific linetypes are assigned.
    - *We will soon cover how to adjust Linetype settings to enhance the impact of the drawing.*

- Click in the upper right corner to close the **Linetypes and Line Widths** category.

Fig. 10

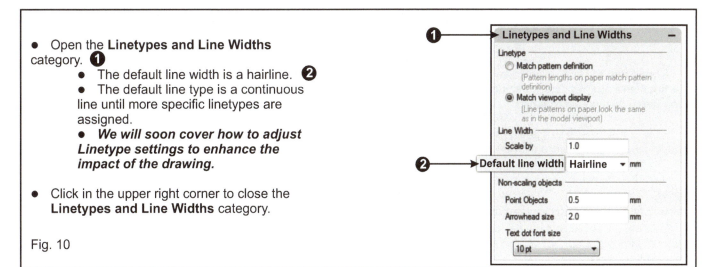

- Click to open the **Visibility** category.

- Note that different options allow other elements to be printed, such as the background color of the viewport, the grid, grid axes, and any picture frame or other background bitmap that may be in the viewport.

- Note the option called **Only Selected Object.**
  - This means that **only objects that are selected** will show in the preview window and be printed.
    - *If you do not see anything in the preview pane and you have not selected anything, check to see if this option is checked!*

Fig. 11

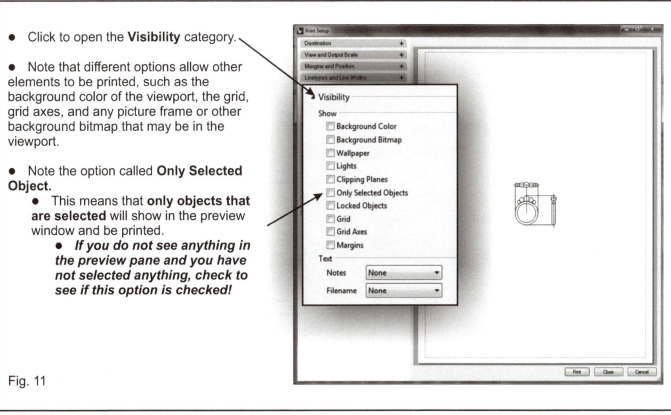

- The final category, **Printer Details,** describes the printer you will be using, it's port into your computer, the paper type and the printable area of the image.

Fig. 12

- Click on the **Print** button to print your drawing.

Fig. 13

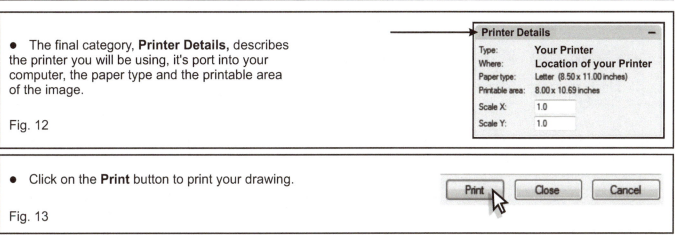

Print Settings for Custom Linetypes, Colors, & Print Width

- Notice that the line widths are, by default, hairlines and all lines are "continuous", rather than being "dotted" or "dashed".

- Now is the time to assign linetypes, colors, and line widths for a more dynamic presentation.

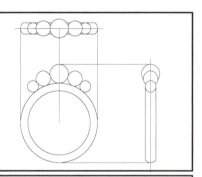

Fig. 14

- Use the cursor to pull the Layers box and column widths out so that you can see all of the column headings.

- We will be working with these categories:
  - **Linetype** ❶
  - **Print Color** ❷
  - **Print Width** ❸

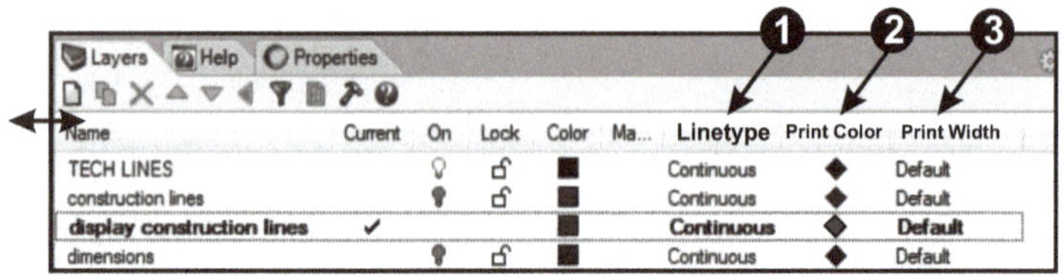

Fig. 15

- If you see something like this, it means that some of the category columns need to be made visible.

Fig. 16

- **Right-click** on the line that shows the column names as shown. ❶

- A drop-down context menu will appear as shown. ❷

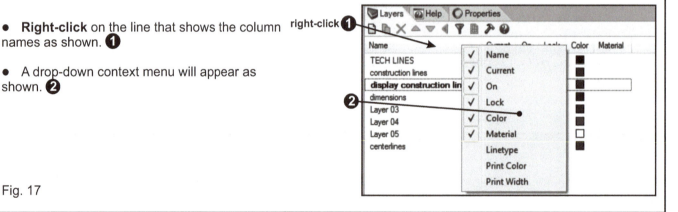

Fig. 17

- Draw the cursor down and click on **Linetype**.❶

- The **Linetype** column will now be showing in the **Layers** box.❷

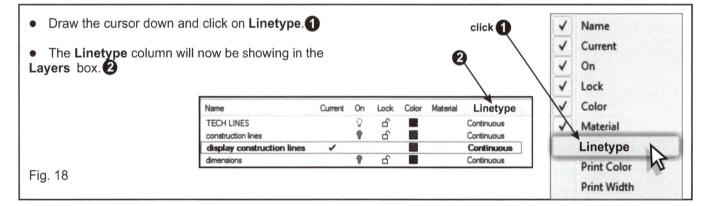

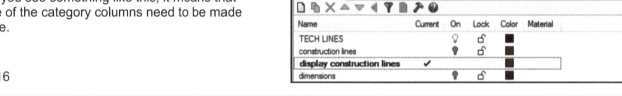

Fig. 18

- Use this process again to make the **Print Color** and **Print Width** category columns visible.

Fig. 19

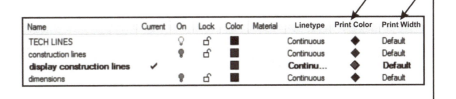

Dotted Linetype

- Click on the word **Continuous** ❶ in the **Linetype** column of the **display construction lines** layer line. ❷

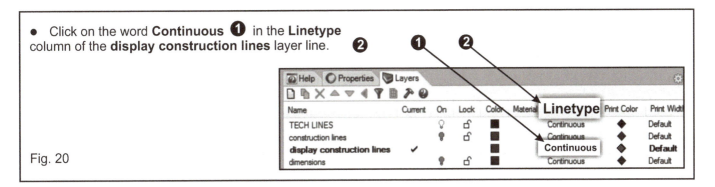

Fig. 20

- When the **Select Linetype** box appears, select the **dots** linetype. ❶

- Click the OK button to exit the box. ❷

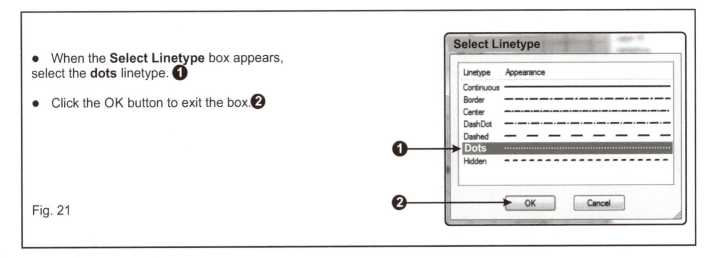

Fig. 21

- The **display construction lines** in the drawing now have a dotted linetype.

- note: You can toggle the grid off by pressing the **F7 Hotkey.** Press again to toggle the grid on again.

F7   **press to toggle grid off**

F7   **press to toggle grid on again**

Fig. 22

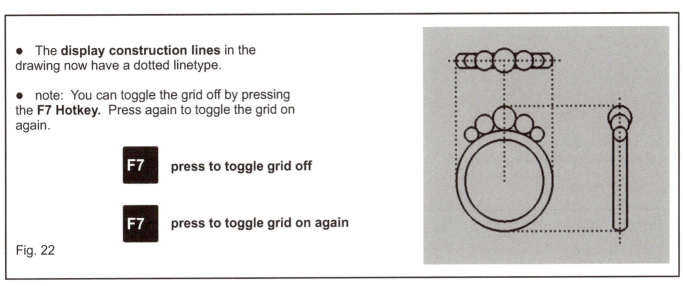

Centerline Linetype

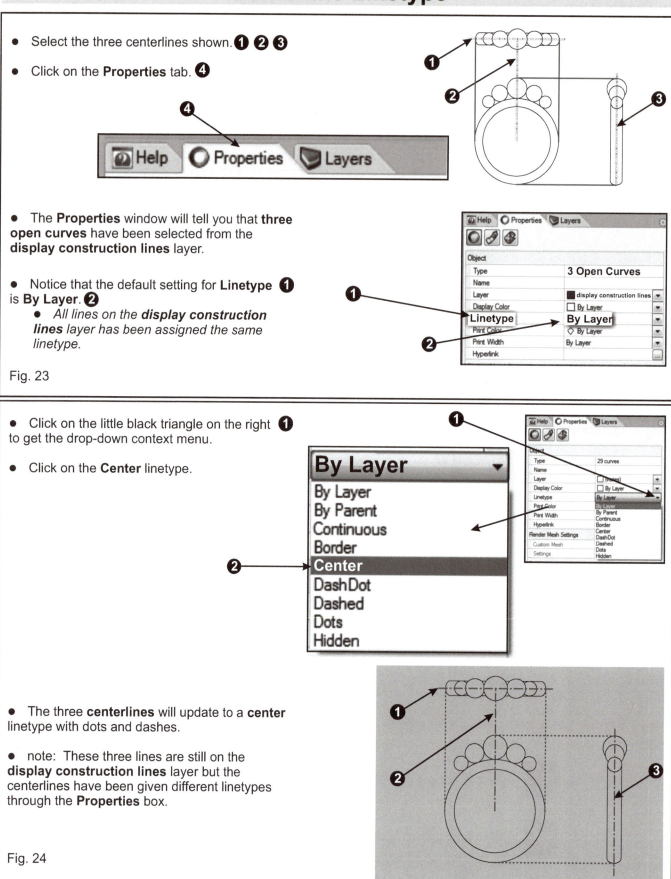

- Select the three centerlines shown. **❶ ❷ ❸**

- Click on the **Properties** tab. **❹**

- The **Properties** window will tell you that **three open curves** have been selected from the **display construction lines** layer.

- Notice that the default setting for **Linetype ❶** is **By Layer**. **❷**
  - *All lines on the display construction lines layer has been assigned the same linetype.*

Fig. 23

- Click on the little black triangle on the right **❶** to get the drop-down context menu.

- Click on the **Center** linetype.

- The three **centerlines** will update to a **center** linetype with dots and dashes.

- note: These three lines are still on the **display construction lines** layer but the centerlines have been given different linetypes through the **Properties** box.

Fig. 24

- The default **dots** linetype may be very faint in the printing.

- In this exercise, a new custom linetype will be created that may show up better in the printed technical drawing.

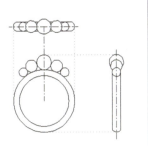

Fig. 25

- **Drafting tabbed toolbar.** `Drafting`

- **Right-click** on the **Document properties page: Linetype** button.

RIGHT-CLICK for
Document properties page: Linetype
button

Fig. 26

- The **Rhino Options** box will open to the **Document Properties** category **Linetypes**. ❶

- Click on the **Add** button. ❷

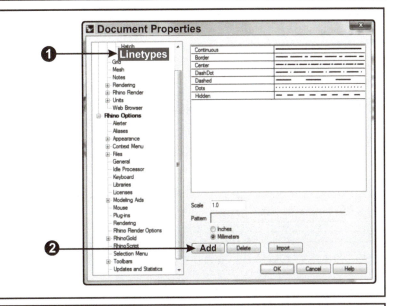

Fig. 27

- A new linetype will appear at the end of the list of linetypes. ❸

- Name the new layer **1mm-1mm.** ❹

new linetype ❸

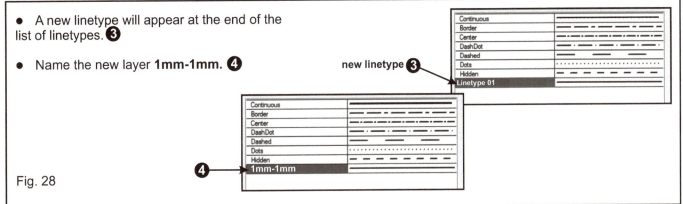

Fig. 28

- Change the **Pattern** setting to read <u>**1.00**</u>, **1.00** ❹

- <u>**1.00**</u> is the **length of each dash**
- **1.00** is the **length of the spaces between the dashes.**

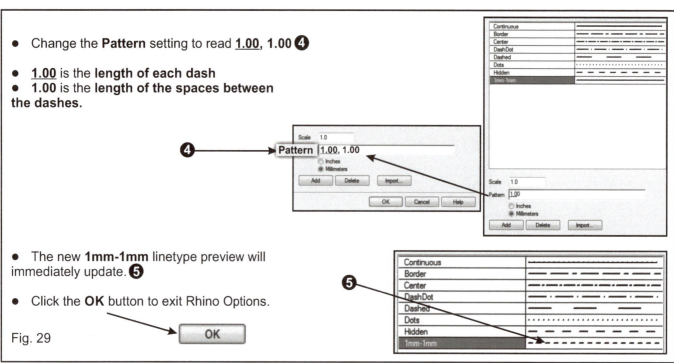

- The new **1mm-1mm** linetype preview will immediately update. ❺

- Click the **OK** button to exit Rhino Options.

Fig. 29

- Click on the word **dots** in the **Linetype** column of the **display construction lines** layer.

- Select the new **1mm-1mm** linetype ❷ that is now one of the listed linetypes in the **Select Linetype** box.

- Click **OK** to exit the **Select Linetype** box.

Fig. 30

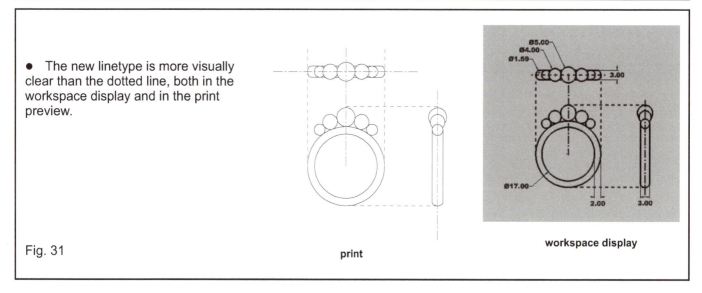

- The new linetype is more visually clear than the dotted line, both in the workspace display and in the print preview.

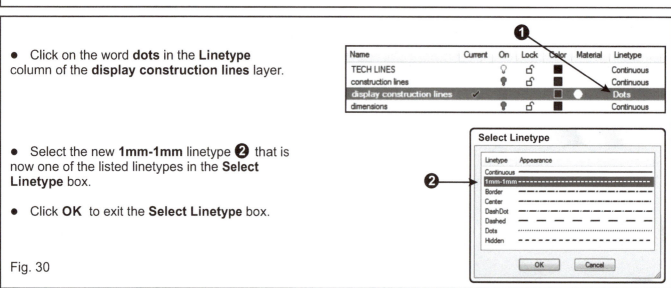

Fig. 31

print   workspace display

147

Print Color

- Default **Print color** will be the same color as the layer. **❶**

- In this example, the layer color of red will also be the **Print Color.** **❷**

- **If you want to change a color for printing, click on the Print Color block for a specific layer.**

Fig. 32

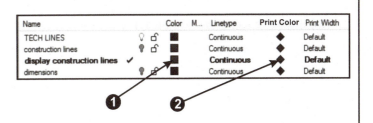

Assigning Print Width

- Click on the word, **default** in the **Print Width** column of the **TECH LINES** layer. **❶**

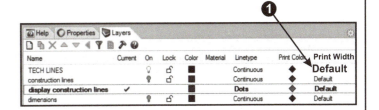

- The **Select Print Width** box will appear.

- Click on the **0.18 width** and click the OK button. **❷**

- This will result in the **TECH LINES** being **printed heavier than the construction lines.**

> - Note: The change in line widths will not show on your workspace display. **_They will only show in the printing._**

Fig. 33

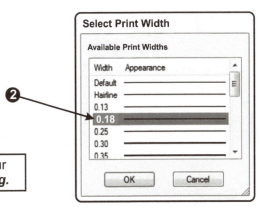

- Print the drawing again, adding dimensions and changing the **Output Color** in the **Destination** category to **Display Color.**

- Looking at the print preview may not show you the difference in line widths but the print itself will show that the main **TECH LINES** are wider than the **construction lines**.

Fig. 34

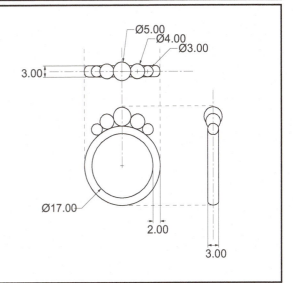

Freeform Curves

Control Point Curves, Interpolate Point Curves

Control Point Curves

- **Curve Tools tabbed toolbar.** Curve Tools
- **Left-click** on the **Control point curve** command.
  - **Start of curve** prompt:
    - Click on the desired location of the start of the curve. ❶

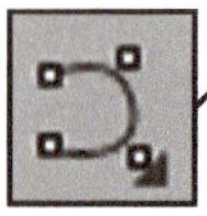

left-click for
Control Point Curve
command

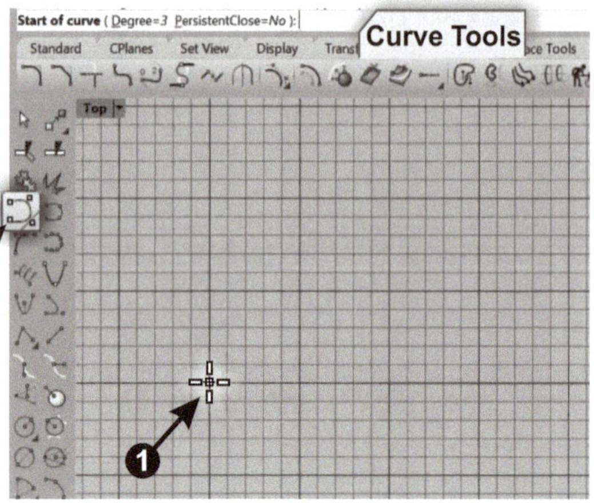

Fig. 1

- **Next point** prompt:
  - Click on the next point of your curve. ❷

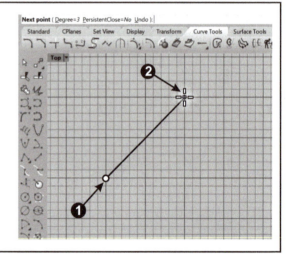

Fig. 2

- **Next point. Press Enter when done** prompt:
  - Notice that when you draw the cursor away to locate the third point, the curve draws away from the second control point.

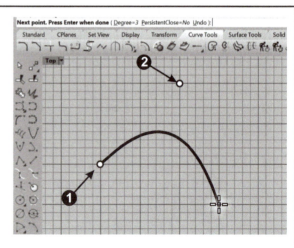

Fig. 3

- Click in desired locations to continue creating the curve and you will see how the curve is controlled by the points but does not pass through them. ❸ ❹ ❺ ❻ ❼

- Click on the **Undo** option in the **Command Line** as shown.

Fig. 4

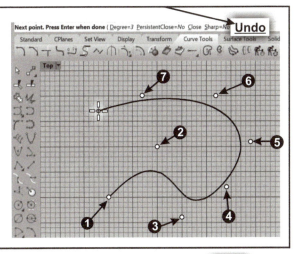

- The last point ❼ will disappear.
- You can click the **Undo** option repeatedly to cancel previous locations in the order in which they were created.

Fig. 5

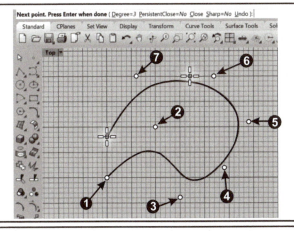

- Click to continue the line a couple of additional times ❼ ❽ until your curve comes around near to the start point.

Fig. 6

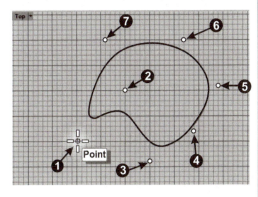

- As you draw the cursor over the start point of the curve, it will automatically snap to the **Point** of the start of the curve. ❶

- *The curve will deform itself to become a totally smooth curve.*

- *Notice how it pulls away from its own start point to achieve this.*

- Click to set the last point and the command will end because you have created a *closed curve.*

Fig. 7

Interpolate Point Curves

- **Curve Tools tabbed toolbar.** ⌐Curve Tools⌐

- **Left-click** on the **Curve: Interpolate points** command.
    - **Start of curve** prompt:
        - Left click on the location for the start of your curve. ❶

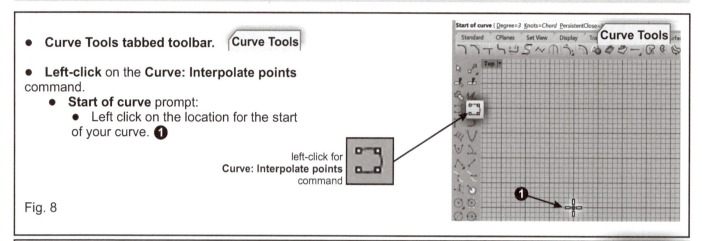

left-click for
Curve: Interpolate points
command

Fig. 8

- As you continue to click to make more points to form your curve, notice that the curve continues to pass through the points where you clicked. ❷ ❸ ❹ ❺ ❻

    - *This is the big difference between the Curve: Interpolate points command and the Control point curve command.*

- In the **Command Line,** click on the **Sharp-No** option to toggle it to **Sharp-Yes** as shown.

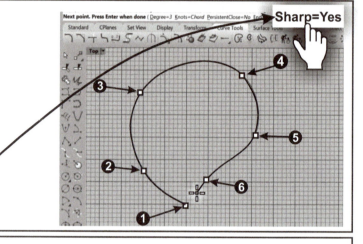

Fig. 9

- Draw your cursor over the first point.
    - The cursor will automatically snap to the **Point** at this location to make a closed curve.
- Click on this location. ❶

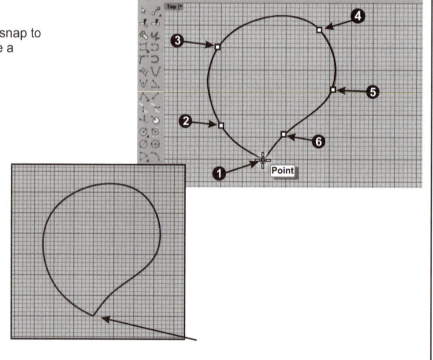

- The point where the beginning and end of the curve meet is a kink, rather than a smooth join.

- This is because you toggled on the **Sharp=Yes** option!

Fig. 10

Adding a Kink to a Curve

Addition of a Kink will enable you to point edit sharp corners into the design of your line.

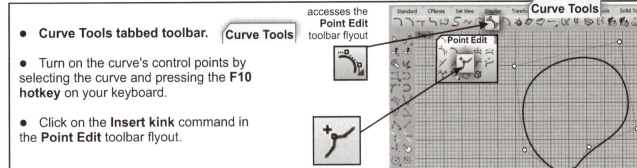

- **Curve Tools tabbed toolbar.** [Curve Tools]

  accesses the **Point Edit** toolbar flyout

- Turn on the curve's control points by selecting the curve and pressing the **F10 hotkey** on your keyboard.

- Click on the **Insert kink** command in the **Point Edit** toolbar flyout.

Insert kink command

Fig. 11

- **Select curve or surface for kink insertion** prompt:
  - Select the curve as shown.

- The curve will not "light up" when selected because the control points are on but that is OK in this command.

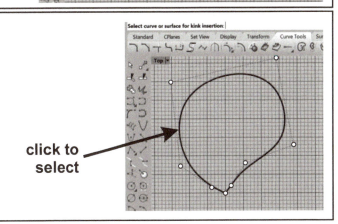

click to select

Fig. 12

- **Point on curve to add a kink** prompt:
  - Click on a location near the top of the curve as shown.

- Notice that during this command, an **On Crv** tooltip shows when the cursor is in contact with the curve.

  - Press **Enter** to end the command.

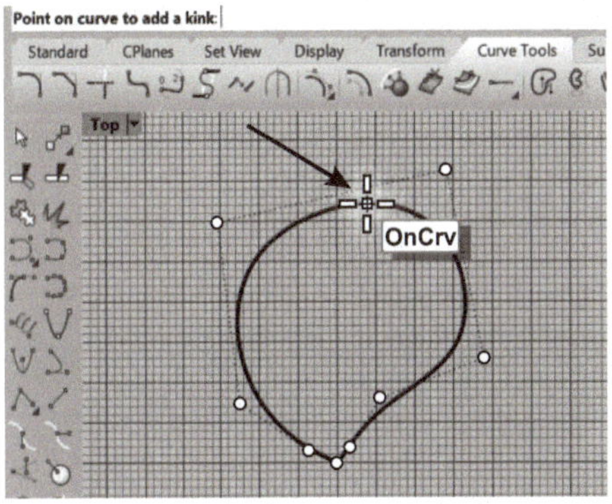

Fig. 13

- A new kink will be created. Notice that control points have moved slightly around the new kink and a couple of new control points have been added right next to the new kink.

- Note: The curve is now a Polycurve and can be exploded into 2 segments.

- You can insert as many kinks as you wish.

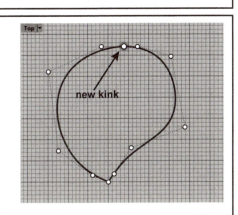

new kink

Fig. 14

- **Move** or **Drag** the new kink to change the design.

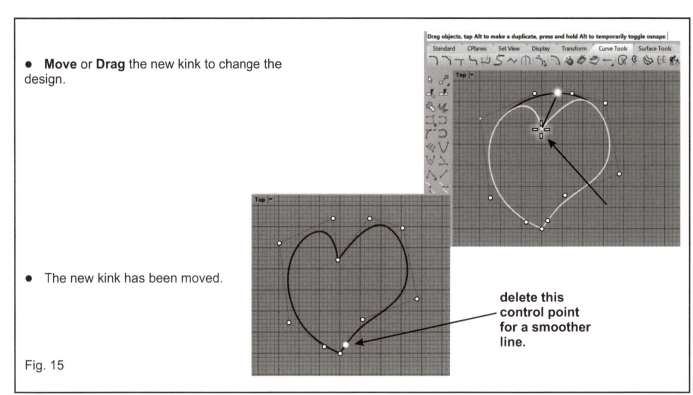

- The new kink has been moved.

delete this control point for a smoother line.

Fig. 15

- Refine your design with further control point manipulation.

- Notice that deleting one of the control points has resulted in a smoother line at the bottom of the heart..

- Save this file as **freeform heart.3dm.** We will use this file again for an **Array Along Curve** exercise.

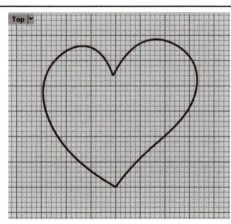

Fig. 16

Open Freeform Curves

- Left-lick on the **Curve: interpolate points** command in the **Curve Tools** tabbed toolbar.

  - **Start of curve** prompt:
    - Type **"0"** in the **Command Line** and press **Enter.**

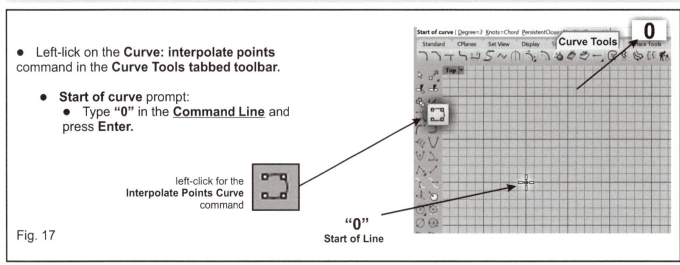

left-click for the
Interpolate Points Curve
command

"0"
Start of Line

Fig. 17

- **Next point. Press enter when done**
prompt:
  - Click a few times to create a rough S shaped curve.
  - After you have clicked enough points to make the S shape, press **Enter** to finish the curve.

- The curve will be completed, stopping at the last point you clicked.

- *You have created an open Freeform curve, instead of the closed curve that you created in the previous examples.*

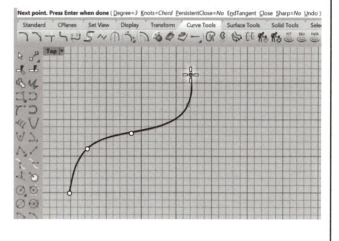

Fig. 18

- Left-click on the **Curve: interpolate points** command in the **Curve Tools tabbed toolbar.**

  - **Start of curve** prompt:
    - Snap to the **End** of the previous curve as shown.
    - Click to set location.

left-click for the **Interpolate Points Curve** command

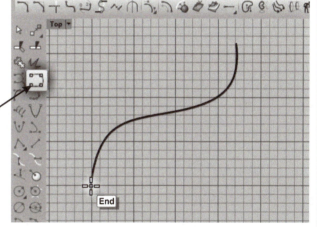

Fig. 19

- **Next point. Press Enter when done**
prompt:
  - After a few clicks, snap to the other **End** of the line.
  - Press **Enter** to finish the line and end the command.

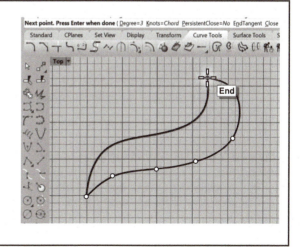

Fig. 20

Joining the Two Curves to Create a Single Closed Curve

- Click on the **Join** command.

  - **Select object for join** prompt:
    - Select one of the curves as shown. **1**

Join
command

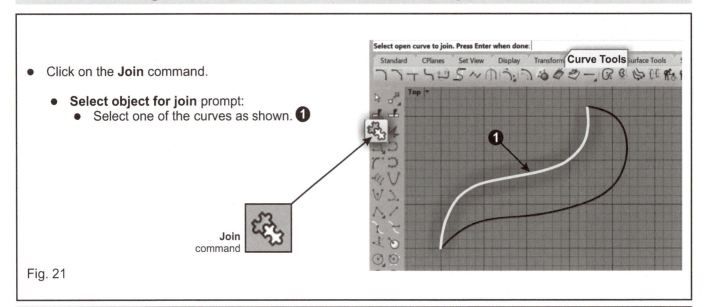

Fig. 21

- **Select curve to join. Press Enter when done** prompt:
  - Select the other curve. **2**

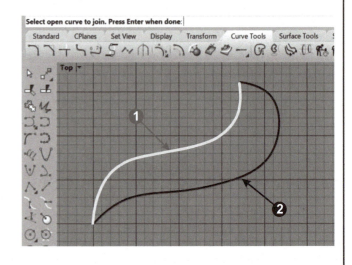

Fig. 22

- The curves will automatically de-select because they are now a closed curve.

- The **History line** will tell you that **2 curves have been joined into one <u>closed curve</u>**.

  - *You can not join another curve to a closed curve or polyline.*

- **This is a closed curve because the Join command was applied to two curves that were touching at both end points.**
  - *If the curves were not touching at both ends. the curve will still be an open curve.*

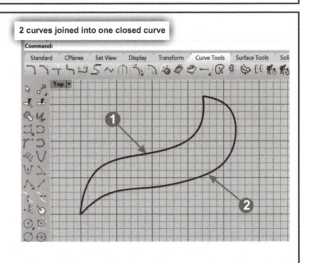

Fig. 23

- **Left-click** on the **Explode** button.

left-click
for the
Explode Command

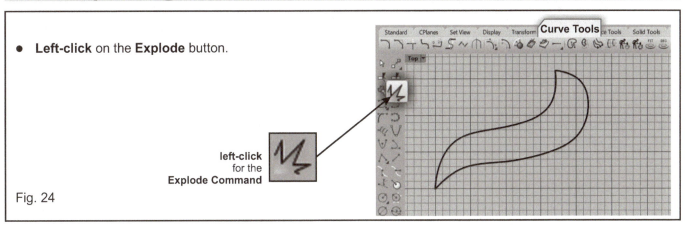

Fig. 24

- **Select objects to explode** prompt:
  - Click to select the closed curve shown.
  - Press **Enter.**

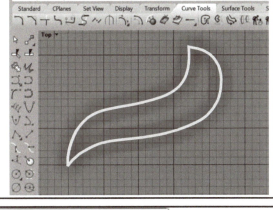

Fig. 25

- If the curves do not de-select, click away to de-select.

- The History line will say **Exploded into 2 segments.**

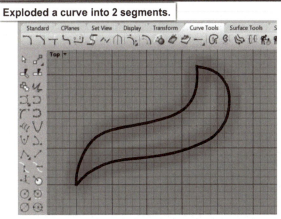

Fig. 26

- You will now be able to select the two lines separately as *they will no longer be joined together.*

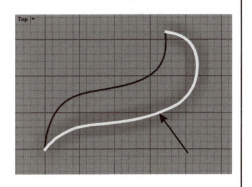

Fig. 27

Picture Plane Command
Placing and Scaling a Design Image in Rhino
Tracing with Freeform Curves

- This is the image that will be used in this chapter that will deal with bringing an image onto the Rhino workspace and tracing it using Rhino's drawing tools.

- It is included in the file library that you can download from the www.rhinoforjewelry.com website.

- See pp. 18-19 for instructions on how to download these files.

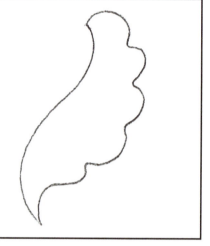

Fig. 1

- **Surface Tools tabbed toolbar.** [Surface Tools]

- **Left-click** on the **Picture Plane** command as shown.

Picture Plane
command

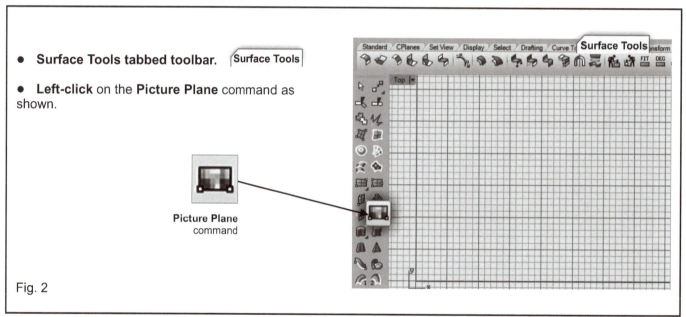

Fig. 2

- The **Open Bitmap** dialog box will open.

- Navigate to the folder in your computer that contains the downloaded texture and Emap files and select **leaf scan for bitmap trace** as shown. ❶

- Click on the **Open** button. ❷

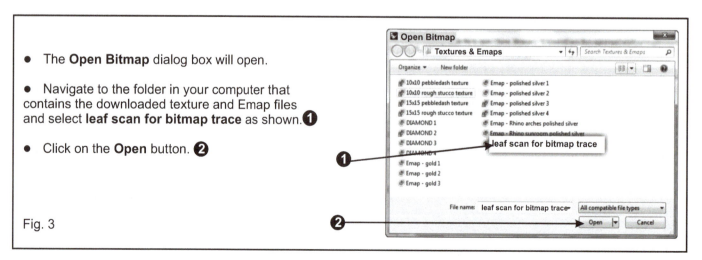

Fig. 3

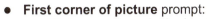

- **First corner of picture** prompt:
  - Click somewhere in the lower left of the viewport as shown. **❶**

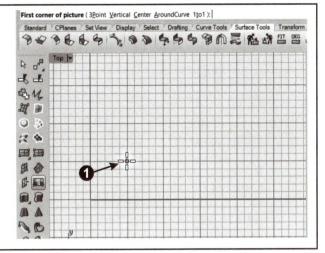

Fig. 4

- **Other corner or length** prompt:
  - Drag the cursor upward at a diagonal across the viewport as shown.
    - *Note: If you want to place the picture plane surface at a diagonal, click on the **3Point** option in the **Command Line.***
  - A preview of the shape of the image will form as you drag the cursor.
  - By default, the picture plane will be placed in line with the grid.

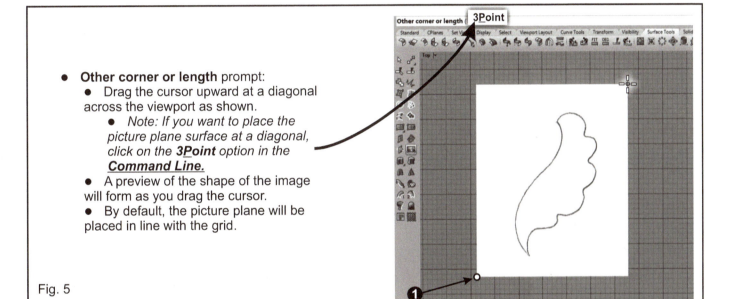

Fig. 5

- **Left click** on the opposite corner to set location. **❷**

- *note: this image will be scaled to the desired size later in this exercise.*

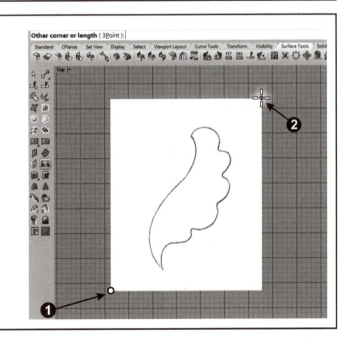

Fig. 6

Making the Image more Transparent
Transparency can make the image easier to trace.

- The sketch that you have placed on the Rhino workspace is a bitmap image that has been "mapped" to a "surface". This will be referred to as the "picture plane".
- Click to select the picture plane surface.**❶**
    - The rectangular border lines are the **edges of the surface.**
    - The lines that cross the middle of the surface are called **isocurves** and are a feature of all surfaces, displaying direction and other geometry.

Fig. 7

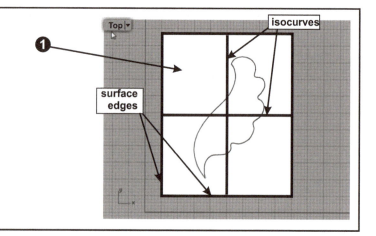

- While the picture frame is still selected, **RIGHT-CLICK** on any tab in the **Layers Panel. ❷**
    - A drop-down menu will appear.
    - **LEFT-CLICK** on **Materials** as shown. **❸**

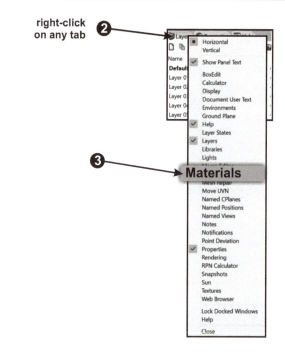

- The **Materials Tab ❹** will appear.

- The name of the material shown will be the same name as the image file that you selected in Fig. 3.
    - This "material" was automatically created in the Picture Plane command.

Fig. 8

● Double-click on the title of the assigned material ❶ to open the Materials window.

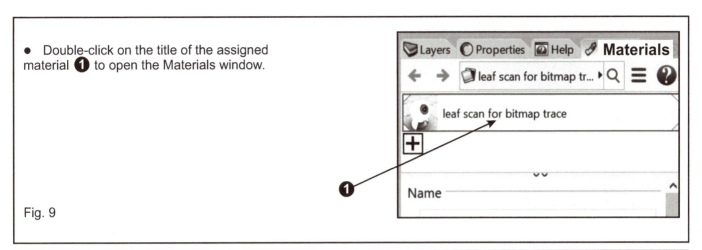

Fig. 9

● The Materials window will open up, displaying the properties of the selected picture surface.

● Click and drag the little triangle on the **Transparency slider** until the percentage of transparency reads about 45%.

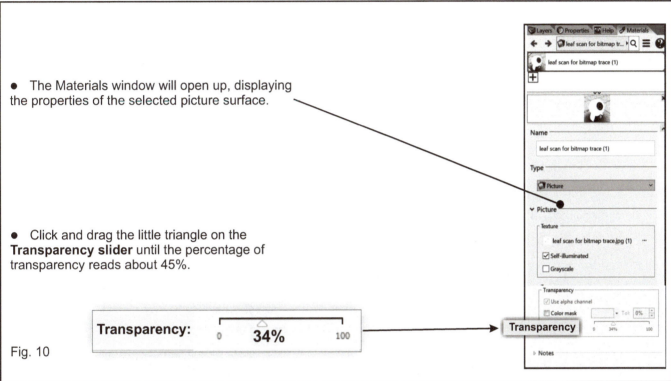

Transparency: 0 △ 34% 100

Fig. 10

● the **Picture Plane** image is now transparent which can make it easier to trace.

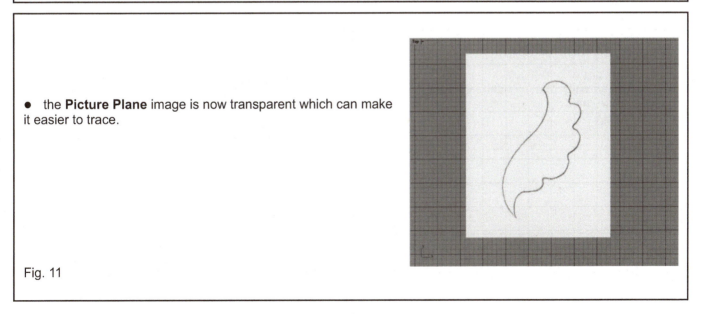

Fig. 11

Tracing the Picture Plane Image
Using a Freeform Curve Command to Trace the Design

- **Standard tabbed toolbar.**   Standard

- Select the picture plane surface and **left click** on the **Lock** command as shown.
    - This "locks" the picture plane so that you can not select it but you can still see it for the tracing that follows.

*[Note: To **Unlock**, just **RIGHT-CLICK** on the **Lock** command button and the surface will be unlocked once again.]*

LEFT-CLICK for
Lock
commaned

Fig. 12

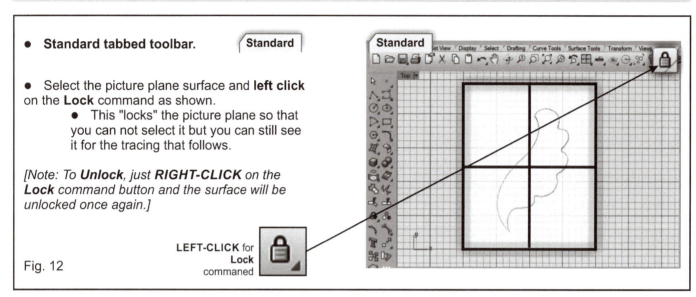

- **Curve Tools tabbed toolbar.**   Curve Tools

- **Left click** on the **Curve: interpolate points** command.

Curve: interpolate points
command

Fig. 13

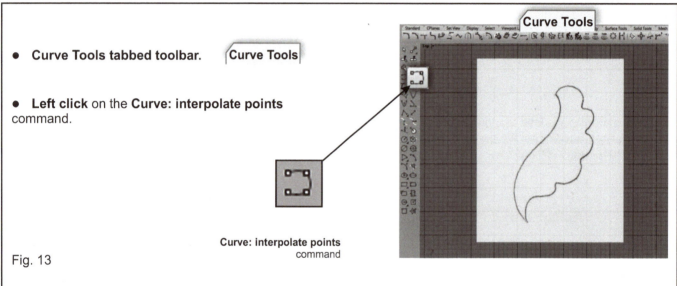

- **Start of curve** prompt:
    - **Left click** on the bottom tip of the leaf to start the tracing, locating this point by eye. ❶

Fig. 14

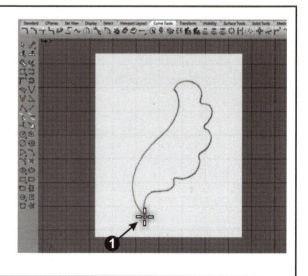

- **Next point** prompt:
  - As you draw the cursor outward, notice the "rubber band" effect.

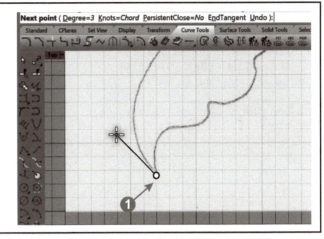

Fig. 15

- **Left click** on the approximate location shown. ❷

- **Next point. Press Enter when done** prompt:
  - Draw the cursor further along the line.
  - Notice the "rubber band" preview line as it curves along the leaf design.

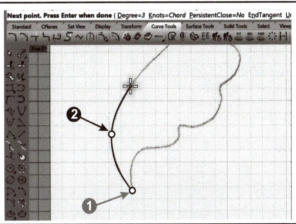

Fig. 16

- **Next point: Press Enter when done** prompt:
  - Keep clicking along the line until you arrive at the top of the leaf.
  - Press **Enter** to end the command.

- *Note: click as few times as possible for a smoother line.*

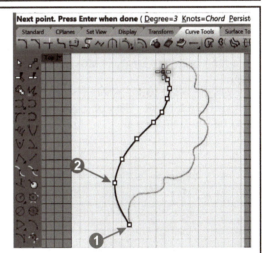

Fig. 17

- View the finished curve.

Fig. 18

- **Select** the curve you just created and **Left click** on the **Edit points on** command as shown.

- **Edit points** will appear along the curve.

Fig. 19

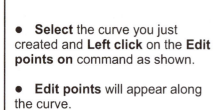
accesses the Point Edit toolbar flyout

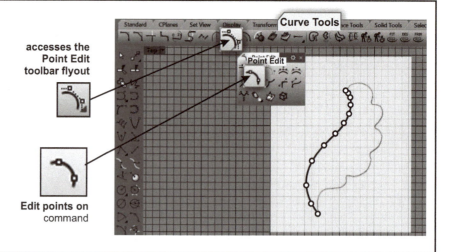

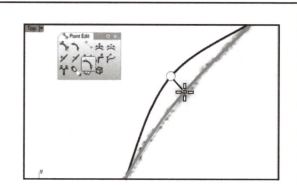
Edit points on command

- **Move** or **Drag** Edit Points to refine the line you just created.
- You also select the **Delete** points by pressing the **Delete key.**

Fig. 20

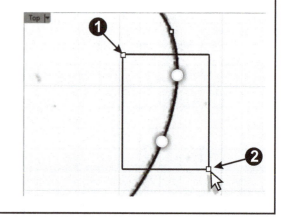

- You can **Window Select** more than one point at a time and then **Drag** or **Move** them together.

- When you finished editing, press the **Esc** key or **right-click** on the **Edit points on** button to turn off the Edit points.

Fig. 21

- **Left click** on the **Curve: interpolate points** command again.

  - **Start of curve** prompt:
    - **Left click** on the end of the curve you just created.
    - Use **End osnap** to make sure that the new curve will start exactly at the endpoint of the existing curve.

Fig. 22

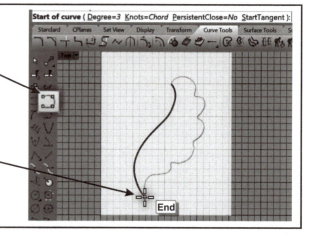
Start of curve (Degree=3 Knots=Chord PersistentClose=No StartTangent):

- **Next point. Press Enter when done** prompt:
  - As you place Edit points, notice how you need more of them to trace lines with sharper curves/more detail.

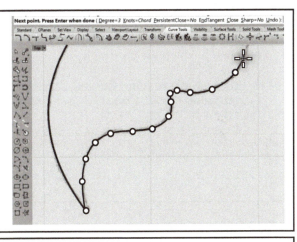

Fig. 23

- **Next point. Press Enter when done** prompt:
  - Snap to the endpoint of the top of the previous line and click to set the last **Edit point** for the curve.
  - Press **Enter** to end the command.

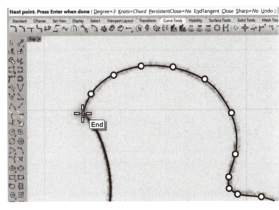

Fig. 24

- The second curve has been created.

- The first and second curves touch each other at both ends and can be later joined together to make them a single **Closed Curve** after point editing.

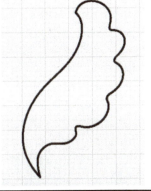

Fig. 25

- Point Edit to refine the curves.

- You can use either **Edit Points** or **Control Points.**

- Click on the little **Disable** box on the status bar at the bottom of the workspace to disable osnap, making editing of the line easier. *Click on it again to enable object snap later.*

Fig. 26

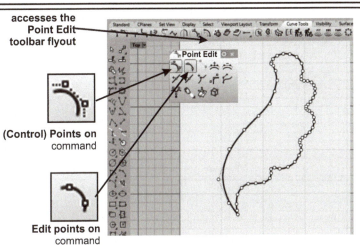

accesses the Point Edit toolbar flyout

(Control) Points on command

Edit points on command

- **Left-click** on the **Join** command.

  - **Select curve to join. Curves, surfaces and polysurfaces must be open. Press Enter when done** prompt:
    - Select one of the curves as shown. **1**

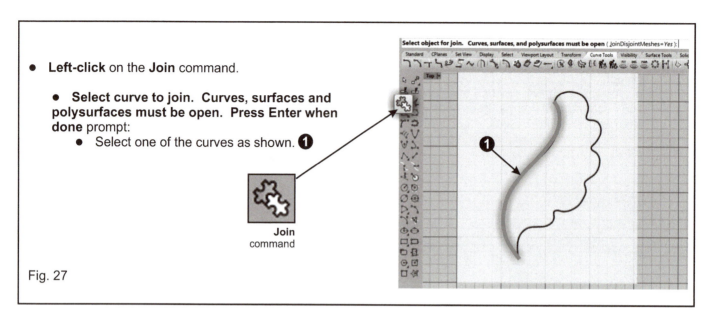

Join
command

Fig. 27

- **Select curve to join. Press Enter when done** prompt:
  - Select the other curve.
  - Both curves will be de-selected.

- The command is ended. *You can not join any more curves to a closed curve.*

- Notice that the **History Window** is stating:
2 curves joined into one closed curve. **2**

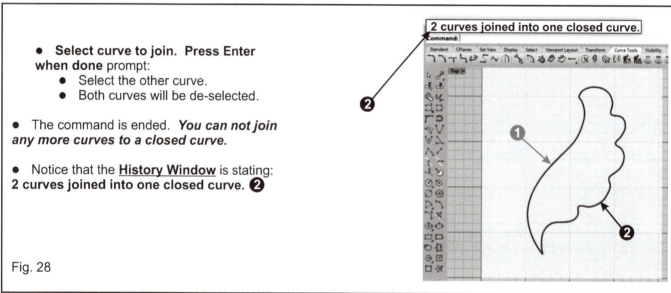

2 curves joined into one closed curve.

Fig. 28

- **Standard tabbed toolbar.** Standard

- **Right-click** on the **Lock** command to unlock the picture plane.
  - The picture plane can now be selected because it is no longer locked.

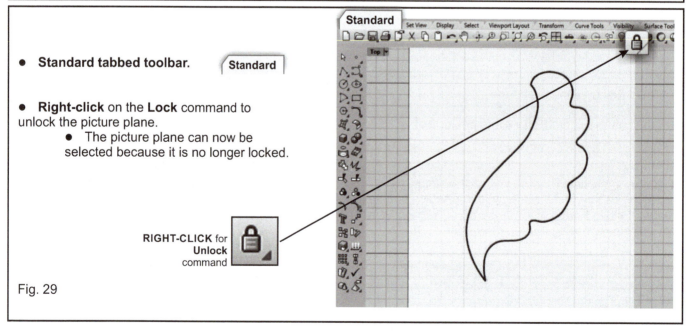

RIGHT-CLICK for
Unlock
command

Fig. 29

Scaling the Tracing and the Picture Plane
Scaling the traced design and the picture frame for accuracy.

- **Transform tabbed toolbar.**

  Transform

- Click on the **Scale 2D** command in the **Scale** toolbar flyout.

  - **Select objects to scale** prompt:
    - Select both the line drawing and the picture plane. **❶**
    - Press **Enter.**

accesses the Scale toolbar flyout

Scale 2D command

Fig. 30

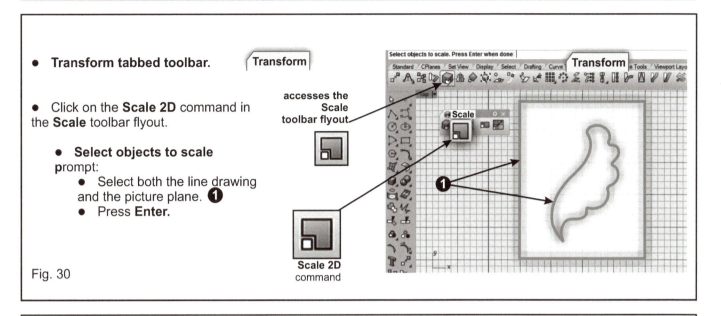

- **Origin Point** prompt:
  - Use **End osnap** to snap to the lower tip of the leaf as shown. **❷**
  - Click to set location.

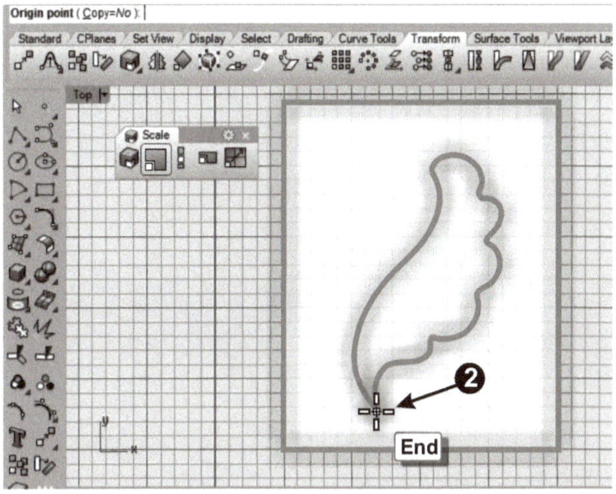

Fig. 31

- **Scale factor or first reference point** prompt:
  - Use **Quad osnap** to snap to the top of the leaf as shown.
  - Click to set location. **❸**

Fig. 32

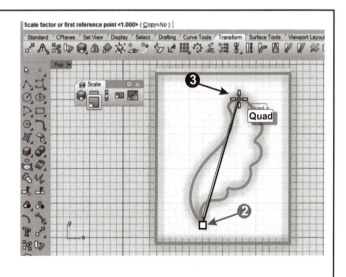

- **Second reference point** prompt:
  - Type **"30"** in the **Command Line.**
  - Press **Enter.**

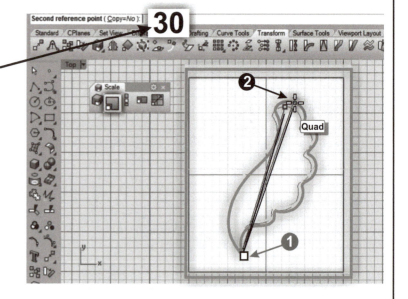

Fig. 35

- The command is ended.

- The dimension of the leaf drawing has now been accurately scaled to a length of 30mm.

- Save this file as: **leaf design.3dm.**

Fig. 34

If your Picture Plane is Missing
Migrating your Picture Plane image when you open your Rhino file on another computer and do not see the image on the Picture Plane surface

- If you re-open this file a different computer and see the **Missing Image files** box with the picture frame image listed, ❶ you need to re-introduce the image to the material properties of the picture frame surface.

- Click on the **Continue** button to complete the opening of the file. ❷

Fig. 35

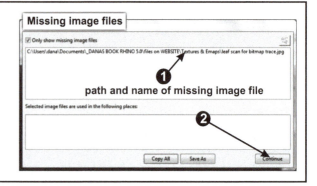

- If you turn off the layer for the linework, you will see a blank picture frame surface.

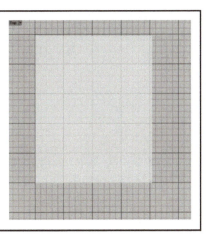

Fig. 36

- Click on the **Materials tab** ❶ to open the **Materials** panel.

- You will see a material listed for the picture frame. ❷

- You will see the **leaf scan for bitmap trace.jpg** file listed under **Textures**. ❸
  - Click on the browse button on the left of the listed texture. ❹

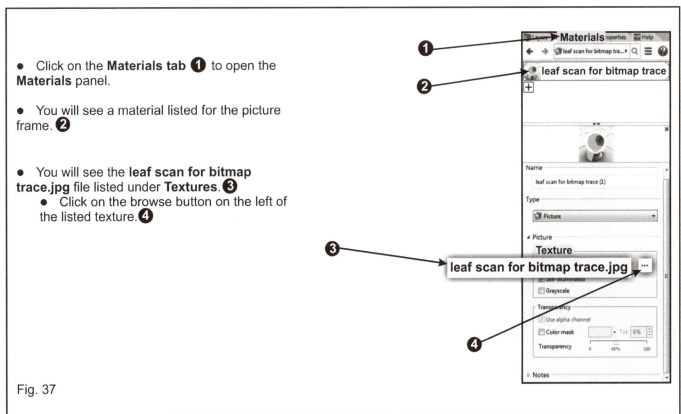

Fig. 37

- Navigate to the folder that contains the image you are using. Select that file ❺ and click on the **Open** button. ❻

- The image will be restored to your picture plane surface.

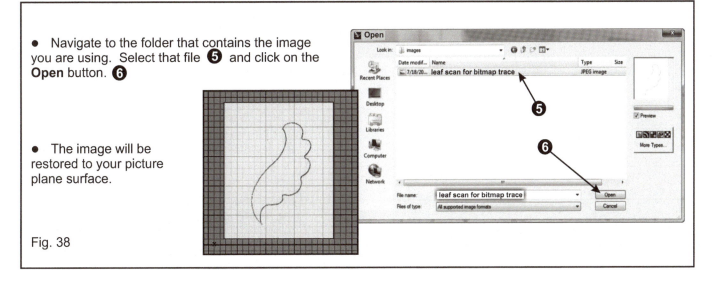

Fig. 38

Move Command
Moving the Picture Plane and Line Drawing

- Open the file **leaf design.3d** that you saved from the previous chapter.

- **Standard tabbed toolbar.**

- Click on **End osnap** to activate it.

- Click on the **Move** command.

Move command

Fig. 1

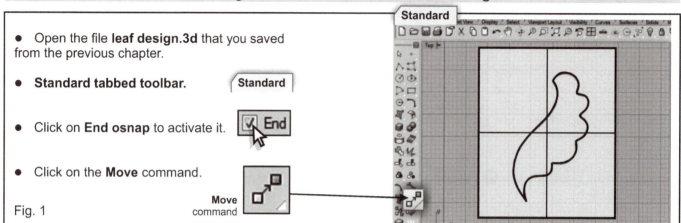

- **Select objects to move** prompt:
  - Select your Picture Plane and line drawing and press **Enter.**

Fig. 2

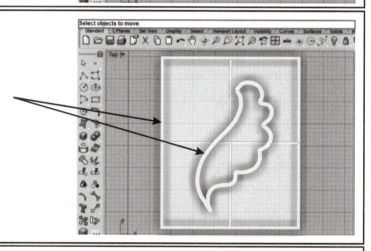

- **Point to move from** prompt:
  - Snap to the **Endpoint** of the bottom of the line drawing.
  - Click to set location.

Fig. 3

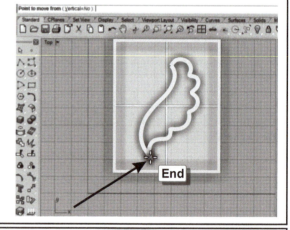

- **Point to move to** prompt:
  - Type a "0" in the **Command Line** and press **Enter.**

Fig. 4

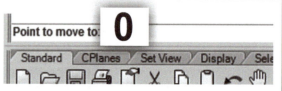

Point to move to: **0**

- The bottom tip of the leaf drawing has been accurately moved to sit on **0,0** which is the center of the grid, **the point where the X and Y axes, come together.**

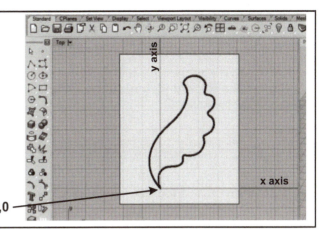

Fig. 5

Hide Objects/Show Objects Commands
Hiding (turning off) the Picture Plane image Showing it again.

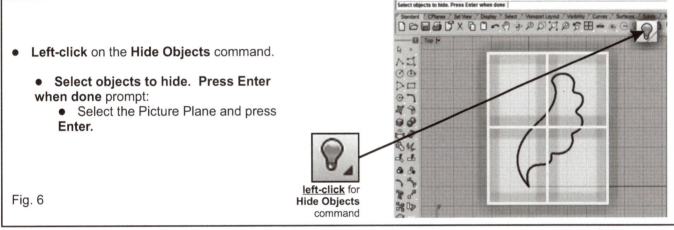

- **Left-click** on the **Hide Objects** command.

  - **Select objects to hide. Press Enter when done** prompt:
    - Select the Picture Plane and press **Enter.**

left-click for
Hide Objects
command

Fig. 6

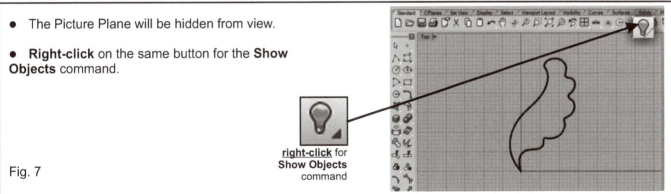

- The Picture Plane will be hidden from view.

- **Right-click** on the same button for the **Show Objects** command.

right-click for
Show Objects
command

Fig. 7

- The Picture Plane will once again be showing on the workspace.

- **Hide** the Picture Plane once again before proceeding to the next step.

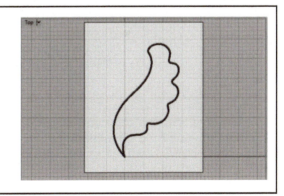

Fig. 8

Mirror Command
Creating Symmetry using the Mirror Command with the History function.

- Click on the **Record History** button at the bottom of the workspace.

Fig. 9

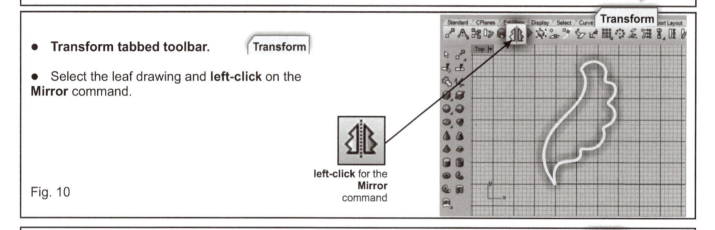

Osnap	SmartTrack	Gumball	Record History

- **Transform tabbed toolbar.** ⌐Transform⌐

- Select the leaf drawing and **left-click** on the **Mirror** command.

left-click for the **Mirror** command

Fig. 10

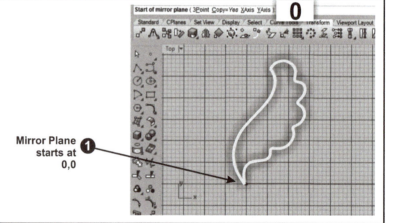

- **Start of mirror plane** prompt:
  - Type "**0**' in the **Command Line** and press **Enter.** ❶

Mirror Plane starts at 0,0 ❶

Fig. 11

- **End of mirror plane** prompt:
  - Draw the cursor straight up, using **ORTHO** so that the mirror plane will be perfectly perpendicular.
  - Click anywhere on this plane to set the direction of the mirror plane. ❷

    - A perfect "mirror image" of the leaf will be created.
      - Both the original and the mirrored copy are the same distance from the mirror plane.

Fig. 12

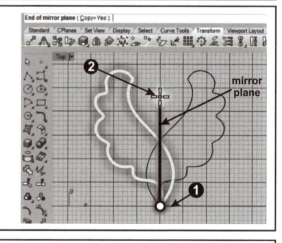

mirror plane

- Notice that after the command is completed, the History button is no longer selected.
- But the **History relationship** between the leaf and its mirrored copy has been established nonetheless.

Fig. 13

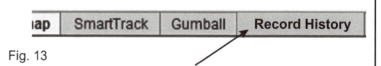

ap	SmartTrack	Gumball	Record History

Rotate, Mirror, Point Editing with History Update
Continuing the design process.

- **Left-click** on the **Rotate 2-D** command.

  - **Center of rotation** prompt:
    - Snap to the **Endpoint** at the bottom of the parent object.
    - Click to set location.❶

left-click for the
Rotate 2-D
command

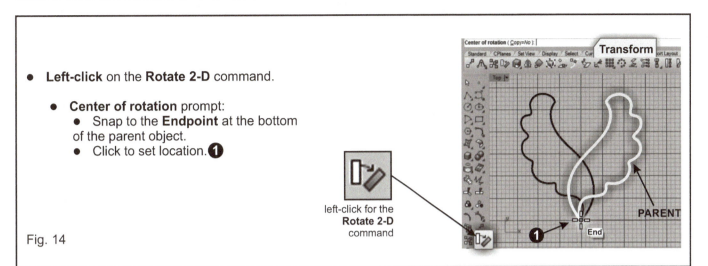

Fig. 14

- **Angle or first reference point** prompt:
  - Draw the cursor upward and click to set the first reference point somewhere on the grid as shown.❷

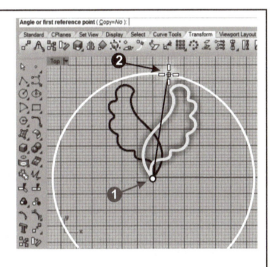

Fig. 15

- **Second reference point** prompt:
  - Draw the cursor around clockwise until the preview of the new location of the leaf is in a position that you like.
  - Click to set this new location.❸

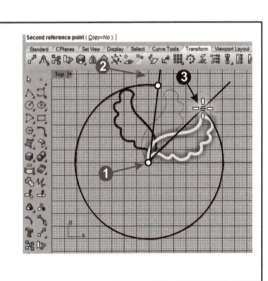

Fig. 16

- The leaf is now rotated into a new position.

- Note: **History** has updated the position of the leaf on the left so that it still is a mirror image of the original leaf that was rotated.
  - The original leaf on the right is called the **PARENT** and the mirror image on the left is called the **CHILD.**

Fig. 17

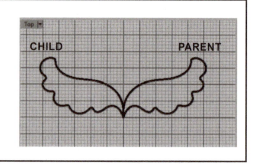

- See how many versions you can make from just point editing the **PARENT** object.

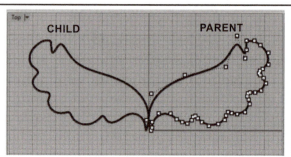

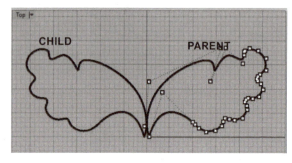

Fig. 18

- Click on the **Record History** button at the bottom of the workspace.

Fig. 19

| Osnap | SmartTrack | Gumball | **Record History** |

- Select both **CHILD** and **PARENT** and left-click on the **Mirror** command.

  - **Start of mirror plane** prompt:
    - Type "0" in the **Command Line** and press **Enter.** ❶

left-click for the
Mirror
command

Fig. 20

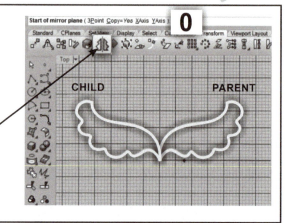

- **End of mirror plane** prompt:
  - Using **ORTHO,** draw the cursor straight over to the right or left and click to set location.❷
  - Two mirror images have been created below the original 2 *and have a History relationship with them.*

Fig. 21

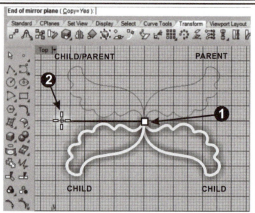

- Select the original **PARENT** object and left-click on the **Rotate 2-D** command.

  - **Center of rotation** prompt.
    - Click in the middle of the leaf as shown. ❶

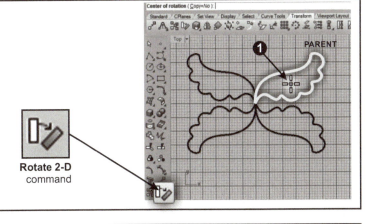

Rotate 2-D
command

Fig. 22

- **Angle or first reference point** prompt:
  - Draw the cursor out and click to set the first reference point as shown. ❷

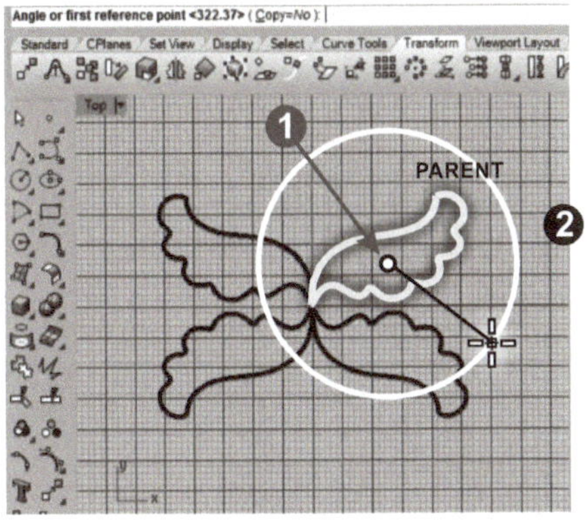

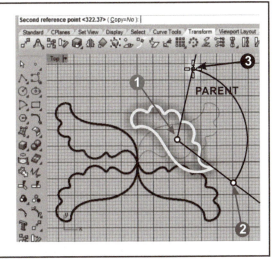

Fig. 23

- **Second reference point** prompt:
  - Rotate the cursor around to the approximate position shown.
  - Click to set the location. ❸

Fig. 24

- The other 3 elements have updated.

- Note how they intersect each other.

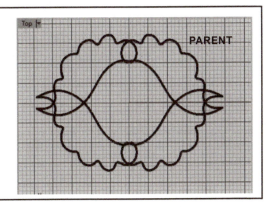

Fig. 25

- **Click and Drag** the original leaf out so that it is within the quadrant made by the X and Y axes as shown.
- Release the cursor.

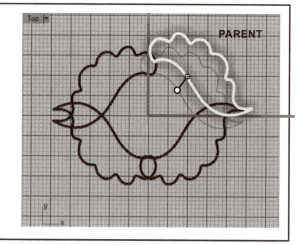

Fig. 26

- The three **CHILD** objects have updated.

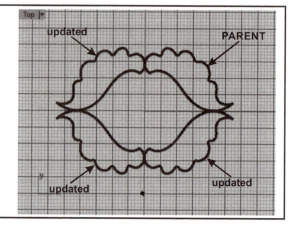

Fig. 27

- Click and drag one of the **CHILD** objects.

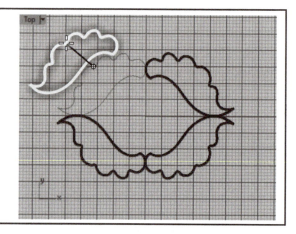

Fig. 28

- As soon as you release the cursor, the **Rhino 6 History Warning** box will appear.

- This will always happen if you edit a **CHILD** object.

- If you want to maintain the History relationship, click OK and then **Undo** the drag.

Fig. 29

- Click on the **Circle: center radius** command.

  - **Center of circle** prompt:
    - Type "0" and press **Enter.** ❶

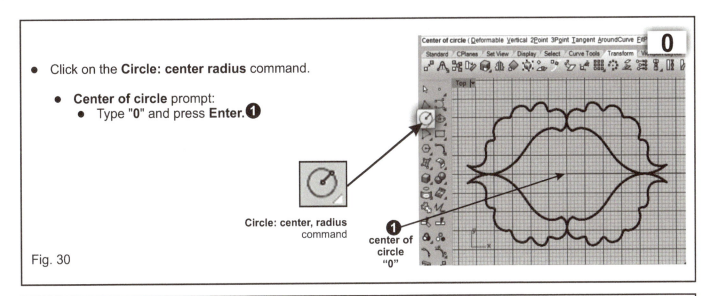

Circle: center, radius
command

center of circle "0"

Fig. 30

- **Diameter (or Radius)** prompt:
  - Draw the cursor out so that it snaps to a point on the design that allows it to sit inside the design without overlapping it.
  - Click to set the location. ❷

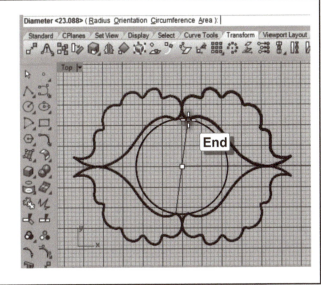

Fig. 31

- Click on the **Record History** button at the bottom of the workspace.

Osnap	SmartTrack	Gumball	Record History

Fig. 32

- Make sure that **End osnap** is checked.

  ☑ End

- **Left-click** on the **Copy** command.
  - **Point to copy from** prompt:
    - Snap to the endpoint shown.
    - Click to set the location. ❶

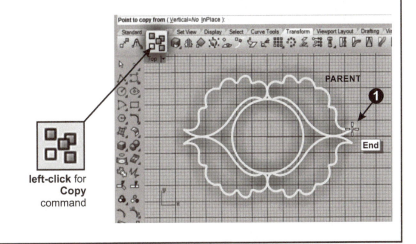

left-click for **Copy** command

Fig. 33

176

- **Point to copy to** prompt:
  - Click on the endpoint on the other side as shown to accurately place the copy. ❷

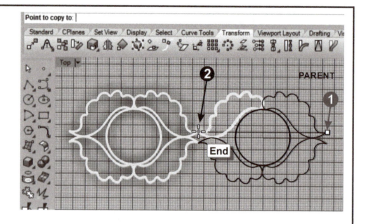

Fig. 34

- Use the same strategy to create another copy.

- Press **Enter** when done.

Fig. 35

- Turn on **Edit Points** for the original **PARENT** object only.

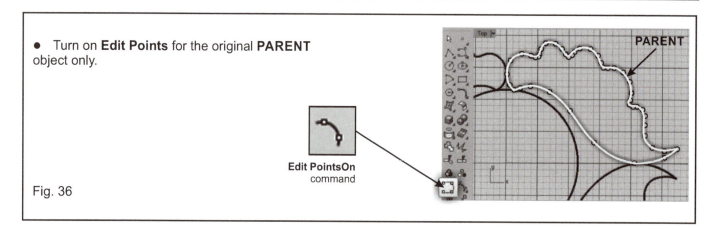

Edit PointsOn
command

Fig. 36

- Click to turn on **Perp osnap**.

☑ Perp

- Select a point and drag it toward the circle until it snaps to a location **Perpendicular** to the original location of the point as shown.

- Release the cursor.

- Do some additional point editing of you want.

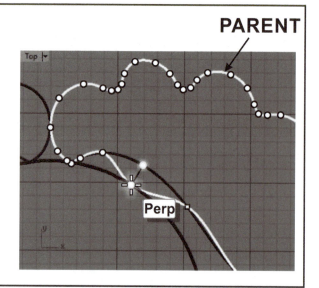

Fig. 37

- All of the other leaves update as you drag control points on the parent object.

PARENT

- History will continue to update the **CHILD** objects if you continue to edit the original **PARENT** object.

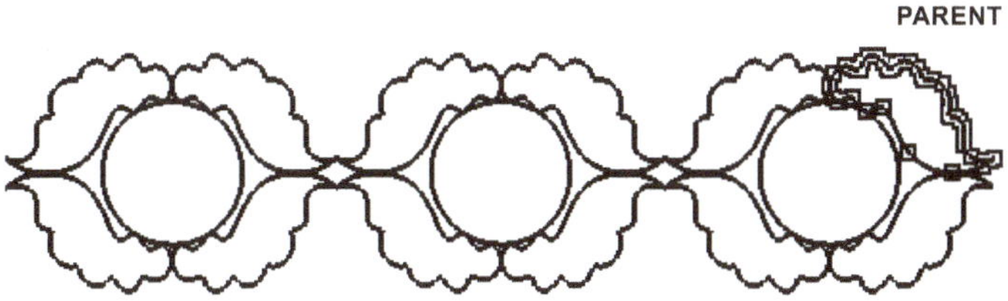

Fig. 38

- Make sure that **Quad osnap** is enabled.

- Select all of the design elements and **left-click** on the **Mirror** command in the **Transform** toolbar flyout.

  - **Start of mirror plane** prompt:
    - Snap to the **Quad** point shown and click to set location. ❶

Fig. 39

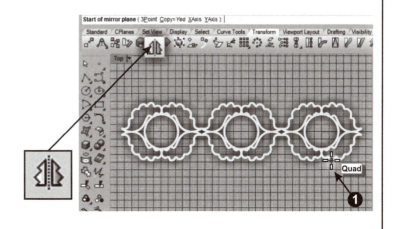

- Click on the **Record History** button at the bottom of the workspace.

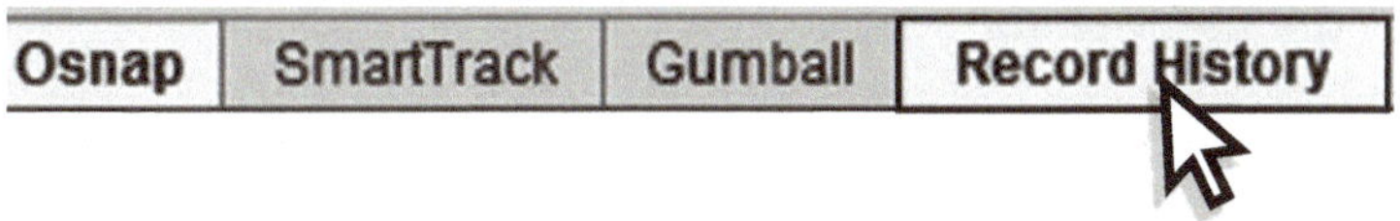

| Osnap | SmartTrack | Gumball | Record History |

- *Note: Even though you have started the Mirror command, you can still decide to use History and enable it while the Mirror command is already in progress.*

Fig. 40

- **End of mirror plane** prompt:
  - Snap to one of the **Quad** points on one of the other leaves.
  - Click to set location. ❷

Fig. 41

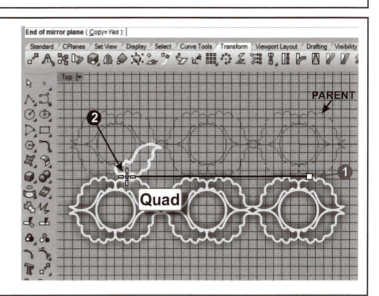

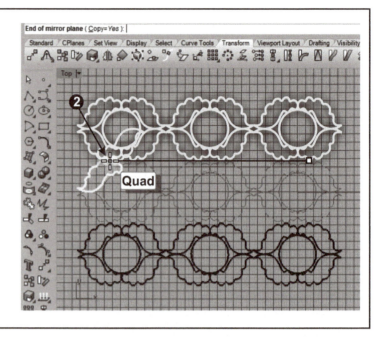

- Use the **Mirror** command again to place another mirror copy on the other side of the original row.

- **Don't forget to enable History once again for this step.**

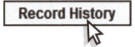

Fig. 42

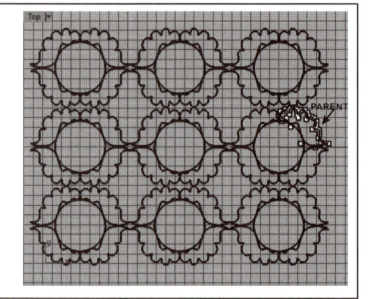

- If you continue to point edit the **PARENT** object, the rest of the leave will update as shown.

- **Save** this file as **mirrored leaf designs.3dm.**

- *The original single leaf sketch will be used in the next section.*

Fig. 43

Polar Array Command
Circular Leaf Design using History

- Open the file **leaf design.3d** once again.

- **Transform tabbed toolbar.** | Transform |

- Move the original leaf design **10mm** straight up above **"0"** as shown.

- Having your two leaf curves joined together is a good idea at this point. (see previous Picture Frame Command chapter, Figs. 30-31)

Fig. 44

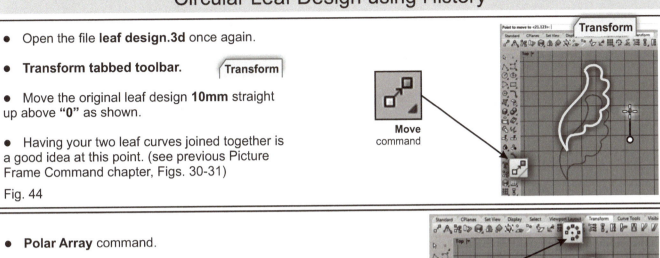

Move command

- **Polar Array** command.

- Make sure to click on **Record History** in the status bar at the bottom of the workspace.

| Record History |

Polar Array command

Fig. 45

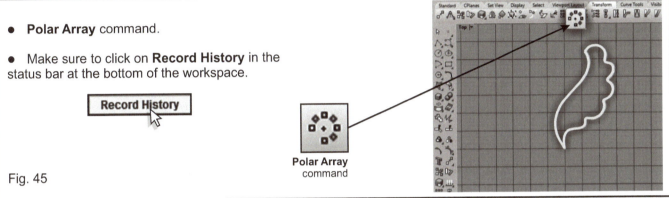

- **Center of polar array** prompt:
  - Type **"0"** and press **Enter**.

Center of polar array: **0**

- **Number if items** prompt:
  - Type **"12"** and press **Enter**.

Number of items <2>: **12**

- **Angle to fill or first reference point** prompt:
  - Press **Enter** to accept the **default 360°**

Angle to fill or first reference point **<360°>**

Fig. 46

- **Press enter to accept** prompt:
  - You will see a circular array preview that shows up in light pink as shown.
  - Click on the **Items=12** link in the **Command Line**.
- **Number of items** prompt:
  - Type **20**.
  - Press **Enter**.
- **Press enter to accept** prompt:
  - Press **Enter**.

Number of items <12>: **20**

Fig. 47

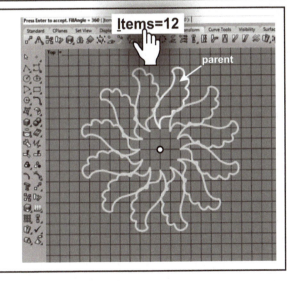

- The command is ended. The polar array has created 20 copies around the designated center of array which, in this case, is **0**.

- Select the original parent object as shown.
- Click on the tab for the **Properties** window. ❶
  - Notice the **Display Color** line. ❷
  - The default setting is that the display color of the parent object is the same as the layer for the child objects - it is **By Layer** as shown.

Fig. 48

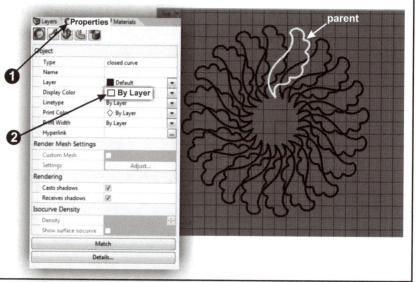

| Changing the color of the Parent object will make it easier to locate among all of the other copies! |

- Access the drop-down menu for the **Display Color** line ❶ and click on a color that is different from the color the parent is now - in this case, the color **Red** is selected. ❷

- The display color will now be seen as Red for the selected parent object.

Fig. 49

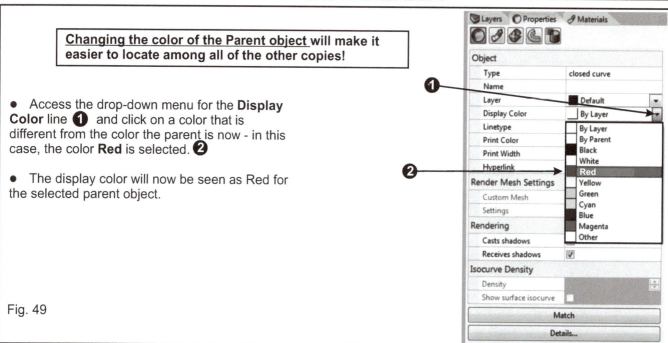

- Click on the grid to de-select the parent object and note that it is now red.

- *Note: it is still on the same layer as the rest of the objects in the array.*

Fig. 50

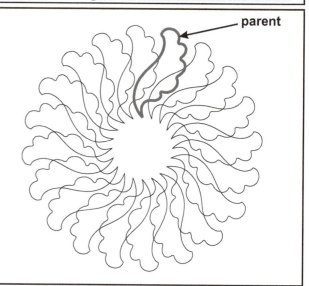

- Drag the **parent object** up about 5mm.

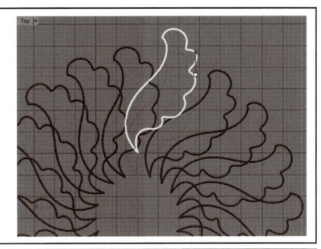

Fig. 51

- When you release the cursor, all of the other leaves will update to maintain the relationship to the parent object.

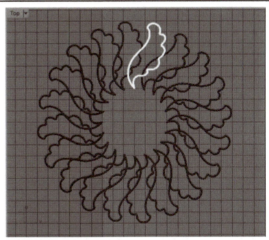

Fig. 52

- Use the **Rotate 2D** command to rotate the **parent object** clockwise as shown.

center of rotation

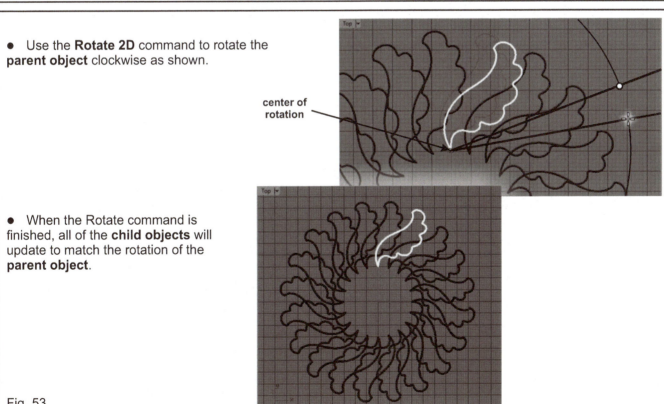

- When the Rotate command is finished, all of the **child objects** will update to match the rotation of the **parent object**.

Fig. 53

- Select a Child object next to the Parent object and click on the **Trim** command.

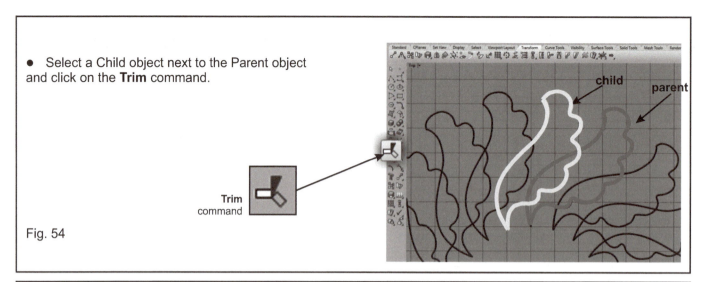

Trim
command

Fig. 54

- **Select object to trim** prompt:
  - Click on a part of the line of the Parent object that is inside the boundary of the selected Child object as shown.
  - When finished trimming, press **Enter**.

click here

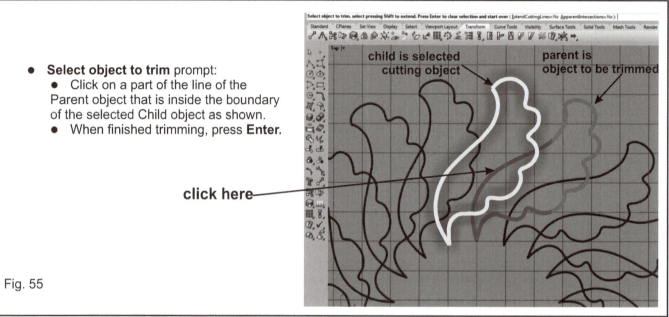

Fig. 55

- The **parent object** has been trimmed and the child objects have all updated.

- Suggestion: do all of your editing of the Parent object before doing this trimming step.

- You can save this design as **leaf design - polar array.3dm**

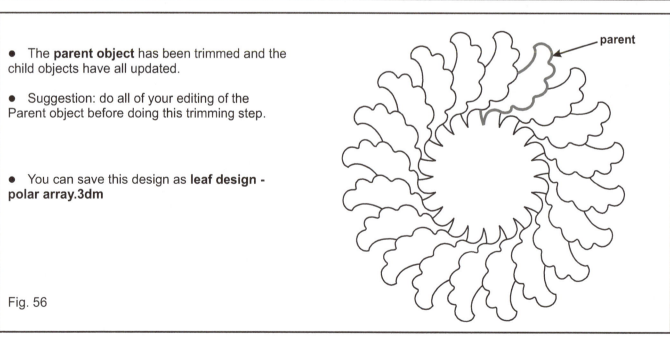

Fig. 56

1-D and 2-D Scaling
Scaling Elements in Drawings and Layouts

Create Objects for Scaling

- Create the squares and circles shown.
  - **squares: 10mm sides**
  - **circles: 6mm diameter**
  - **lge circle: Ø10mm**

  - Use **Grid Snap** to quickly create these simple objects.

    Grid Snap

- Click to toggle off Grid Snap when you are finished drawing these objects.

    ~~Grid Snap~~

Fig. 1

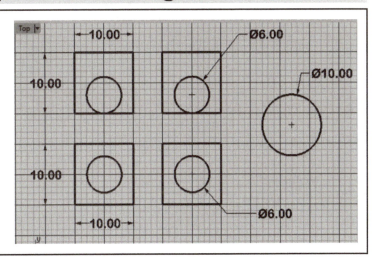

Scale 1-D Command - 1-Dimensional Scaling

- **Standard tabbed toolbar.**

    Standard

- Zoom in on the square in the upper left corner.

- Click on the **Scale 1-D** command in the **Scale** toolbar flyout.

    accesses the **Scale** toolbar flyout

    Scale 1-D command

Fig. 2

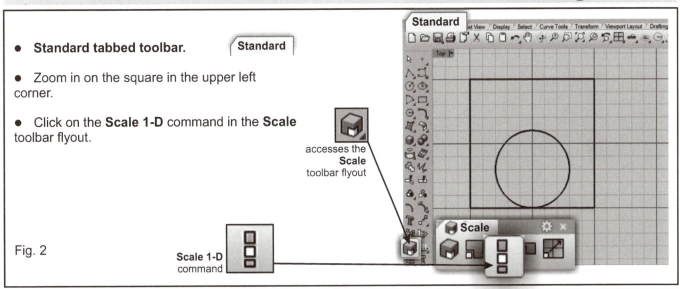

- **Select objects to scale. Press Enter when done** prompt:
  - Select the circle and press **Enter.**

Fig. 3

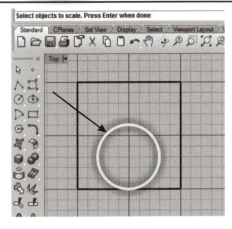

- **Origin point. Press Enter for automatic** prompt:
  - Snap to the **Mid** point of the bottom of the square as shown.
    - *[Note: **Intersection** or **Quad** osnap will also work here.]*
  - Click to set location. ❶

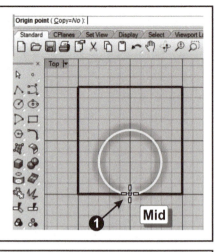

Fig. 4

- **Scale factor or first reference point** prompt:
  - Drag the cursor up to the top of the circle and snap to the top **Quad** point as shown.
  - Click to set location. ❷

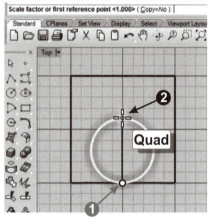

Fig. 5

- **Second reference point** prompt:
  - Snap to the **Mid** point of the top of the square as shown.
  - Click to set location. ❸

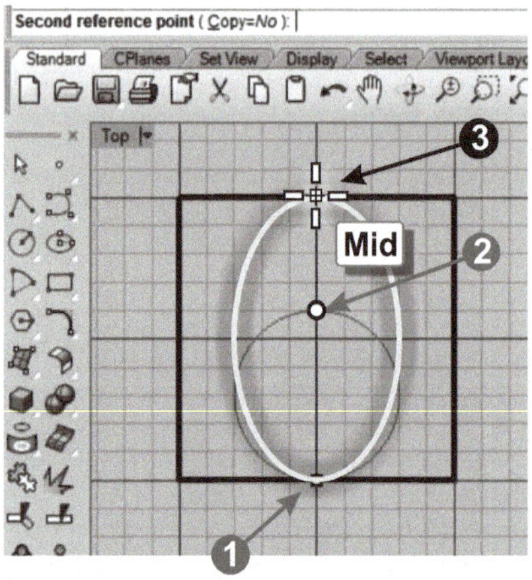

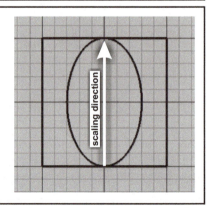

Fig. 6

- The circle has been scaled in 1 direction to form an elongated shape as shown.

Fig. 7

- Zoom in on the square and circle in the lower left corner.

- Click on the **Scale 1-D** command.

    - **Select objects to scale** prompt:
        - Select the circle as shown.
        - Press **Enter.**

Scale 1-D
command

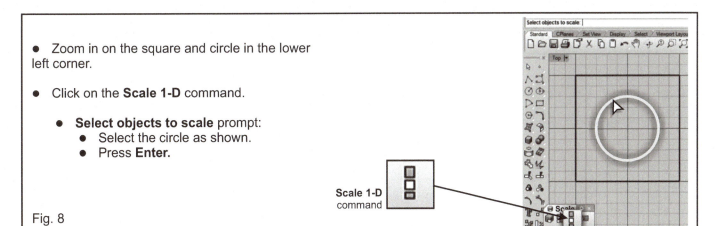

Fig. 8

- **Origin point** prompt:
    - Use **Center osnap** to select the center of the circle as shown.
    - Click to set location.❶

origin point ❶

Fig. 9

- **Scale factor or first reference point** prompt:
    - Draw the cursor up to snap to the top **Quad** of the circle as shown.
    - Click to set location.❷

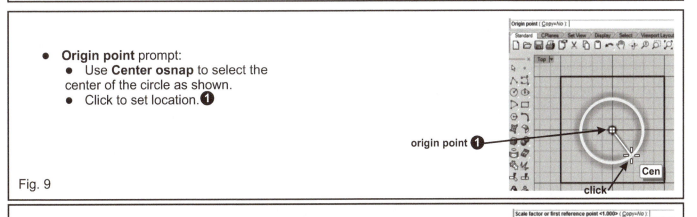

Fig. 10

- **Second reference point** prompt:
    - Draw the cursor up to the **Mid** point at the top line of the square as shown.
    - Click to set location. ❸

- The **Scale 1-D** command has created another elongated shape because it scaled in only one direction from the origin point.

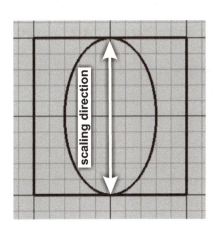

scaling direction

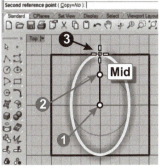

Fig. 11

- Zoom out so that you can see the two sets of squares and circles in the top row.

- Click on the **Scale 2-D** command in the **Scale** toolbar flyout.

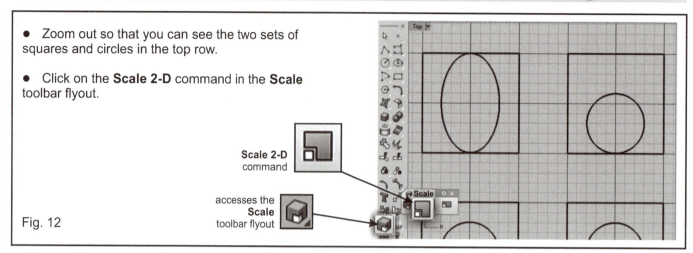

Scale 2-D command

accesses the **Scale** toolbar flyout

Fig. 12

- **Select objects to scale** prompt:
  - Select the circle shown and press **Enter.**

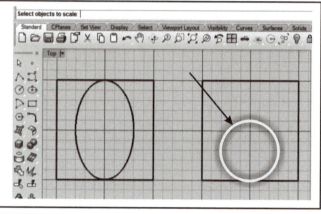

Fig. 13

- **Origin point** prompt:
  - Snap to the lower **Mid** point of the square.
    - *[Notice that, because **Quad** osnap is also enabled, both snaps show up in the cursor tooltip.]*
  - Click to set location. ❶

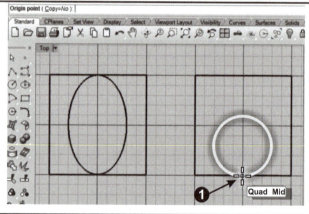

Fig. 14

- **Scale factor or first reference point** prompt:
  - Draw the cursor up to the top **Quad** point of the circle as shown.
  - Click to set location. ❷

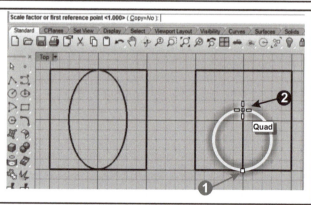

Fig. 15

- **Second reference point** prompt:
  - Draw the cursor up to the top of the square and snap to the **Midpoint** of the top line as shown.
  - Click to set location.

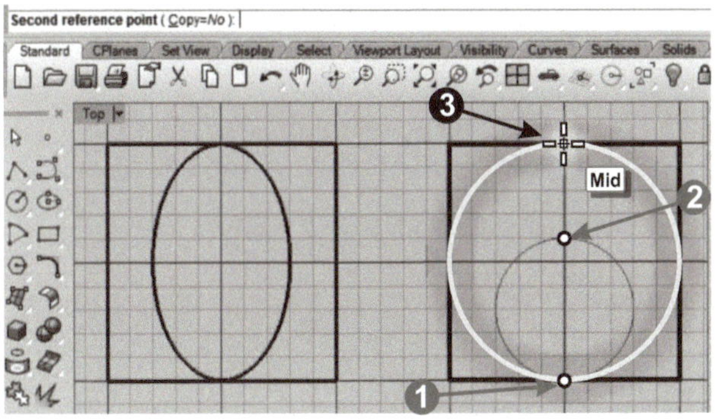

Fig. 16

- The scaled circle fills the surrounding square and is still a circle.

- Scale 2-D has scaled the circle *in all directions* from the **Origin Point.** ❶

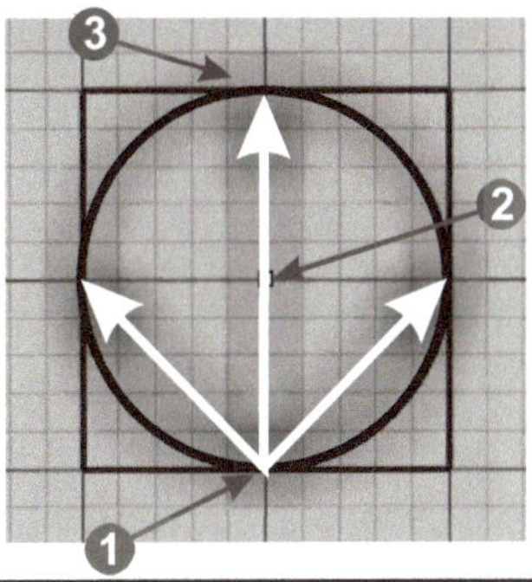

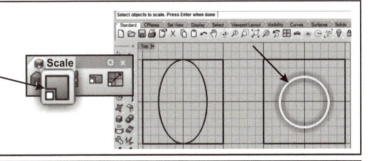

Fig. 17

- Pan downward so that you can see the two lower squares and circles.

- Click on the **Scale 2-D** command again.

  - **Select objects to scale** prompt:
    - Select the circle shown and press **Enter.**

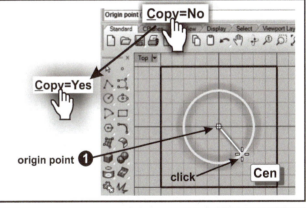

Fig. 18

- **Origin point** prompt:
  - Click on the **Copy=No** option in the **Command Line** to toggle the setting to **Copy=Yes.**
  - Use **Center osnap** to snap to the center of the circle as shown.
  - Click to set location. ❶

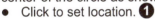

origin point ❶

click   Cen

Fig. 19

- **Scale factor or first reference point** prompt:
  - Draw the cursor up to snap to the upper **Quad** point of the circle as shown.
  - Click to set location. ❷

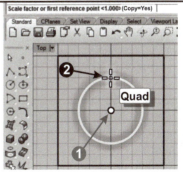

Quad

Fig. 20

- **Second reference point** prompt:
  - Draw the cursor up and snap to the **Midpoint** of the top line of the square as shown.
  - Click to set location.

Fig. 21

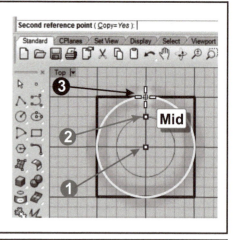

- **Second reference point** prompt:
  - Press **Enter** to end the command.

    - *[Note: You can continue to click in different locations to make more copies if you want. You press **Enter** to end the command when you have made all of the copies that you want.]*

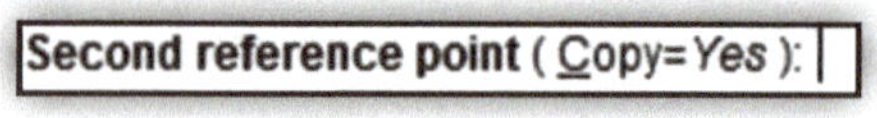

Fig. 22

Second reference point (<u>C</u>opy=*Yes*):

- The original circle and the scaled **Copy**.

- With the origin point in the center of the circle, the **Scale 2-D** command scaled the circle out from its center point.

Fig. 23

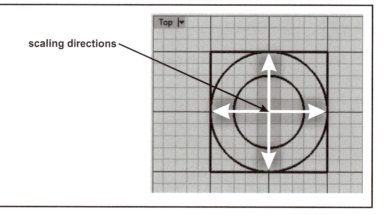

scaling directions

Specifying a Scale Factor
Scaling by Percentage

- Zoom in on the single **Ø10mm** circle on the right.

- Click on the **Scale 2-D** command.

  - **Select objects to scale** prompt:
    - Select the circle and press **Enter**.

Fig. 24

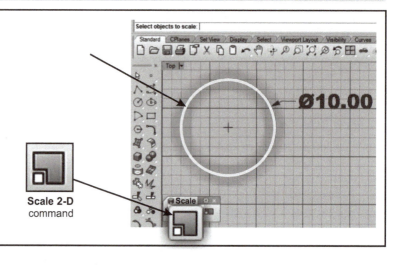

Scale 2-D
command

Ø10.00

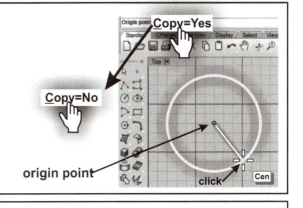

- Click to toggle the **Copy=Yes** option to **Copy=No** in the **Command Line** as shown.

- **Origin point** prompt:
  - Snap to the **Center** of the circle.
  - Click to set location.

origin point

click

Cen

Fig. 25

- **Scale factor or first reference point** prompt:
  - Type **"1.5"** in the **Command Line** and press **Enter.**

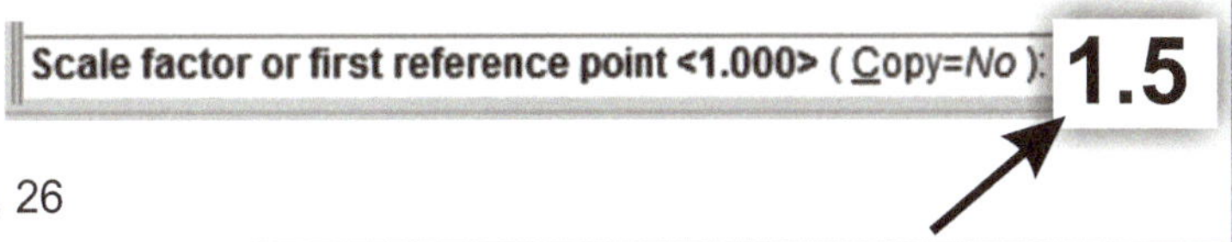

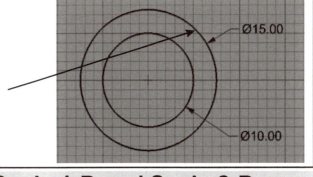

Scale factor or first reference point <1.000> (Copy=No): **1.5**

Fig. 26

- The circle has been scaled up by a factor of **1.5 (150%)**

Ø15.00

Ø10.00

Fig. 27

Control Point Editing with Scale 1-D and Scale 2-D

- **Pre-select** the circle and then press the **F10 Hotkey** to turn on its control points. **F10**

- Click on the **Scale 1-D** command.

  - **Select objects to scale** prompt:
    - Select the two control points shown.
    - Press **Enter.**

Scale 1-D command

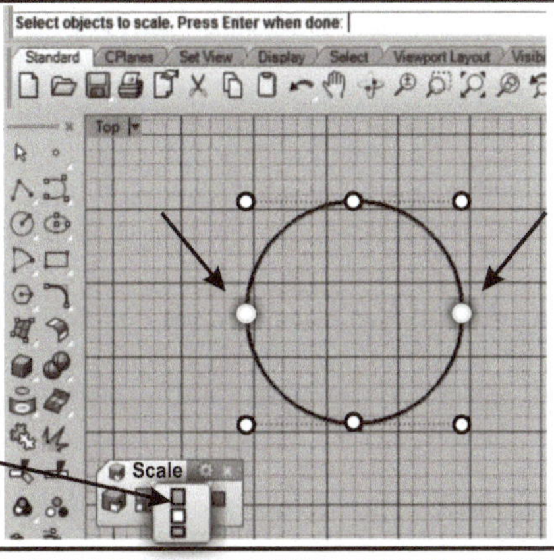

Select objects to scale. Press Enter when done:

Fig. 28

- **Origin point** prompt:
  - Snap to the **Center** of the circle and click to set location. ❶

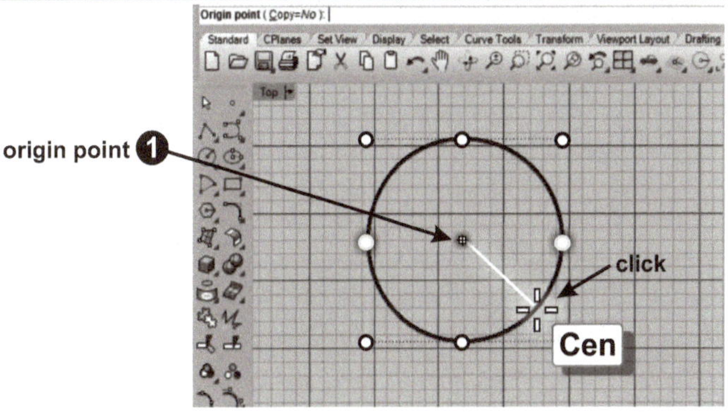

origin point ❶

click

Cen

Origin point (Copy=No):

Fig. 29

190

- **Scale factor or first reference point** prompt:
  - Draw the cursor to the side and snap to the **one of the selected points** on the side as shown. ❷

Fig. 30

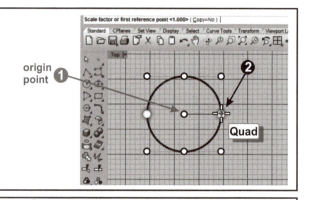

- **Second reference point** prompt:
  - Draw the cursor out further and notice that a preview appears, showing the scaling of the two control points outward and the way the circle is changing.
  - Click when your preview shows the shape you want. ❸

Fig. 31

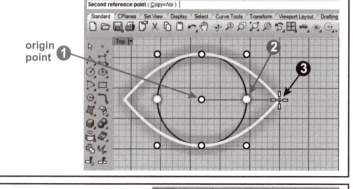

- Two points have been scaled out in one horizontal direction to create the finished shape.

- Turn off control points by pressing the **Esc Key** twice, once to de-select selected points and the second time to turn off the control points.

Fig. 32

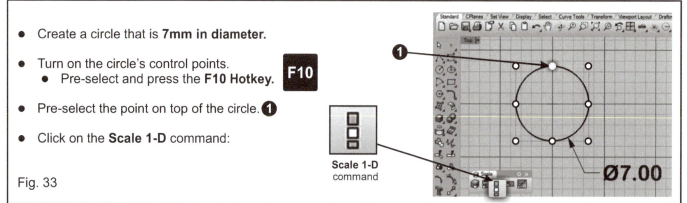

- Create a circle that is **7mm in diameter.**

- Turn on the circle's control points.
  - Pre-select and press the **F10 Hotkey.**

- Pre-select the point on top of the circle. ❶

- Click on the **Scale 1-D** command:

Scale 1-D
command

Fig. 33

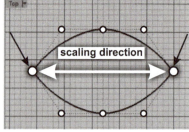

- **Origin point** prompt:
  - Snap to the **Point** on the bottom of the circle.
  - Click to set location. ❷

Fig. 34

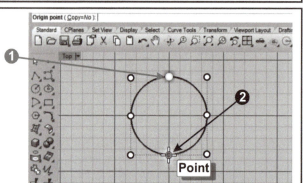

191

- **Scale factor or first reference point** prompt:
  - Snap again to the original selected point on the top as shown.
  - Click to set location. ❸

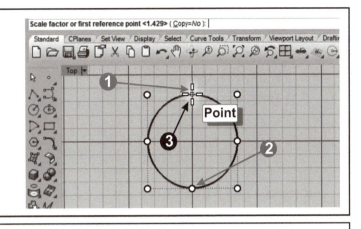

Fig. 35

- **Second reference point** prompt:
  - Type **"10"** in the **Command Line.**
  - Press **Enter.**

Fig. 36

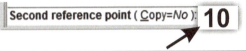

- The selected point has been scaled upward to a distance that is **10mm** away from the origin point at the bottom of the circle.

- Press the **Esc key** a couple of times to turn off control points.

- A drawing of a **7mm x 10mm pear shaped stone** has been created.

Fig. 37

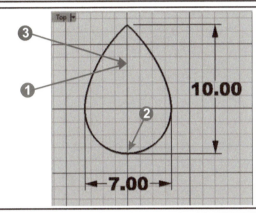

- Create another circle **and turn on its control points.** Diameter dimension does not matter.

- Pre-select the **4 outer control points** shown.

- Click on the **Scale 1-D** command.

  - **Origin Point** prompt:
    - Snap to the **Point** at the bottom of the circle as shown.
    - Click to set location. ❶

Fig. 38

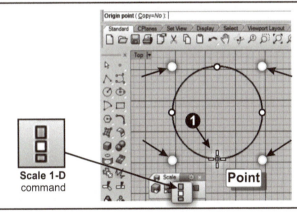

Scale 1-D
command

- **Scale factor or first reference point** prompt:
  - Draw the cursor to the right and snap to the lower right point shown.
  - Click to set location. ❷

Fig. 39

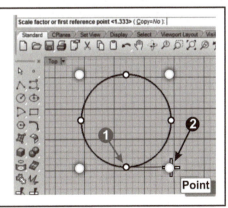

192

- **Second reference point** prompt:
  - Draw the cursor over to the right until the preview line shows you the shape you want.
  - Click to set location. **3**

Fig. 40

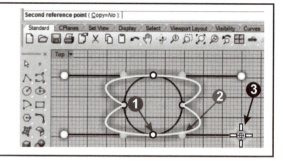

- The finished shape shows how the **origin point** can also be above or below the object being edited, as long as it is at the middle of your object as shown.

Fig. 41

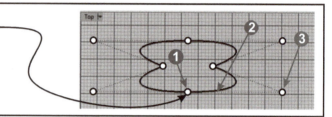

- Undo the last scale or create another circle.

- Pre-select and press the **F10 Hotkey** to turn on control points.

  F10

- Click on the **Scale 2-D** command.

  - **Origin point** prompt:
    - Snap to the **Center** of the circle as shown.
    - Click to set location. **1**

Fig. 42

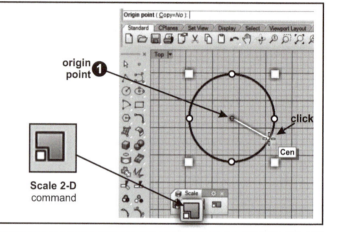

Scale 2-D
command

- **Scale factor or first reference point** prompt:
  - Draw the cursor out and click on a random location as shown. **2**

Fig. 43

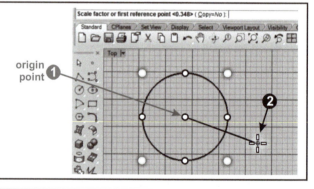

origin point **1**

- **Second reference point** prompt:
  - Draw the cursor out until the preview curve shows the shape you want.
  - Click to set.

- The selected control points have been evenly scaled out as shown.

Fig. 44

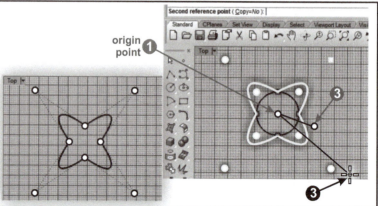

origin point **1**

- **Curve Tools tabbed toolbar.**   Curve Tools

- **Rebuild** the circle to 16 control points.

- Pre-select and press the **F10 Hotkey** to turn on control points.   **F10**

Fig. 45

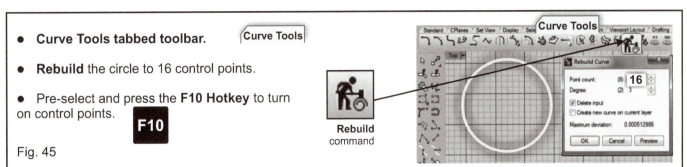

Rebuild
command

- **Standard tabbed toolbar.**   Standard

- Click on the **Scale 2-D** command.

  - **Select objects to scale. Press Enter when done** prompt:
    - Select *alternate control points* as shown.
    - Press **Enter.**

Fig. 46

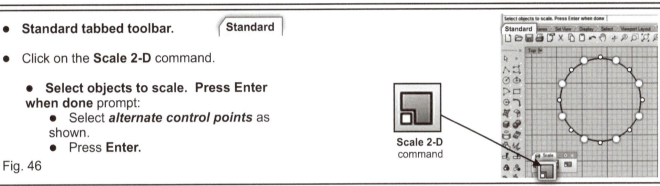

Scale 2-D
command

- **Origin point** prompt:
  - Snap to the **Center** of the circle.
  - Click to set location. ❶

Fig. 47

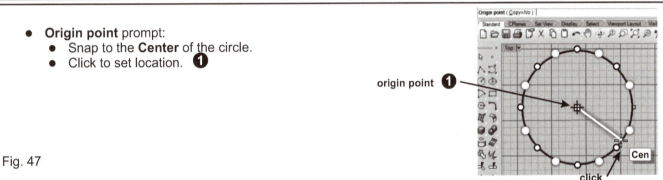

origin point ❶

Cen
click

- **Scale factor or first reference point** prompt:
  - Draw the cursor out of the circle and click on the approximate location shown. ❷

Fig. 48

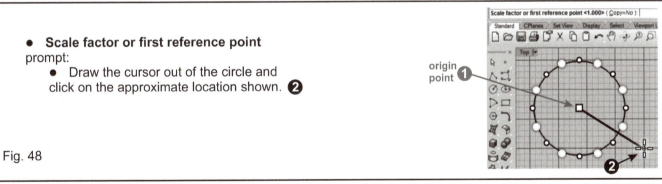

origin point ❶

❷

- **Second reference point** prompt:
  - Draw the cursor out further until the preview shows the desired shape.
  - Click to set location.❸

- Because the origin point was the center of the circle, the selected control points all scaled out evenly from it to create a symmetrical final shape.

Fig. 49

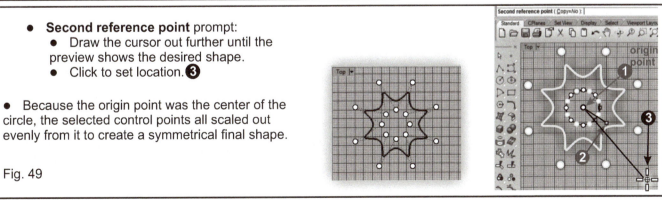

origin point

❶
❷
❸

- In this example, **Scale 2-D** is creating a different shape because the **origin point** is on the bottom of the circle as shown.

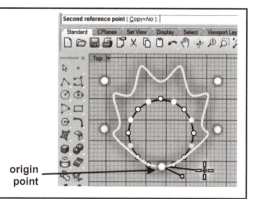

origin
point

Fig. 50

Control Point Editing the Butterfly with Scale Commands

- Open the file **polyline for butterfly**.3dm original drawing and create a line down the middle of the drawing, **snapping to mid points** for accuracy.

- Turn on Control Points of the polyline.
  - Select the polyline and press the **F10** hotkey. **F10**

Fig. 51

new line
Mid
Mid

- Click on the **Scale 2-D** command.

  - **Select objects to scale. Press Enter when done** prompt:
    - Select the two control points at the top as shown.
    - Press **Enter**.

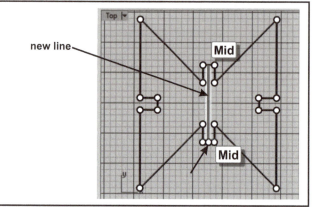

Scale 2-D
command

Fig. 52

- **Origin point** prompt:
  - Snap to the **Mid point** on the center line just created. **1**

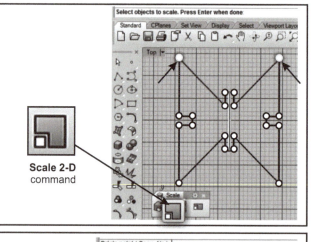

origin point **1**

Mid

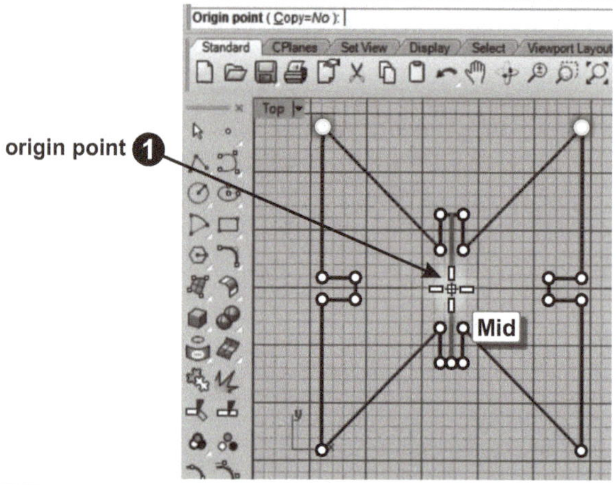

Fig. 53

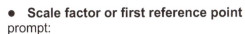
- **Scale factor or first reference point** prompt:
    - Using **ORTHO** for symmetry, draw the cursor out to the side as shown.
    - Click to set location. ❷

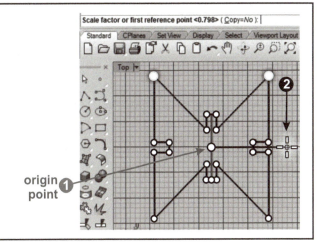

Fig. 54

- **Second reference point** prompt:
    - Draw the cursor out further.
    - The selected control points will scale outward and upward, **scaling from the origin point in a symmetrical arrangement.**
    - Click when the preview shows approximately as shown. ❸

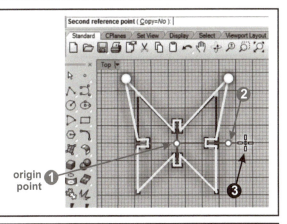

Fig. 55

- The newly edited shape of the polyline is still symmetrical.

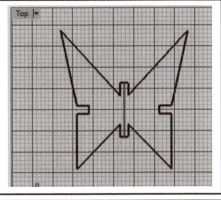

Fig. 56

- Select the two lower control points as shown.

- Click on the **Scale 1-D** command as shown.

    - **Origin point** prompt:
        - Snap to the **Mid point** on the center line as shown.
        - Click to set location. ❶

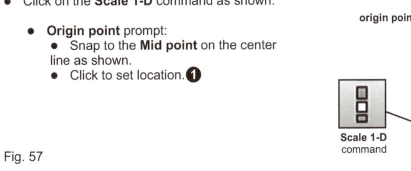

Scale 1-D
command

Fig. 57

196

- **Scale factor or first reference point** prompt:
  - Using **ortho** for symmetry, draw the cursor outward.
  - Click in the approximate location shown. ❷

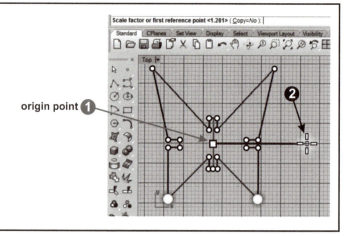

Fig. 58

- **Second reference point** prompt:
  - Draw the cursor inward.
  - Click to set location when the desired shape is created approximately as shown. ❸

- Press the **Esc** key a couple of times to turn off control points. **Esc**

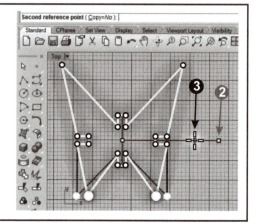

Fig. 59

- **Scale 2-D** and **Scale 1-D** have created a rough symmetrical butterfly shape.

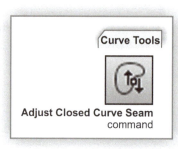

Fig. 60

- **Rebuild** the polyline to 30 control points.

- ***Don't forget to adjust the closed curve seam (Adjust Closed Curve Seam command in the Curve Tools tabbed toolbar) so that you get an even and symmetrical distribution of control points!***

- Turn on Control Points by pre-selecting and pressing the **F10 Hotkey**. **F10**

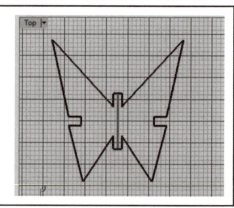

Curve Tools

Adjust Closed Curve Seam
command

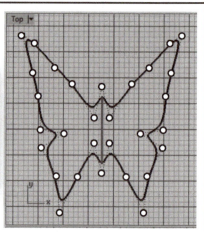

Fig. 61

- Select the two control points shown.

- Click on the **Scale 1-D** command.

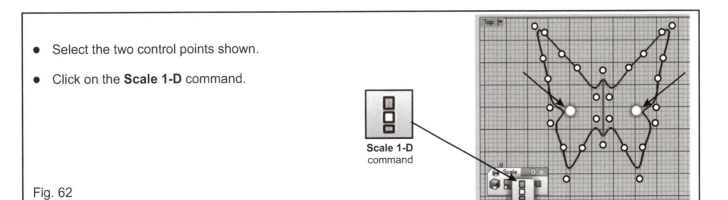

Scale 1-D
command

Fig. 62

- **Origin point** prompt:
  - Snap to a point on the center line and click to set location. **1**

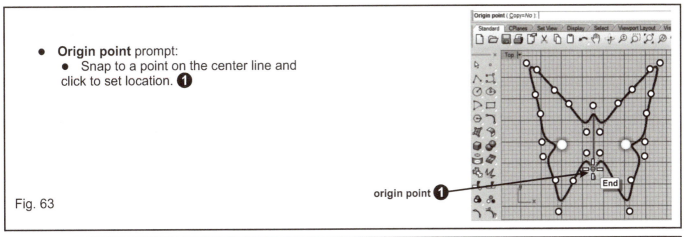

origin point **1**

Fig. 63

- **Scale factor or first reference** prompt:
  - Draw the cursor outward and click to set location. **2**

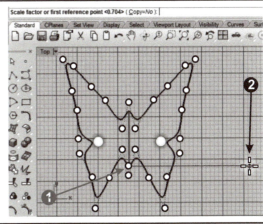

Fig. 64

- **Second reference point** prompt:
  - Draw the cursor in as shown and click in the desired location. **3**

- The result is symmetrical point editing.

- Press the **Esc** key a couple of times to turn off the control points.

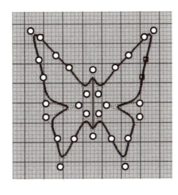

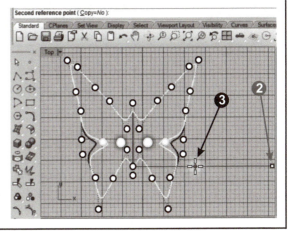

Fig. 65

198

Arc Commands

Arc: Center, Start, Angle command

- **Curve Tools tabbed toolbar.** | Curve Tools |

- Using **ORTHO,** draw two line segments, **15mm each**, to create the polyline shown.

- Turn off **ORTHO.**

Fig. 1

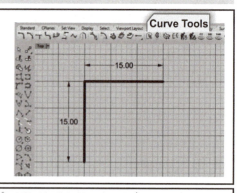

- Click on the **Arc: Center, Start, Angle** command as shown.

  - **Center of arc** prompt:
    - Snap on the **Midpoint** of the line **1** shown.
    - Click to set location.

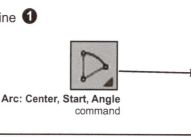

Arc: Center, Start, Angle
command

Fig. 2

- **Start of arc** prompt:
  - Snap to one of the **Endpoints** of the line as shown.
  - Click to set location. **2**

Fig. 3

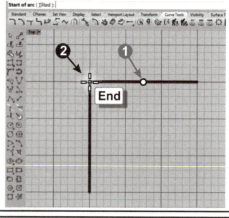

- **End point or angle** prompt:
  - Draw the cursor around in a counterclockwise direction toward the other end other end of the line.
  - Notice preview arc and line.

- *Make sure that ORTHO is turned off so that the cursor will move smoothly around to the other side of the line.*

Fig. 4

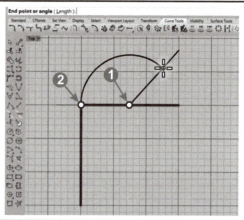

- **End point or angle** prompt:
  - Snap to the **Endpoint** shown.
  - Click to set location. ❸

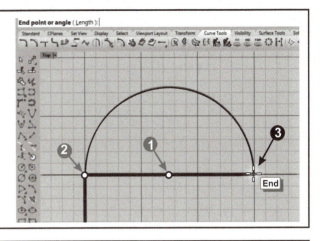

Fig. 5

- The diameter of the new arc is exactly 15mm, the length of the line it was built on.

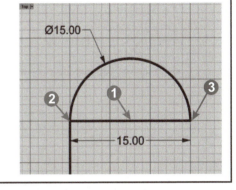

Fig. 6

Arc: Start, End, Point on Arc command

- Create a line, **approximately 3mm long**, up from the **midpoint** of the horizontal line as shown.

- **Left-click** on the **Arc: Start, End, Point on Arc** command.

left-click for
Arc: Start, End, Point on Arc
command

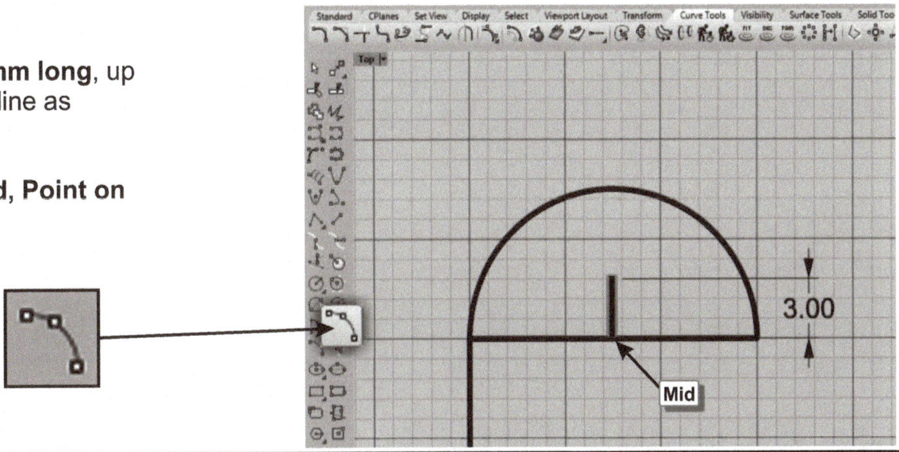

Fig. 7

- **Start of arc** prompt:
  - Snap to one of the endpoints of the horizontal line as shown.
  - Click to set location. ❶

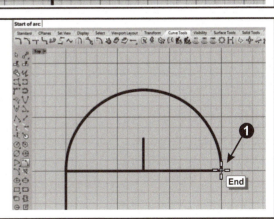

Fig. 8

- **End of arc** prompt:
  - Snap to the other end of the line as shown.
  - Click to set location. ❷

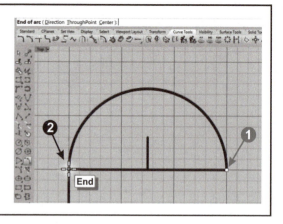

Fig. 9

- **Point on arc** prompt:
  - Snap to the **Endpoint** of the little 3mm perpendicular line as shown.
  - Click to set location. ❸

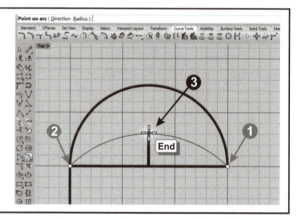

Fig. 10

- The finished arc has been created by clicking on 3 designated points.

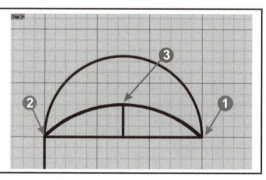

Fig. 11

Arc: Start, End, Direction at Start Command

- Click on the **Arc: Start, End, Direction at Start** command in the **Arc** toolbar flyout.

  - **Start of arc** prompt:
    - Snap to the lower endpoint of the vertical line as shown.
    - Click to set location. ❶

left-click for
Arc: Start, End, Direction at Start
command

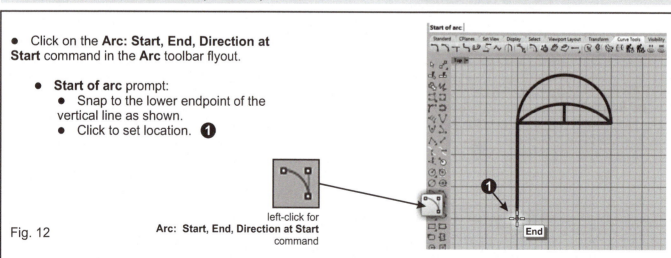

Fig. 12

- **End of arc** prompt:
  - Snap to the endpoint of the horizontal line as shown.
  - Click to set location.

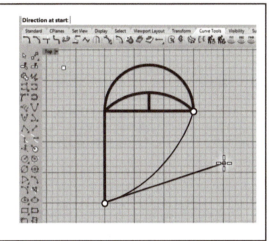

Fig. 13

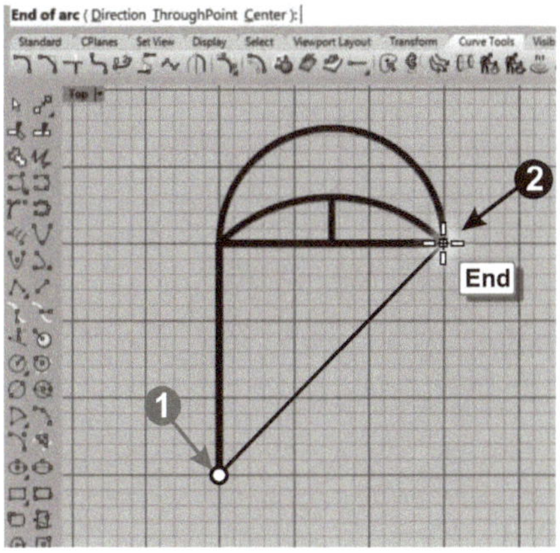

- **Direction at start** prompt:
  - Draw the cursor down and see a preview of the arc and a straight direction guideline that follows the cursor.

Fig. 14

- **Direction at start** prompt:
  - Use **ORTHO** to ensure that the arc direction guideline is perfectly horizontal.
  - Click to set location. ❸

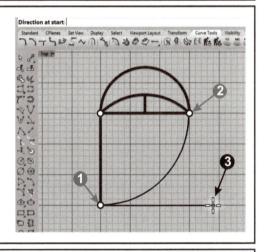

Fig. 15

- The finished arc touches two designated locations and the radius is determined by the direction control of the final location.

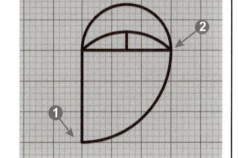

Fig. 16

Technical Drawing - Necklace Layout
Using Arcs and Scaling

- Create the layers shown.

- **ref geo** layer current.

Fig. 1

TECH LINES
ref geo
hidden lines

Creating the Basic Motif

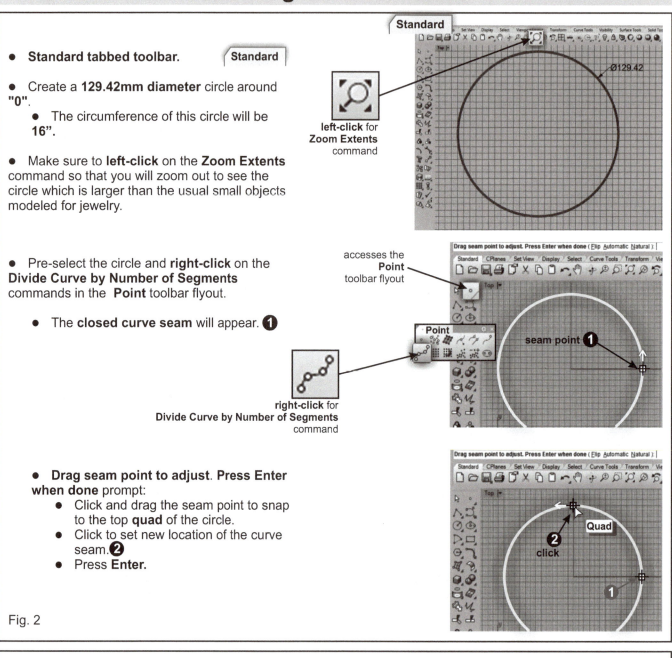

- **Standard tabbed toolbar.** *Standard*

- Create a **129.42mm diameter** circle around **"0"**.
    - The circumference of this circle will be **16"**.

- Make sure to **left-click** on the **Zoom Extents** command so that you will zoom out to see the circle which is larger than the usual small objects modeled for jewelry.

left-click for
Zoom Extents
command

Ø129.42

- Pre-select the circle and **right-click** on the **Divide Curve by Number of Segments** commands in the **Point** toolbar flyout.

    - The **closed curve seam** will appear. ❶

accesses the
Point
toolbar flyout

seam point ❶

right-click for
Divide Curve by Number of Segments
command

- **Drag seam point to adjust. Press Enter when done** prompt:
    - Click and drag the seam point to snap to the top **quad** of the circle.
    - Click to set new location of the curve seam.❷
    - Press **Enter.**

Quad

❷
click

❶

Fig. 2

- **Number of segments** prompt:
    - Type **"60"** and press **Enter.**

Number of segments <3> (Length Split=*No* MarkEnds=*Yes* GroupOutput=*No*) **60**

Fig. 3

- The circle will be divided into 60 equal segments by the placement of point objects.

- These are **"point objects"**, not control points.

Fig. 4

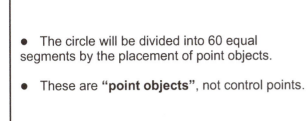

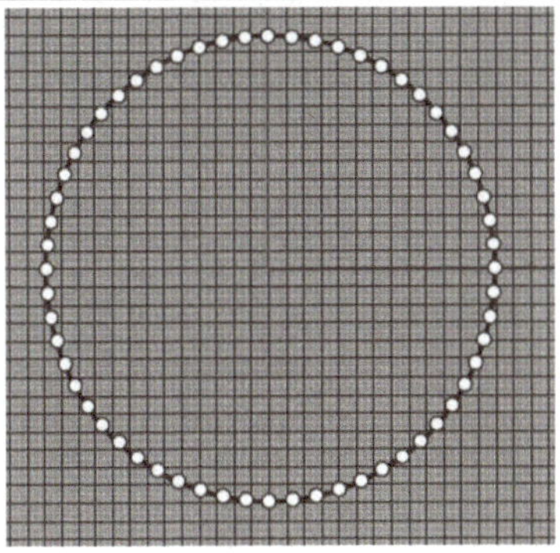

- **TECH LINES** layer current.

Fig. 5

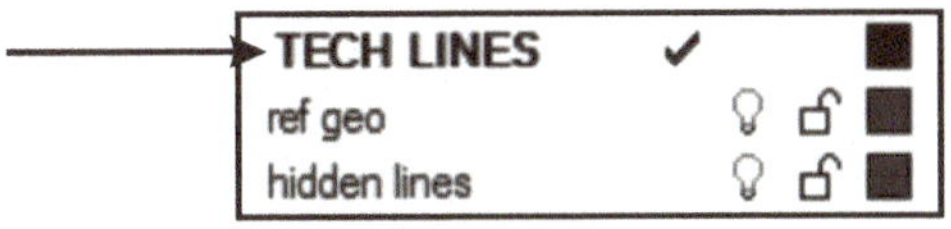

TECH LINES	✔	■
ref geo	♀ 🔓	■
hidden lines	♀ 🔓	■

- Create a **Ø2mm diameter** circle around the second point from the top point.
  - Use **Point osnap** for accuracy.

Fig. 6

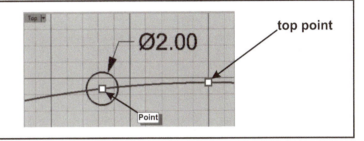

- **Curve Tools tabbed toolbar.**   `Curve Tools`

- Use **Curve Offset** to offset the original Ø129.42 mm circle at a 1mm distance , using the **B**oth**S**ides option to put offsets inside and outside the circle.

Fig. 7

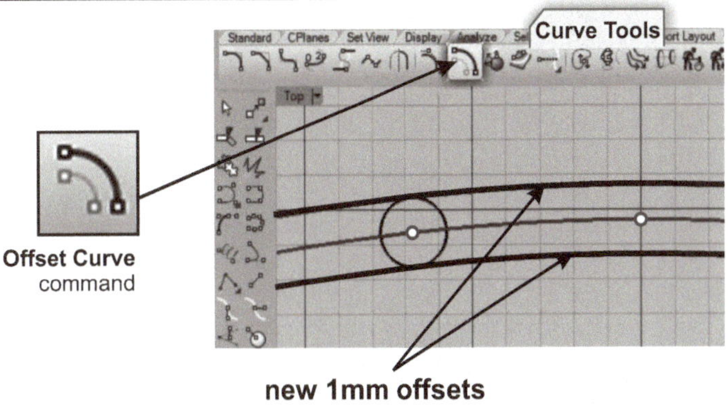

Offset Curve
command

new 1mm offsets

- **hidden lines** layer current.

TECH LINES	♀ 🔓	■
ref geo	♀ 🔓	■
hidden lines	✔ 🔓	■
Layer 04	♀ 🔓	■

- Use the **Offset Curve** command again to offset the original 129.42 diameter circle to a distance of **.5mm** with the **B**oth**S**ides option again.

new .5mm offsets

Fig. 8

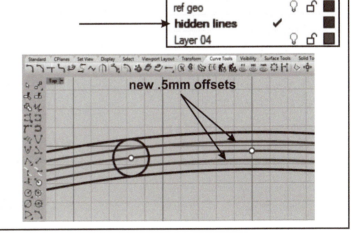

- **TECH LINES** current.

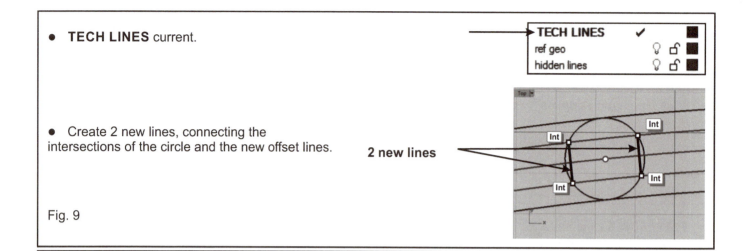

- Create 2 new lines, connecting the intersections of the circle and the new offset lines.

2 new lines

Fig. 9

- Click on the **Extend Curve** command.
  - Click on the **ToBoundary** option ❶ in the **Command Line.**
  - **Select boundary objects. Press Enter when done** prompt:
    - Select the two outer curves ❷ and press **Enter.**

Extend Curve command

- **Select curve to extend** prompt:
  - Click near the end of one of the little lines.❸

- The end of the curve that you selected will extend out, stopping at the designated boundary object. ❹

- You will continue to be prompted to **Select curve to extend. Use the same procedure to extend the other 3 curve ends.**

- Press **Enter** to end the command when all 4 curve ends have been extended to the boundary objects as shown.

Fig. 10

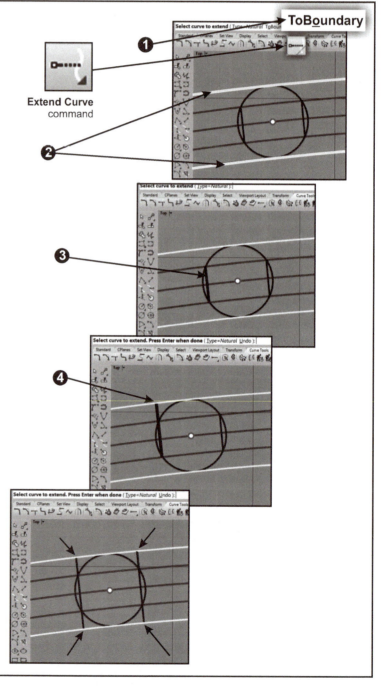

● Select the circle and click on the **Split** command.

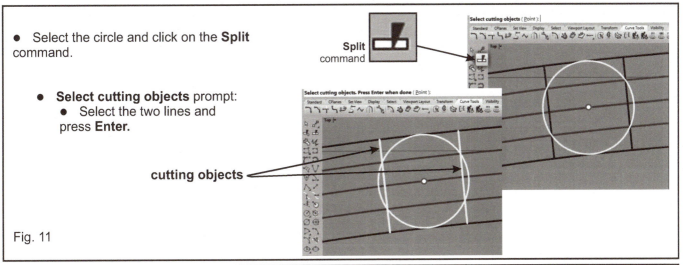

Split
command

- **Select cutting objects** prompt:
  - Select the two lines and press **Enter.**

cutting objects

Fig. 11

● Select the two split-off sides of the circle and change them to the **hidden lines** layer.

TECH LINES	✓	⬛
ref geo	♀ 🔒	⬛
hidden lines	♀ 🔓	⬛

Fig. 12

● **Transform tabbed toolbar.** `Transform`

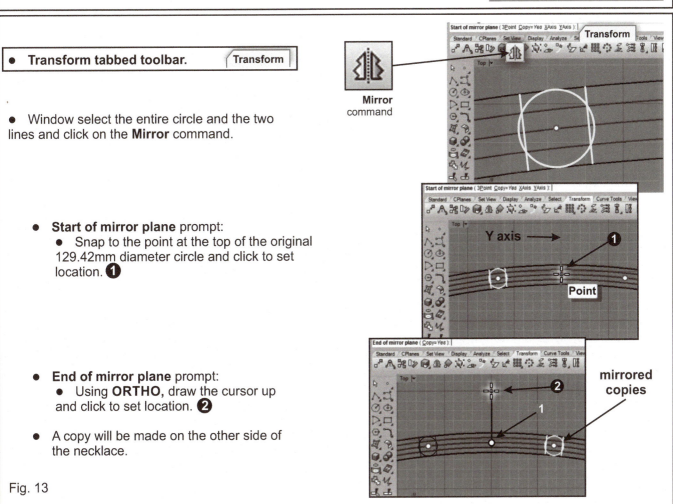

Transform

Mirror
command

● Window select the entire circle and the two lines and click on the **Mirror** command.

- **Start of mirror plane** prompt:
  - Snap to the point at the top of the original 129.42mm diameter circle and click to set location. ❶

Y axis

Point

- **End of mirror plane** prompt:
  - Using **ORTHO,** draw the cursor up and click to set location. ❷

mirrored copies

- A copy will be made on the other side of the necklace.

Fig. 13

- Select the two little inner lines and click on the **Trim** command.

Trim command

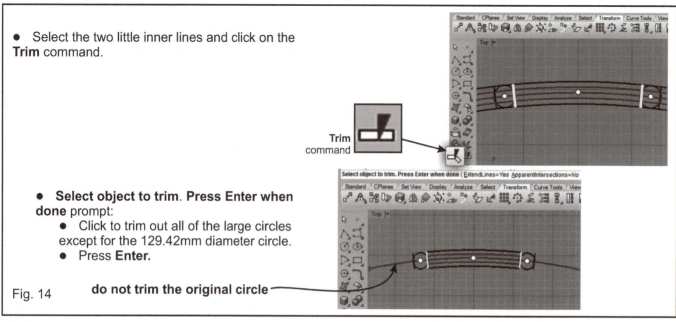

- **Select object to trim. Press Enter when done** prompt:
    - Click to trim out all of the large circles except for the 129.42mm diameter circle.
    - Press **Enter.**

Fig. 14   **do not trim the original circle**

- Select the two larger arcs and the two little lines and click on the **Join** command to join these 4 curves into one **closed curve**.

Join command

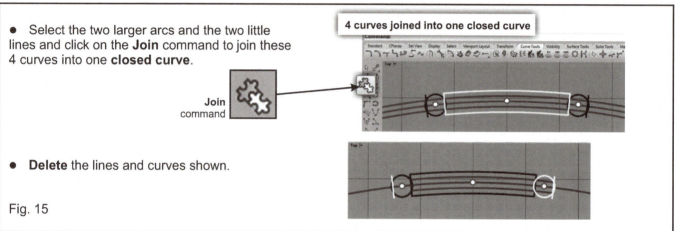

4 curves joined into one closed curve

- **Delete** the lines and curves shown.

Fig. 15

- Turn off the **ref geo** layer.

Fig. 16

TECH LINES ✓ ■
ref geo
hidden lines

- Select all of the objects shown and click on the **Polar Array** command.
    - **Center of Polar Array** prompt:
        - Type **"0"** and press **Enter.**
    - **Number of items** prompt:
        - Type **"30"** and press **Enter.**
    - **Angle to fill or first reference point <360>** prompt:
        - Press **Enter** to accept the default **360°** angle to fill.
    - **Press Enter to accept** prompt:
        - Press **Enter.**

Polar Array command

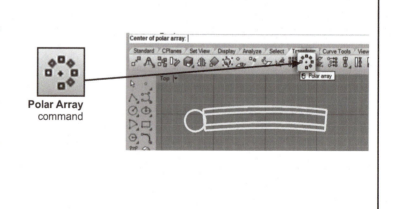

Fig. 17

- **ref geo** layer current.

- Turn off **hidden lines** layer.

Fig. 18

- The suctions of 2mm tubing and the 2mm beads will be polar arrayed into place.

Fig. 19

- Using **ORTHO,** create a 15mm long vertical line from the top quad of the necklace as shown.

Fig. 20

- **TECH LINES** current.

Fig. 21

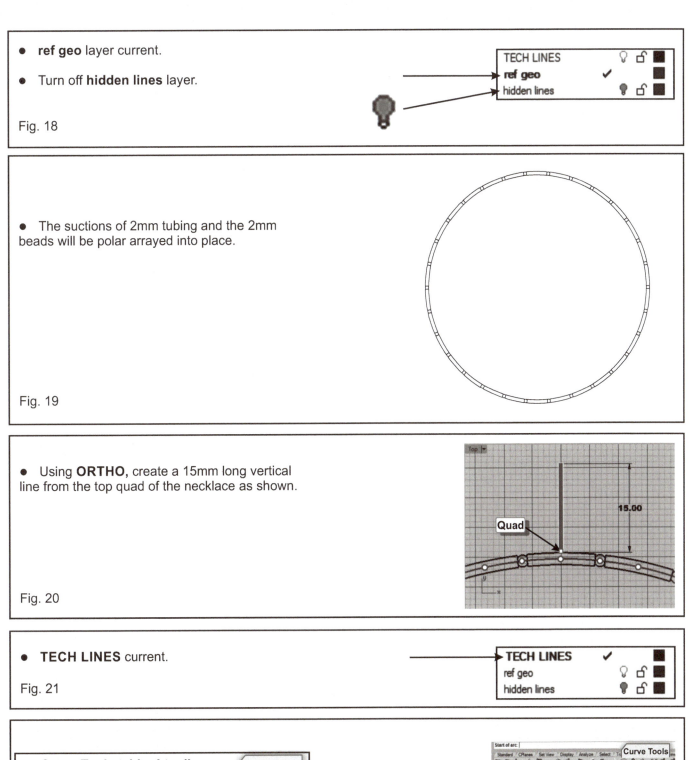

- **Curve Tools tabbed toolbar.** Curve Tools

- Click on the **Arc: Start, End, Direction at Start** command.
  - **Start of arc** prompt:
    - Snap to the top end point of the tube segment on the top of the necklace.
    - Click to set location. ❶

Arc: Start, End,
Direction at Start
command

Fig. 22

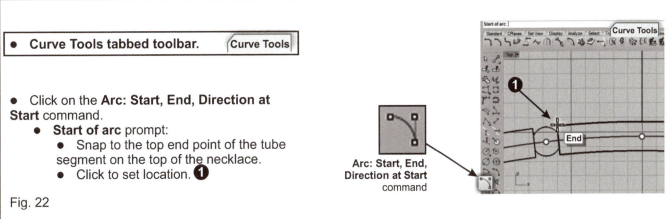

208

- **End of arc** prompt:
  - Snap to the top of the new 15mm line.
  - Click to set location. ❷

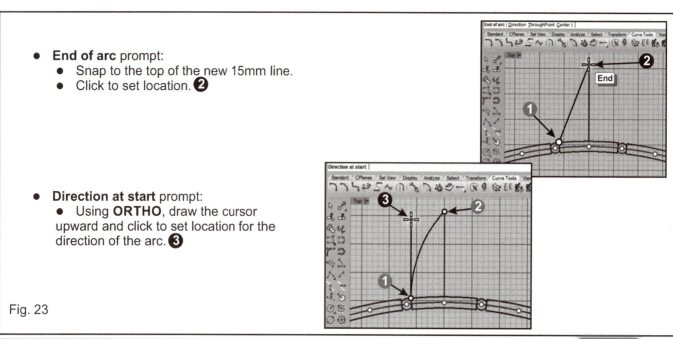

- **Direction at start** prompt:
  - Using **ORTHO**, draw the cursor upward and click to set location for the direction of the arc. ❸

Fig. 23

- **Transform tabbed toolbar.** [Transform]

- **Mirror** the new arc over to the other side.

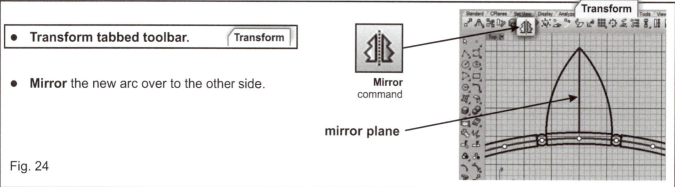

Mirror
command

mirror plane

Fig. 24

- Select the two arcs and click on the **Join** command to create a single open curve.

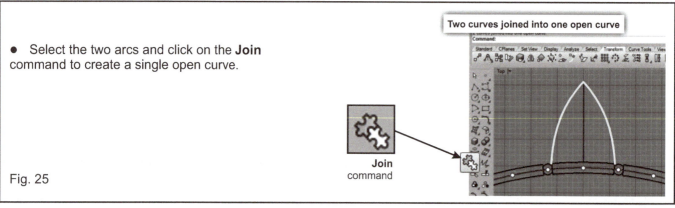

Two curves joined into one open curve

Join
command

Fig. 25

- **Transform tabbed toolbar.** [Transform]

- Select the new design motif and click on the **Polar Array** command.

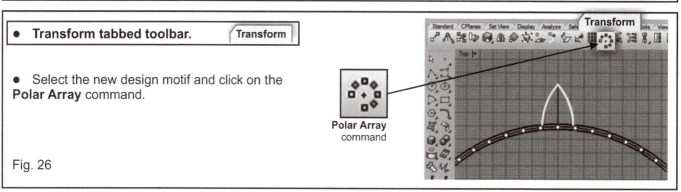

Polar Array
command

Fig. 26

- **Center of polar array** prompt:
  - Type "**0**" and press **Enter**.
- **Number of items** prompt:
  - Type "**30**" and press **Enter**.
- **Angle to fill or first reference point <360>** prompt:
  - Press **Enter** to accept the default **360° angle to fill.**
- **Press Enter to accept** prompt:
  - Press **Enter**.

- The design motif will be Polar Arrayed into place, in proper alignment with the tubing sections.

Fig. 27

- Create a new layer called **ref geo 2** and make that layer current.
- This layer will be a reference for the scaling of the design motifs.

Fig. 28

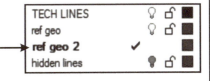

- **Curve Tools tabbed toolbar.** | Curve Tools

- Create a **Line** between the **end points** of the arcs of the new motif.

Fig. 29

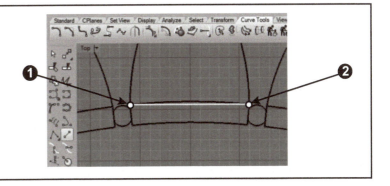

- **Transform tabbed toolbar.** | Transform

- **Polar Array** the new line.
  - **Center of polar array** prompt:
    - Type "**0**" and press **Enter**.
  - **Number if items** prompt:
    - Type "**30**" and press **Enter**.
  - **Angle to fill or first reference point** prompt:
    - Press **Enter** to accept the default **360°.**
  - **Press Enter to accept** prompt:
    - Press **Enter**.

Fig. 30

Polar Array command

line to be arrayed

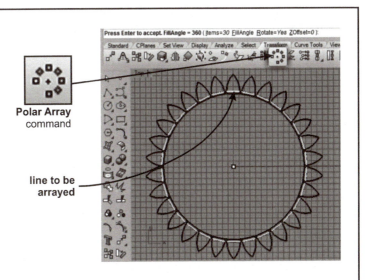

- Create a **30mm perpendicular line** at the bottom of the necklace, starting at the mid point of the newly polar arrayed line.

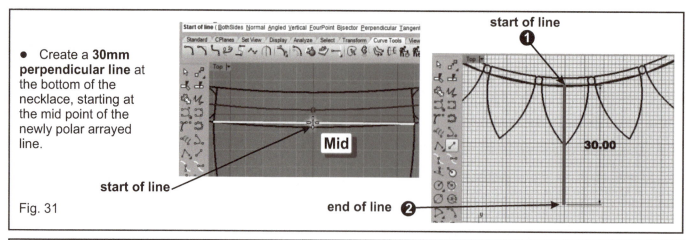

Fig. 31

- **Curve Tools tabbed toolbar.** Curve Tools

- Use the **Circle: diameter** command to create a circle from the top of the necklace to the end of the new 30mm line at the bottom.

Circle: diameter
command

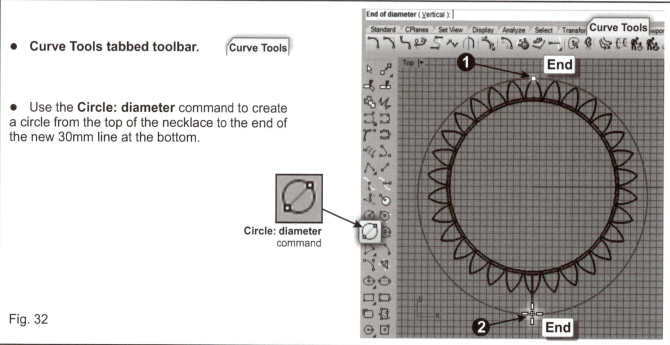

Fig. 32

accesses the **Scale** toolbar flyout

- Select the design motif at the bottom of the necklace and click on the **Scale 1-D** command in the **Scale toolbar flyout**.
  - **Origin point** prompt:
    - Snap to the **end point** of the new 30mm line at the top of the motif.
    - Click to set location.❶

Scale 1-D
command

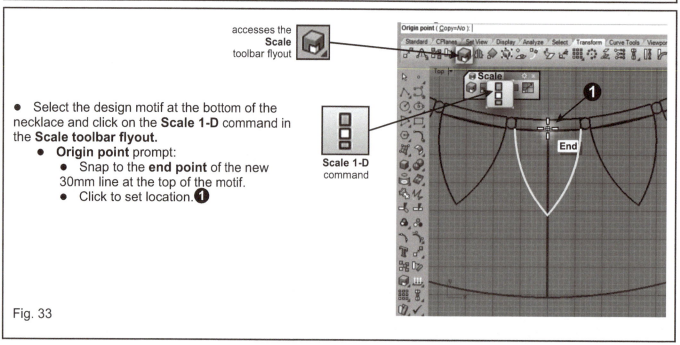

Fig. 33

- **Scale factor or first reference point** prompt:
  - Draw the cursor down and snap to the **End point** of the design motif.
  - Click to set location. ❷

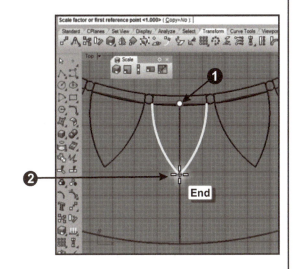

- **Second reference point** prompt:
  - Draw the cursor down and snap to the **end point** of the **30mm line**.
  - Click to set location. ❸

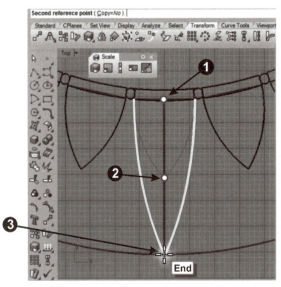

Fig. 34

- Select the next design motif up from the one just scaled and click on the **Scale 1-D command** again.
  - **Origin point** prompt:
    - Snap to the **mid point** of the straight line that was polar arrayed previously in Fig. 30.
    - Click to set location. ❶

Scale 1-D
command

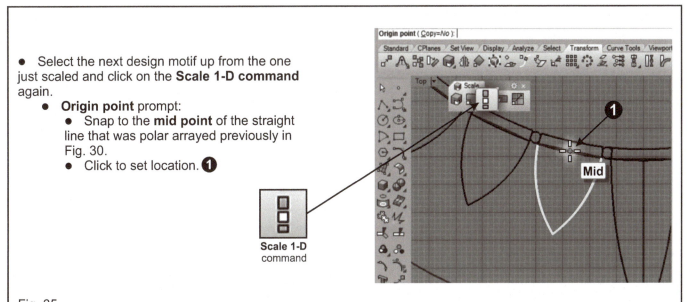

Fig. 35

- **Scale factor or first reference point** prompt:
    - Draw the cursor down and snap to the **End point** of the design motif.
    - Click to set location. ❷

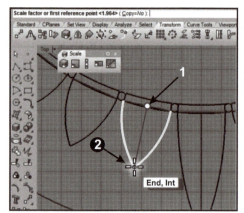

- **Second reference point** prompt:
    - Draw the cursor down and snap to the **intersection** with the outer circle.
    - Click to set location. ❸

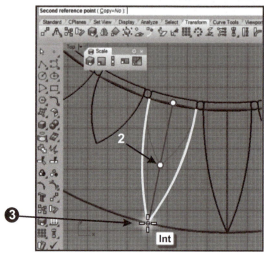

Fig. 36

- The rest of the design motifs have been scaled, using the same technique.

- The motifs on the other side of the necklace have been deleted.

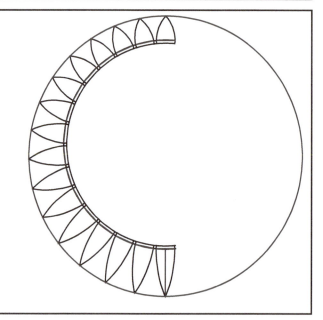

Fig. 37

- Turn off the **ref geo 2** layer.

- **TECH LINES** layer current.

Fig. 38

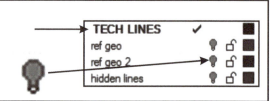

- Select all of the design motifs, tubing sections, and beads, **except for the motifs and tubing sections on the top and bottom of the necklace** and click on the **Mirror** command.

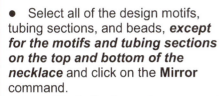

Mirror command

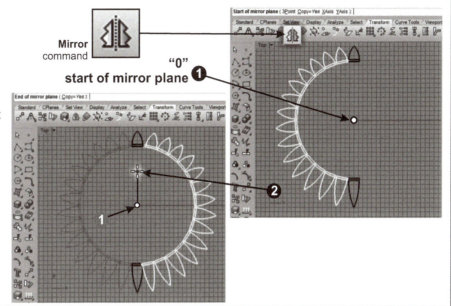

"0" start of mirror plane ❶

  - **Start of mirror plane** prompt:
    - Type **"0"** and press **Enter.** ❶

  - **End of mirror plane** prompt:
    - Using **ORTHO**, draw the cursor up and click to set location. ❷

Fig. 39

- **Curve Tools tabbed toolbar.**  Curve Tools

- Click on the **Circle: diameter** command.
  - **Start of diameter** prompt:
    - Snap to the top **Quad** of the inner edge of the tubing segment at the top of the necklace.
    - Click to set location. ❶

Circle: diameter command

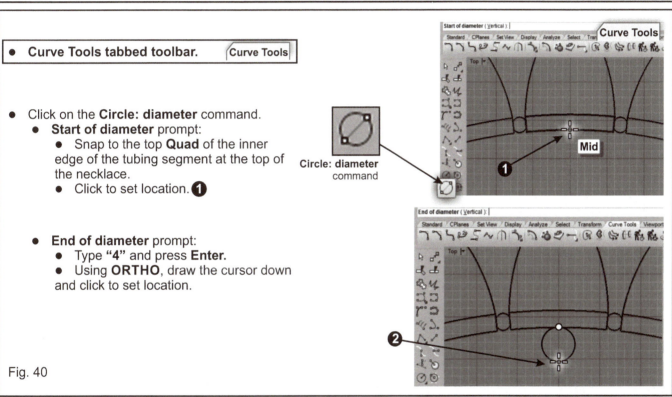

  - **End of diameter** prompt:
    - Type **"4"** and press **Enter.**
    - Using **ORTHO**, draw the cursor down and click to set location.

Fig. 40

- Click on the **Offset Curve** command.
  - **Select curve to offset** prompt:
    - Select the **4mm circle** just created.
  - **Offset distance**: .5
  - **Side to offset** prompt:
    - Offset to the inside of the circle.

- A top view technical of a 3mm stone with a .5mm bezel has been created.

new offset

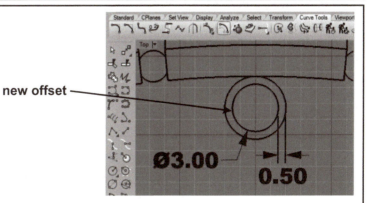

Fig. 41

- **Polar Array** the new bezel with stone around the inside of the necklace, creating 30 copies that align with the tubing sections.

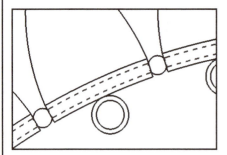

- You can turn on the **hidden lines** layer for a detail view.
  - The hidden lines layer has been assigned a custom linetype of .5.00,.5.00.

Fig. 42

- In this version, an additional circle allows for alternate scaling.

- Notice that the top motif has been replaced by a basic shape for a clasp.

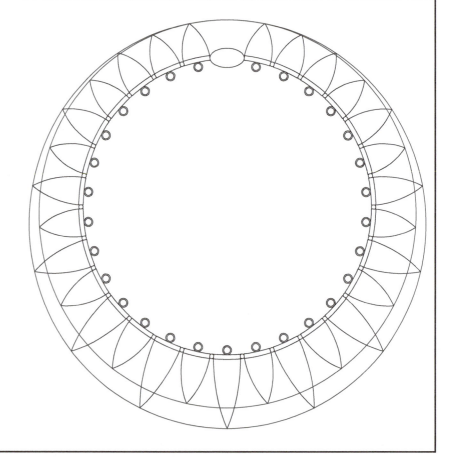

Fig. 43

Arraying Around a Square
Array Along Curve and Polar Array Commands

- Create the layers shown.

- **CENTER STONE** layer current.

Fig. 1

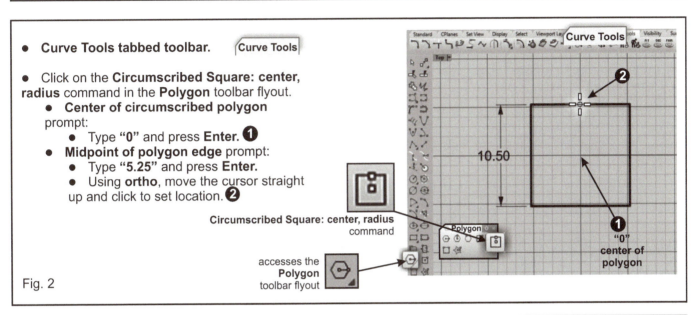

- **Curve Tools** tabbed toolbar. Curve Tools

- Click on the **Circumscribed Square: center, radius** command in the **Polygon** toolbar flyout.
    - **Center of circumscribed polygon** prompt:
        - Type **"0"** and press **Enter.** ❶
    - **Midpoint of polygon edge** prompt:
        - Type **"5.25"** and press **Enter.**
        - Using **ortho**, move the cursor straight up and click to set location. ❷

Circumscribed Square: center, radius command

accesses the **Polygon** toolbar flyout

Fig. 2

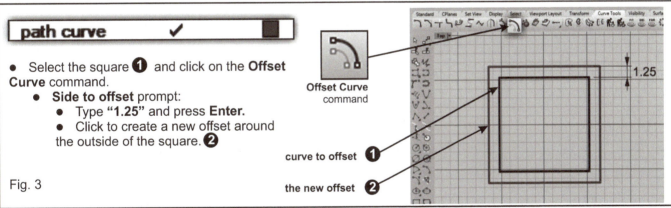

- Select the square ❶ and click on the **Offset Curve** command.
    - **Side to offset** prompt:
        - Type **"1.25"** and press **Enter.**
        - Click to create a new offset around the outside of the square. ❷

Offset Curve command

curve to offset ❶

the new offset ❷

Fig. 3

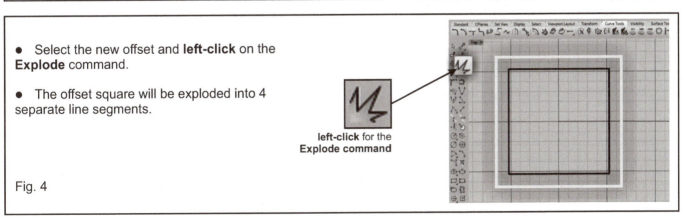

- Select the new offset and **left-click** on the **Explode** command.

- The offset square will be exploded into 4 separate line segments.

left-click for the **Explode command**

Fig. 4

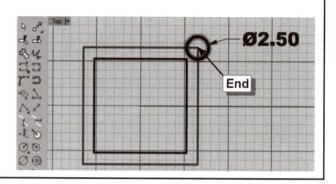

CLUSTER STONES ✔ ■

- Create a **Ø2.5mm circle** around the endpoint shown..

Fig. 5

- **Transform tabbed toolbar.** 〔Transform〕

- Click on the **Array Along Curve** command in the **Array** toolbar flyout.

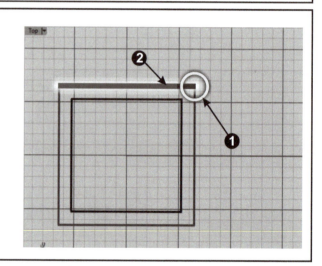

accesses the **Array** toolbar flyout

Array Along Curve command

Fig. 6

- **Select objects to array** prompt:
  - Select the circle. ❶
  - Press **Enter.**
- **Select path curve** prompt:
  - **Click near the right end** of the horizontal line at the top as shown. ❷

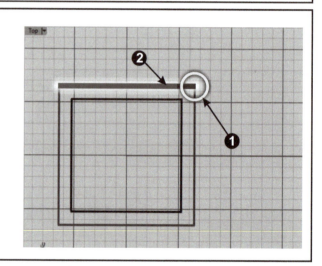

Fig. 7

- As soon at the **path curve** is selected, the **Array Along Curve Options** box will appear.

  - Type the number **"6"** in the **Number of Items** category as shown.
  - Click on the **OK** button to exit the dialog box.

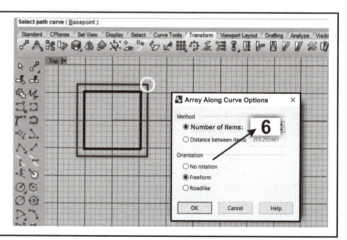

Fig. 8

- After you exit the dialog box, 6 circles will appear evenly spaced along the assigned path curve.

- **Delete** the circle on the far left.

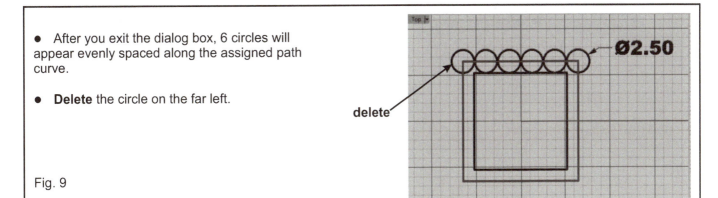

Fig. 9

- Click on the **Polar Array** command.
  - **Select objects to array** prompt:
    - Select all of the circles and press **Enter.**

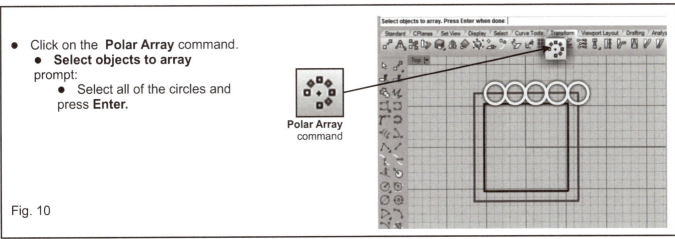

Polar Array command

Fig. 10

- **Center of polar array** prompt:
  - Type **"0"** and press **Enter.**
- **Number of items** prompt:
  - Type **"4"** and press **Enter.**
- **Angle or first reference point** prompt:
  - Press **Enter** to accept the **360°** default or type **"360"** in the **Command Line** and press **Enter.**

Center of polar array: **0**

Number of items **4**

Angle to fill or first reference point <360> (

- A number of pink **preview circles** appear.

- Press **Enter** to accept.

- The finished array.

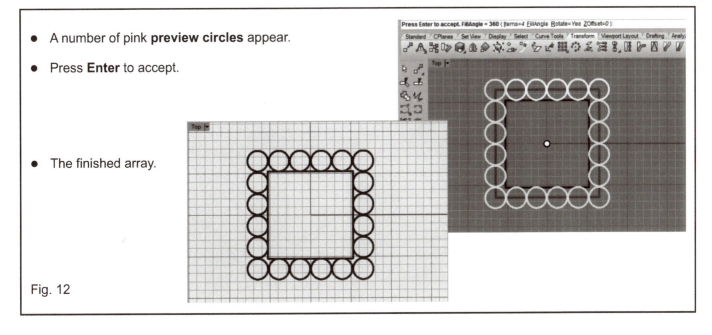

Fig. 12

218

Cluster Around an Oval Center Stone
Array Along Curve command

- Create the layers shown.

- **OVAL STONE** layer current.

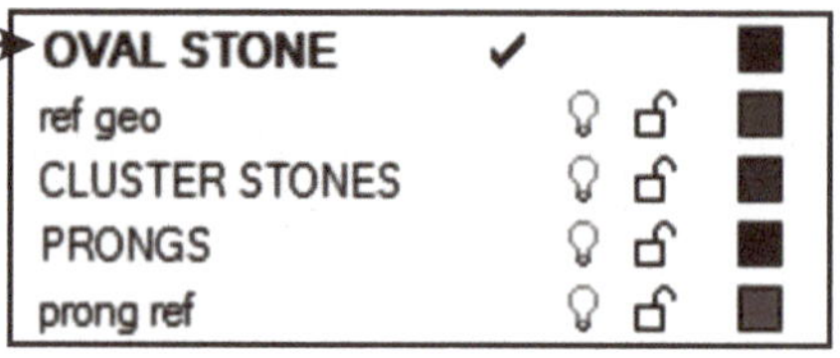

OVAL STONE	✔		■
ref geo		💡 🔓	■
CLUSTER STONES		💡 🔓	■
PRONGS		💡 🔓	■
prong ref		💡 🔓	■

Fig. 1

- **Curve Tools tabbed toolbar.** | Curve Tools |

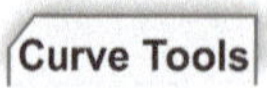

- Click on the **Ellipse: from center** command.
  - **Ellipse center** prompt:
    - Type **"0"** and press **Enter.** ❶
  - **End of first axis** prompt:
    - Type **"4"** and press **Enter.**
    - Using **ORTHO**, draw the cursor over to the right and click to set location. ❷
  - **End of second axis** prompt:
    - Type **"5"** and press **Enter.**
    - Using **ORTHO**, draw the cursor straight up and click to set location. ❸

Ellipse: from center command

"0" ellipse center

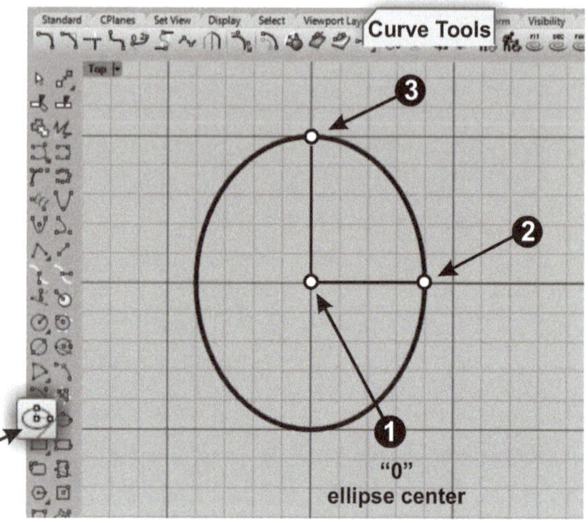

Fig. 2

- The finished 8mm x 10mm oval.

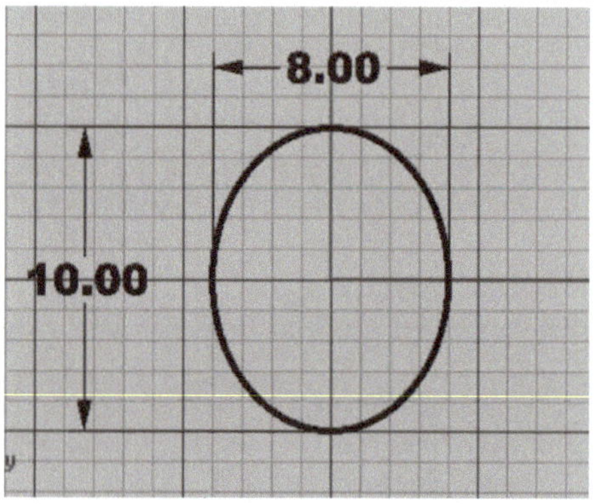

← 8.00 →

10.00

Fig. 3

CLUSTER STONES ✔   ■

- Click on the **Circle: Diameter** command:
  - **Start of diameter** prompt:
    - Snap to the **Quad** of the top of the oval and click to set location. ❶
  - **End of diameter** prompt:
    - Type **"2"** and press **Enter.**
    - Using **ORTHO**, draw the cursor up and click to set location. ❷

Circle: diameter command

Quad

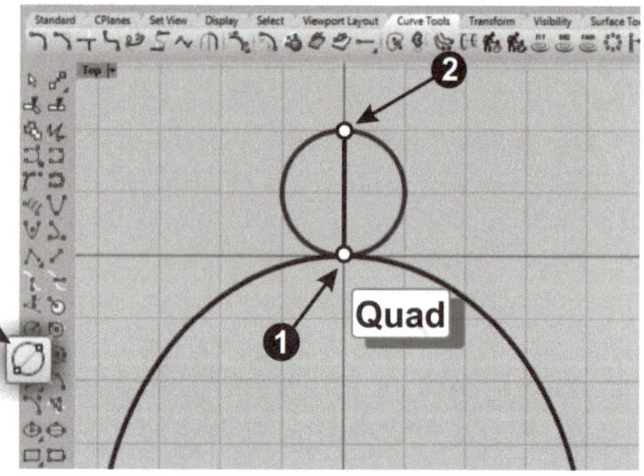

Fig. 4

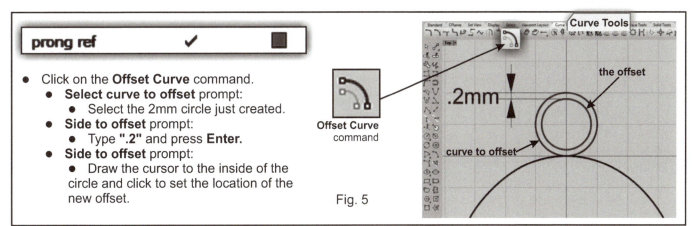

prong ref ✓ ■

- Click on the **Offset Curve** command.
  - **Select curve to offset** prompt:
    - Select the 2mm circle just created.
  - **Side to offset** prompt:
    - Type **".2"** and press **Enter**.
  - **Side to offset** prompt:
    - Draw the cursor to the inside of the circle and click to set the location of the new offset.

Offset Curve
command

Fig. 5

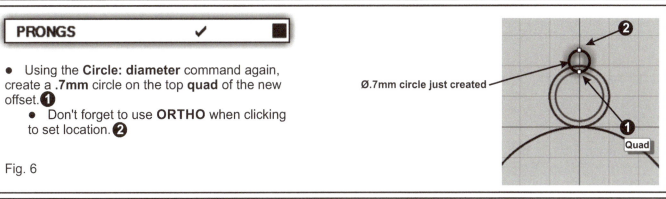

PRONGS ✓ ■

- Using the **Circle: diameter** command again, create a **.7mm** circle on the top **quad** of the new offset. **❶**
  - Don't forget to use **ORTHO** when clicking to set location. **❷**

Ø.7mm circle just created

Fig. 6

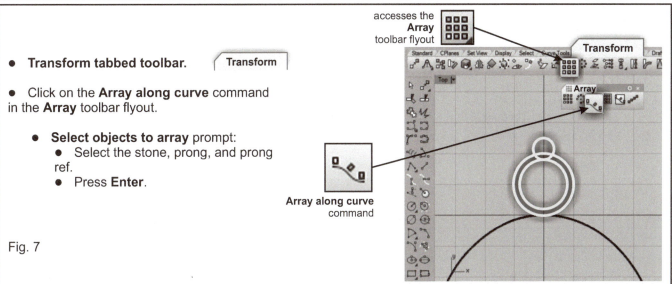

- **Transform tabbed toolbar.** `Transform`

- Click on the **Array along curve** command in the **Array** toolbar flyout.

  - **Select objects to array** prompt:
    - Select the stone, prong, and prong ref.
    - Press **Enter**.

accesses the **Array** toolbar flyout

Array along curve
command

Fig. 7

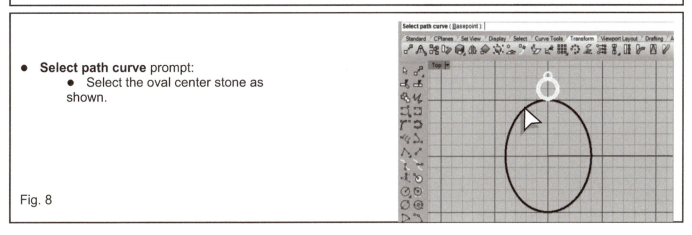

- **Select path curve** prompt:
  - Select the oval center stone as shown.

Fig. 8

- The **Array Along Curve Options** box will appear.
  - **Number of items** category: type **"16"** and click on the OK button.

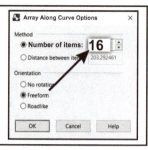

Fig. 9

- The array is completed - 16 items have been arrayed around the oval center stone.

- **But this is not an accurate spacing of stones - the gaps between them are inconsistent.**

- **Undo** this array (Ctrl + Z on your keyboard or click on the **Undo** button in **Standard tabbed toolbar**.)

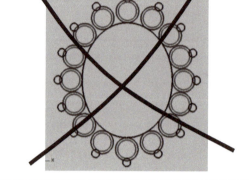

Undo
command

Fig. 10

---

prong ref ✔ ⬛

- **Curve Tools tabbed toolbar.** [Curve Tools]

- Select the **Oval** ❶ and click on the **Offset** ❷ **Curve** command.
  - **Side to offset** prompt:
    - Click on the **ThroughPoint** option in the **Command Line.**

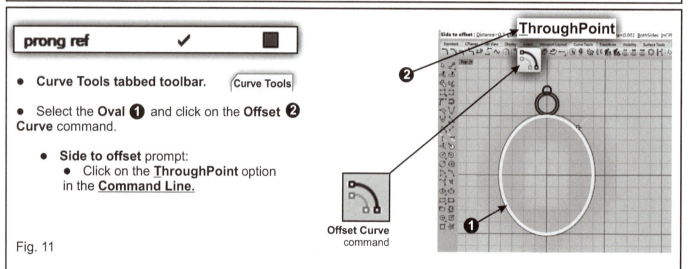

Offset Curve
command

Fig. 11

- **Through point** prompt:
  - Draw the offset out until it snaps to the **center of the circle** at the top of the oval as shown.
  - Remember that the cursor has to be over the curve of a circle to deploy **Center snap.**
  - Click to set location.

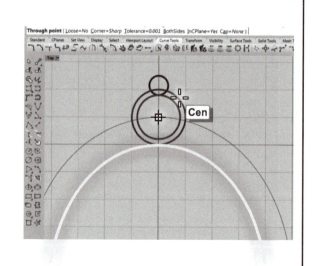

Fig. 12

- Use the **Array Along Curve** command again to array the little circles as before.

- This time, use the new offset as the **path curve.**

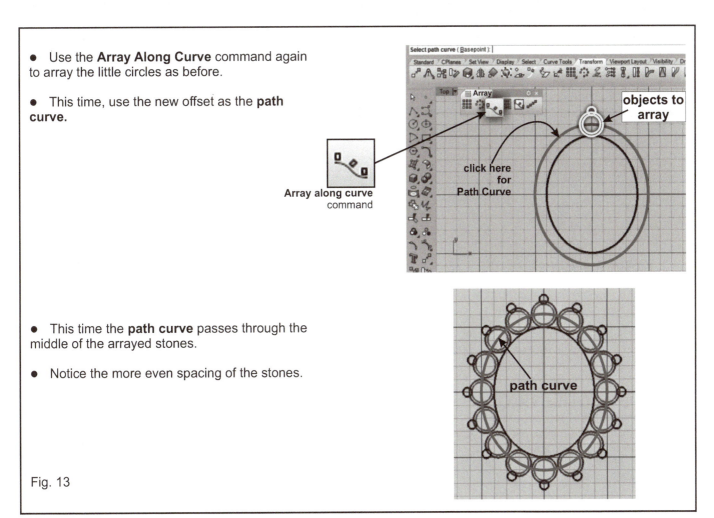

Array along curve
command

objects to array

click here for Path Curve

- This time the **path curve** passes through the middle of the arrayed stones.

- Notice the more even spacing of the stones.

path curve

Fig. 13

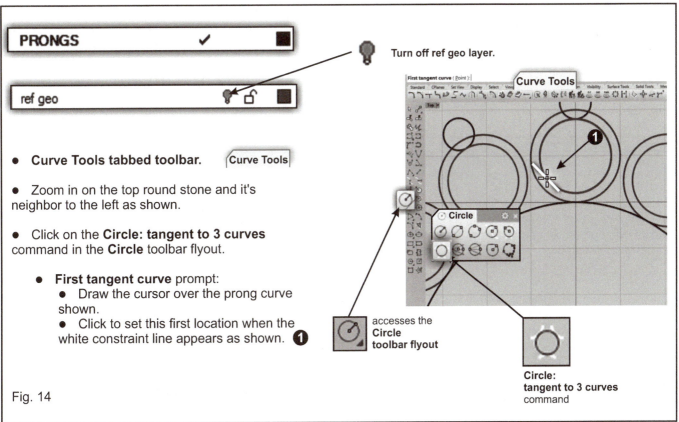

PRONGS ✓ ■

Turn off ref geo layer.

ref geo 🔓 ■

Curve Tools

- **Curve Tools tabbed toolbar.** Curve Tools

- Zoom in on the top round stone and it's neighbor to the left as shown.

- Click on the **Circle: tangent to 3 curves** command in the **Circle** toolbar flyout.

- **First tangent curve** prompt:
  - Draw the cursor over the prong curve shown.
  - Click to set this first location when the white constraint line appears as shown. ❶

accesses the **Circle** toolbar flyout

Circle: tangent to 3 curves command

Fig. 14

222

- **Second tangent curve or radius** prompt:
  - Draw the cursor across to the inner offset of the neighboring circle as shown.
  - Click when the white constraint line appears. ❷

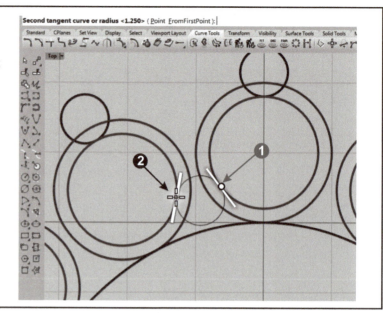

Fig. 15

- **Third tangent curve. Press Enter to draw circle from first two points.** prompt:
  - Draw the cursor over to the curve of the oval center stone.
  - Click when the white constraint line appears. ❸

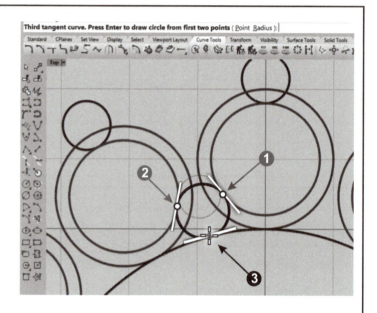

Fig. 16

- The new prong curve is tangent to both neighboring prong ref geo curves as well as to the oval center stone.

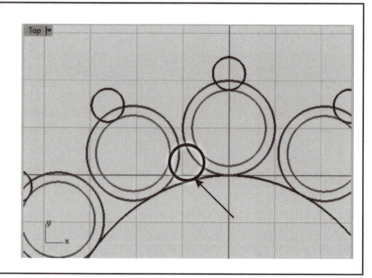

Fig. 17

223

- Create 3 more prongs, using the same technique.

- **Stop with these prongs.** *You do not have to create prongs for the rest of the stones.*

Fig. 18

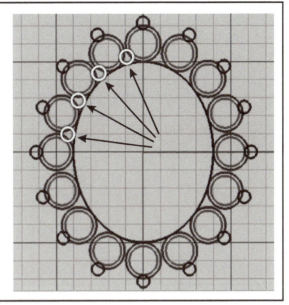

Trim
command

turn off

prong ref

- Select all of the prongs shown and click on the **Trim** command.

- **Select object to trim** prompt:
  - Trim the lines out of all of the prong circles as shown.
  - This makes the prongs look like they are in front of the stones which is the right way to perceive them.

Fig. 19

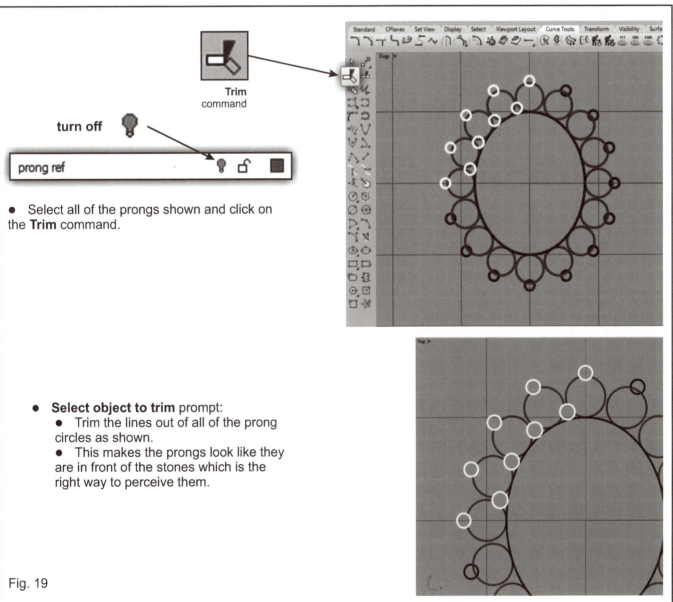

224

- Using **Grid Snap** mode, draw a polyline along the X and Y axes on the grid as shown.

- The angle of this polyline is at **0** and the lines are perfectly vertical and horizontal.

- Turn off **grid snap.**

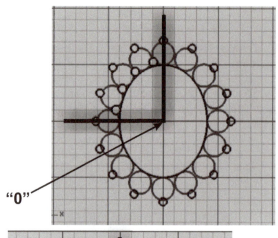

"0"

- Select all stones and prongs that are outside of the angle of the polyline as shown.

- **Delete** these selected objects.

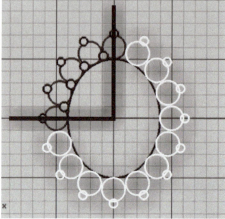

- Select the polyline and click on the **Trim** command.

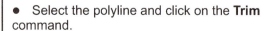

Trim
command

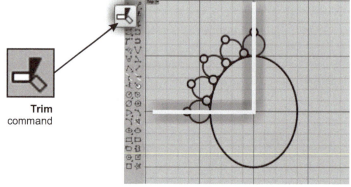

- Trim away everything that is on the outside of the angle of the polyline as shown.

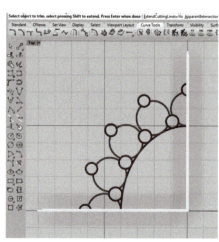

Fig. 20

- **Transform tabbed toolbar.** `Transform`

- **Hide** or **Delete** the polyline.

- Select all remaining objects and **Mirror** them across the Y axis to make a **horizontal mirror copy** as shown.

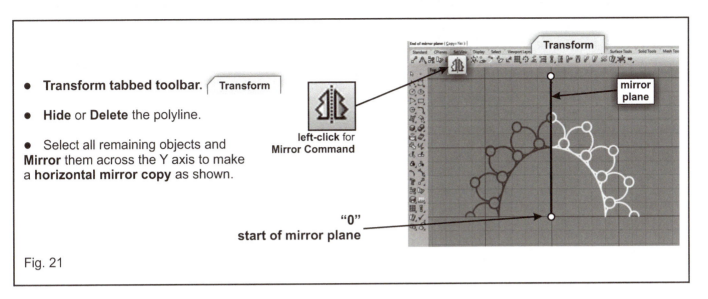

left-click for **Mirror Command**

mirror plane

"0" start of mirror plane

Fig. 21

- Select all objects again and **Mirror** across the X axis to create a **vertical mirror copy** as shown.

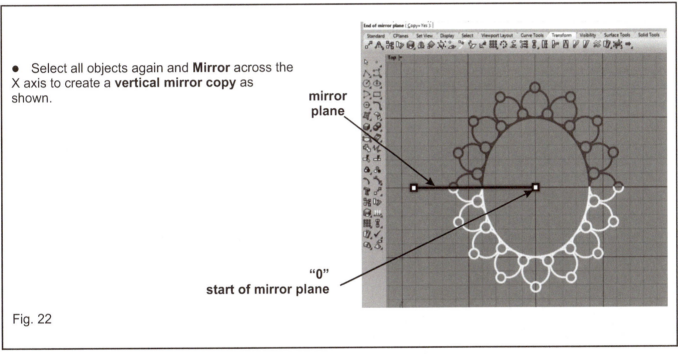

mirror plane

"0" start of mirror plane

Fig. 22

- The finished oval cluster.

- Remember, you can toggle the grid on and off by pressing the F7 key. **F7**

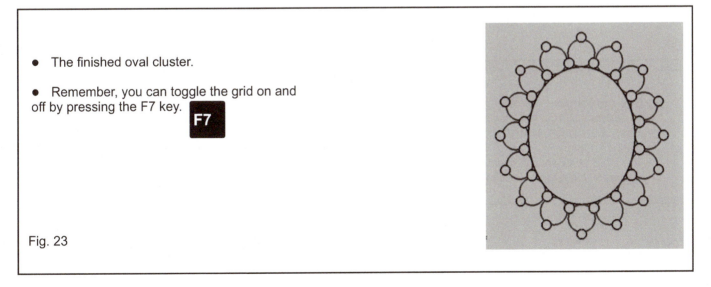

Fig. 23

Arraying Along a Freeform Curve
Arraying Stones Around a Heart Shape

- Open the **freeform heart.3dm** file that you made in the **Freeform Curves** chapter.

  - If you do not have this file, use freeform curves to create the heart shown, making sure to use **End osnap** so that the curves touch each other end to end at top and bottom.

  - Make your heart approximately the same height as the one shown.

Fig. 1

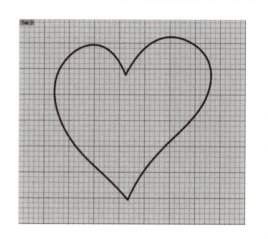

- Create the layers shown with the **STONES** layer current.

Fig. 2

HEART		♀	☐	■
path curve	✓			■
STONES		♀	☐	■
PRONGS		♀	☐	■
prong ref		♀	☐	■

- **Curve Tools tabbed toolbar.** ⌐Curve Tools⌐

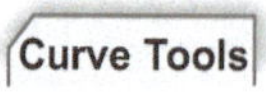

- Zoom in on the top of the heart and click on the **Circle: tangent, tangent, radius** command.

  - **First tangent curve** prompt:
    - Draw the cursor over to the curve shown. A white constraint line will appear when you are close enough.
    - Click to set location. ❶

Circle: **tangent, tangent, radius** command

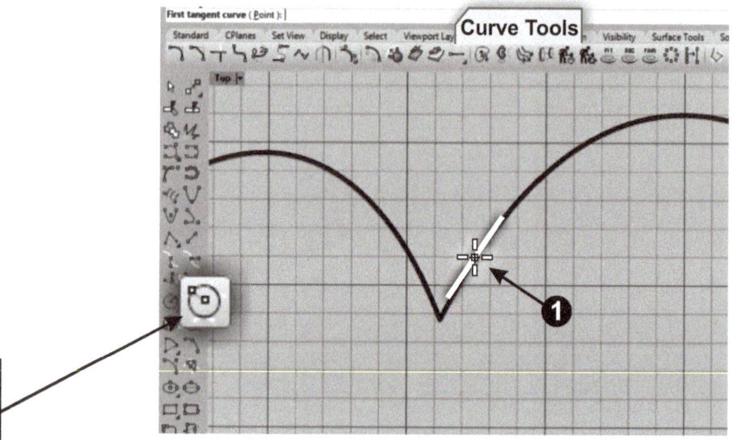

Fig. 3

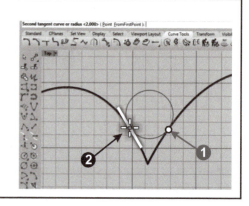

- **Second tangent curve or radius** prompt:
  - Draw your cursor over to the other side of the heart so that it touches the curve shown.
  - When the white constraint line appears, click to set location. ❷

Fig. 4

- **Radius** prompt:
  - Type **"1"** and press **Enter**.

- A 2mm round stone has been placed in the angle of the heart, tangent to both curves.

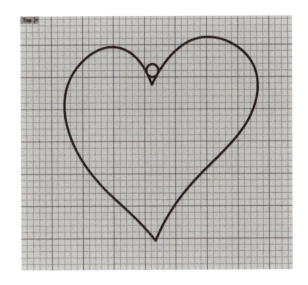

Fig. 5

- Click on the **Offset Curve** command.

  - **Select curve to offset** prompt:
    - Select the heart curve. ❶

  - **Side to offset** prompt:
    - Click on the **ThroughPoint** option ❷ in the **Command Line.**

  - **Through point** prompt:
    - Draw the cursor over to the 2mm circle until the cursor touches it and snaps to the **Center** of the circle as shown. ❸ (You must use **Center osnap**.)
    - Click to set location.

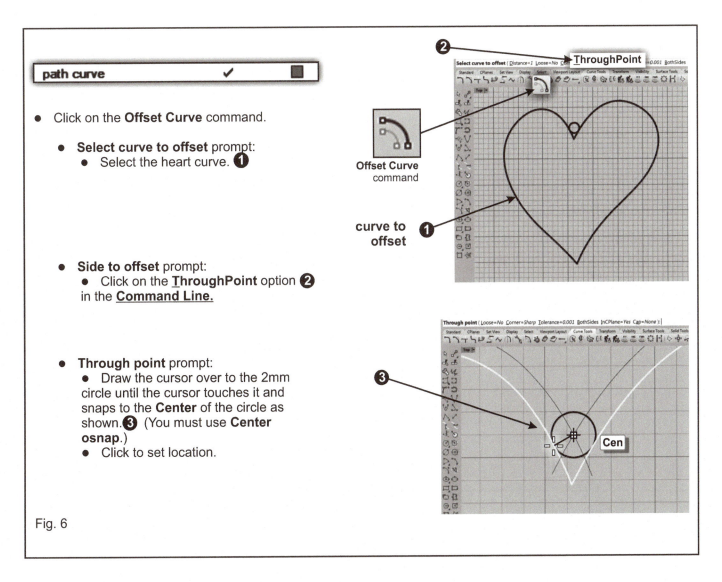

Offset Curve command

curve to offset ❶

Fig. 6

228

- The finished 1mm offset.

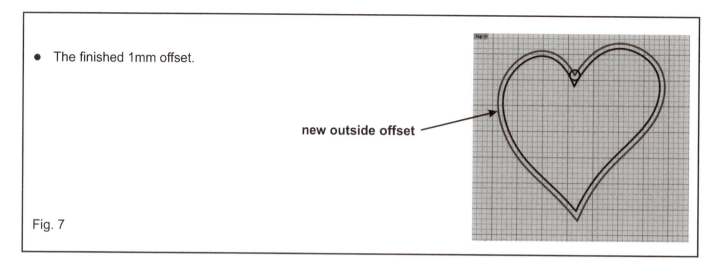

new outside offset

Fig. 7

- **Explode** the offset curve.

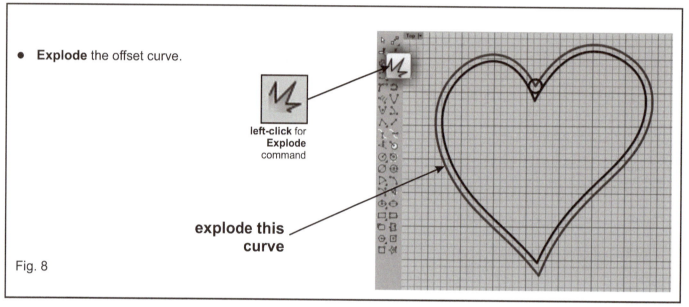

left-click for
Explode
command

**explode this
curve**

Fig. 8

- **Join** curve segments together as shown.
  - The offset command created these extra pieces.

- You should end up with 2 separate curves, one on each side of the heart.

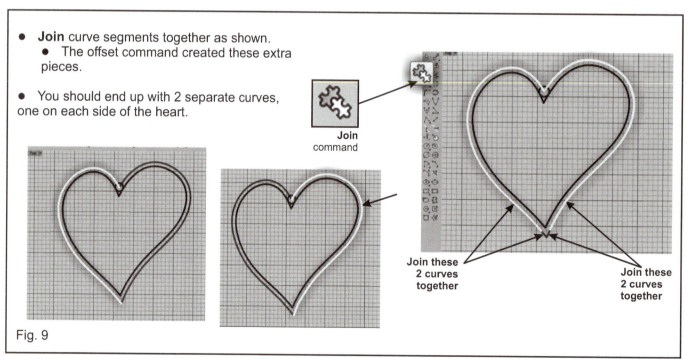

Join
command

**Join these
2 curves
together**

**Join these
2 curves
together**

Fig. 9

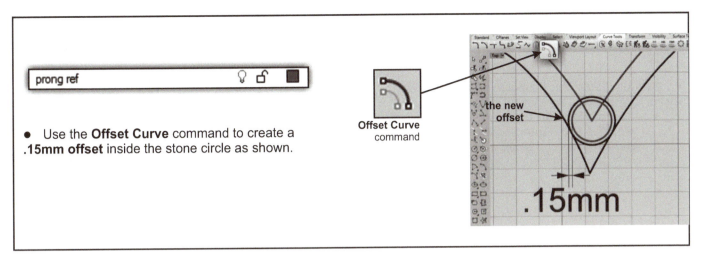

prong ref

- Use the **Offset Curve** command to create a
  .15mm offset inside the stone circle as shown.

Offset Curve
command

the new
offset

.15mm

- Click on the **Line** command.

  - **Start of line** prompt:
    - Snap to the **intersection** of the stone
    circle and the heart curve shown.
    - Click to set location. ❶

Line
command

Int
❶

- **End of line** prompt:
  - Type **"3"** in the **Command Line.**
  - Press **Enter.**

End of line (BothSides) 3

- **End of line** prompt:
  - Snap to the **perpendicular** of either
  the stone circle or the offset prong curve
  inside it.
  - The end of the line will extend beyond
  the boundary of the stone circle on the
  upper left as shown.
  - Click to set location. ❷

Perp
❷
❶

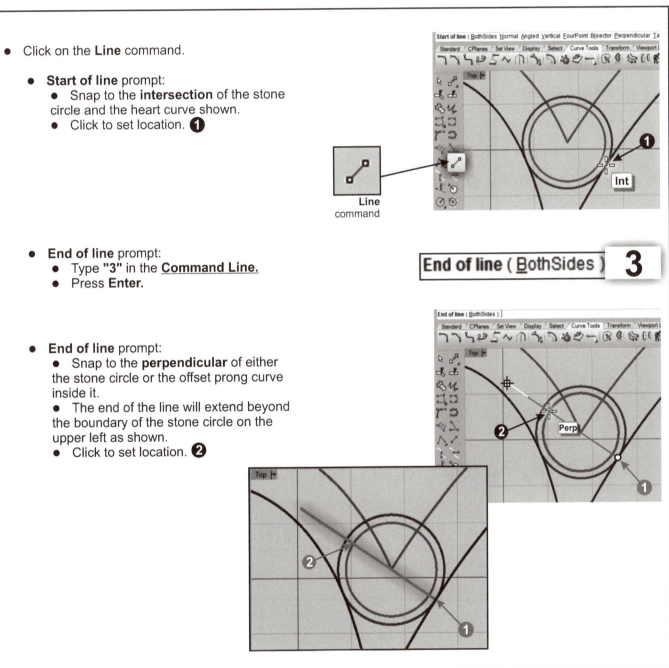

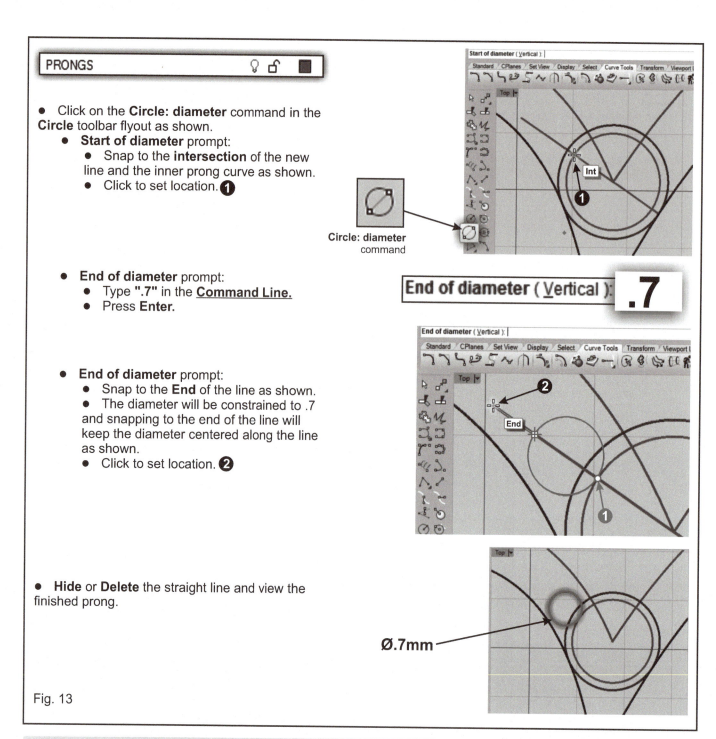

PRONGS ♀ 🔓 ■

- Click on the **Circle: diameter** command in the **Circle** toolbar flyout as shown.
  - **Start of diameter** prompt:
    - Snap to the **intersection** of the new line and the inner prong curve as shown.
    - Click to set location. **1**

Circle: diameter command

- **End of diameter** prompt:
  - Type **".7"** in the <u>Command Line.</u>
  - Press **Enter.**

End of diameter (Vertical): **.7**

- **End of diameter** prompt:
  - Snap to the **End** of the line as shown.
  - The diameter will be constrained to .7 and snapping to the end of the line will keep the diameter centered along the line as shown.
  - Click to set location. **2**

- **Hide** or **Delete** the straight line and view the finished prong.

Ø.7mm

Fig. 13

Arraying the Stones Along the Heart Curves

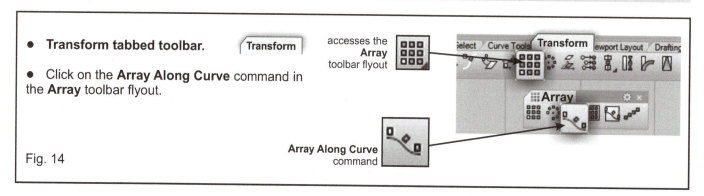

- **Transform tabbed toolbar.** `Transform` accesses the **Array** toolbar flyout

- Click on the **Array Along Curve** command in the **Array** toolbar flyout.

Array Along Curve command

Fig. 14

- **Select objects to array** prompt:
  - Select the 3 circles shown.
  - Press **Enter**. ❶

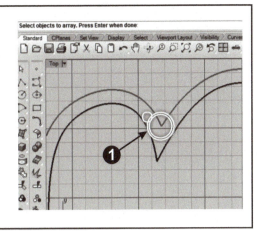

Fig. 15

- **Select path curve** prompt:
  - Select the offset on the right.
  - Click on the approximate location shown. ❷

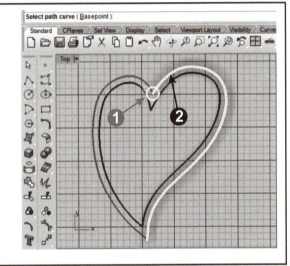

Fig. 16

- The **Array Along Curve Options** box will appear.
  - For **Number of Items**, try typing **"21"** and click on the OK button.

Fig. 17

- The stone will array evenly along the specified path curve.

> - **Remember! Everyone's heart design will be different.**
>
> - **You may have to undo the array and then repeat it, trying <u>another number of items</u> until you have a good number for your own original design.**

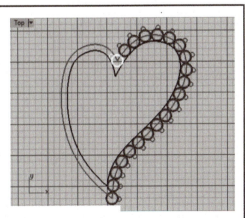

Fig. 18

- **Delete** the prong on the original stone and create a new prong on the other side as shown.

- Create a prong on the other side of the original stone as shown.

Fig. 19

- Delete the stone at the bottom and click on the **Array along Curve** command again.

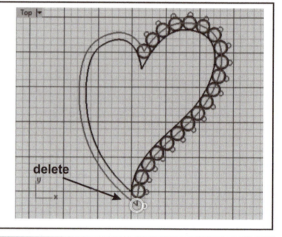

delete

Fig. 20

- **Select objects to array** prompt:
  - Select the stone, prong, and prong curve at the top as shown and press **Enter.** ❶

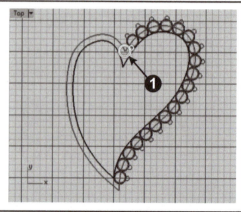

Fig. 21

- **Select path curve** prompt:
  - Select the offset, this time on the left of the heart as shown.❷
  - *Make sure to select near the top* as shown.

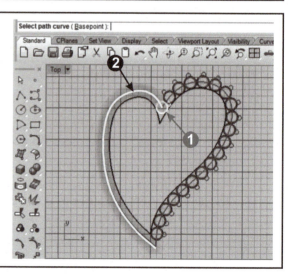

Fig. 22

- In this example, **"18"** is the number specified for **Number of items.**

Fig. 23

- The finished array.

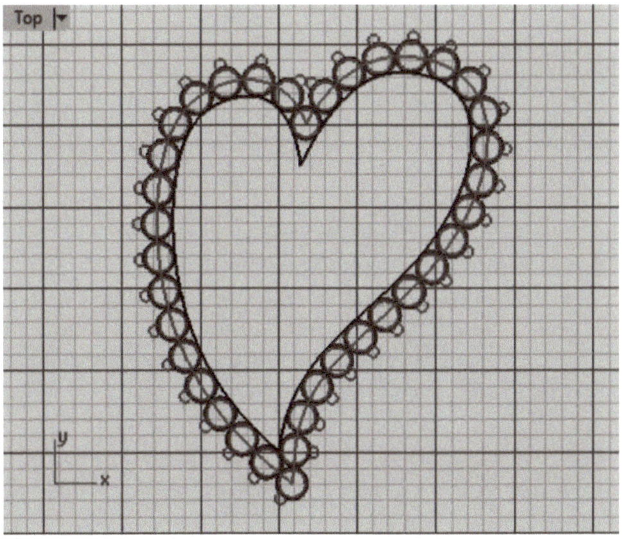

Fig. 24

- **Rotate** the bottom prong to adjust position for a pleasing arrangement.
  - **Center of rotation: ❶**
    - Use **center osnap**
  - **First reference point: ❷**
  - **Second reference point ❸**

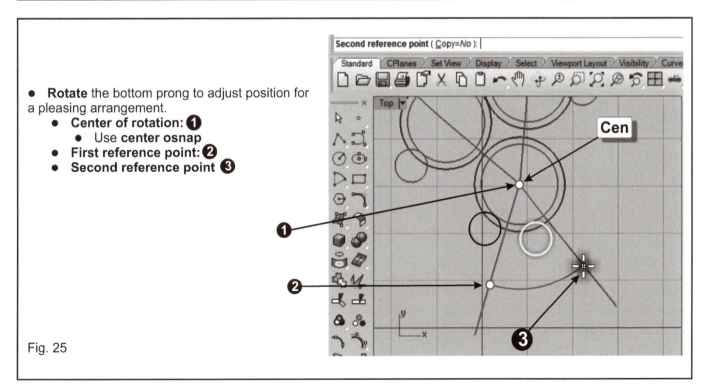

Fig. 25

234

- Some stones may intersect each other.

- You can either drag them away from each other or slightly reduce the diameter of one or both of the stones.

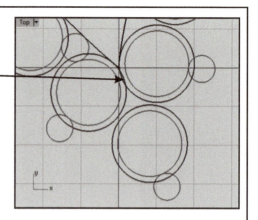

Fig. 26

- Create inner prongs as shown, using the **Circle: tangent to 3 curves** command.
  - See the previous chapter, pp. 218-219

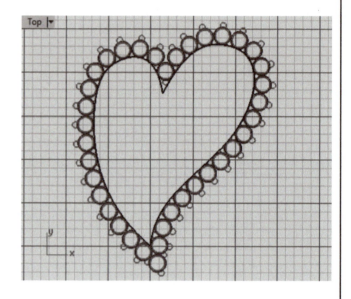

Fig. 27

- Trim out all of the prongs.

Fig. 28

- Make a teardrop shape with a freeform curve, making sure that the **Sharp=Yes** option is toggled on in the **Command Line.**
  - With the Sharp option on, when your curve is closed, it will close with a point as shown.

- Make your offset curve before placing a stone on it. In this example, the offset is 1mm and the stone is 2mm in diameter.

- This array was done along the single path curve that runs around the teardrop shape.

- The original prong's orientation is along the side so that the prongs run along the piece in a good formation. Rotate this prong into position after the array.

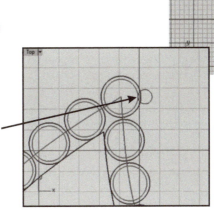

Fig. 29

Introduction to 3D Space
Viewports: Navigation and Display Modes

The Default 4-Viewport Layout

- Each viewport represents a different view of your work area and the object that you create.

- In addition to the different views, these viewports represent 3 separate construction planes - the TOP, FRONT, and RIGHT construction planes upon which the grid for each view rests.

- The default perspective viewport uses the TOP construction plane, also known as **"World TOP"**.

- **Standard Tabbed toolbar.**　　Standard

- **Right-click twice** on the **4 Default Viewports** command as shown.

right-click twice for
4 Default Viewports
command

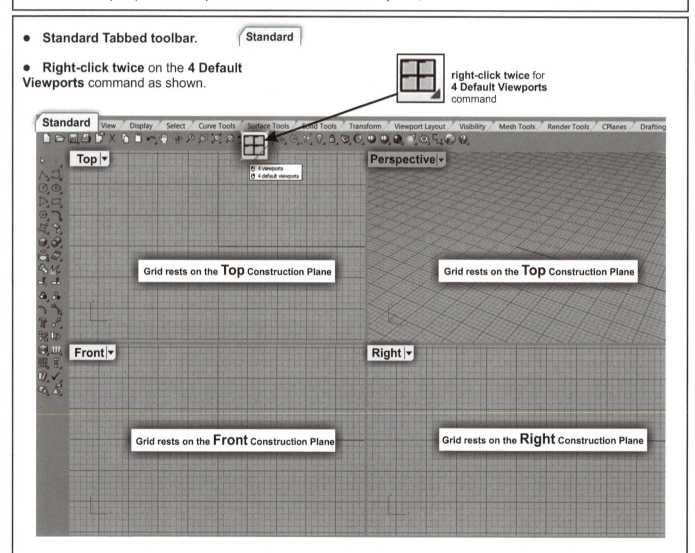

★ **Note**: Anything that you draw in a viewport will be placed directly on that viewport's construction plane unless you are using Object Snap to override this default.

Fig. 1

Anatomy of a Viewport

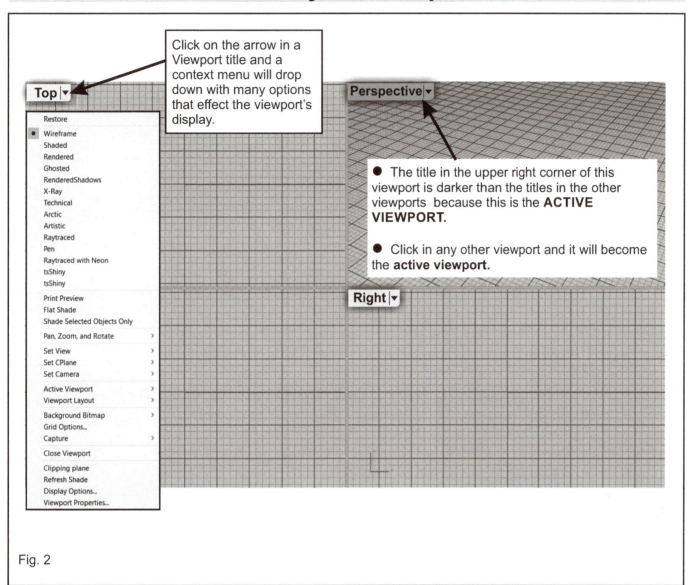

Click on the arrow in a Viewport title and a context menu will drop down with many options that effect the viewport's display.

Top ▾

- Restore
- Wireframe
- Shaded
- Rendered
- Ghosted
- RenderedShadows
- X-Ray
- Technical
- Arctic
- Artistic
- Raytraced
- Pen
- Raytraced with Neon
- tsShiny
- tsShiny

- Print Preview
- Flat Shade
- Shade Selected Objects Only

- Pan, Zoom, and Rotate   ›

- Set View   ›
- Set CPlane   ›
- Set Camera   ›

- Active Viewport   ›
- Viewport Layout   ›

- Background Bitmap   ›
- Grid Options...
- Capture   ›

- Close Viewport

- Clipping plane
- Refresh Shade
- Display Options...
- Viewport Properties...

Perspective ▾

● The title in the upper right corner of this viewport is darker than the titles in the other viewports because this is the **ACTIVE VIEWPORT.**

● Click in any other viewport and it will become the **active viewport.**

Right ▾

Fig. 2

● Click anywhere on the Grid of a Viewport to make it the **active viewport..** ❶

● Click on the **Properties** tab ❷ in the pane on the right of the screen as shown.

    ● Here you will see a lot of information about the active viewport.

● The **Projection** category ❸ shows that the mode of this viewport is **Perspective.**

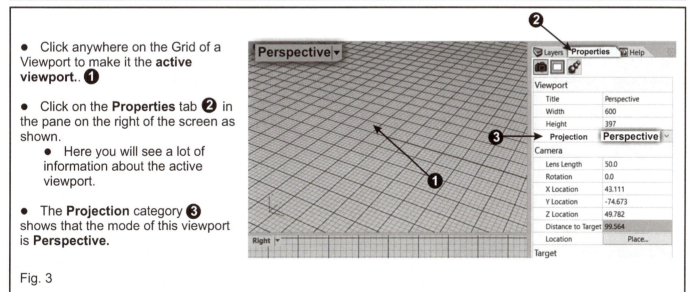

Fig. 3

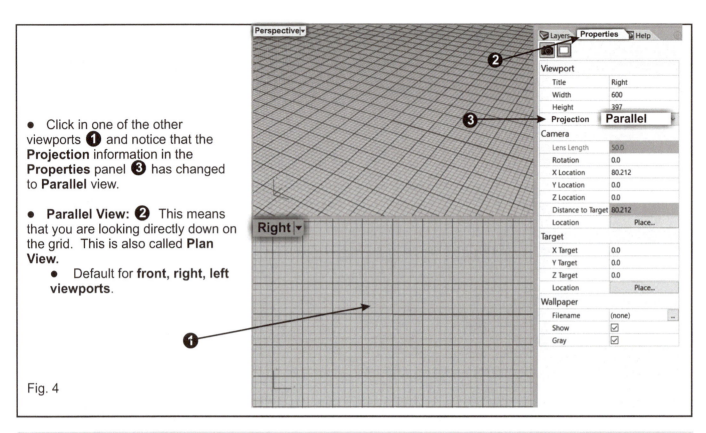

- Click in one of the other viewports ❶ and notice that the **Projection** information in the **Properties** panel ❸ has changed to **Parallel** view.

- **Parallel View:** ❷ This means that you are looking directly down on the grid. This is also called **Plan View.**
  - Default for **front, right, left** viewports.

Fig. 4

Navigating in a Perspective Viewport
Rotating, Panning, and Zooming the View In 3D Space

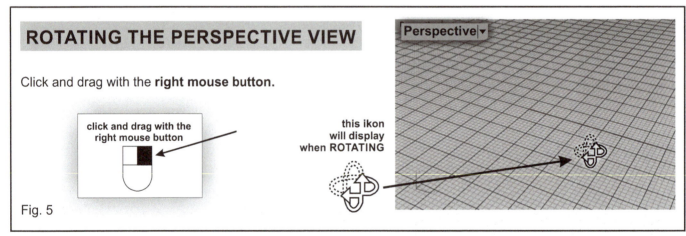

ROTATING THE PERSPECTIVE VIEW

Click and drag with the **right mouse button.**

click and drag with the
right mouse button

this ikon
will display
when ROTATING

Fig. 5

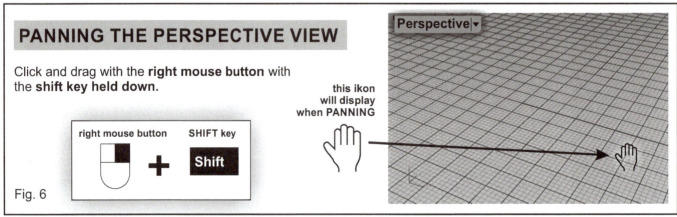

PANNING THE PERSPECTIVE VIEW

Click and drag with the **right mouse button** with the **shift key held down.**

right mouse button   SHIFT key

Shift

this ikon
will display
when PANNING

Fig. 6

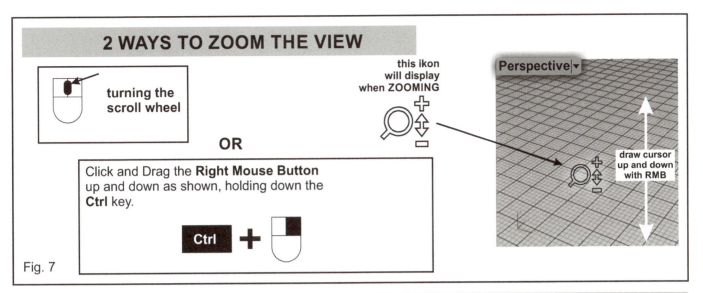

2 WAYS TO ZOOM THE VIEW

turning the scroll wheel

OR

this ikon will display when ZOOMING

Click and Drag the **Right Mouse Button** up and down as shown, holding down the **Ctrl** key.

Ctrl +

Perspective ▾

draw cursor up and down with RMB

Fig. 7

Viewing an Object in Different Viewports

Creating a Torus object for the exercise

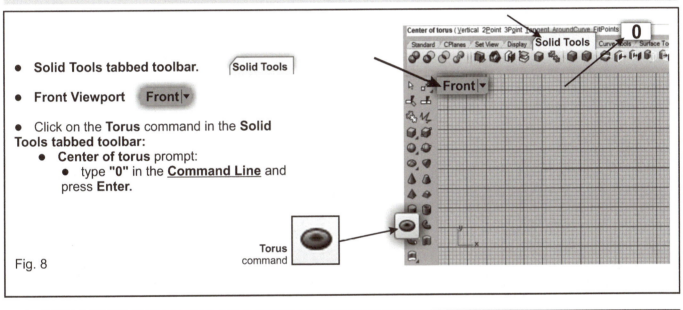

- **Solid Tools tabbed toolbar.**   Solid Tools

- **Front Viewport**   Front ▾

- Click on the **Torus** command in the **Solid Tools tabbed toolbar:**
  - **Center of torus** prompt:
    - type **"0"** in the **Command Line** and press **Enter.**

Center of torus (Vertical 2Point 3Point Tangent AroundCurve FitPoints   **0**
Standard CPlanes Set View Display **Solid Tools** Curve Tools Surface To
Front ▾

Torus command

Fig. 8

- **Radius** prompt:
  - type **"9.5"** in the **Command Line** and press **Enter.**

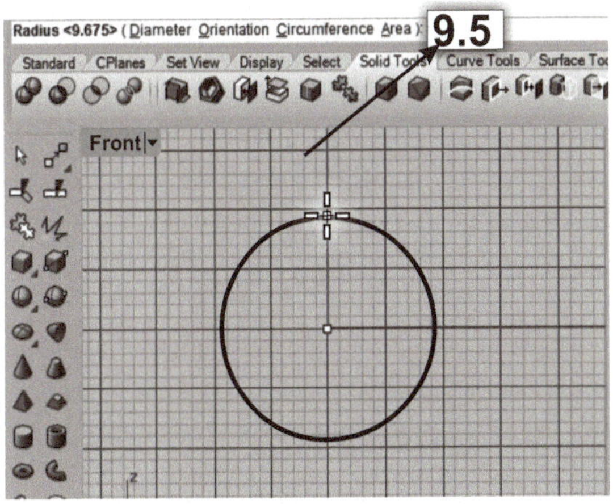

Radius <9.675> (Diameter Orientation Circumference Area) **9.5**
Standard CPlanes Set View Display Select Solid Tools Curve Tools Surface Too
Front ▾

Fig. 9

240

- **Second radius** prompt:
  - Click on the **Diameter** option in the **Command Line.**
    - Type **"3"** in the **Command Line** and press **Enter.**

Fig. 10

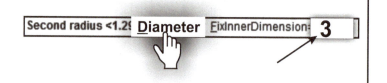

- The finished torus shown in **Wireframe Mode.**

- **You will see thicker lines, representing the seams and edges of surfaces.**

- The thinner lines, called Isocurves, represent the shape and the geometry of the objects but are just indicators, not real curve objects.

Fig. 11

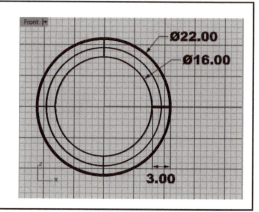

- The Torus object will be visible in all 4 viewports, all viewed from a different angle - seen here in the default **Wireframe Mode.**

Fig. 12

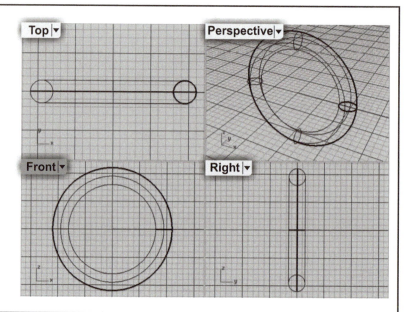

Display Modes

- **Display tabbed toolbar.**   Display

- **Perspective viewport.**   Perspective ▾

- Click on the **Shaded Viewport** command.
  - Objects in the **active viewport** will now show in **Shaded Mode.**

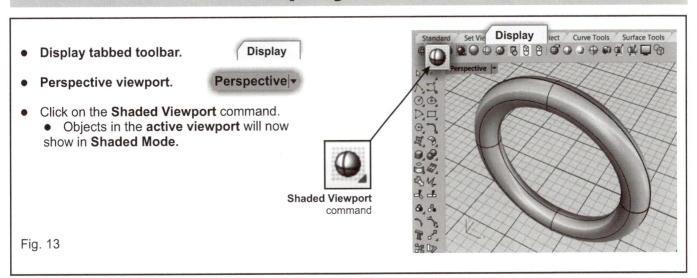

Shaded Viewport
command

Fig. 13

- If you **right-click** on this command, *all viewports will go into Shaded mode.*

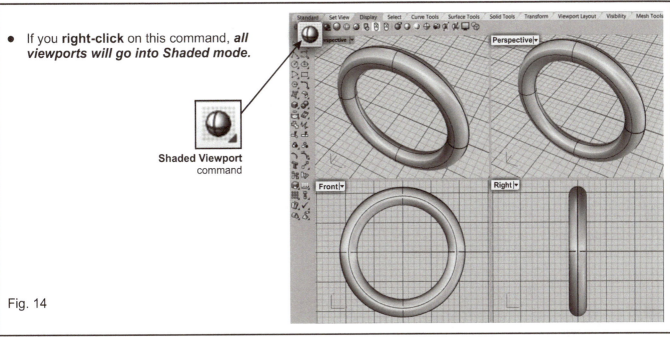

Shaded Viewport
command

Fig. 14

- Click on the **Wireframe Viewport** command .

- The view will now show in **Wireframe Viewport Mode.**

- **Right-click** on this button to show all viewports in **Wireframe Viewport Mode.**

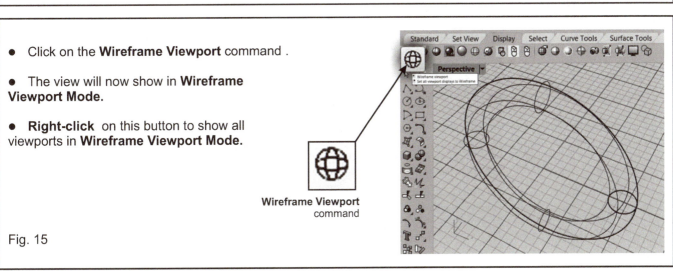

Wireframe Viewport
command

Fig. 15

- Click on the **Shade** command in the **Display** toolbar flyout as shown.

- The view will now show in **Shade Mode.**
  - **Right-click** on this button to show all viewports in **Shade Mode.**

- By default, **Shade** mode looks a lot like **Shaded Viewport Mode.** But you can change the options in the <u>**Command Line**</u> to change the appearance.

- *Click away and your display mode will revert back to the mode you were viewing before clicking on the Shade command.*

Fig. 16

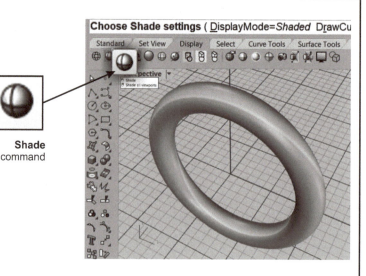

Choose Shade settings (<u>D</u>isplayMode=*Shaded* DrawCu

Shade
command

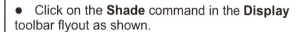

- Click on the **Rendered Viewport** command in the **Display tabbed toolbar**.
- **Raytraced Viewport** mode will show the same visual characteristics.

- The view will now show in **Rendered (or Raytraced) Viewport Mode.**
  - **Right-click** on this button to show all viewports in **Rendered (or Raytraced) Viewport Mode.**

- By default, this will shade the object without showing curves or isocurves.

- *Adjusting Render and Raytraced settings will make these display mode more usable.*

Fig. 17

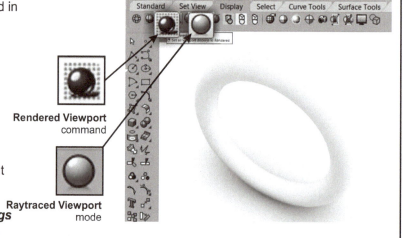

Rendered Viewport
command

Raytraced Viewport
mode

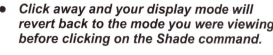

- Click on the **Ghosted Viewport** command in the **Display tabbed toolbar**.

- The view will now show in **Ghosted Viewport Mode.**
  - **Right-click** on this button to show all viewports in **Ghosted Viewport Mode.**

- Surfaces will appear transparent, with the forward parts showing more intensely.
  - This is a good modeling mode as you can see what is happening on all sides of the piece at once.

Fig. 18

Ghosted Viewport
command

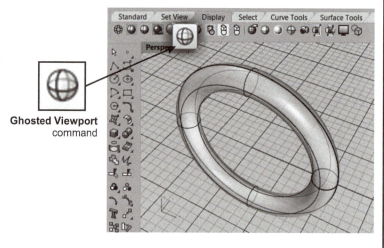

- Click on the **X Ray Viewport** command in the **Display tabbed toolbar**.

- The view will now show in **X Ray Viewport Mode**.
  - **Right-click** on this button to show all viewports in **X Ray Viewport Mode**.

- Like **Ghosted** mode, you can see through the surfaces but all lines are seen in the same intensity. This can sometimes be confusing.

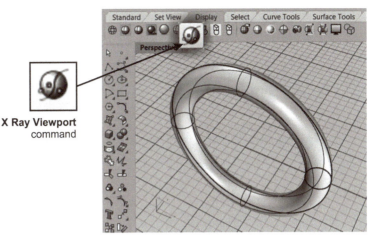

X Ray Viewport
command

Fig. 19

- Click on the **Technical Viewport** command in the **Display tabbed toolbar**.

- The view will now show in **Technical Viewport Mode**.
  - **Right-click** on this button to show all viewports in **Technical Viewport Mode**.

- The display will show continuous lines and dotted lines, representing shapes and hidden lines.

- *Note: This file, the **star shaped signet ring**, is from a future chapter and has been brought in to this exercise for illustration purposes.*

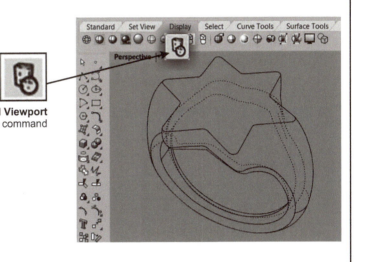

Technical Viewport
command

Fig. 20

- Click on the **Pen Viewport** command in the **Display tabbed toolbar**.

- The view will now show in **Pen Viewport Mode**.

- **Right-click** on this button to show all viewports in **Pen Viewport Mode**.

- The display will show lines that have the look of drawing with a pen, rather than the usual look of CAD's vector lines.

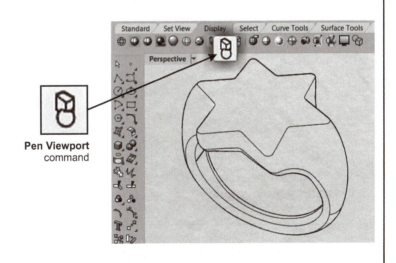

Pen Viewport
command

Fig. 21

- Click on the **Artistic Viewport** command in the **Display tabbed toolbar**.

- The view will now show in **Artistic Viewport Mode**.
  - **Right-click** on this button to show all viewports in **Artistic Viewport Mode**.

- The view will have the appearance of a pencil drawing.

Fig. 22

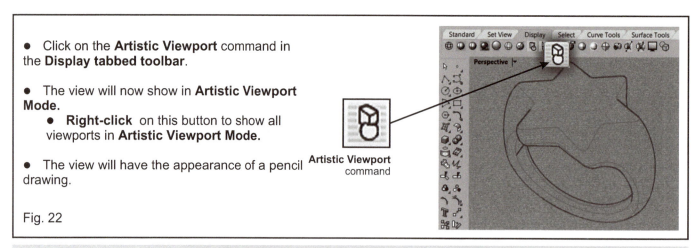

Artistic Viewport
command

Clearing Render Meshes
This command is essential for reducing file size.

- **Standard tabbed toolbar.** | Standard |

- Click on the **Clear All Meshes (tooltip says "Clear All Render and Analysis Meshes")** in the **Utilities** toolbar flyout.

- Note: you can also generate this command by typing **"clearallmeshes"** and pressing **Enter.**

- The viewport will show in **Wireframe view.**

- All of the render "meshes" which have been "mapped" to surfaces will have been eliminated, reducing the file size.

- This is good for saving your work to a smaller file size, especially if you have to email a file to someone.

Fig. 23

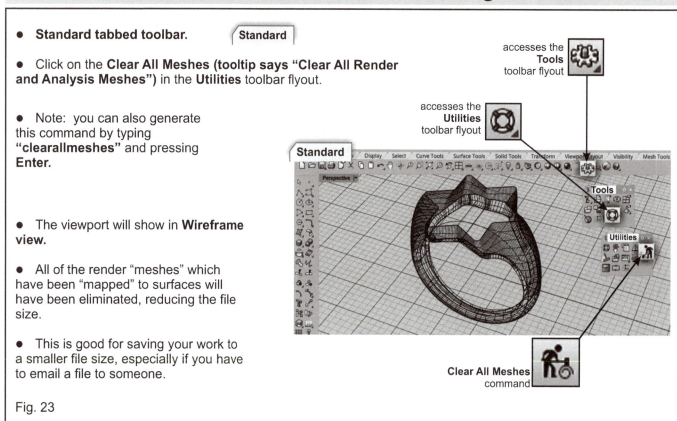

accesses the
Tools
toolbar flyout

accesses the
Utilities
toolbar flyout

Clear All Meshes
command

Additional Commands

- **Display tabbed toolbar.**

- Click on the **Render Mesh Settings in the Display tabbed toolbar** to adjust the resolution of your render meshes in order to get the clarity and definition you need.
  - The default **Jagged and Faster** setting is usually sufficient.

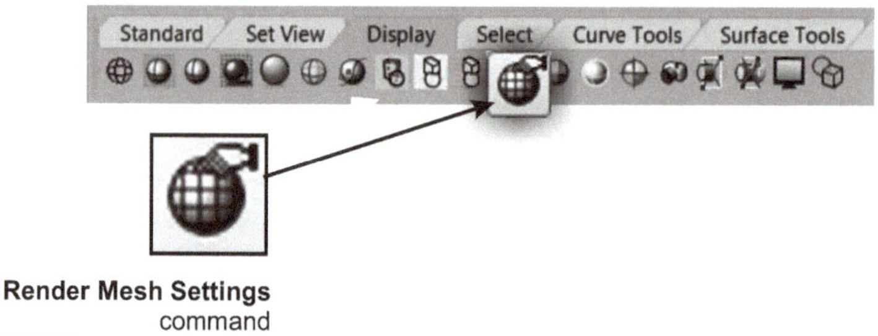

Fig. 24

Render Mesh Settings
command

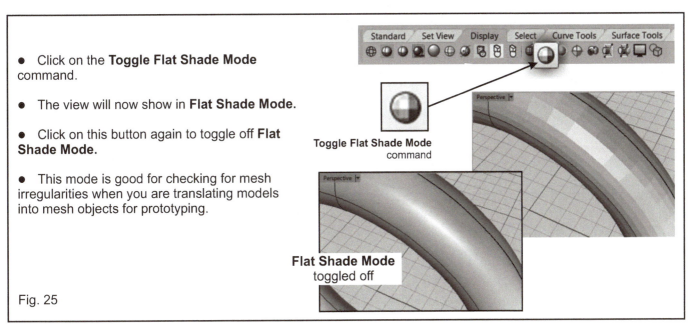

- Click on the **Toggle Flat Shade Mode** command.

- The view will now show in **Flat Shade Mode**.

- Click on this button again to toggle off **Flat Shade Mode.**

- This mode is good for checking for mesh irregularities when you are translating models into mesh objects for prototyping.

Toggle Flat Shade Mode
command

Flat Shade Mode
toggled off

Fig. 25

- If you click on the **Toggle Shade Selected Mode** command, every object you select will be shaded until it is de-selected.

⊙ **Warning**: This mode can be **very confusing**.

⊙ **Click on this command again to toggle this mode off!!**

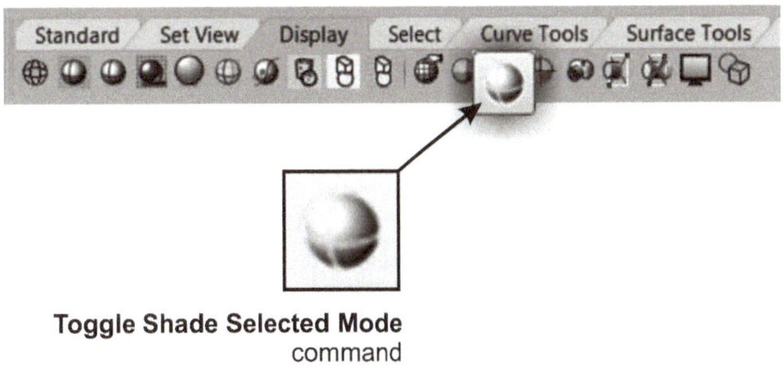

Toggle Shade Selected Mode
command

Fig. 26

The Quickest Way to Change Display Modes

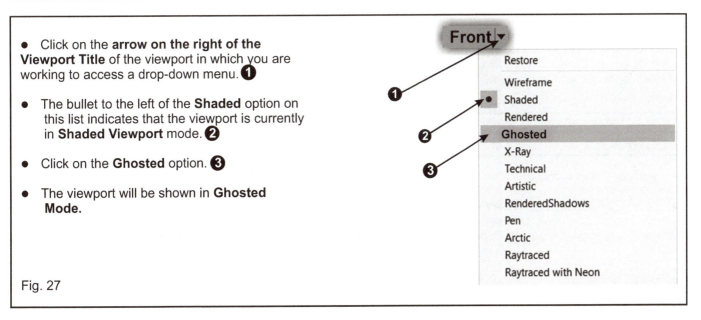

- Click on the **arrow on the right of the Viewport Title** of the viewport in which you are working to access a drop-down menu. ❶

- The bullet to the left of the **Shaded** option on this list indicates that the viewport is currently in **Shaded Viewport** mode. ❷

- Click on the **Ghosted** option. ❸

- The viewport will be shown in **Ghosted Mode.**

Front ▾

Restore
Wireframe
• Shaded
Rendered
Ghosted
X-Ray
Technical
Artistic
RenderedShadows
Pen
Arctic
Raytraced
Raytraced with Neon

Fig. 27

Working in Different Viewports

Working with the Top, Front, and Right Construction Planes

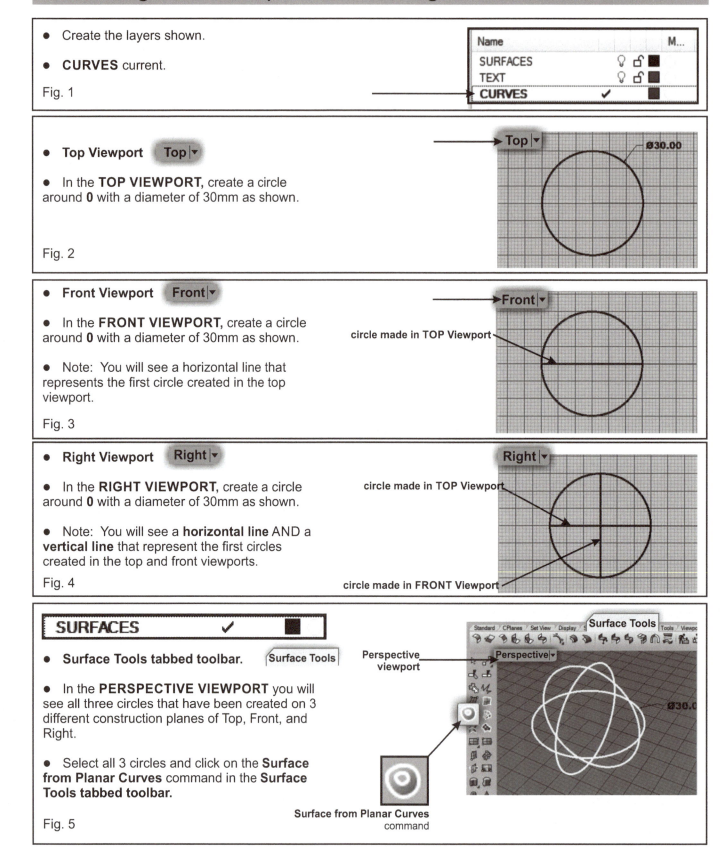

- Create the layers shown.

- **CURVES** current.

Fig. 1

Name		M...
SURFACES	♀ 🔓 ■	
TEXT	♀ 🔓 ■	
CURVES	✓ ■	

- **Top Viewport** Top ▾

- In the **TOP VIEWPORT,** create a circle around **0** with a diameter of 30mm as shown.

Fig. 2

Top ▾   Ø30.00

- **Front Viewport** Front ▾

- In the **FRONT VIEWPORT,** create a circle around **0** with a diameter of 30mm as shown.

- Note: You will see a horizontal line that represents the first circle created in the top viewport.

Fig. 3

Front ▾

circle made in TOP Viewport

- **Right Viewport** Right ▾

- In the **RIGHT VIEWPORT,** create a circle around **0** with a diameter of 30mm as shown.

- Note: You will see a **horizontal line** AND a **vertical line** that represent the first circles created in the top and front viewports.

Fig. 4

Right ▾

circle made in TOP Viewport

circle made in FRONT Viewport

SURFACES ✓ ■

- **Surface Tools tabbed toolbar.** Surface Tools

- In the **PERSPECTIVE VIEWPORT** you will see all three circles that have been created on 3 different construction planes of Top, Front, and Right.

- Select all 3 circles and click on the **Surface from Planar Curves** command in the **Surface Tools tabbed toolbar.**

Fig. 5

Perspective viewport   Perspective ▾

Ø30.0

Surface from Planar Curves command

247

- A surface has been created inside each circle as shown.

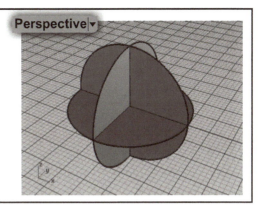

Fig. 6

TEXT ✓ ■

- **TOP VIEWPORT**

- **Drafting tabbed toolbar.** `Drafting`

- **Left-click** on the **Create Text** command in the **Dimension** toolbar flyout as shown.

TEXT

Left-click for **Create Text** command

Fig. 7

- The **Text** box will appear.
  - Note the settings that are indicated by the arrows.
  - In the text box, type the word **TOP** as shown.
  - Click the OK button.

- The text will appear in the upper left corner of the surface seen in the **Top Viewport** as shown.

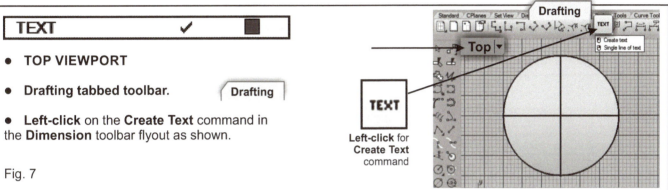

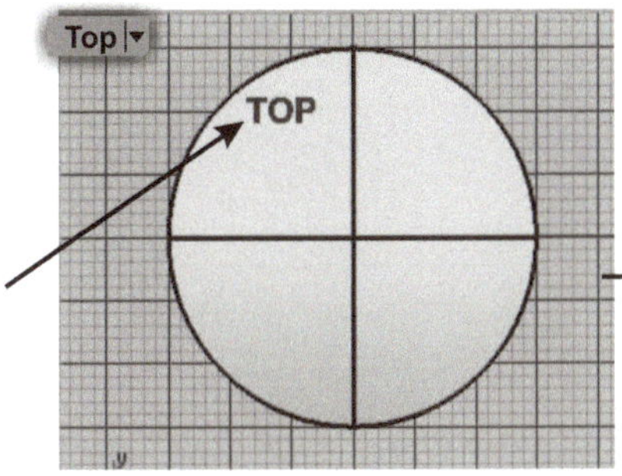

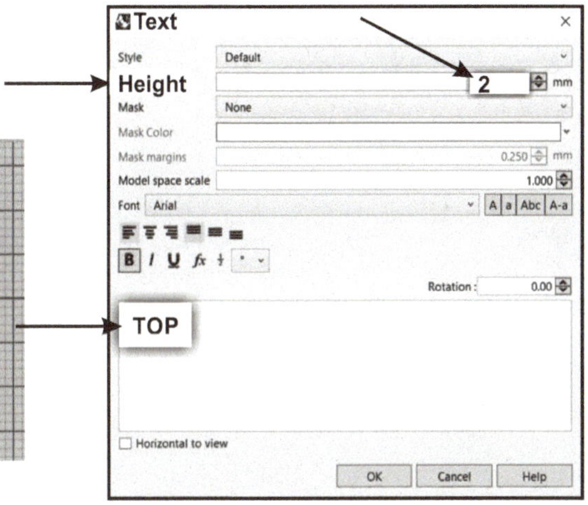

Fig. 8

- **Pick point** prompt:
  - Click on the desired location for the text.

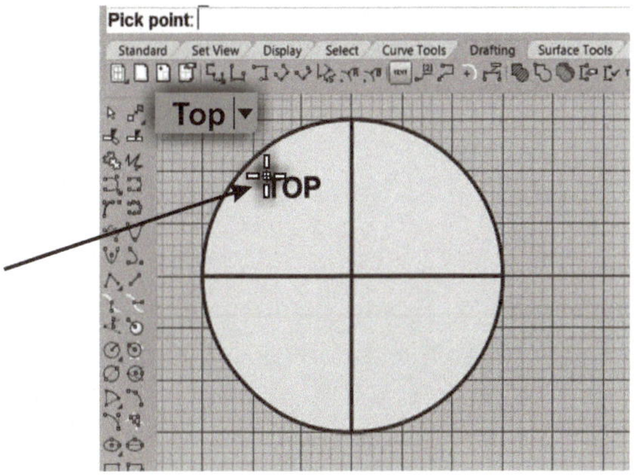

Fig. 9

- Use the **Create Text** command again in the **Front** and **Right** viewports in turn as shown.

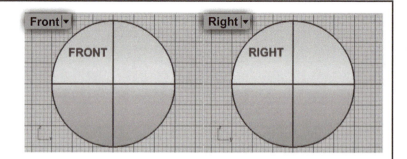

Fig. 10

- Rotate the view in the **Perspective Viewport** for an illustration on how working in different viewports places the circular surfaces and the text you created.

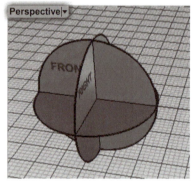

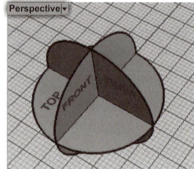

Fig. 11

The Set View Toolbar
Changing from One Viewport to Another

- **Front Viewport.** `Front|▼`

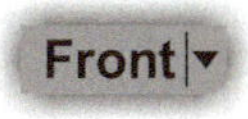

- Use the **Shaded Viewport** display mode.

- Create the same **Torus** as in pp. 245-246.

- Access the **Set View tabbed toolbar.** `Set View`

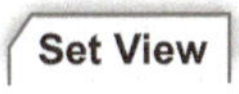

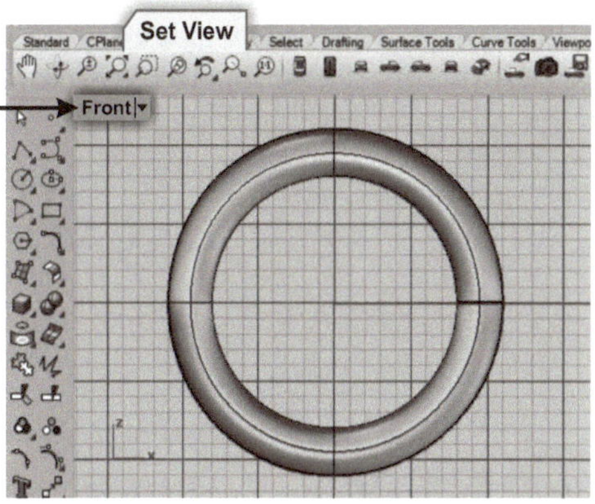

Fig. 1

- The **Right View** button takes you to the **Right viewport**.

Right View command

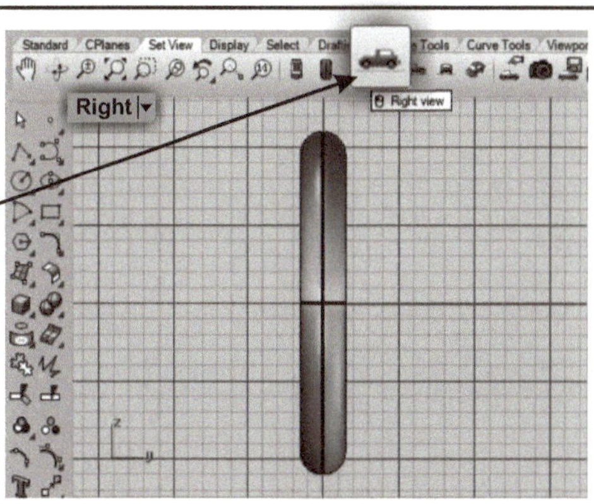

Fig. 2

- The **Front View** button takes you to the **Front viewport**.

Front View command

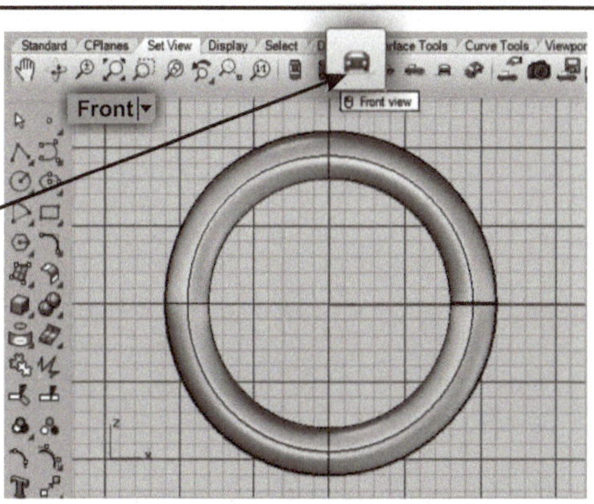

Fig. 3

- Click on the **Perspective View** button.

- The viewport will show the **Perspective View** of the **Front Viewport..**

- **By default, the Perspective View** command will show the **Perspective View** of any construction plane in which you are working (the Current Viewport)

Perspective View of the **current viewport**

left-click for **Perspective View** command

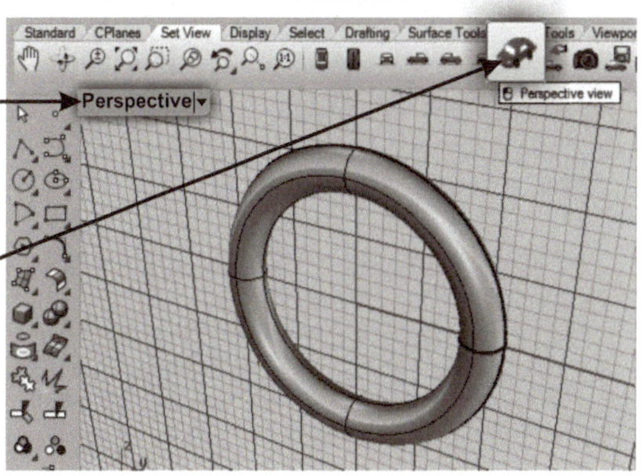

Fig. 4

Changing to the Default Perspective Viewport
The two steps needed

- Click on the **Top View** button as shown. **1**
  - You are now in the **Top Viewport.**
  - This will set the default top Construction Plane.

Top View
command

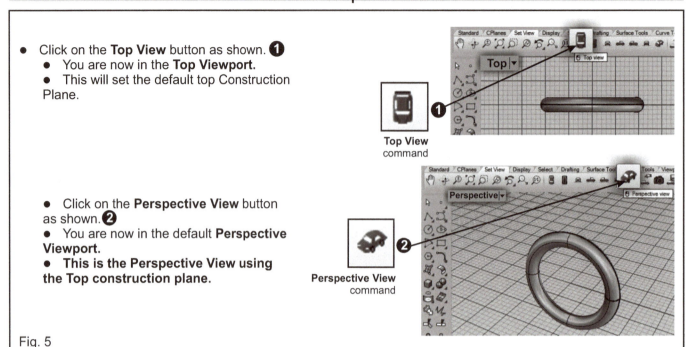

- Click on the **Perspective View** button as shown. **2**
- You are now in the default **Perspective Viewport.**
- **This is the Perspective View using the Top construction plane.**

Perspective View
command

Fig. 5

Creating a quick 1-Click Return to Default Top Perspective
Adding Functionality to the Perspective Viewport Command Button

- **Hold down the SHIFT key** and **RIGHT-CLICK** on the **Perspective View** command button.

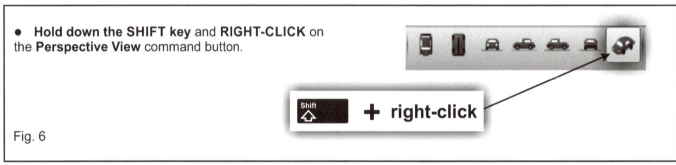

Shift **+** right-click

Fig. 6

- The **Button Editor** window will open.

- The **Tooltip** line **1** over the column that controls the **left mouse button** shows the text of the tooltip that appears when you roll your cursor over the **Perspective View** button.

- In the **Command** box below, is the script **2** that controls the command.

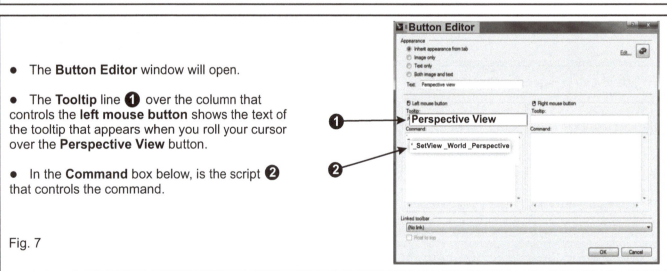

Fig. 7

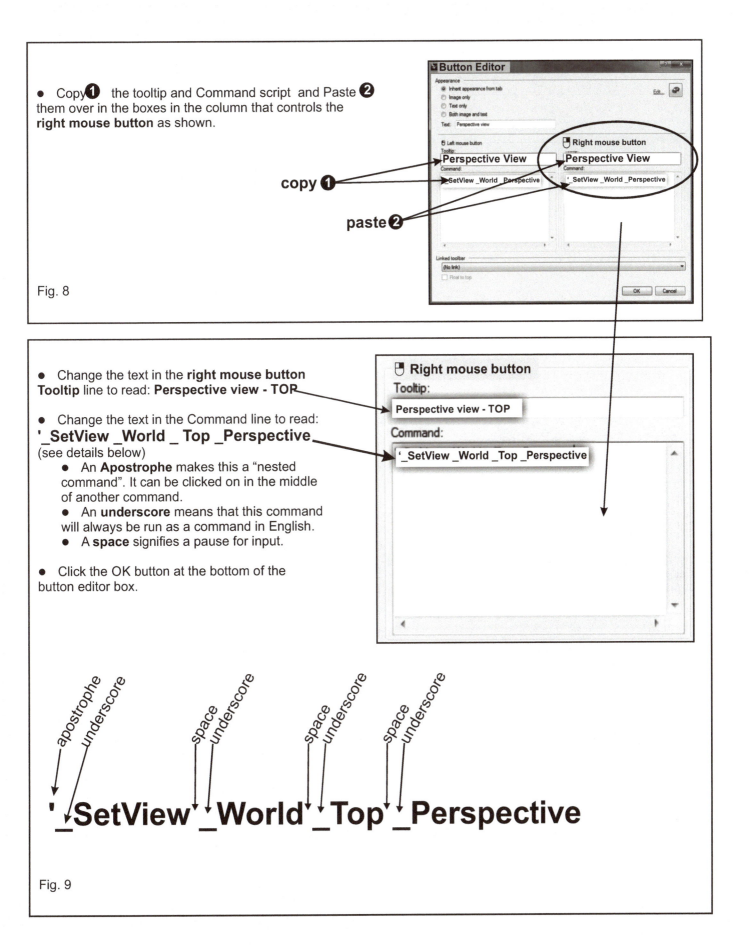

- Copy ❶ the tooltip and Command script and Paste ❷ them over in the boxes in the column that controls the **right mouse button** as shown.

Fig. 8

Button Editor

Appearance
- Inherit appearance from tab
- Image only
- Text only
- Both image and text

Text: Perspective view

🖱 Left mouse button
Tooltip:
Perspective View

Command:
_SetView _World _Perspective

🖱 Right mouse button
Tooltip:
Perspective View

Command:
'_SetView _World _Perspective

Linked toolbar
(No link)
☐ Float to top

OK   Cancel

copy ❶

paste ❷

- Change the text in the **right mouse button Tooltip** line to read: **Perspective view - TOP**

- Change the text in the Command line to read:
'_SetView _World _ Top _Perspective
(see details below)
  - An **Apostrophe** makes this a "nested command". It can be clicked on in the middle of another command.
  - An **underscore** means that this command will always be run as a command in English.
  - A **space** signifies a pause for input.

- Click the OK button at the bottom of the button editor box.

🖱 **Right mouse button**

Tooltip:
Perspective view - TOP

Command:
'_SetView _World _Top _Perspective

apostrophe underscore   space underscore   space underscore   space underscore

'_SetView _World _Top _Perspective

Fig. 9

252

Using the New Top Perspective Button Command

- Click on the **Front View** button to take you to the **Front viewport** as shown. **1**

Front View command

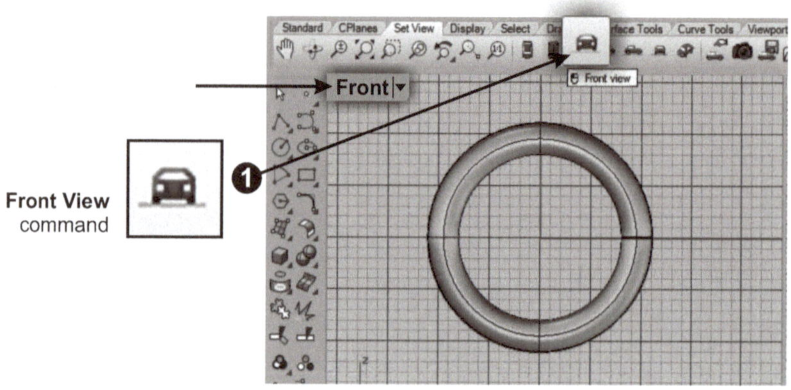

Fig. 10

- **RIGHT-CLICK** on the **Perspective View** button. **2**

- The viewport will show the **default Perspective View** using the **Top construction Plane.**

- **This is because of the new command for Perspective View - Top that you have programmed for the Right Mouse Button.**

RIGHT-CLICK for new **Perspective View - TOP** command

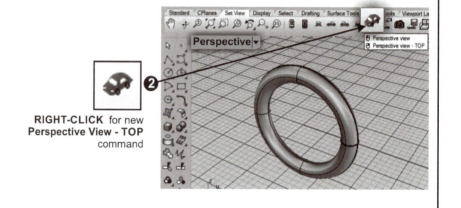

Fig. 11

- ***WITH ONE CLICK***, you have been taken to the default **Perspective View** in the **top construction plane** as shown.

Fig. 12

Introduction to Simple Solid Objects

A solid is a volume that is completely enclosed by a single surface or two or more surfaces. Solids are essential for prototyping.

The Box

- Open Rhino and save the file as **solid objects.3dm**.

- **Default Perspective viewport.** Perspective ▾

- **Solid Tools tabbed toolbar.** Solid Tools

- Click on the **Box: corner to corner, height** command.

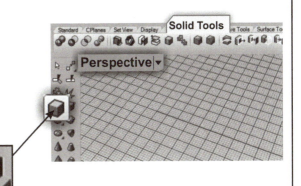

Box: corner to corner, height command

Fig. 1

- **First corner of base** prompt:
  - Type "**0**" and press **Enter**.

First corner of base (Diagonal 3Point Vertical Center): **0**

Fig. 2

- **Other corner of base or length** prompt:
  - Type **15** and press **Enter**.
- **Width. Press Enter to use length** prompt:
  - Draw the cursor upward along the grid and note the preview lines.
  - Type **12.75** and press **Enter**.

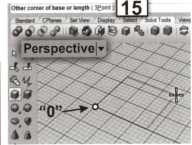

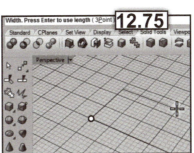

- **Height. Press Enter to use width** prompt:
  - Draw the cursor up and note the vertical preview line..
  - Press **Enter** to use the same value for the height as you used for the width.
  - This will end the command.

- ***Dimensioning 3D objects will be covered in a later chapter.***

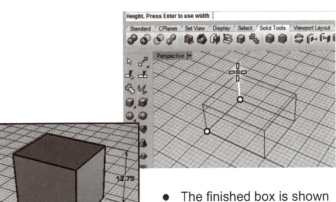

- The finished box is shown in **Shaded Viewport Mode**.

Fig. 3

254

- By default, the **Box Commands** will create **Simple Lightweight Extrusions.**
  - A **Box** will have 6 surfaces.
  - But you will only see surface Edges and Seams by default on an **Extrusion**.

- Creating Polysurfaces with this command will be covered in the next chapter.

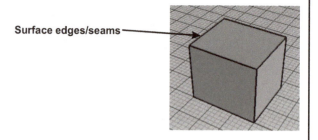
Surface edges/seams

- *Lightweight extrusion objects use less memory than the more traditional form of surface modeled objects, polysurfaces.*

Fig. 4

- The **Box toolbar flyout**.
  - More ways to make a box.
  - The button on the end is the **Bounding Box** command.

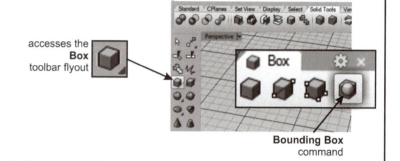

accesses the **Box** toolbar flyout

Bounding Box command

Fig. 5

The Sphere

- Click on the **Sphere: center, radius** command in the **Solid tabbed toolbar.**
  - **Center of sphere** prompt:
    - Click on the desired location on the construction plane.
  - **Diameter** prompt:
    - Click on the **Diameter** option in the **Command Line.**
    - Type **"15"** and press **Enter.**
    - *Note that you need to specify whether you are entering a value for the diameter or the radius.*

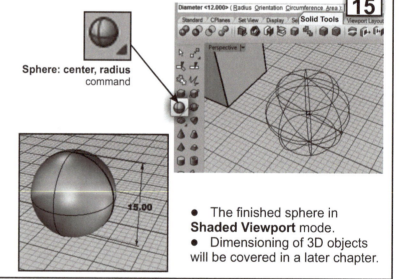

Sphere: center, radius command

15.00

- The finished sphere in **Shaded Viewport** mode.
- Dimensioning of 3D objects will be covered in a later chapter.

Fig. 6

- A sphere is a **Single Closed Surface.** It has one surface that encloses the space inside perfectly, making it a **Solid object.** It has only 1 seam as shown.

- A sphere has two visible attributes:
  - **A Seam** that describes a perfect arc from top to bottom of the sphere.
  - **Isocurves**: As with other surfaces, the isocurves show direction and geometry of the suface.

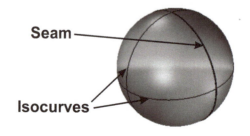

Seam

Isocurves

Fig. 7

- The **Sphere** toolbar flyout
  - These commands for different ways to make a sphere mostly relate to the varied ways to create a circle.

accesses the **Sphere** toolbar flyout

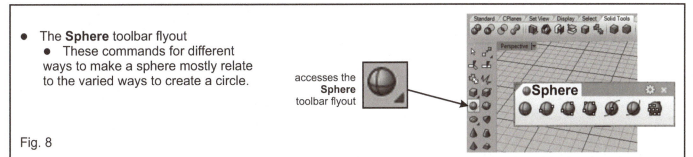

Fig. 8

The Ellipsoid

- Click on the **Ellipsoid: from center** command in the **Solid Tools tabbed toolbar**.

  - **Ellipsoid center** prompt:
    - Click on the desired location. ❶

Ellipsoid: from center command

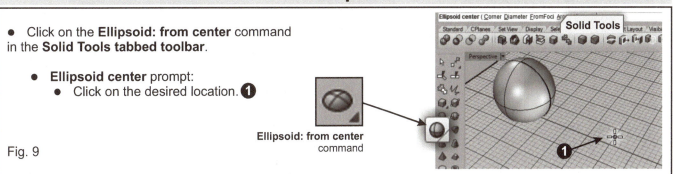

Fig. 9

- **End of first axis** prompt:
  - Type **"10"** and press **Enter.**
  - Click to set to location of the end of the first axis as shown. ❷

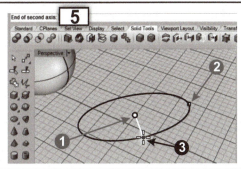

Fig. 10

- **End of second axis** prompt:
  - Type **"5"** and press **Enter.**
  - Click to set the location of the end of the second axis as shown. ❸

Fig. 11

- **End of third axis** prompt:
  - Your cursor will be constrained to a direction that is vertical to the construction plane as shown.
  - Type **"5"** and press **Enter.**

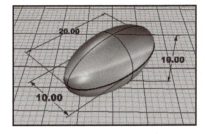

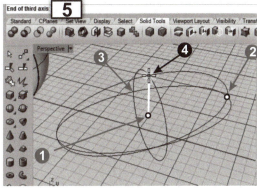

Fig. 12

- The finished **Ellipsoid**.

- Like the Sphere, this is a **single closed surface** with only **one surface** and **one seam**.

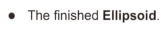

Fig. 13

- The **Ellipsoid** toolbar flyout.
  - These commands are reminiscent to the commands in the 2-D Ellipse commands.

accesses the **Ellipsoid** toolbar flyout

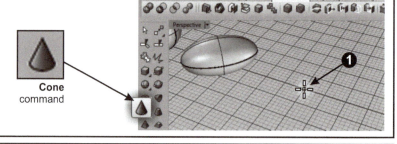

Fig. 14

The Cone

- Click on the **Cone** command in the **Solid Tools tabbed toolbar.**

  - **Base of cone** prompt:
    - Click on a desired location.❶

Cone command

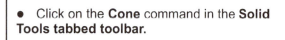

Fig. 15

- **Radius** prompt:
  - Type **"5"** and press **Enter.**❷
  - This defines the radius/diameter of the base of the cone.

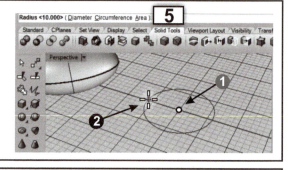

Fig. 16

- **End of cone** prompt:
  - Draw the cursor up and type **10.** ❸
  - Press **Enter.**

- Finished **Cone** viewed in **Shaded Mode.**
- Dimensioning for 3D objects will be covered in a later chapter.

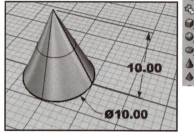

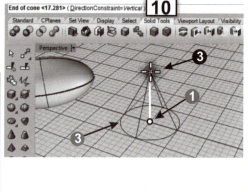

Fig. 17

257

- Click on the **Truncated Cone** command in the **Solid Tools tabbed toolbar.**

  - **Base of truncated cone** prompt:
    - Click in the desired location. **❶**

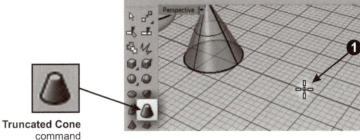

Truncated Cone
command

Fig. 18

- **Radius at base** prompt (notice that you can click on the diameter option in the **Command Line**):
  - Type **"7.5"** and press **Enter. ❷**

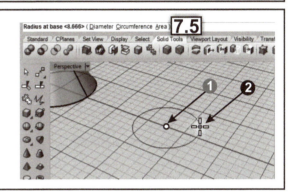

Fig. 19

- **End of truncated cone** prompt (this is prompt is for the *height of the cone)*:
  - Type **10** and press **Enter. ❸**

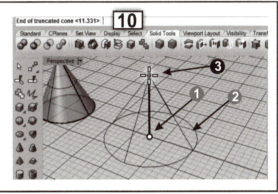

Fig. 20

- **Radius at top** prompt:
  - Type **4** and press **Enter. ❹**

- The finished **Truncated Cone** seen in **Shaded Viewport mode.**
- Dimensioning 3D objects will be covered in a later chapter.

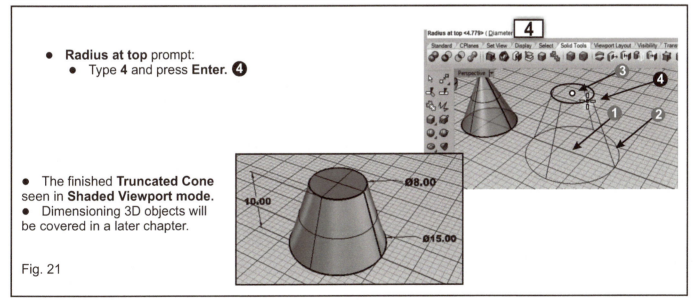

Fig. 21

Pyramid, Truncated Pyramid, Star, Truncated Star
Polygon Based Solids with Similar Polygon Options

The Pyramid

- Click on the **Pyramid** command in the **Solid Tools tabbed toolbar.**

    - **Center of inscribed pyramid** prompt:
        - Click on the desired location.**❶**

Pyramid command

Fig. 22

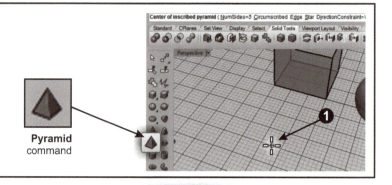

- **Corner of pyramid** prompt:
    - Click on the **NumSides** option in the **Command Line** as shown.
- **Number of sides** prompt:
    - Type **8** and press **Enter.**   Fig. 23

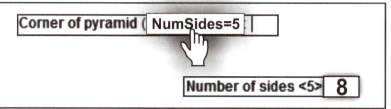

Corner of pyramid (NumSides=5)

Number of sides <5> **8**

- **Corner of pyramid** prompt:
    - Type **7** and press **Enter.**
    - Click to set location.**❷**
        - Use **ortho** for accurate lining up the grid.

Fig. 24

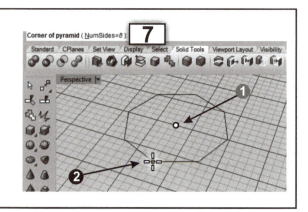

- **Pick point** prompt:
    - This sets the height of the pyramid.
    - Draw the cursor downward as shown.
    - Type **10** and press **Enter.**
    - Click to set location.**❸**

- The pyramid's tip is facing downward because of the position of the cursor when clicking on the location of the pick point.

Fig. 25

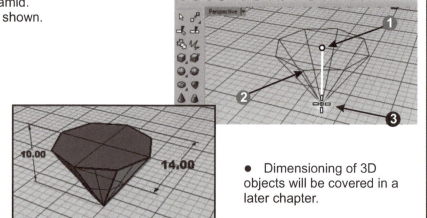

- Dimensioning of 3D objects will be covered in a later chapter.

The Truncated Pyramid

- Click on the **Truncated Pyramid** command in the **Solid Tools tabbed toolbar**.

  - **Center of inscribed pyramid** prompt:
    - Click on the **NumSides=5** option in the **Command Line.**
    - **Number of sides** prompt: type **"6"** and press **Enter.**

Number of sides <5>: **6**

Truncated Pyramid command

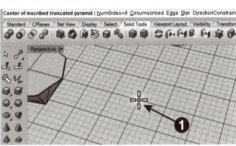

Fig. 26

- **Center of inscribed truncated pyramid** prompt:
  - Click on the desired location. **1**

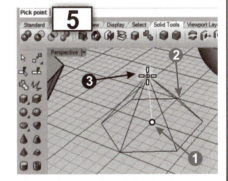

- **Corner of truncated pyramid** prompt:
  - Type **"5"** and press **Enter.**
  - Click to set location. **2**

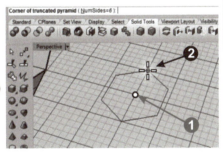

- **Pick point** prompt:
  - Type **"5"** and press **Enter.**
  - Click to set location. **3**

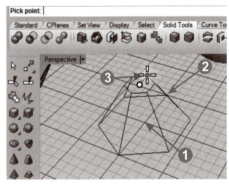

Fig. 27

- **Pick point** prompt:
  - This sets the radius of the upper surface of the Truncated Pyramid.
  - Type **"2"** and press **Enter.**

- The finished **truncated pyramid.**
- Dimensioning of 3D objects will be covered in a later chapter.

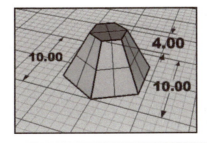

10.00   4.00   10.00

Fig. 28

The Star Pyramid

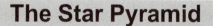

Click on the **Pyramid** command in the **Solid Tools tabbed toolbar.**

- Click on the **Star** option in the <u>Command Line</u>.
- **Number of sides: 5**

Fig. 29

Pyramid command

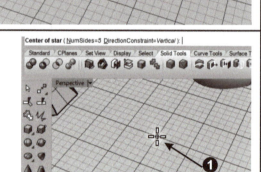

- **Center of star** prompt:
  - Click on desired location. **1**

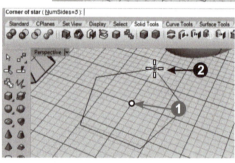

- **Corner of star** prompt:
  - Type **"8"** and press **Enter.**
  - Click to set location. **2**

- **Second star radius. Press Enter for automatic** prompt:
  - Move the cursor in slightly so that the points of the star do not get too sharp looking.
  - Click to set location by eye. **3**

Fig. 30

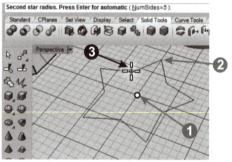

- **Pick point** prompt:
  - Type **"5"** and press **Enter.**
  - Click to set location. **4**

- The finished **Star Pyramid.**

- Dimensioning of 3D objects will be covered in a later chapter.

Fig. 31

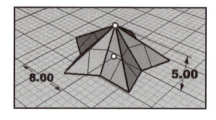

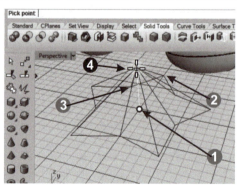

The Truncated Star Pyramid

- Click on the **Truncated Pyramid** command in the **Solid Tools tabbed toolbar.**

  - Click on the **Star** option in the **Command Line**.
  - **Number of sides:** 5

Truncated Pyramid command

- **Center of star** prompt:
  - Click on desired location. ❶

Fig. 32

- **Corner of star** prompt:
  - Type **"8"** and press **Enter.**
  - Click to set location. ❷

- **Second star radius. Press Enter for automatic** prompt:
  - Move the cursor in slightly so that the points of the star do not get too sharp looking.
  - Click to set location by eye. ❸

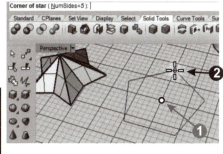

Fig. 33

- **Pick point** prompt:
  - Type **"5"** and press **Enter.** Click to set location. ❹
  - Defines the pyramid height.

- **Pick point** prompt:
  - Type **"2"** and press **Enter.** Click to set location. ❺
  - Defines the outer radius at the top of the truncated star.

- **Pick point** prompt:
  - Type **"1"** and press **Enter.**
  - Defines the inner radius at the top of the truncated star.

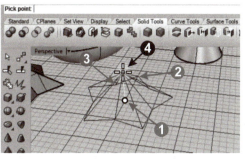

- The finished **Truncated Star Pyramid.**

- Dimensioning of 3D objects will be covered in a later chapter.

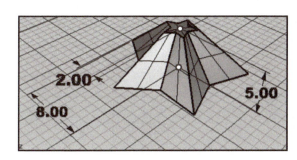

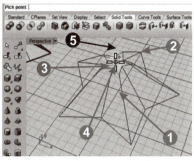

Fig. 34

- Click on the **Cylinder** command in the **Solid Tools tabbed toolbar.**.
  - **Base of cylinder** prompt:
    - Click to set location.

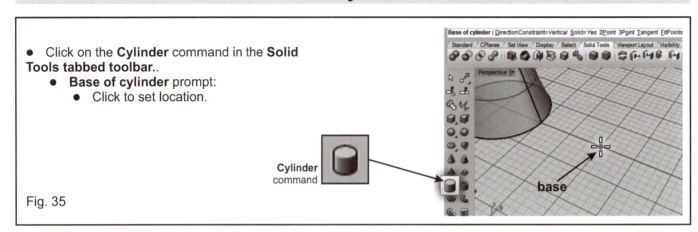

Cylinder command

Fig. 35

- Make sure that the **Diameter** option is enabled in the command line.
- **Diameter** prompt:
  - Draw the cursor out from the designated base as shown. Note the preview lines.
    - Type **"10"** and press Enter

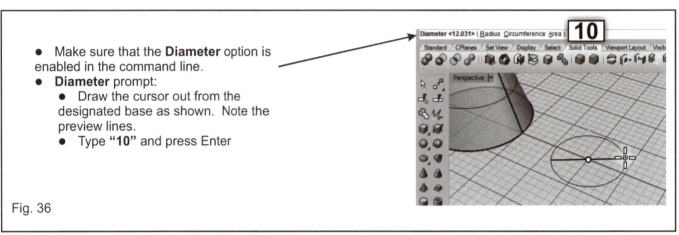

Fig. 36

- Draw the cursor up or down and note the preview lines.
  - Note that you can select a **bothsides** option in the Command Line.
- **End of cylinder** prompt:
  - Type **15** and press **Enter.**

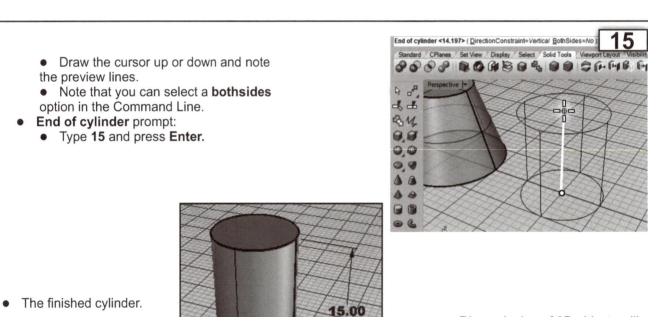

- The finished cylinder.

- Dimensioning of 3D objects will be covered in a later chapter.

Fig. 37

- Click on the **Tube** command in the **Solid Tools tabbed toolbar**.

  - **Base of tube** prompt:
    - Click on the desired location.

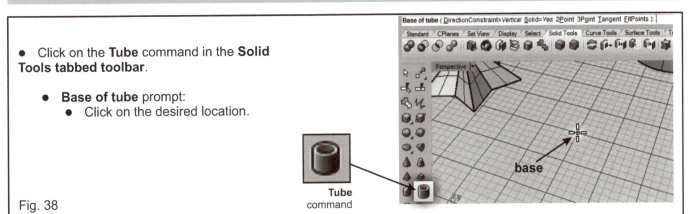

Tube
command

Fig. 38

- **Diameter** prompt (make sure that the **Diameter** option is chosen in the **Command Line** if you want to specify a diameter, not a radius:
  - Type **"10"** and press **Enter**.
  - This will set the **inner diameter** of the tube.

Fig. 39

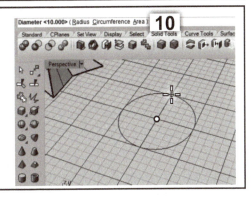

- **Diameter** prompt:
  - Click on the **WallThickness=1** option in the **Command Line.**
- **Wall Thickness** prompt:
  - Type **1.2** and press **Enter**.

Fig. 40

- **End of tube** prompt:
  - Type **10** and press **Enter**.

- The finished **Tube**

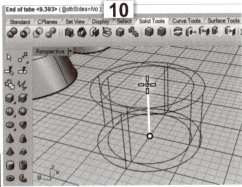

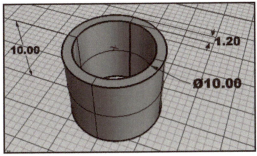

Fig. 41

The Torus

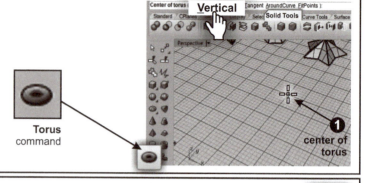

- Click on the **Torus** command in the **Solid Tools tabbed toolbar.**.

  - **Center of torus** prompt:
    - Click on the **Vertical** option in the **Command Line** so that the Torus will stand up vertical to the construction plane.
    - Click on the desired location for the center of the torus. ❶

Torus
command

Fig. 42

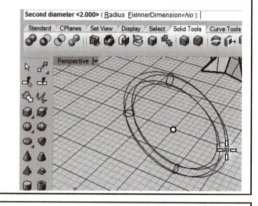

- **Diameter** prompt (make sure the diameter option is active):
  - Type **18.1** and press **Enter.**
  - Click to set location using **ORTHO** to line the diameter of the circle up with the grid if this is the position you want. ❷

Fig. 43

- **Second diameter** prompt (make sure that the diameter option is active):
  - Type **2** and press **Enter.**

Fig. 44

- The finished **Torus** is sitting vertical to the construction plane.

- It is viewed here in **Shaded Viewport mode.**

- Save your file as **solid objects.3dm.**

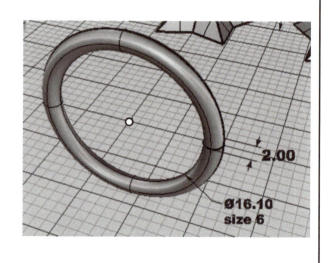

Fig. 45

Extrusions, Polysurfaces, and Surfaces
Differences and characteristics

- Open the file that you created, **solid objects.3dm.**

- These are all **solid objects, valid for prototyping.**

- List of objects suitable for prototyping:
  - **Closed surfaces**
  - **Closed Polysurfaces**
  - **Closed Extrusions**

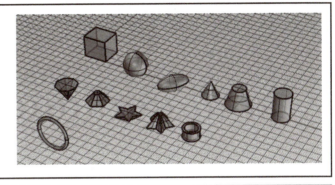

Fig. 1

- **Select tabbed toolbar.**   Select

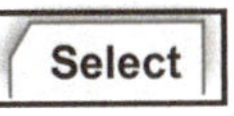

- Open the **Select Polysurfaces** ❶ and the **Select Surfaces** ❷ **toolbar flyouts** from the **Select tabbed toolbar.**

Fig. 2

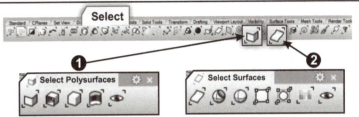

Extrusions & Polysurfaces

- **Top Perspective view.** ❶ ❷

- Click on the **Select Closed Polysurfaces** command in the **Select Polysurfaces** toolbar.

- *The Sphere, Ellipsoid and Torus will not select because they are single surfaces.*

- Click away to de-select.

Select Closed Polysurfaces
command

Fig. 3

2 Extrusions, 7 polysurfaces added to selection

- Click on the **Select lightweight extrusion objects** command in the **Select tabbed toolbar.**

- Only the **Box** and the **Cylinder** will be selected.

Select lightweight extrusion objects
command

Fig. 4

Command: '_SelExtrusion
2 extrusions added to selection.

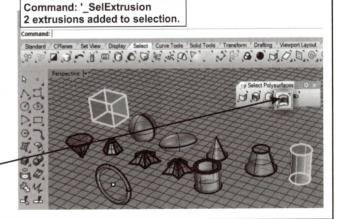

- **Solid Tools tabbed toolbar.** `Solid Tools`

- Create a **15mm diameter** circle.

- Click on the **Extrude Closed Planar Curve** command.

Extrude closed planar curve command

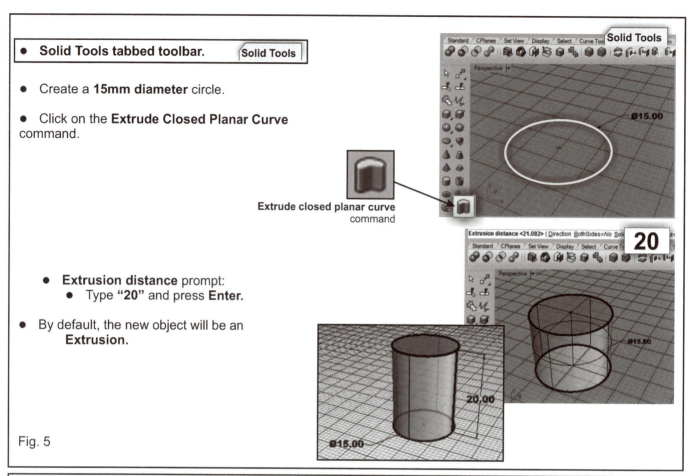

- **Extrusion distance** prompt:
    - Type **"20"** and press **Enter.**

- By default, the new object will be an **Extrusion.**

Fig. 5

- The default **Box** is an **Extrusion (Lightweight Extrusion Object)**

- **This is a solid object.**

- **Extrusion benefits:**
    - They use less memory.
    - They save smaller.
    - They "mesh faster" for quicker shading and rendering.

Fig. 6

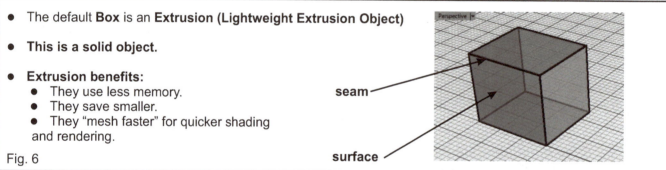

seam

surface

- **Solid Tools tabbed toolbar.** `Solid Tools`

- **RIGHT-CLICK** on the **Extract Surfaces** command.

    - Click to select top surface of the box. ❶
    - The surface will be selected.
    - Press **Enter** to end the command.

- The two pieces of the box are a **single surface** and an **open polysurface.**

- Editing of the Extrusion has converted the elements to a **Surface** and a **Polysurface.**

    - Click away to de-select.

Fig. 7

RIGHT-CLICK for Extract Surfaces command

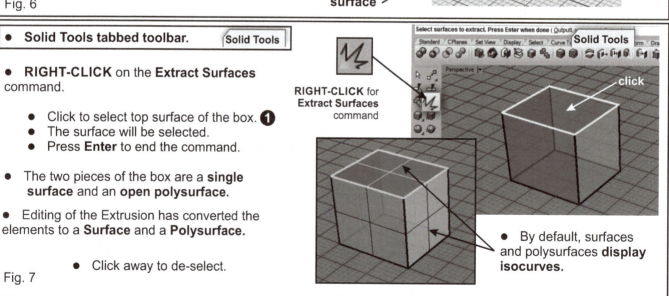

click

- By default, surfaces and polysurfaces **display isocurves.**

- Click on the **Select Polysurfaces** command.
  - Only the bottom part of the box will select because the extracted top surface is now a **Single Surface**, not a **Polysurface.**

- Click away to de-select.

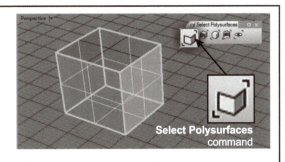

Select Polysurfaces
command

- Click on the **Select Open Polysurfaces** command.
  - Only the bottom of the box will select because it is both **open** (because the top surface was extracted) and a **polysurface** because it is comprised of more than one surface.
    - **This is not a solid object.**

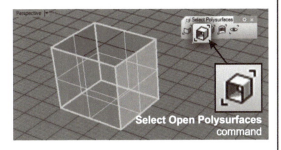

Select Open Polysurfaces
command

- Click on the **Select Closed Polysurfaces** command.
  - No part of the box will select because, with the extraction of the top surface, the box is not longer a single closed polysurfaces.

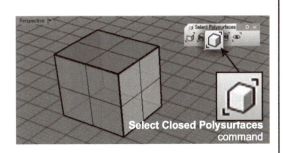

Select Closed Polysurfaces
command

Fig. 8

- Select the **two Box surfaces** and click on the **Join** command.

- The separate surfaces of the box will be joined together again to make a **Closed Polysurface.**

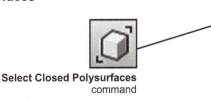

Join
command

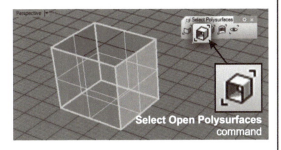

- Click on the **Select Closed Polysurfaces** command again.
  - The box will select, along with the other closed polysurfaces, including the extrusions.

- **Closed Polysurfaces are solid objects.**

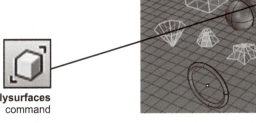

Select Closed Polysurfaces
command

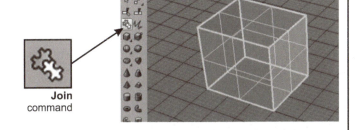

Fig. 9

268

Closed Surfaces and Open Surfaces

- Click on the **Select Closed Surfaces** command in the **Select Surfaces** toolbar.

- Notice that only the **Sphere, Ellipsoid, and the Torus** are selected.

- These are *closed single surfaces.*

- **These closed surfaces are solids.**

Fig. 10

Select Closed Surfaces command

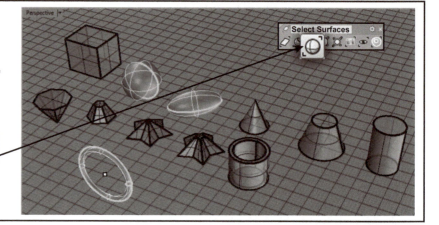

- Select the **Cone** and **LEFT-CLICK** on the **Explode** command.

- Click away to de-select.

Explode command

- Click on the **Select Open Surfaces** command.

- **2 surfaces** will be selected because the cone was exploded out into **2 separate open surfaces.**

- These open surfaces are **not solids.**

Fig. 11

2 surfaced added to selection
Command:

Select Surfaces

Select Open Surfaces command

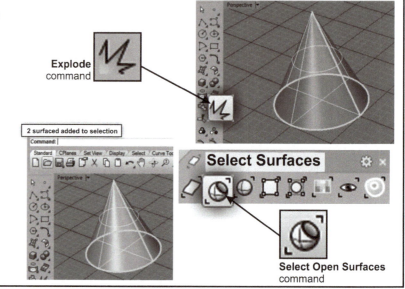

Information About Selected Objects
Checking Objects and Getting Object Details

- Select the **Cylinder** or the **new extrusion** and type **"check"** in the **Command Line** and press **Enter.**

- The **Check** window will open to inform you that this object is an extrusion with no bad geometry ("valid").
  - The button for this command is in the **Standard tabbed toolbar.**

Fig. 12

Check

Rhino extrusion object is valid.

Copy All   Save As..   Close

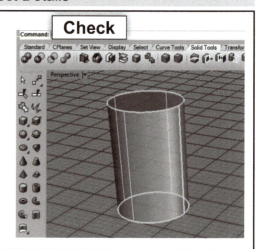

- Select one of the **Polysurfaces.**

- Type **"what"** in the **Command Line** and press **Enter.**

- The **Object Description** window will open to give a detailed description of the selected object.

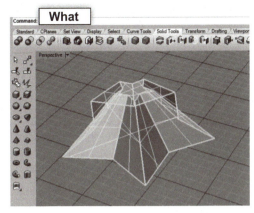

Fig. 13

Control Points for Surfaces & Polysurfaces

- Select all of the objects shown and press the **F10 key to turn on Control Points.**

F10

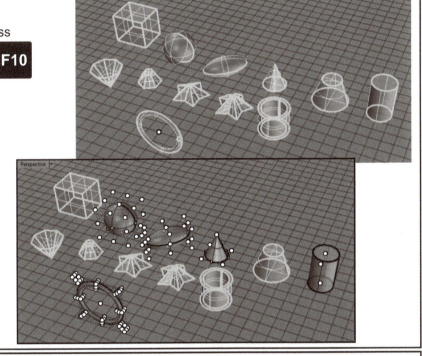

- Only the **single surfaces** will have control points.
    - *(notice that the two single surfaces of the cone have control points.)*
    - The points you see on the **Cylinder** are **Extrusion Points.**

- Click to de-select.

Fig. 14

- **Solid Tools tabbed toolbar.**  Solid Tools

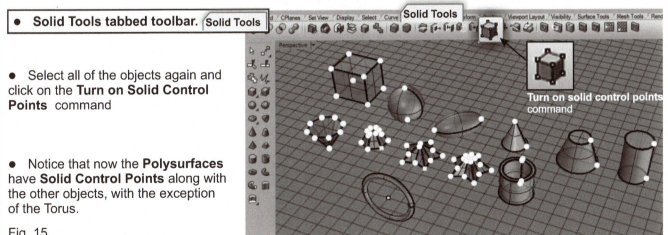

- Select all of the objects again and click on the **Turn on Solid Control Points** command

- Notice that now the **Polysurfaces** have **Solid Control Points** along with the other objects, with the exception of the Torus.

Fig. 15

Point Editing Basic Solid Objects

Solid Point Editing a Polysurface

- **Solid Tools tabbed toolbar.** `Solid Tools`

- **Top Perspective view.** ❶ 🖥 ❷ 🎨

- Click on the **Box: Corner to Corner, Height** command.

  - Click on the **Center** option in the **Command Line**.

  - **Center of Base** prompt:
    - Type **"0"** and press **Enter.**
  - **Other corner of base or length** prompt:
    - Type **"15"**
  - **Width. Press Enter to use length** prompt:
    - Press **Enter.**
  - **Height. Press Enter to use width** prompt:
    - Press **Enter.**

- A **15x15x15 box extrusion** has been created with its base centered on **0.**

Fig. 1

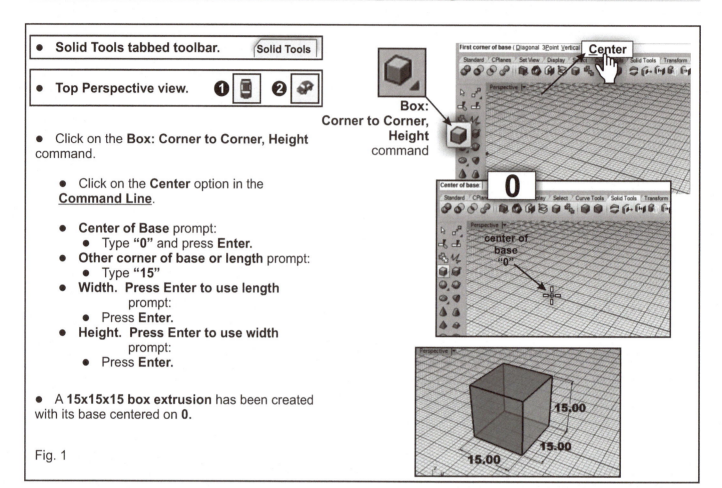

- Click on the **Turn on Solid Control Points** command.

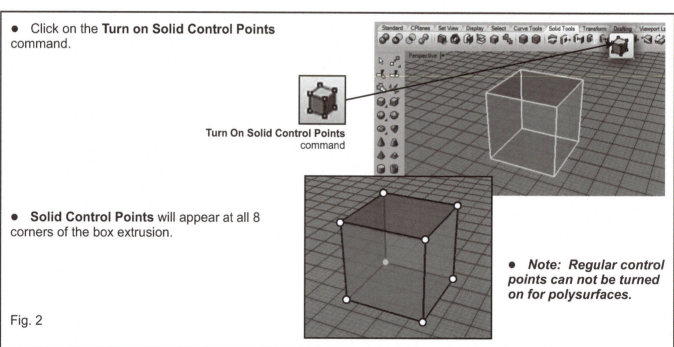

Turn On Solid Control Points
command

- **Solid Control Points** will appear at all 8 corners of the box extrusion.

- *Note: Regular control points can not be turned on for polysurfaces.*

Fig. 2

- **Transform tabbed toolbar.** `Transform`

- Select all **4 points** on the top of the box and **left-click** on the **Rotate 2-D** command.

  - **Center of rotation** prompt:
    - Type **"0"** and press **Enter.** ❶

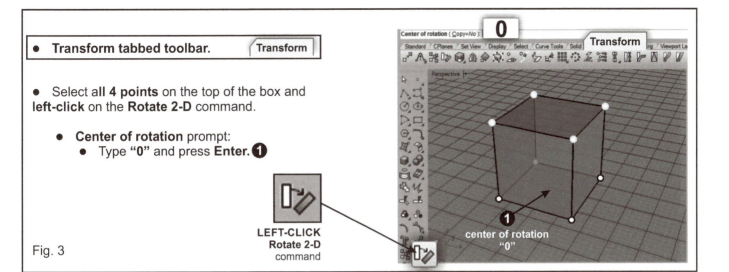

**LEFT-CLICK
Rotate 2-D
command**

Fig. 3

- **Angle or first reference point** prompt:
  - Using **ORTHO**, draw the cursor out and click to set location. ❷

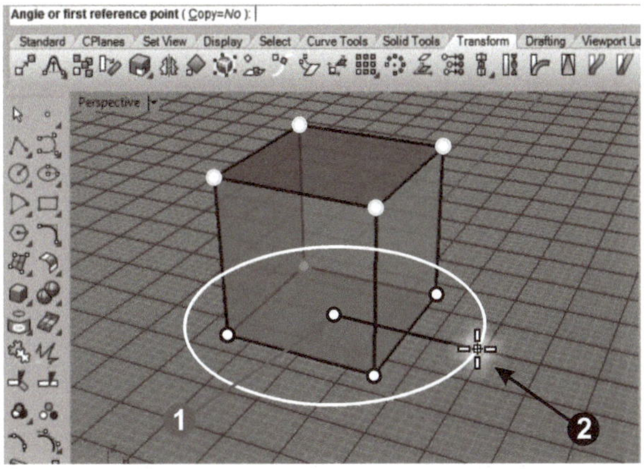

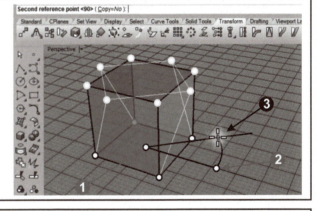

Fig. 4

- **Second reference point** prompt:
  - **Turn off ortho**
  - Draw the cursor around until preview lines show the desired twisted shape.
  - Click to set location. ❸

Fig. 5

- The twisted box shape has been converted into a **Polysurface.**

- **Editing of an extrusion will result in it being converted into a Polysurface.**

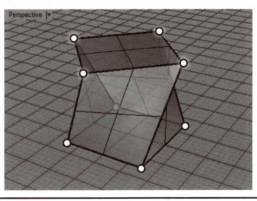

Fig. 6

- **Solid Tools tabbed toolbar.** `Solid Tools`

- **Front Viewport.** `Front|▾`

- Click on the **Torus** command.

  - **Center of torus** prompt:
    - Type **"0"** and press **Enter**.
  - **Diameter of torus** prompt:
    - Make sure that the **Diameter** option is enabled in the **Command Line.**
    - Type **"18.1"** and press **Enter**.

  - **Second diameter** prompt:
    - Type **"2"** and press **Enter**.

- **Top Perspective view.** ❶ 🚗 ❷ 🚙

- The finished **torus** will be a ring band with an **inner diameter of 16.1mm (size 6)** and a **band thickness of 2mm.**

Fig. 7

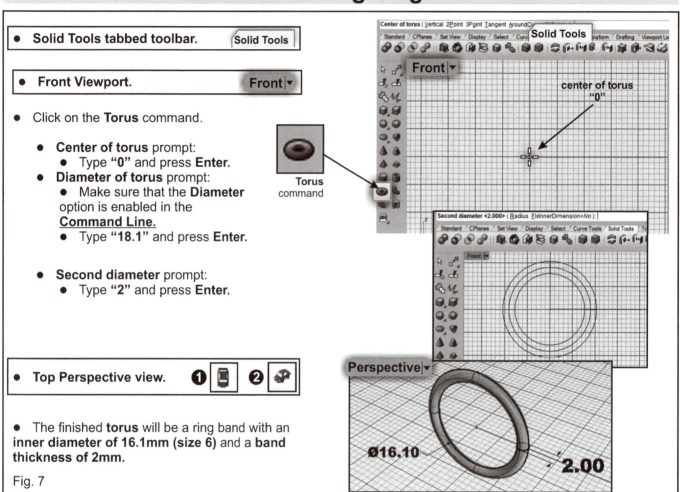

- Click on the **Sphere: Center, Radius** command.

  - **Center of sphere** prompt:
    - Snap to the **Quad** at the top of the Torus and click to set location.
      - The seam that goes around the outside of the torus allows you to click to this quad point.

  - **Diameter** prompt:
    - Type **"3"** and press **Enter**.

- The finished sphere will be accurately placed at the top of the torus.

Fig. 8

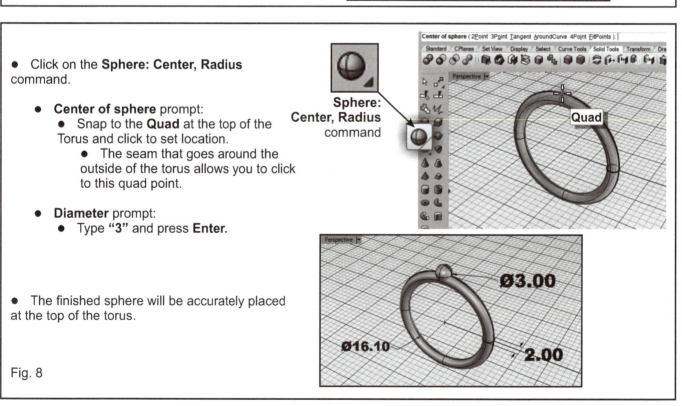

- **Transform tabbed toolbar.** `Transform`

- **Front Viewport.** `Front ▼`

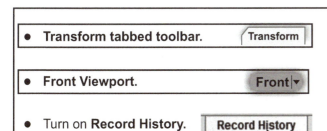

- Turn on **Record History.** `Record History`

- Select the **Sphere** and click on the **Polar Array** command.

  - **Center of polar array** prompt:
    - Type **"0"** and press **Enter.**

  - **Number of items: 16**
  - **Angle to fill or first reference point: 360°**
  - **Press Enter to accept the polar array preview.**

center of polar array
"0"

- **Top Perspective view.** ❶ 🖥 ❷ 🚗

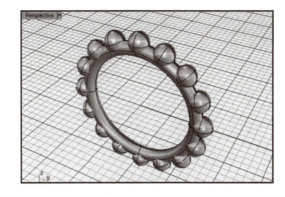

- The finished polar array.

Fig. 9

- Select the torus and all of the spheres **except for the original sphere which is the PARENT OBJECT.**

- Type **"lock"** in the **Command Line** and press **Enter.**

- All objects are **locked** except for the sphere on the top of the ring.

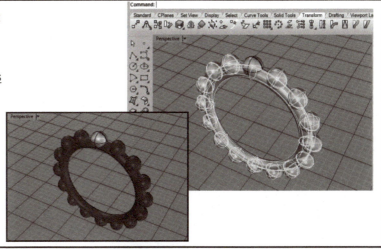

Fig. 10

- Select the sphere and **press the F10 key** to turn on **control points**.

  `F10`

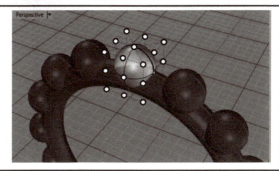

Fig. 11

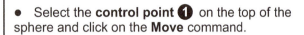

- Select the **control point ❶** on the top of the sphere and click on the **Move** command.

  - **Point to move from** prompt:
    - Click on the **<u>Vertical</u>** option **❷** in the <u>Command Line</u>.
      - *The direction of the move will be constrained to a direction vertical to the construction plane.*

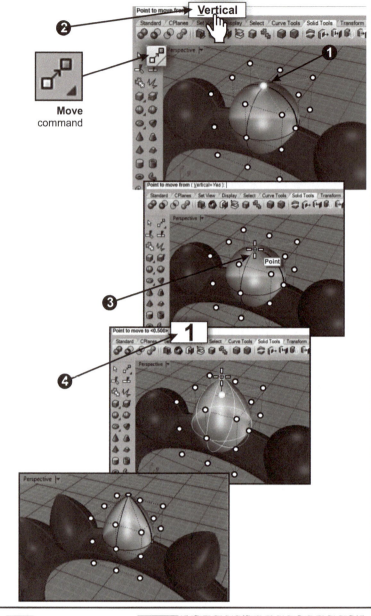

Move command

  - **Point to move from** prompt:
    - Snap to the selected **Point ❸** at the top of sphere and press **Enter**.

  - **Point to move to** prompt:
    - Type **"1"** and press **Enter. ❹**
    - *Notice the preview.*

- *The point has been moved 1mm upward, vertical to the construction plane.*

- **History** has updated the rest of the spheres.

Fig. 12

- Press the **Esc** key to turn off control points.

Esc

- Type **"unlock"** and press **Enter** to unlock all locked objects.

- You can **Delete** a number of the edited spheres on the lower part of the ring for a different look that will be also more comfortable to wear.

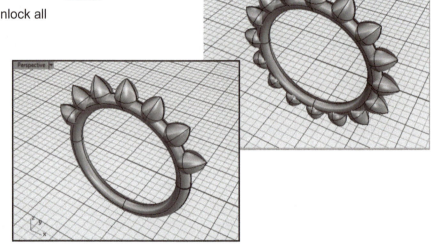

Fig. 13

Mirror and Polar Array Commands in 3D Space

Mirror Command in 3-D Space

- **Solid Tools tabbed toolbar.**   Solid Tools

- **Perspective viewport.**   Perspective ▾

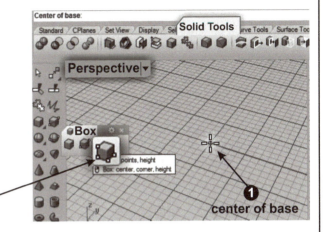

- **RIGHT-CLICK** for the **Box: center: corner, height** command in the **Box** toolbar flyout.

  - **Center of base** prompt:
    - Type **"0"** and press **Enter. ❶**

  RIGHT-CLICK for
  Center: corner, height
  command.

- **Other corner of base or length** prompt:
  - Type **"10"** and press **Enter. ❷**
- **Width. Press Enter to use length** prompt:
  - Press **Enter** to use the same dimension as the length. **❸**
- **Height. Press Enter to use width** prompt
  - Press **Enter** to use the same dimension of the length and width measurements. **❹**

❷ | Other corner of base or length (3Point): **10**

❸ | Width. Press Enter to use length (3Point):

❹ | Height. Press Enter to use width:

- The finished box measures **10mm x 10mm x 10mm**

- This box is a **Simple Lightweight Extrusion** which is the default solid for this command. (more about this in the next chapter).

Fig. 1

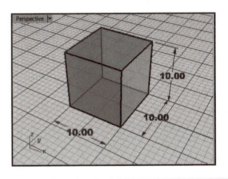

- Click on the **Sphere: center, radius** command in the **Solid Tools tabbed toolbar.**

  - **Center of sphere** prompt:
    - Snap to the **Endpoint ❶** of one of the corners of the box.
    - Click to set location.

    - *Notice that you can snap to seams and surface edges as if they were lines or curves.*

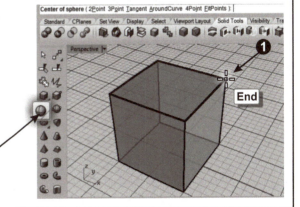

Sphere: center, radius
command

Fig. 2

- **Diameter** prompt:
  - Notice the wireframe preview lines when you draw the cursor outward.
  - Make sure that you are being prompted for the diameter, not the radius.
  - Type **"3"** ❷ in the **Command Line** and press **Enter.**

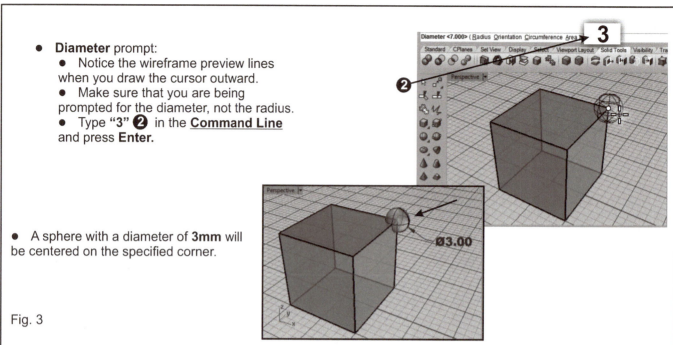

- A sphere with a diameter of **3mm** will be centered on the specified corner.

Fig. 3

- **Transform tabbed toolbar.**

- Select the new sphere and ❶ click on the **Mirror command.**

  - **Start of mirror plane** prompt:
    - Type **"0"** ❷ and press **Enter.**

  Mirror
  command

  - **End of mirror plane** prompt:
    - Using **ORTHO,** draw the cursor upward along the **Y Axis** ❸ and click to set location.

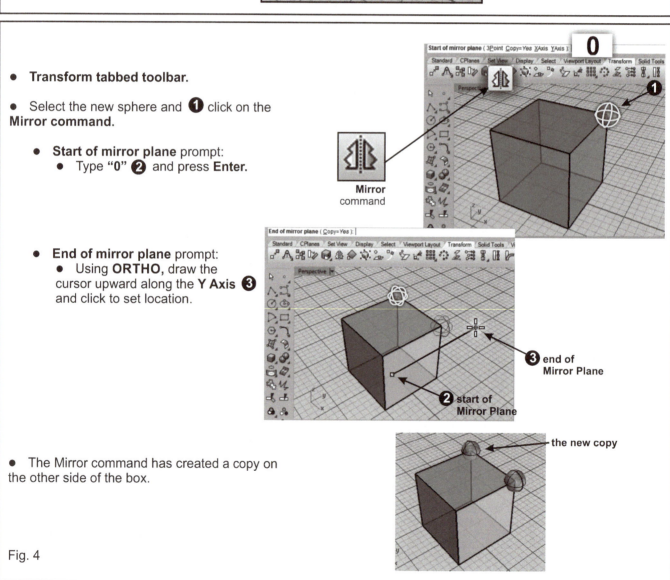

- The Mirror command has created a copy on the other side of the box.

Fig. 4

- Select the two spheres and click on the **Mirror** command again.

  - **Start of mirror plane** prompt:
    - Type "0" ❶ and press **Enter**.

  - **End of mirror plane** prompt:
    - Using **ORTHO**, draw the cursor upward along the **X Axis** ❷ and click to set location.

- The Mirror command has created copies on the front corners of the box.

new copies

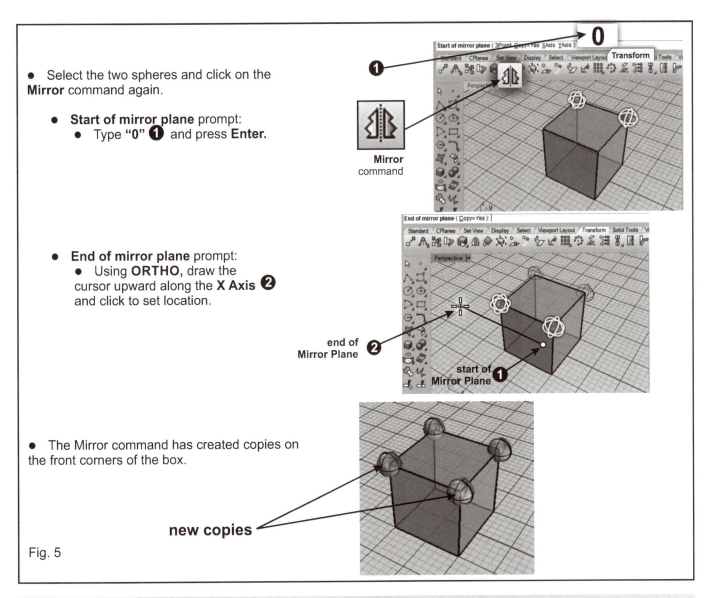

Mirror command

end of Mirror Plane ❷

start of ❶ Mirror Plane

Fig. 5

Changing to the Front Perspective View

- **Set View tabbed toolbar.** Set View

- Click on the **Front View** ❶
- Then the **Perspective View.** ❷

- You will now be in **Front Perspective** view, even though the viewport title will just read **"Perspective"**.

- Notice that the view is in *Perspective* but the *Construction Plane* is for the *Front View*.

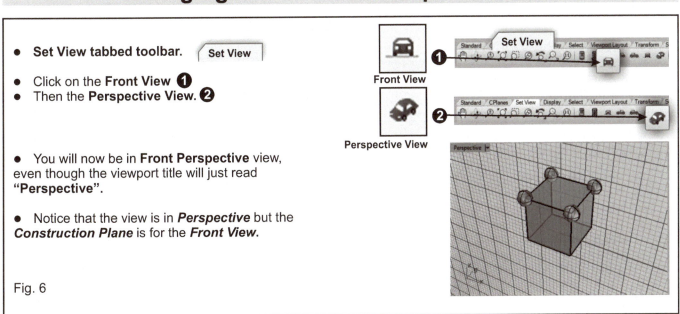

Front View

Perspective View

Fig. 6

- **Transform tabbed toolbar.** `Transform`

- Select the two spheres and click on the **Mirror** command.

  - **Start of mirror plane** prompt:
    - Snap to the **Midpoint ❶** of the vertical seam as shown.
    - Click to set location.

  - **End of mirror plane** prompt:
    - Snap to the **Midpoint ❷** of the neighboring vertical seam as shown.

- The top 4 spheres have been mirrored down to the bottom of the box.

- It was necessary to change to the **Front Perspective** view.

- *The mirror command creates copies in a direction **parallel to the Construction Plane**.*

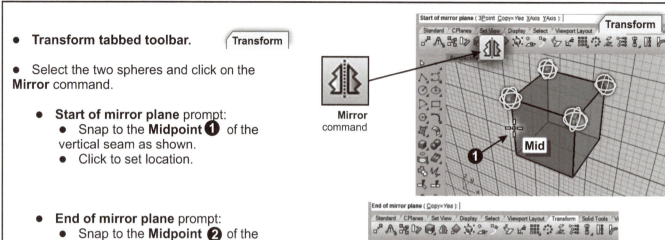

Mirror
command

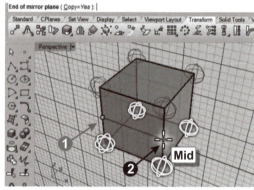

Fig. 7

Polar Array Command in 3-D space

- **Set View** tabbed toolbar. `Set View`

- **Default Perspective view.**
  - Click on the **Top View** command. ❶
  - Click on the **Perspective View** command. ❷

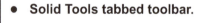

- **Solid Tools tabbed toolbar.**

- Click on the **Torus** command.

  - **Center of torus** prompt:
    - Click on the **Vertical** option in the **Command Line.**
  - **Center of torus** prompt:
    - Type **"0"** and press **Enter. ❶**

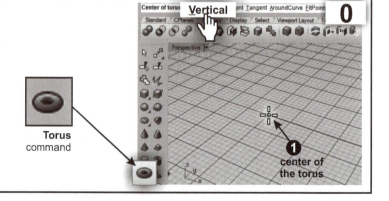

Torus
command

Fig. 8

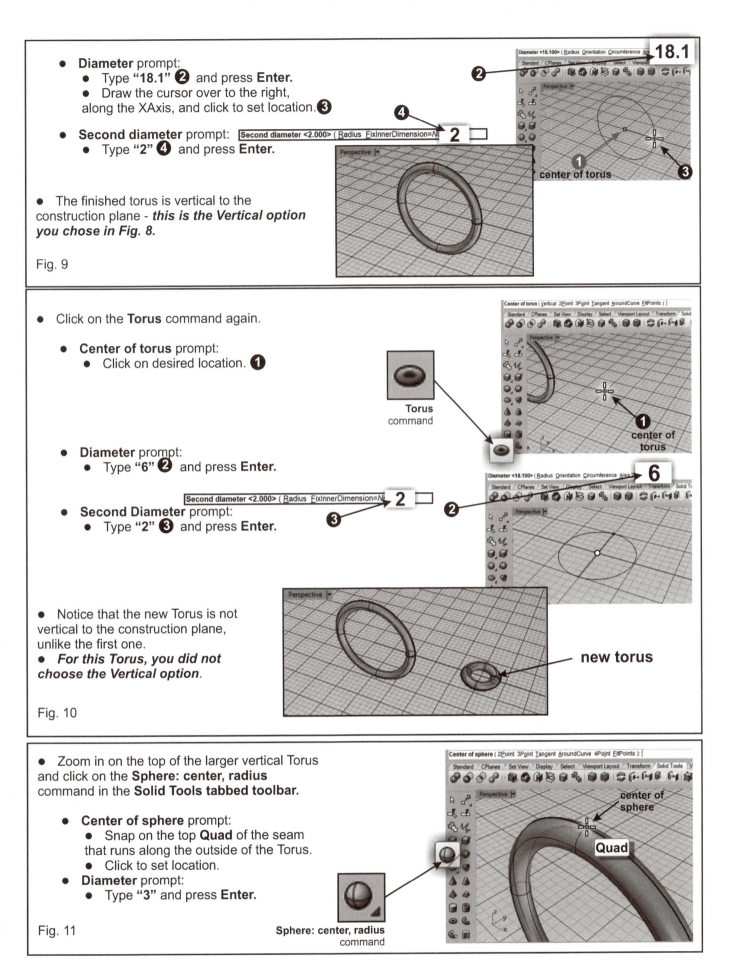

- **Diameter** prompt:
  - Type "18.1" ❷ and press **Enter.**
  - Draw the cursor over to the right, along the XAxis, and click to set location. ❸

- **Second diameter** prompt:
  - Type "2" ❹ and press **Enter.**

- The finished torus is vertical to the construction plane - *this is the Vertical option you chose in Fig. 8.*

Fig. 9

- Click on the **Torus** command again.

  - **Center of torus** prompt:
    - Click on desired location. ❶

Torus
command

  - **Diameter** prompt:
    - Type "6" ❷ and press **Enter.**

  - **Second Diameter** prompt:
    - Type "2" ❸ and press **Enter.**

- Notice that the new Torus is not vertical to the construction plane, unlike the first one.
- *For this Torus, you did not choose the Vertical option.*

new torus

Fig. 10

- Zoom in on the top of the larger vertical Torus and click on the **Sphere: center, radius** command in the **Solid Tools tabbed toolbar.**

  - **Center of sphere** prompt:
    - Snap on the top **Quad** of the seam that runs along the outside of the Torus.
    - Click to set location.
  - **Diameter** prompt:
    - Type "3" and press **Enter.**

Sphere: center, radius
command

Fig. 11

- The sphere is **3mm** in diameter and sits with its center on the top quad point of the seam that runs along the outside of the sphere.

Fig. 12

- Zoom in on the right side of the small Torus that is lying flat on the Construction Plane - *the vertical option was not clicked when making this sphere.*

- Click on the **Sphere: center, radius** command.

  - **Center of sphere** prompt:
    - Snap to the **Quad location** that is at the crossing of the two seams of the torus.
    - Click to set location.
  - **Diameter** prompt:
    - Type **"2"** and press **Enter.**

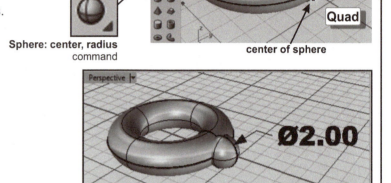

Sphere: center, radius
command

center of sphere

- The new sphere is **2mm** in diameter and sits with its center on the quad point at the crossing of the two seams of the Torus.

Fig. 13

- **Transform tabbed toolbar.** [Transform]

- Select the **2mm sphere** and click on the **Polar Array** command.

  - **Center of polar array** prompt:
    - Snap to the **Center** of the outer seam of the Torus.
    - Click to set location. ❶
  - **Number of items** prompt:
    - Type **"16"** and press **Enter.**

  - **Angle: 360**
  - **Press Enter to accept array preview.**

- The arrayed copies are sitting on the construction plane.

- *note: Polar Array is construction plane specific.*
- *It will always make it's array parallel to the construction plane.*

Fig. 14

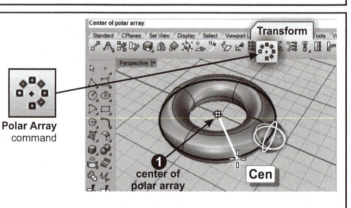

Polar Array
command

center of
polar array

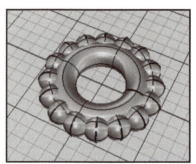

- **Set View tabbed toolbar.**

- Click on the **Front View** command. ❶
- Click on the **Perspective View** command. ❷

Front View   Perspective View

Fig. 15

- **Transform tabbed toolbar.**

- Zoom in on the **large torus** and notice that it is now sitting flat on the **construction plane of the Front Perspective** view.

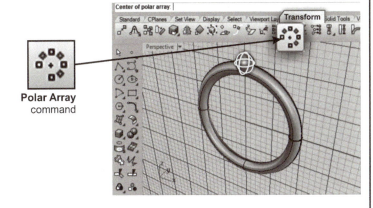

Polar Array
command

- Click on the **Polar Array** command.

  - **Center of Polar Array** prompt:
    - Type "0" and press **Enter.**
  - **Number of items: 16**
  - **Angle: 360**
  - **Press Enter to accept array preview.**

- 16 spheres have been arrayed around the center of the Torus.

Fig. 16

- Two different polar arrays have been created.
  - One on the **default top perspective view** ❶
  - and the other on the **Front Perspective view.** ❷

- *note: Polar Array is <u>construction plane specific.</u>*
- *It will always make it's array <u>parallel to the construction plane.</u>*

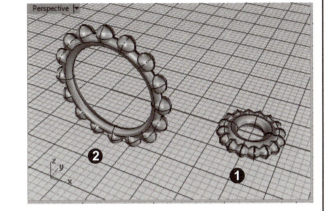

Fig. 17

Ring from Basic Solid Objects

Solid Commands: Booleans, Pipe, and Solid Fillet

- Create the layers shown.

- **ring band ref** layer current.

current → RING BAND 💡 🔓 ■
ring band ref ✓ ■

Fig. 1

- **Front Viewport.** Front ▾

- **Curve Tools tabbed toolbar.** Curve Tools

- Create a **Ø17.35mm circle** around **"0"**.

Front ▾   Ø17.35

Fig. 2

- Select the circle and click on the **Offset Curve** command.

  - **Side to offset** prompt:
    - Type **"1"** and press **Enter.**
    - Draw the cursor to the outside of the circle and click to set location. ❶

Offset Curve command

1   --1.00   ❶   new offset

- Select the new offset curve and offset to the outside again with the same offset distance as before, **1mm.** ❷

❶
❷ new offset

Fig. 3

- **RING BAND** layer current.

RING BAND ✓ ■
ring band ref 💡 🔓 ■

Fig. 4

- **Top Perspective view.** ❶ 🔲 ❷ 🔳

- **Solid Tools tabbed toolbar.** Solid Tools

Pipe: flat caps command

- Select the middle circle and click on the **Pipe: flat caps** command.

Fig. 5

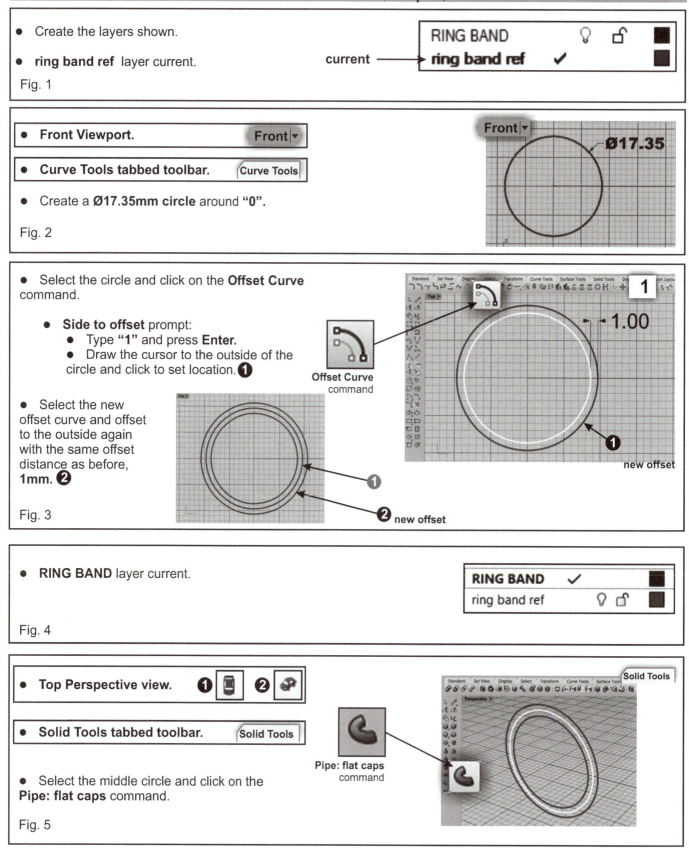

- **Radius for closed pipe** prompt:
  - Draw the cursor out and snap to the **Quad** of the outer circle as shown.
    - This is done where the preview line of the pipe appears.
  - Click to set location.

- **Point of next radius. Press Enter for none** prompt:
  - Press **Enter.**

- A tubular surface, the ring band, will form around the designated circle with a consistant band thickness of **2mm.**

Fig. 6

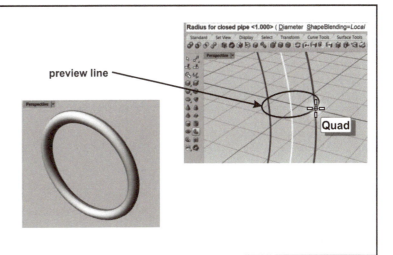

preview line

- Click on the **Ellipsoid: from center** command.

  - **Ellipsoid center** prompt:
    - Snap to the **upper Quad** of the middle circle and click to set location. ❶

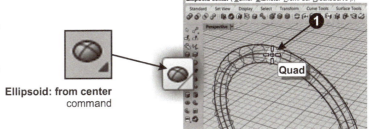

Ellipsoid: from center
command

  - **End of first axis** prompt:
    - Type **"2"** and press **Enter.**
    - Using **ortho,** draw the cursor out and click to set location. ❷

  - **End of second axis** prompt:
    - Type **"2"** and press **Enter.**
    - Using **ortho,** draw the cursor out to the side shown and click to set location. ❸

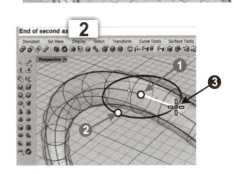

  - **End of third axis** prompt:
    - Type **"1.5"** and press **Enter.**
    - Draw the cursor upward and click to set location. ❹

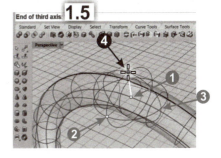

Fig. 7

- An ellipsoid that is round when viewed from the top and flatter when viewed from the side has been created around the center of the diameter of the tube.

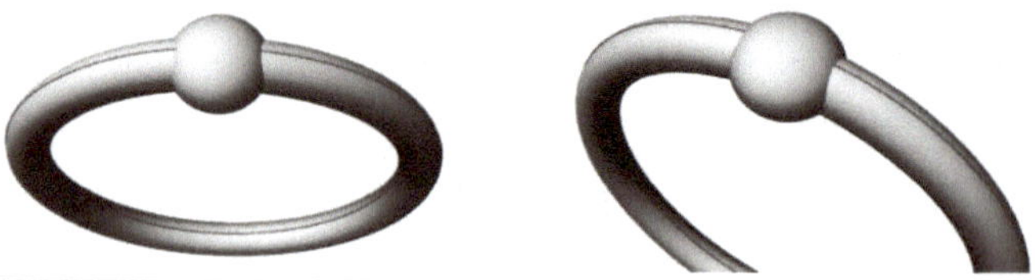

Fig. 8

- Turn off the **ring band ref** layer.

Fig. 9

RING BAND	✓	■
ring band ref	💡 🔓	■

- **Front Viewport.** `Front ▼`

- **Transform tabbed toolbar.** `Transform`

- Select the new **ellipsoid** and click on the **Polar Array** command.

  - **Center of polar array: 0**
  - **Number of items: 6**
  - **Angle to fill: 360**
  - **Press Enter.**
  - **Press Enter to accept preview of array**

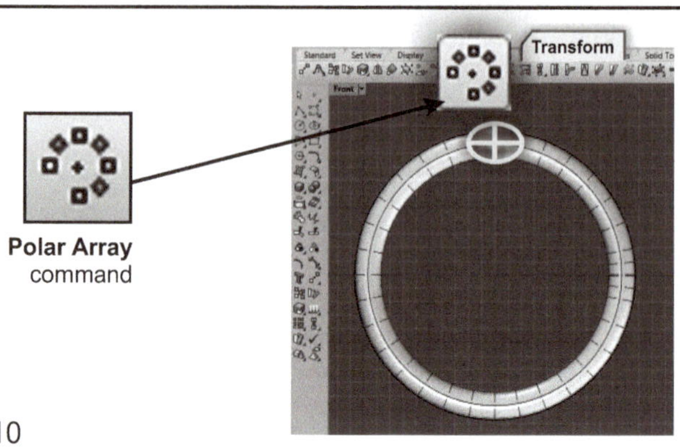

Polar Array command

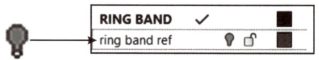

Fig. 10

- The finished array.

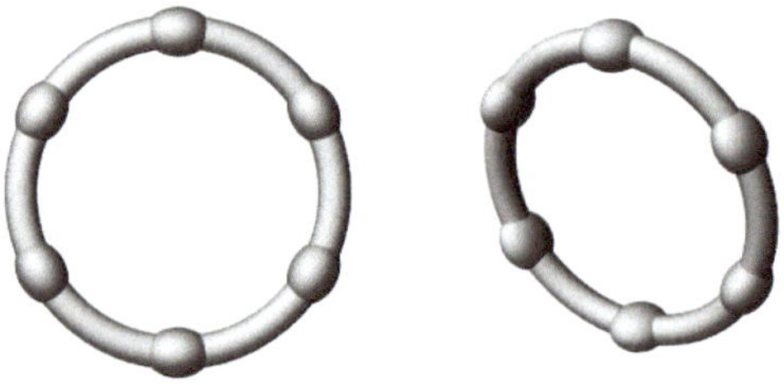

Fig. 11

- Change to **Top Perspective view.** ❶ ❷

- **Solid Tools tabbed toolbar.** `Solid Tools`

- Select all objects and click on the **Boolean Union** command.

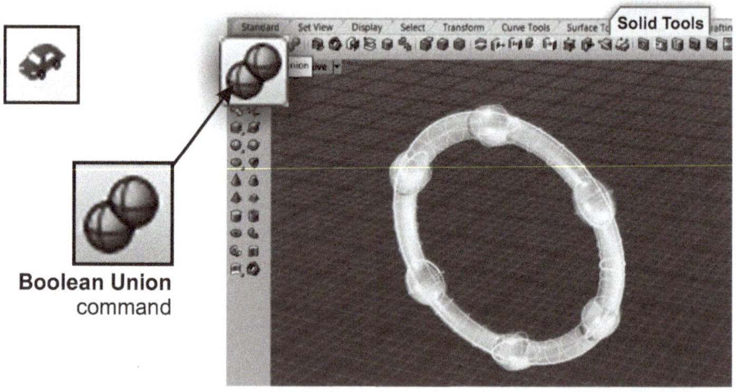

Boolean Union command

- The ring and the ellipsoids are now **a single closed polysurface.**

- **Notice the seams where the band and the ellipsoids have trimmed and joined each other.**

Fig. 12

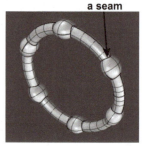

a seam

before Boolean Union

after Boolean Union

- **Left-click** on the **Variable Radius Solid Fillet** command.

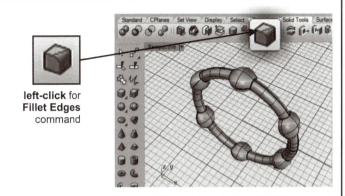

left-click for
Fillet Edges
command

- **Select edges to fillet. Press Enter when done** prompt:
- Type "**.5**" and press **Enter.**
    - This sets the radius of the fillets.
  - Draw a selection window around the entire piece as shown.

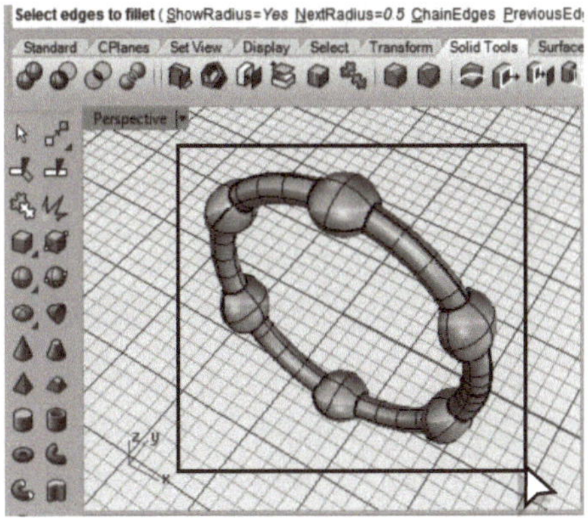

- When you release the cursor, all of the edges will be selected.
- You will also see the radius for each fillet in white numbers.

- **Select fillet handle to edit. Press Enter when done** prompt.
  - Press **Enter** because you don't want to change any of the fillet values.

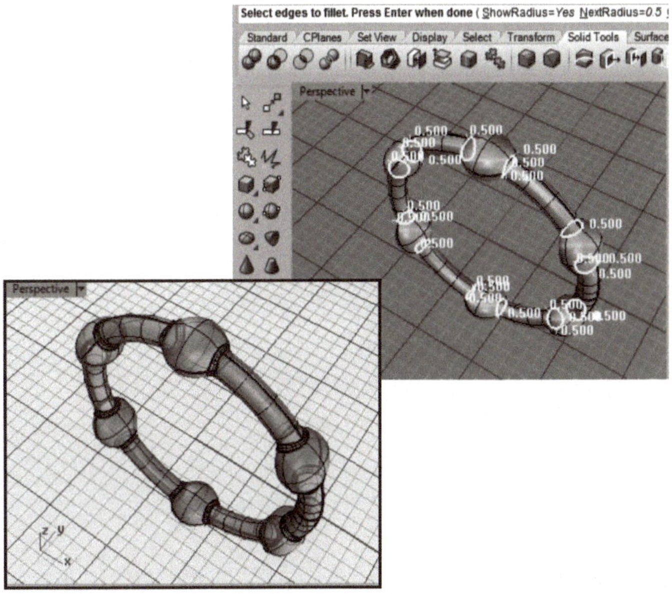

- Each seam has been softened with an additional fillet surface added.

Fig. 13

- These two illustrations show the ring before and after the fillets.

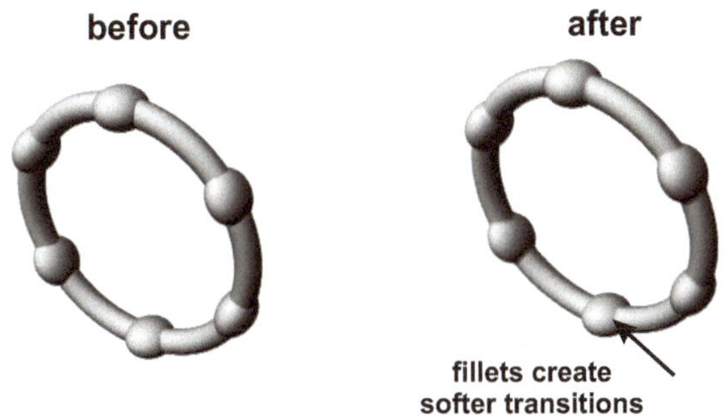

before

after

fillets create
softer transitions

Fig. 14

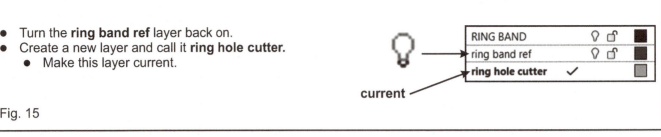

- Turn the **ring band ref** layer back on.
- Create a new layer and call it **ring hole cutter.**
  - Make this layer current.

RING BAND	♀ 🔓 ■
ring band ref	♀ 🔓 ■
ring hole cutter	✓ □

current

Fig. 15

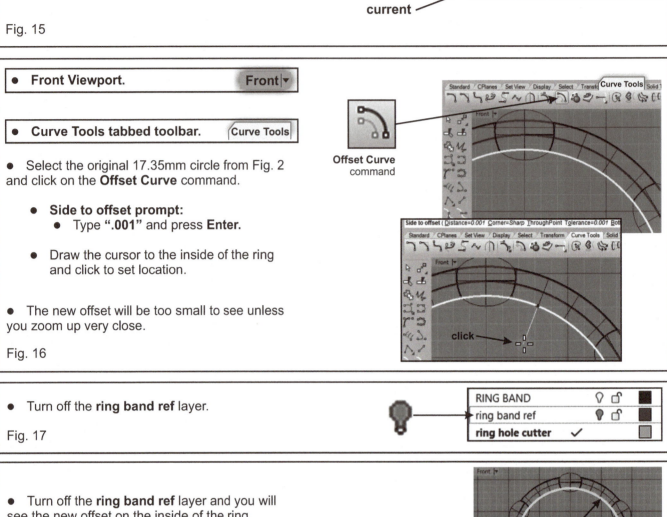

- **Front Viewport.**   Front ▾

- **Curve Tools tabbed toolbar.**   Curve Tools

- Select the original 17.35mm circle from Fig. 2 and click on the **Offset Curve** command.

  - **Side to offset prompt:**
    - Type "**.001**" and press **Enter.**

  - Draw the cursor to the inside of the ring and click to set location.

- The new offset will be too small to see unless you zoom up very close.

Offset Curve
command

click

Fig. 16

- Turn off the **ring band ref** layer.

RING BAND	♀ 🔓 ■
ring band ref	♀ 🔓 ■
ring hole cutter	✓ □

Fig. 17

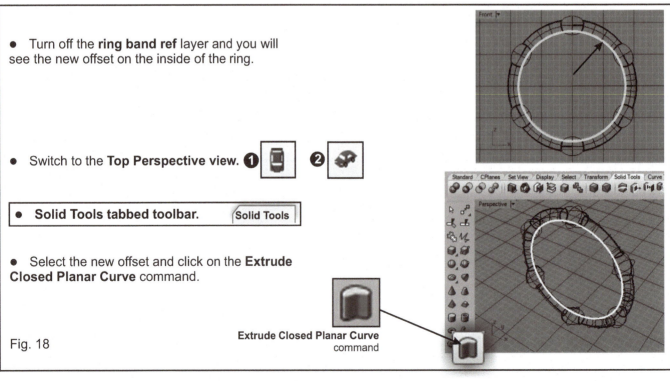

- Turn off the **ring band ref** layer and you will see the new offset on the inside of the ring.

- Switch to the **Top Perspective view.** ❶ ❷

- **Solid Tools tabbed toolbar.**   Solid Tools

- Select the new offset and click on the **Extrude Closed Planar Curve** command.

Extrude Closed Planar Curve
command

Fig. 18

287

- Draw the cursor out with the **Both Sides** option enabled.
  - Click to set the extrusion when both sides are clear of the shank.

- Because of the **.001** offset, this cutter is .001 away from the shank to avoid bad geometry when cutting out the finger hole.
- *If this cutter were touching the round shank, this would cause the boolean difference in the next step to fail.*

Fig. 19

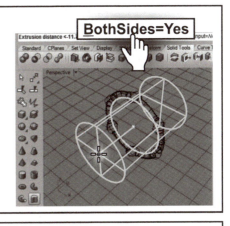

- Click on the **Boolean Difference** command.

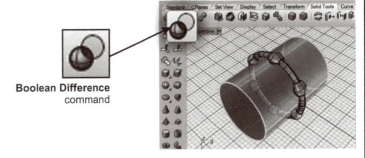

Boolean Difference command

- **Select surfaces or polysurfaces to subtract from. Press Enter to continue** prompt:
  - Select the ring and press **Enter**.

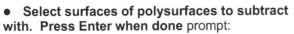

- **Select surfaces of polysurfaces to subtract with. Press Enter when done** prompt:
  - Make sure to click to toggle **Deleteinput=Yes** to **Deleteinput=No** so that your cutting object is not deleted at the end of this command!
  - Select the extrusion you just made and press **Enter**.

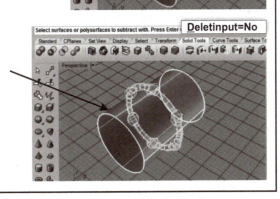

Fig. 20

- Turn off the **ring hole cutter** layer and notice that the inside of the ellipsoids has been cut away in the smooth shape of the cutting object.

- Save this file as: **pipe & ellipsoid ring.3dm**

Fig. 21

Sculpting Simple Rings
Control Point Editing a Torus

- **Solid Tools tabbed toolbar.** | Solid Tools |

- **Front Viewport.** | Front ▾ |

- Click on the **Torus** command.

  - **Center of torus** prompt:
    - Type **"0"** and press **Enter.**
  - **Diameter of torus** prompt:
    - Make sure that the **Diameter** option is enabled in the **Command Line.**
    - Type **"19.35"** and press **Enter.**

  - **Second diameter** prompt:
    - Type **"2"** and press **Enter.**

Torus command

- **Top Perspective view.** ❶ 🚗 ❷ 🚙

- A size 7 ring band has been created.

Fig. 1

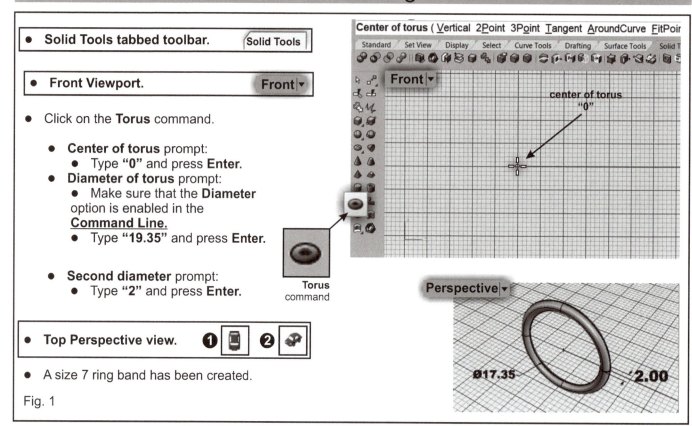

center of torus "0"

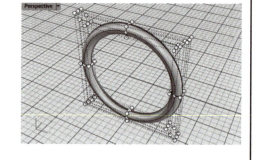

Ø17.35 · 2.00

- Select the torus and turn on its control points. You can press the **F10** hotkey to turn on control points if you have selected the torus.

F10

- You will see the same squared off conformation of control points that you see on a simple circle before control point editing.

Fig. 2

- Multi select the control points in all 4 corners and drag them back along the Y axis using ortho.

- Notice the sharpness of the bends in the torus. Notice the sharper kink in the location where the surface seam is located.

- To get a more even and graceful shape after point editing it is necessary to **Rebuild** this torus.

- **Undo** the drag to restore the torus to its original shape.

Fig. 3

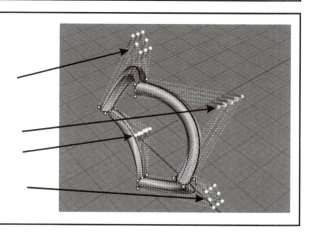

- Select the torus and type **Rebuild** in the **Command Line.**

- A series of **green** and **red** arrows will show over the surface of the torus - **they show the two directions of the surface.**
  - **Red arrows:** show the **U Direction.**
  - **Green arrows:** show the **V Direction.**

- Assign the value of **8** to both **U** and **V** directions. ❶
- Assign a Degree of **3** to both directions to maintain surface smoothness. ❷

Fig. 4

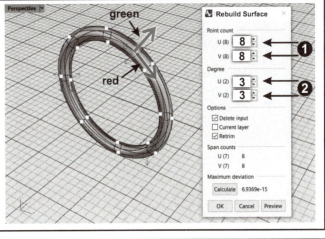

- The torus now has more isocurves, reflecting the change in its number of control points.

- Turn on control points.

- Notice how the distribution of control points has changed to show an even pattern.
  - Moving control points now will result in more even and graceful control point editing.

Fig. 5

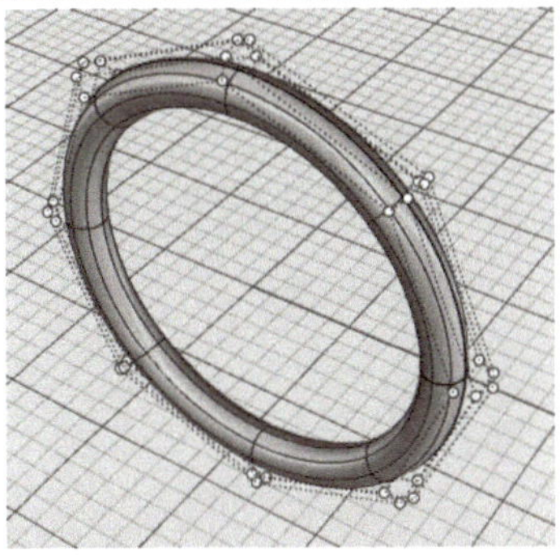

Double Domed Ring

- **Transform tabbed toolbar.** [Transform]

accesses the **Scale** toolbar flyout

Scale 1D command

- Multi select the top 3 rows of control points as shown.

- Click on the **Scale 1D** command in the **Scale** toolbar flyout.

Fig. 6

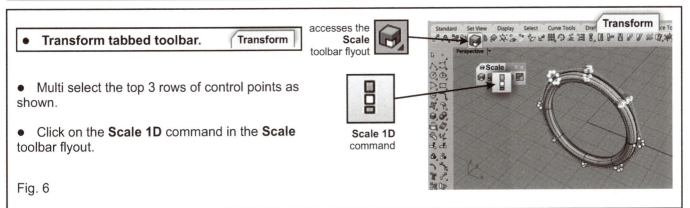

- **Origin point. Press Enter for automatic** prompt:
  - Snap to the point at the top of the row that is at the top of the torus and click to set location. ❶

Fig. 7

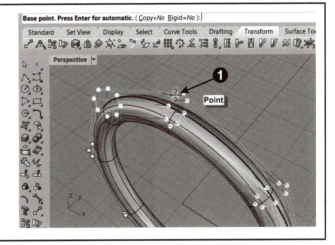

- **Scale factor or first reference point** prompt:
  - Using **ortho,** move the cursor outward as shown.
  - Click on a location as shown. ❷

Fig. 8

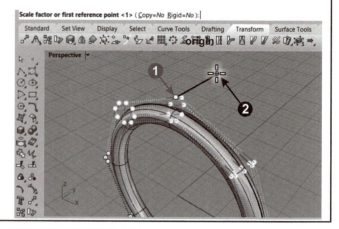

- **Second reference point** prompt:
  - Pull the cursor out further until the preview shows the desire shape.
  - Click to set the second reference point. ❸

Fig. 9

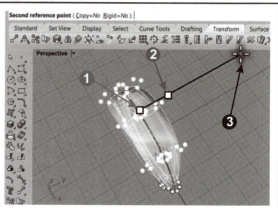
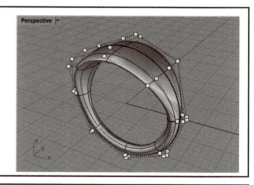

- The top of the ring will now be wider than the bottom.

Fig. 10

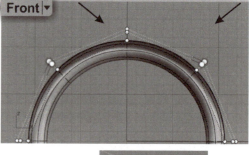

- **Front Viewport.**  Front |▼

- **Window select the 2 top control points** on either side of the top row as shown.

- Looking in the Perspective viewport, notice that you are actually selecting **3 control points** on each side!

Fig. 11

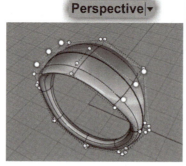
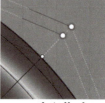

detail view

- Using **ortho,** drag the selected control points straight up.

- When the preview shows the desired shape, click to set location.

- Press the **Esc** key a couple of times to turn off control points.

- The ring is viewed here in Rendered Viewport display mode.

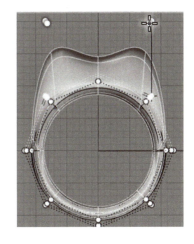

Fig. 12

- Moving the control points at the top of the ring can create variations in shape.

- Save this file as: **double domed ring.3dm**

Fig. 13

Square Ring

- Create another Torus and rebuild it, using the same dimensions and control point settings as before.

- Turn on control points.

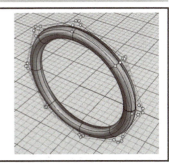

Fig. 14

- **Front Viewport.**   Front ▾

- Multi select **2 control points in each of the 4 corners**.

- Note: In the perspective view, notice that you have actually selected 3 control points in each of these 4 locations.

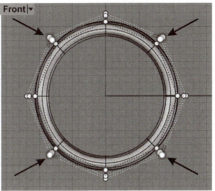

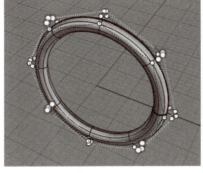

Fig. 15

- Click on the **Scale 2D** command in the **Scale** toolbar flyout.

  - **Base point. Press Enter for sutomaticOrigin point** prompt:
    - Type **"0"** and press **Enter.**❶

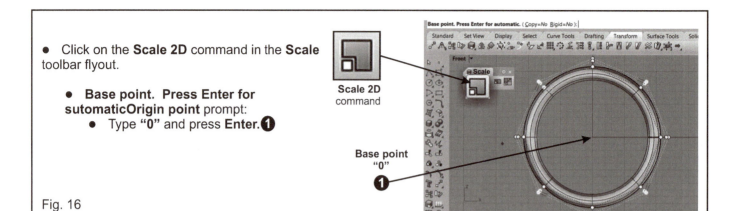

Scale 2D
command

Base point
"0"
❶

Fig. 16

- **Scale factor or first reference point** prompt:
  - Draw the cursor out and click somewhere on the grid as shown.❷

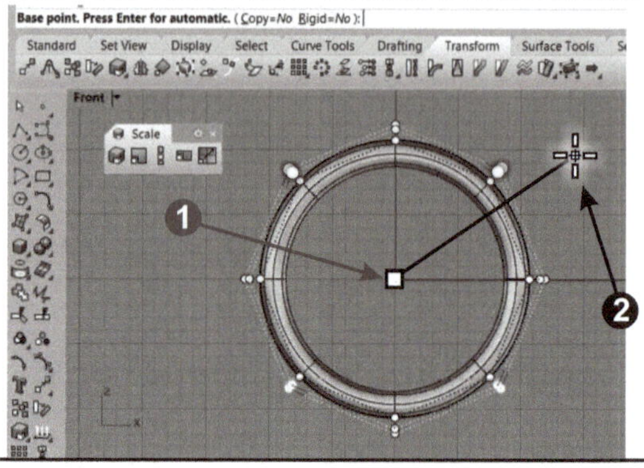

Fig. 17

- **Second reference point** prompt:
  - Draw the cursor out and click when the preview shows the desired shape.❸

- Turn off control points

- In the perspective view the ring now has a soft squared silhouette.

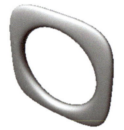

- Viewed in Rendered mode. Press the **F7** key to toggle off the grid.

Fig. 18

- **Top Perspective view.** ❶ 🔲 ❷ 🔲

- To make the ring a little thicker, click on the **Scale 1D** command in the **Scale** toolbar flyout.

  - **Base Point. Press Enter for automotic** prompt:
    - Snap to the **quad** point on the top of the ring and click to set location.❶

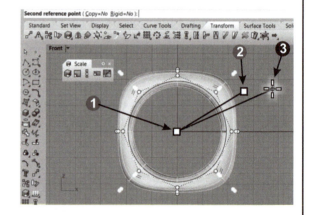

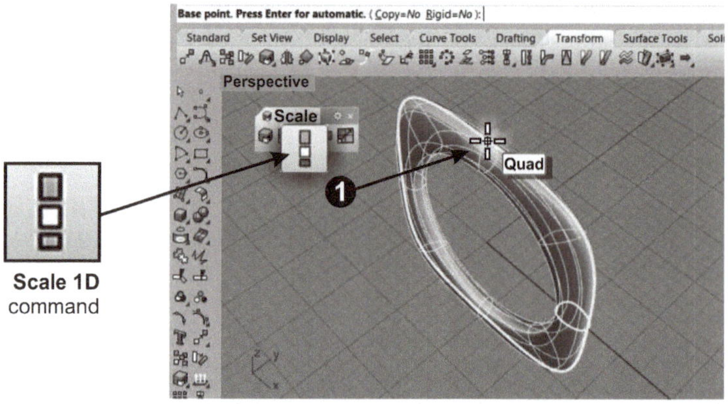

Scale 1D
command

Fig. 19

- **Scale factor or first reference point** prompt:
  - Draw the cursor out, using **ortho**, and click a short distance away. ❷

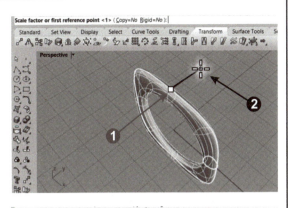

- **Second reference point** prompt:
  - Draw the cursor further out until the preview shows the desired width.
  - Click to set location.

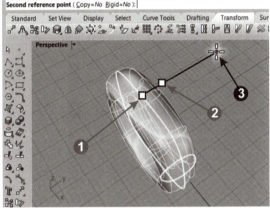

- The finished ring is a soft square and has been made a little thicker.

- Shown in Rendered Viewport mode with the grid toggled off.

- Save this file as: **square band ring.3dm.**

Fig. 20

Rippled Ring

- Create a new torus with the same dimensions again.

- Rebuild the torus:
  - **U direction: 24 pts**
  - **V direction: 8 pts**

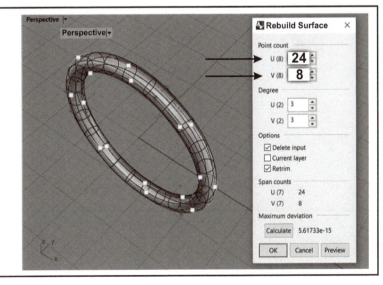

Fig. 21

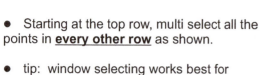

- Starting at the top row, multi select all the points in **every other row** as shown.

- tip: window selecting works best for selecting these - and remember to zoom in to make it easier to select the points.

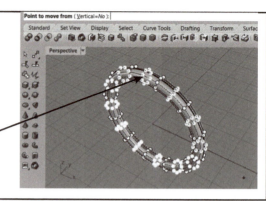

- Start by selecting the row at the top of the ring.

Fig. 22

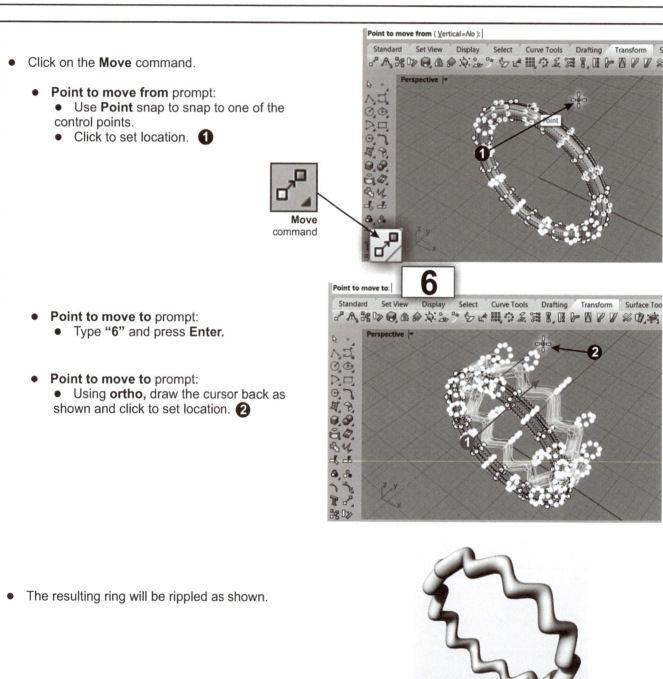

- Click on the **Move** command.

  - **Point to move from** prompt:
    - Use **Point** snap to snap to one of the control points.
    - Click to set location. ❶

  Move command

  - **Point to move to** prompt:
    - Type **"6"** and press **Enter.**

  - **Point to move to** prompt:
    - Using **ortho,** draw the cursor back as shown and click to set location. ❷

- The resulting ring will be rippled as shown.

Fig. 23

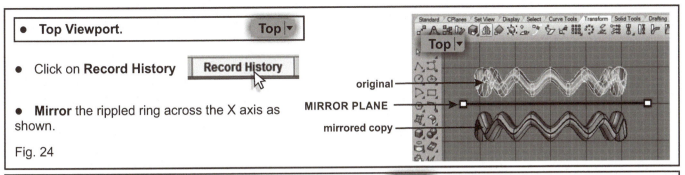

- **Top Viewport.** Top ▼

- Click on **Record History** [Record History]

- **Mirror** the rippled ring across the X axis as shown.

Fig. 24

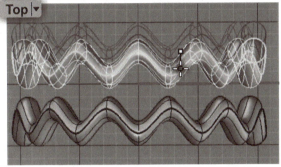

original →
MIRROR PLANE →
mirrored copy →

- **Move** or **Drag** the original ring straight down so that it slightly overlaps the X axis.

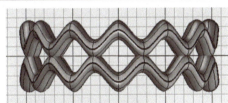

- The **Child** object below will update and the two rippled rings will overlap as shown.

- **Top Perspective view.**

- The double ring viewed in perspective.

Fig. 25

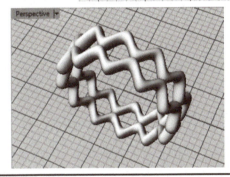

- **Solid Tools tabbed toolbar.** [Solid Tools]

- Select both rings and click on the **Boolean Union** command.

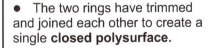
Boolean Union
union

- The two rings have trimmed and joined each other to create a single **closed polysurface.**

- Save this file as: **rippled band ring.3dm**

Fig. 26

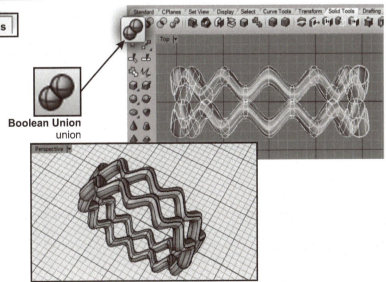

- Create a torus with the same dimensions as the previous examples.

- **Rebuild:**
  - **U direction: 8 pts**
  - **V direction: 8 pts**

- Select rows of control points at the 4 locations as shown.

- Click on the **Move** command.

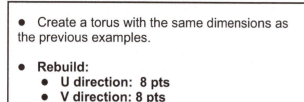

Move
command

  - **Point to move from** prompt:
    - Snap to a **Point** at the top of the ring and click to set location. ❶

  - **Point to move to** prompt:
    - Type **"10"** in the **Command Line** and press **Enter.**
    - Draw the cursor outward, using **Ortho,** and click to set location. ❷

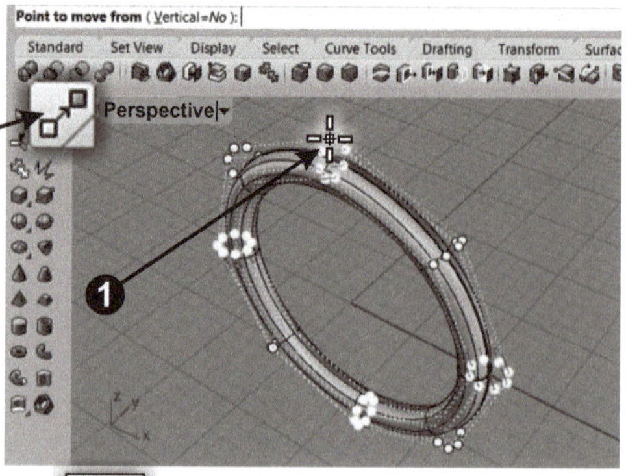

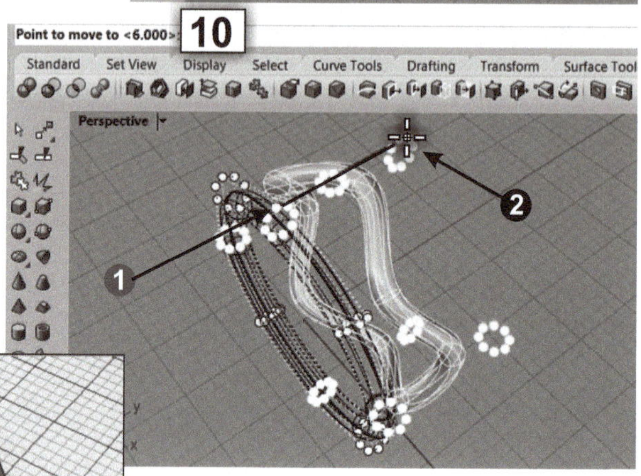

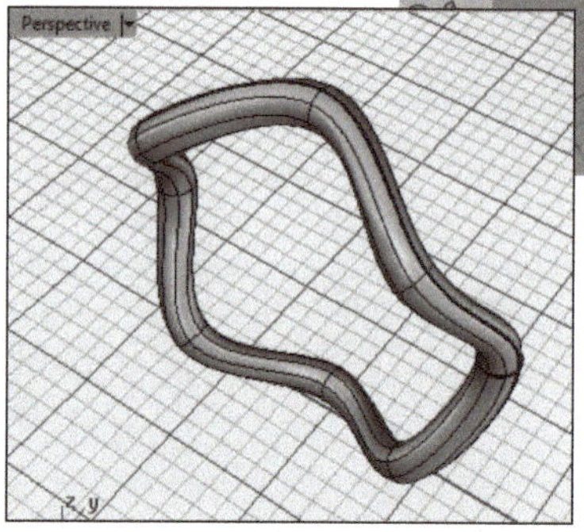

- The ring will have a wavy shape.

Fig. 27

- **Rebuild** the torus to **16 points** in the **U direction and 8 points in the V direction.**

Fig. 28

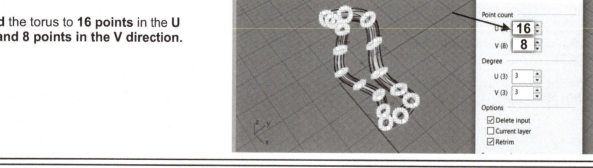

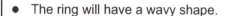
- **Top Viewport.**　　　　　Top ▾

- **Move** the ring band straight down **5mm**, using **ORTHO** for accuracy.

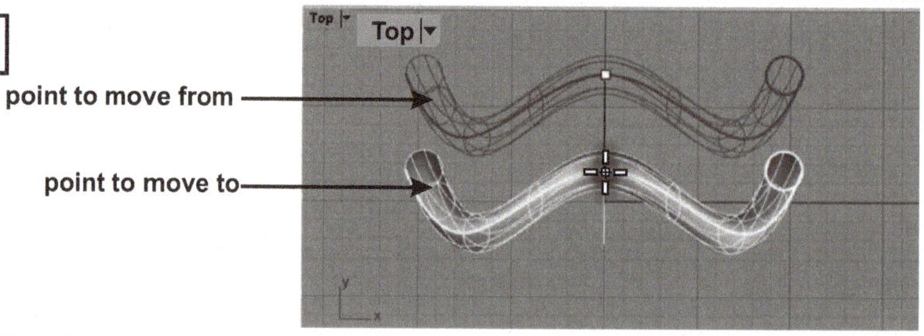

Fig. 29

point to move from ⟶

point to move to ⟶

- **Mirror** the ring band vertically across the X axis as shown.

Fig. 30

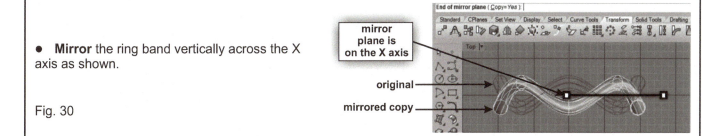

mirror plane is on the X axis

original

mirrored copy

- Select the new mirrored band and type **"lock"**.
- Press **Enter** to end the command.

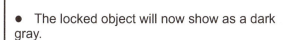

- The locked object will now show as a dark gray.

- Viewed in **Shaded Viewport Mode**.

Fig. 31

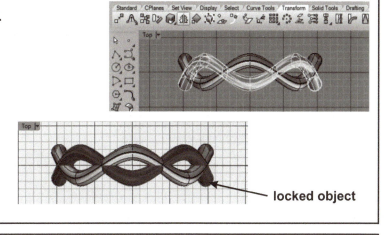

locked object

- **Front Viewport.**   `Front ▼`

- Turn on control points for the torus that is not locked.

- Window select the three outer points at all 4 locations shown.
  - *It will look like you have selected two points until you look at the selection in perspective view.*

- Notice how all of the selected points are at locations where the two ring elements cross each other.   Fig. 32

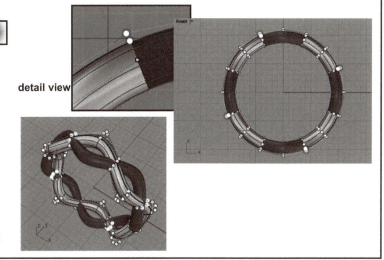

detail view

- **Transform tabbed toolbar.**   `Transform`

- Turn on **Grid Snap**.

- Click on the **Scale 2D** command in the **Scale toolbar flyout.**

Scale 2D command

Fig. 33

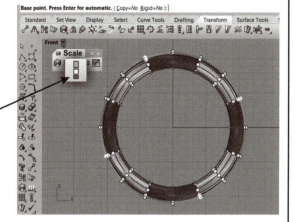

- **Base point. Press Enter for automatic**
prompt:
  - Type **"0"** and press **Enter.** ❶

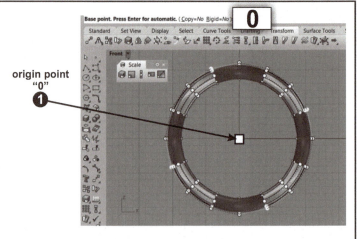

origin point "0"

❶

- **Scale factor or first reference point**
prompt:
  - Draw the cursor straight out with **ORTHO** engaged.
  - Snap on a grid intersection nearby.
  - Click to set location. ❷

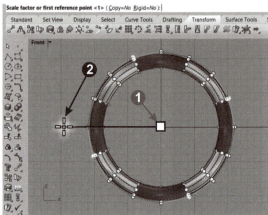

- **Second reference point** prompt:
  - Snap on the next grid intersection.
  - Click to set location. ❸

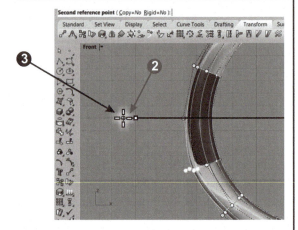

- Notice that where the points were edited to move outward, you can see the start of the interwoven effect of the two bands.

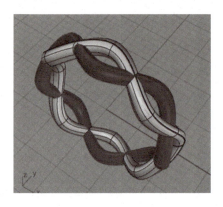

Fig. 34

- **Standard tabbed toolbar.**　〔Standard〕

accesses the
Lock
Toolbar

〔Standard〕

- Click on the **Lock Swap** command in the **Lock toolbar flyout**.

- This command **swaps locked and unlocked objects**.

- *Compare this image to the previous one and notice that what was locked is now unlocked and vise versa!*

Fig. 35

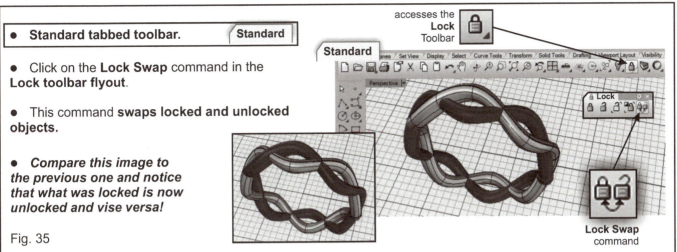

Lock Swap
command

- **Front Viewport.**　〔Front ▾〕

- Turn on control points and select the three outer points at all 4 locations shown.
  - *These points are located in areas that have not had points scaled outward yet.*

- Notice how all of the selected points are at locations where the two rings cross each other.

Fig. 36

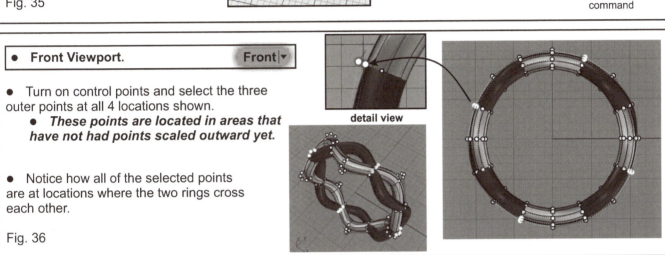

detail view

- **Transform tabbed toolbar.**　〔Transform〕

- **Front Viewport.**　〔Front ▾〕

- Click on the **Scale 2D** command in the **Scale toolbar flyout**.

  - **Base point. Press Enter for automatic** prompt:　❶
    - Type **"0"** and press **Enter**.

  - **Scale factor or first reference point** prompt:
    - Draw the cursor straight out with **ORTHO** engaged.
    - Snap on a grid intersection nearby and click to set location. ❷

Fig. 37

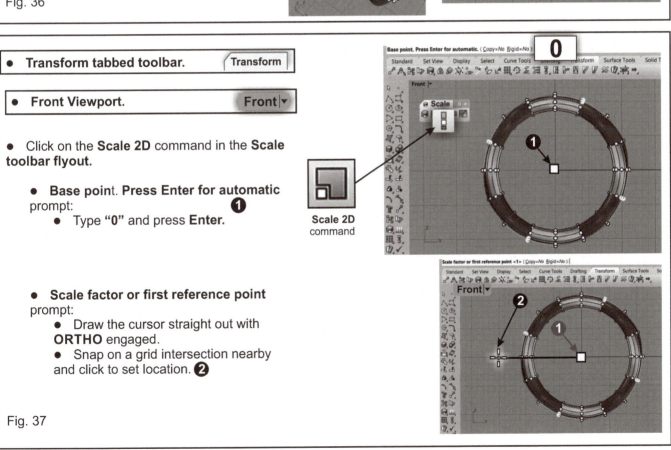

Scale 2D
command

- **Second reference point** prompt:
  - Snap on the next grid intersection and click to set location. ❸

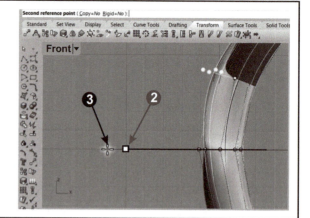

Fig. 38

- Turn off control points.

- Type **"unlock"** and press **Enter** to unlock all locked objects.

Fig. 39

Boolean Union - Making the 2 Rings a Single Closed Polysurface

- **Solid Tools tabbed toolbar.** `Solid Tools`

- **Front Perspective view.** ❶ 🚗 ❷ 🚙

- Select both parts of the ring and click on the **Boolean Union** command.

Boolean Union
command

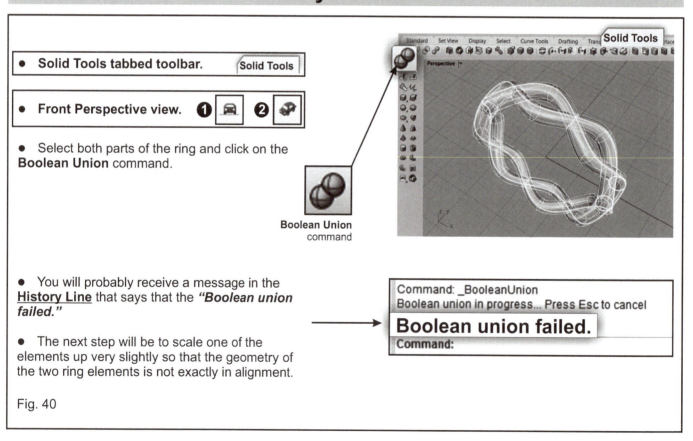

- You will probably receive a message in the **History Line** that says that the *"Boolean union failed."*

- The next step will be to scale one of the elements up very slightly so that the geometry of the two ring elements is not exactly in alignment.

```
Command: _BooleanUnion
Boolean union in progress... Press Esc to cancel
Boolean union failed.
Command:
```

Fig. 40

- **Transform tabbed toolbar.** [Transform]

- Select one of the ring elements and click on the **Scale 3D** in the **Scale** toolbar flyout.

    - **Base point. Press Enter for automatic** prompt:
        - Press **Enter** and Rhino will automatically make the base point in the center of the selected object.

    - **Scale factor or first reference point** prompt:
        - Type "**1.001**" and press **Enter.**

- **The ring element has been scaled up 1/1000 of a millimeter which is so tiny a difference that it is not visible to the naked eye.**

Fig. 41

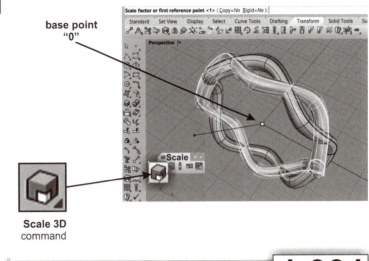

base point "0"

Scale 3D
command

Scale factor or first reference point <1.000> (Cop **1.001**

- **Solid Tools tabbed toolbar.** [Solid Tools]

- Select both parts of the ring and click on the **Boolean Union** command.

Fig. 42

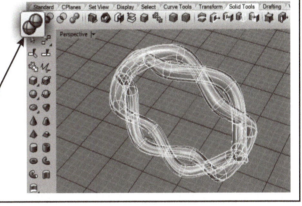

Boolean Union
command

- This time the Boolean Union is successful.

- The geometries of the two elements needed to be slightly moved off of each other.

- Notice the new seams where the two ring's elements cross each other.

- *The two elements have trimmed and joined each other for a single closed polysurface.*

- Save this file as: **woven band ring.3dm**

Fig. 43

seams

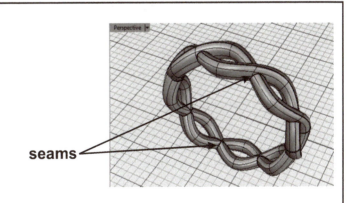

Applying Dimensions to 3D Objects
Using different viewports to get different dimension locations

- **Drafting tabbed toolbar.** `Drafting`

- **Top Perspective view.** ❶ 🚗 ❷ 🚙

- Open the file that you saved previously: **solid objects.3dm.**

- Create **Linear Dimensions** (ref. **Applying Dimensions** chapter) for the length and width of the box. using **End Osnap** for accuracy.

Fig. 1

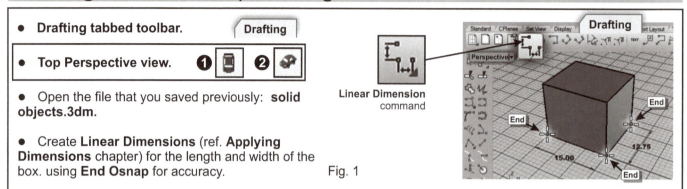

Linear Dimension
command

- <u>**Front**</u> **Perspective Viewport.** ❶ 🚗 ❷ 🚙

- Add the **12.75** dimension for the height of the box, using End Osnap as before.

- *Note: dimensions always need to be created on or parallel to the active construction plane.*

Fig. 2

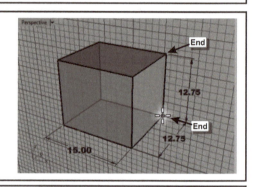

- **Top Perspective view** ❶ 🚗 ❷ 🚙

- The dimensions are still in position and will stay that way if you rotate your view.

Fig. 3

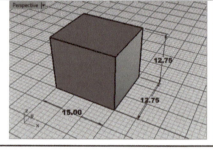

- **Front Perspective view.** ❶ 🚗 ❷ 🚙

- Zoom in on the **Sphere.**

- Click on the **Linear Dimension** command.

  - **First dimension point** prompt:
    - Snap to one of the end points of the seam of the sphere as shown.
    - Click to set location. ❶
  - **Second dimension point** prompt:
    - Snap to the other end of the seam and click to set location. ❷

Fig. 4

Linear Dimension
command

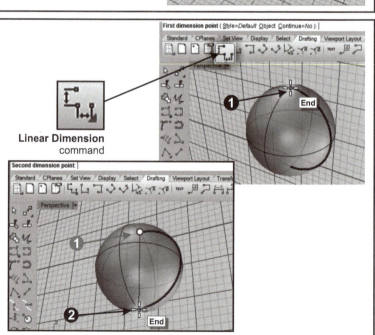

- **Dimension location** prompt:
  - Draw the cursor out and click to set the location of the dimension text and extension lines. ❸

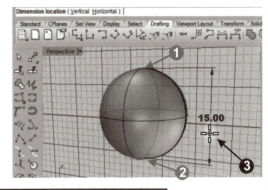

- **Top Perspective view.** ❶ 🖳 ❷ 🚗

- The dimension has been created.

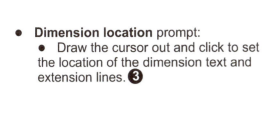

Fig. 5

- Zoom in on the **Cylinder.**

- Click on the **Diameter Dimension** command.

  - **Select curve for diameter dimension** prompt:
    - Click on the edge of the bottom seam as shown. ❶
  - **Dimension location** prompt:
    - Draw the cursor out and click to set location. ❷

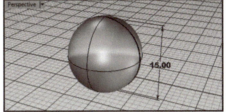

Diameter Dimension command

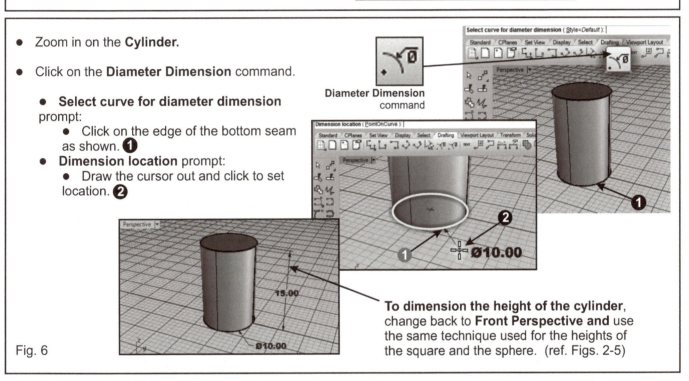

To dimension the height of the cylinder, change back to **Front Perspective and** use the same technique used for the heights of the square and the sphere. (ref. Figs. 2-5)

Fig. 6

- Use the **Aligned Dimension** command to dimension the length of the ellipsoid, **snapping to the two ends of the seam** as shown in steps ❶ & ❷
  - The **Aligned Dimension** command is needed because the tilted ellipsoid is not in line with the grid.

- *To get the width and height dimensions, we will need to create reference geometry because there are no other seams to snap to.*

Aligned dimension

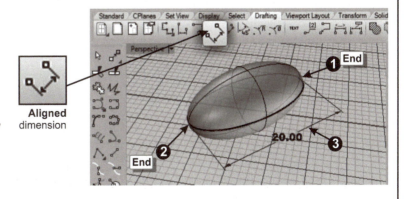

Fig. 7

Creating Curves on the Surface of an Object
Extract Isocurve Command

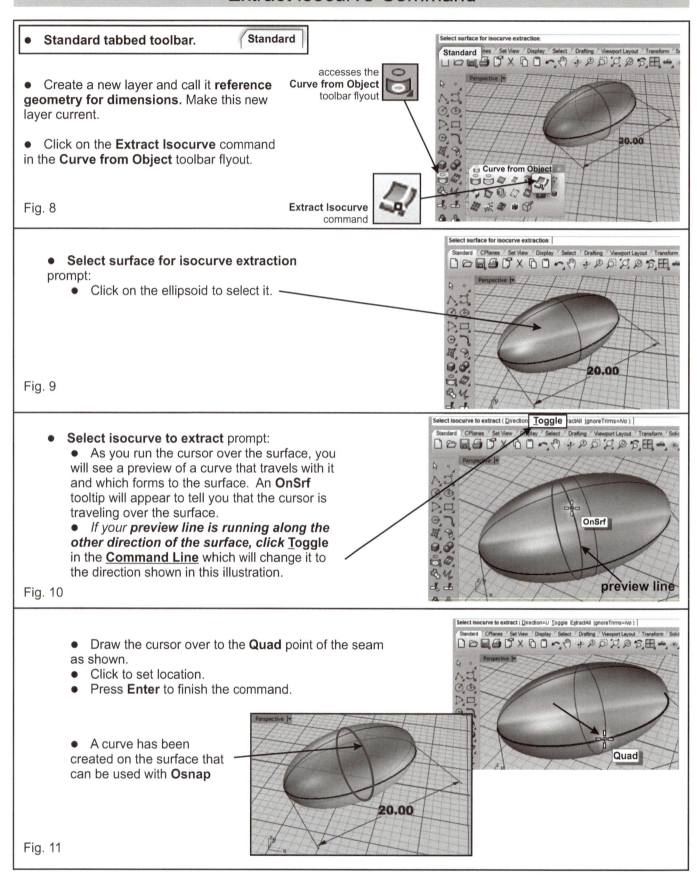

- **Standard tabbed toolbar.** 〔 Standard 〕

- Create a new layer and call it **reference geometry for dimensions.** Make this new layer current.

- Click on the **Extract Isocurve** command in the **Curve from Object** toolbar flyout.

accesses the **Curve from Object** toolbar flyout

Extract Isocurve command

Fig. 8

- **Select surface for isocurve extraction** prompt:
    - Click on the ellipsoid to select it.

Fig. 9

- **Select isocurve to extract** prompt:
    - As you run the cursor over the surface, you will see a preview of a curve that travels with it and which forms to the surface. An **OnSrf** tooltip will appear to tell you that the cursor is traveling over the surface.
    - *If your **preview line is running along the other direction of the surface, click** Toggle* in the **Command Line** which will change it to the direction shown in this illustration.

Fig. 10

preview line

- Draw the cursor over to the **Quad** point of the seam as shown.
- Click to set location.
- Press **Enter** to finish the command.

- A curve has been created on the surface that can be used with **Osnap**

Fig. 11

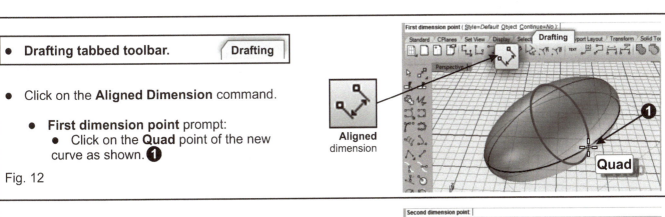

- Drafting tabbed toolbar. ⟨ Drafting ⟩

- Click on the **Aligned Dimension** command.

  - **First dimension point** prompt:
    - Click on the **Quad** point of the new curve as shown. ❶

Fig. 12

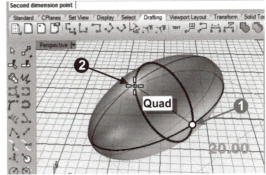

- **Second dimension point** prompt:
  - Click on the **Quad** at the other side of the curve as shown. ❷

Fig. 13

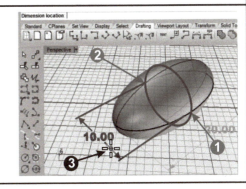

- **Dimension location** prompt:
  - Draw the cursor out and click on desired location. ❸

Fig. 14

- Front Perspective viewport. ❶ 🚗 ❷ 🚗

- Click on the **Linear Dimension** command.

  - **First dimension point** prompt:
    - Snap to the **Quad** on the top of the new curve. ❶
    - Click to set location.

Linear Dimension command

Fig. 15

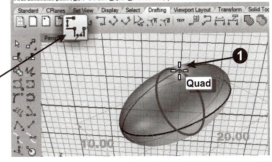

- **Second dimension point** prompt:
  - Snap to the **Quad** at the bottom of the ellipsoid as shown. ❷

Fig. 16

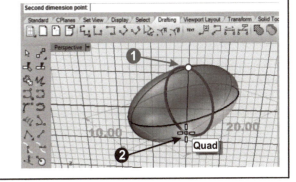

- **Dimension location** prompt:
  - Draw the cursor out and click to set location.

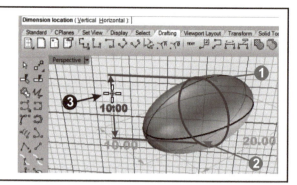

Fig. 17

Rotating a Dimension for Better Orientation

- **Standard toolbar flyout.** `Standard`

- Select the new dimension and **LEFT-CLICK** on the **Rotate** command.

  - **Center of rotation** prompt:
    - Click on the **Quad** at the top of the new curve.
    - Click to set location. **1**

  LEFT-CLICK for **Rotate 2-D** command

Fig. 18

- **Angle or first reference point** prompt:
  - Snap to the **End** of one of the dimension leader lines as shown.
  - Click to set location. **2**

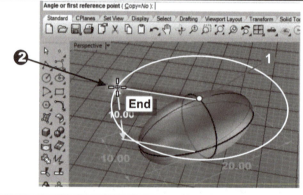

Fig. 19

- **Second reference point** prompt:
  - Snap to the back **Quad** of the new curve.
  - Click to set location. **3**

- Rotating the final dimension for better orientation completes the creating of length, width, and height dimensions for the ellipsoid.

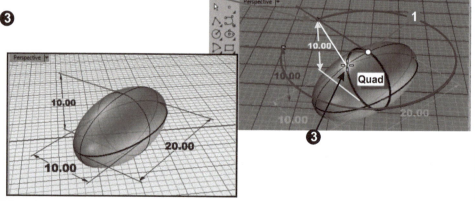

Fig. 20

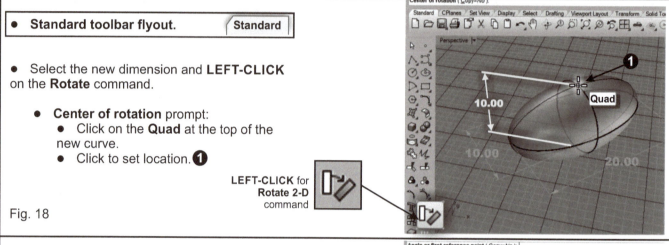

- Open the ET Ring file.

- The stones being used here are the plain Maquette stones. Turn off the faceted stone layer and turn on the maquette stone layer.

Fig. 1

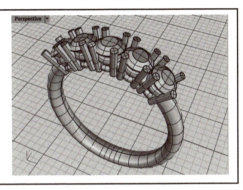

- **Top Viewport.**   Top ▼

- **Drafting tabbed toolbar.**   Drafting

- Click on the **Make 2-D Drawing** command.

Fig. 2

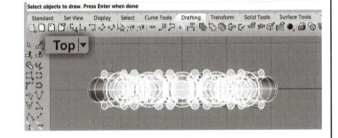

Make 2-D Drawing command

- **Select objects to draw. Press Enter when done** prompt:
  - Select the ring and press **Enter**.

- The **2-D Drawing Options** box will open.

- Select the following options:
  - **Third angle projection.** ❶
  - **Hidden Lines** ❷
  - **Keep the other default settings.** ❸

- Click the **OK button** to exit.

Fig. 3

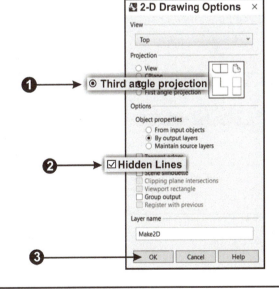

- A drawing will be generated.

- The top, front, and side views will be to exact 1:1 scale.
  - The gray lines are the **hidden lines.**

- If you have a perspective viewport open, a perspective view will be generated as well but this will not be to scale.

- Drag the drawing upward on the construction plane so that it is not intersecting with the model

Fig. 4

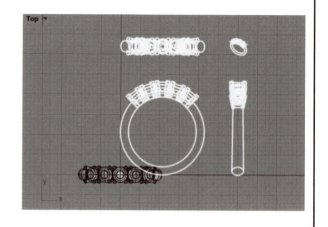

- Visible curves will be black but hidden curves will be gray and will be dashed lines (which is the Hidden linetype).

Fig. 5

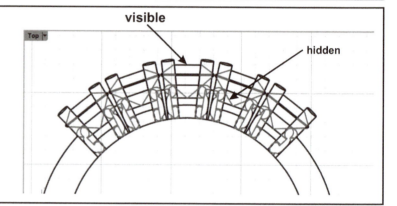

visible

hidden

- The Make 2D layers have been added to the layers panel.
  - Note the sub layers and sub sub layers
  - Change the two hidden layers to red which is easier to see than the default gray.

Fig. 6

change to red

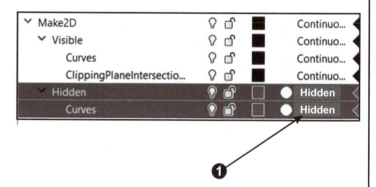

- Select the two Hidden layers and click on the words. "Hidden" ❶ that are the default linetype and which are in the Linetype column.

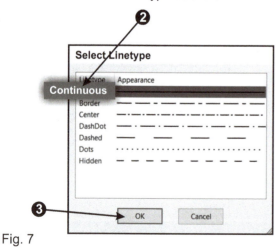

Select Linetype

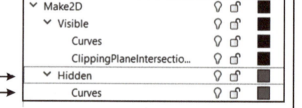

- The **Select Linetype** box will open.

- Click to select the **Continuous** linetype ❷ which is a straight line.
- Click on the OK button ❸ to exit.

Fig. 7

- Hidden lines will now be red and will be easier to see.

Fig. 8

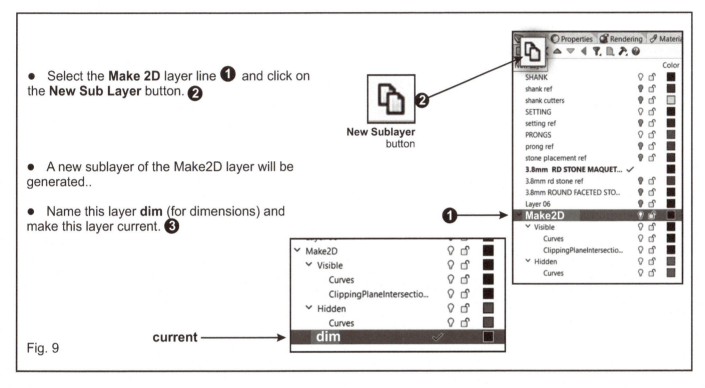

- Select the **Make 2D** layer line ❶ and click on the **New Sub Layer** button. ❷

New Sublayer
button

- A new sublayer of the Make2D layer will be generated..

- Name this layer **dim** (for dimensions) and make this layer current. ❸

		Color
SHANK	♀ ♂	■
shank ref	♀ ♂	■
shank cutters	♀ ♂	☐
SETTING	♀ ♂	■
setting ref	♀ ♂	■
PRONGS	♀ ♂	■
prong ref	♀ ♂	■
stone placement ref	♀ ♂	■
3.8mm RD STONE MAQUET... ✓		■
3.8mm rd stone ref	♀ ♂	■
3.8mm ROUND FACETED STO...	♀ ♂	■
Layer 06	♀ ♂	■
▼ Make2D	♀ ⋒	■
▼ Visible	♀ ♂	■
Curves	♀ ♂	■
ClippingPlaneIntersectio...	♀ ♂	■
▼ Hidden	♀ ♂	■
Curves	♀ ♂	■

❶ →

▼ Make2D	♀ ♂	■
▼ Visible	♀ ♂	■
Curves	♀ ♂	■
ClippingPlaneIntersectio...	♀ ♂	■
▼ Hidden	♀ ♂	■
Curves	♀ ♂	■
dim	✓	■

current →

Fig. 9

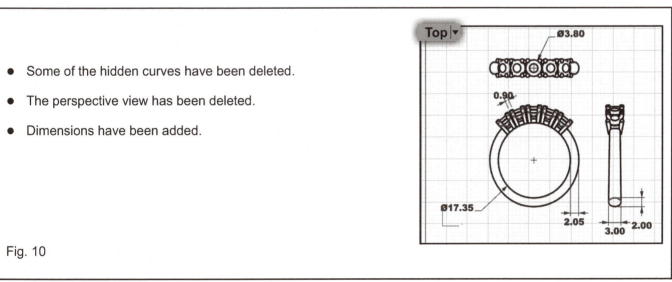

- Some of the hidden curves have been deleted.

- The perspective view has been deleted.

- Dimensions have been added.

Fig. 10

Rhino Rendering
With Raytrace, Raytrace with Neon
and Rendered Viewport Modes

- **Top Perspective view.** ❶ 🔲 ❷ 🎨

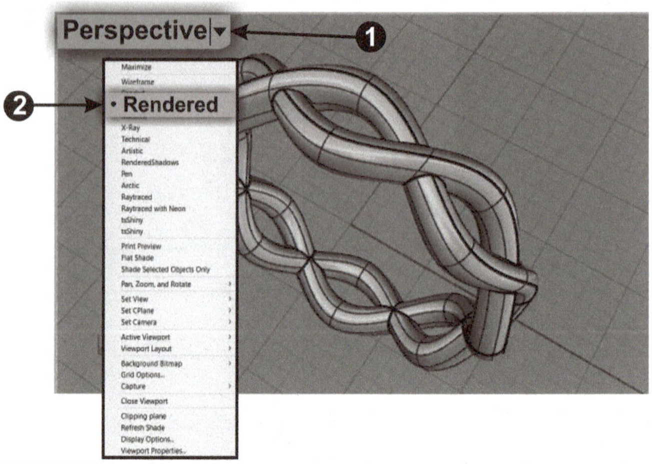

- Open up the Woven Band ring model from the end of the chapter, **Sculpting Simple Rings.**

- Click ❶ to access the viewport dropdown.
- Change to **Rendered** display mode. ❷

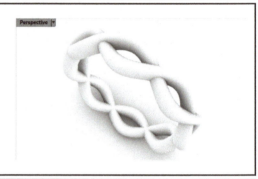

Fig. 1

- The viewport will display in the default Render Mode.

Fig. 2

- **RIGHT CLICK** on one of the tabs on the panel at the right of the workspace. ❶

- Click on the **Rendering** option in the resulting drop down context menu. ❷

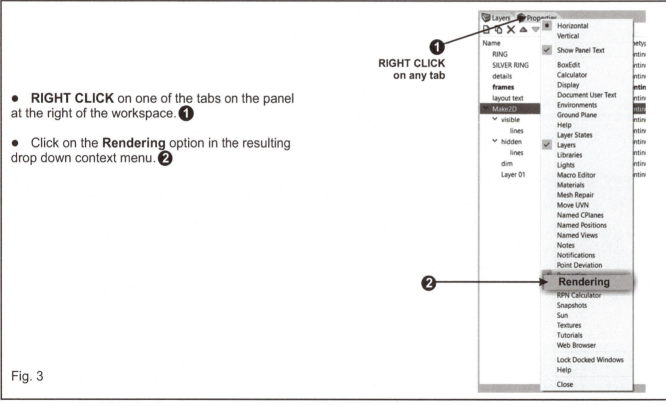

Fig. 3

311

- The top section of the **Rendering** panel will be displayed.

- Click on the **Reset to Defaults** button ❷ at the bottom of the panel as shown.

- In the **Backdrop category,** ❸ click on the color swatch ❹ in the **Solid Color** line.❺
  - Select the color **Gray** ❻ in the **Select Color** box and click on the OK button ❼ at the bottom.

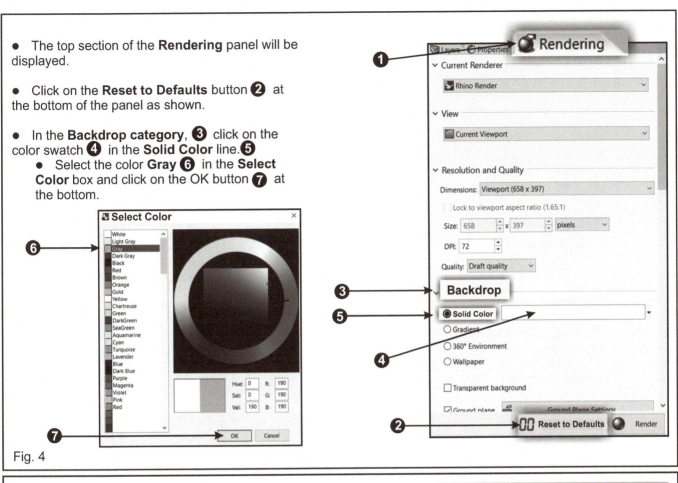

Fig. 4

- The background color will now be Gray.

Fig. 5

- Click to access the viewport's context menu to change to **Raytraced** mode.

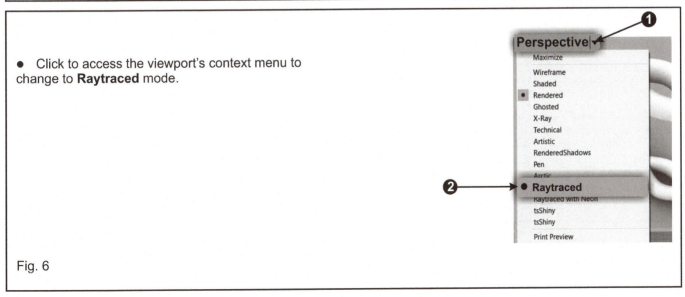

Fig. 6

312

- **Raytraced** is the mode to use for final **Rhino rendering.**

- **Ray tracing traces the path of light as pixels.**
  - For this reason, it cycles through different steps (which you can see at the bottom of the viewport) to get the final resolution.

- This mode gives a beautiful final rendered image but will pixilate during viewport navigation in the process of creating a model.

Fig. 7

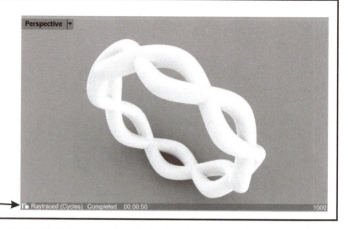

- The **Raytraced with Neon** mode will generate a different type of image.

- This mode and **Rendered** mode are easier to work with when you are inspecting your model during its creation because the images do not pixilate.

Fig. 8

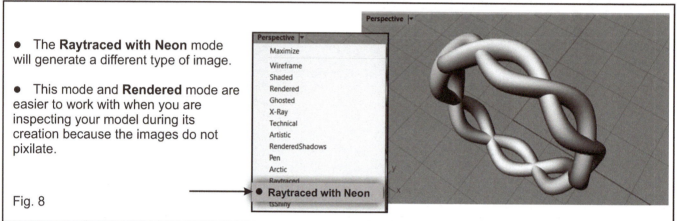

- Change back to **Raytraced** mode.

Fig. 9

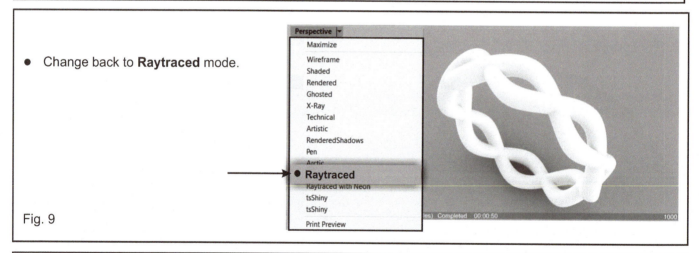

- Click on the faint round circle in the **RING** line of the Layers Panel.
  - Make sure that you are clicking in the **ring line** so that the render materials will be applied to the ring which is on this layer!

Fig. 10

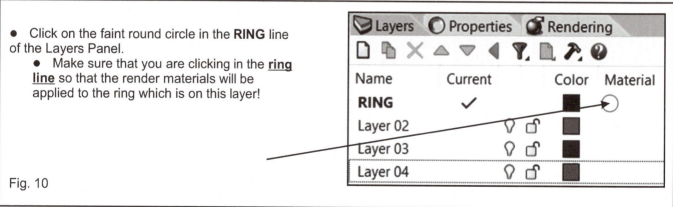

- The **Layer Material** window will open.

Fig. 11

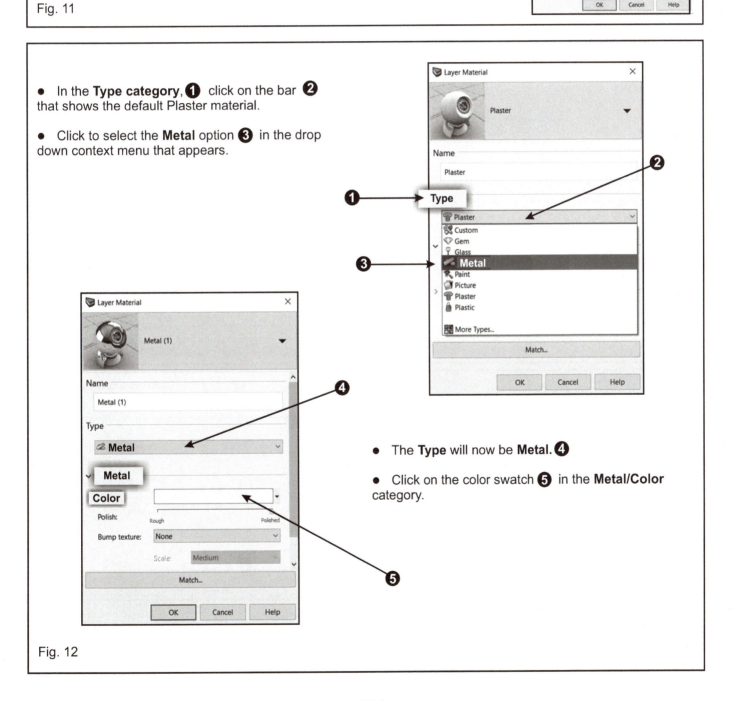

- In the **Type category,** ❶ click on the bar ❷ that shows the default Plaster material.

- Click to select the **Metal** option ❸ in the drop down context menu that appears.

- The **Type** will now be **Metal.** ❹

- Click on the color swatch ❺ in the **Metal/Color** category.

Fig. 12

314

- The colors displayed in the **Select Color** box will be different types of metal.
  - Choose the **Gold** option.
  - Click the OK button at the bottom of the box.

- The Layer Material box will reflect your choice of metal color.

- Click the OK button at the bottom of the box to exit.

Fig. 13

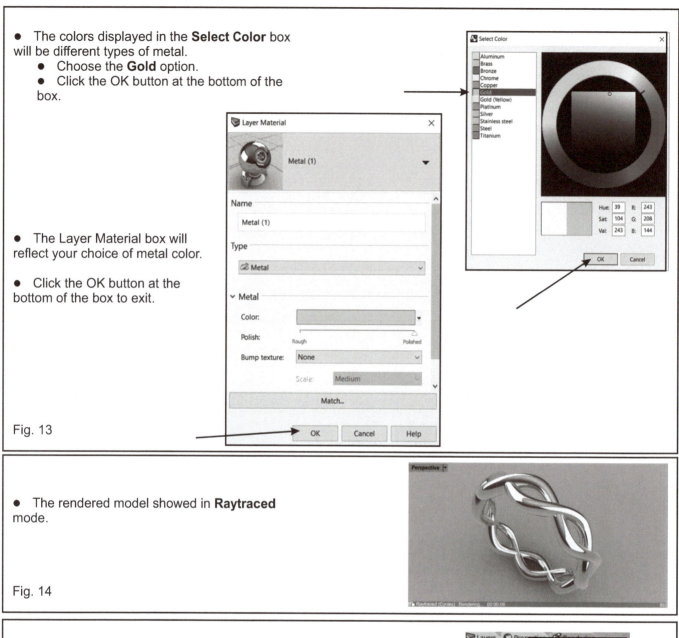

- The rendered model showed in **Raytraced** mode.

Fig. 14

- **RIGHT CLICK** on one of the tabs. ❶

- Click on the **Materials** option in the resulting drop down context menu. ❷

Fig. 15

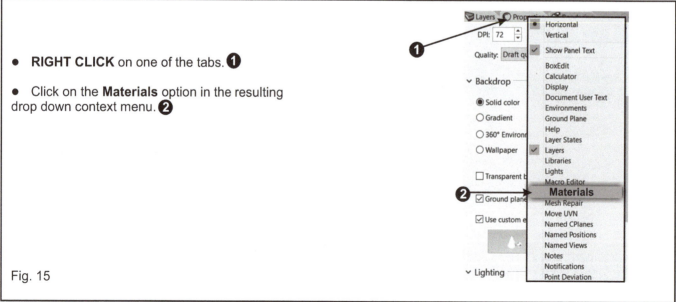

- The **Materials** panel will be displayed.
  - The only material on the list will be the polished gold ❶ that you just created.
  - You can change the name of this material to **polished gold** by slowly clicking two times on the title of the material and typing your own name for it.

- Click on the **plus sign** ❶ to add a new rendering material.
  - Click on the **Metal** option ❷ in the drop down context menu.

- Name the new material **polished silver.**
  - Because the default color is white, it is not necessary to change the color.

Fig. 16

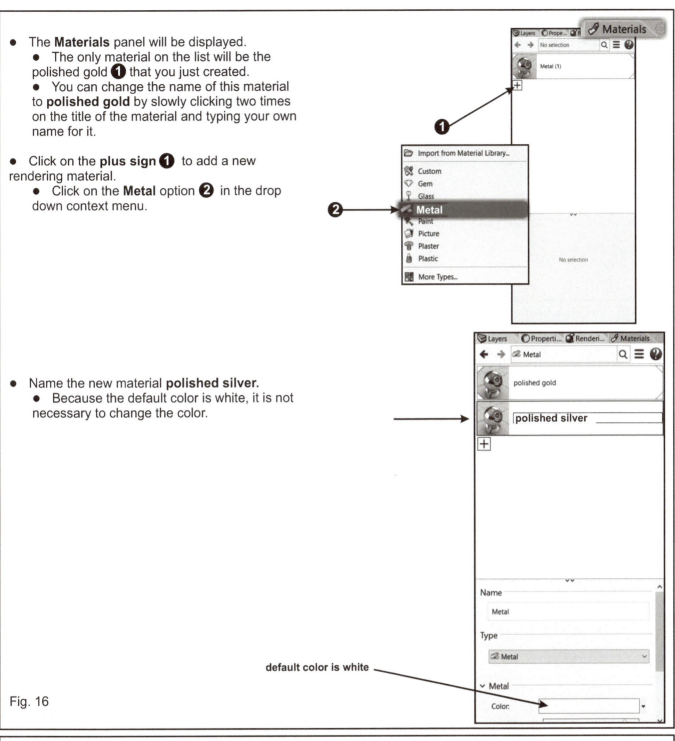

- **Top Viewport.** Top ▼

- Copy the ring model as shown.

new copy

Copy command

Fig. 17

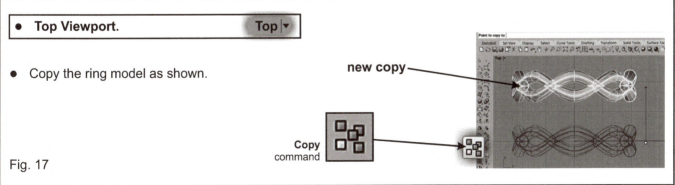

- **Perspective Viewport.**　　Perspective ▾

- **Raytrace viewport mode**

- Click and drag the polished silver material ❶ over to one of the copies of the ring ❷ until the object selects and you see a tooltip that says **"Assign"**.

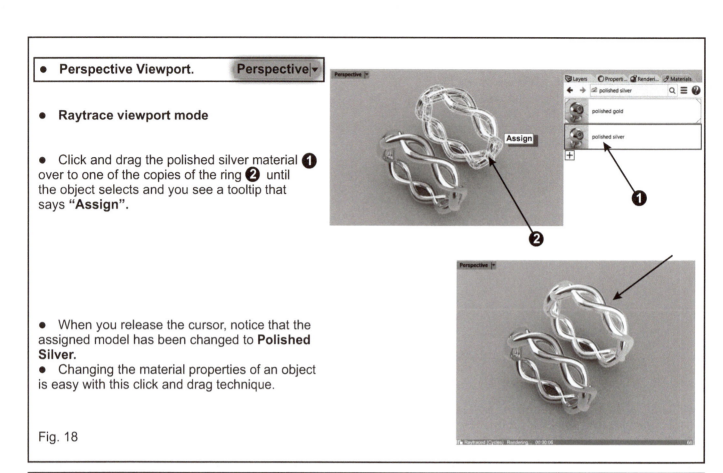

- When you release the cursor, notice that the assigned model has been changed to **Polished Silver.**
- Changing the material properties of an object is easy with this click and drag technique.

Fig. 18

Changing the Ground Plane

- Click on the **Rendering** tab to open the window.

- Scroll down to the **Ground Plane Settings.**
  - Click on the **Ground Plane Settings** button. ❶

- When the **Ground Plane** box opens, click on the **Use a Material** option. ❷

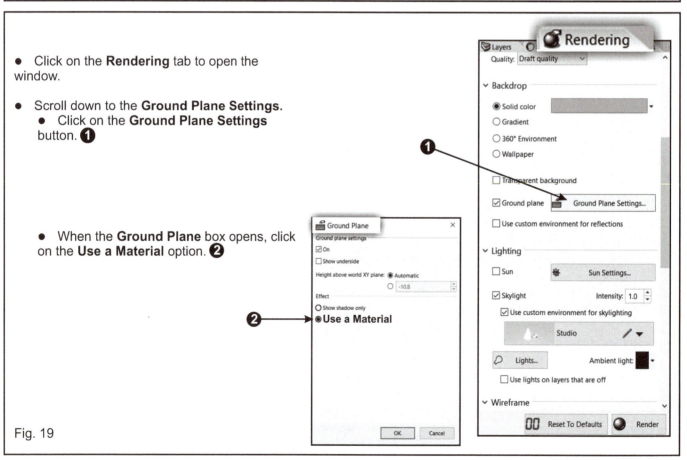

Fig. 19

- Click on the default **Plaster**.
  - Click to select the **Glass** option ❸ in the drop down menu.

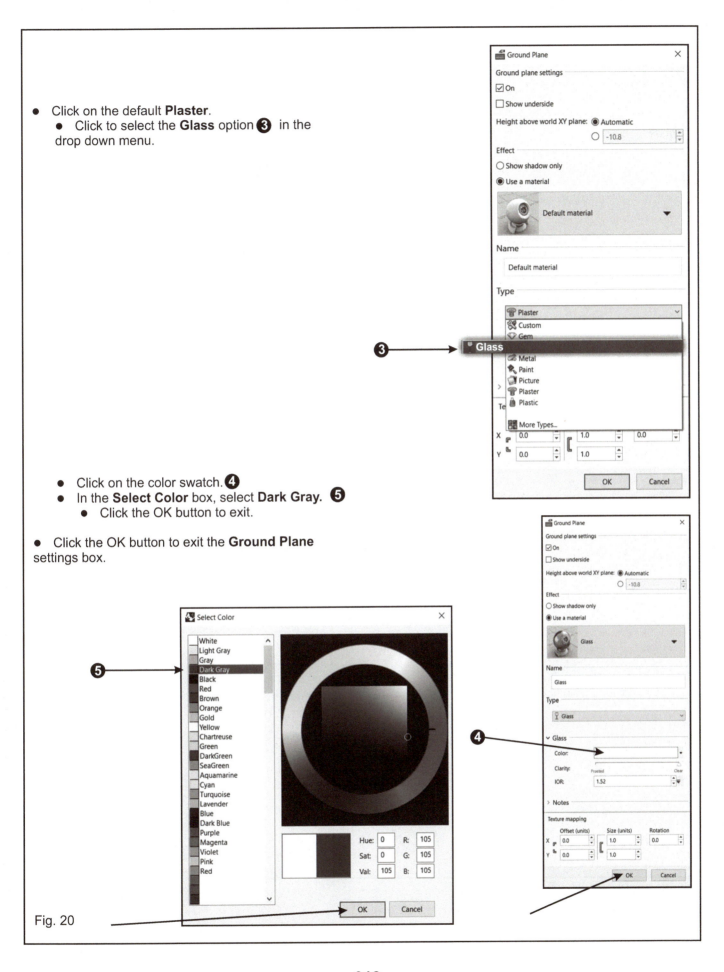

- Click on the color swatch. ❹
- In the **Select Color** box, select **Dark Gray.** ❺
  - Click the OK button to exit.

- Click the OK button to exit the **Ground Plane** settings box.

Fig. 20

318

- The ground plane is now reflecting the two models.

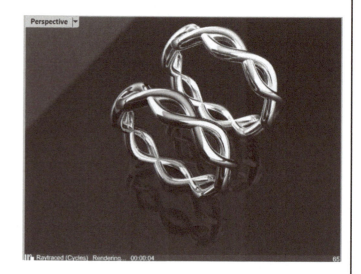

Fig. 21

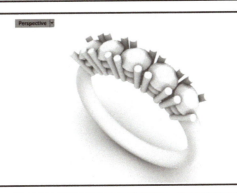

- Open the **ET Band** file (from a later chapter in the book).

- This is displayed in default **Render** mode.

Fig. 22

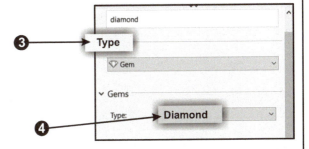

- Apply a polished silver material to the ring shank layer. (Ref: Figs. 15-18)

- Refer to Figs. 4-5 to set the background color.

Fig. 23

- Click on the plus sign ❶ to create an additional material.
    - Select the **Gem** option ❷ in the drop down context menu.

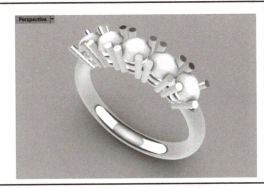

- Scroll down to the **Type category.** ❸
    - Notice that the default is **diamond.** ❹

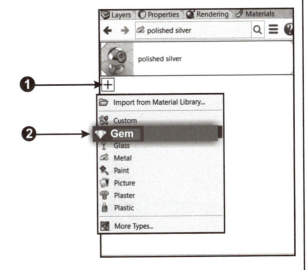

Fig. 24

- **RIGHT CLICK** on the **Diamond** material. ❶
  - Click to select the **Assign to Layers** option ❷ in the drop down context menu.

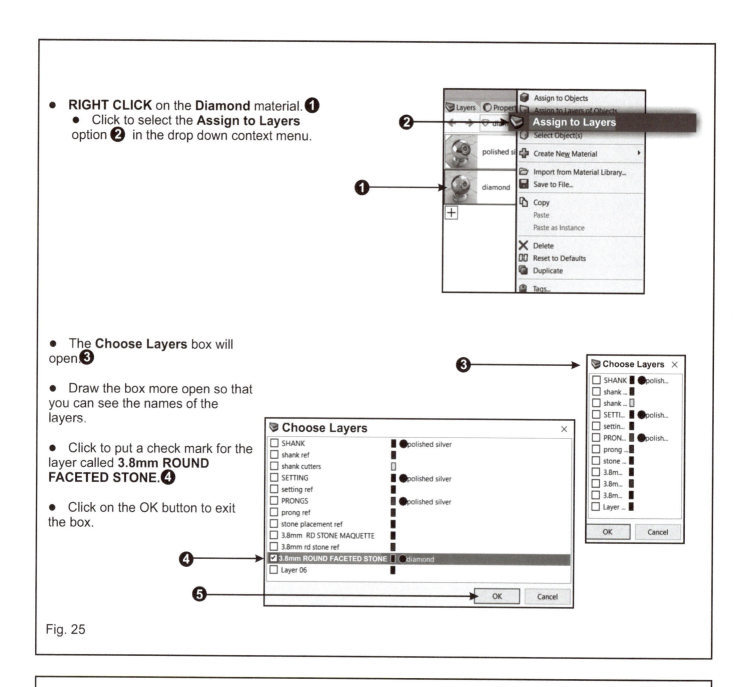

- The **Choose Layers** box will open. ❸

- Draw the box more open so that you can see the names of the layers.

- Click to put a check mark for the layer called **3.8mm ROUND FACETED STONE.** ❹

- Click on the OK button to exit the box.

Fig. 25

- Make sure that you are in the **Raytraced** viewport mode.

- The stones will now have the diamond material assigned to them.

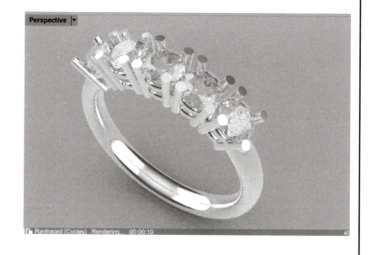

Fig. 26

- Click on the plus sign **1** to create an additional material.
  - Select the **Gem** option **2** in the drop down context menu.

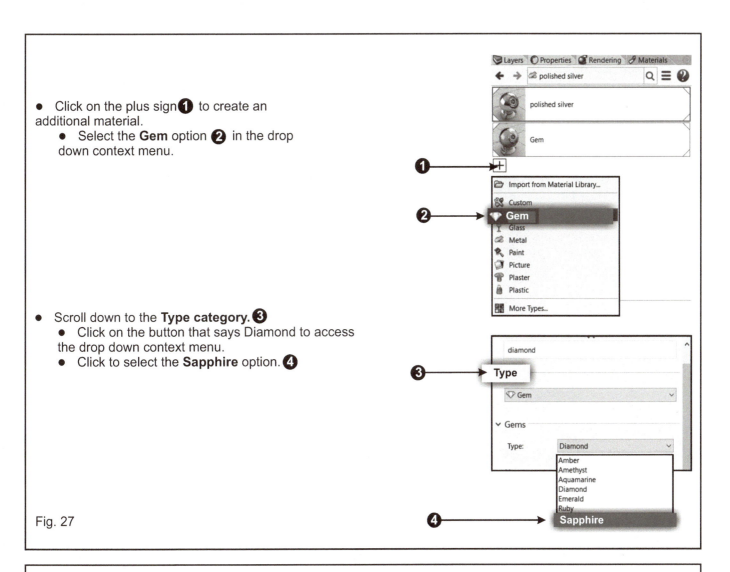

- Scroll down to the **Type category. 3**
  - Click on the button that says Diamond to access the drop down context menu.
  - Click to select the **Sapphire** option. **4**

Fig. 27

- Carefully click and drag the new **Sapphire 1** material over to one of the diamonds **2** releasing when the **Assign** tooltip appears.

- The designated diamond will now be a Sapphire color.

Fig. 28

Custom Materials

- Click on the plus sign **1** to create another material.

Select **Custom** **2** on the drop down context menu.

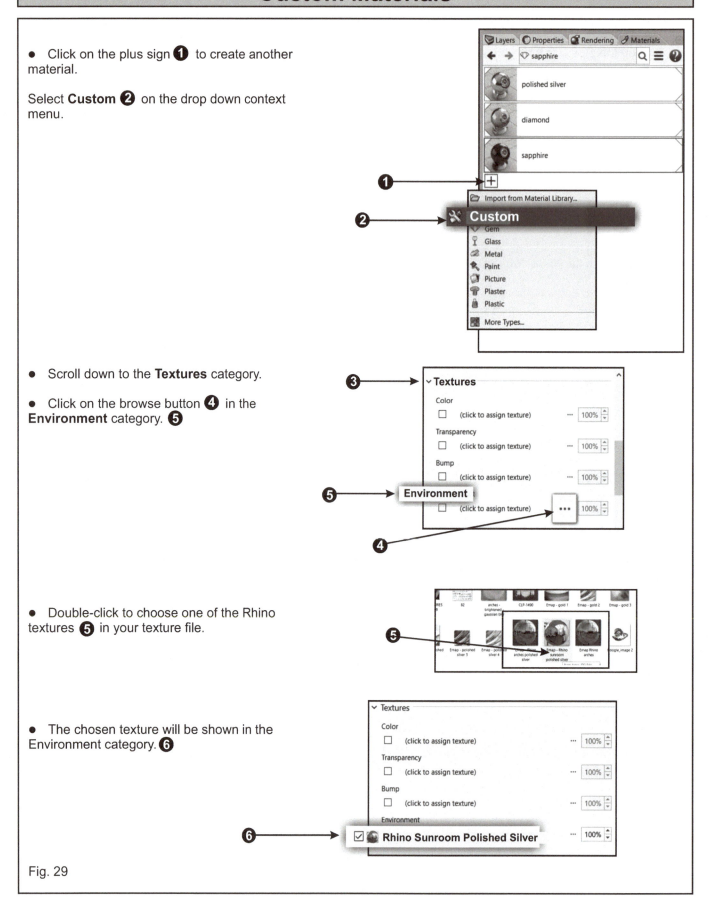

- Scroll down to the **Textures** category.

- Click on the browse button **4** in the **Environment** category. **5**

- Double-click to choose one of the Rhino textures **5** in your texture file.

- The chosen texture will be shown in the Environment category. **6**

Fig. 29

- Assign the new custom material to the layers of the metal elements of the ring.

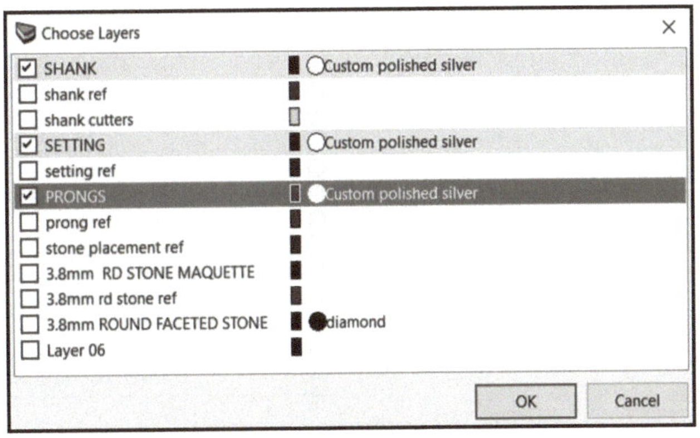

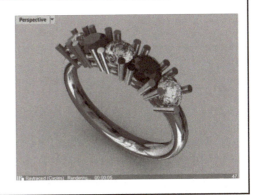

Fig. 30

- The ring now has a new material assigned to the metal elements with a different appearance.

Fig. 31

Custom Gemstones
Diamonds

- Click on the plus sign ❶ to create an additional material.
- Name this layer **custom diamond.**
  - Select the **Custom** option ❷ in the drop down context menu.

- Scroll down to **Custom Settings.** ❸
  - **Gloss finish: 7%** ❹
  - **Transparency: 16%** ❺

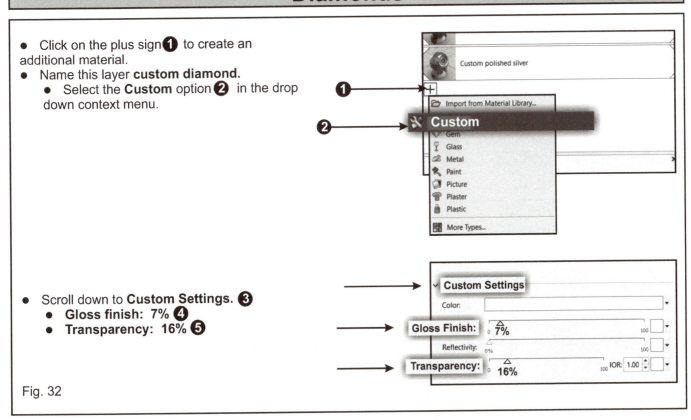

Fig. 32

- Scroll down to the **Textures** category. ❶

- Click on the browse button ❷ in the **Color** category.

- Double-click to choose **Diamond 3** ❸ in your texture file.

- The chosen texture will be shown in the **Color** category. ❺

- Use the same method to assign the same material ❻ to the **Environment** category. ❼

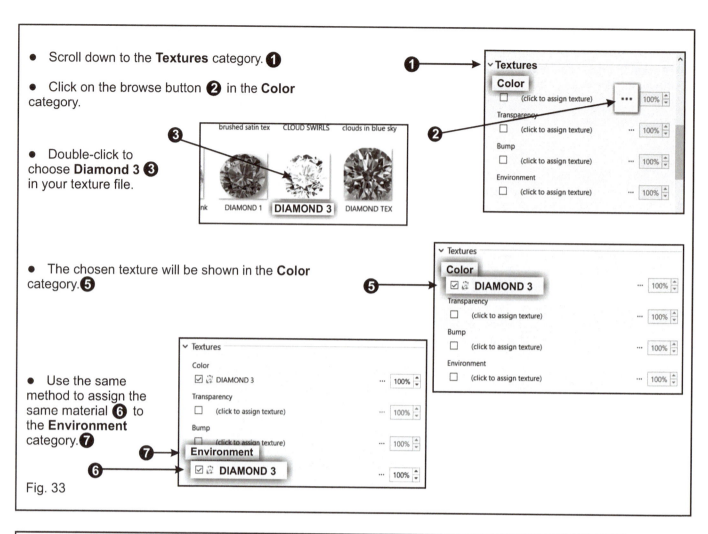

Fig. 33

- **RIGHT-CLICK** on the new **custom diamond** layer. ❶
  - Click to select the **Assign to Layers** option ❷ in the drop down context menu.

- Click to select the **3.8mm ROUND FACETED STONE** layer ❸ in the **Choose Layers** box.
- Click the OK button to exit box.

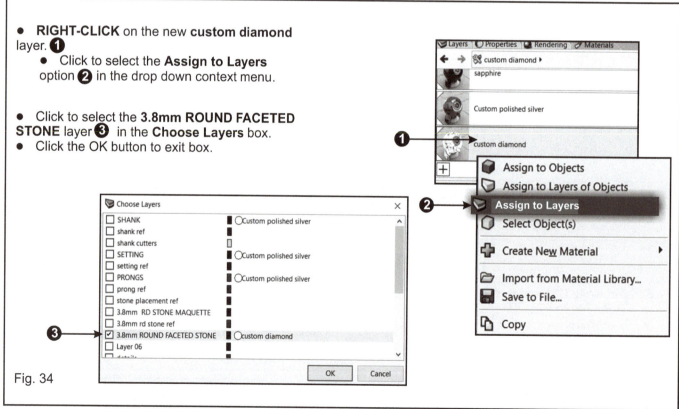

Fig. 34

325

- Click on the plus sign **1** to create an additional material.
- Name this layer **custom sapphire.**
  - Select the **Custom** option **2** in the drop down context menu.

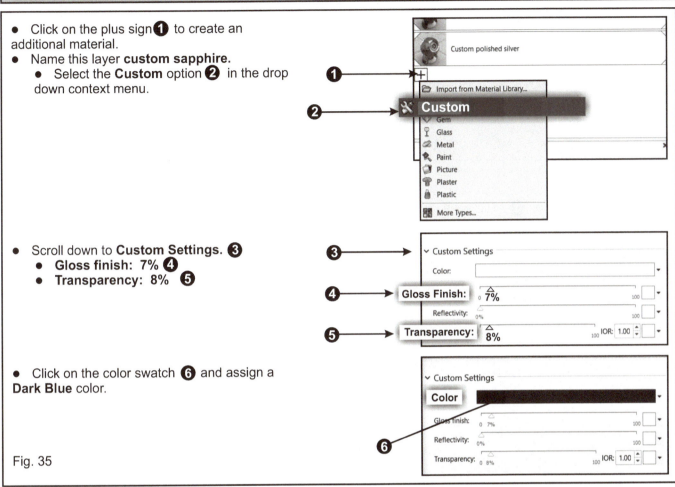

- Scroll down to **Custom Settings. 3**
  - **Gloss finish: 7% 4**
  - **Transparency: 8% 5**

- Click on the color swatch **6** and assign a **Dark Blue** color.

Fig. 35

- **RIGHT-CLICK** on the new **custom sapphire** layer. **1**
  - Click to select the **Assign to Objects** option **2** in the drop down context menu.

- **Select objects. Press Enter when done** prompt:
  - Select the two **sapphires 3** that have been previously colored with the Rhino materials.

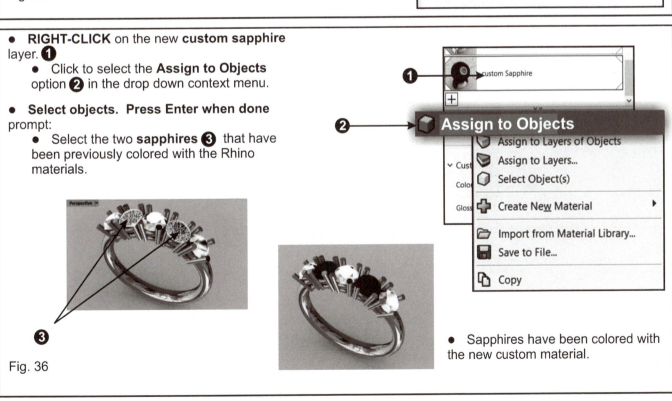

- Sapphires have been colored with the new custom material.

Fig. 36

Rendering Cabochons

- Open the Round Cabochon in Bezel Setting file from a chapter further in the book.

- A polished gold material has already been assigned to the bezel.

Fig. 37

- Click on the plus sign ❶ to create a new material.

- Click to choose the **Paint** option ❷ in the drop down context menu.

- Click on the color swatch ❸ in the **Paint/Color** category.
  - Choose a color in the **Select Color** box.❹
  - Click OK button to exit. ❺
- Notice that you can also adjust the glossiness in the line ❻ below the color line.

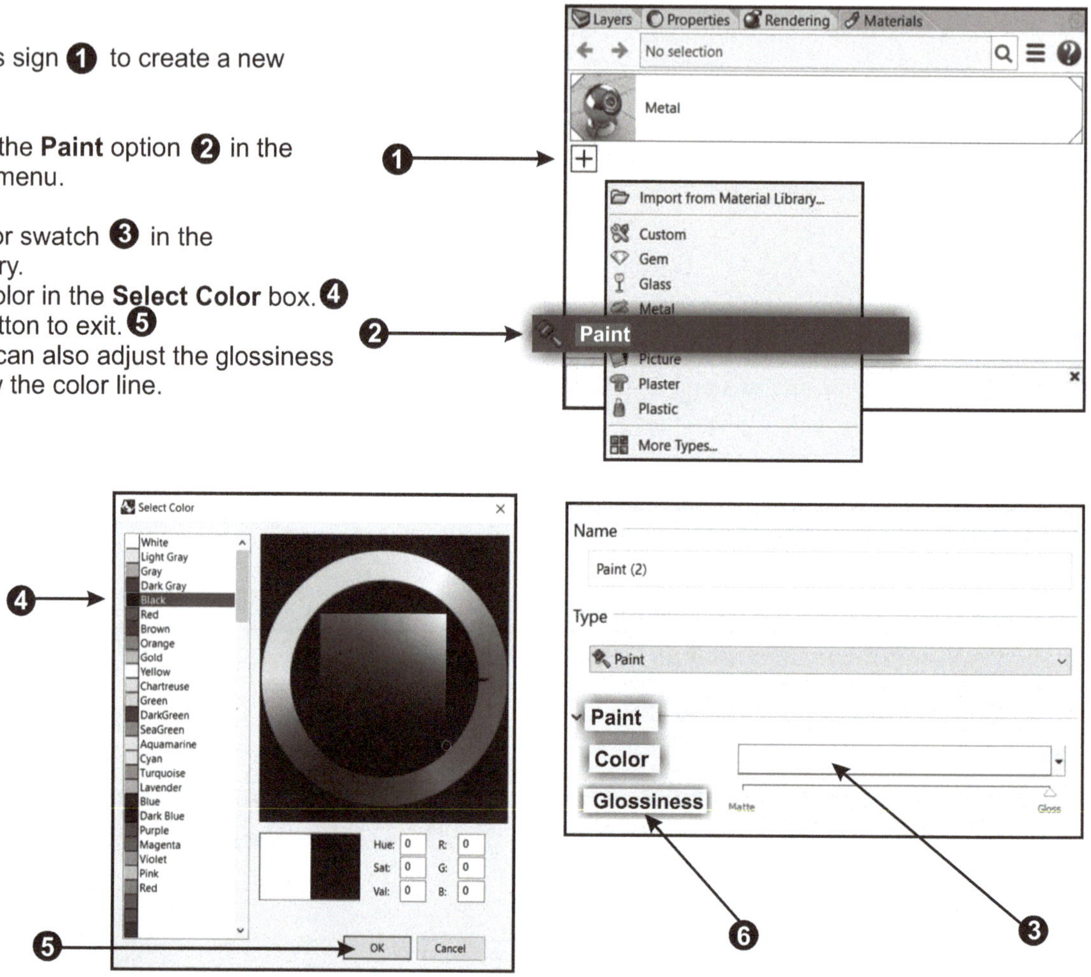

Fig. 38

- Click and drag the new material over to the cabochon to assign.

- The cabochon with have color and gloss.

Fig. 39

Display - Layout Command
A print layout viewport of a project

- Open this file from the previous chapter: **ET bandz.3dm.**

- Both the model and the generated technical drawing from the previous chapter will be shown in the layout sheet (or "print layout viewport") that will be created in this chapter.

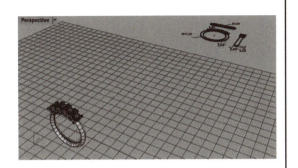

Fig. 1

Starting the Layout - Unit Settings
Making Sure that the Model and the Layout are using the same Unit of Measurement

- Click on the **Tools** category in the **Menu Bar** at the top of the workspace. ❶

- Click on **Options** in the drop-down context menu. ❷

- The **Rhino Options** box will open.

- Click to open up the **Units** category.❶
   - Notice that the units are set to millimeters.

- Now, click to access the **Model**❷ and then the **Layout** ❸ pages.

- *Both of these pages need to display the same unit settings.*

- Click on the **OK button** to exit the Rhino Options box.

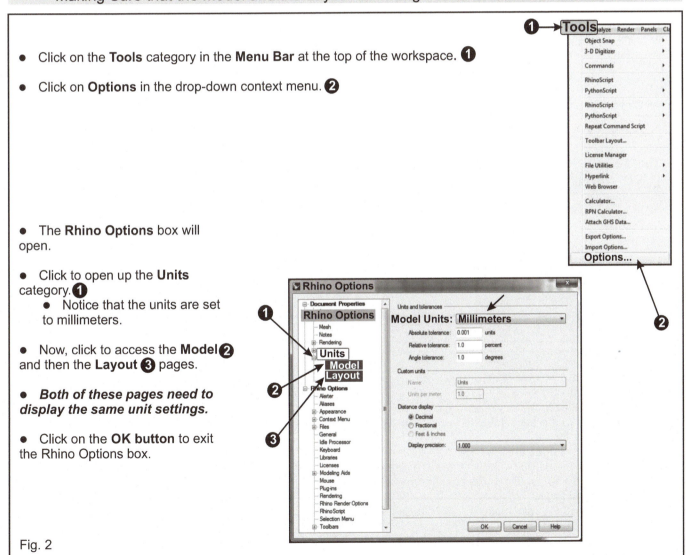

Fig. 2

- Check to make sure that the **Viewport Tabs** are showing below the viewports.

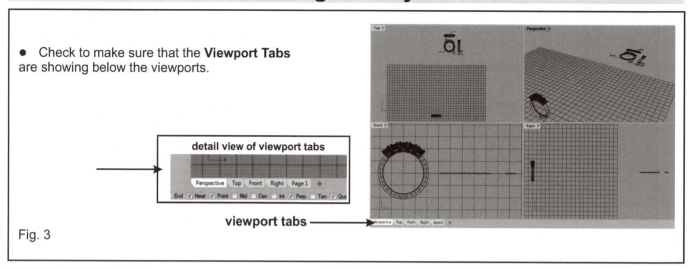

detail view of viewport tabs

viewport tabs

Fig. 3

- If the **Viewport Tabs** are not showing:

  - **Viewport Layout tabbed toolbar.** [Viewport Layout]

    - **Right-click** on the **Viewport Tab Controls** button to toggle on the viewport tabs.

RIGHT-CLICK on
Viewport Tab Controls
button

Fig. 4

- **Right-click** on any of the viewport tabs to get a context menu. ❶

- Click on the **New Layout** option. ❷

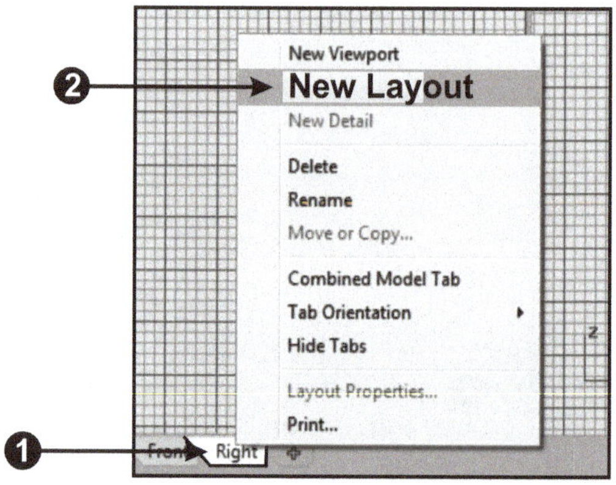

Fig. 5

- The **New Layout** box will open.

  - You can rename the new layout ❶ if you want.
  - **Printer**: use the drop-down to assign the printer of your choice. ❷
  - **Width and Height** are the size of an 8.5 x 11 piece of paper by default - shown here in millimeters.
    - *You can adjust this to the size of paper that you are using.*
  - **Initial Detail Count:** Make this **0**. The detail windows will be added manually. ❸

Fig. 6

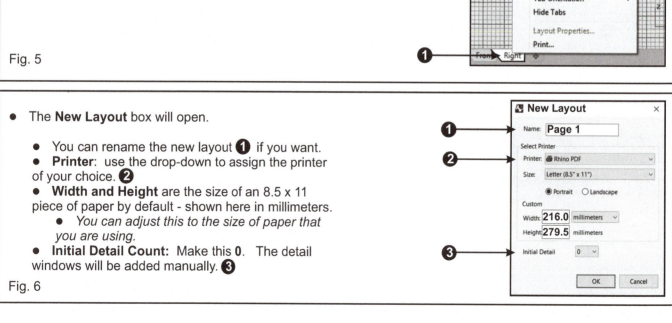

- A new **Layout Viewport** will be created.

- The **Viewport Title** ❶ and the **Viewport Tab** ❷ will show the name you assigned to the layout.

Fig. 7

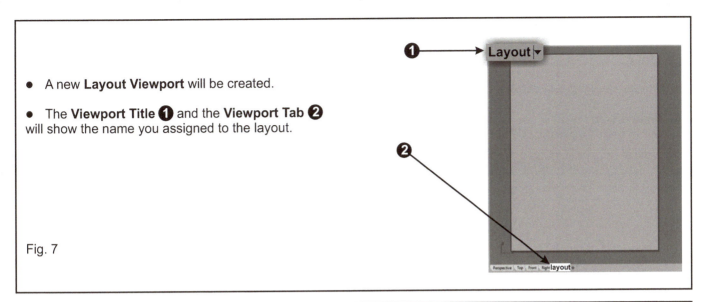

- Access the **Rhino Options** Box.

- Click to open the **Appearance category.** ❶

- Click on **Colors.** ❷
  - Notice that the default color for the layout is light gray.

- Click on the color block and change this color to **white.** ❸

- Click the **OK button** to exit.

change this color
to white

Fig. 8

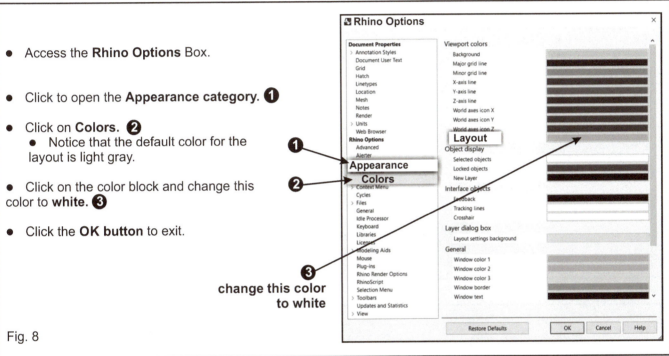

- The Layout will now have a white background.

Fig. 9

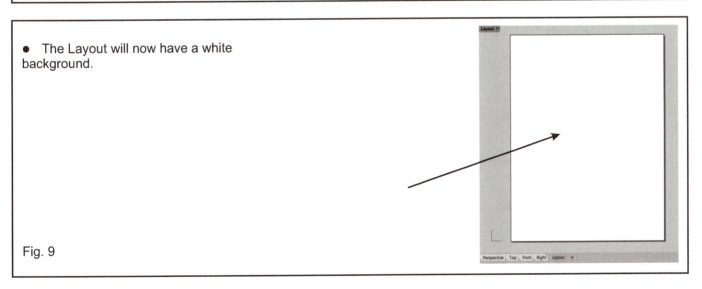

Creating Details - windows on the model

- Create 3 new layers, **details, frames,** and **layout text**.

- **details** layer current.
  - For clarity, assign a different color for the details layer.

details	✓		■
frames		♀ 🔓	■
layout text		♀ 🔓	■

Fig. 10

- **Right-click** on the **Layout tab.** ❶

- Select the **New Detail** command in the context menu.

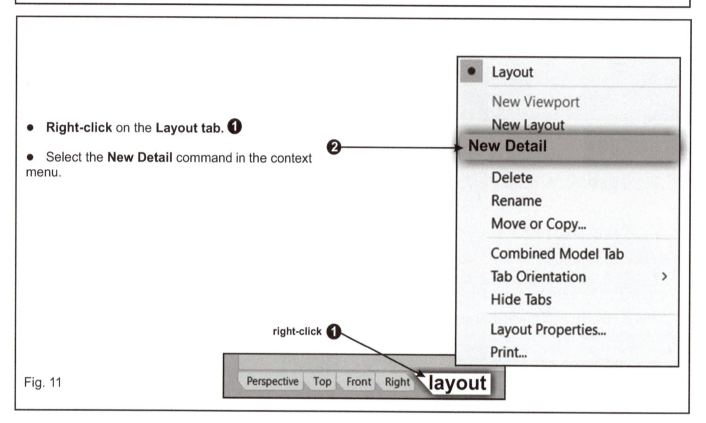

Fig. 11

- **First corner of rectangle** prompt:

  - Click near the top left of the layout sheet.❶

- **Other corner or length** prompt:

  - Draw the cursor down as if you were drawing a corner to corner rectangle. ❷
  - Click to set location.

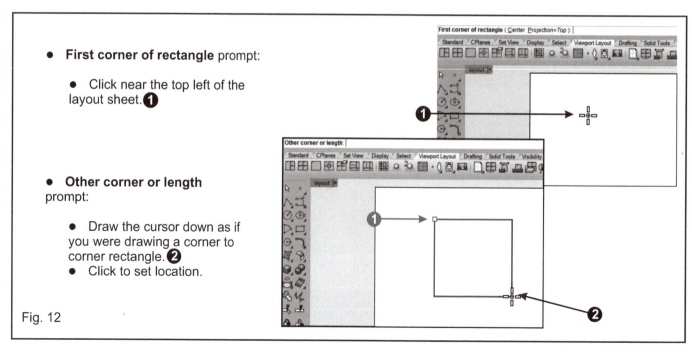

Fig. 12

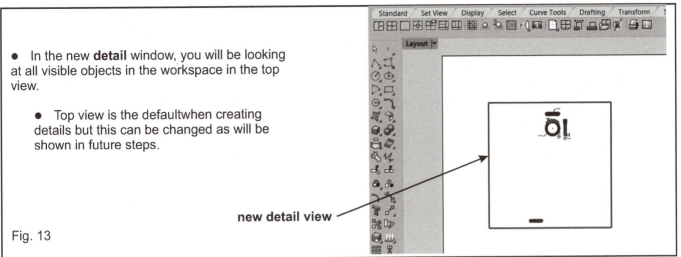

- In the new **detail** window, you will be looking at all visible objects in the workspace in the top view.

  - Top view is the defaultwhen creating details but this can be changed as will be shown in future steps.

← new detail view

Fig. 13

- **Double-click** inside the detail window as shown.

- The **Detail** view will become **"enabled"** or **"active"**.

  - You will see the grid and background color of the construction plane as well as the model and other objects.
  - The detail will display in **Wireframe Viewport mode.**

- When the detail is enabled, note that the viewport title refers to the new detail.

layout - Detail (Top)

double-click
to make detail window active

Fig. 14

Navigating in an Active Detail Window
Navigation is the same as in the regular viewports.

- **Click and Drag with the right mouse button** to pan the viewport and center the technical drawing in the middle of the detail.

- You can also **zoom** the view in an active detail window in the same way that you would zoom in a regular viewport.

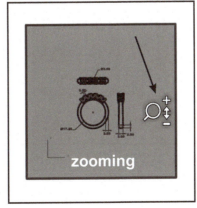

zooming

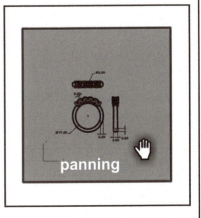

panning

Fig. 15

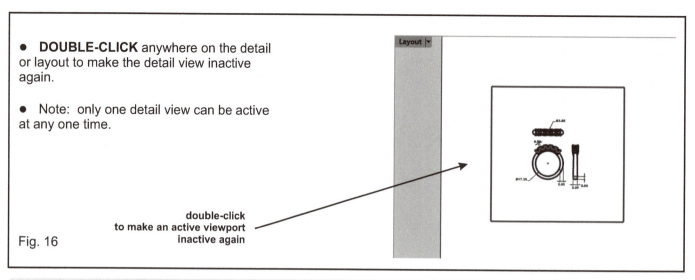

- **DOUBLE-CLICK** anywhere on the detail or layout to make the detail view inactive again.

- Note: only one detail view can be active at any one time.

**double-click
to make an active viewport
inactive again**

Fig. 16

Precision Scaling of the Detail Window

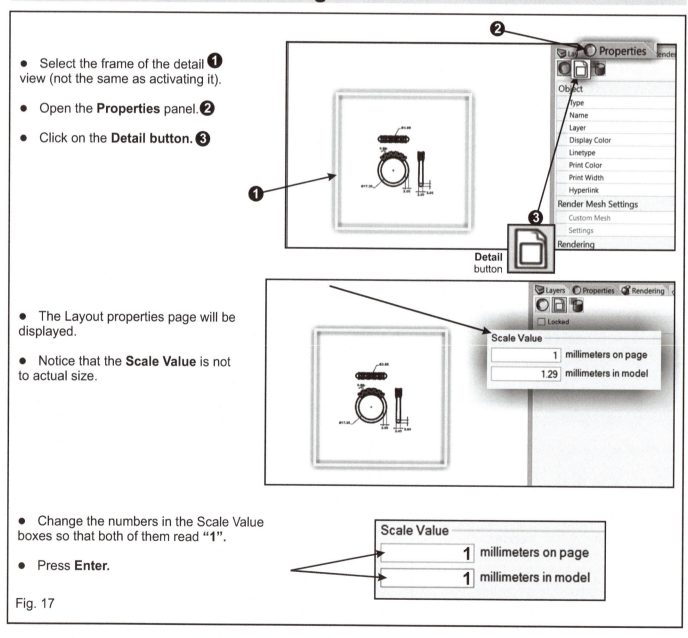

- Select the frame of the detail ❶ view (not the same as activating it).

- Open the **Properties** panel. ❷

- Click on the **Detail button.** ❸

Detail button

- The Layout properties page will be displayed.

- Notice that the **Scale Value** is not to actual size.

- Change the numbers in the Scale Value boxes so that both of them read **"1"**.

- Press **Enter.**

Fig. 17

- The scale of the objects in the selected detail will now be actual size, 1:1.

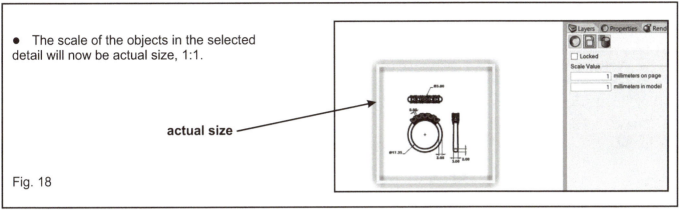

actual size

Fig. 18

- Click and drag the detail window further up into the upper left corner of the layout sheet.

- *note: a detail view must be <u>disabled by double-clicking in it's window</u> or <u>elsewhere on the layout</u> before it can be dragged, copied, or point edited.*

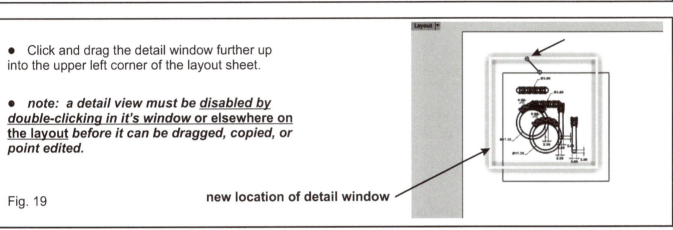

Fig. 19

new location of detail window

Copying the Detail Window

- Drag the detail window down.

- As you are dragging, **lightly tap the Alt key.**

Alt
lightly tap

- **A little plus sign** will appear next to the cursor, **informing you that you are making a copy**.

- Release the cursor to finish the copy.

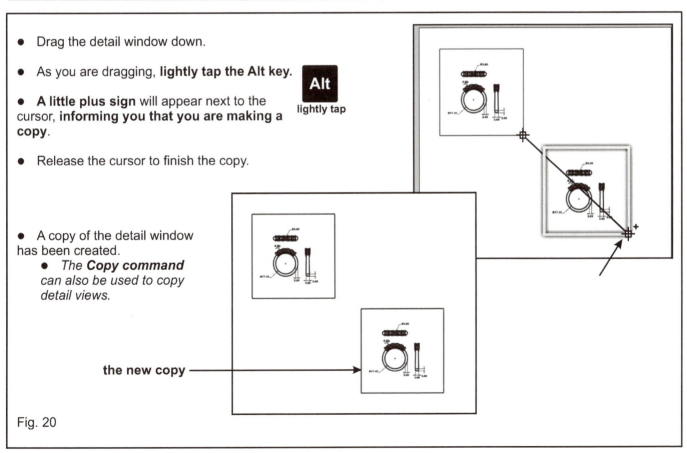

- A copy of the detail window has been created.
  - *The **Copy command** can also be used to copy detail views.*

the new copy

Fig. 20

- Select the new detail window.

- View the **Properties/Layout window.**
  - *Notice that the scale is 1:1 because this is a duplicate of the originally scaled detail window.*

- Change the Scale Value millimeters on page to **1.5.** ❷

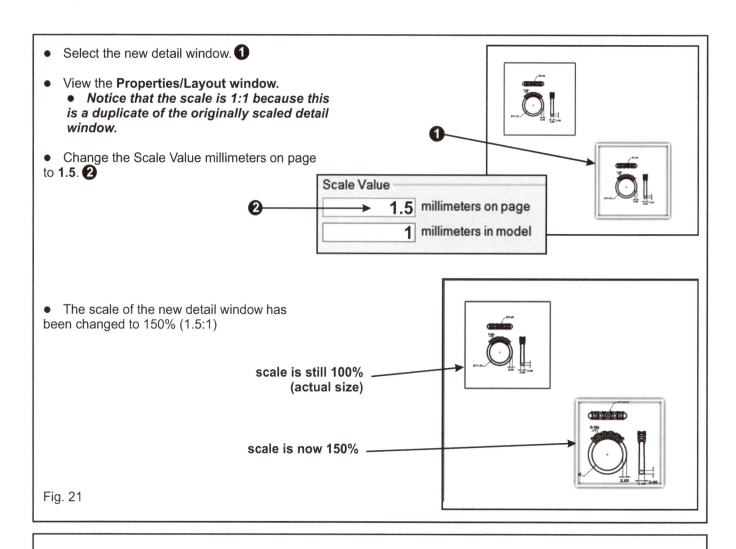

Scale Value	
❷ → **1.5**	millimeters on page
1	millimeters in model

- The scale of the new detail window has been changed to 150% (1.5:1)

scale is still 100%
(actual size)

scale is now 150%

Fig. 21

- Notice that the detail window is now too small to show all of the scaled up technical drawing.

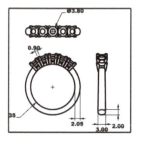

Fig. 22

Point Editing the Size and Shape of the Detail Window

- Click on the frame of the **detail window** to select it.
  - This is not the same as making the detail window enabled.

- **Turn on the detail window's control points.**
  - Press the **F10** key
  - or type **"PointsOn"** and press **Enter**.

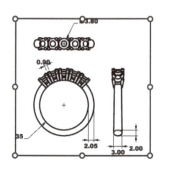

Fig. 23

335

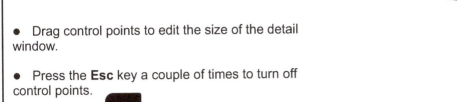

- Drag control points to edit the size of the detail window.

- Press the **Esc** key a couple of times to turn off control points.

Esc

Fig. 24

- Detail windows can be dragged to reposition them on the layout.
  - *Remember: to drag a detail window, it must be de-activated!*

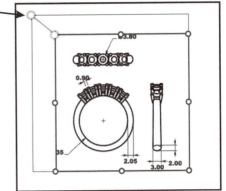

Fig. 25

- **Right-click** on the **Layout tab.** ❶

- Select the **New Detail** command in the context menu. ❷

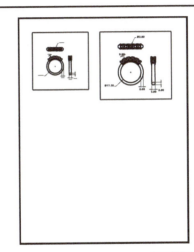

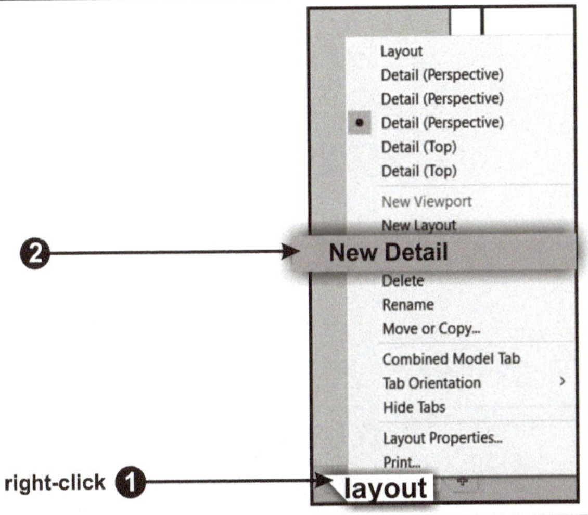

❷ →

right-click ❶

Fig. 26

- The new detail window will be created in **perspective view (projection).**

  - **First corner of rectangle** prompt:
    - Click on the **Projection=*Top*** option in the **Command Line.** ❶

First corner of rectangle (Center **Projection=*Top***

❶

  - **Projection** prompt:
    - Click on the **Perspective** option. ❷

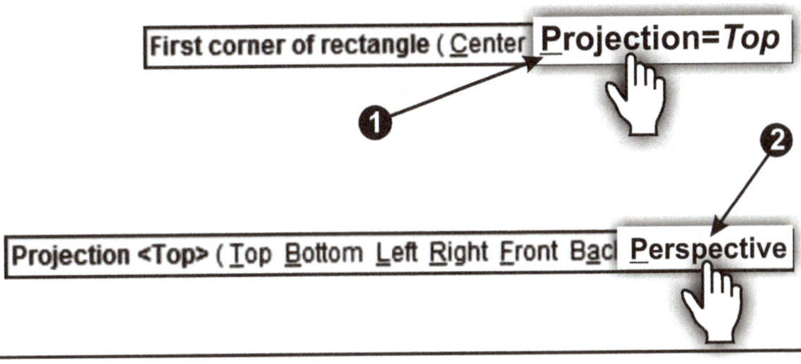

❷

Projection <Top> (Top Bottom Left Right Front Bac **Perspective**

Fig. 27

- Draw an outline for the new detail window.

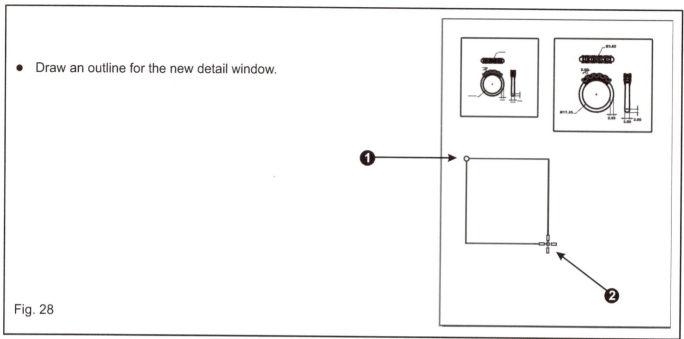

Fig. 28

- The new detail window is in perspective view and shows all objects in the workspace.

- With the new detail window activated, navigate to the desired view.
  - You can **pan, zoom, and rotate the view** in the same way as you would do to navigate in regular perspective viewports.

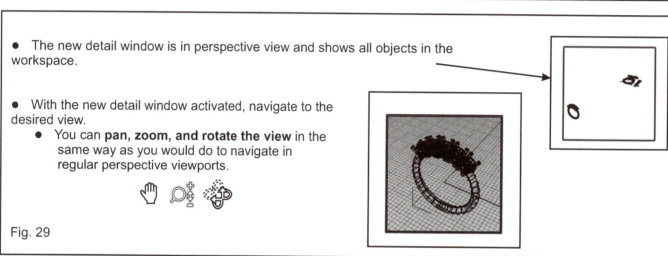

Fig. 29

- Click on the arrow in the viewport title for the drop-down context menu.

- Select the **Raytraced** option to change to Rendered Viewport display mode.

- The detail window is now in **Raytraced Viewport display mode.**

- Remember to turn off the **stone maquette layer** and turn on the **faceted stone layer.**

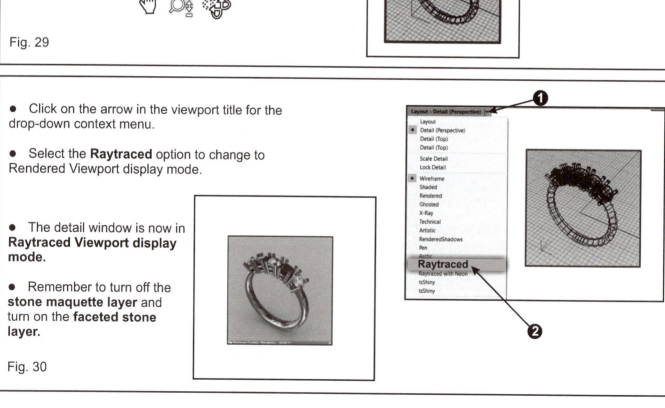

Fig. 30

337

- Double-click make the Detail view inactive.

- **Note: Custom render materials for the gemstones may work better in a layout using Raytraced mode than some of the Rhino presets.**
  - **This is bug that needs to be fixed by the developer.**

- **You can also switch to Rendered viewport mode.**

Fig. 31

- Click to select the **SHANK** layer in the Layers panel.
- Click on the **New Layer button ❶** on the Layers Panel.
  - A new layer ❷ will be created under the selected layer.
  - Name this new layer **GOLD SHANK.**

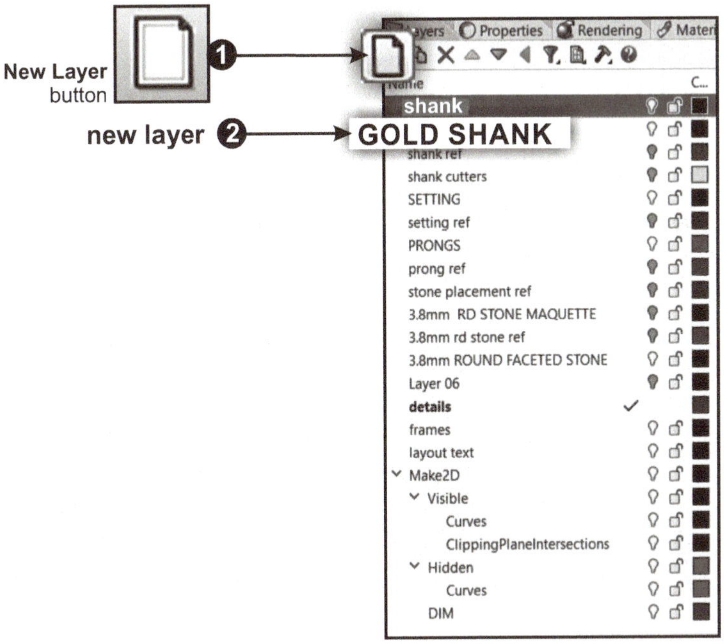

New Layer button ❶

new layer ❷ **GOLD SHANK**

Layers ○ Properties ☑ Rendering ✐ Materi

Name		C...
shank	♀ ♂ ■
GOLD SHANK	♀ ♂ ■
shank ref	♀ ♂ □
shank cutters	♀ ♂ □
SETTING	♀ ♂ ■
setting ref	♀ ♂ ■
PRONGS	♀ ♂ ■
prong ref	♀ ♂ ■
stone placement ref	♀ ♂ ■
3.8mm RD STONE MAQUETTE	♀ ♂ ■
3.8mm rd stone ref	♀ ♂ ■
3.8mm ROUND FACETED STONE	♀ ♂ ■
Layer 06	♀ ♂ ■
details	✓
frames	♀ ♂ ■
layout text	♀ ♂ ■
Make2D	♀ ♂ ■
Visible	♀ ♂ ■
Curves	♀ ♂ ■
ClippingPlaneIntersections	♀ ♂ ■
Hidden	♀ ♂ ■
Curves	♀ ♂ ■
DIM	♀ ♂ ■

Fig. 32

- **Top Viewport.**   Top ▾

- **Copy** the ring and its stones about 20mm to the back.

point to copy to ❷

point to copy from ❶

Copy command

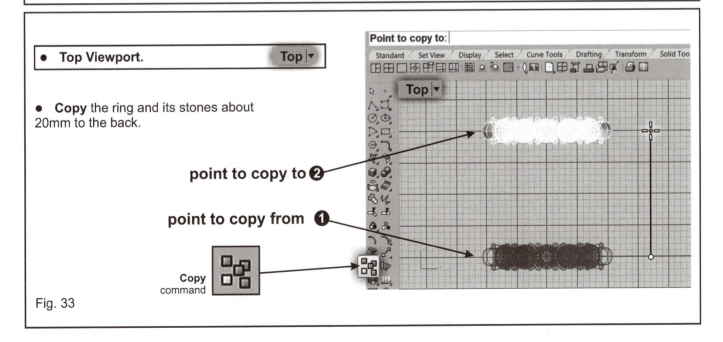

Fig. 33

338

- Change the metal elements of the new copy to the **GOLD SHANK** layer.

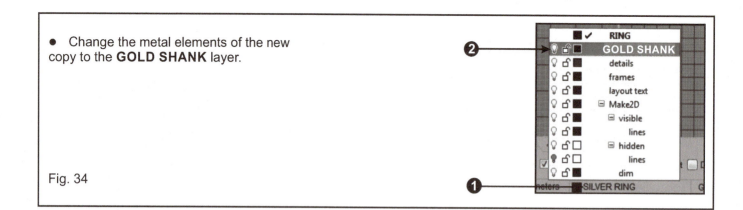

Fig. 34

- In a Rendered viewport, the two rings sit side-by-side in polished gold and polished silver.

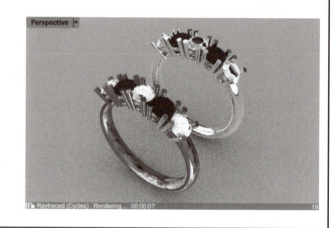

Fig. 35

- **Double-click** to disable the detail window.

- Click and drag the new detail window, making a copy as before.

the new copy

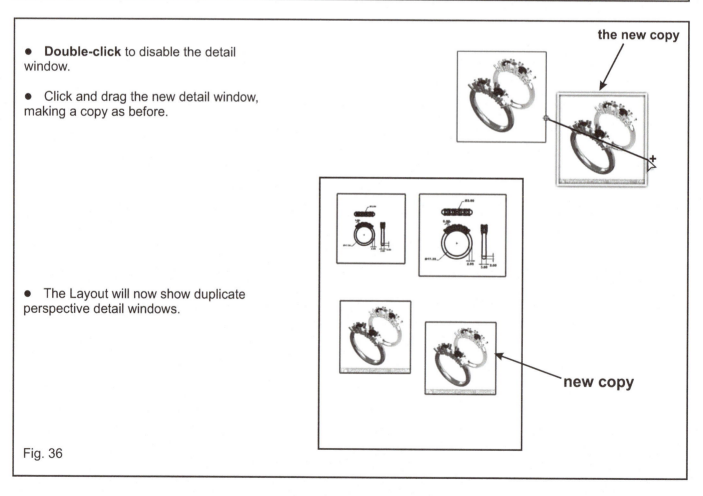

- The Layout will now show duplicate perspective detail windows.

new copy

Fig. 36

Managing Layers in Detail Windows

- In some windows, you might not want to see all elements.

- Managing detail windows allows you to hide unwanted objects just in a designated detail window.

Fig. 37

- Pull **1** the layers pane boundary out to the left until you see **additional columns on the right** that **control layer visibility and other properties for the detail windows. 2**
  - *The columns that control the detail windows are slightly shaded..*
  - *These columns will show only when you are viewing a layout page.*

- You can turn off some of the columns by left-clicking at the heads of the columns to uncheck these options on the drop-down context menu.

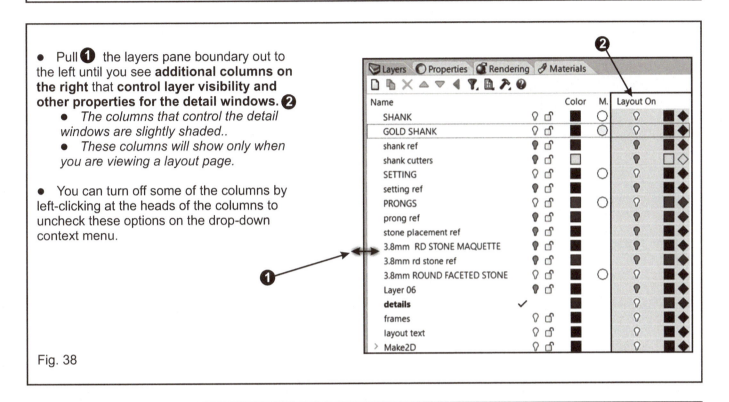

Fig. 38

- If the Detail Layer columns are not showing in the layers panel, click on the **View button** above the layers list. **1**

- Click on the **View all layer settings** option **2** in the drop-down context menu.

- The Detail Layer columns will then be visible.

Fig. 39

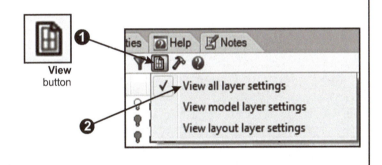

- On the **GOLD SHANK** layer line **1**

- **With the new copy of the detail window from Fig. 36 enabled, click to turn off the GOLD SHANK layer. 2**
  - Make sure that you are clicking in the **Layout On** column.
  - **warning:** If you click to turn off the layer in the regular **GOLD SHANK** column, you will turn off the **GOLD RING** in all detail views!c

Fig. 40

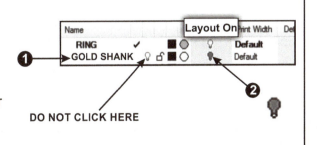

DO NOT CLICK HERE

- The **SILVER RING** is not longer visible in the enabled detail view.

- The stones for the GOLD SHANK will still be visible as their layer was not changed.

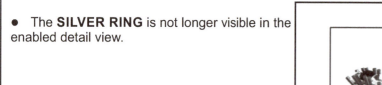

stones still visible

Fig. 41

- Select the remaining stones **1** for the Gold Shank that has been turned off in the detail window.

- Type **HideInDetail** and press **Enter.**

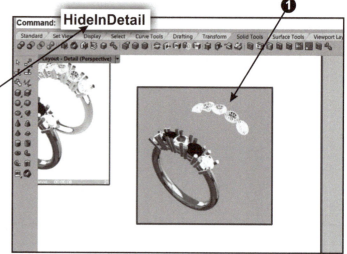

select stones
1

2

stones are now hidden

- The selected stones will now be hidden only in this detail window.

- To see the stones again, type **ShowInDetail** and the stones will once again be visible.

Fig. 42

- Double-click inside or outside the detail view to de-activate it.

detail window de-activated

Fig. 43

- Detail window has been activated again.

- Regular perspective viewport navigation has adjusted the view of the ring.

Fig. 44

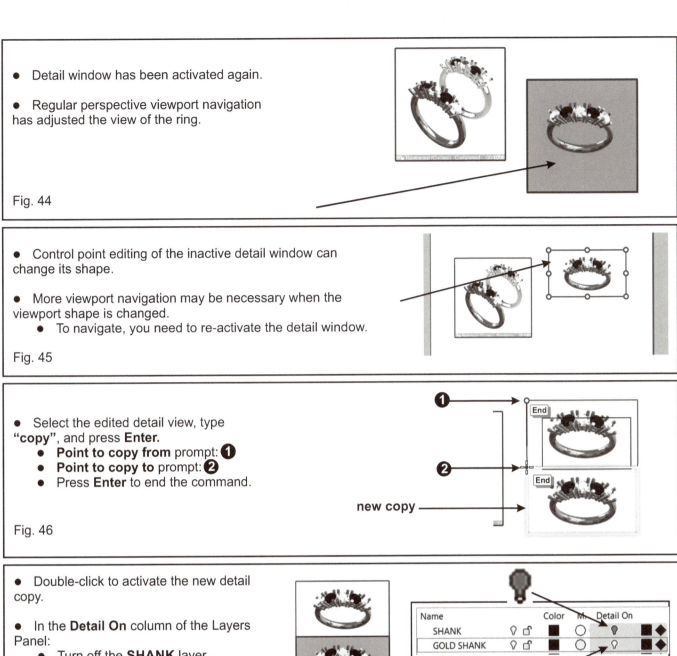

- Control point editing of the inactive detail window can change its shape.

- More viewport navigation may be necessary when the viewport shape is changed.
  - To navigate, you need to re-activate the detail window.

Fig. 45

- Select the edited detail view, type **"copy"**, and press **Enter.**
  - **Point to copy from** prompt: **1**
  - **Point to copy to** prompt: **2**
  - Press **Enter** to end the command.

Fig. 46

new copy

- Double-click to activate the new detail copy.

- In the **Detail On** column of the Layers Panel:
  - Turn off the **SHANK** layer.
  - Turn on the **GOLD SHANK** layer.

Fig. 47

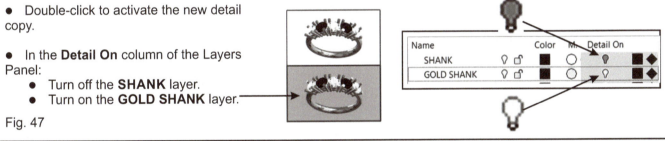

- The new detail view now displays only the **GOLD SHANK**.

- Navigate so that the ring sits in the middle of the detail window.

- If you want to display the stones that were hidden in Fig. 42, activate the detail window, type **ShowInDetail** and press **Enter.**
  - The stones will be visible again.

Fig. 48

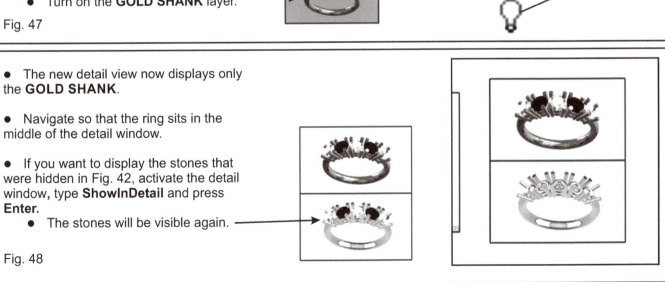

- **frames** layer current.

Fig. 49

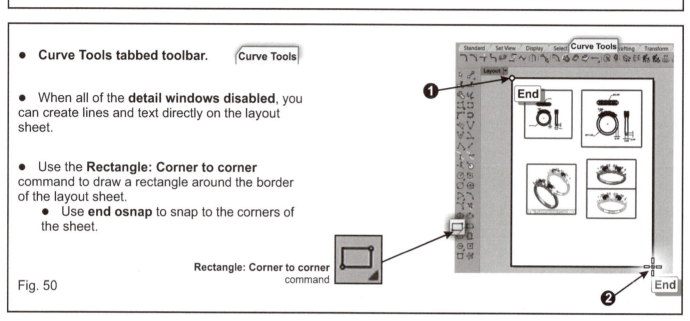

current ——→ | details | 🔆 🔓 ⬛ |
| **frames** | ✓ ⬛ |
| layout text | 🔆 🔓 ⬛ |

- **Curve Tools tabbed toolbar.** ⌐Curve Tools⌐

- When all of the **detail windows disabled**, you can create lines and text directly on the layout sheet.

- Use the **Rectangle: Corner to corner** command to draw a rectangle around the border of the layout sheet.
    - Use **end osnap** to snap to the corners of the sheet.

Rectangle: Corner to corner
command

Fig. 50

- Select the new rectangle and click on the **Offset Curve** command.
    - Offset to the inside of the layout sheet.
    - **Offset distance: 12.7**

- This will create a border that is ½" in from the edge of the layout sheet.

- **Delete** the original rectangle.

Fig. 51

Offset Curve
command

new 12.7mm offset

delete

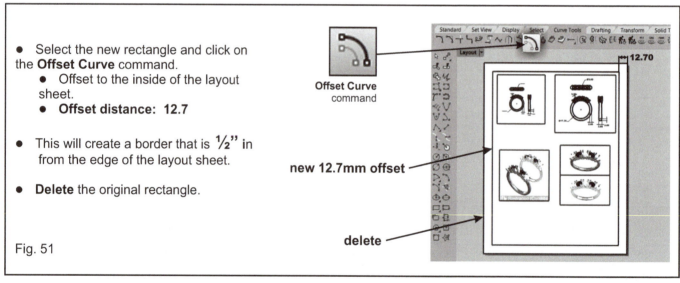

- Use **end osnap** and **near osnap** to create a rectangle at the bottom of the the new offset rectangle.

Rectangle: 3 Points
command

Fig. 52

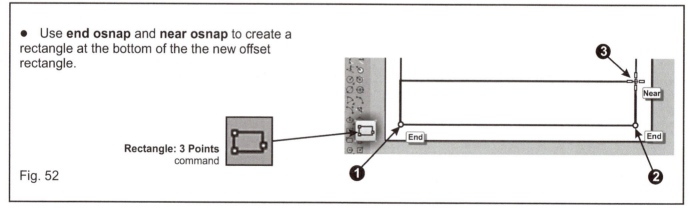

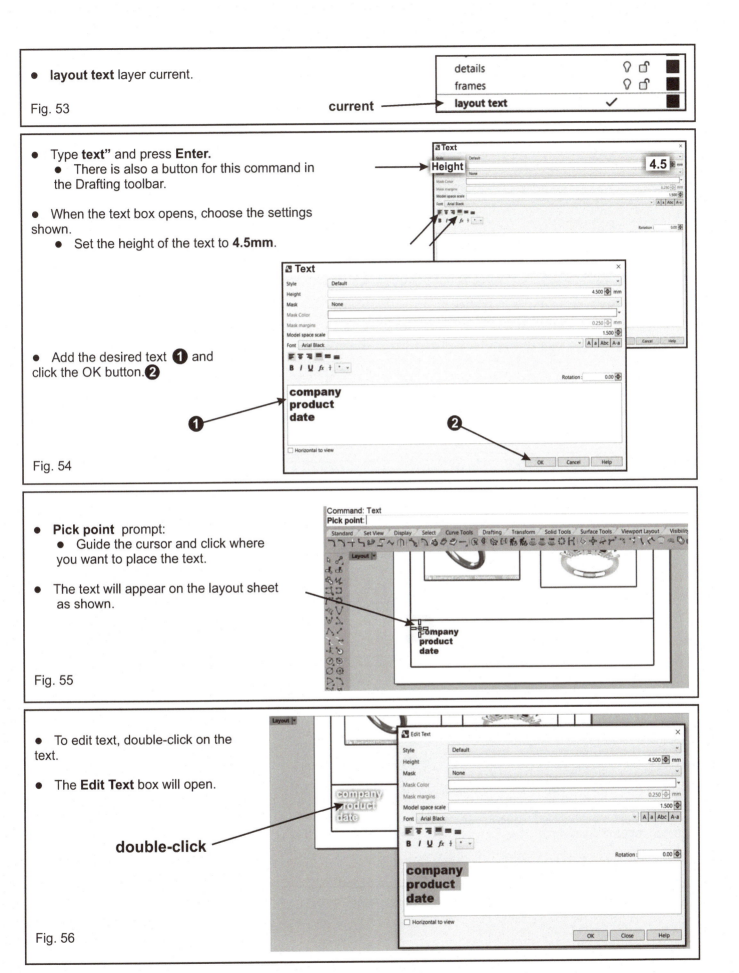

- **layout text** layer current.

Fig. 53

current ——

- Type **text"** and press **Enter.**
  - There is also a button for this command in the Drafting toolbar.

- When the text box opens, choose the settings shown.
  - Set the height of the text to **4.5mm**.

- Add the desired text ❶ and click the OK button. ❷

❶

❷

Fig. 54

- **Pick point** prompt:
  - Guide the cursor and click where you want to place the text.

- The text will appear on the layout sheet as shown.

Fig. 55

- To edit text, double-click on the text.

- The **Edit Text** box will open.

double-click

Fig. 56

344

- Text has been added in this illustration to indicate that one detail window is diaplaying in actual size and the other is scaled up to 150%.

Fig. 57

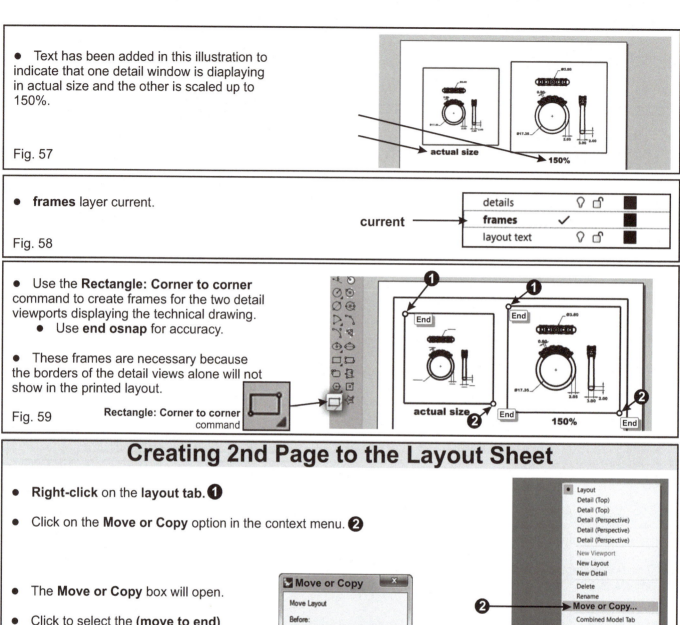

- **frames** layer current.

Fig. 58

current ⟶ details 🔆 🔓 ⬛
frames ✓ ⬛
layout text 🔆 🔓 ⬛

- Use the **Rectangle: Corner to corner** command to create frames for the two detail viewports displaying the technical drawing.
  - Use **end osnap** for accuracy.

- These frames are necessary because the borders of the detail views alone will not show in the printed layout.

Fig. 59

Rectangle: Corner to corner command

Creating 2nd Page to the Layout Sheet

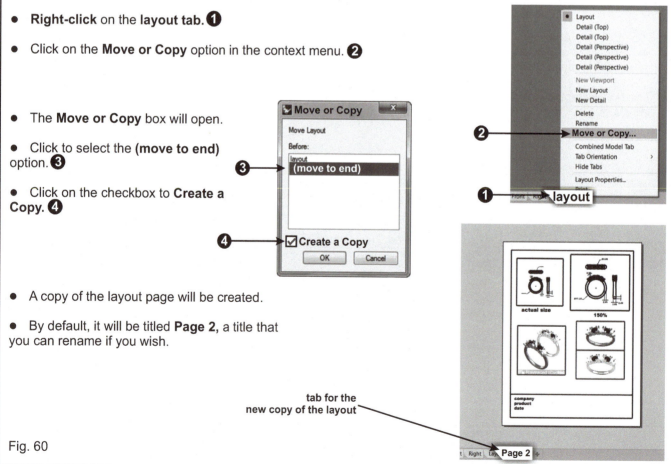

- **Right-click** on the **layout tab.** ❶

- Click on the **Move or Copy** option in the context menu. ❷

- The **Move or Copy** box will open.

- Click to select the **(move to end)** option. ❸

- Click on the checkbox to **Create a Copy.** ❹

- A copy of the layout page will be created.

- By default, it will be titled **Page 2,** a title that you can rename if you wish.

tab for the
new copy of the layout

Fig. 60

- On the new layout page, **Select** and **Delete** ❶ the two larger detail views.

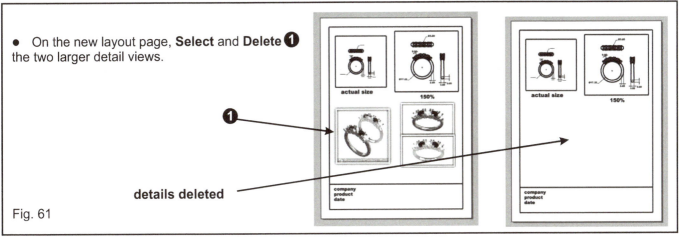

❶

details deleted

Fig. 61

- **details** layer current

Fig. 62

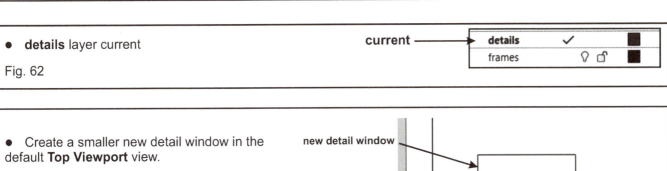

current ⟶ details ✓ ■
frames ♀ 🔓 ■

- Create a smaller new detail window in the default **Top Viewport** view.

- Scale the detail window to **1:1. (ref. Figs. 18-23)**
    - Edit the size/shape of the detail if necessary.

- **Rendered or Raytrace Viewport Mode.**

- Activate the detail and turn off the **GOLD SHANK** layer in the **Layout On** column of the Layers Panel.

Fig. 63

new detail window

Name			Color	M.	Layout On		
SHANK	♀	🔓	■	○	♀	■	◆
GOLD SHANK	♀	🔓	■	○	♀	■	◆

- Use the **HideInDetail** command to hide the stones on the gold ring image.

- Navigate the silver ring to the center of the detail window.
    - Make sure that the scale stays at 1:1.

- You can point edit the shape of the new detail window after you de-activate it.

top view of ring

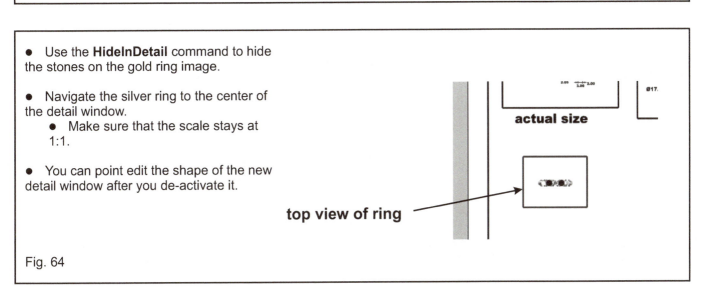

actual size

Fig. 64

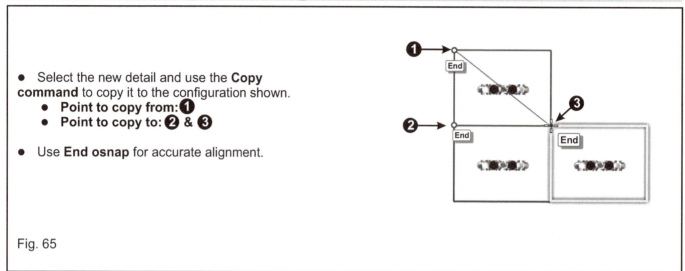

- Select the new detail and use the **Copy command** to copy it to the configuration shown.
  - **Point to copy from: ❶**
  - **Point to copy to: ❷ & ❸**

- Use **End osnap** for accurate alignment.

Fig. 65

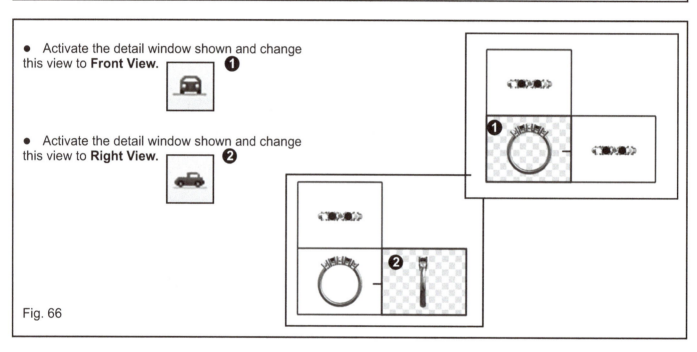

- Activate the detail window shown and change this view to **Front View.** ❶

- Activate the detail window shown and change this view to **Right View.** ❷

Fig. 66

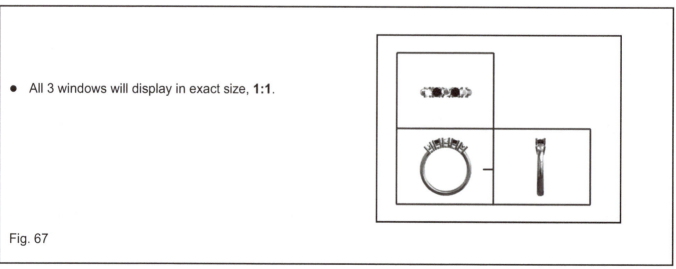

- All 3 windows will display in exact size, **1:1**.

Fig. 67

- Select the 3 new detail windows and **copy** to the other side of the layout.

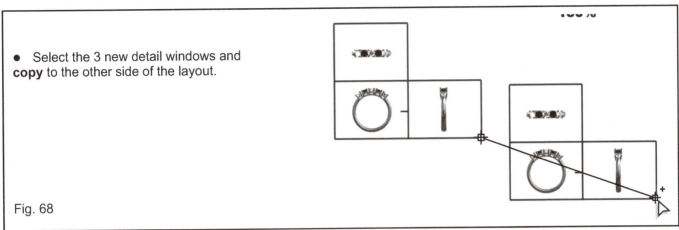

Fig. 68

- Double-click to activate the new copied top view, ❶ click to view the Properties Panel, ❷ and click on the **Detail** button.❸

- **Millimeters on page**❹
  - Type "**1.5**" and press **Enter.**

- **Millimeters in model**
  - This should be 1.

- The detail view will be scaled up 150%.

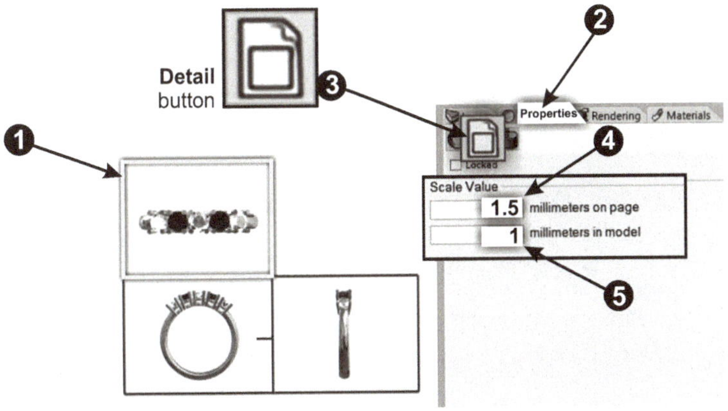

Detail button

Properties | Rendering | Materials

Scale Value
1.5 | millimeters on page
1 | millimeters in model

Fig. 69

- Repeat this command to scale up the front and side views.

- Point edit the scaled up detail windows to make them larger if necessary.

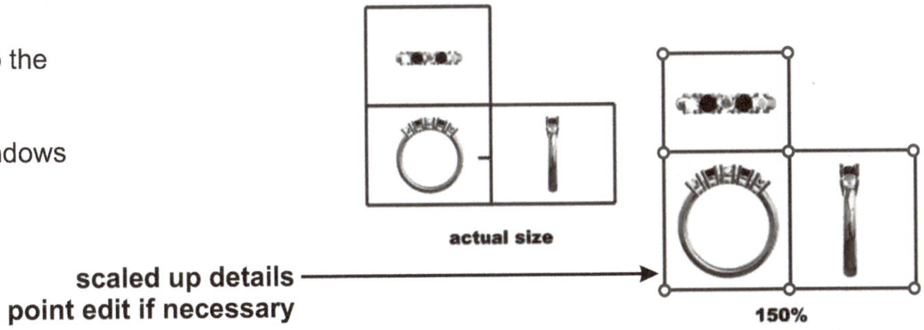

actual size

scaled up details ──
point edit if necessary

150%

Fig. 70

- Draw frames around the new detail views.

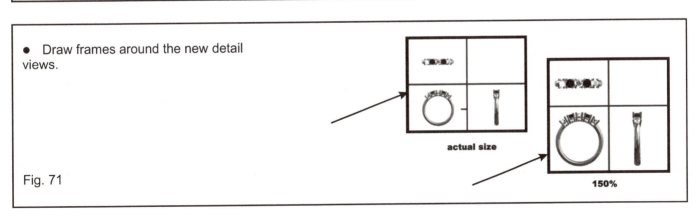

actual size

150%

Fig. 71

- Use the File drop down menu for the **Print** command. The **Ctrl+P** shortcut will work as well.
  - The **Print Setup** box will open.

- For **Destination,** you can specify a printer or a PDF file, as well as varous image files.

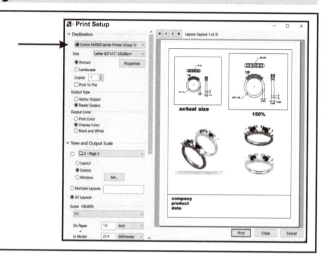

Fig. 72

- **View and Output Scale** category: ❶
  - Make sure that the **All Layouts** option ❷ is selected as there are 2 pages to this layout.
  - Make sure that the scale is set at 100% (1:1) ❸

- Click on the **Print** button. ❹

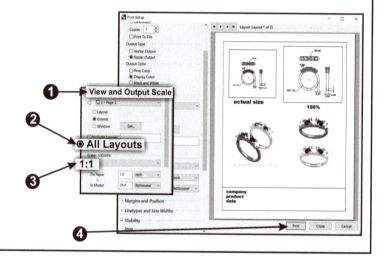

Fig. 73

- The layout will print in exact size, as specified.

- If you are printing to a PDF file or other image format, you will be asked for a file location.

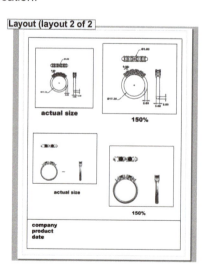

Layout (layout 2 of 2)

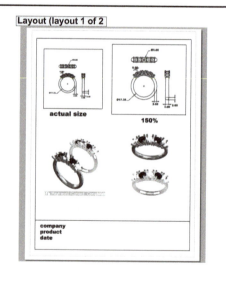

Layout (layout 1 of 2)

Fig. 74

Zebra Surface Analysis
Evaluating Surface Smoothness and Tangency using a Zebra Stripe Map

- Applying a "Stripe Map" to a surface or a polysurface is useful for surface analysis.

- You can check to see if your surface is perfectly smooth and that surfaces are perfectly tangent to each other.

- Open the Rhino file: **double-domed ring.3dm** from the chapter **Sculpting Simple Rings**.

Fig. 1

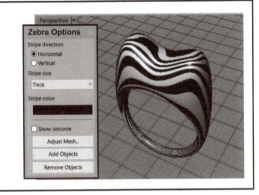

- **Perspective Viewport.** Perspective ▾

- **Analyze tabbed toolbar.** Analyze

- **Shaded** viewport mode.

- Select the ring and click on the **Zebra Analysis** command.

Fig. 2

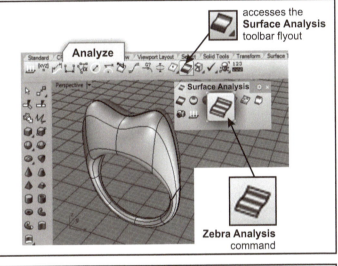

accesses the **Surface Analysis** toolbar flyout

Analyze

Zebra Analysis command

- A striped "map" will be applied to the surface.

- As you turn the ring, the stripes will flow over the surface.

- An **Emap Options** box will also open in the extreme upper left corner of the workspace. You can drag it down for easier access.

- The size and distance of stripes from one another will vary according to the acuteness of the bends in the surface.

Fig. 3

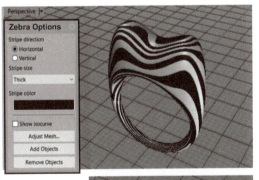

Zebra Options

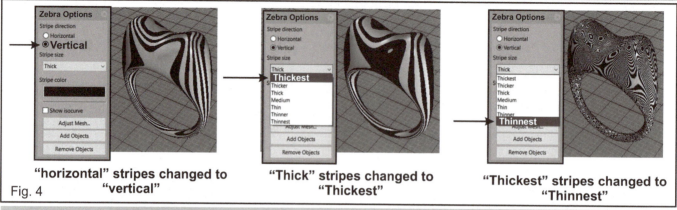

"horizontal" stripes changed to "vertical"

"Thick" stripes changed to "Thickest"

"Thickest" stripes changed to "Thinnest"

Fig. 4

Zebra Analysis for Non Tangent Elements

- **Solid Tools tabbed toolbar.**   [Solid Tools]

- Click on the **Sphere: center, radius** command.
  - Create a sphere with a **20mm diameter.**

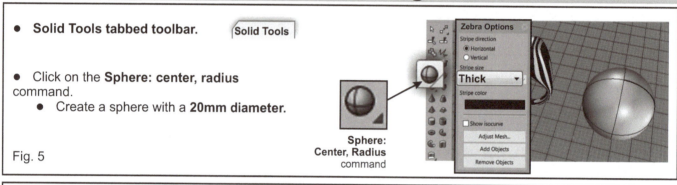

Sphere: Center, Radius command

Fig. 5

- Select the **sphere** and click on the **Add Objects** button in the **Zebra Options** box.
  - The stripe map will now be applied to the sphere.

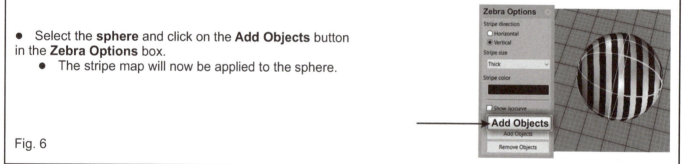

Fig. 6

- Select the **sphere** and press **F10** to turn on its control points. ❶

- Window select the center line of control points as seen from the top. ❷

- Using **ORTHO,** drag the selected control points downward a few millimeters. ❸

- The point editing has created a crease down the shape, breaking up the smoothness of the stripe map.

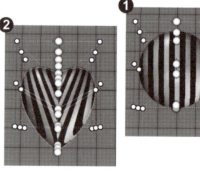

- To exit, **Zebra Analysis**, either **RIGHT-CLICK** on the command button or click to **"X"** out of the **Zebra Options** box.

Fig. 7

Extruded Jewelry Shapes
Extruding Curves and Surfaces
Extruded Ring

- Create the layers shown.

- **ref geo** layer current.

Fig. 1

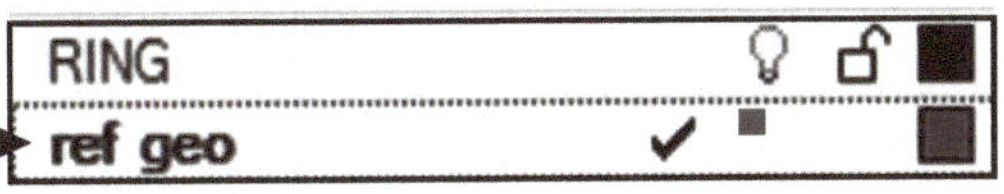

RING   💡 🔓 ■
ref geo   ✓ ■ ■

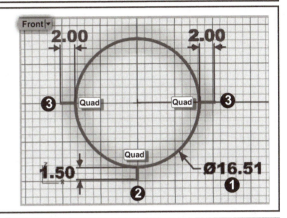

- **Front Viewport.**   Front ▾

- Create a **16.51mm diameter circle** around "0". **1**

- Create a **1.5mm line** vertically down from the bottom **Quad** point of the circle. **2**

- Create a **2mm horizontal line** from each side **Quad** of the circle. **3**

Fig. 2

- Use the **Arc: start, end, point on arc** command to create an arc that touches the ends points of all 3 lines just created.

Arc: start, end, point on arc command

Fig. 3

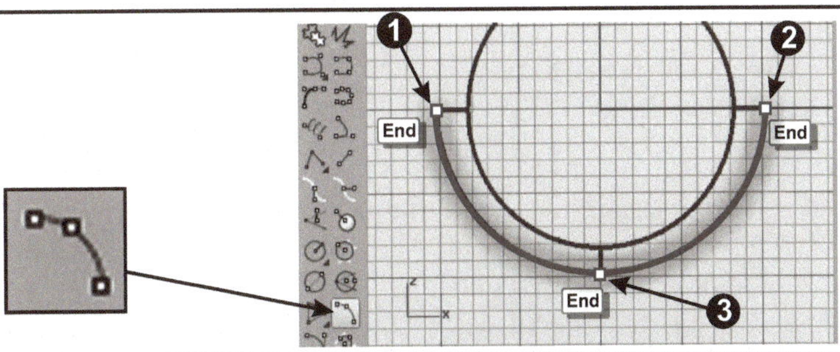

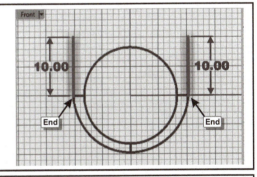

- Create two **10mm vertical lines** up from the end points of the arc as shown.

Fig. 4

- From the **End** point of one line to the **End** point of the other line, draw a curve of your own design.

- In this example, the **Curve: interpolate points** command was used.

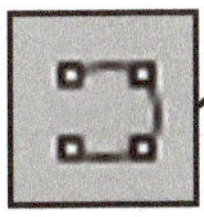

Curve: interpolate points command

Fig. 5

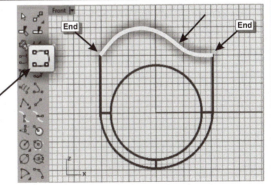

- Use the **Join** command to make a single closed curve of the arc, two straight vertical lines, and the freeform curve at the top.

- Make sure that the **History Line** says that the 4 curves are joined into **one closed curve**.

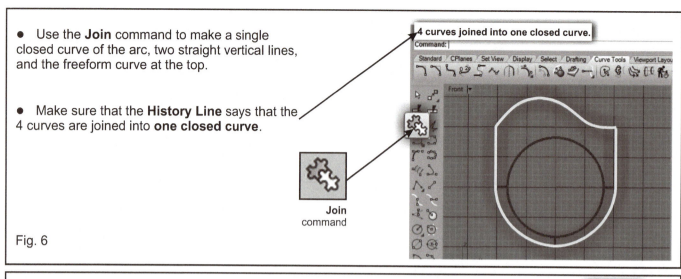

Fig. 6

Join
command

- **Solid Tools tabbed toolbar.** | Solid Tools |

- **Top Perspective view.** ❶ ❷

RING ✓ ▮

- **Turn on Record History.** | Record History |

- Select both inner ❶ and outer ❷ curves and click on the **Extrude closed planar curve** command.

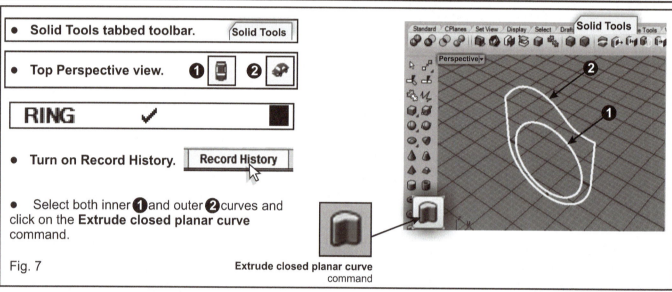

Fig. 7

Extrude closed planar curve
command

- **Extrusion distance** prompt:
  - Click on the **BothSides=No** option in the **Command Line** to toggle it to a **BothSides=Yes** option. ❶
  - Type **"1.5"** in the **Command Line** and press **Enter.** ❷

- A simple flat ring with a thickness of **3mm** has been created.

- This is called an **Extrusion** (or **Simple Light Extrusion.**

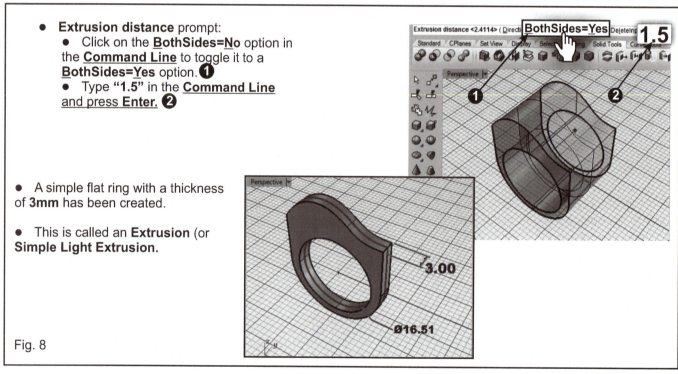

Fig. 8

- **Front Perspective view.** ❶ ❷

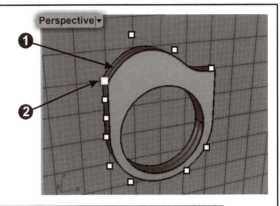

- Select the outer curve ❶ and press the **F10** `F10` hotkey to **turn on Control Points**.

- Select the control point in the corner as shown.❷

- Press the **Delete** key.

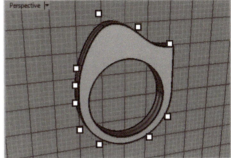

- The silhouette of the ring has been changed because **History** was enabled for the extrusion of the ring.

- Continue to point edit the curves to transform the shape of the ring.

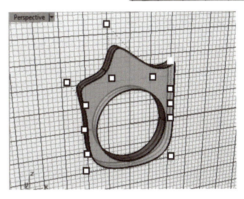

Fig. 9

- See how many shapes you can create with this simple Extrusion strategy and your own designs.

- Save this file as **simple extruded rings.**

Fig. 10

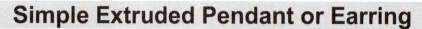

Simple Extruded Pendant or Earring

- Create the layers shown.

- **ref geo** layer current.

Fig. 11

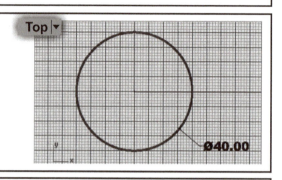

- **Curve Tools tabbed toolbar.** `Curve Tools`

- **Top Viewport.** `Top ▼`

- Create a **40mm diameter circle** around **"0"** as shown.

Fig. 12

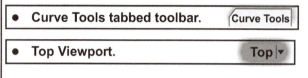

Top ▼

Ø40.00

- Click on the **Ellipse: diameter** command.
  - **Start of first axis** prompt:
    - Click on the lower **Quad** of the circle. **1**

Fig. 13

Ellipse: diameter
command

Quad

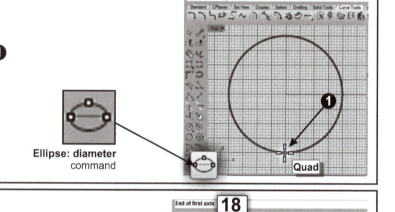

- **End of first axis** prompt:
  - Type **"18"** and press **Enter.**
  - Using **ORTHO,** draw the cursor up and click to set location. **2**
- **End of second axis** prompt:
  - Type **"7"** and press **Enter**
  - Draw the cursor to the side and click to set location. **3**

- The finished ellipse touches the bottom **Quad** of the circle.

Fig. 14

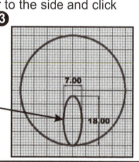

7.00

18.00

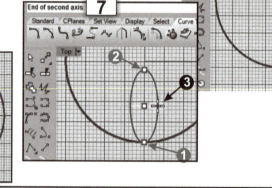

- Click on the **Offset Curve** command in the **Curve Tools** toolbar.

- Create a **1.5mm** offset on the inside of the ellipse as shown.

Fig. 15

Offset Curve
command

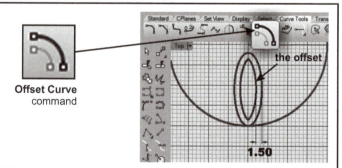

the offset

1.50

- **Transform tabbed toolbar.** `Transform`

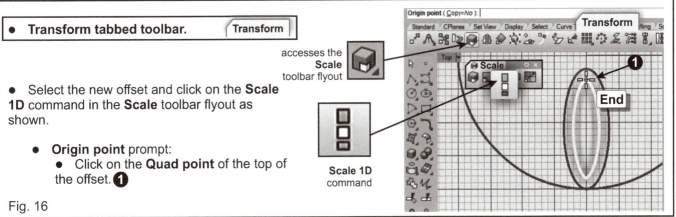

accesses the
Scale
toolbar flyout

- Select the new offset and click on the **Scale 1D** command in the **Scale** toolbar flyout as shown.

  - **Origin point** prompt:
    - Click on the **Quad point** of the top of the offset. ❶

Scale 1D
command

Fig. 16

- **Scale factor or first reference point** prompt:
  - Click on the **Quad point** of the bottom of the oval. ❷
  - Type "**13**" and press **Enter**.

- The inner oval will now be **13mm high.**

- **Rebuild** the inner oval to **12 control points.**
  - *This will now make a smoother curve with no kinks.*

Fig. 17

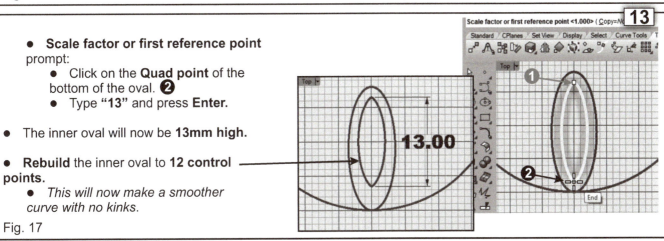

13.00

13

- **Polar Array** the ellipse and the offset.
  - **Center of Polar Array:** "0"
  - **Number of items:** "7"
  - **Angle to fill:** 360
  - **Press Enter to accept** preview prompt: press **Enter**

- Select the inner oval offsets and the large circle and type **Lock** in the **Command Line**.
  - Press **Enter**.
  - All of the inner ovals will be locked.

Fig. 18

Polar Array
command

**inner ovals are
locked**

- Select the large ovals and **Trim** them out.

- Use the **Join** command to join the trimmed curves into two closed polycurves. ❶ & ❷

Join
command

Trim
command

Fig. 19

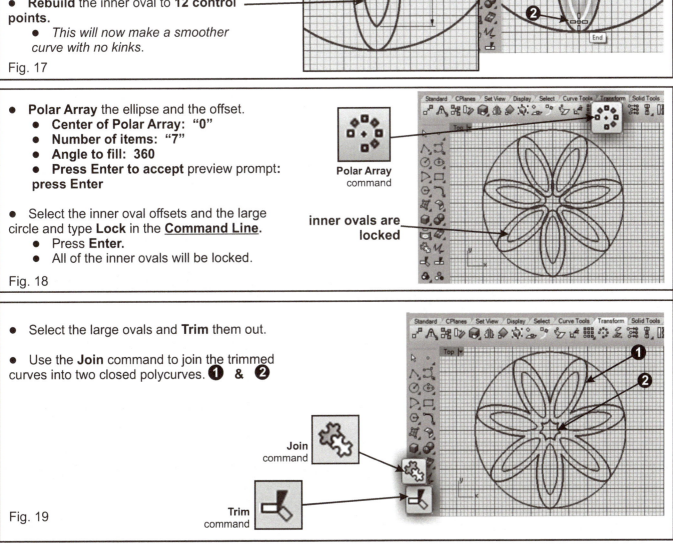

- **Curve Tools tabbed toolbar.** `Curve Tools`

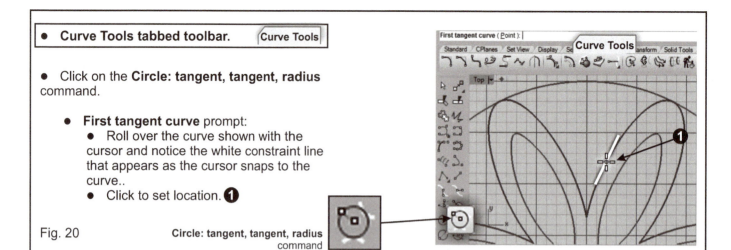

- Click on the **Circle: tangent, tangent, radius** command.

  - **First tangent curve** prompt:
    - Roll over the curve shown with the cursor and notice the white constraint line that appears as the cursor snaps to the curve..
    - Click to set location. ❶

Fig. 20   **Circle: tangent, tangent, radius** command

- **Second tangent curve or radius** prompt:
  - Type **"2.2"** and press **Enter.**
  - Roll over the curve on the opposite side and notice the white constraint line and the faint preview of the circle being created as the cursor snaps to the curve.
    - Click to set location. ❷

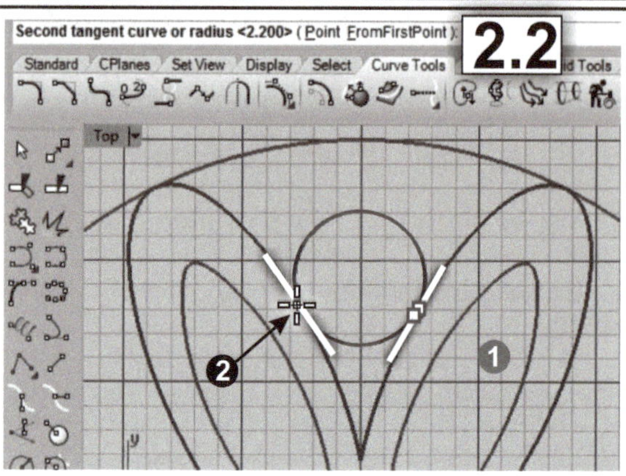

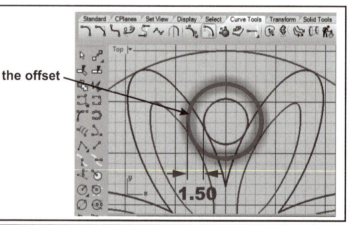

Fig. 21

- **Offset** the circle just created at a distance of **1.5mm**.

the offset

Fig. 22

- Select the two smaller circles and the polycurve as shown and **Trim** them out as shown.

- **Join** the trimmed curves.

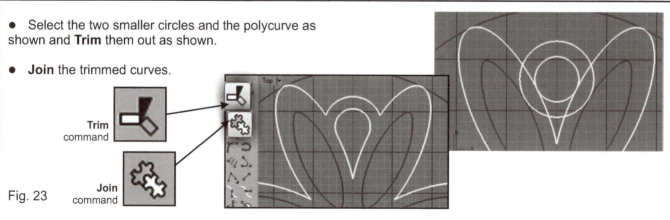

Trim command

Join command

Fig. 23

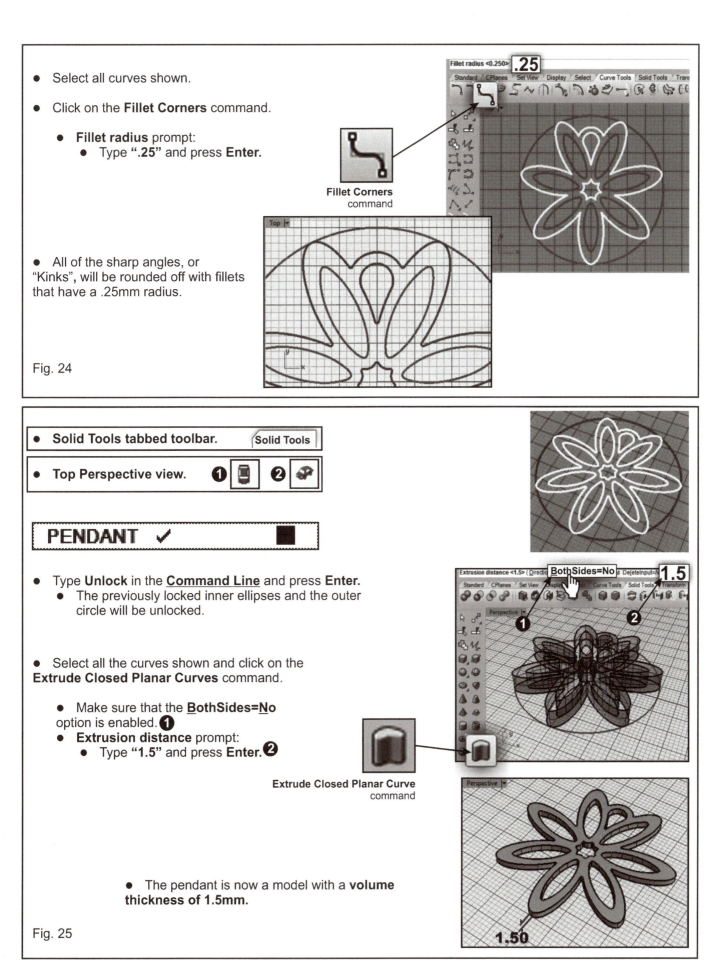

- Select all curves shown.

- Click on the **Fillet Corners** command.

  - **Fillet radius** prompt:
    - Type "**.25**" and press **Enter**.

Fillet Corners
command

- All of the sharp angles, or "Kinks", will be rounded off with fillets that have a .25mm radius.

Fig. 24

- **Solid Tools tabbed toolbar.**   Solid Tools

- **Top Perspective view.**   ❶ [ ] ❷ [ ]

PENDANT ✓

- Type **Unlock** in the **Command Line** and press **Enter.**
  - The previously locked inner ellipses and the outer circle will be unlocked.

- Select all the curves shown and click on the **Extrude Closed Planar Curves** command.

  - Make sure that the **BothSides=No** option is enabled. ❶
  - **Extrusion distance** prompt:
    - Type "**1.5**" and press **Enter.** ❷

Extrude Closed Planar Curve
command

  - The pendant is now a model with a **volume thickness of 1.5mm.**

Fig. 25

Simple Extruded DOMED Pendant or Earring

- Turn off the **PENDANT** layer. ❶
- Create a new layer called **DOMED PENDANT** and make ❷ **current.**
- Turn on the **ref geo** layer. ❸

Fig. 26

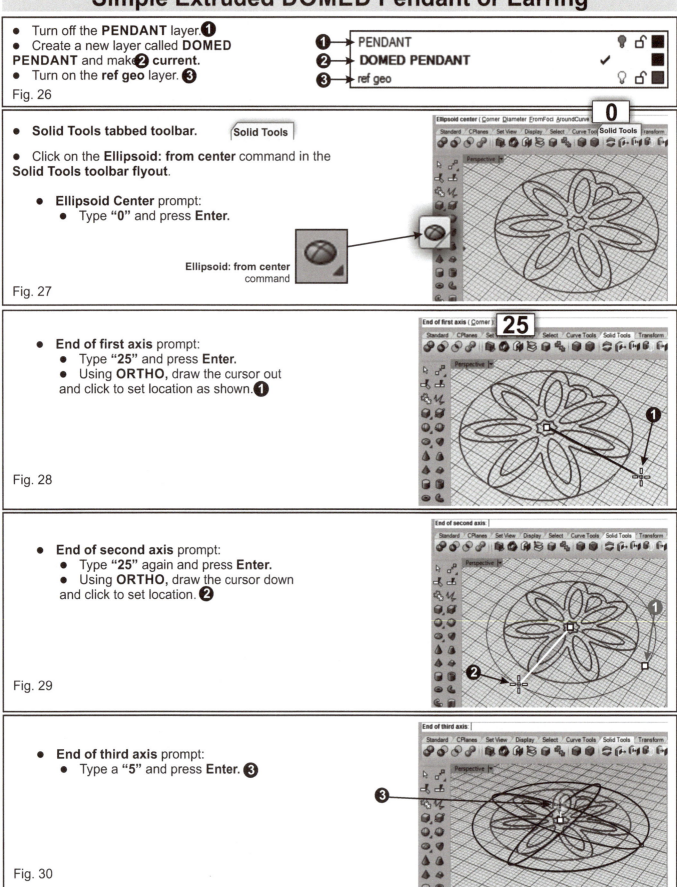

- **Solid Tools tabbed toolbar.**   Solid Tools

- Click on the **Ellipsoid: from center** command in the **Solid Tools toolbar flyout**.

  - **Ellipsoid Center** prompt:
    - Type **"0"** and press **Enter.**

    Ellipsoid: from center
    command

Fig. 27

- **End of first axis** prompt:
  - Type **"25"** and press **Enter.**
  - Using **ORTHO,** draw the cursor out and click to set location as shown. ❶

Fig. 28

- **End of second axis** prompt:
  - Type **"25"** again and press **Enter.**
  - Using **ORTHO,** draw the cursor down and click to set location. ❷

Fig. 29

- **End of third axis** prompt:
  - Type a **"5"** and press **Enter.** ❸

Fig. 30

359

- An Ellipse that measures 25 x 25 x 10 has been created around the reference geometry of the pendant as shown in **Ghosted Viewport Mode.**

Fig. 31

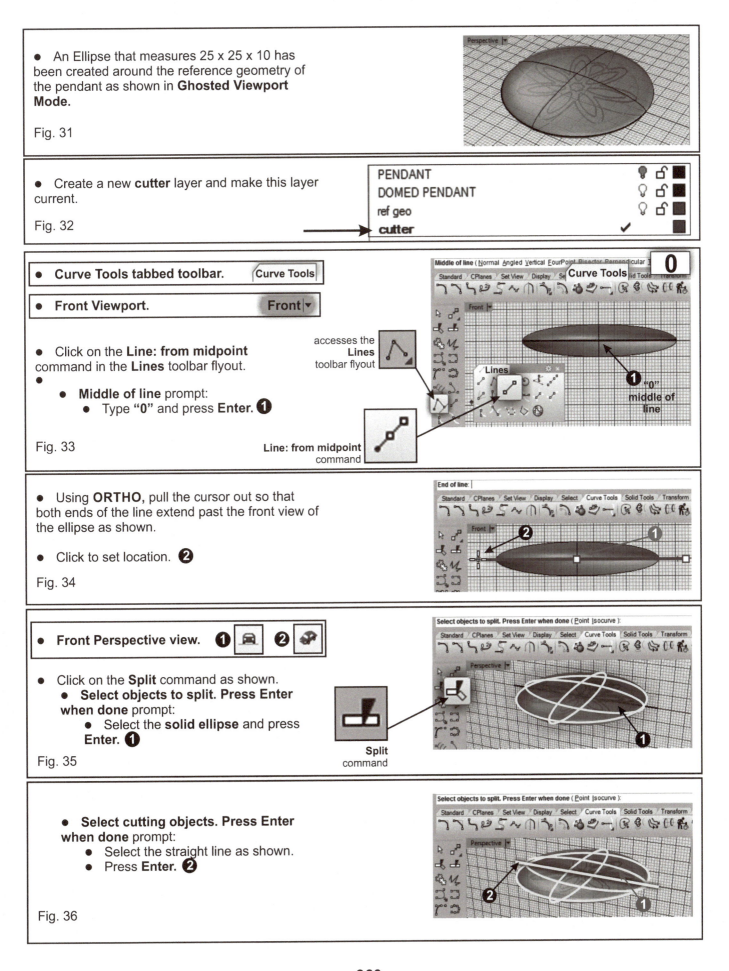

- Create a new **cutter** layer and make this layer current.

Fig. 32

PENDANT		💡 🔓 ■
DOMED PENDANT		💡 🔓 ■
ref geo		💡 🔓 ■
cutter	✓	■

- **Curve Tools tabbed toolbar.**   `Curve Tools`

- **Front Viewport.**   `Front ▾`

- Click on the **Line: from midpoint** command in the **Lines** toolbar flyout.
-
  - **Middle of line** prompt:
    - Type **"0"** and press **Enter.** ❶

accesses the **Lines** toolbar flyout

Line: from midpoint command

Fig. 33

- Using **ORTHO,** pull the cursor out so that both ends of the line extend past the front view of the ellipse as shown.

- Click to set location. ❷

Fig. 34

- **Front Perspective view.** ❶ 🚗 ❷ 🚙

- Click on the **Split** command as shown.
  - **Select objects to split. Press Enter when done** prompt:
    - Select the **solid ellipse** and press **Enter.** ❶

Split command

Fig. 35

- **Select cutting objects. Press Enter when done** prompt:
  - Select the straight line as shown.
  - Press **Enter.** ❷

Fig. 36

- The Ellipse will be split horizontally into 2 pieces.

- *The "cutting object" line projected itself vertically from the construction plane to split the designated ellipse.*

- Select the bottom piece and press the **Delete** key.

- Only the top half of the ellipse will remain.

Fig. 37

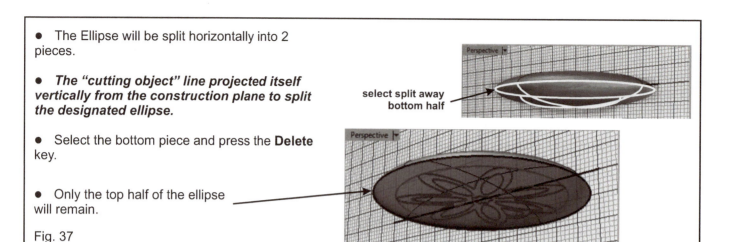

select split away bottom half

- **Top Perspective view.** ❶ ❷

- You can turn off the **cutter** layer.

- Click on the **Split** command.
  - **Select objects to split. Press Enter when done** prompt:
  - Select the domed surface and press **Enter.** ❶

Fig. 38

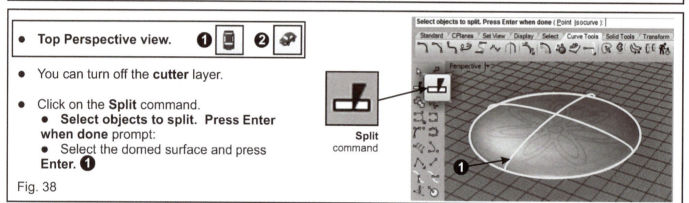

Split command

- **Select cutting objects. Press Enter when done** prompt:
  - Select all of the reference geometry of the pendant as shown and press **Enter.**

Fig. 39

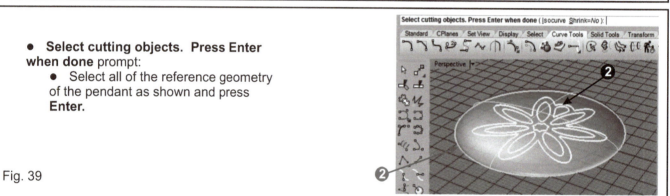

- Lines will appear on the surface showing where *the designated cutting objects projected themselves vertically from the construction plane to split the designated object.*
  - *The lines you see are actually the surface edges of the split out pieces.*

Fig. 40

- Turn off the **ref geo** layer.

- Only the **DOMED PENDANT** layer will be on.

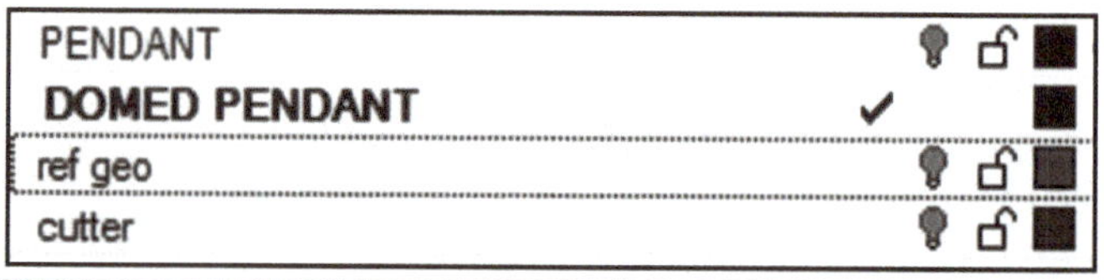

Fig. 41

PENDANT
DOMED PENDANT ✓
ref geo
cutter

- Select the outer piece of the split dome and press the **Delete** key.

- Carefully select the delete other pieces until only the shape of the pendant is left as shown.

Fig. 42

- **Solid Tools tabbed toolbar.** 〔Solid Tools〕

- Select the trimmed surface and click on the **Extrude Surface** command.

Fig. 43

 Extrude Surface
command

- **Extrusion distance** prompt:
  - Toggle **DeleteInput=<u>No</u>** to **DeleteInput=<u>Yes</u>**. **❶**
  - Type **"-2"** and press **Enter**. **❷**

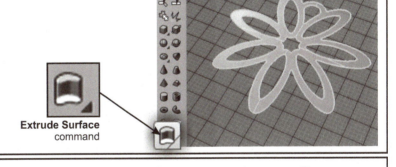

Fig. 44

- The designated surface has been extruded into a 2mm thick domed pendant.

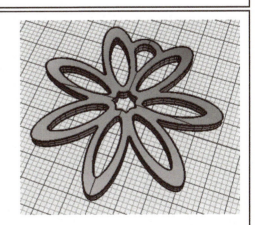

Fig. 45

362

- To soften the edges, left-click on the **Variable Radius Fillet** command.

  - **Select edges to fillet**. **Press Enter when done** prompt:
    - Type "**.4**" and press **Enter**.
    - **Window select** the whole pendant so that all of it's edges will be selected.
    - Press **Enter**.

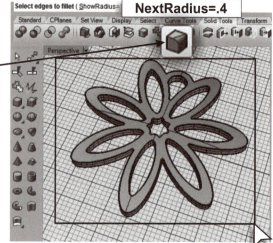

left-click for **Fillet Edges** command

Fig. 46

- When you window select the pendant, *all of the edges will be highlighted, along with little notations showing the radius of each fillet to be created.*
- Press **Enter** twice to finish the command.

- The edges will all be softened.

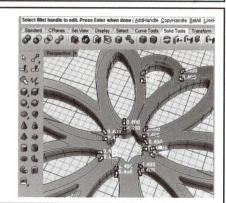

- Press the **F7 Hotkey** to toggle the grid off and on.

- Viewed in **Rendered Viewport** mode.

Fig. 47

Briolette - Step Cut
Using Lines and Surfaces to create faceted objects.

- Create the layers shown.

- **briolette ref 1** layer current.

Fig. 1

BRIOLETTE	☿ 🔓 ■
briolette ref 1	✓ ■
briolette ref 2	☿ 🔓 ■

Creating the Linear Framework for the Facets

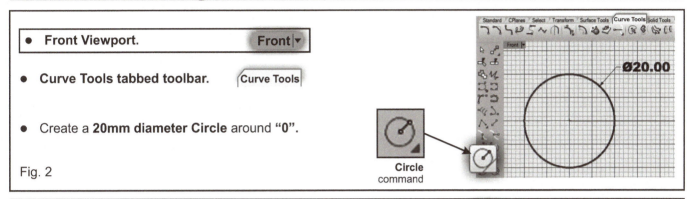

- **Front Viewport.**   Front ▾

- **Curve Tools tabbed toolbar.**   Curve Tools

- Create a **20mm diameter Circle** around **"0"**.

Fig. 2

Circle
command

Ø20.00

- Select the circle and press **F10** to turn on it's control points.   **F10**

- With **ORTHO** enabled use the **Move** command to move the top control point upwards **10mm**.

  - **Point to move from:** ❶
  - **Point to move to:** ❷

Fig. 3

Move
command

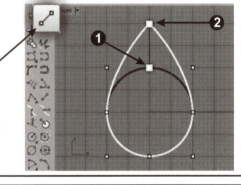

- Create a **Line** from the top **end point** to the bottom **quad point**.

Fig. 4

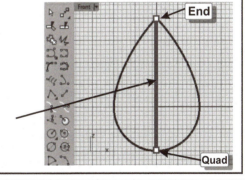

End

Quad

- Select the new line, type **"divide"**, and press **Enter**.

  - **Number of segments** prompt:
    - Type **"6"** and press **Enter**.

- Point objects will be created along the line, dividing it into 6 equal segments.

Fig. 5

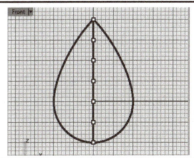

- Use the **Line: from midpoint** command in the **Lines toolbar flyout** to draw contour lines out from each point object to intersect with the pear-shaped outline.
    - Use **Point Osnap** to accurately place the lines.
    - Use **ORTHO** to keep the lines perfectly horizontal.

    - **Middle of line: ❶**
    - **End of line: ❷**

Fig. 6

- Start to **Drag** the bottom line down and tap the **Alt** key to make a copy.

- Drag the line down about halfway to the bottom of the pear shape. Release the cursor at the desired location for the copy.

copy

Fig. 7

- **Top Perspective view.** ❶ ❷

- The linework is sitting up vertically to the top construction plane.
    - This is because it was created in the **Front viewport** on the **Front construction plane**.

Fig. 8

- Switch to the **briolette ref 2** layer.

BRIOLETTE
briolette ref 1
briolette ref 2 ✓

Fig. 9

- Click on the **Polygon: Center, Radius** command.

    - **Center of inscribed polygon** prompt:
        - Snap to the **intersection** of the bottom contour line and the vertical center line and click to set location.

    - Click on the **NumSides=5** option in the **Command Line.**
        - **Number of sides** prompt:
            - Type **"12"** and press **Enter.**

Polygon: Center, Radius
command

❶ Int

Fig. 10

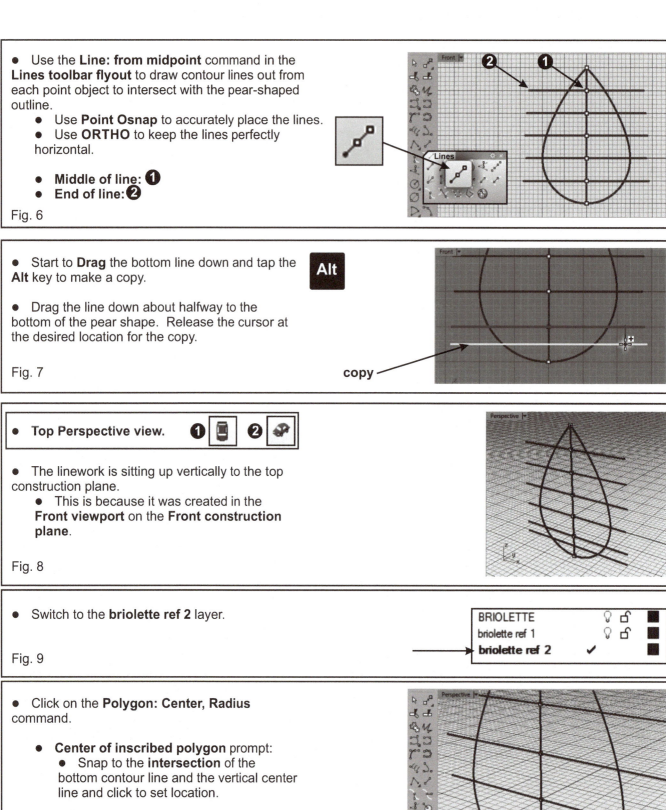

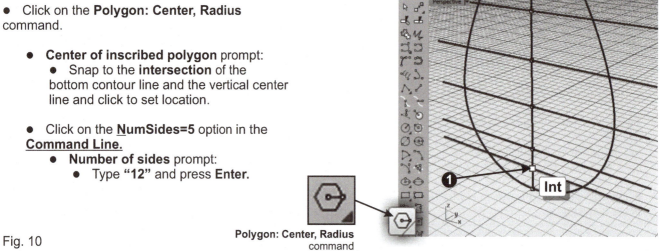

- **Corner of polygon** prompt:
  - Draw the cursor out and snap to the **intersection** of the contour line and the outer pear shaped line.

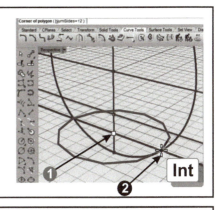

Fig. 11

- Use the same technique to create a polygon on each of the contour lines.

Fig. 12

- Place **Point objects** at the very top and the very bottom of the perpendicular line you created in Fig. 4, using **end osnap.**

  - There are already points at these locations that were created with the Divide command in Fig. 5 but they are on a layer that is about to be turned off.

Fig. 13

Creating the Surfaces for the Briolette

- Turn off the **briolette ref 1** layer.

- Make the **BRIOLETTE** layer current.

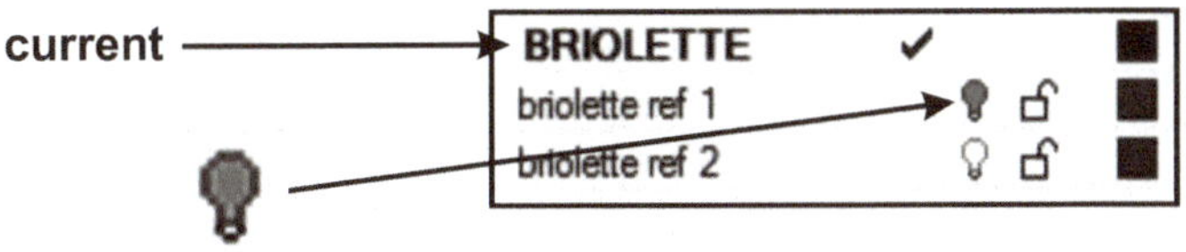

Fig. 14

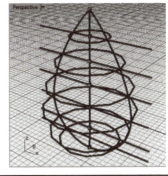

- **Surface Tools tabbed toolbar.** [Surface Tools]

- Click on the **Surface from 3 or 4 corner points** command.
  - Use **end osnap** for accurate placement.

  - **First corner of surface:** ❶
  - **Second corner of surface:** ❷
  - **Third corner of surface:** ❸
  - **Fourth corner of surface:** ❹

Surface from 3 or 4 corner points command

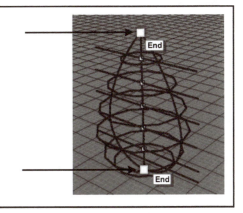

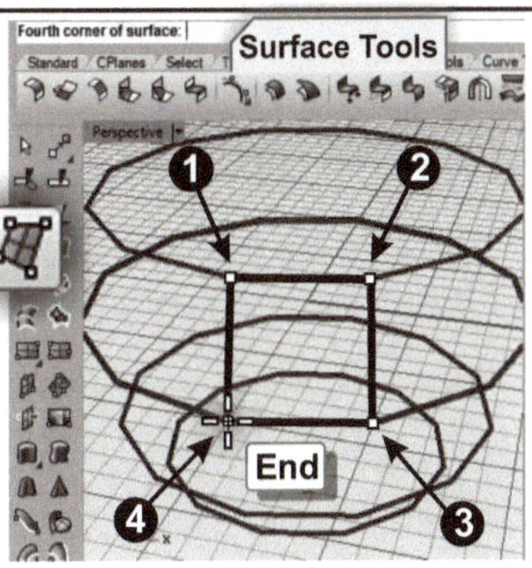

Fig. 15

- The first surface has been created. **1**

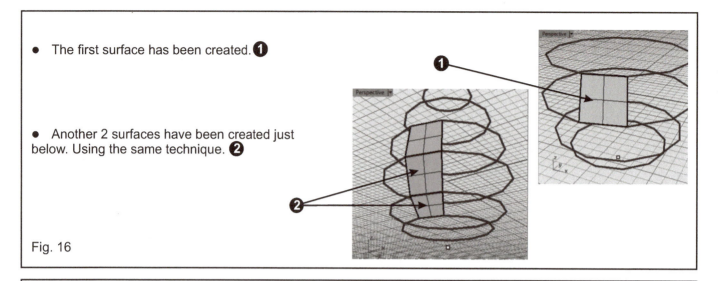

- Another 2 surfaces have been created just below. Using the same technique. **2**

Fig. 16

- At the bottom and top of the piece, triangular surfaces will be necessary but you can use the same command.
  - Use **end** and **point osnap** for accurate placement.

  - **First corner of surface: 1**
  - **Second corner of surface: 2**
  - **Third corner of surface: 3**
  - **Fourth corner of surface** prompt:
    - Press **Enter** to end the command at 3 corners, creating a triangular surface.

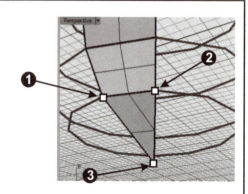

Fig. 17

- Continue up the column until a line of surfaces is created from top to bottom of the piece.

Fig. 18

- **Select tabbed toolbar.** `Select`

- Click on the **Select Surfaces** command to quickly select all of the surfaces.

- Click on the **Join** command to join all of the surfaces to make an **open polysurface**.

Join command

Select Surfaces command

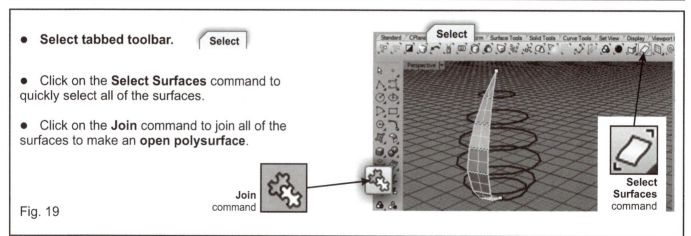

Fig. 19

- **Transform tabbed toolbar.**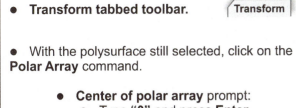

- With the polysurface still selected, click on the **Polar Array** command.

  - **Center of polar array** prompt:
    - Type **"0"** and press **Enter.**
  - **Number of items** prompt:
    - Type **"12"** and press **Enter.**
  - **Angle to fill or first reference point** prompt:
    - Press **Enter** to accept the default value of **360°.**
  - **Press Enter to accept** prompt:
    - Press **Enter** to accept the preview of the finished polar array.

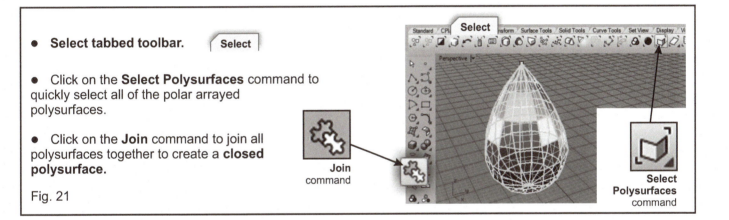

Polar Array
command

Fig. 20

- **Select tabbed toolbar.** Select

- Click on the **Select Polysurfaces** command to quickly select all of the polar arrayed polysurfaces.

- Click on the **Join** command to join all polysurfaces together to create a **closed polysurface.**

Join
command

Select
Polysurfaces
command

Fig. 21

- Save this file as: **Briolette - step cut.3dm**

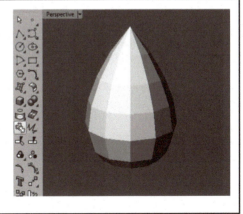

Fig. 22

Briolette - Brilliant Cut
Using Lines and Surfaces to create faceted objects.

- Open your saved Rhino file from the previous chapter: **Briolette, Step Cut.3dm.**

- Save this file as: **Briolette - Brilliant Cut.3dm.**

- Select and **Delete** the briolette.
  - Do not delete the reference geometry.

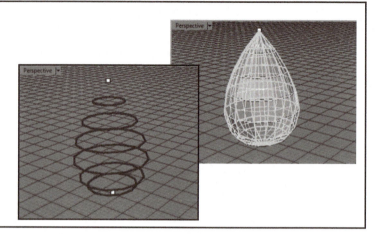

Fig. 1

- **BRIOLETTE** layer current.

Fig. 2

Adjusting the Linear Framework for the Facets

- **Transform tabbed toolbar.**   `Transform`

- Select every other polygon as shown.

- **LEFT-CLICK** on the **Rotate** command.
  - **Center of rotation** prompt:'
    - Type **"0"** and press **Enter.** ❶
  - **Angle or first reference point** prompt:
    - Draw the cursor outward and snap to one of the angles of one of the polygons.
    - Click to set location. ❷

  - **Second reference point** prompt:
    - Draw the cursor around and snap to the **midpoint** of one of the polygon's edges.
    - Click to set location. ❸

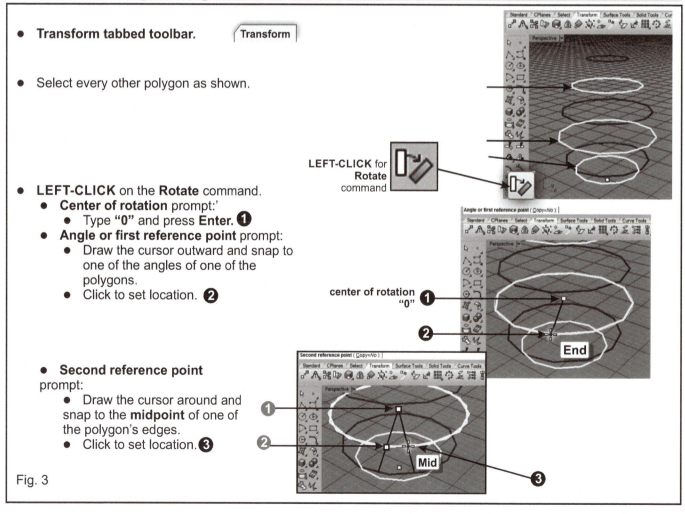

Fig. 3

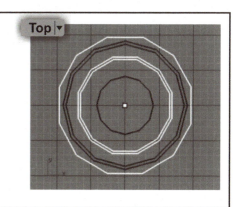

● **Top Viewport.** Top ▾

● A quick look at the top view will show that all 3 rotated polygons (seen highlighted here) are staggered now in their alignment with the other polygons.

● Their angles are exactly in line with the mid points of the polygons that were not rotated.

Fig. 4

● **Top Perspective view.** ❶ 🖥 ❷ 🖨

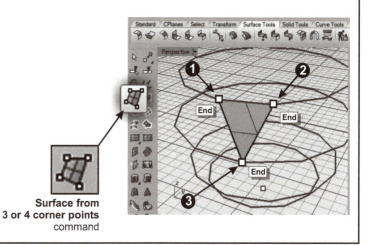

● With **end osnap** enabled, use the **Surface from 3 or 4 corner points** command to create a new triangular surface.
  ● **First corner of surface:** ❶
  ● **Second corner of surface:** ❷
  ● **Third corner of surface:** ❸
  ● **Fourth corner of surface** prompt:
    ● Press **Enter** to end the command at 3 corners, creating a triangular surface.

Surface from 3 or 4 corner points command

Fig. 5

● Create another surface next to the first surface as shown.

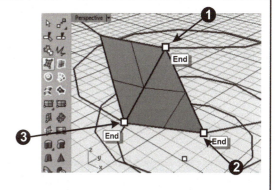

Fig. 6

● Because the position of the polygons has been changed, it is now necessary to create two little triangular surfaces on each level as shown.

● Only one triangular surface is needed at top and bottom.

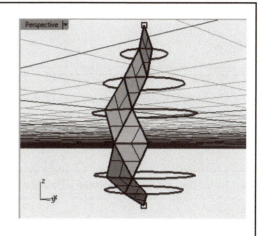

Fig. 7

370

- **Select tabbed toolbar.** `Select`

- Click on the **Select Surfaces** command to quickly select all of the surfaces.

- Click on the **Join** command to join all of the surfaces to make an **open polysurface**.

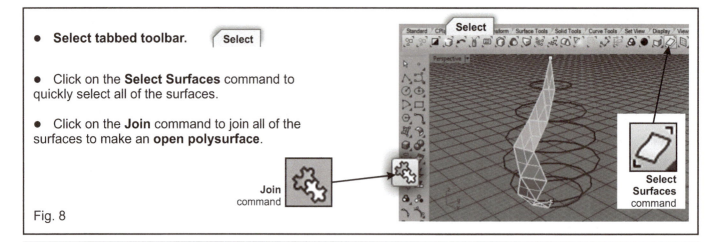

Join
command

Fig. 8

Select
Surfaces
command

- **Transform tabbed toolbar.** `Transform`

- With the polysurface still selected, click on the **Polar Array** command.
    - **Center of polar array** prompt:
        - Type **"0"** and press **Enter.**
    - **Number of items** prompt:
        - Type **"12"** and press **Enter.**
    - **Angle to fill or first reference point** prompt:
        - Press **Enter** to accept the default value of **360°.**
    - **Press Enter to accept** prompt:
        - Press **Enter** to accept the preview of the finished polar array.

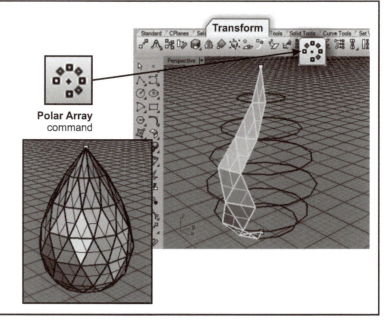

Polar Array
command

Fig. 9

- **Select tabbed toolbar.** `Select`

- Click on the **Select Polysurfaces** command to quickly select all of the polar arrayed polysurfaces.

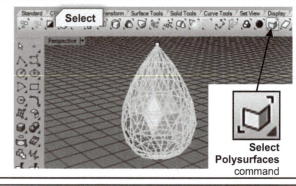

Select
Polysurfaces
command

Fig. 10

- Click on the **Join** command to create a **closed polysurface.**
    - You can also just type **"join"** and press **Enter.**

- Save this file as: **Briolette - Brilliant Cut.3dm**

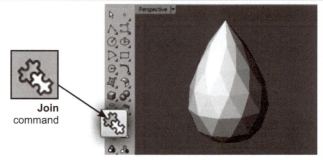

Join
command

Fig. 11

371

Revolved Ring Band
Revolve Command with History

- Create the layers shown.

- **ref geo** layer current.

Fig. 1

RING   ♀   🔓   ■

→ **ref geo**   ✔   ■

- **Front Viewport.**   Front ▾

- Create a **Ø17.35** circle around **0** as shown.

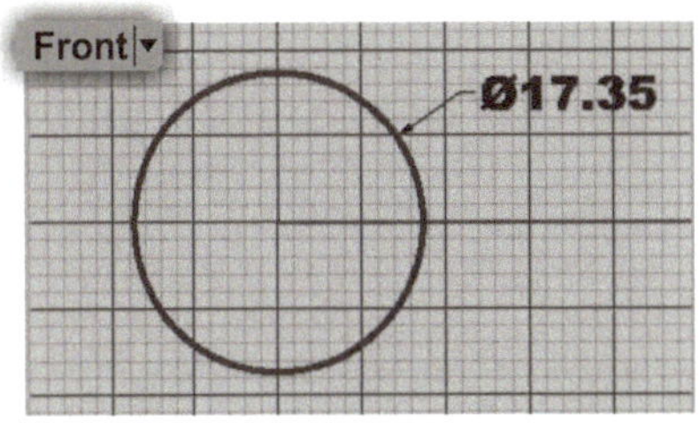

Fig. 2

Front ▾

Ø17.35

Creating a Profile Curve

- Using **quad osnap** and **ORTHO**, create a **2mm vertical line** from the top **quad** of the circle as shown.

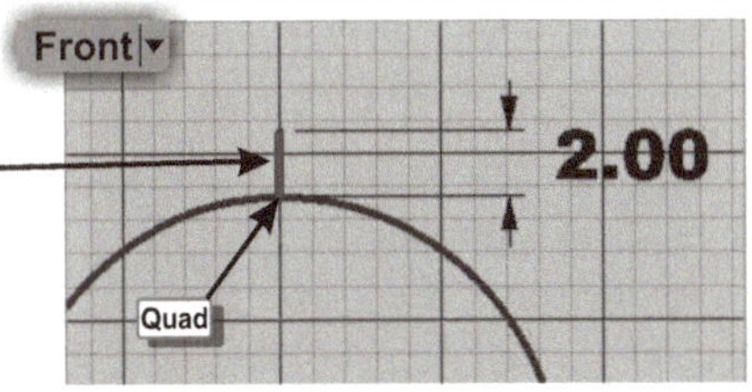

Fig. 3

Front ▾

2.00

Quad

- Select the new 2mm line.
- Press the **F10 hotkey** but turn on the line's control points.

F10

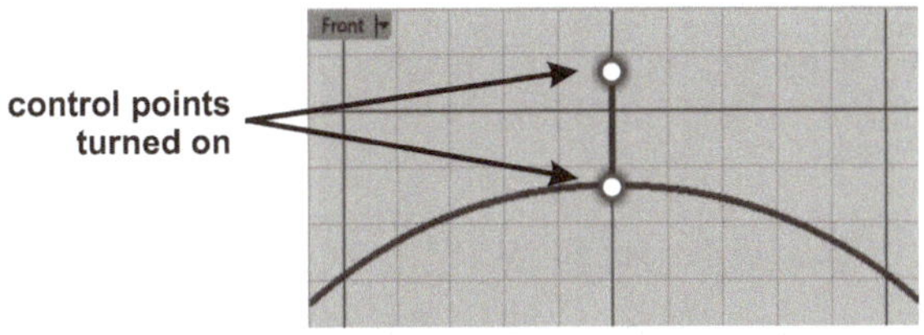

Fig. 4

control points turned on

Front ▾

- **Curve Tools tabbed toolbar.**   Curve Tools

- **Right Viewport.**   Right ▾

- Click on the **Arc: Center, Start, Angle** command.
  - **Center of arc** prompt:
    - Snap to the **bottom control point** of the new 2mm line.
    - Click to set location. ❶

Fig. 5

Center of arc (Deformable StartPoint Tangent Extension)

Standard CPlanes Set View Display Sel **Curve Tools** Transform Solid

Right ▾

❶

Point

Arc: Center, Start, Angle command

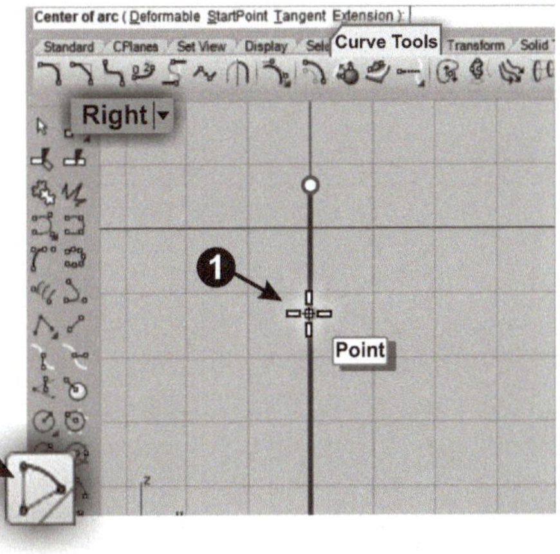

- **Start of arc** prompt:
  - Type **"3"** and press **Enter.**
  - Use **ORTHO** to draw the cursor out to the right and click to set location **2**

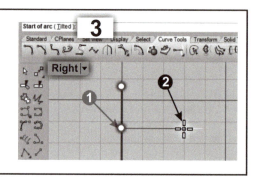

Fig. 6

- **End point or angle** prompt:
  - Type **"180"** and press **Enter.**

- The finished arc is an exact semi-circle.

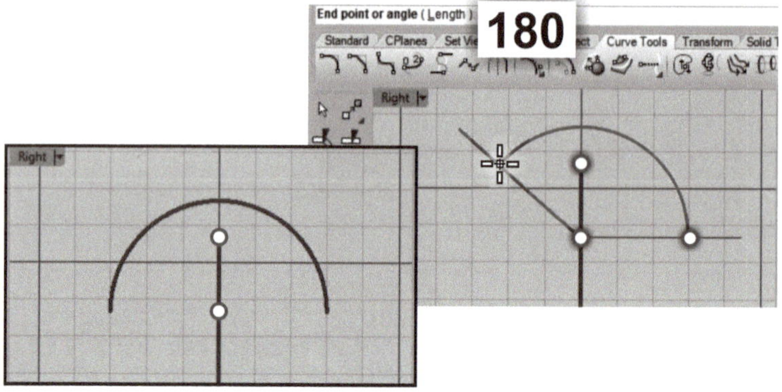

Fig. 7

- Press the **Esc** key to turn off the control points for the 2mm line.

- Select the new Arc and press the **F10 hotkey** to turn on it's control points.

- Select the top 3 control points as shown.

- **Drag** the middle control point down until it snaps to the end of the 2mm vertical line as shown.

- Click to set location.

- The arc has been edited down to a height of 2mm.

- Turn off control points.

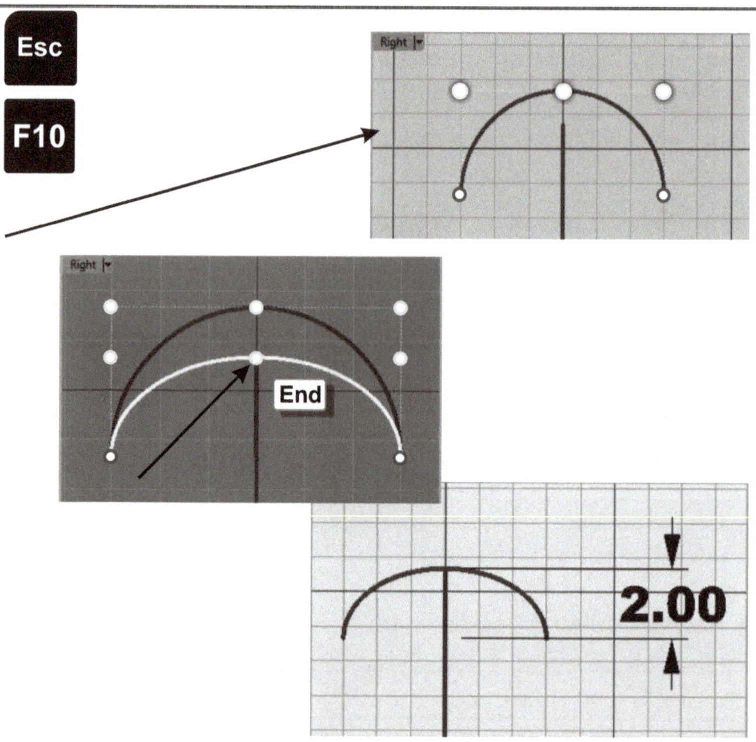

Fig. 8

- Using **End osnap,** create a line between the two ends of the arc as shown.

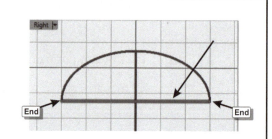

Fig. 9

Revolving to Create the Ring Surfaces

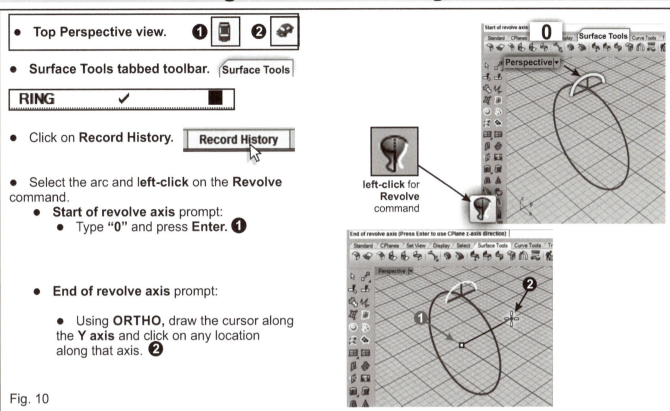

- **Top Perspective view.** ❶ 🖥 ❷ 🚗

- **Surface Tools tabbed toolbar.** [Surface Tools]

RING ✓ ■

- Click on **Record History.** [Record History]

- Select the arc and **left-click** on the **Revolve** command.
  - **Start of revolve axis** prompt:
    - Type **"0"** and press **Enter.** ❶

  - **End of revolve axis** prompt:

    - Using **ORTHO,** draw the cursor along the **Y axis** and click on any location along that axis. ❷

left-click for **Revolve** command

Fig. 10

- **Start angle** prompt:

  - Click on the **FullCircle** option in the **Command Line.**

    Start angle <0> (DeleteInput=No Deformable= **FullCircle** ForStartAngle=Yes SplitAtTangents=No): |

    Fig. 11

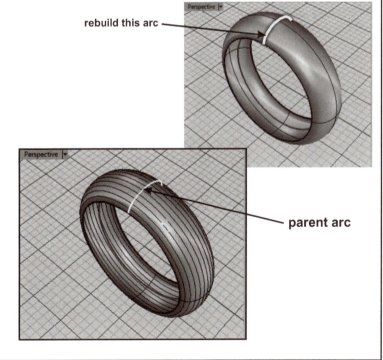

rebuild this arc

parent arc

- The resulting ring band's outer surface has been created.

- Select the parent arc and **rebuild to 15 control points.**

- **NOTE: DO NOT REBUILD THE SURFACE. JUST REBUILD THE ARC!!**

- After the Rebuild, notice that the number of isocurves in the U Direction of the surface has increased to reflect the larger number of control points of the parent arc.
  - This is because History was enabled for the revolve, making the Arc the Parent object and the ring surface the Child object.

Fig. 12

- Select the ring band and type **"lock"** in the **Command Line**.
- Press **Enter** and note the dark grey color of the ring band when it is locked.

Fig. 13

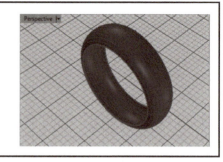

- **Right Viewport.** `Right ▼`

- Select the arc, type **"EditPtOn"**, and press **Enter**.
  - The button for this command is in the **Standard tabbed toolbar** but typing saves you the extra step of changing tabbed toolbars.

  - *Edit points remain exactly on the line, making for very accurate editing.*

`Right ▼`

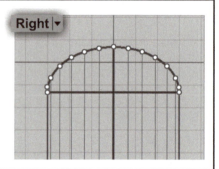

Fig. 14

- Select the edit points shown. ─────────────→

- Drag the selected points down slightly and release the cursor.

Fig. 15

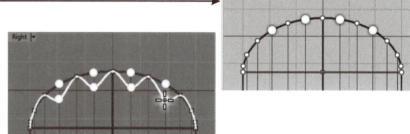

- **History** will update the ring band, shown here in **Rendered Viewport mode**.

- Viewed in d**efault perspective viewport**.

- Press the **F7** hotkey to toggle the grid off and on.

Fig. 16

- **Curve Tools tabbed toolbar.** `Curve Tools`

- Click on the **Fillet curves** command.

  - **Select first curve to fillet** prompt:
    - Type **".5"** in the **Command Line** and press **Enter**.
    - Click on **Join=No** to change the option to **Join=Yes**.

Fillet curves command

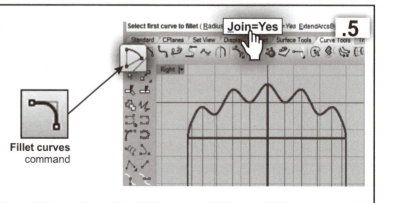

Fig. 17

- **Select first curve to fillet** prompt:
    - Click near the end of the edited arc as shown. ❶

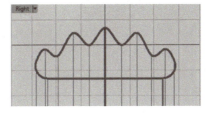

- **Select second curve to fillet** prompt:
    - Click near the end of the straight line as shown. ❷

- Fillet the curves on the other side in the same way.
- History has updated the ring and has created an inner surface from the straight line that was filleted with the edited parent curve.

- Because there are no kinks in the filleting of the curves, a **single closed surface** has been created which makes the ring a **solid object.**

Fig. 18

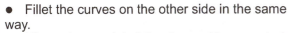

- Select control points on the straight line and drag them upwards a short distance.

- The ring will update with a more hollowed shape.

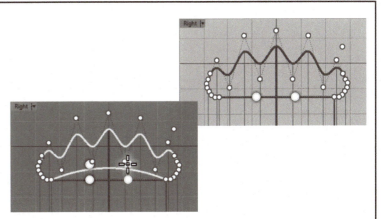

Fig. 19

accesses the
Scale toolbar flyout

- **Transform** tabbed toolbar.　　　Transform

- **Right** Viewport.　　　Right ▾

Scale 1-D
command

- Select the two control points shown and click on the **Scale 1D** command in the **Scale** toolbar flyout.

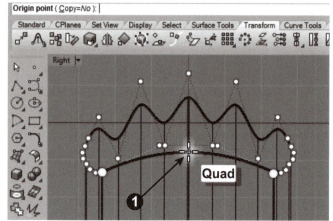

- **Origin point** prompt:
  - Snap to the **Quad** point of the lower line as shown.
  - Click to set location. ❶

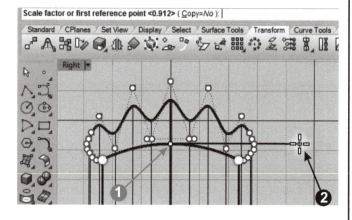

- **Scale factor or first reference point** prompt:
  - Using **ORTHO**, draw the cursor out and click on the approximate location shown. ❷

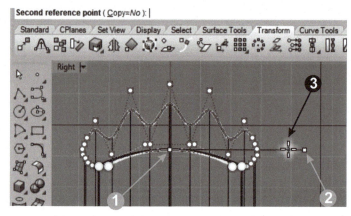

- **Second reference point** prompt:
  - Using **ORTHO**, draw the cursor slightly back toward the ring and click at the approximate location shown. ❸

Fig. 20

377

- The shape of the inner part of the ring has been slightly thickened at the edges.

Fig. 21

Creating a Matching Band in a Different Size

- **Top Perspective view.** ❶ ❷

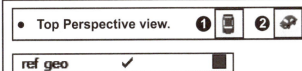
ref geo ✓ ■

- To **unlock** the ring: type **"unlock"** and press **Enter.**

- Select both the ring band and its reference geometry and copy it up along the Y axis at a distance of about 20mm as shown.

Select the copy and it's reference geometry.

- Type **"hide"** and press **Enter.**

- The new copy will be hidden from view.

Fig. 22

- **Front Viewport.** Front ▾

- Create a **19.84 diameter circle** around **0.**

- This is the diameter of a size 10 ring. It will guide the changing of the size of this band from a size 7 to a size 10.
  - You can temporarily turn off the **RING** layer during this step for better visibility.

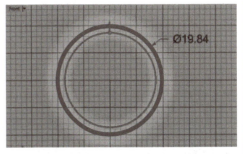

Fig. 23

- **Top Perspective view.** ❶ ❷

- Select the profile curve as shown and click on the **Move** command.

  - **Point to move from** prompt:
    - Click on the upper **quad** of the smaller size 7 circle as shown. ❶

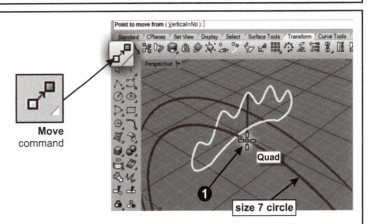

Fig. 24

- **Point to move to** prompt:
  - Click on the upper quad of the new larger size 10 circle as shown.

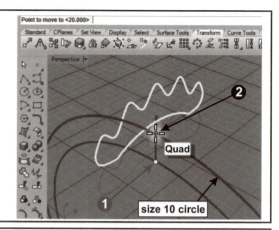
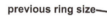

Fig. 25

- Turn on the **RING** layer to see that History has updated the ring band to a larger ring size *even though the RING layer was turned off.*

previous ring size

- Type **"show"** and press **Enter.**

- The ring in the back will be visible once again.

- Notice the difference in ring sizes.

Fig. 26

- Try some profile curves of your own design. Here are some examples.

- Use your knowledge of curves and their editing and transformation to create many variations!

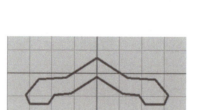
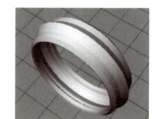

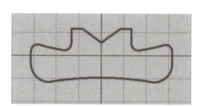

Fig. 27

Revolve Command
Round Cabochon in Bezel Setting

Creating the Round Cabochon

- Create the layers shown.

- **rd cab ref** layer current.
  - [*this is an abbreviation for* ***"round cabochon reference geometry"***]   Fig. 1

ROUND CAB		💡 🔓	⬛
rd cab ref	✓		⬛
RD BEZEL		💡 🔓	⬛
rd bezel ref		💡 🔓	⬛

- **Top Viewport.**   `Top ▾`

- **Curve Tools tabbed toolbar.**   `Curve Tools`

- Create a **10mm diameter** circle around **"0"**.

Fig. 2

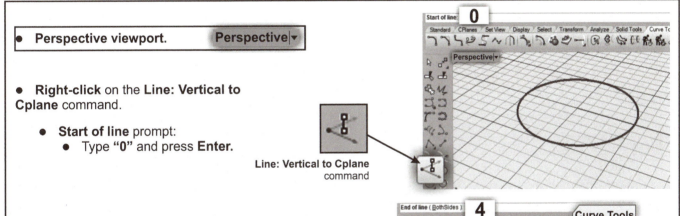

- **Perspective viewport.**   `Perspective ▾`

- **Right-click** on the **Line: Vertical to Cplane** command.

  - **Start of line** prompt:
    - Type **"0"** and press **Enter**.

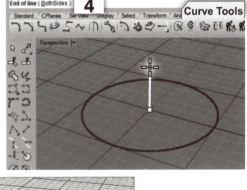

Line: Vertical to Cplane
command

  - Draw the cursor upwards and notice the white vertical direction constraint line.
  - **End of line** prompt:
    - Type **"4"** and press **Enter**.
    - Click to set location.

- A new 4mm vertical line sitting on the center of the 10mm circle has been created.

Fig. 3

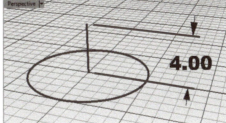

- Click on the **Arc: start, end, point on arc** command.

  - **Start of arc** prompt:
    - Click on one of the **quads** of the circle. ❶
  - **End of arc** prompt:
    - Click on the **quad** on the opposite side of the circle. ❷
  - **Point on arc** prompt:
    - Click on the **End** of the vertical line as shown. ❸

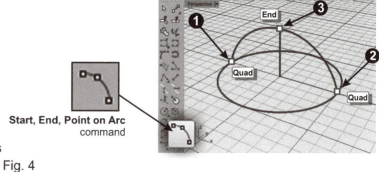

Start, End, Point on Arc command

Fig. 4

- Click on the **Trim** command.

  - **Select cutting objects** prompt:
    - Select the vertical line shown and press **Enter.** ❶
  - **Select object to trim. Press Enter to clear selection and start over** prompt:
    - Click on the section of the arc shown. ❷
    - Press **Enter** to end the command.

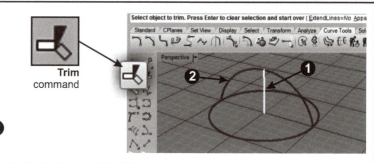

Trim command

- One half of the arc has been trimmed away.

cutting object

Fig. 5

ROUND CAB ✔

- **Surface Tools tabbed toolbar.** ⌐Surface Tools⌐

- **Left-click** on the **Revolve** command.

  - **Select curves to revolve**. Press **Enter** when done prompt:
    - Select the arc segment and press **Enter.** ❶
  - **Start of revolve axis** prompt:
    - Click on one end of the vertical line using **End osnap.** ❷
  - **End of revolve axis** prompt:
    - Click on the other end of the vertical line using **End osnap** as before. ❸
  - **Start angle** prompt:
    - Click on the **FullCircle** option in the **Command Line.**

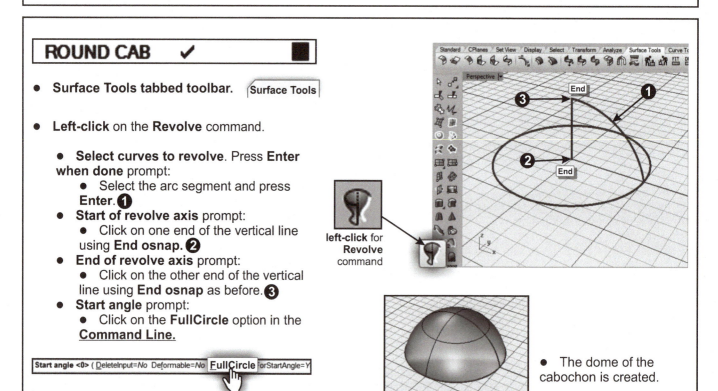

left-click for **Revolve** command

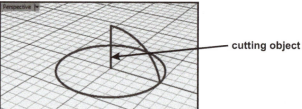

- The dome of the cabochon is created.

Fig. 6

381

- Select the new revolved surface.
- Type **"cap"** and press **Enter**.
  - FYI: The actual command button for this is in the **Solid Tools** tabbed toolbar.

- A flat surface will form to close the open planar hole at the bottom of the surface.
  - The new surface is called a **"cap"**.
  - The stone is now a closed polysurface.

Fig. 7

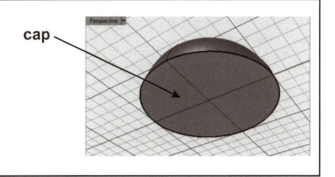

cap

Creating the Bezel Setting

rd bezel ref ✓ ■

- Type **"point"** and press **Enter**.
  - FYI: The actual command button is in the **Standard tabbed toolbar**.

- **Location of point object** prompt:
  - Using **Point osnap**, click to place the point on the left quad point of the circle.

Fig. 8

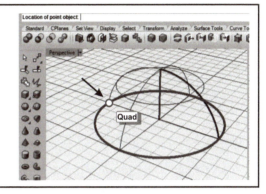

- **Front Viewport.**   Front ▼

- **Curve Tools tabbed toolbar.**   Curve Tools

- Click on the **Rectangle: Corner to corner** command.

  - **First corner of rectangle** prompt:
    - Snap to the point as shown and click to set location.

  - **Other corner or length** prompt:
    - Type **"-.6"** and press **Enter**.

  - **Width. Press Enter to use length** prompt:
    - Type **"1.5"** and press **Enter**.

- The finished rectangle will measure 1.5mm x .6mm.

Fig. 9

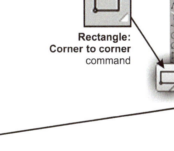
Rectangle: Corner to corner command

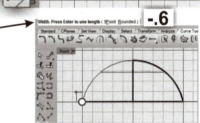
-.6

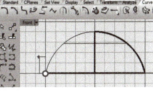
1.5

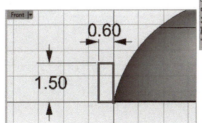
0.60
1.50

- Click on the **Rectangle: Corner to corner** command again.
  - **First corner of rectangle** prompt:
    - Use **End osnap** to click on the corner of the first rectangle shown.
  - **Other corner or length** prompt:
    - Type **"2"** and press **Enter.**
  - **Width. Press Enter to use length** prompt:
    - Type **"-.8"** and press **Enter.**

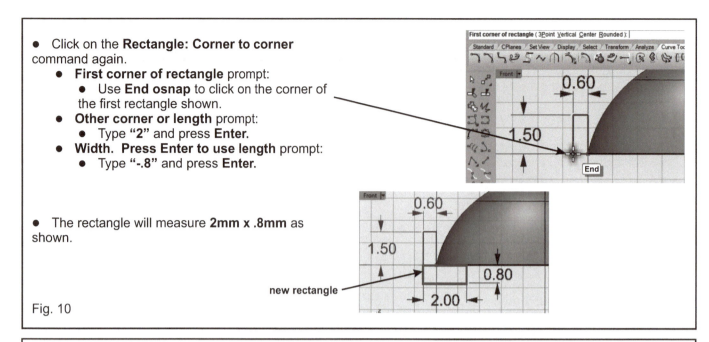

- The rectangle will measure **2mm x .8mm** as shown.

new rectangle

Fig. 10

- Select the two rectangles and click on the **Curve Boolean** command.

  - **Click inside regions to keep. press Enter when done** prompt:
    - Click on **DeleteInput=None** option in the **Command Line.**
      - **DeleteInput** prompt: Click on the **All** option.

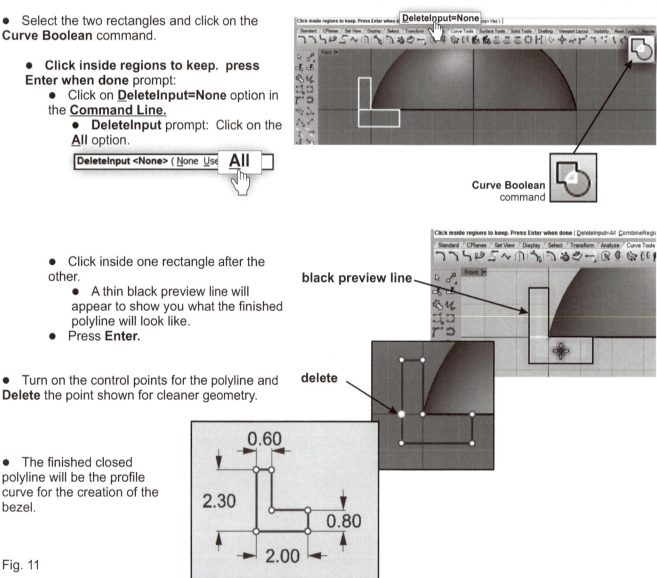

Curve Boolean command

  - Click inside one rectangle after the other.
    - A thin black preview line will appear to show you what the finished polyline will look like.
  - Press **Enter.**

black preview line

- Turn on the control points for the polyline and **Delete** the point shown for cleaner geometry.

delete

- The finished closed polyline will be the profile curve for the creation of the bezel.

Fig. 11

- **Perspective viewport.** ❶ 🔲 ❷ 🔲

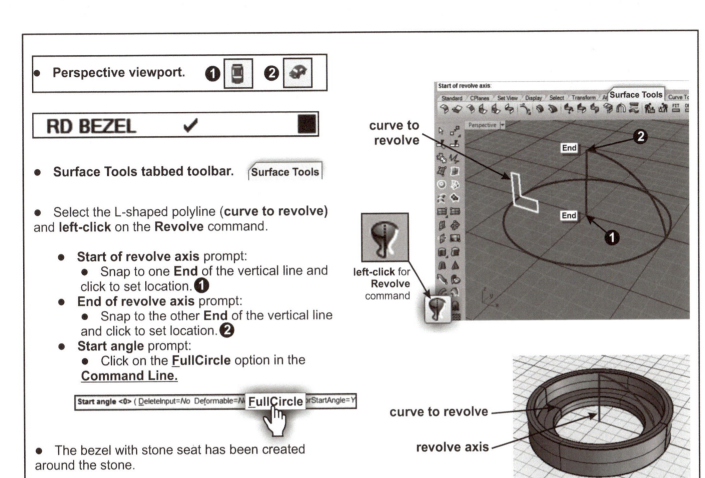

RD BEZEL ✓ ⬛

- **Surface Tools tabbed toolbar.** `Surface Tools`

- Select the L-shaped polyline (**curve to revolve)** and **left-click** on the **Revolve** command.

  - **Start of revolve axis** prompt:
    - Snap to one **End** of the vertical line and click to set location. ❶
  - **End of revolve axis** prompt:
    - Snap to the other **End** of the vertical line and click to set location. ❷
  - **Start angle** prompt:
    - Click on the **FullCircle** option in the **Command Line.**

`Start angle <0> ( DeleteInput=No  Deformable=M  FullCircle  orStartAngle=Y`

- The bezel with stone seat has been created around the stone.

Fig. 12

curve to revolve
revolve axis

- Both bezel and cabochon stone now have render properties.

- Save this file as: **bezel set 10mm RD cabochon.3dm**

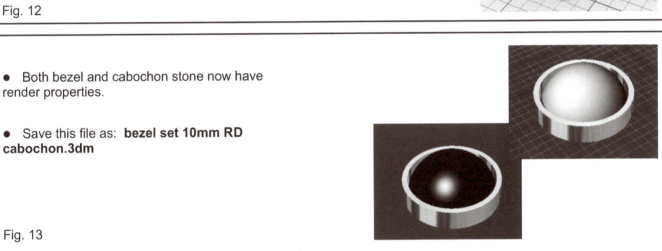

Fig. 13

384

Rail Revolve and Sweep 1 Rail Commands
Oval Cabochon in Bezel Setting

- Create layers shown.

- **oval cab ref** layer current.

Fig. 1

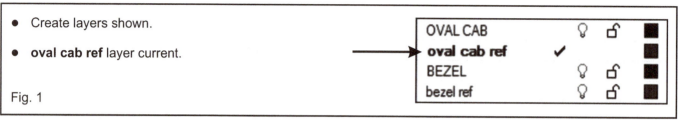

OVAL CAB		💡	🔓	⬛
oval cab ref	✓			⬛
BEZEL		💡	🔓	⬛
bezel ref		💡	🔓	⬛

- **Top Viewport.**   Top ▾

- **Curve Tools tabbed toolbar.**   Curve Tools

- Create an **8mm x 10mm Ellipse.**
  - **Ellipse center** prompt: Type **"0"** and press **Enter.**
  - **End of first axis** prompt: Type **"4"** and press **Enter.**
  - **End of second axis** prompt: Type **"5"** and press **Enter.**

Fig. 2

Ellipse: from center command

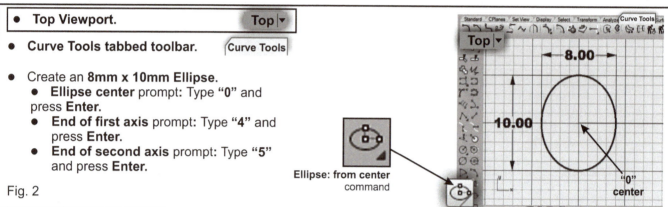

- **Perspective viewport.**   Perspective ▾

- Create a **4mm line** from the center of the ellipse using the **Line: Vertical to Cplane** command.

  - **Start of line prompt**: Type **"0"** and press **Enter.**
  - **End of line** prompt: Type **"4"** and press **Enter.**
  - Draw the cursor up and click to set location.

Fig. 3

Line: Vertical to Cplane command

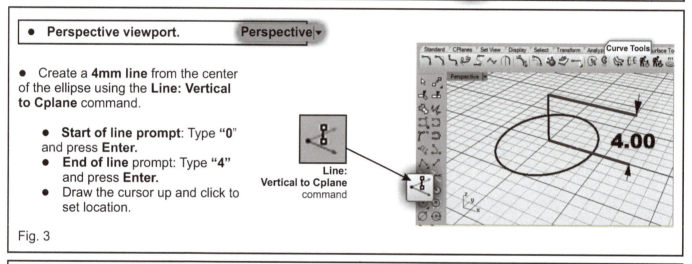

- Create an arc using the **Arc: start, end, point on arc** command.

  - **Start of arc:** ❶
  - **End of arc :** ❷
  - **Point on arc :** ❸

Fig. 4

Arc: start, end, point on arc command

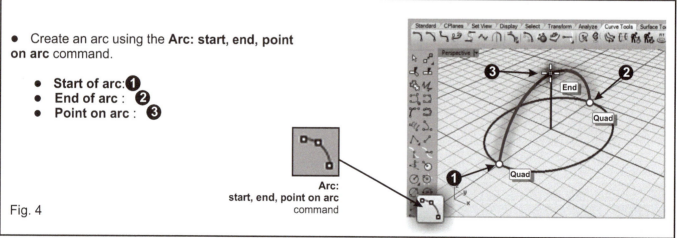

- Use the **Trim** command to trim away one half of the arc.
  - **Select cutting objects** prompt:
    - Select the perpendicular line ❶ and press **Enter.**
  - **Select object to trim** prompt:
    - Click on one end of the arc ❷ and press **Enter.**

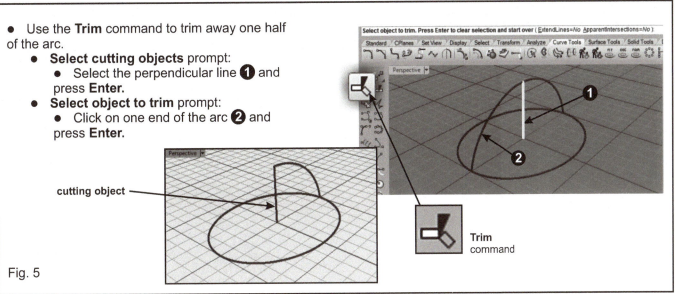

cutting object

Trim
command

Fig. 5

OVAL CAB ✔ ■

- **Right-click** on the **Rail Revolve** command.

  - **Select profile curve** prompt:
    - Select the trimmed arc. ❶
  - **Select rail curve** prompt:
    - Select the ellipse. ❷
  - **Start of rail revolve axis** prompt:
    - Click on one end of the vertical line, using **end osnap.** ❸
  - **End of rail revolve axis** prompt:
    - Click on the other end of the vertical line, using **end osnap.** ❹

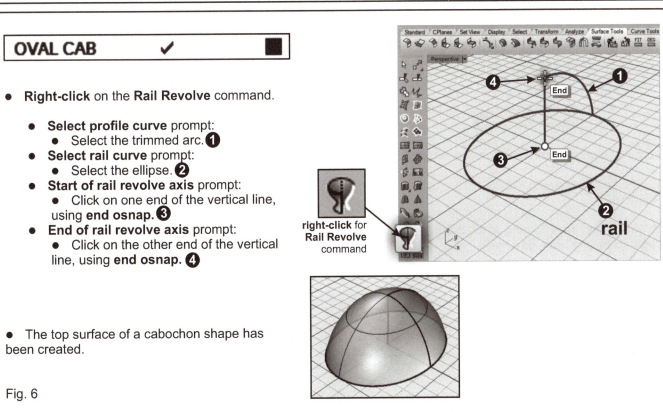

right-click for
Rail Revolve
command

rail

- The top surface of a cabochon shape has been created.

Fig. 6

- Select the new revolved surface.
- Type **"cap"** and press **Enter.**

  - A flat surface will form to close the open planar hole at the bottom of the surface.
  - The new surface is called a **"cap"**.
  - The stone is now a closed polysurface.

cap

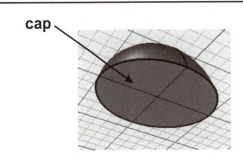

Fig. 7

- Create a bezel profile curve, using the same method as in the previous chapter, **Revolve Command - Round Cabochon in Bezel Setting**.
  - Ref: Figs. 8-11.

- You can turn off the **OVAL CAB layer** for more clarity in the next step.

Fig. 8

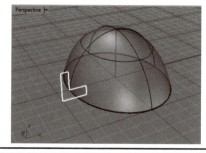

BEZEL ✓ ■

- **Surface Tools tabbed toolbar.** [Surface Tools]

- **Right-click** on the **Rail Revolve** command.

  - **Select profile curve** prompt:
    - Select the bezel profile curve. ❶
  - **Select rail curve** prompt:
    - Select the ellipse.❷
  - **Start of rail revolve axis** prompt:
    - Using **End osnap,** click on one end of the vertical line.❸
  - **End of rail revolve axis** prompt:
    - Using **End osnap,** click on the other end of the vertical line,❹

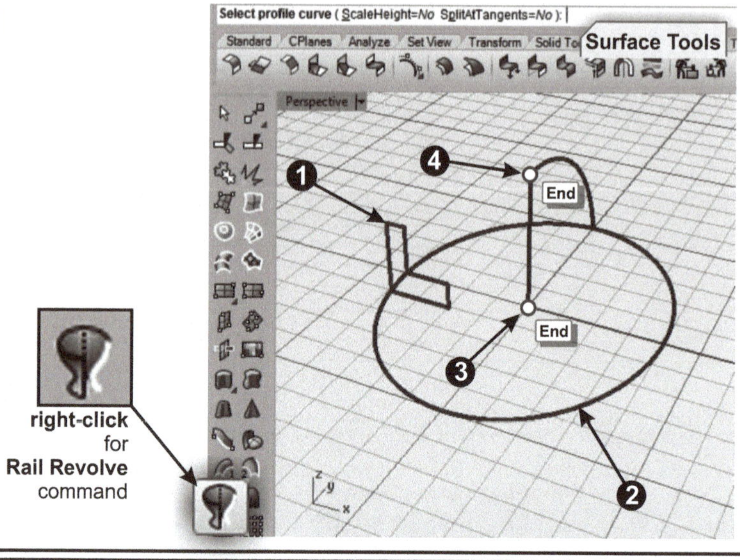

Fig. 9

right-click
for
Rail Revolve
command

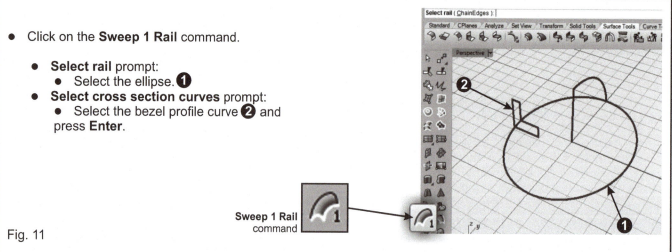

- The finished bezel has followed the oval shape of the rail curve.

- Notice that the thickness of the bezel is **not consistent at middle and ends.**

- Another strategy needs to be used to create a bezel of consistent thickness.

- **Delete** or **Undo** the Rail Revolve.

Fig. 10

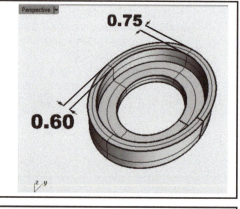

0.75

0.60

- Click on the **Sweep 1 Rail** command.

  - **Select rail** prompt:
    - Select the ellipse.❶
  - **Select cross section curves** prompt:
    - Select the bezel profile curve ❷ and press **Enter**.

Sweep 1 Rail
command

Fig. 11

- **Drag seam point to adjust. Press Enter when done** prompt:
  - Make sure that the seam point is on one of the corners of the profile curve.
  - Press **Enter.**

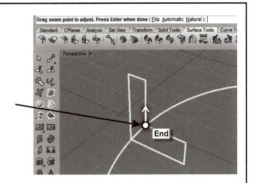

- The **Sweep 1 Rail Options** dialog box will appear.
  - Keep the options shown in the dialog box. ❶
  - Click on the OK button. ❷

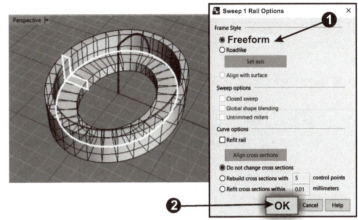

- Now the thickness of the bezel will be entirely consistent.

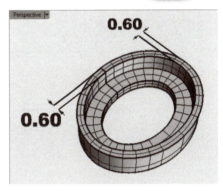

Fig. 12

- The finished stone and bezel are shown in **Rendered Viewport mode** with an **Environment Map** applied to the bezel.
  - These are custom render materials.

- Render colors have been assigned to the cabochon layer:
  - Color: **Aquamarine**
  - Gloss Finish: **approx 10%**

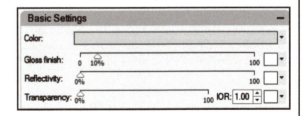

Fig. 13

Rail Revolve Command - Puffed Heart

Creating the Rail Curve for the Heart

- Create the layers shown.

- **ref geo** layer current (abbreviation for *reference geometry*)

Fig. 1

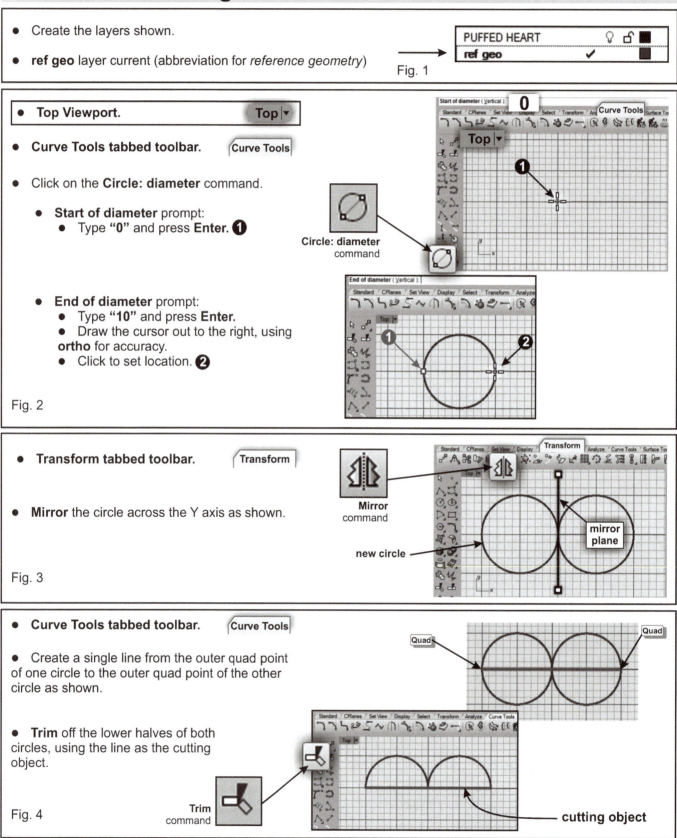

- **Top Viewport.** `Top ▼`

- **Curve Tools tabbed toolbar.** `Curve Tools`

- Click on the **Circle: diameter** command.

  - **Start of diameter** prompt:
    - Type **"0"** and press **Enter.** ❶

  Circle: diameter command

  - **End of diameter** prompt:
    - Type **"10"** and press **Enter.**
    - Draw the cursor out to the right, using **ortho** for accuracy.
    - Click to set location. ❷

Fig. 2

- **Transform tabbed toolbar.** `Transform`

- **Mirror** the circle across the Y axis as shown.

  Mirror command

  new circle

  mirror plane

Fig. 3

- **Curve Tools tabbed toolbar.** `Curve Tools`

- Create a single line from the outer quad point of one circle to the outer quad point of the other circle as shown.

  Quad   Quad

- **Trim** off the lower halves of both circles, using the line as the cutting object.

  Trim command

  cutting object

Fig. 4

- **Delete** the cutting object so that there are just the two arcs left as shown.

- Type **"point"** and press **Enter**.
  - The actual command button is in the **Standard tabbed toolbar.**

  - **Location of point object** prompt:
    - click on **Grid Snap** | Grid Snap |

    - Click on the grid intersection that is **15 mm** below **"0"** to place a point as shown.

- Click to toggle off **Grid Snap.**

Fig. 5

accesses the
Extend
toobar flyout

- Click on the **Extend by Arc to Point** command in the **Extend toolbar flyout.**

  - **Select curve to extend** prompt:
    - Click near the outer end of one of the arcs.❶

**Extend
by Arc to Point**
command

  - **End of extension. Press Enter to use the radius of curvature of the curve** prompt:
    - Draw the cursor downward toward the point and notice the preview line the follows it.

    - Snap to the point you created earlier and click to set location.

    - Then click to extend the arc on the other side in the same way.

    - Press **Enter** to end the command.

- Both arcs have been extended down to the point below.

Fig. 6

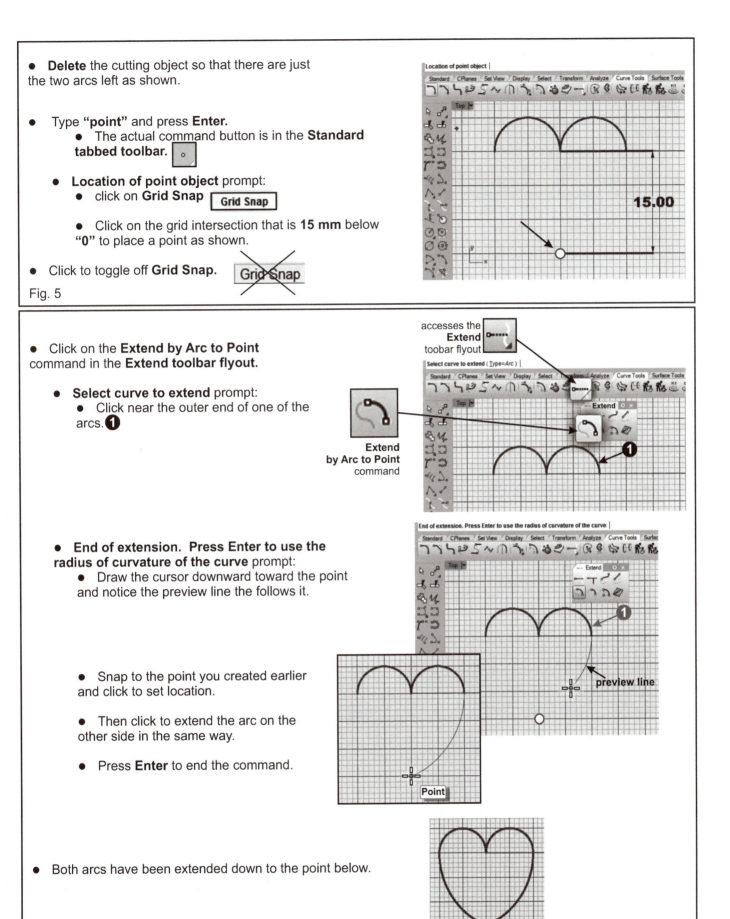

- Click on the **Fillet Curves** command.
  - Click on the **Join=No** option in the **Command Line** so that it reads **Join=Yes** as shown.
  - The fillet radius should be 1mm which is the default.
    - **Select first curve to fillet** prompt:
      - Click on the curve on one side of the angle of the two curves as shown. **❶**
    - **Select second curve to fillet** prompt:
      - Click on the curve on the other side as shown. **❷**

- The finished fillet will round off the sharp angle at the cleft of the heart with an arc that has a radius of **.5mm**.

- The sharp corner at the bottom has been filleted with a 4mm fillet radius.

- The result is a **closed curve**. If it is open, use the **Join** command to close all segments.

- The point at the bottom has been deleted.

Fig. 7

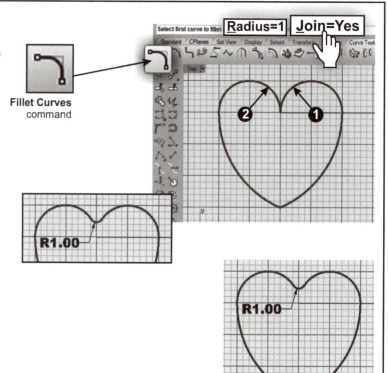

Fillet Curves
command

Reference Geometry and the Rail Revolve

- *It is now necessary to re-locate the curve seam along the middle of the heart curve so that the rebuild will be symmetrical.*

- Select the heart and click on the **Adjust Closed Curve Seam** command.

  - An arrow and a point will appear at the curve seam. It will be at one of the join points where a fillet meet the heart outline. **❶**

Fig. 8

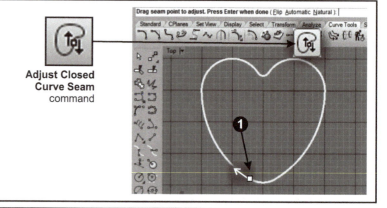

Adjust Closed
Curve Seam
command

- **Drag seam point to adjust. Press Enter when done** prompt:
  - Click on the point of the seam and drag it down to the lower **quad** point of the heart.
  - Click on the **quad** point to set the new location for the curve seam. **❷**
  - Press **Enter** to end the command.

Fig. 9

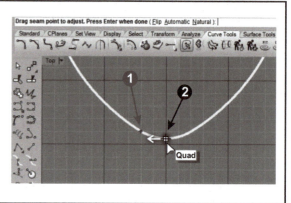

- **Rebuild** the heart to **26 control points**.

- Notice the symmetrical arrangement of the control points.

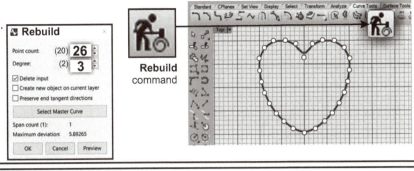

Fig. 10

- Create a line that **connects the two quad points** of the heart shown.

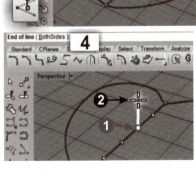

Fig. 11

- Select the line, type **"divide"**, and press **Enter**.
    - The button for this command, **Divide by Number of Segments** is in the **Point toolbar flyout** in the **Standard tabbed toolbar**.

- **Number of segments** prompt:
    - *Make sure that the prompt says "Number of segments". If it says "length", click on the* **"Number of segments"** *option in the* **Command Line.**
    - Type **"5"** and press **Enter**.

- Points will appear on the line, dividing it into 5 equal segments.

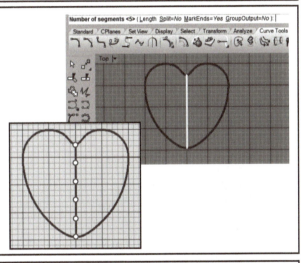

Fig. 12

- **Perspective viewport.**

Perspective ▾

- Click on the **Line: Vertical to Cplane**.

    - **Start of line** prompt:
        - Snap to the **3rd point down from the top** and click to set location. ❶

    - **End of line** prompt:
        - Draw the cursor upwards and *notice the vertical white constraint line.*
        - Type **"4"** and press **Enter**.
        - Click to set location. ❷

- A 4mm vertical line has been created.

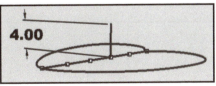

4.00

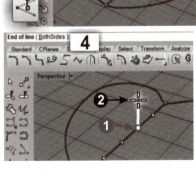

Fig. 13

- (Right) Perspective viewport. ❶ 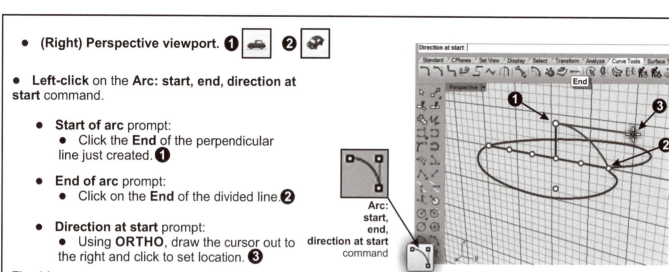 ❷

- **Left-click** on the **Arc: start, end, direction at start** command.

  - **Start of arc** prompt:
    - Click the **End** of the perpendicular line just created. ❶

  - **End of arc** prompt:
    - Click on the **End** of the divided line. ❷

  - **Direction at start** prompt:
    - Using **ORTHO**, draw the cursor out to the right and click to set location. ❸

Arc: start, end, direction at start command

Fig. 14

- Turn on the control points for the arc just created.

- **Rebuild** the arc to **4 control points.**

- **Hide** or **Delete** the center line and its points.

Fig. 15

- **Right Viewport.**   Right ▼ <image />

- Select the 2nd point from the bottom of the arc and click on the **Move** command.

Move command

  - **Point to move from** prompt:
    - Click on the **Point** that has been selected, using **Point Osnap.** ❶

  - **Point to move to** prompt:
    - Using **ORTHO**, draw the cursor to the right and **Tap the Tab key.**

    Tab ⇥

      - The direction of the move will be constrained.

      - Click on the **Point (or End)** at the bottom end of the arc. ❷

- Because of the direction constraint used, the moved point is now directly over the point at the bottom that you snapped to. ❷

Fig. 16

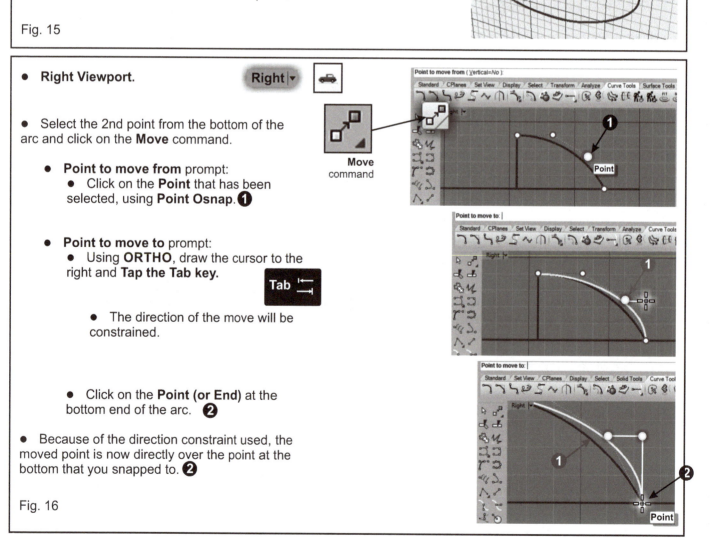

393

- Use the **Move** command again to move the next point up to the right **1mm.**

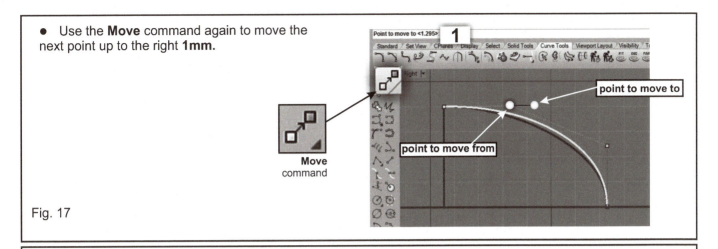

Move
command

Fig. 17

- Use the **Offset Curve** command to make a **.8mm** offset of the arc.

- **Rebuild** the new offset curve to **5 control points.**

Offset Curve
command

0.80

the new offset rebuilt to 5 control points

Fig. 18

- **Zoom** in to see that the upper end of the offset line does not quite touch the vertical revolve axis.

- This gap must be closed.

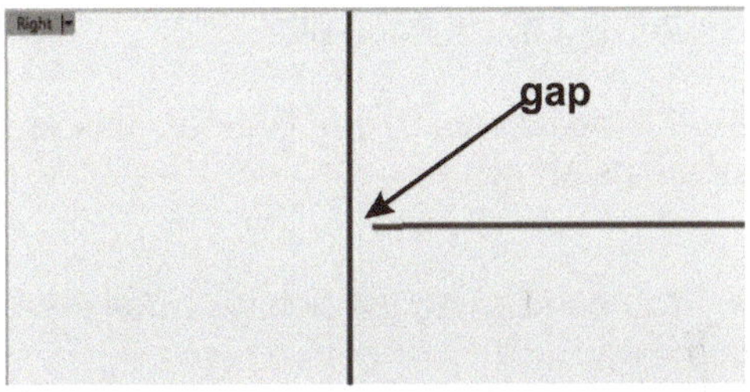

Fig. 19

gap

- Click on the **Extend Curve** command.
  - Click to select the **ToBoundary** option **1** in the **Command Line.**
  - **Select boundary objects. Press Enter when done** prompt:
    - Select the vertical line and press **Enter.2**

  - **Select curve to extend** prompt:
    - Click near the end of the horizontal line. **3**
    - The curve will extend to touch the designated vertical line.**4**
    - Press **Enter** to end the command.

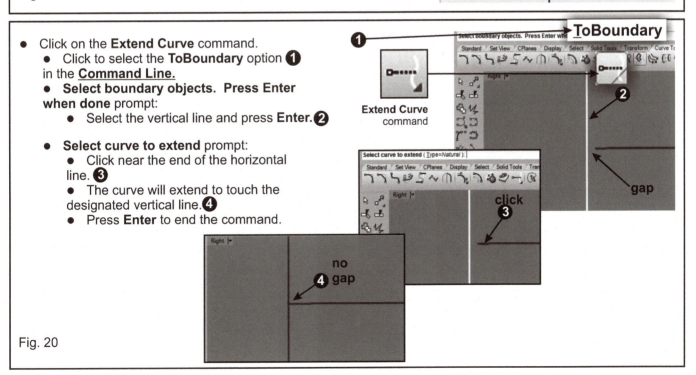

Extend Curve
command

ToBoundary

click
3

gap

no
4 gap

Fig. 20

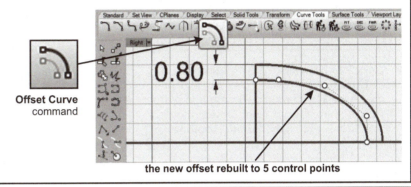

- **Top Perspective view.** ❶ ❷

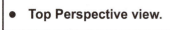

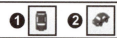

- Select the heart and create an **.8mm** offset to the inside.

- Rebuild the offset to **50 control points.**

Fig. 21

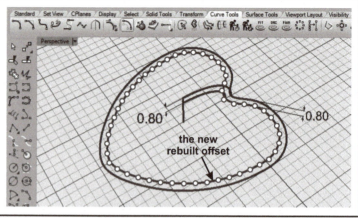

- The two arcs need to be touching ("intersecting") both the **vertical revolve axis** and the two hearts which will be the **rail curves**.

- Select all 5 curves, type **"Intersect"**, and press **Enter.**
  - **FYI:** The actual command button is in the **Curve from Objects** toolbar in the **Standard tabbed toolbar.**

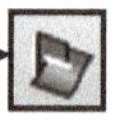

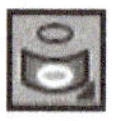

- Points will appear at the intersections of all curves that touch each other.

- It is necessary to see intersections at all 4 locations shown.

- You can **Delete** the points or use the **Undo** command.

Fig. 22

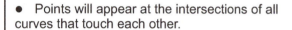

Creating the Inner Surface of the Heart

- **Surface Tools tabbed toolbar.** Surface Tools

PUFFED HEART ✔

- **Right-click** on the **Rail Revolve** command in the **Surface Creation** toolbar flyout.

  - **Select profile curve** ❶
  - **Select rail curve** ❷
  - **Start of RailRevolve axis:** snap to one **End** of the vertical line. ❸
  - **End of RailRevolve axis:** snap to the other **End** of the vertical line ❹

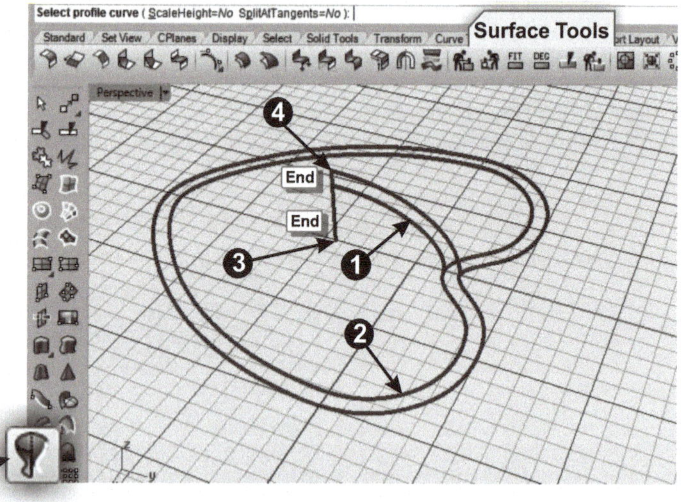

right-click for **Rail Revolve** command

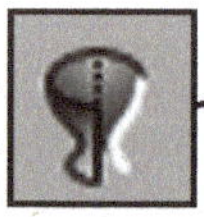

Fig. 23

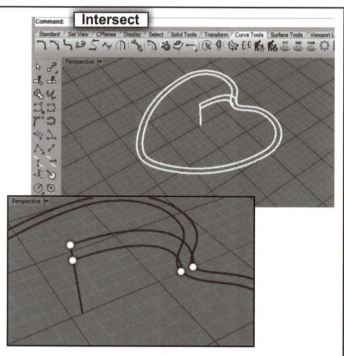

- The inner surface of the heart has been created.

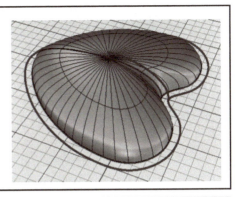

Fig. 24

Creating the Outer Surface of the Heart

- Select the outer curves shown when revolving the outer surface of the heart.

- **Right-click** on the **Rail Revolve** command in the **Surface Creation** toolbar flyout.

    - **Select profile curve ❶**
    - **Select rail curve ❷**
    - **Start of RailRevolve axis:** snap to one **End** of the vertical line. ❸
    - **End of RailRevolve axis:** snap to the other **End** of the vertical line. ❹

    right-click for **Rail Revolve** command

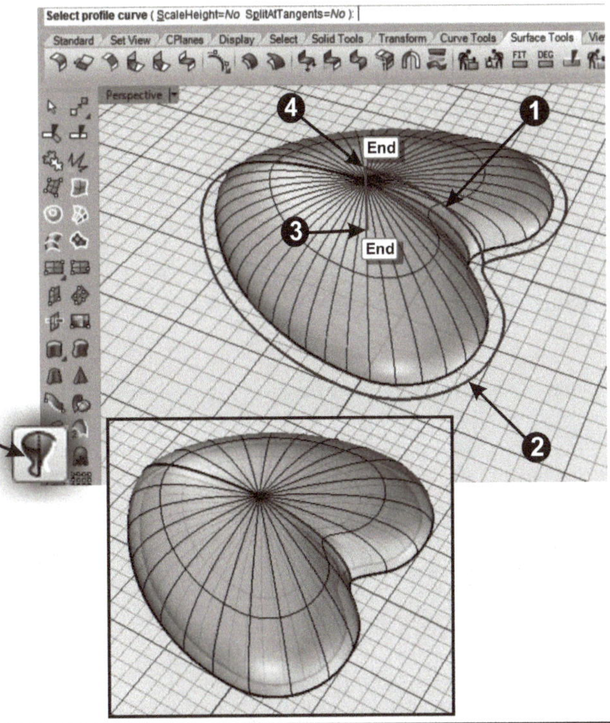

- The outer surface of the heart has been created.

Fig. 25

- Click on the **Surface from Planar Curves** command.

    - **Select planar curves to build surface. Press Enter when done** prompt:
        - Select the edges of both inner and outer heart surfaces as shown.
        - Press **Enter**.

    Surface from Planar Curves command

- A new surface has been created that fills in the gap between the inner and outer surfaces of the heart.

- Use the **Join** command to join these three surfaces together to complete a **single closed polysurface** that will be a solid.

- Save this file as: **hollow puffed heart.3dm**

Fig. 26

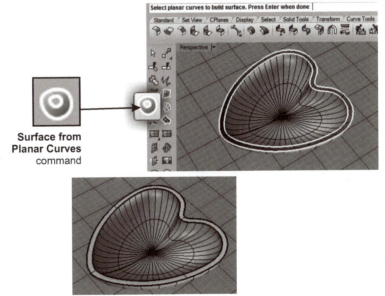

- **Explode** the heart into single surfaces.

- Retain the outer surface.

Fig. 27

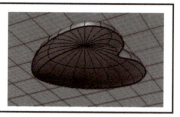

- **Right Viewport.** `Right |▼`

- **Transform tabbed toolbar.** `Transform`

- Select the puffed heart surface and **Mirror** it across the X axis (vertical mirror).

Fig. 28

`Right |▼`

mirror plane

new mirrored copy

- Select the new mirrored copy and click on the **Scale 1-D** command in the **Scale** toolbar flyout.

  - **Origin point** prompt:
    - Type "0" and press **Enter. ❶**
  - **Scale factor or first reference point** prompt:
    - Using **ORTHO,** draw the cursor down and click approximately in the same location shown. ❷

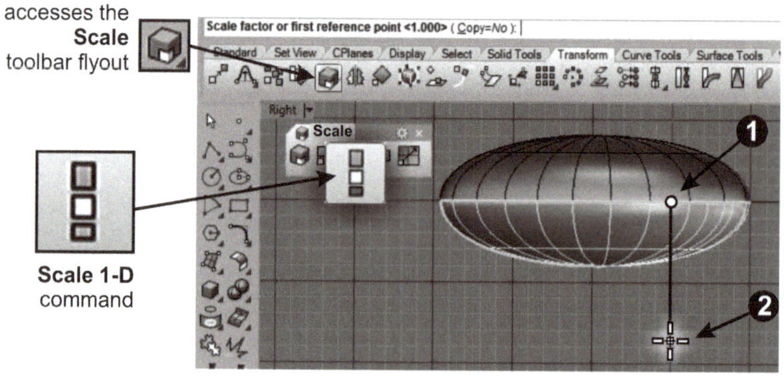

accesses the **Scale** toolbar flyout

Scale 1-D command

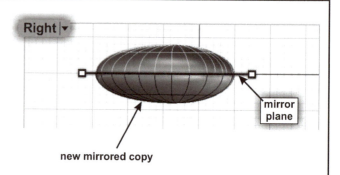

  - **Second reference point** prompt:
    - Draw the cursor up and click on a second reference point as shown.

- The bottom of the double heart will be shallower than the top.

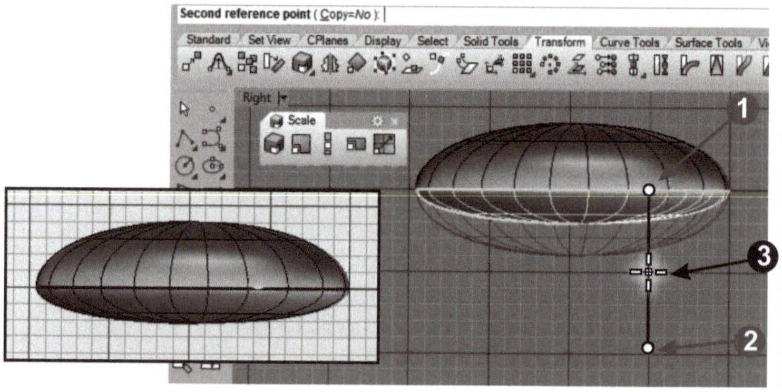

- Use the **Join** command to join the front and back surfaces of the heart to make a closed polysurface that will be a solid object.

- Save this file as **double puffed heart.3dm.**

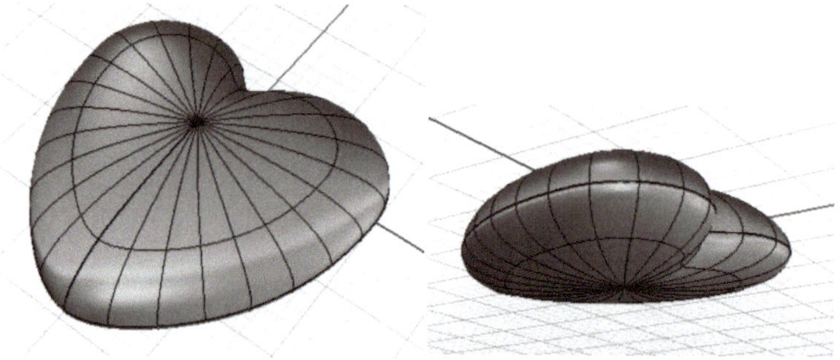

Fig. 29

Creating a Heart with a Flat Back - Cap Command

- **Explode** the heart and retain the outer surface.

- **Solid Tools tabbed toolbar.** ⌐Solid Tools⌐

Fig. 30

- Select the heart surface and click on the **Cap Planar Holes** command in the **Solid Tools** toolbar flyout.

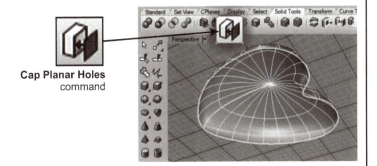

Cap Planar Holes command

- A new surface - the **"Cap"** will be created that closes off the opening at the back.

- The new **cap** automatically joins the existing surface to create a **closed polysurface** which is a solid object.

- Save this file as: **flat backed puffed heart.3dm.**

the new cap

Fig. 31

Rail Revolve Exercises

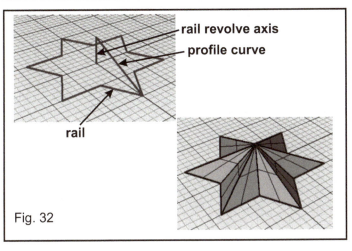

rail revolve axis
profile curve
rail

Fig. 32

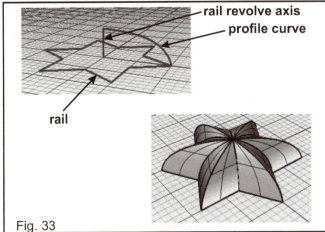

rail revolve axis
profile curve
rail

Fig. 33

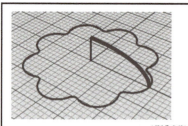

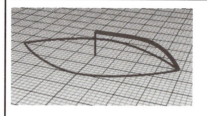

- **Rail Curve** made from Polar Arrayed and filleted arcs. See the chapter on the **Necklace Layout** for reference. Fillet with **Fillet Corners** command.

Fig. 34

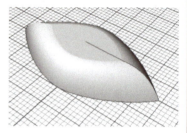

- **Rail Curve** point edited from a circle.

Fig. 35

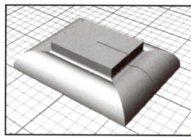

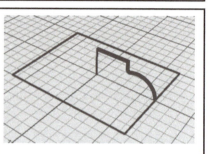

- A **polyline** and an **Arc** were joined and then **filleted** with the **Fillet Curve** command.

RIGHT-CLICK for **Extract Surface** command

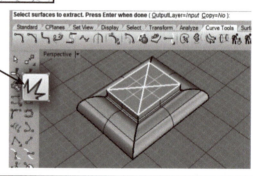

- For cleaner geometry, **right-click** on the **Explode** button to get the **Extract Surface** command.

- Select the 4 top surfaces shown and press **Enter.**

- Press the **Delete** key to delete the selected surfaces.

Fig. 35

- Select the polysurface, type **"cap"**, and press **Enter.**

- The planar openings at both top and bottom will be "capped". The model will be **closed polysurface.**

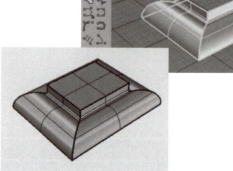

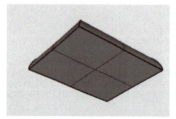

Fig. 36

Sweep 1 Rail Command
Simple Ring with History

- Create the layers shown.

- **ref** layer current.

Fig. 1

| RING | | 💡 | 🔓 | ⬛ |
| **ref** | ✔ | | | ⬛ |

- **Front Viewport.** **Front** ▾

- Create a **Circle** around **"0"** with a diameter of **17.35mm.**

Fig. 2

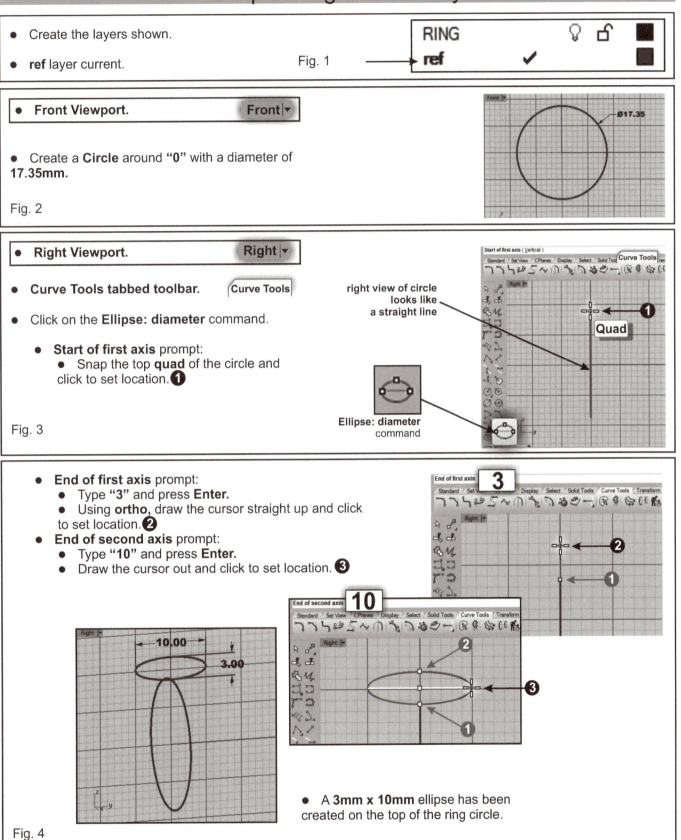

- **Right Viewport.** **Right** ▾

- **Curve Tools tabbed toolbar.** **Curve Tools**

- Click on the **Ellipse: diameter** command.

  - **Start of first axis** prompt:
    - Snap the top **quad** of the circle and click to set location. ❶

Fig. 3

right view of circle looks like a straight line

Quad

Ellipse: diameter command

- **End of first axis** prompt:
  - Type **"3"** and press **Enter**.
  - Using **ortho**, draw the cursor straight up and click to set location. ❷
- **End of second axis** prompt:
  - Type **"10"** and press **Enter**.
  - Draw the cursor out and click to set location. ❸

- A **3mm x 10mm** ellipse has been created on the top of the ring circle.

Fig. 4

- Use the same technique to create a **2mm x 4mm** ellipse at the bottom of the ring.

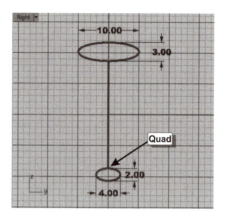

Fig. 5

- **Top Perspective view.** ❶ 🔲 ❷ 🎨

RING ✓ ⬛

- **Surface Tools tabbed toolbar.** ⌐Surface Tools

⌐Record History

- Click on the **Sweep 1 Rail** command.

  - **Select rail** prompt:
    - Select the circle. ❶
  - **Select cross section curves** prompt:
    - Select the two ovals and press **Enter**. ❷ & ❸   Fig. 6

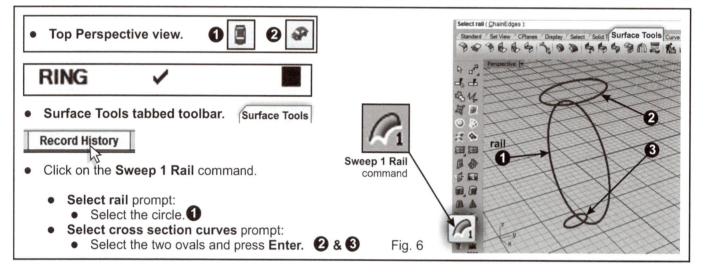

- *Because the cross section curves are **closed curves**, you will be prompted for the **seam location**.*

Fig. 7

- **Drag seam to adjust. Press Enter when done** prompt:
  - Click on the top seam point and drag, snapping to bottom **quad** of the large ellipse as shown - click to set location. ❶
  - Move the bottom seam point so that is rests on the top **quad** point of the small ellipse. ❷
  - Press **Enter**.

    - **IMPORTANT: both** curve points need to be either inside the ring or outside the ring because this guides the location of the resulting closed surface's seam.

both curve points are on the inside the ring

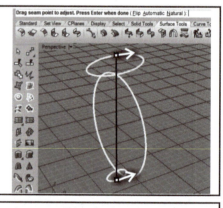

Fig. 8

401

- The **Sweep 1 Rail Options** box will open.

- The surface formed has only been created between the two designated cross section curves.

  - Click in the check box to engage **Closed Sweep.** ❶

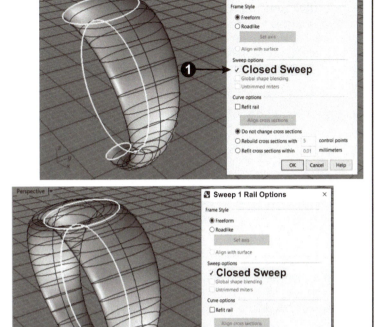

- The preview, viewed here in **Shaded Viewport Mode** will update showing the sweep forming a full ring, rather than just half of one.

- Click on the **OK button** to complete the command.

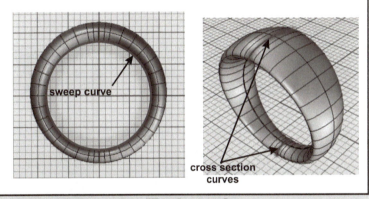

Fig. 9

Sweep 1 Rail Explained

- The **sweep curve** has guided the direction of the surface creation.

- The **cross sections curves (there is no limit on how many cross section curves you can designate)** guide the ring's height and the modulation of the surface.

- The width and height of the ring have been gracefully flowed from one cross section curve to the other.

Fig. 10

If the Preview of the Ring is Twisted

- Note the twisted shape of the ring in this **Preview example.**

- To fix this, click on the **Align Cross Sections button.**

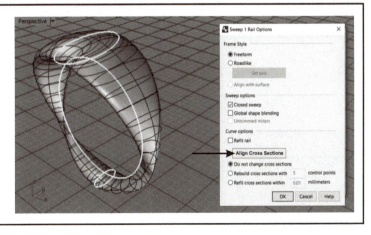

Fig. 11

- **Click end of shape curve to reverse.
Press Enter when done** prompt:
  - Click on the point of one of the shape curve points as shown.

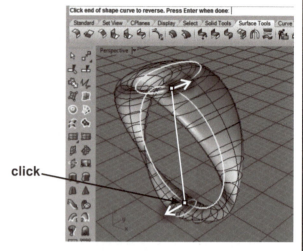

click

- The arrow will switch direction.

- The preview ring will immediately straighten out.

- Press **Enter.**

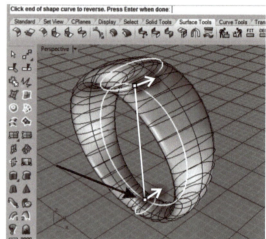

- Click the **OK button** to end the command.

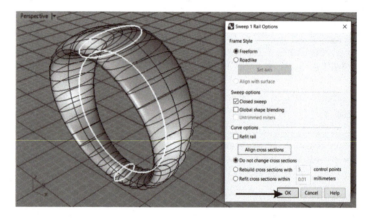

Fig. 12

Using History to Edit the Ring's Shape

- **ref** layer current.

- **Lock** the **RING** layer.

Fig. 13

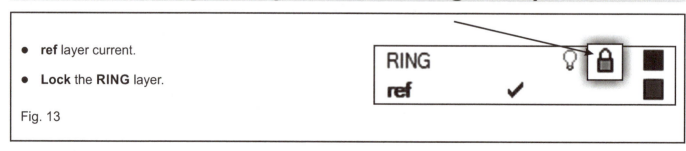

- Select both ellipses and **Rebuild** to **32 control points.**

- It is better geometry for all cross section curves to have the same number of control points if possible.
  - But this may not be feasible if cross section curves are radically different shapes from each other.

- Note how the amount of isocurves increases. This is because of the **History relationship** between the **curves (PARENTS)** and the **surface (CHILD).**
  - Ref. Fig. 6 where **History was enabled.**

Fig. 14

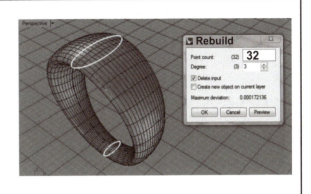

Right ▼

- **Right Viewport.**   **Right ▼**

- Turn on the control points for the upper ellipse. **F10**

- Select **control points** shown.

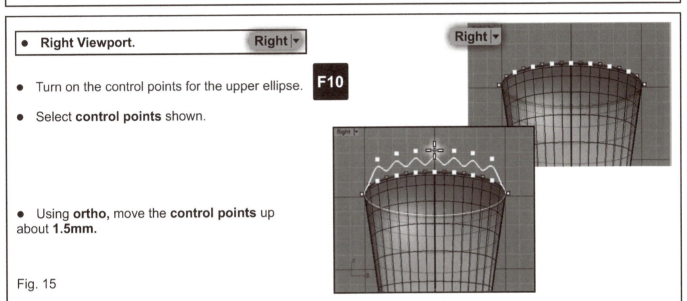

- Using **ortho,** move the **control points** up about **1.5mm.**

Fig. 15

- **History** has updated the ring to be rippled on top and smooth on the bottom where there was no editing.

- The ripples have gradually flattened out as they modulate from the top of the ring to the bottom, guided by the different shapes of the two cross section curves.

Fig. 16

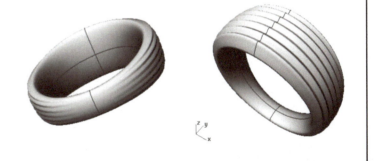

- Many variations can be made by point editing the cross section curves.

- The **Set XYZ Coordinates/Set Points** command used the **Right Viewport** made the flat top of this ring.

Fig. 17

Sweep 2 Rails Command
Band Ring to Specifications

- Create the layers shown.

- **ref** layer current.

Fig. 1

| RING | 💡 🔓 ⬛ |
| **ref** | ✔ ⬛ |

- This model will be made to the specifications of this technical drawing.

6.00 widest point | 4.00 narrowest point

3.00

Ø16.51

1.50

2.00

6.00

4.00

Fig. 2

- **Front Viewport.**   Front ▾

- **Curve Tools tabbed toolbar.**   Curve Tools

- Create a **16.51mm diameter circle** around "**0**".

- Rebuild to **32 control points.**

Fig. 3

Rebuild ×

Point count: (8) **32**

Degree: (2) 3

☑ Delete input
☐ Create new object on current layer
☐ Preserve end tangent directions

Select Master Curve

Span count (7): 32
Maximum deviation: 3.22394e-05

OK   Cancel   Preview

Ø16.51

- Draw the 4 lines shown from the 4 **quads** of the circle.
    - Line from top quad: **3mm** ❶
    - Line from bottom quad: **1.5mm** ❷
    - Lines from left and right quads: **2mm** ❸

Fig. 4

3.00   2.00

Quad

2.00   1.50

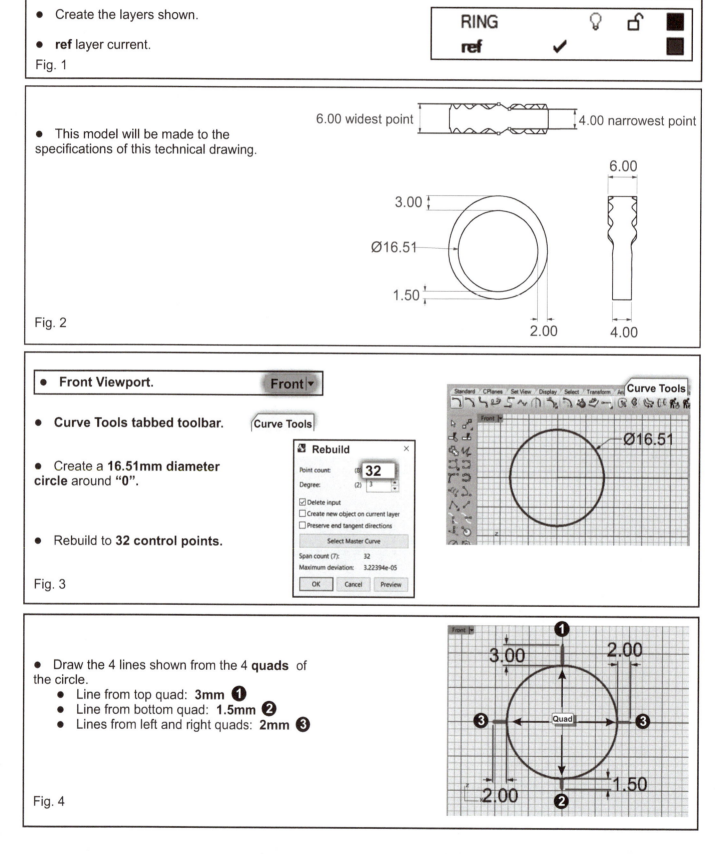

Creating the 2 Rails for the 2-Rail Sweep

- **Top Perspective view.** ❶  ❷

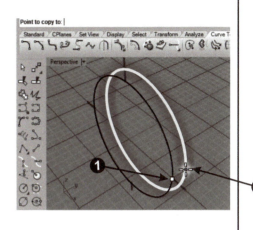

- Select the circle, type **"copy"**, and press **Enter.**

    - **Point to copy from** prompt:
        - Snap to one of the **quads** of the circle and click to set location. ❶

    - **Point to copy to** prompt:
    - Type **"2"** and press **Enter.**
    - Using **ortho**, draw the cursor back and click to set location.
    - Press **Enter** to end the command. ❷

Fig. 5

- **Left-click** on the **Line: from Midpoint** command in the **Lines** toolbar flyout.

    - **Middle of line** prompt:
        - Snap to the top **quad** of the original circle that was created around "0" in the first step. Click to set location. ❶

    - **End of line** prompt:
        - Type **"3"** and press **Enter.**
        - Using **ortho,** draw the cursor to the back and click to set location. ❷

- The new line is centered on the **top quad** of the original circle and is **6mm long.**

Fig. 6

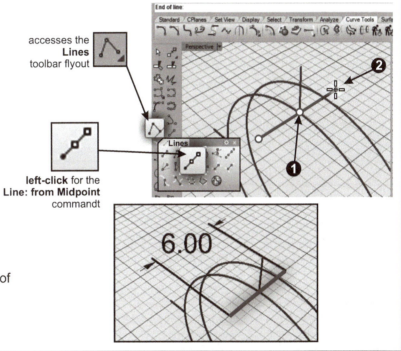

accesses the
Lines
toolbar flyout

left-click for the
Line: from Midpoint
commandt

- **Standard tabbed toolbar.** ⌐ Standard ⌐

- Select the circle shown and click on the **Edit Points On** command.
    - *This is not the same as control points. Make sure you click on the Edit Points button, not the Control Points button.*

- Unlike Control Points, Edit Points will always be located on the curve or line to be edited.

Fig. 7

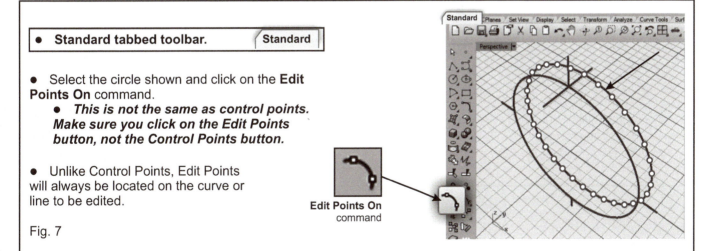

Edit Points On
command

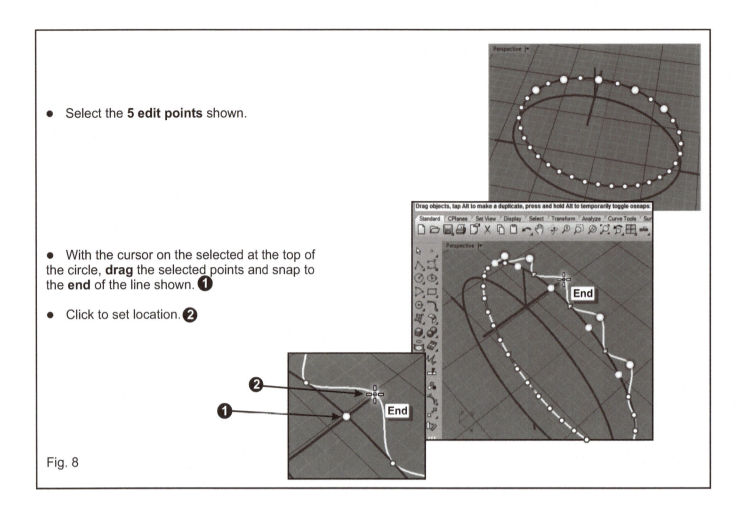

- Select the **5 edit points** shown.

- With the cursor on the selected at the top of the circle, **drag** the selected points and snap to the **end** of the line shown. ❶

- Click to set location. ❷

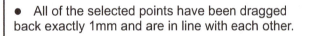

Fig. 8

- All of the selected points have been dragged back exactly 1mm and are in line with each other.

- Edit points will give you this precision because they are always in contact with the line edited.
    - Control points would not have worked for this.

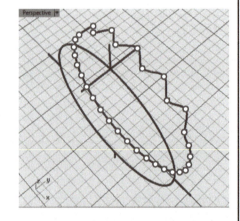

- **Mirror** the newly edited wavy line to the other side of the middle circle.
    - Use the **X Axis** as your **mirror plane.**

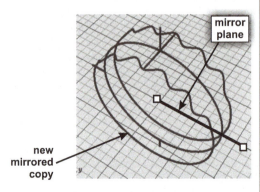

mirror plane

new mirrored copy

Fig. 9

- **Curve Tools tabbed toolbar.** (Curve Tools)

- Click on the **Rectangle: 3 Points** command.

  - **Start of edge** prompt:
    - Click on one of the **ends** of the 6mm line at the top of the ring. ❶

  - **End of edge** prompt:
    - Click on the other end of the 6mm line. ❷

  - **Width. Press Enter to use length** prompt:
    - Draw the rectangle upward to snap to the end of the perpendicular 3mm line at the top of the ring..
    - Click to set location. ❸

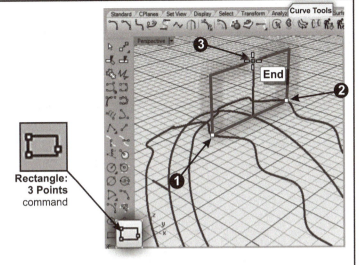

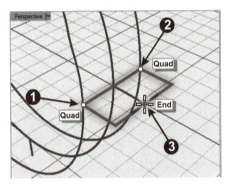

Rectangle:
3 Points
command

- Use the same technique to create a rectangle on the side of the ring.

- Use the same technique once more to create a rectangle on the bottom quad of the ring.

Fig. 10

- **Mirror** the rectangle on the side over to the other side of the two rails.

- Select all of the elements, except for the two rails and the 4 rectangle cross sections, type **"hide",** and press **Enter.**

- You just want to see the 2 rails and the 4 cross sections as shown.

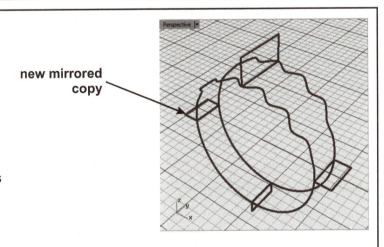

new mirrored
copy

Fig. 11

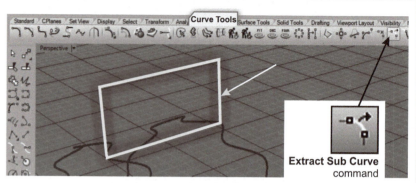

- Select the top rectangle and click on the **Extract Sub Curve** command.

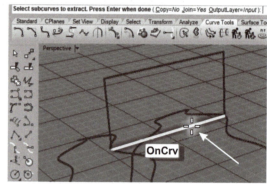

Extract Sub Curve
command

- **Select subcurves to extract. Press Enter when done** prompt:
  - Click on the bottom edge of the rectangle.
  - Press **Enter.**

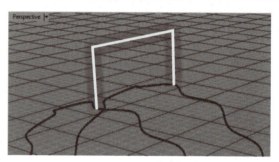

OnCrv

- **Hide** or **Delete** the extracted curve.

- The cross section curve is now an open curve.

Fig. 12

- Repeat this process with the 3 other cross section curves to make them all open curves.

- Note: cross section curves must be all open or all closed curves, never a combination of open and closed curves in a single sweep command.

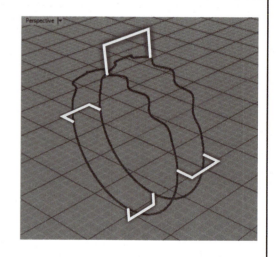

Fig. 13

RING ✔ ■

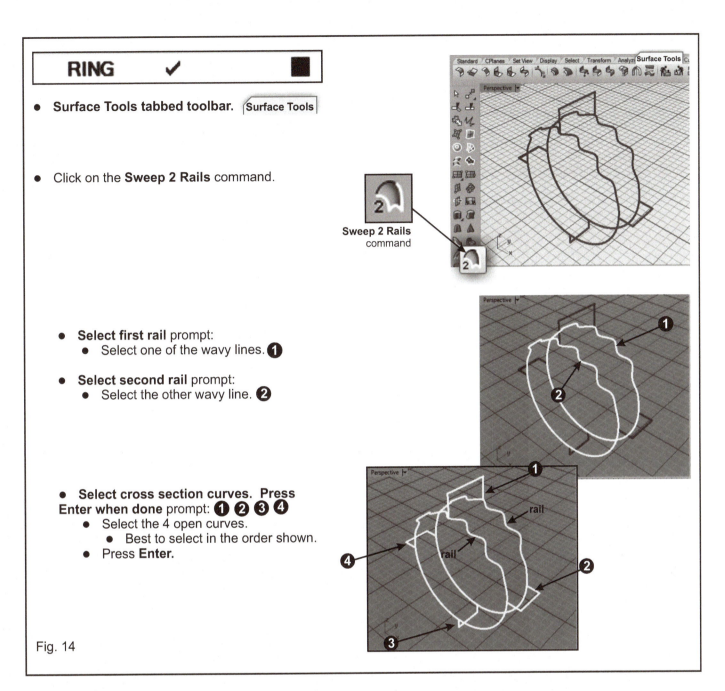

- **Surface Tools tabbed toolbar.** Surface Tools

- Click on the **Sweep 2 Rails** command.

Sweep 2 Rails command

- **Select first rail** prompt:
  - Select one of the wavy lines. ❶

- **Select second rail** prompt:
  - Select the other wavy line. ❷

- **Select cross section curves. Press Enter when done** prompt: ❶ ❷ ❸ ❹
  - Select the 4 open curves.
    - Best to select in the order shown.
  - Press **Enter.**

Fig. 14

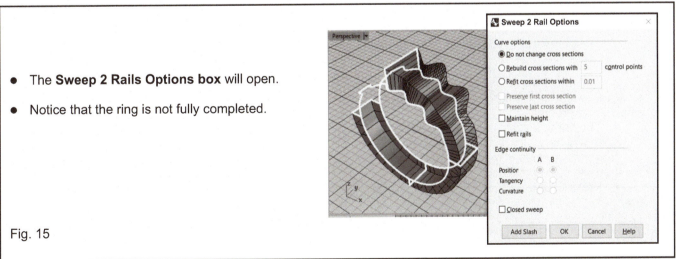

- The **Sweep 2 Rails Options box** will open.

- Notice that the ring is not fully completed.

Fig. 15

- Click to put a check mark on the **Maintain Height option.** ❶
  - This will keep the height of the surface to the heights of the cross section curves.

- Click to put a check mark on the **Closed Sweep** option. ❷
  - This will close up the ring at the top.

- You can click on the **Preview** button to update the view of the piece. ❸

Fig. 16

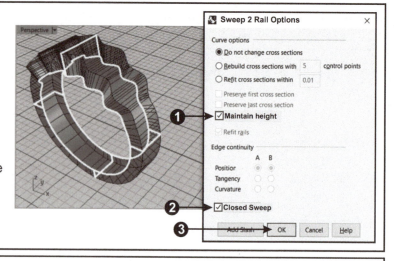

- Click the **OK button** to complete the ring.

Fig. 17

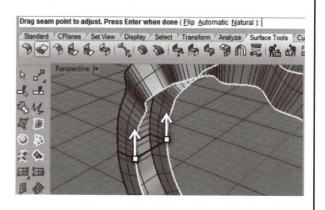

Lofting the Inside Surface of the Ring

Loft command

- Click on the **Loft** command.

  - **Select curves to loft** prompt:
    - Click on one of the open surface edges of the inside of the ring as shown. ❶

  - **Select curves to loft. Press Enter when done** prompt:
    - Click to select the open surface edge on the other side of the ring. ❷
    - Press **Enter.**

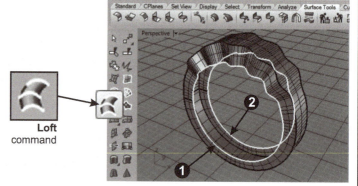

- **Drag seam point to adjust. Press Enter when done** prompt.
  - The surface seam needs to be straight as shown here. If it is not, you need to drag the two ends of the seam so that they line up with other.
    - Press **Enter.**

Fig. 18

- The **Loft Options** box will open.

- The **Straight Sections** style is the default when only lofting two curves.

- Press the **OK button.**

- The inner surface of the ring has been created.

Fig. 19

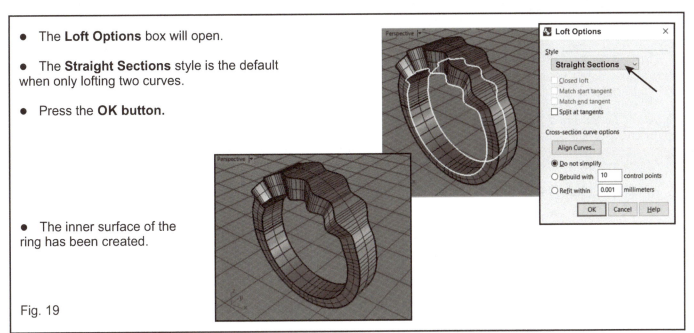

- Select both the outer and inner parts of the ring and click on the **Join** command.

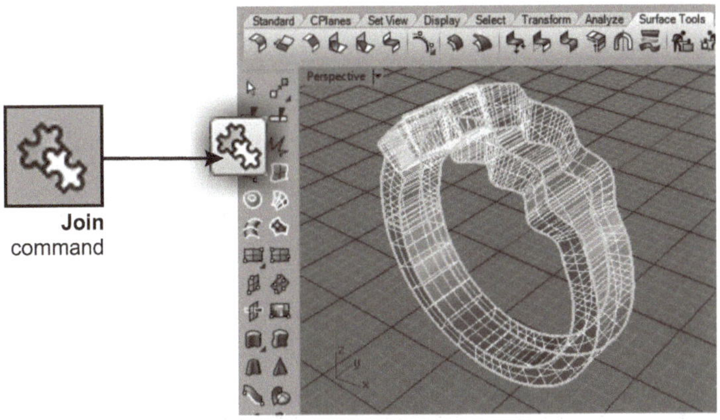

Join
command

Fig. 20

2 surfaces or polysurfaces joined into one closed polysurface

- The History line will inform you that the join is resulted in **one closed polysurface.**
  - **This is now a solid model.**

Fig. 21

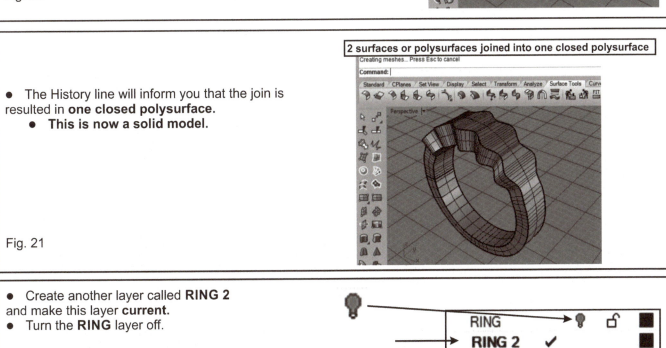

- Create another layer called **RING 2** and make this layer **current.**
- Turn the **RING** layer off.

- Turn the **ref** layer back on.

Fig. 22

RING

RING 2 ✓

ref

- Click on the **Sweep 2 Rails** command and choose the same sweep curves and cross section curves as before.

- When the **Sweep 2 Rail Options box** opens up, **uncheck the Maintain Height option.**

- Check the **Closed Sweep option** as before.

- Click on the **OK button.**

Fig. 23

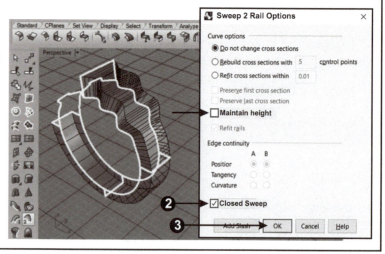

- The height of the cross section curves has not been maintained, resulting in an intuitive modulation in the silhouette of the ring.

Fig. 24

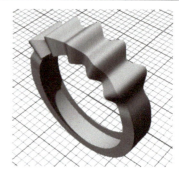

- When **Lofting** the inner surface of the ring, notice that the seam is crooked.

- Now, one of the seam points has been dragged to be in line with the other, using **Quad osnap** to anchor location.

- Make sure to click to set the new location and the seam end.

- When the seam is straight, press **Enter** to finish the inner surface of the ring.

- Use the **Join** command to create a **closed polysurface.**

- Save these rings as 2 separate files:
  - **Sweep 2 Rails ring 1.3dm**
  - **Sweep 2 Rails ring 2.3dm**

Fig. 25

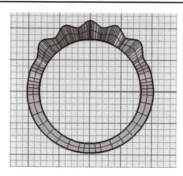

Naked Edges
Surface/Polysurface Edges that can not Join to other Edges

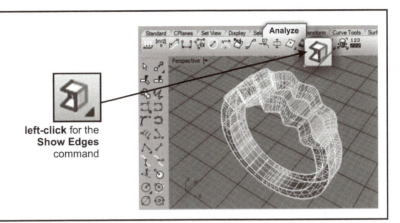

left-click for the
Show Edges
command

- Open the file: **Sweep 2 Rails Ring 1.3dm** from the previous chapter.

- **Analyze tabbed toolbar.** [Analyze]

- Select the ring and **left-click** on the **Show Edges** command.

Fig. 1

Found 9 edges total; no naked edges, no non-manifold edges.

- The History line will inform you about the number of edges and whether there are any Naked Edges as well as whether you have more than two surfaces joined at one seam.

- All seams will be illuminated in pink with points at the ends of seams.

- The **Edge Analysis** box will appear as well.

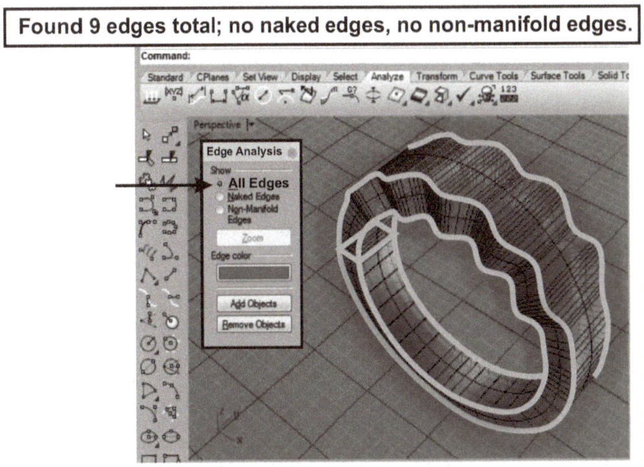

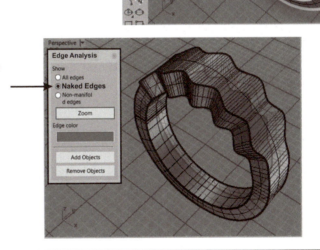

- Click to choose the **Naked Edges** option in the **Edge Analysis** box.

- All of the pink lines will disappear because there are no Naked Edges on this piece.

- This piece is a **closed polysurface** and is, therefore, a **Solid.**

Fig. 2

- Note: **Closed Surfaces** or **Closed Polysurface** are solid objects.

- A **closed surface** has a seam with no openings.

- **Closed Polysurfaces** are multiple surfaces that are **Joined** together with no openings.

Fig. 3

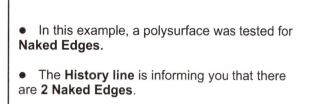

- In this example, a polysurface was tested for **Naked Edges**.

- The **History line** is informing you that there are **2 Naked Edges**.

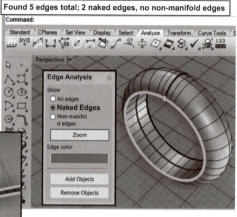

- A detail view shows the **2 separate naked edges** at the gap between these two surfaces.

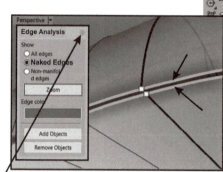

Fig. 4

- Click to close out the **Edge Analysis** box and turn off the layer that contains the surfaces so that you can see only the **reference geometry**.

- Notice that there is a gap between the end of the arc and the end of the line which is the reason that, when the surfaces were created, their edges were not in contact with each other.

- This gap needs to be closed, either by point editing or checking the dimensions and re-doing the arc or the line.

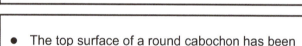

gap

Fig. 5

- The top surface of a round cabochon has been revolved.

- When tested for **Naked Edges,** the bottom edge of this surface is a **Naked Edge.** This is still an **open surface.**

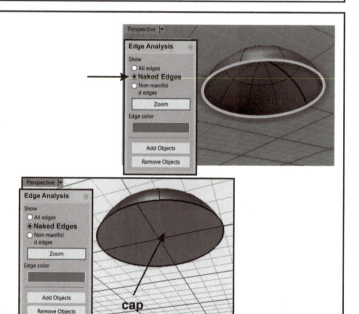

- Now the surface has been **Capped.**

- The cap has closed the opening on the bottom of the cabochon and the piece now does not have **Naked Edges.**

- It is now a **closed polysurface.**

cap

Fig. 6

415

Bombé Ring

Surface from a Network of Curves command

Creating the Curve Network

- Create the layers shown.

- **bombe ring ref** layer current.

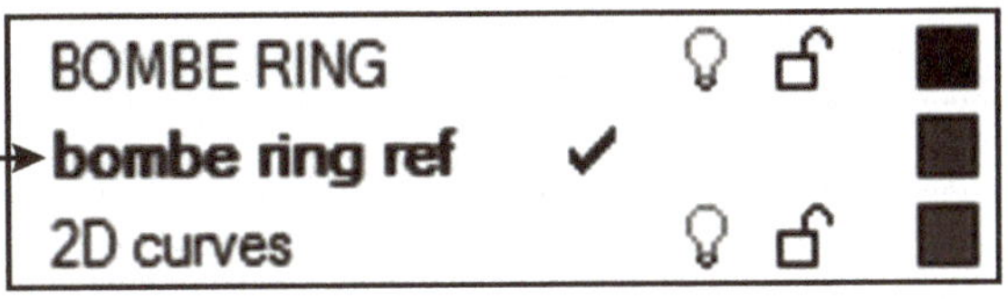

Fig. 1

BOMBE RING		💡 🔓 ⬛
bombe ring ref	✓	⬛
2D curves		💡 🔓 ⬛

- **Front Viewport.**   Front ▾

- **Curve Tools tabbed toolbar.**   Curve Tools

- Create a **17.35mm diameter circle** around **"0"**.

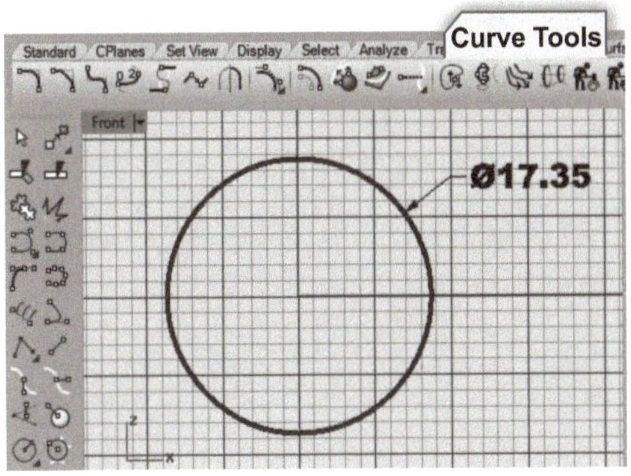

Ø17.35

Fig. 2

- Using **ORTHO**, draw **2mm straight lines** from the two side **quads** of the circle. ❶

- Using **ORTHO**, draw **one 1.5mm line** down from the bottom **quad** of the circle. ❷

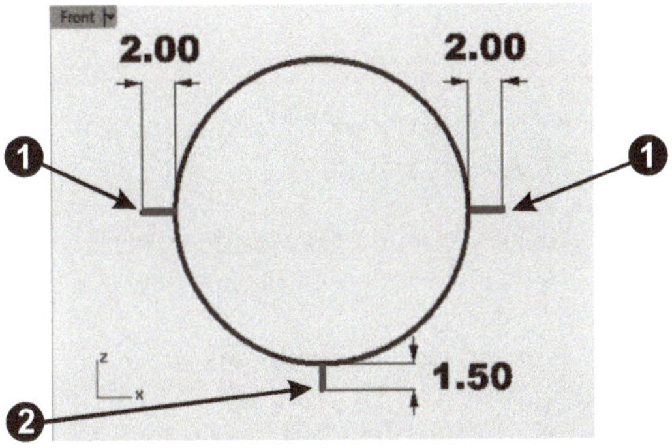

2.00   2.00

1.50

Fig. 3

- Click on the **Arc: start, end, point on arc** command.

  - Using **End Osnap**, follow <u>Command Line</u> prompts:
    - **Start of Arc:** ❶
    - **End of Arc:** ❷
    - **Point on Arc:** ❸

Arc: start, end, point on arc
command

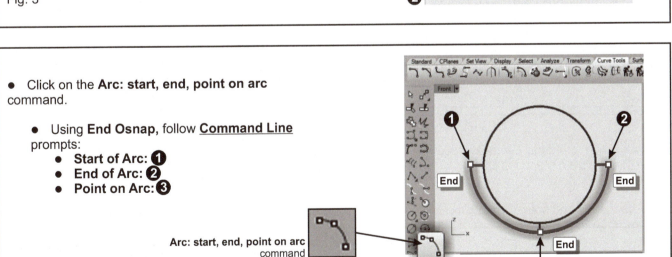

Fig. 4

- Click on the **Arc: start, end, direction at start** command.

  - Follow prompts for:
    - **Start of Arc:** ❶
    - **End of Arc:** ❷
    - **Direction at Start:** ❸ (Use ORTHO)

Fig. 5

Arc: start, end, direction at start
command

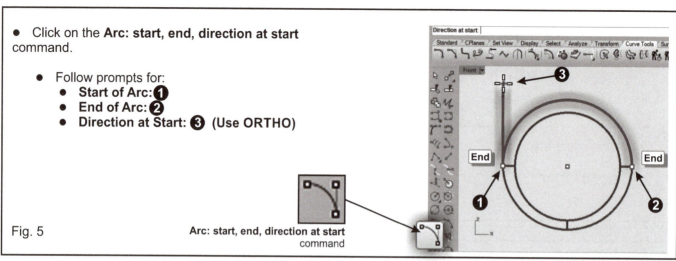

- Use the **Move** command to move the new arc **upward 3mm.**

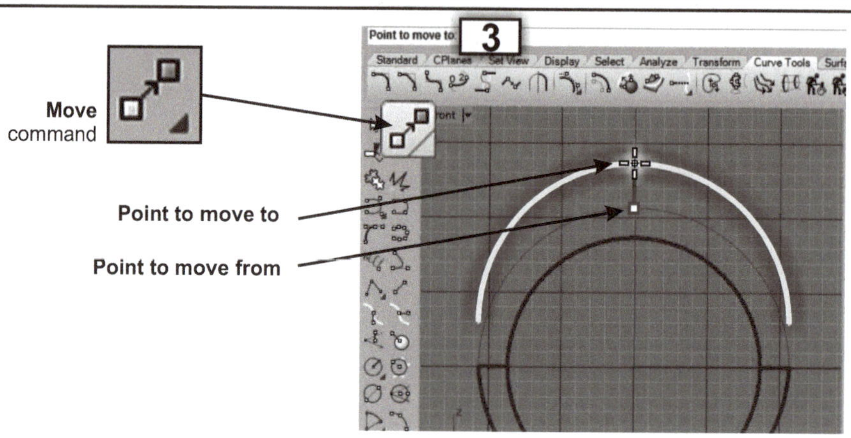

Move
command

Point to move to

Point to move from

Fig. 6

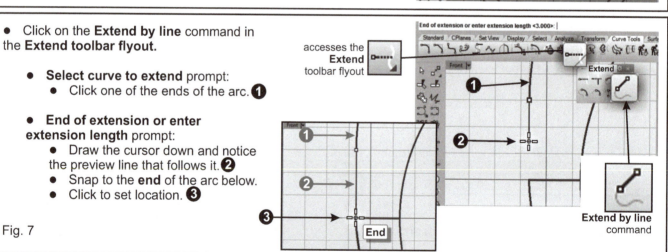

- Click on the **Extend by line** command in the **Extend toolbar flyout.**

  - **Select curve to extend** prompt:
    - Click one of the ends of the arc. ❶

  - **End of extension or enter extension length** prompt:
    - Draw the cursor down and notice the preview line that follows it. ❷
    - Snap to the **end** of the arc below.
    - Click to set location. ❸

Fig. 7

accesses the
Extend
toolbar flyout

Extend by line
command

- When the top arc has been extended on both sides, press **Enter** to end the **Extend by line** command.

- **Join** the top and bottom arcs to make a **closed polycurve.**

Fig. 8

Join
command

closed polycurve

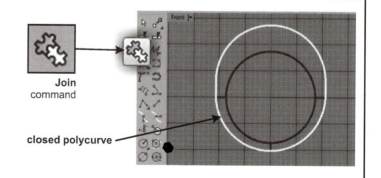

- If you turn on the control points for the new polycurve, note that some points are right on the curve while others show the characteristic default square configuration for arcs and circles.

- It is necessary to rebuild for a more even distribution of points that will ensure smooth even geometry.

Fig. 9

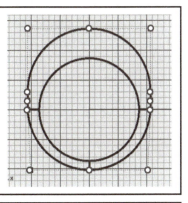

- The next step will be to rebuild the new polycurve. But before that, the curve seam needs to be in a perfectly central location for symmetry in the rebuild.

- Select the polycurve and click on the **Adjust closed curve seam** command.
  - The seam indicator, **a point and a white arrow**, will be at one of the locations where the two elements of the polycurve joined each other in the previous step.

Adjust closed curve seam command

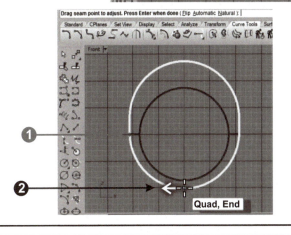

- **Drag seam point to adjust. Press Enter when done** prompt:
  - Click one the curve seam's single point ❶ and drag the seam indicator down to snap to the lower **quad point**.
    - Notice that the osnap tooltip says **quad, end** because both of those snaps are enabled.
    - Click to set location. ❷

Fig. 10

- **Rebuild** to **44 control points.**

- **Points will be evenly distributed** with a minimum deviation from the original shape.

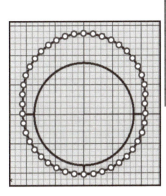

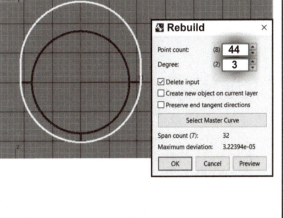

Fig. 11

- Select the two 2mm lines **❶** on the side quads of the inner circle and click on the **Split** command.

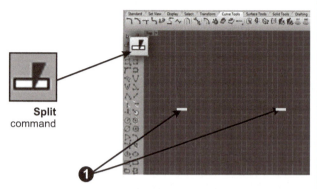

Split
command

- **Select cutting objects. Press Enter when done** prompt:
  - Select the large outer closed curve **❷** and press **Enter.**

- If you zoom in on either end of the 2mm lines, you will see a very short segment that has been split off from the line.
  - **Delete** both of these small split off segments.

delete

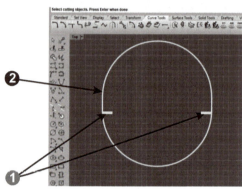

- When the large outer curve was rebuilt, it deformed slightly, creating an intersection with the two 2mm lines which might cause inaccuracies further into the project. This is why the two 2mm lines needed to be split.

Fig. 12

- **Top Perspective view.**   **❶** 🖾   **❷** 🖾

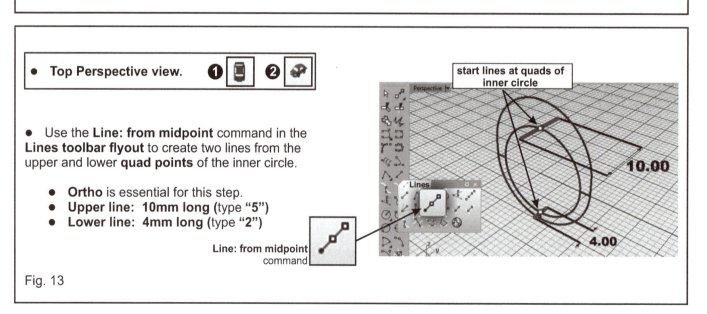

start lines at quads of inner circle

- Use the **Line: from midpoint** command in the **Lines toolbar flyout** to create two lines from the upper and lower **quad points** of the inner circle.

  - **Ortho** is essential for this step.
  - **Upper line: 10mm long** (type **"5"**)
  - **Lower line: 4mm long** (type **"2"**)

Line: from midpoint
command

10.00

4.00

Fig. 13

- Using the **Arc: start, end, point on arc** command, create arcs on the top and bottom of the ring.

  - **Start of arc:** ❶
  - **End of Arc:** ❷
  - **Point on Arc:** ❸

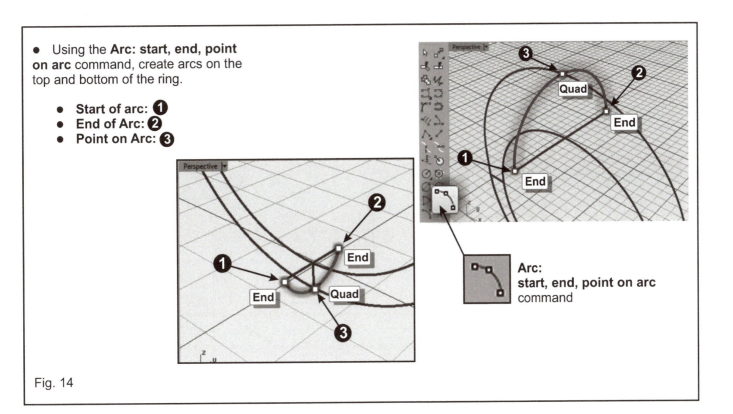

Arc:
start, end, point on arc
command

Fig. 14

- **2D curves** layer current.

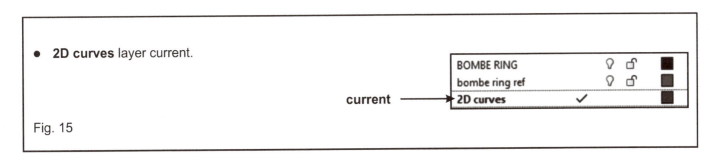

current ──→

Fig. 15

- **Right Viewport.**   Front ▼

- The next step will determine the silhouette of the ring from the side view.

- Use the **Arc: start, end, direction at start** command to map out the silhouette curve shown.

  - **Start of arc:** ❶
  - **End of arc:** ❷
  - **Direction of arc:** ❸ (use ORTHO)

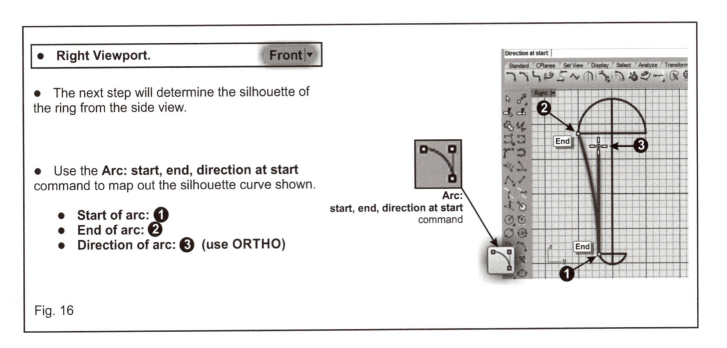

Arc:
start, end, direction at start
command

Fig. 16

- Extending this new arc by **1mm** on each end will ensure good geometry in the next step.

- Click on the **Extend curve, smooth** command in the **Extend toolbar flyout.**

  - **Select curve to extend. Press Enter when done** prompt:
    - Click near the end of the line. ❶
    - Draw the cursor upward and notice the smoothness of the extend. ❷
    - Type "1" and press **Enter.**

- The curve will be smoothly extended by **1mm.**

  - **Select curve to extend. Press Enter when done** prompt:
    - Extend the bottom of the line by 1mm, using the same procedure as above.

  - Press **Enter** to end the command.

Fig. 17

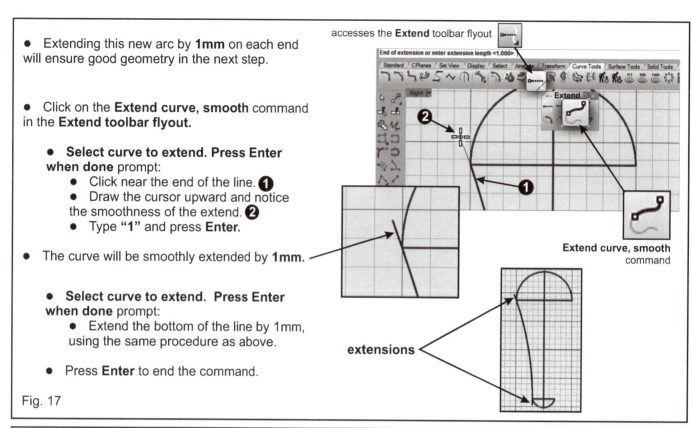

extensions

Extend curve, smooth
command

- **bombe ring ref** layer current.

current ⟶

BOMBE RING		♀ 🔓	■
bombe ring ref	✓		■
2D curves		♀ 🔓	■

Fig. 18

- The next step will be the creation of a curve by combining two separate planar curves.

- Click on the **Curve from 2 views** command.

  - **Select first curve** prompt:
    - Click on the circle. ❶
  - **Select second curve** prompt:
    - Click on the new arc. ❷

- A new curve will immediately appear. It is combination of the two selected curves. ❸

Curve from 2 views
command

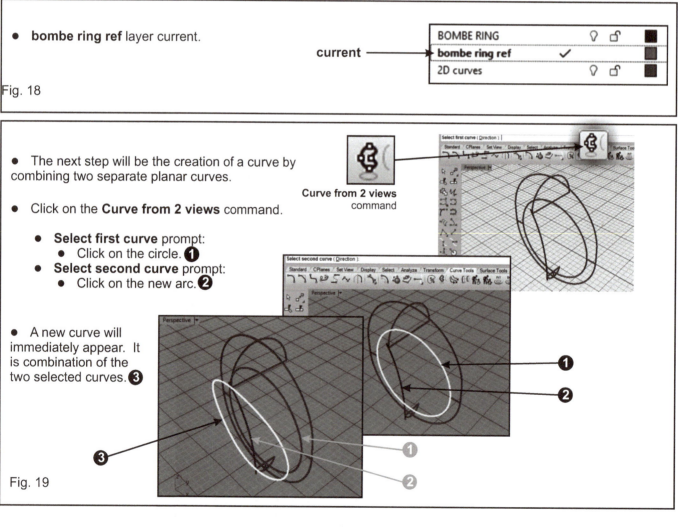

Fig. 19

421

- This is the way the new curve looks from the **Front** and from the **Right**.

- **The new curve is a combination of these two views.**

- **If the two curves had been extruded to intersect each other, the new curve would be a line along their intersection.**

Fig. 20

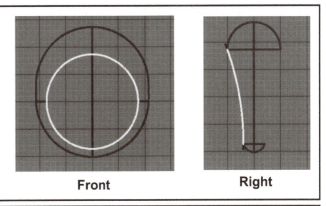

Front   **Right**

2D curves

- Use **Line: from midpoint** to create a curve from the **end point** shown ❶ out to snap to the **Quad, end** of the two outer curves. ❷

- **Mirror** the line over to the other side of the ring.

new mirrored copy

Fig. 21

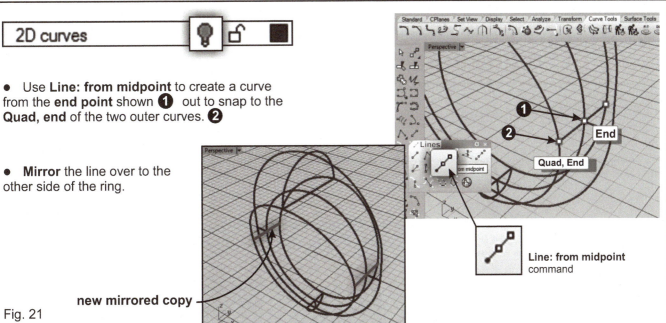

Line: from midpoint
command

- Use the **Start, end, point on arc** command to create an arc on the side of the ring as shown.

  - **Start of arc:** ❶
  - **End of arc:** ❷
  - **Point on arc:** ❸

Start, end, point on arc
command

Fig. 22

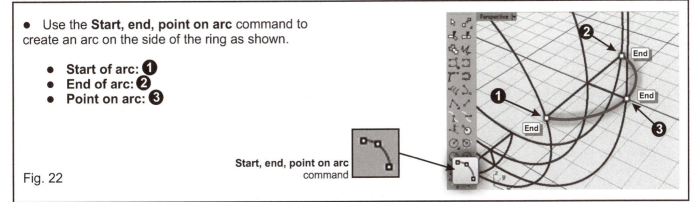

---

mirrored copy

- **Mirror** the new arc across the ring to the other side.

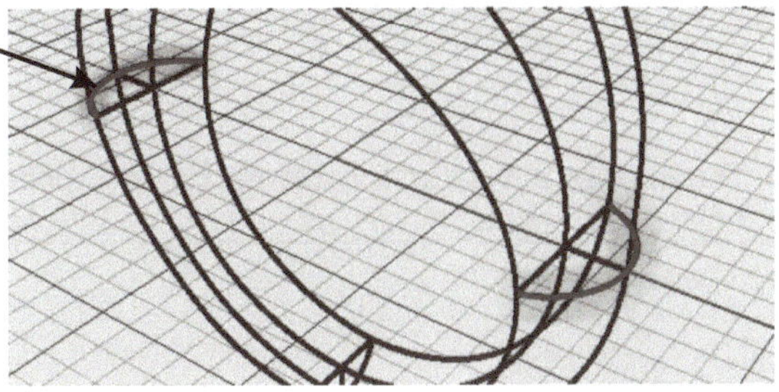

Fig. 23

- Select the **11 curves shown**, type **"hide"** and press **Enter**.

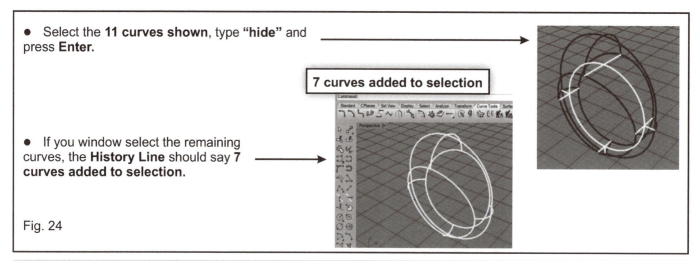

7 curves added to selection

- If you window select the remaining curves, the **History Line** should say **7 curves added to selection.**

Fig. 24

Creating the Surfaces of the Ring

- **BOMBE RING** layer current.

Fig. 25

current

BOMBE RING	✓		■
bombe ring ref	♀	⌂	■
2D curves	♀	⌂	■

- Window select all 7 curves and click on the **Surface from network of curves** command.

Surface from network of curves command

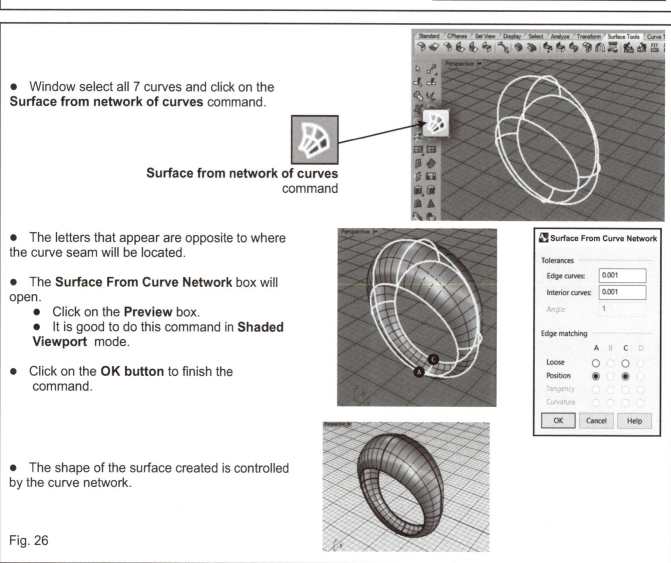

- The letters that appear are opposite to where the curve seam will be located.

- The **Surface From Curve Network** box will open.
    - Click on the **Preview** box.
    - It is good to do this command in **Shaded Viewport** mode.

- Click on the **OK button** to finish the command.

- The shape of the surface created is controlled by the curve network.

Fig. 26

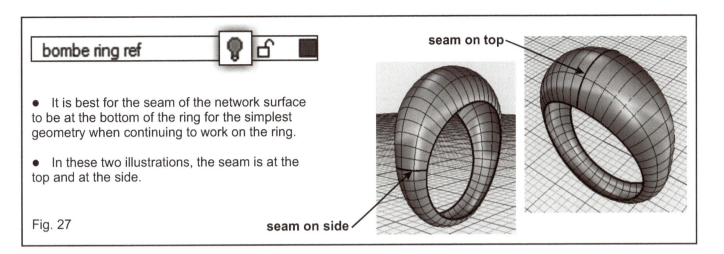

bombe ring ref

seam on top

- It is best for the seam of the network surface to be at the bottom of the ring for the simplest geometry when continuing to work on the ring.

- In these two illustrations, the seam is at the top and at the side.

seam on side

Fig. 27

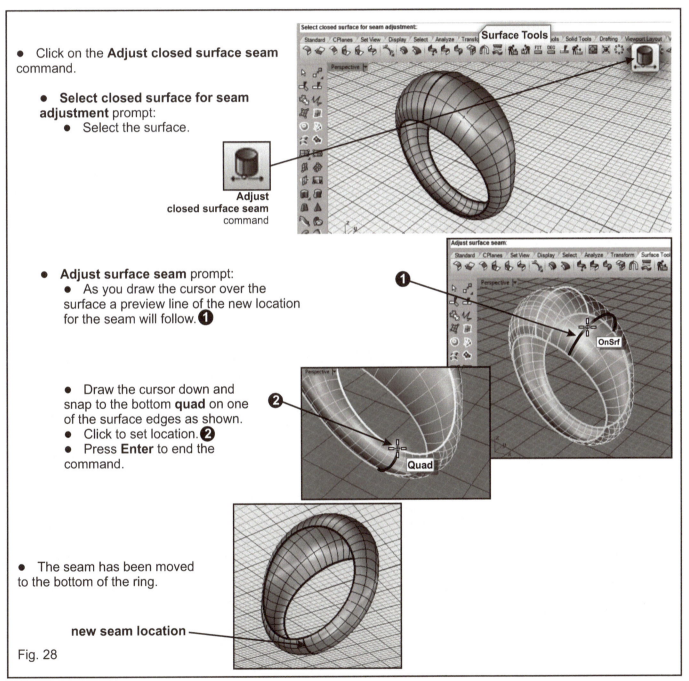

- Click on the **Adjust closed surface seam** command.

  - **Select closed surface for seam adjustment** prompt:
    - Select the surface.

Adjust closed surface seam command

- **Adjust surface seam** prompt:
  - As you draw the cursor over the surface a preview line of the new location for the seam will follow. **1**

  - Draw the cursor down and snap to the bottom **quad** on one of the surface edges as shown.
  - Click to set location. **2**
  - Press **Enter** to end the command.

- The seam has been moved to the bottom of the ring.

new seam location

Fig. 28

- Click on the **Loft** command.

    - **Select curves to loft** command.
        - In this example, only half of the surface edge has been selected.

- *Sometimes, when moving a surface seam, the surface edges can become split.*

- Press the **Esc** key to cancel the command.

Fig. 29

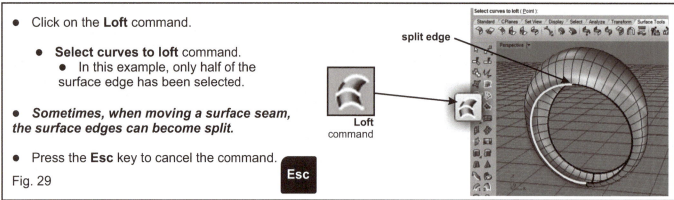

split edge

Loft
command

Esc

- **Analyze tabbed toolbar.** Analyze

- **RIGHT-CLICK** on the **Merge All Edges** command.
    - *Will repair all split edges on the piece.*

    - **Select surfaces or polysurfaces. Press Enter when done** prompt:
        - Select the ring and press **Enter**.

- The edges will all be mended **("merged")**

Fig. 30

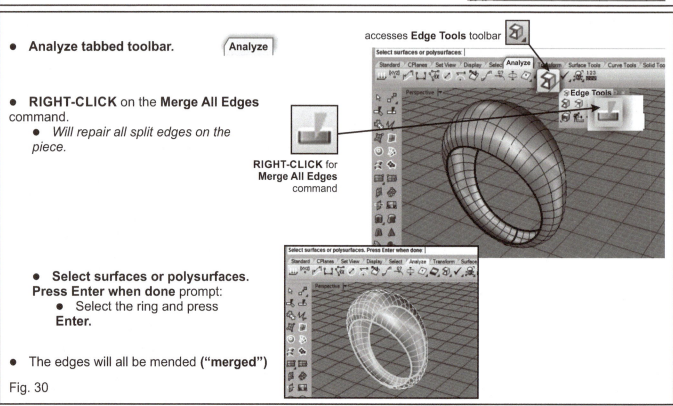

accesses **Edge Tools** toolbar

RIGHT-CLICK for
Merge All Edges
command

- **Surface Tools tabbed toolbar.** Surface Tools

- Click on the **Loft** command.

    - **Select curves to loft. Press Enter when done** prompt:
        - Select the two surface edges as shown and press **Enter**.

    - **Drag seam point to adjust. Press Enter when done** prompt:
        - The seam points should be touching the ends of the surface seam.
        - Click and drag if necessary.
        - Press **Enter**.

Fig. 31

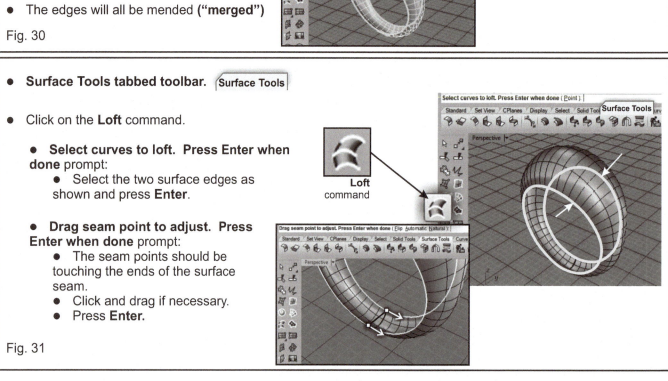

Loft
command

- Click on the **OK button** in the **Loft Options** box to accept the settings shown.

- The inside surface of the ring has been created.

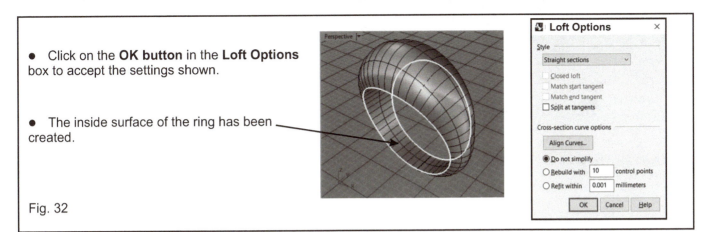

Fig. 32

- Select both outer and inside surfaces of the ring and click on the **Join** command.

- The **History Line** will inform you that you have created a **closed polysurface.**

- Save this file as: **bombe ring.3dm**

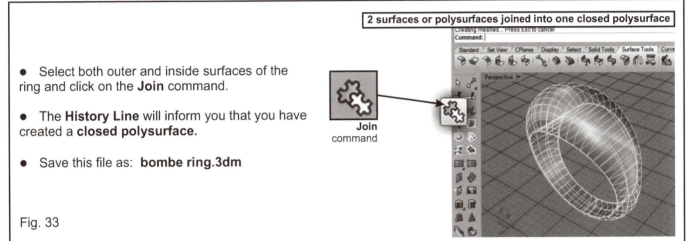

Fig. 33

Changing Curves for Design Variations

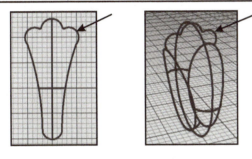

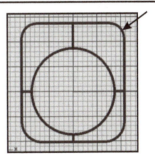
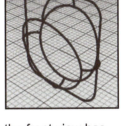

- Use **Arc from 3 Points** and **Fillet Curve** to replace the top arc.

- The new soft filleted curve changes the nature of the ring.

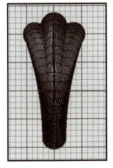

Fig. 34

- The profile curve created in the front view has been changed to a rectangle with fillets on the corners.

- The new soft rectangle touches all of the arcs.

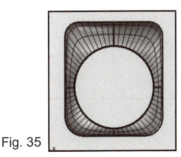

Fig. 35

426

Surface Offset - Creating the Cutting Object

- Open the file, **Bombe Ring.3dm** saved from the previous chapter.

Fig. 1

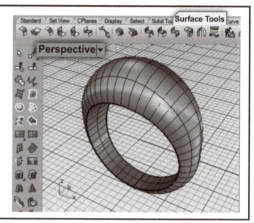

- Create a new layer called **cutter** and make this layer current.

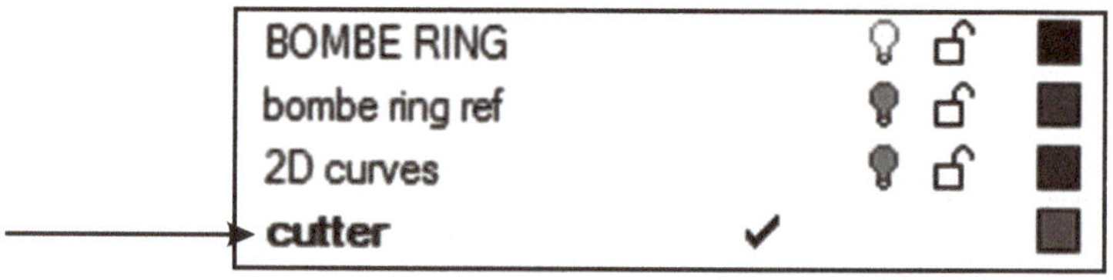

Fig. 2

BOMBE RING	♀ 🔓	■
bombe ring ref	♀ 🔓	■
2D curves	♀ 🔓	■
→ cutter	✔	■

- Select the ring and click on the **Explode** command to explode the ring into 2 surfaces.

- Note the update in the **History Line** after you have exploded the ring.

Fig. 3

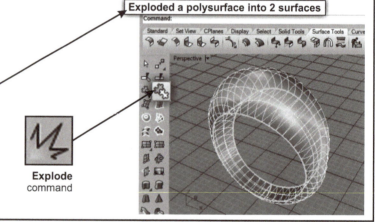

Exploded a polysurface into 2 surfaces

Explode command

- Select the inner surface of the ring, type **"hide"**, and press **Enter**.

- The inner surface will be hidden from view.

- *The next steps will deal with the outer surface only to create the cutting object that will hollow out the ring.*

Fig. 4

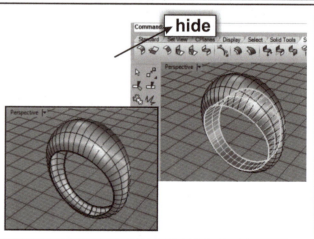

hide

- **Surface Tools tabbed toolbar.** Surface Tools

- Select the ring and click on the **Offset Surface** command.

Offset Surface
command

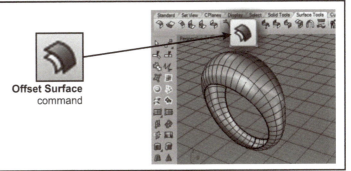

Fig. 5

- A series of **offset direction arrows** will appear, all normal (perpendicular) to the surface of the ring.

- Click the **FlipAll** option in the **Command Line** to change the direction of all of the arrows.

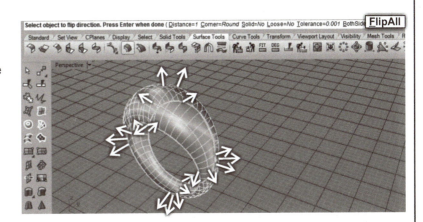

- The arrows will now point inward.
  - *The direction arrows indicate the direction of the offset. This offset needs to be to the inner part of the ring.*

- click on the **Solid=Yes** option to toggle it to **Solid=No** ❶

- Type ".8" ❷ and press **Enter.**

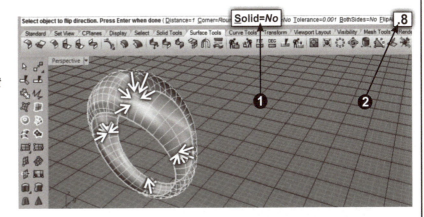

- Press **Enter** again to complete the **offset surface** command.

- A new .8mm offset surface will appear inside of the ring.

new offset

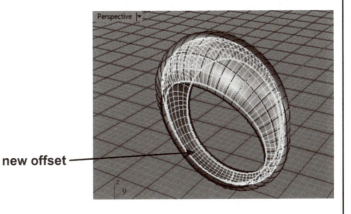

Fig. 6

428

• Notice that, when viewed from the front viewport, the new offset surface only shows on the inside of the ring at the bottom, not at the top.

• To make this a cutting object that will hollow out the ring, this surface must be protruding into the inner part of the ring **all the way around.**

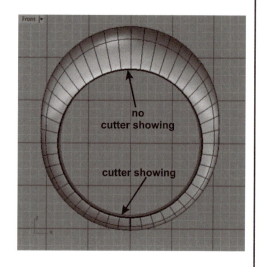

Fig. 7

• **Top Perspective view.** ❶ 📱 ❷ 🚗

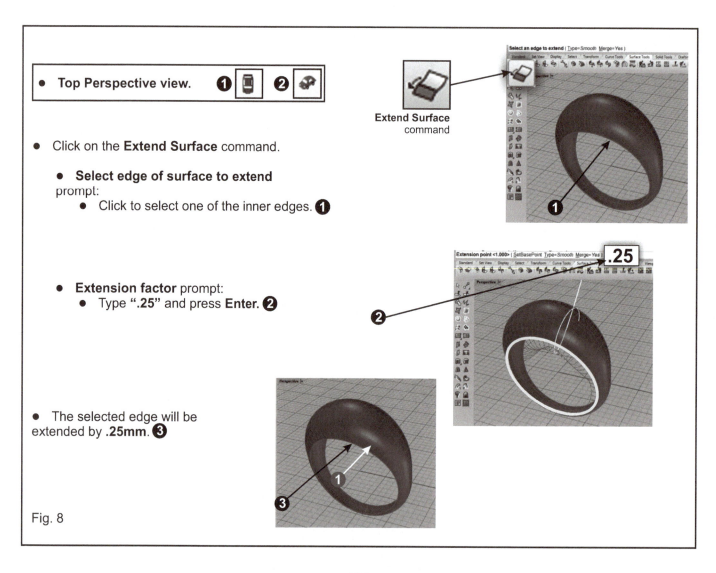

Extend Surface
command

• Click on the **Extend Surface** command.

  • **Select edge of surface to extend**
  prompt:
    • Click to select one of the inner edges. ❶

  • **Extension factor** prompt:
    • Type "**.25**" and press **Enter.** ❷

• The selected edge will be extended by **.25mm.** ❸

Fig. 8

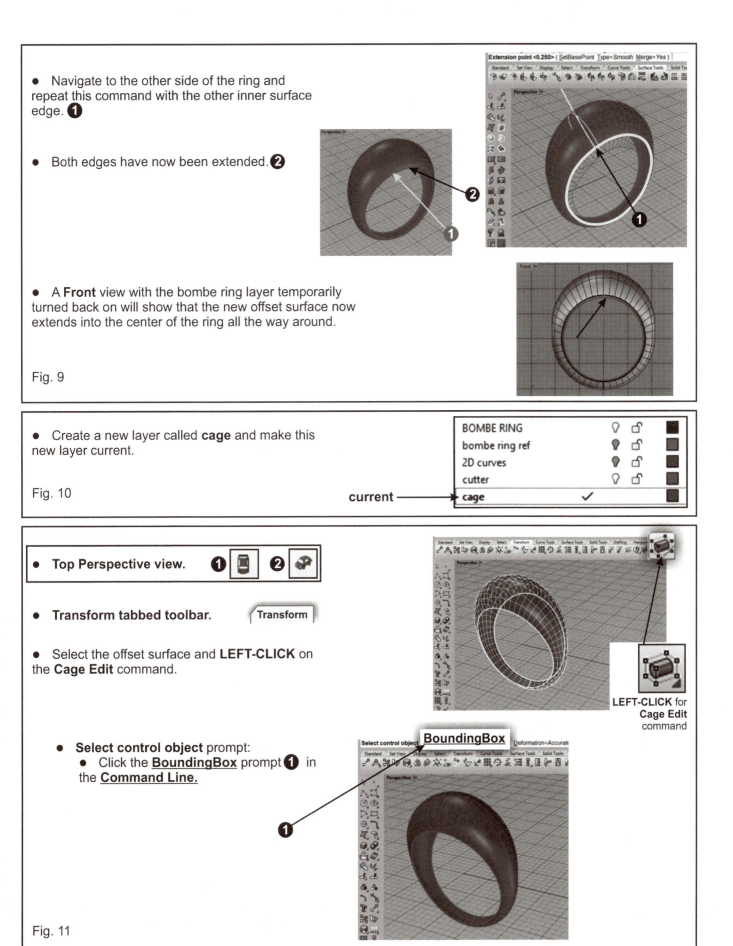

- Navigate to the other side of the ring and repeat this command with the other inner surface edge. ❶

- Both edges have now been extended. ❷

- A **Front** view with the bombe ring layer temporarily turned back on will show that the new offset surface now extends into the center of the ring all the way around.

Fig. 9

- Create a new layer called **cage** and make this new layer current.

Fig. 10

current ⟶ cage ✓

BOMBE RING	💡	🔓	⬛
bombe ring ref	💡	🔓	⬛
2D curves	💡	🔓	⬛
cutter	💡	🔓	⬛
cage		✓	⬛

- **Top Perspective view.** ❶ 🔲 ❷ 🚗

- **Transform tabbed toolbar.** Transform

- Select the offset surface and **LEFT-CLICK** on the **Cage Edit** command.

LEFT-CLICK for **Cage Edit** command

- **Select control object** prompt:
  - Click the **BoundingBox** prompt ❶ in the **Command Line.**

BoundingBox

Fig. 11

430

- **Coordinate System** prompt:
  - Press **Enter** to accept the default **World** setting.❷

Coordinate system <World> (CPlane World 3Point):

❷

- **Cage Parameters** prompt:❸
  - Press **Enter** to accept the default settings showing control points and degrees for the bounding box that will be created.

❸

Cage parameters (XPointCount=4 YPointCount=4 ZPointCount=4 XDegree=3 YDegree=3 ZDegree=3):

❹

- **Region to edit** prompt:
  - Press **Enter** to accept the default **Global** setting. ❹

Region to edit <Global> (Global Local Other):

- A cage object around the selected surface will be created.

- Notice the control points in X, Y and Z directions.

- Point editing this bounding box will effect the shape of the surface it surrounds.

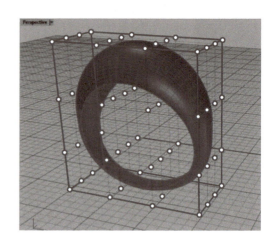

Fig. 12

- Turn on the **BOMBE RING** layer.

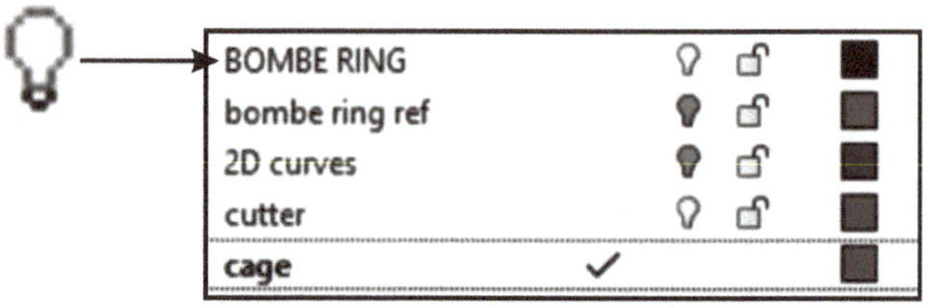

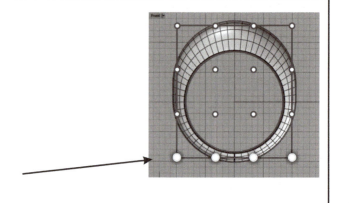

BOMBE RING		♀	⌂	■
bombe ring ref		♀	⌂	■
2D curves		♀	⌂	■
cutter		♀	⌂	■
cage	✓			■

Fig. 13

- **Front Viewport.**　　　　　Front ▾

- Window select the bottom row of control points for the editing cage.

- Each point actually represents 4 points. 3 additional points are right behind each single point that you see. You need to select all points in the rows shown.

Fig. 14

- **Move** or **Drag** the selected points upward, using **ORTHO** to constrain the move in a vertical direction.

- Notice that the cutter is being drawn up out of the ring at the bottom as its shape is controlled by the cage.

- Click to set the location of the point when the cutter is raised to the desired level.

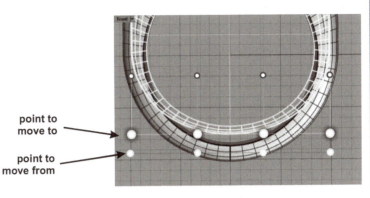

point to move to

point to move from

- **Top Perspective view.**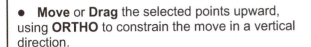

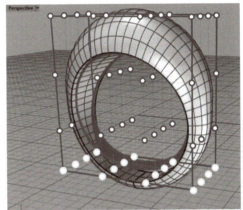

- Moving the bottom row of control points has caused the bottom of the cutter to be moved upward.

- You can press the **Esc** key to turn off the control points.

Esc

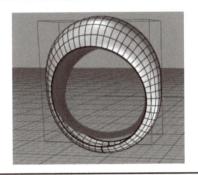

Fig. 15

- Turn off the **cutter** and **cage** layers.

- **BOMBE RING** layer current.

Fig. 16

current ———→

BOMBE RING	✓		■
bombe ring ref		💡 🔓	■
2D curves		💡 🔓	■
cutter		💡 🔓	■
cage		💡 🔓	■

- Type **"show"** and press **Enter** to bring the inside surface of the bombe ring back to visibility.

Inside surface is now visible again. ———→

Fig. 17

- Select the inner and outer surfaces of the ring to create a single closed polysurface.

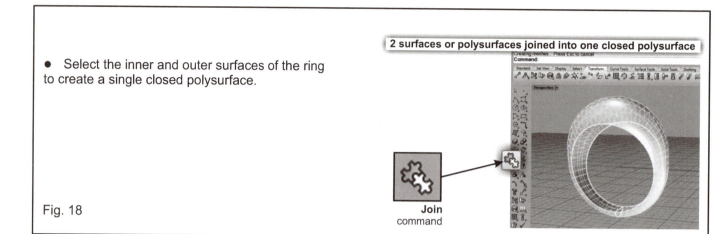

Join
command

Fig. 18

- Turn the cutter layer back on.

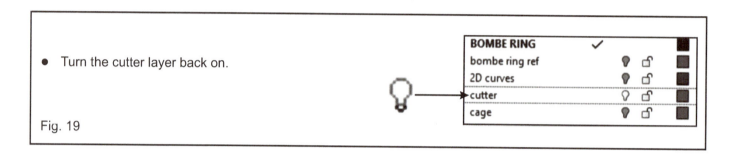

Fig. 19

- Select the **cutter,** type **"Dir",** and press **Enter.**

  - **Note:** The **Direction** command button can be found in the **Analyze tabbed toolbar** or the **Analyze** toolbar flyout.

- A series of white **arrows (surface normals)** will appear vertical (**normal**) to the surface.

- These **arrows need to be pointing outward** as shown for the **Boolean Difference** command to cut out the inside of the ring.
  - Click on the **Flip** option in the **Command Line** if necessary.

- Press **Enter** to finish the command when the surface normals are facing inward as shown.

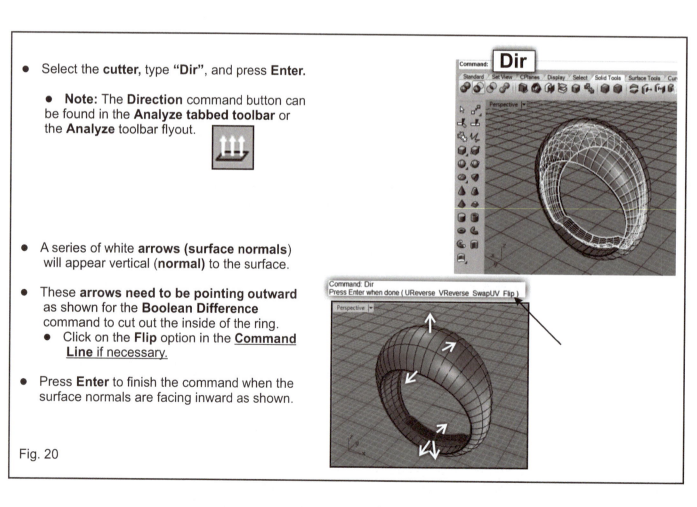

Fig. 20

- **Solid Tools tabbed toolbar.** `Solid Tools`

- Click on the **Boolean Difference** command.

Boolean Difference
command

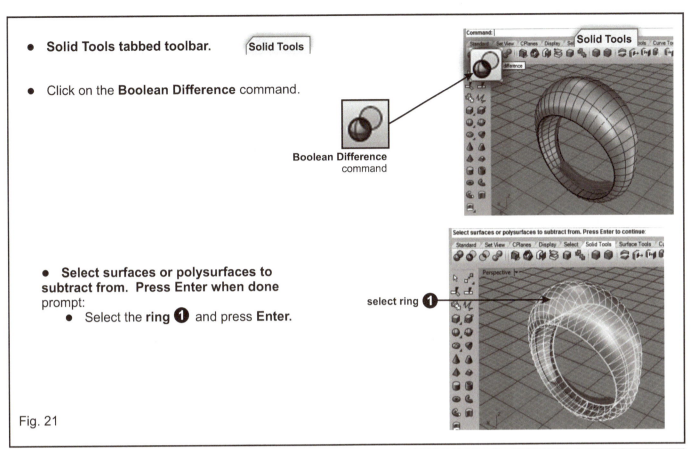

- **Select surfaces or polysurfaces to subtract from. Press Enter when done** prompt:
  - Select the **ring ❶** and press **Enter.**

select ring ❶

Fig. 21

- **Select surfaces or polysurfaces to subtract with. Press Enter when done** prompt:
  - Select the **cutter ❷** and press **Enter.**

- The cutter has hollowed out the ring.

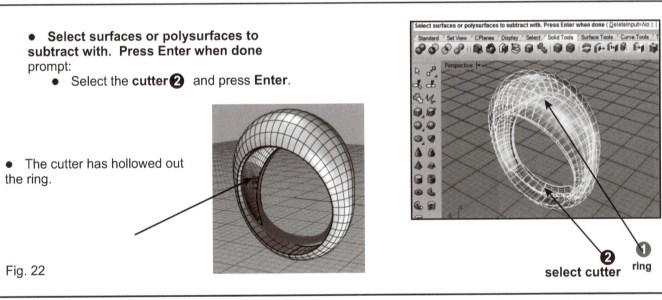

select cutter ❷   ring ❶

Fig. 22

- Turn off the **cutter layer** and view the hollowed out interior of the ring.

- Save this file as: **bombe ring hollowed out.3dm.**

Fig. 23

8 x 10mm Oval Signet Ring
Curve Network

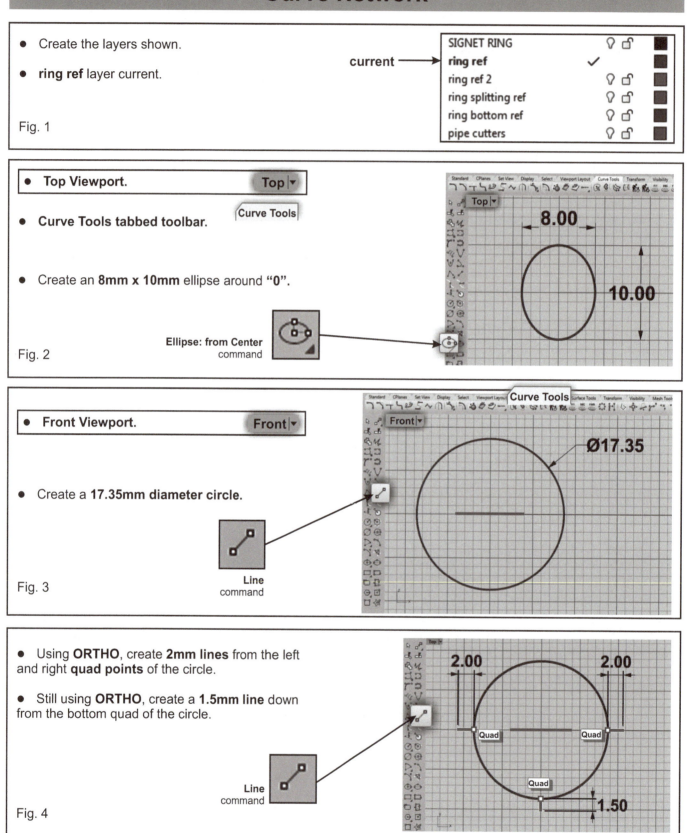

- Create the layers shown.

- **ring ref** layer current.

current ⟶

SIGNET RING		🔒	⬛
ring ref	✓		⬛
ring ref 2	💡	🔓	⬛
ring splitting ref	💡	🔓	⬛
ring bottom ref	💡	🔓	⬛
pipe cutters	💡	🔓	⬛

Fig. 1

- **Top Viewport.**   Top ▾

- **Curve Tools tabbed toolbar.**   Curve Tools

- Create an **8mm x 10mm** ellipse around **"0"**.

Ellipse: from Center command

8.00

10.00

Fig. 2

- **Front Viewport.**   Front ▾

- Create a **17.35mm diameter circle**.

Ø17.35

Line command

Fig. 3

- Using **ORTHO**, create **2mm lines** from the left and right **quad points** of the circle.

- Still using **ORTHO**, create a **1.5mm line** down from the bottom quad of the circle.

Line command

2.00   2.00

Quad   Quad

Quad

1.50

Fig. 4

- **LEFT-CLICK** on the **Arc: Start, Center, Point on Arc** command.
  - **Start of Arc:** Use **end osnap.** ❶
  - **End of Arc:** Use **end osnap.** ❷
  - **Point on Arc:** Use **end osnap.** ❸

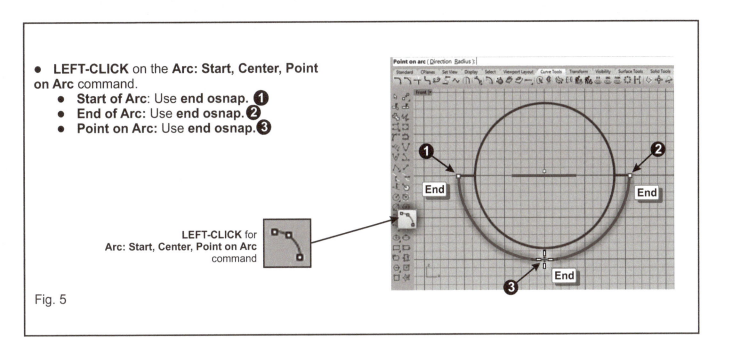

LEFT-CLICK for
Arc: Start, Center, Point on Arc
command

Fig. 5

- Using **ORTHO**, create a **3mm line** from the top **quad** of the circle.
  - **Start of line:** Use **quad osnap.** ❶
  - **End of line:** ❷

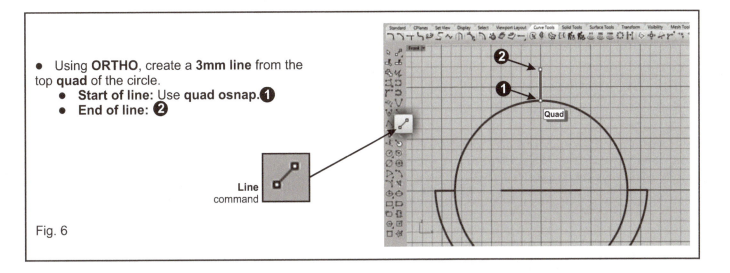

Line
command

Fig. 6

- Using **ORTHO,** use the **Line: from Midpoint** command in the **Lines toolbar flyout** to create lines on the top and bottom **quad points** of the ring circle.
  - **Middle of line** prompt:
    - Snap to the upper **quad** of the circle. ❶
  - **End of line** prompt:
    - Type **"5"** and press Enter.
    - Draw the cursor out in the direction shown and click to set location ❷ to make a **10mm line.**
  - Repeat these steps for the line at the bottom, typing **"1.5"** at the **End of Line** prompt to make a **3mm line.**

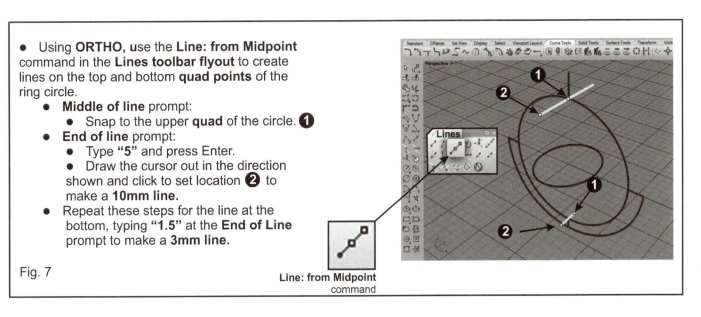

Line: from Midpoint
command

Fig. 7

- **Top Perspective view.** ❶ ❷

- Select the **8 x 19mm oval** and click on the **Move** command.
  - **Point to move from** prompt:
    - Type **"0"** and press **Enter.**

Move
command

"0"
point to
move from ❶

- **Point to move to** prompt:
  - Snap to the **End** of the 3mm line (created in Fig. 6) on top of the circle. ❷
  - Click to set location.

"0" ❶

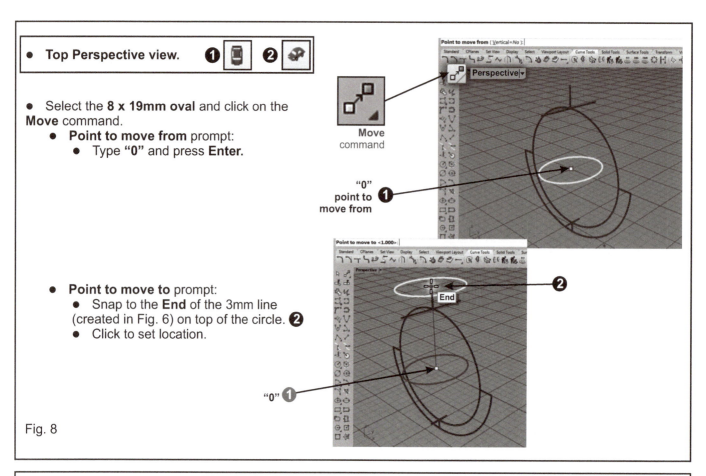

Fig. 8

- Click on the **Extend by Arc: to Point** command in the **Extend toolbar flyout.**
  - **Select curve to extend** prompt:
    - Click near one of the ends ❶ of the new arc at the bottom of the ring.

accesses the
Extend
toolbar flyout

Extend by Arc: to Point
command

- **End of extension** prompt:
  - Draw the cursor up and snap to the **quad** at the side of the oval.
  - Click to set location. ❷

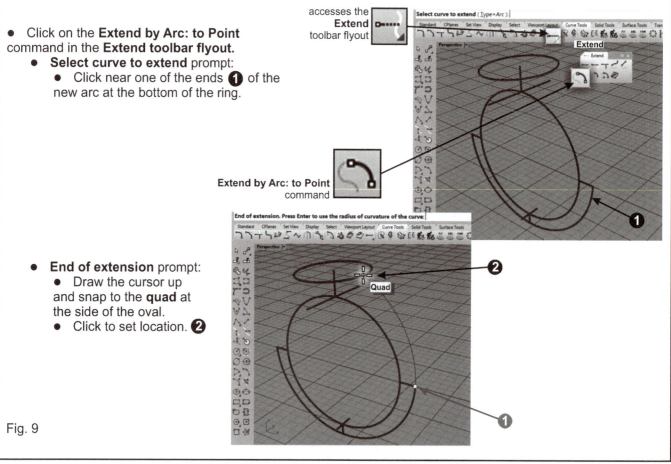

Fig. 9

437

- **End of extension** prompt:
  - Repeat the first step on the other side of the ring. **❸**

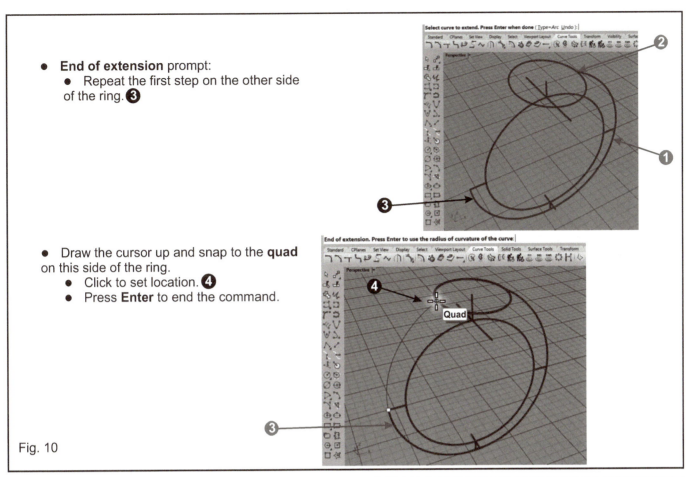

- Draw the cursor up and snap to the **quad** on this side of the ring.
  - Click to set location. **❹**
  - Press **Enter** to end the command.

Fig. 10

- **Right Viewport.**　　　　　　　**Right ▾**

- **LEFT-CLICK** on the **Arc: Start, End, Direction at Start** command.
  - **Start of arc** prompt:
    - Snap to the **end** of the 3mm line at the bottom of the ring. **❶**
    - Click to set location.

LEFT-CLICK for
Arc: Start, End, Direction at Start
command

- **End of arc** prompt:
  - Snap to the end of the **10mm line. ❷**
  - Click to set location.

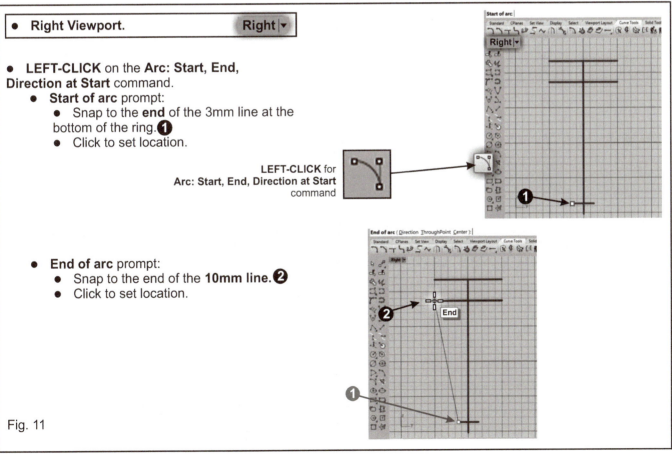

Fig. 11

- **Direction at start** prompt:
  - Using **ORTHO**, draw the cursor straight up and click to set the direction at start. ❸

Fig. 12

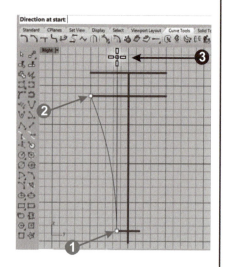

- **Top Perspective view.** ❶ ❷

- The new arc.

Fig. 13

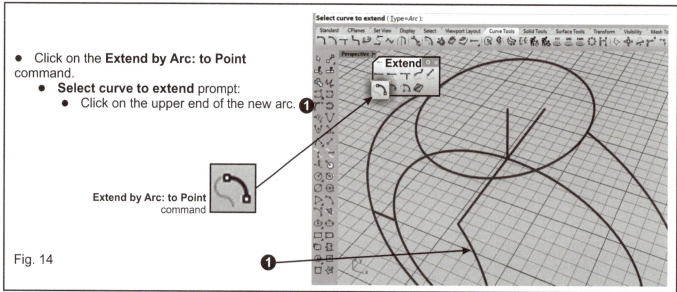

- Click on the **Extend by Arc: to Point** command.
  - **Select curve to extend** prompt:
    - Click on the upper end of the new arc. ❶

Extend by Arc: to Point
command

Fig. 14

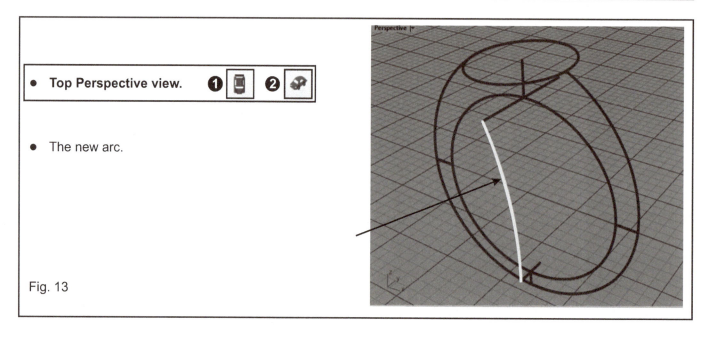

439

- **End of extension** prompt:
  - Draw the cursor up and snap to the **quad** of the front end of the ellipse. ❷
  - Click to set location.
  - Press **Enter** to end the command.

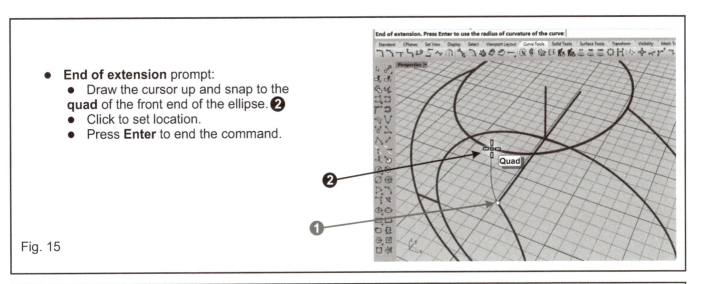

Fig. 15

- Select the newly extended arc, type **"mirror"** and press **Enter.**
  - **Start of mirror plane** prompt:
    - **Type "0"** and press **Enter.** ❶
  - **End of mirror plane** prompt:
    - Using **ORTHO**, draw the cursor out along the Xaxis and click to set location. ❷

new mirrored copy

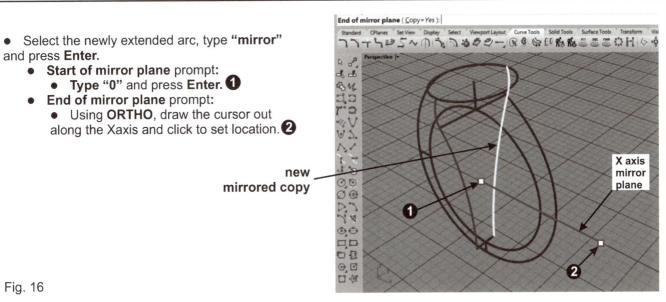

Fig. 16

- Use the **Arc: Start, End, Point on Arc** command to create an arc that snaps to the **ends** of the lines shown at the bottom of the ring.

  - **Start of Arc:** ❶
  - **End of Arc:** ❷
  - **Point on Arc:** ❸

LEFT-CLICK for
Arc: Start, Cetner, Point on Arc
command

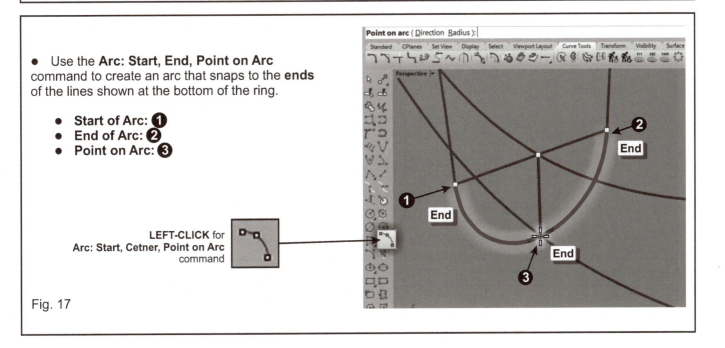

Fig. 17

- Click on the **Curve from 2 views** command.

    - **Select first curve** prompt:
        - Select the extended arc curve. **❶**
    - **Select second curve** prompt:
        - Select the original 17.35mm diameter circle created in Fig. 3. **❷**

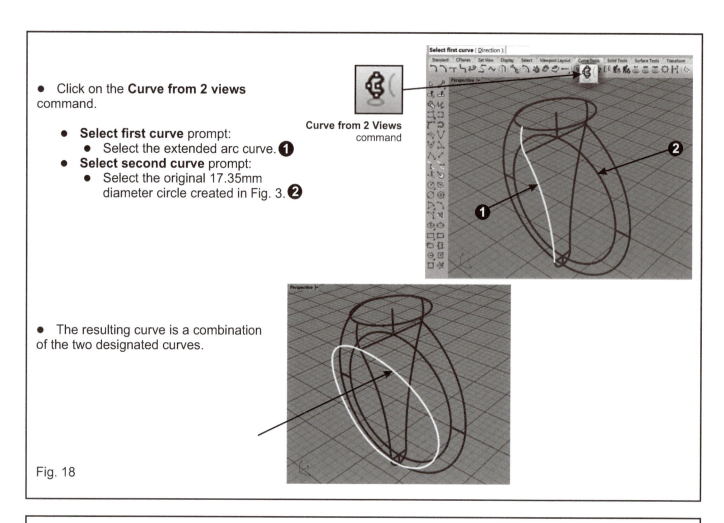

Curve from 2 Views command

- The resulting curve is a combination of the two designated curves.

Fig. 18

- The curve is created by the selection of two curves that are each planar to their different construction planes and that will look like the respective curves on their construction planes.

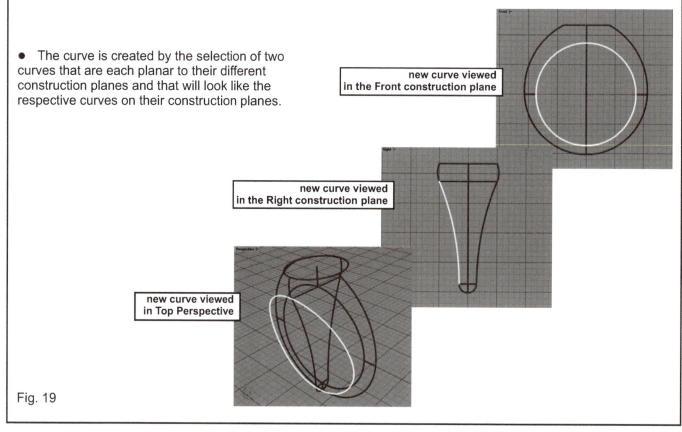

new curve viewed in the Front construction plane

new curve viewed in the Right construction plane

new curve viewed in Top Perspective

Fig. 19

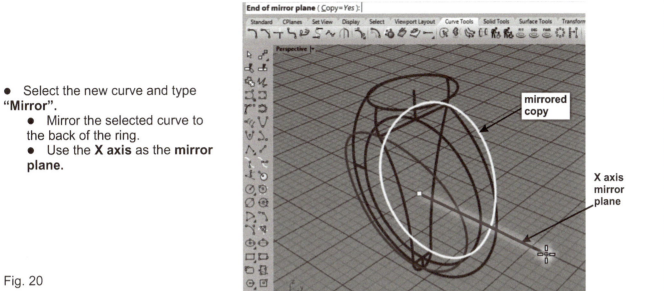

- Select the new curve and type **"Mirror".**
  - Mirror the selected curve to the back of the ring.
  - Use the **X axis** as the **mirror plane.**

Fig. 20

mirrored copy

X axis mirror plane

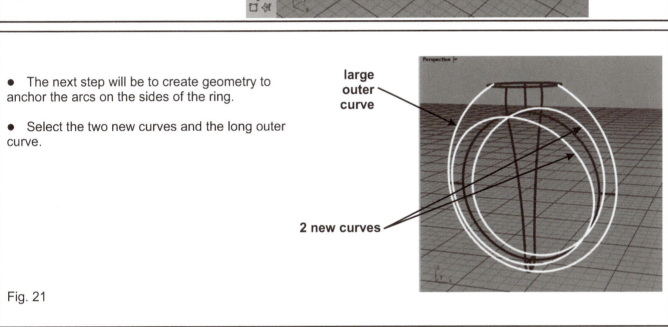

- The next step will be to create geometry to anchor the arcs on the sides of the ring.

- Select the two new curves and the long outer curve.

large outer curve

2 new curves

Fig. 21

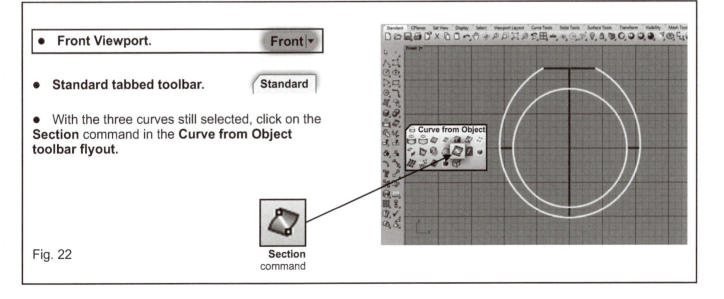

- **Front Viewport.** Front ▾

- **Standard tabbed toolbar.** Standard

- With the three curves still selected, click on the **Section** command in the **Curve from Object** toolbar flyout.

Curve from Object

Section command

Fig. 22

- **Start of section** prompt:
  - Type "**0**" and press **Enter.** ❶

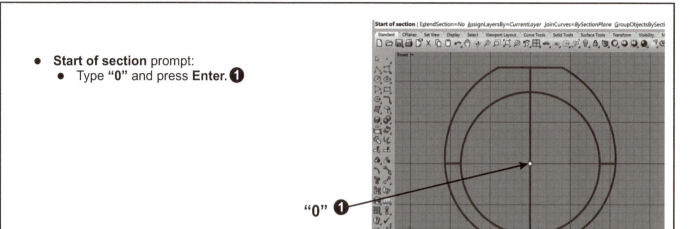

"0" ❶

- **End of section** prompt:
  - Using **ORTHO**, draw the cursor to the right, along the Xaxis.
  - The cursor must pass through the ring curves and out the other side as shown. ❷
  - Press **Enter** to end the command.

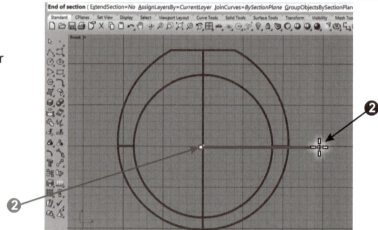

- You can see two control points that have been created in the exact path of the section.

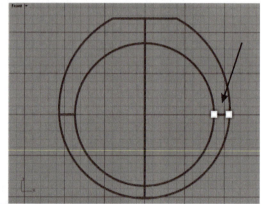

- When you change to the Top Perspective viewport, you can see that 3 points were actually created.

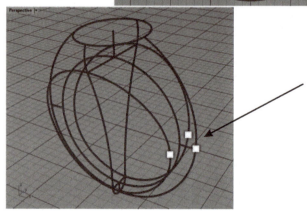

Fig. 23

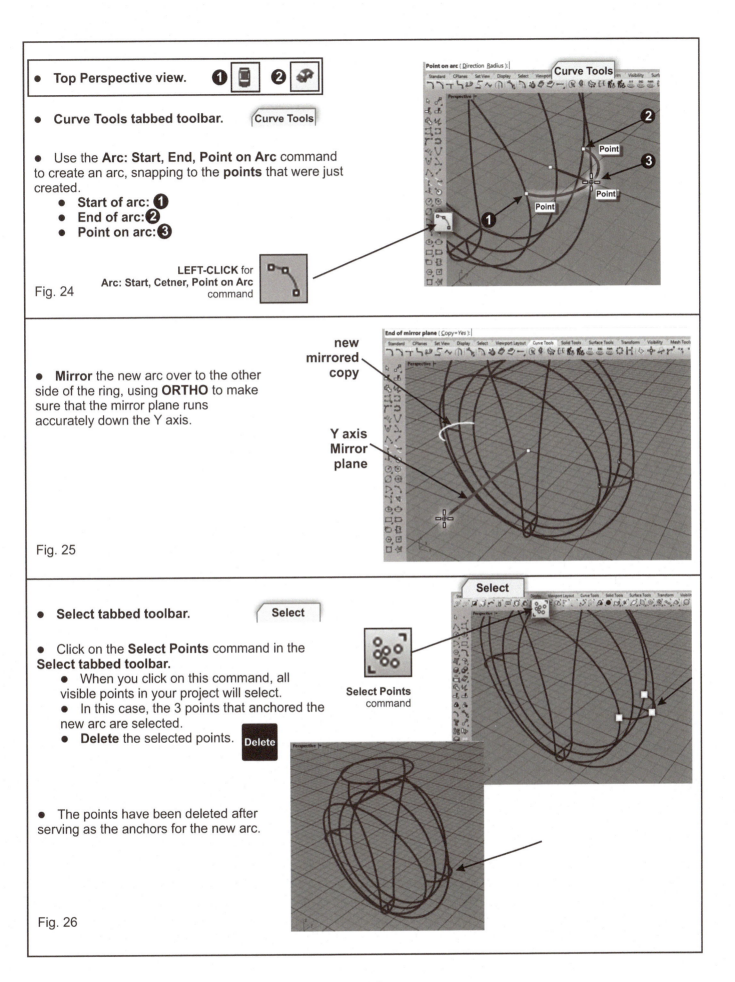

- **Top Perspective view.** ❶ ❷

- **Curve Tools tabbed toolbar.** ⟨Curve Tools⟩

- Use the **Arc: Start, End, Point on Arc** command to create an arc, snapping to the **points** that were just created.
  - **Start of arc:** ❶
  - **End of arc:** ❷
  - **Point on arc:** ❸

LEFT-CLICK for
Arc: Start, Cetner, Point on Arc
command

Fig. 24

- **Mirror** the new arc over to the other side of the ring, using **ORTHO** to make sure that the mirror plane runs accurately down the Y axis.

new mirrored copy

Y axis Mirror plane

Fig. 25

- **Select tabbed toolbar.** ⟨Select⟩

- Click on the **Select Points** command in the **Select tabbed toolbar.**
  - When you click on this command, all visible points in your project will select.
  - In this case, the 3 points that anchored the new arc are selected.
  - **Delete** the selected points. [Delete]

Select Points
command

- The points have been deleted after serving as the anchors for the new arc.

Fig. 26

- Select the curves shown.

- **RIGHT-CLICK** on the **ring ref 2** layer line.❶

- Click on the **Change Object Layer** option in the drop-down context menu.❷

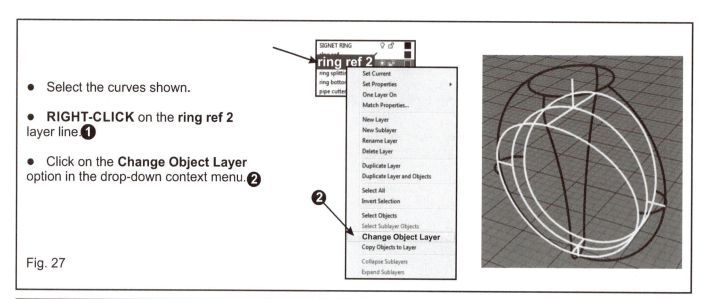

Fig. 27

- **Turn off** the **ring ref 2** layer as these objects are not needed for the next step.

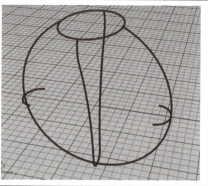

Fig. 28

- The remaining visible curves will be used for the curve network.

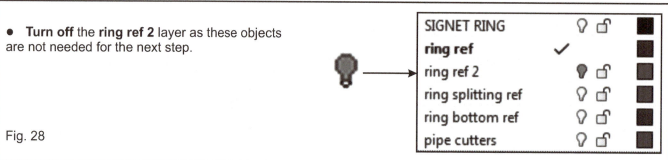

Fig. 29

- Create a line between the end points of the two new arcs on the sides of the ring.
  - Use **End osnap.**

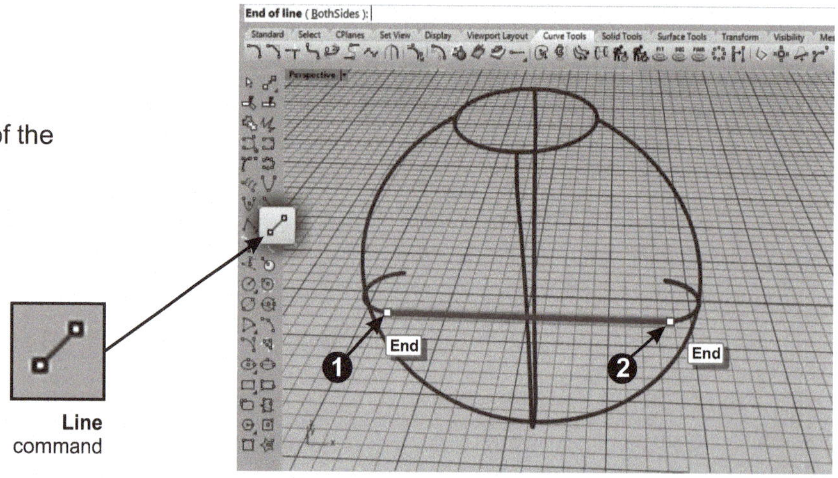

Line command

Fig. 30

- **Mirror** the new line to the back of the ring, using the **X axis** for the **mirror plane.**

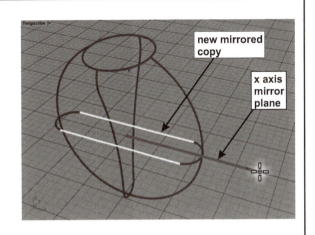

new mirrored copy

x axis mirror plane

Fig. 31

- Select the two arcs and the lines that now connect them at front and back of the ring.

- Click on the **Join** command
  - (or just type **"join"** and press **Enter).**

- In the History line, you will read **"4 curves joined into one closed curve"**

Fig. 32

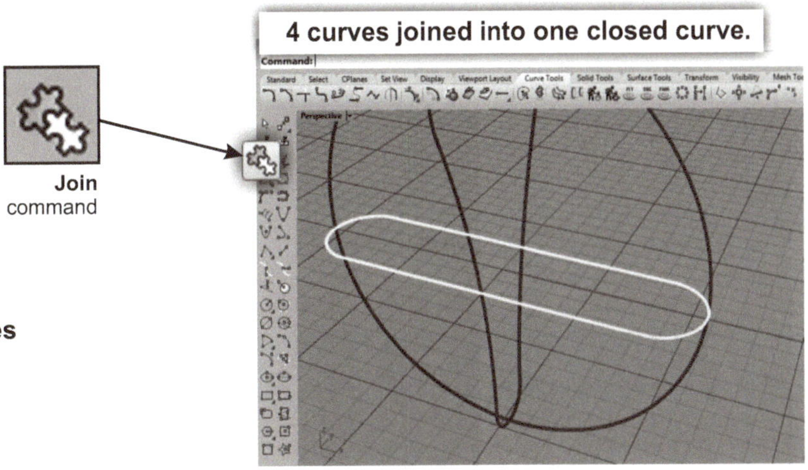

Join command

4 curves joined into one closed curve.

- Select the large outer curve ❶ and click on the **Split** command.
  - Or you can just type **"split"** and press **Enter.**

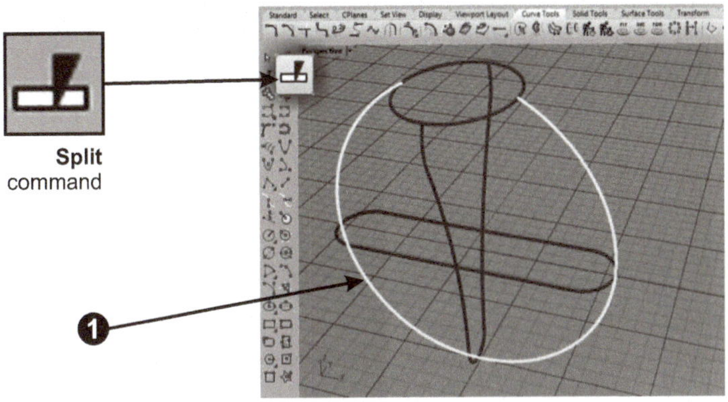

Split command

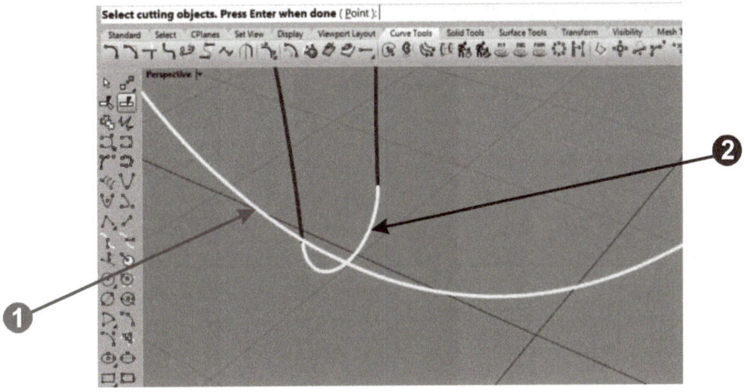

- **Select cutting objects. Press Enter when done** prompt:
  - Select the **arc** ❷ at the bottom of the ring and press **Enter.**

Fig. 33

446

- The large outer silhouette curve will be split into 2 pieces.

Fig. 34

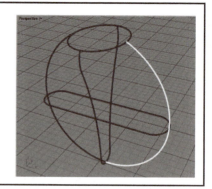

- Select the arc at the bottom of the ring ❶
- and click on the **Split** command.

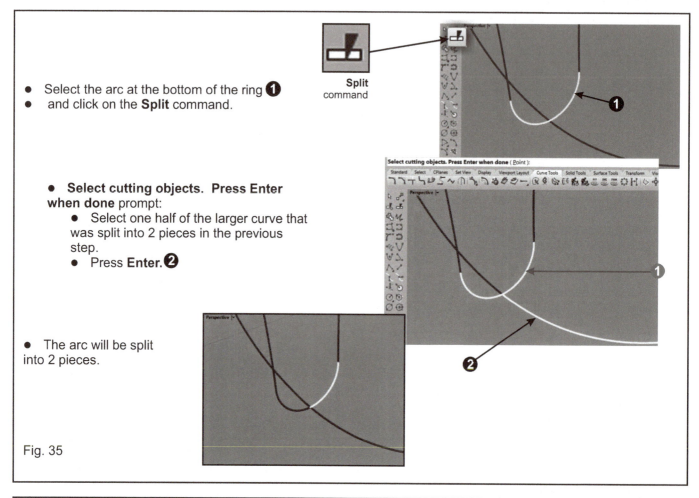

Split
command

- **Select cutting objects. Press Enter when done** prompt:
    - Select one half of the larger curve that was split into 2 pieces in the previous step.
    - Press **Enter.** ❷

- The arc will be split into 2 pieces.

Fig. 35

- **Join** the long curve at the back of the ring with ½ of the arc that was split in the previous step.

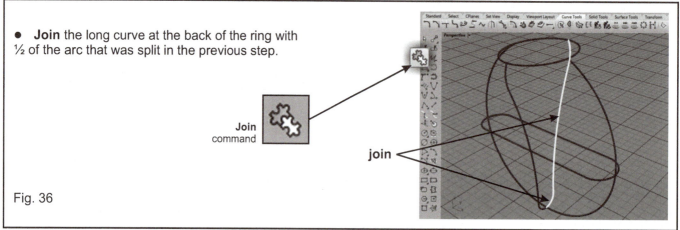

Join
command

join

Fig. 36

- **Join** the front two curves shown.

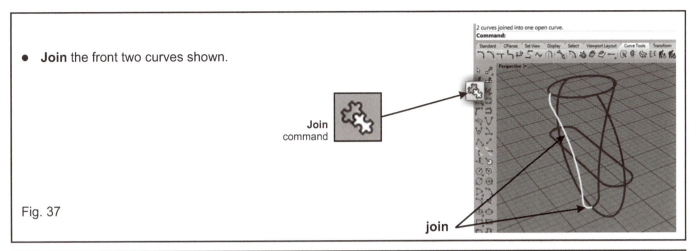

Fig. 37

join

- The **Join** command has created two single open curves.

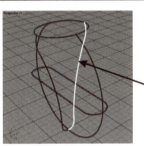

Fig. 38

---

6 curves added to selection

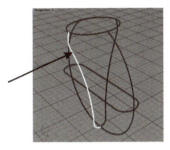

- Select all curves at once.

- The **History** line should read: **"6 curves added to selection"**

- If your History line reads that more curves than 6 have been selected:
  - Look for duplicates on top of each other - delete all duplicates.
  - Look for lines that should have been transferred to the **ring ref 2 layer.**

Fig. 39

Found 14 intersections.

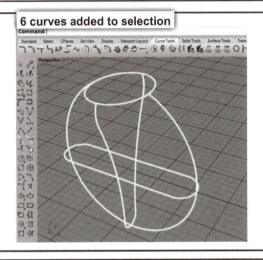

- Select all 6 curves, type **"intersect"**, and press **Enter.**

- A point object will appear at each intersection.
- The History line will tell you: **"Found 14 intersections."**

- **Undo** this command. The reason for this was to make sure that curves were intersecting as they should.

Fig. 40

- **SIGNET RING** layer current.

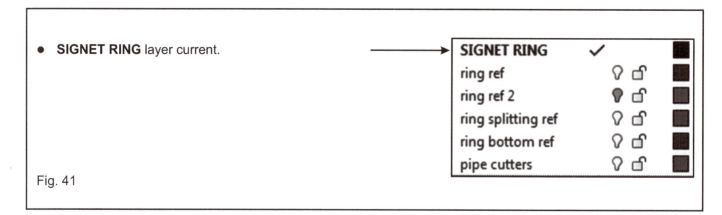

Fig. 41

- **Surface Tools tabbed toolbar.** Surface Tools

- Click on the **Surface from network of curves** command.

Surface from
Network of Curves
command

- The **Surface from Curve Network** box will open.

  - It is best to be in **Ghosted** or **Shaded** mode for this step so that you can better see the preview.

- Click on the **OK button** to complete the command.

Fig. 42

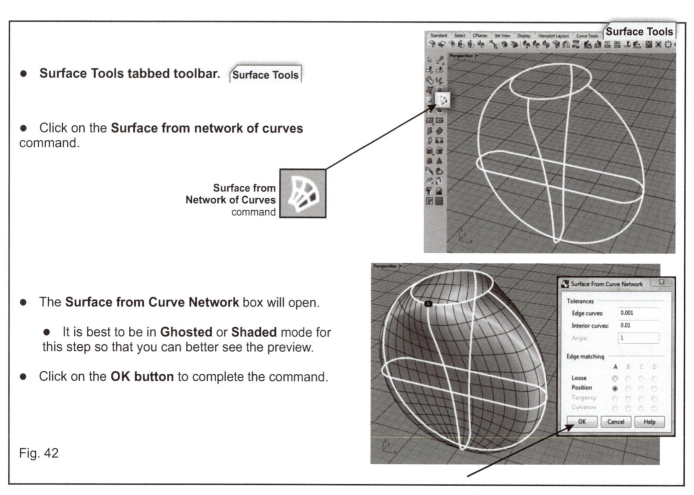

- Turn off the **ring ref** layer.

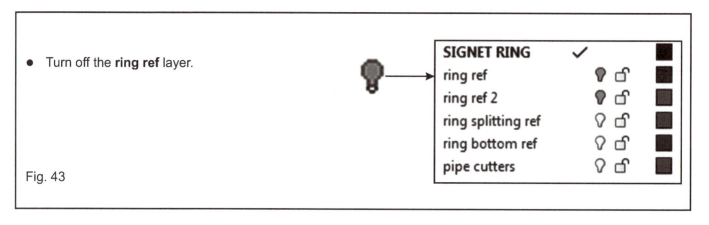

Fig. 43

- Navigate around the finished curve network until you can see the surface seam.

- It is necessary for this seam to be located in the center of the piece, not on the side as shown in this illustration.
  - The surface seam on your project may be on the other side, which is OK, or even in the center of the piece already!

Fig. 44

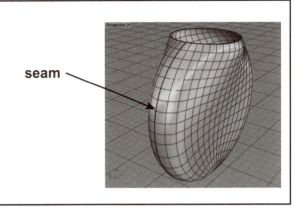

seam

- Click on the **Adjust closed surface seam** command.

  - **Select closed surface for seam adjustment** prompt:
    - note: a **"closed surface"** needs to have one seam but can be an "open" or "closed" surface in terms of whether it is a solid or not. *This surface is not a solid but is a closed surface for this command.*

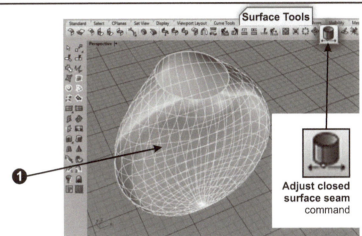

Adjust closed surface seam command

- After the closed surface is selected, move the cursor over the surface and notice that the a preview of the new seam location follows it.

- Snap to the front **Quad** of the oval opening at the top of the ring and click to set location.

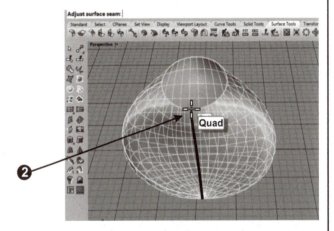

Quad

- The seam will now be accurately located down the front center of the ring surface.

new location of seam

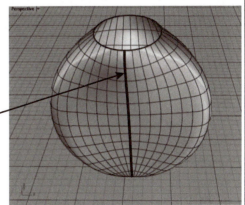

Fig. 45

450

- Select the surface, type **"cap"**, and press **Enter**.

- The opening at the top at the ring will now be **"capped"** and the object will be a **closed polysurface**.

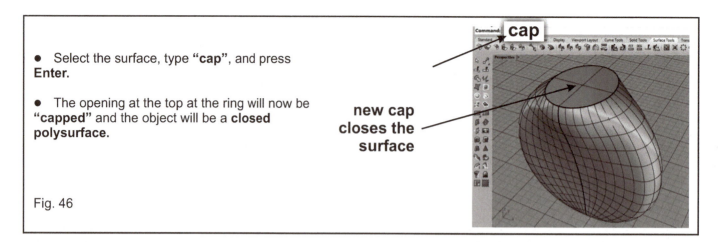

new cap closes the surface

Fig. 46

- Turn on the **ring ref 2** layer.

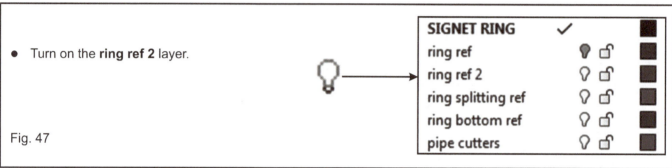

Fig. 47

- Switch to **ghosted display mode**.

- **Ghosted mode** will let you see the curves on the **ring ref 2** layer that are now visible.

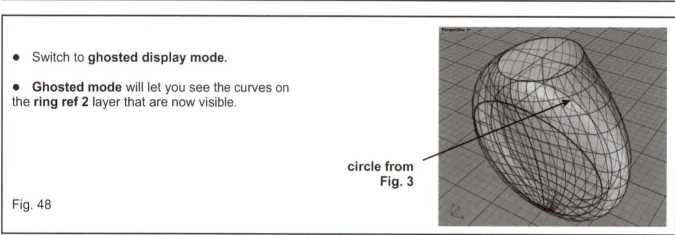

circle from Fig. 3

Fig. 48

- **Solid Tools tabbed toolbar.** | Solid Tools |

- Click on the **Wire Cut** command.

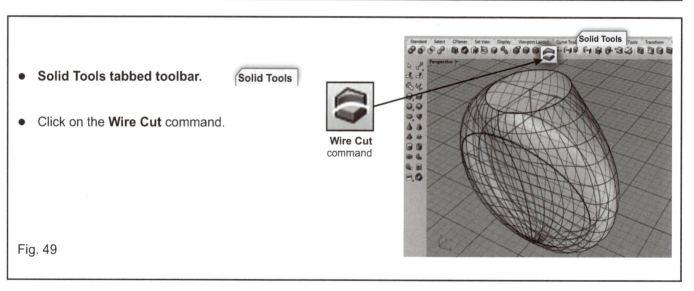

Wire Cut command

Fig. 49

- **Select cutting curve** prompt:
  - Select the **original 17.35mm circle** from Fig. 3 which is now inside the ring object.

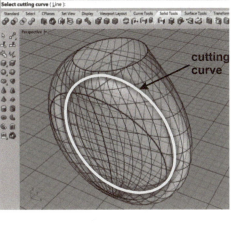

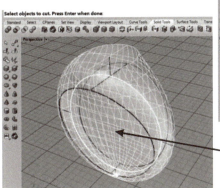

cutting curve

- **Select objects to cut. Press Enter when done** prompt:
  - Select the ring polysurface and press **Enter.**

the surface of the ring is the object to cut

- **Cut depth point. Press Enter to cut through object** prompt:
  - A preview of the cut direction will appear and will follow the cursor.
  - Press **Enter** to opt for cutting through the object.

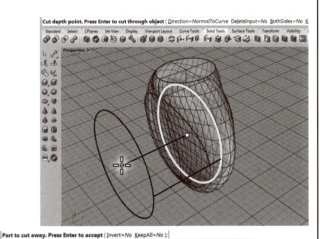

- **Part to cut away. Press Enter to accept** prompt:
  - If your preview shows the finger hole being cut away, press **Enter.**

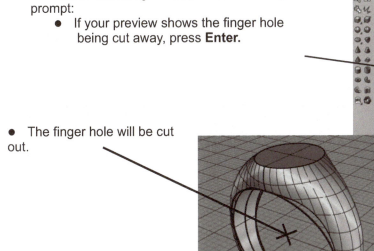

- The finger hole will be cut out.

Fig. 50

- **If** your preview shows that the outside of the ring will be cut away, click the **Invert=No** option ❶ to read **Invert=Yes.** ❷
  - Then press **Enter.**

- The preview will be inverted to show that the finger hole will be cut out which is the desired option.
  - Press **Enter.**

Fig. 51

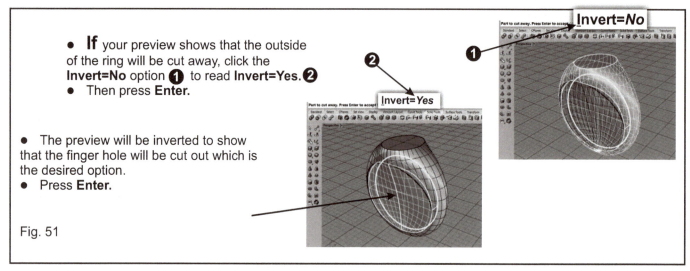

- A finger opening has been created.

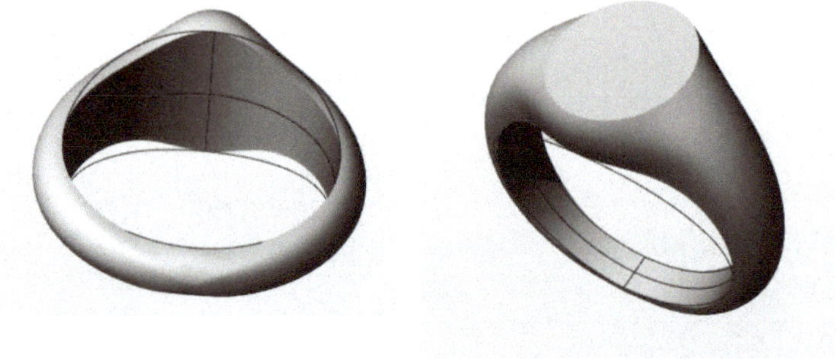

Fig. 52

- Turn off the **ring ref 2** layer.

- **ring splitting ref** layer current.

current

SIGNET RING			
ring ref	♀	⌂	■
ring ref 2	♀	⌂	■
ring splitting ref	✓		■
ring bottom ref	♀	⌂	■
pipe cutters	♀	⌂	■

Fig. 53

- Notice that the bottom of the ring has an awkward bulge - and the surface is not perfectly smooth.

- It is necessary to rebuild the bottom of the ring so that it will blend gracefully with the rest of the shank and will have a smooth surface.

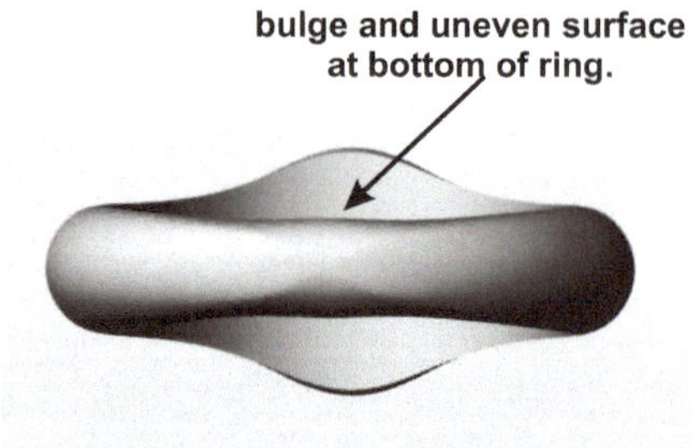

Fig. 54

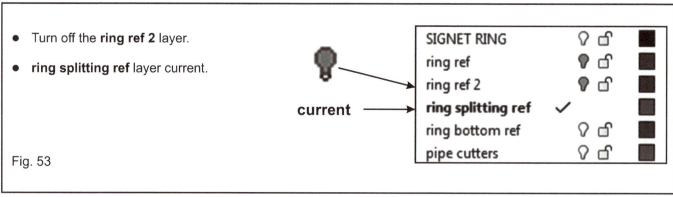

bulge and uneven surface at bottom of ring.

- **Front Viewport.** `Front ▾`

- **Curve Tools tabbed toolbar.** `Curve Tools`

Line: from Midpoint command

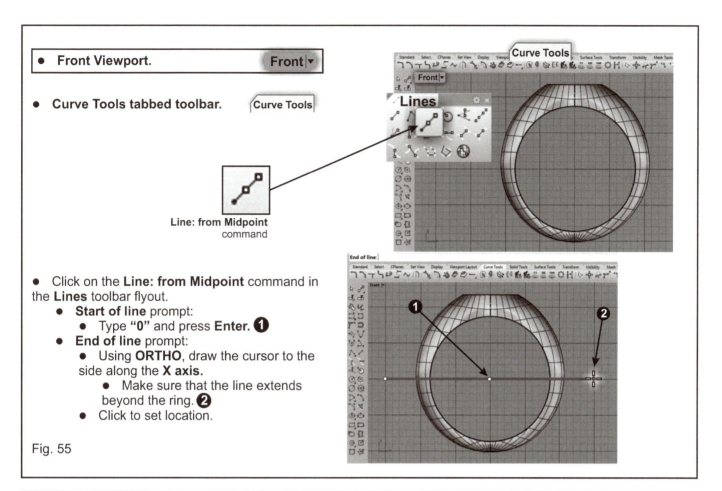

- Click on the **Line: from Midpoint** command in the **Lines** toolbar flyout.
    - **Start of line** prompt:
        - Type **"0"** and press **Enter. ❶**
    - **End of line** prompt:
        - Using **ORTHO**, draw the cursor to the side along the **X axis.**
            - Make sure that the line extends beyond the ring. **❷**
        - Click to set location.

Fig. 55

- **Front Perspective view.** ❶ 🚗 ❷ 🚗

Split command

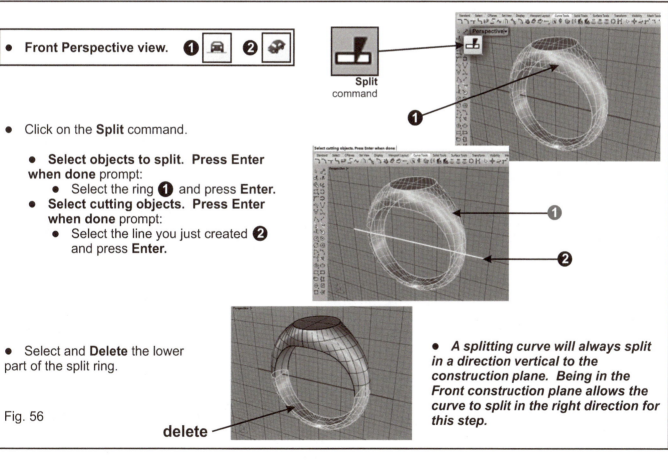

- Click on the **Split** command.

    - **Select objects to split. Press Enter when done** prompt:
        - Select the ring ❶ and press **Enter.**
    - **Select cutting objects. Press Enter when done** prompt:
        - Select the line you just created ❷ and press **Enter.**

- Select and **Delete** the lower part of the split ring.

Fig. 56

delete

- *A splitting curve will always split in a direction vertical to the construction plane. Being in the Front construction plane allows the curve to split in the right direction for this step.*

- Turn on the **ring ref** layer.

- Turn off the **ring splitting ref** layer.

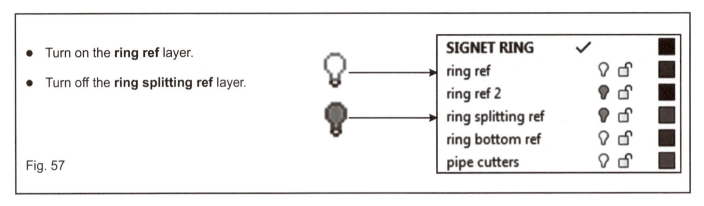

Fig. 57

- Turn the **ring ref** layer back on and select the four main silhouette curves shown.

- **RIGHT-CLICK** on the **ring bottom ref** layer in the layers panel.

- Click on the **Copy Objects to Layer** option in the drop-down context menu.

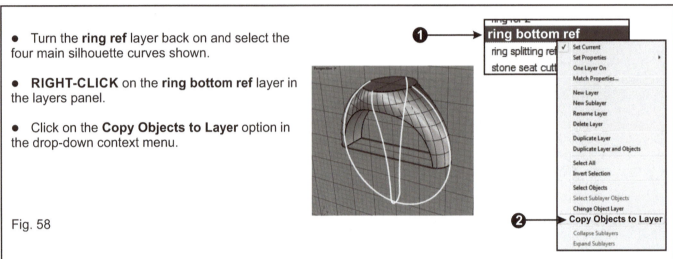

Fig. 58

- Turn off the **ring ref** layer.

- **ring bottom ref** layer current.

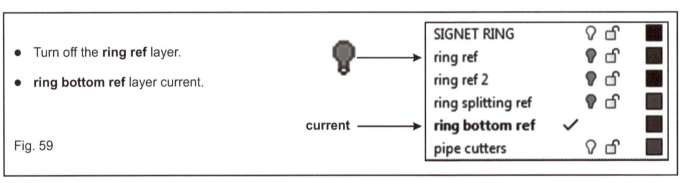

current

Fig. 59

- Select and **Explode** the curves shown.

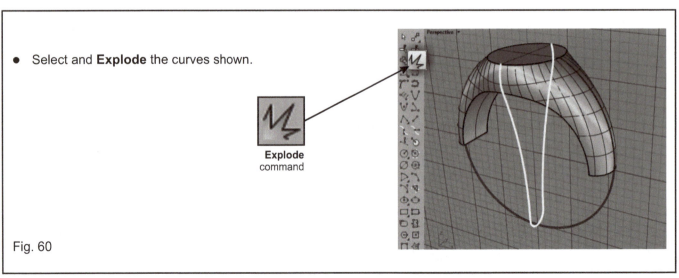

Explode
command

Fig. 60

- Select the **Delete** the upper parts of the curves as shown.

- Only the small arc at the bottom will remain.

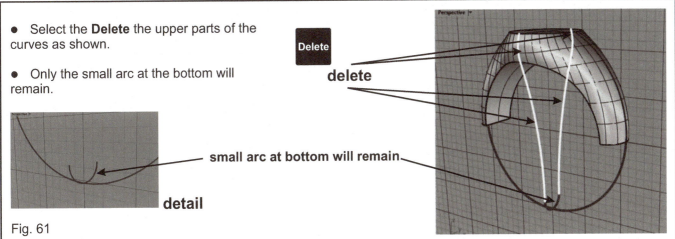

delete

small arc at bottom will remain

detail

Fig. 61

- Select the two outer silhouette curves ❶ and click on the **Join** command.

  - **Select cutting objects Press Enter when done** prompt:
    - Select the ring and press **Enter.** ❷

Join
command

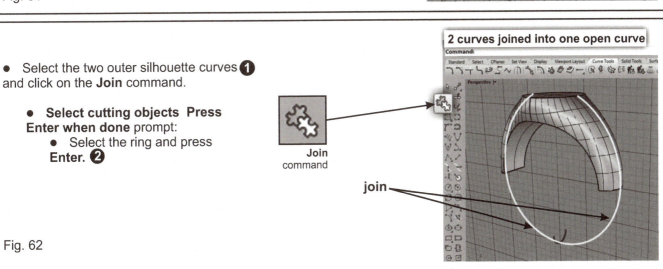

2 curves joined into one open curve

join

Fig. 62

- Click on the **Split** command.
  - **Select objects to split. Press Enter when done** prompt:
    - Select the single curve that was just joined from two separate curves.

Split
command

- **Select cutting objects** prompt:
  - Select the ring ❷ and press **Enter.**

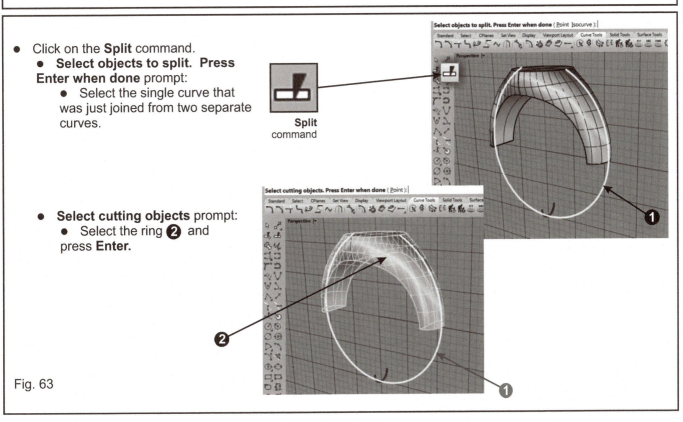

Fig. 63

- Select and **Delete** the split away curves lying along the ring surface.

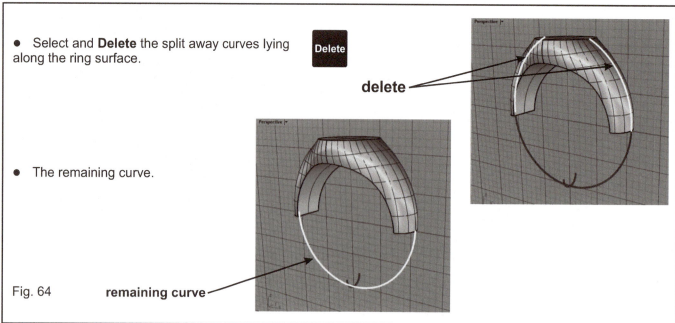

delete

- The remaining curve.

Fig. 64   remaining curve

- Select the two sides of the small arc at the bottom of the ring and click on the **Join** command.

- The History line will say **2 curves joined into one open curve.**

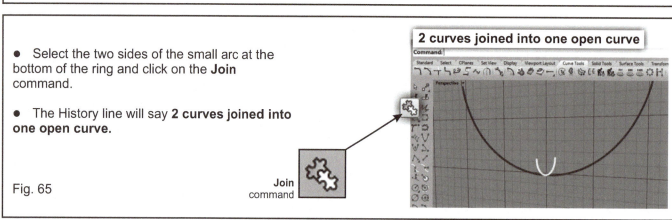

2 curves joined into one open curve

Fig. 65

Join
command

- Click on the **Arc: Start, End, Point on Arc** command.
  - Use **end osnap** to anchor the arc as shown.
    - **Start of arc:** ❶
    - **End of arc:** ❷
    - **Point on arc:** ❸

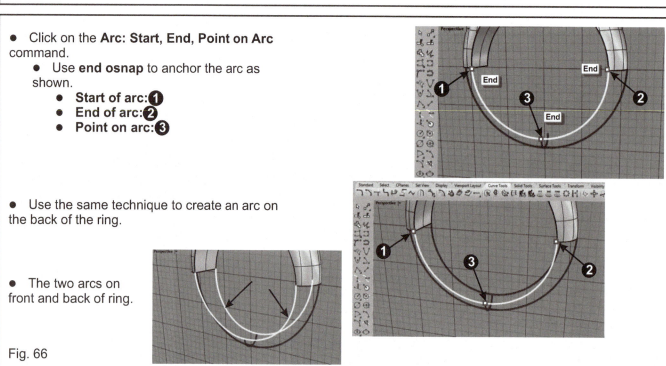

- Use the same technique to create an arc on the back of the ring.

- The two arcs on front and back of ring.

Fig. 66

457

- Select the ring and all bottom curves.
  - The History line will read: **4 curves, 1 polysurface added to selection.** ❶

- With all objects still selected, type **"intersect"** ❷ and press **Enter.**

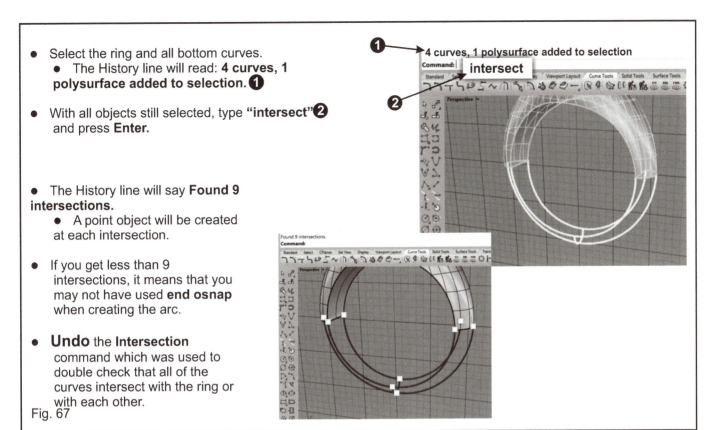

- The History line will say **Found 9 intersections.**
  - A point object will be created at each intersection.

- If you get less than 9 intersections, it means that you may not have used **end osnap** when creating the arc.

- **Undo** the **Intersection** command which was used to double check that all of the curves intersect with the ring or with each other.

Fig. 67

- **SIGNET RING** layer current.

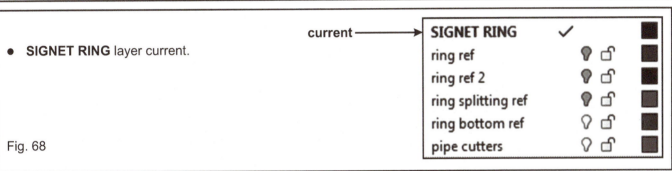

Fig. 68

- **Top Perspective view.** ❶ ❷

- **Surface Tools tabbed toolbar.** [Surface Tools]

- Click on the **Surface from network of curves** command.

  - **Select curves in network. Press Enter when done** prompt:
    - Select the 4 network curves plus the edges on both sides of the ring as shown.
    - Press **Enter.**

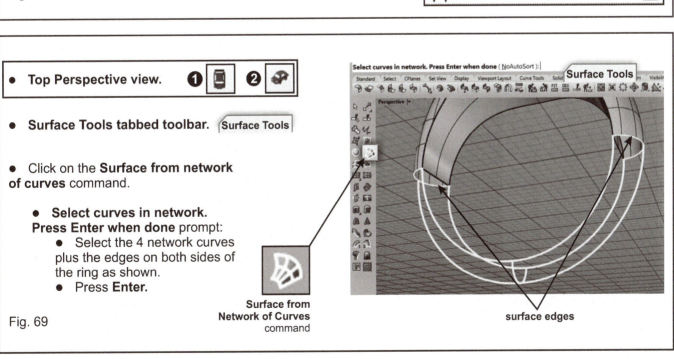

Surface from Network of Curves command

surface edges

Fig. 69

- In the **Surface from Curve Network** box, notice that tangency is possible at the surface edges that were selected as part of the curve network.

- Click the **OK button** to complete the command.

Fig. 70

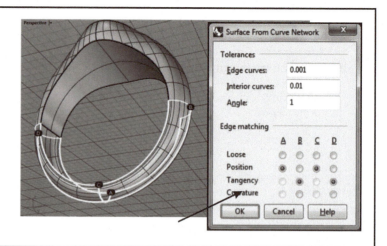

- Turn off the **ring bottom ref** layer.

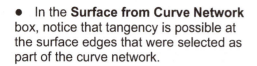

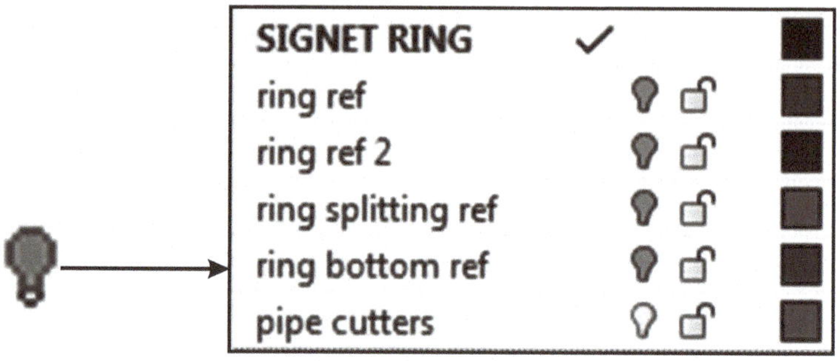

SIGNET RING	✓		■
ring ref	💡	🔓	■
ring ref 2	💡	🔓	■
ring splitting ref	💡	🔓	■
ring bottom ref	💡	🔓	■
pipe cutters	💡	🔓	■

Fig. 71

- Notice that the shape and surface of the bottom of the ring is now smooth and consistent.

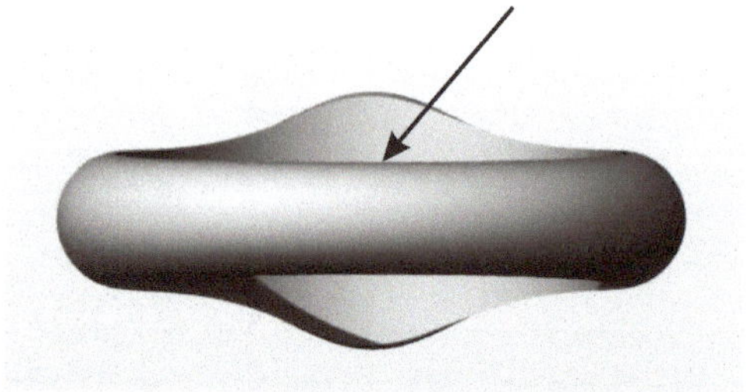

Fig. 72

- Select the ring and the new bottom surface.

- Click on the **Join** command.

- The result will be an open polysurface.

Join command

Fig. 73

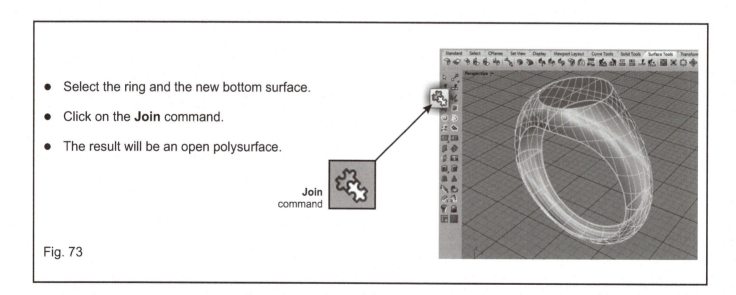

459

- Click on the **Sweep 2 Rails** command.

  - **Select first rail** prompt:
    - Select one of the long surface edges. ❶
  - **Select second rail** prompt:
    - Select the other long surface edge. ❷

Sweep 2 Rails command

  - **Select cross section curves** prompt:
    - Select the two short surface edges. ❸ ❹
    - Press **Enter.**

- Press the **OK button** to accept the default options in the **Sweep 2 Rails** dialog box.

- A new surface will be created to close up the inside of the ring.

new surface

Fig. 74

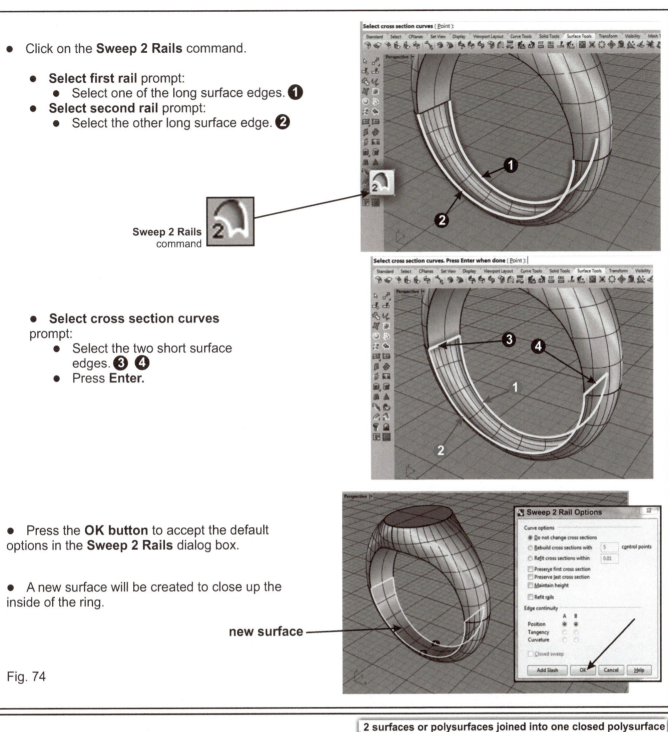

- Select the ring and the new surface.

- Click on the **Join** command (or type **"join"** and press **Enter**) to join these two objects and make a **closed polysurface.**

- The History line will say **2 surfaces or polysurfaces joined into one closed polysurface.**

Fig. 75

Join command

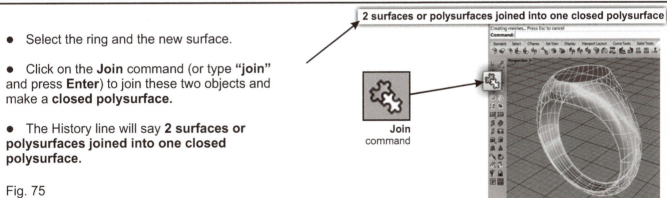

- **pipe cutters** layer current

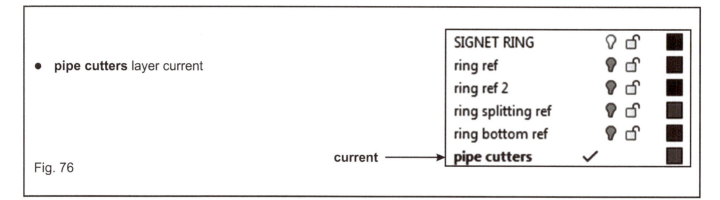

current ⟶ **pipe cutters** ✓

Fig. 76

- **Standard tabbed toolbar.** [Standard]

- Click on the **Duplicate Edge** command in the **Curve from Object toolbar flyout.**

  - **Select edges to duplicate. Press Enter when done** prompt:
    - Select the edges on one side of the ring as shown and press **Enter.**

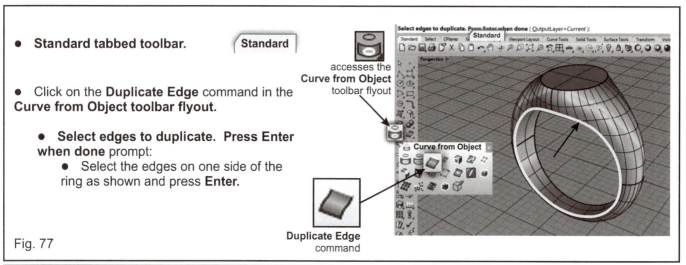

accesses the **Curve from Object** toolbar flyout

Curve from Object

Duplicate Edge command

Fig. 77

- Click on the **Join** command to make a single curve on the inside of the ring.

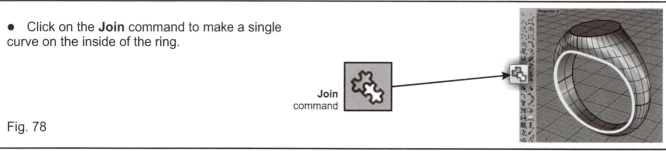

Join command

Fig. 78

- **Curve Tools tabbed toolbar.** [Curve Tools]

- Click on the **Adjust closed curve seam** command.

  - **Drag seam point to adjust. Press Enter when done** prompt:
    - Click on the seam point that will appear at one of the ring's seams. ❶ On your project, the location of this seam may be in a different location but that is OK.
    - Drag the seam point down to the bottom of the ring.
    - Snap to the **quad point** shown ❷ and click to set seam point's new location.
    - Press **Enter** to end the command.

Adjust closed curve seam command

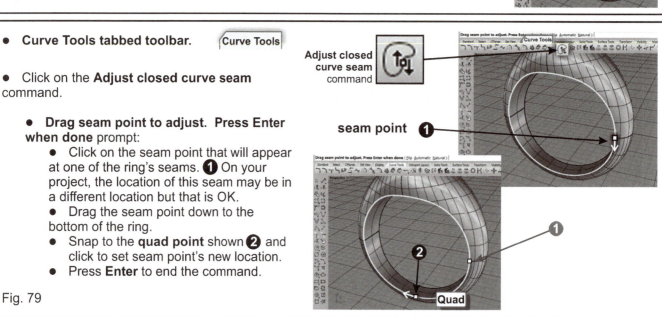

seam point ❶

Fig. 79

461

- Select the new curve, type **"rebuild"**, and press **Enter.**

  - **Rebuild** the curve to **30 control points.**

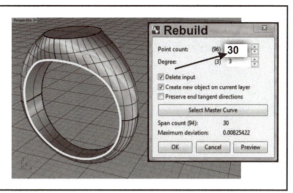

Fig. 80

- **Solid Tools tabbed toolbar.**   Solid Tools

- Click on the **Pipe** command.
  - **Select rail** prompt:
    - Select the curve along the edge of the ring that you just created.

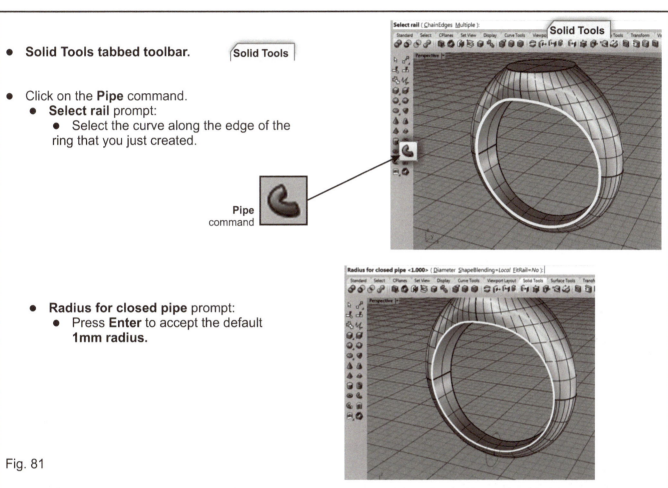

Pipe
command

- **Radius for closed pipe** prompt:
  - Press **Enter** to accept the default **1mm radius.**

Fig. 81

- **Point for next radius. Press Enter for none** prompt:
  - Press **Enter** because you only want one radius for the pipe.

- A **2mm diameter pipe** surface will be created around the curve.

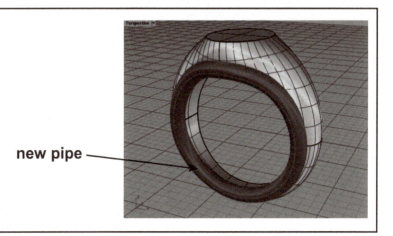

new pipe

Fig. 82

- **Mirror** the pipe surface to the back of the ring, using the **X axis** for the **mirror plane**.

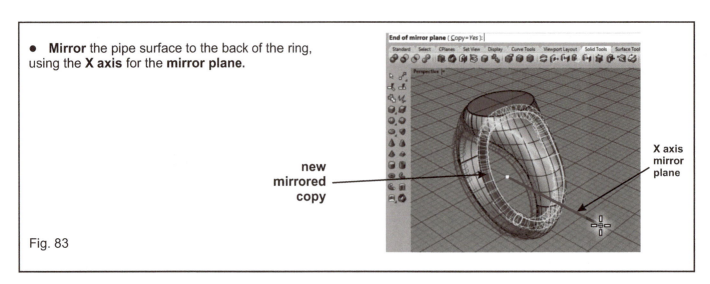

new
mirrored
copy

X axis
mirror
plane

Fig. 83

- Click on the **Split** command.

  - **Select objects to split. Press Enter when done** prompt:
    - Select the ring and press **Enter.** ❶

Split
command

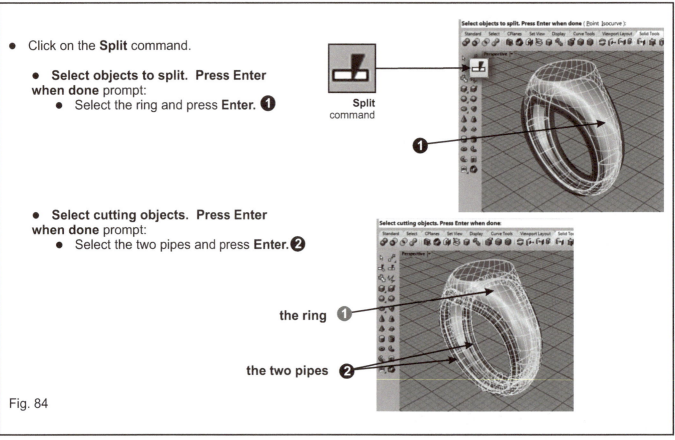

  - **Select cutting objects. Press Enter when done** prompt:
    - Select the two pipes and press **Enter.** ❷

the ring ❶

the two pipes ❷

Fig. 84

- **SIGNET RING** layer current.

- Turn off the **pipe cutters** layer.

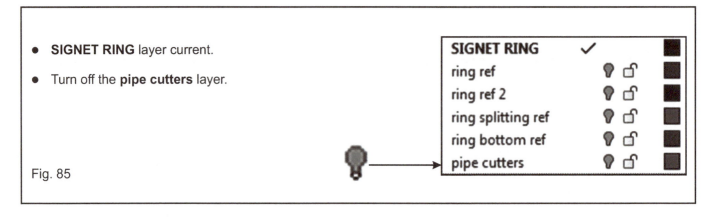

SIGNET RING	✓	■
ring ref	♀ 🔓	■
ring ref 2	♀ 🔓	■
ring splitting ref	♀ 🔓	■
ring bottom ref	♀ 🔓	■
pipe cutters	♀ 🔓	■

Fig. 85

- **Delete** the two strips on either side of the ring that have been split from the rest of the ring.

Fig. 86

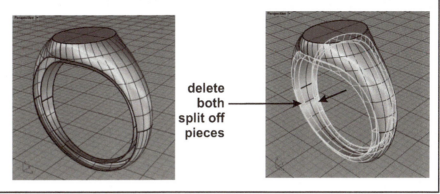

delete
both
split off
pieces

- **Surface Tools tabbed toolbar.**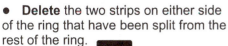

- Click on the **Blend Surface** command.
  - **Select first edge** prompt:
    - Click on the **ChainEdges ❶** prompt in the **Command Line.**
      - This will open up the rest of the Command Line options.
      - Notice that the **AutoChain=Yes** option has been toggled on. ❸

  - **Select segment for first edge** prompt:
    - Select the edge shown ❷ and notice that all 3 edges will be selected because the AutoChain option is enabled. ❸

  - **Select segment for second edge** prompt:
    - Select the edge of the inner surface. Both edges will select. ❹

Blend Surface command

all 3 edges
select as one

second edge ❹

- **Drag seam points to adjust. Press Enter when done** prompt:
  - Click and drag the seam points so that the seam is straight.
  - The seam on your model may be in a different location but that is OK.
  - Press **Enter.**

seam

detail view

Fig. 87

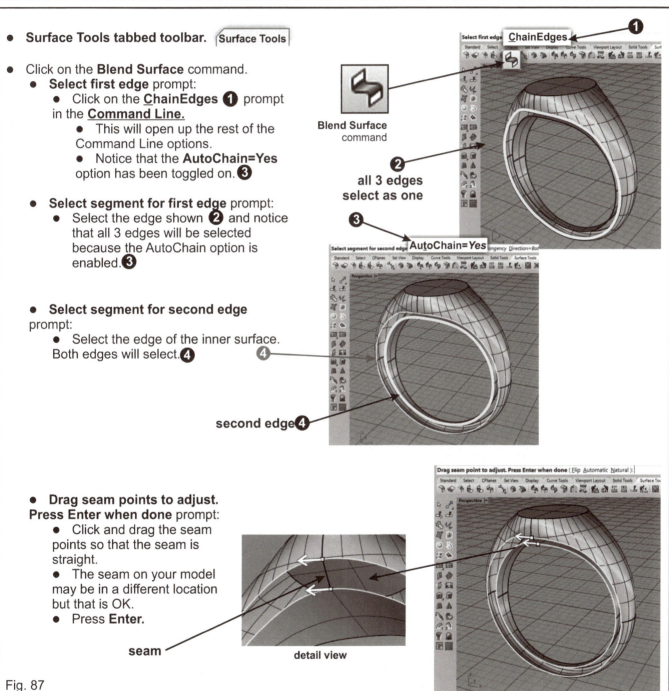

464

- If your seam is on the side of the ring, make sure that the seam points are on the **ends** of the seams of both outside and inside surfaces.

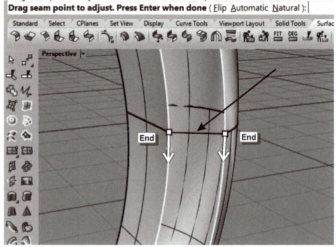

- Click to select the **Tangency** option in the **Adjust Surface Blend** box.
- Click the **OK button** to complete the command.

- If you wish, you can experiment with **curvature** or other settings offered that will determine the final shape of the blend surface.

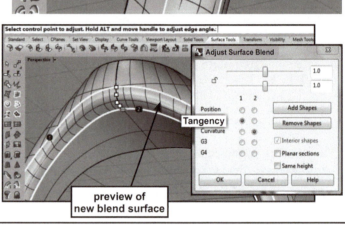

Fig. 88

- **Join** the new surface to the rest of the ring.
  - Use the same **Blend Surface** technique to soften the other side of the ring.

- The inner edges of the ring have been softened.

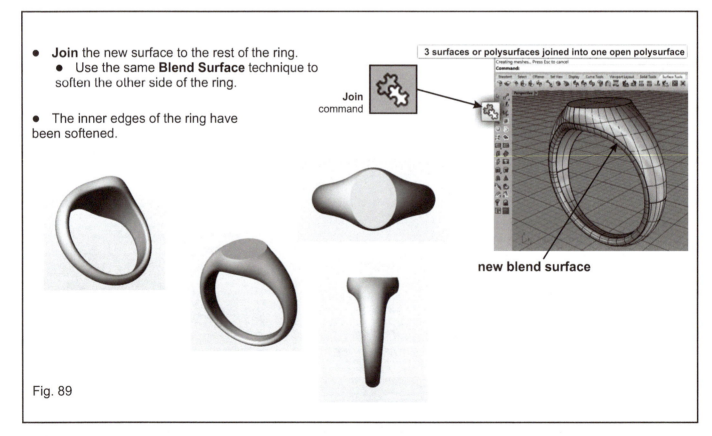

Fig. 89

Hollowing Out the Signet Ring
Offset of Original Untrimmed Curve Network

- Open the 8 x 10 Signet Ring.

- **Delete** the ring, leaving the curve network.

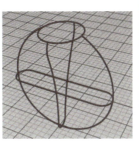

delete

Fig. 1

- Create a new layer and call it **CUTTER.**

- Make this new layer current.

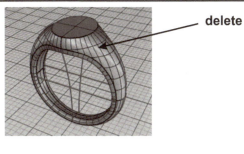

SIGNET RING		🔦	🔓	⬛
ring ref		🔦	🔓	⬛
ring ref 2		🔦	🔓	⬛
ring splitting ref		🔦	🔓	⬛
ring bottom ref		🔦	🔓	⬛
pipe cutters		🔦	🔓	⬛
CUTTER		✓		⬛

current ➜

Fig. 2

- Create the Signet Ring again but do not soften the edges.

- Hollowing comes out better without extremely softened edges.

do not fillet edges ⟶

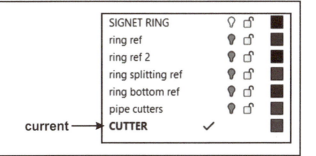

Fig. 3

- **RIGHT-CLICK** on the **Explode** button for the **Extract Surface** command.
  - **Select surfaces to extract** prompt:
    - **RIGHT-CLICK** to select the outer surface on the top half the ring as shown.
    - Press **Enter** to end the command.

RIGHT-CLICK for **Extract Surface** command

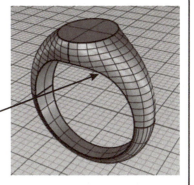

extracted surface

Fig. 4

- With the extracted surface still selected, **①**
RIGHT-CLICK on the **CUTTER** layer. **②**
  - Click on the **Copy Objects to Layer** **③**
  option in the context menu that appears.

Extracted surface still seleted ①

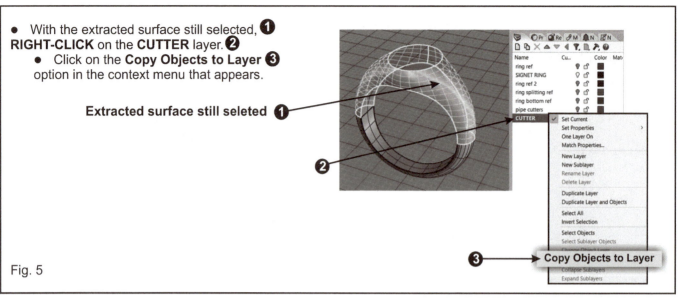

Fig. 5

- Turn off the **SIGNET RING** layer.

- **CUTTER** layer current.

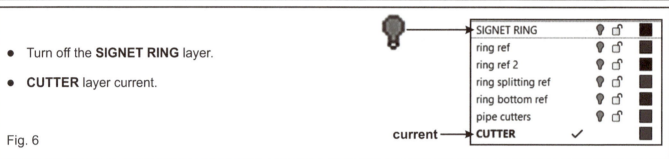

current

Fig. 6

- If you turn on the control points for the trimmed surface that you just extracted, you will see that Rhino remembers the original shape of this "trimmed" surface.

Fig. 7

- **Surface Tools tabbed toolbar.** [Surface Tools]

- **LEFT-CLICK** for the **Untrim** command.
  - **Select edge to untrim** prompt:
    - Click on the inside edge on the extracted surface.

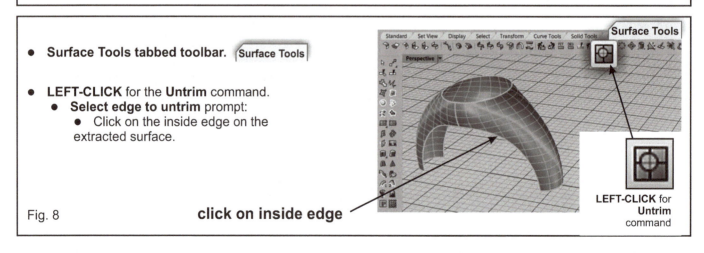

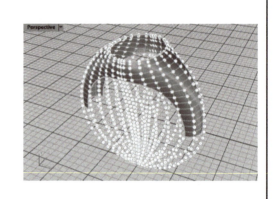

LEFT-CLICK for
Untrim
command

Fig. 8   **click on inside edge**

467

- The original shape of this surface will be restored.

Fig. 9

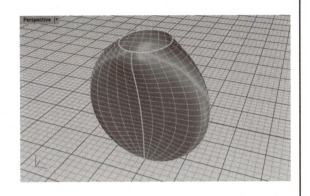

- Click on the **Offset Surface** command.
  - **Select surfaces or polysurfaces to offset. Press Enter when done** prompt:
    - Select the surface and press **Enter**.

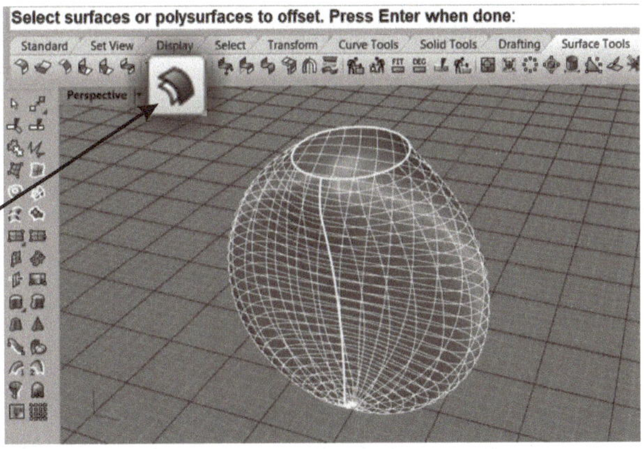

Offset Surface
command

Fig. 10

Select surfaces or polysurfaces to offset. Press Enter when done:

❷

Select object to flip direction. Press Enter when done (Distance=0.8 C... .8

- **Select object to flip direction. Press Enter when done** prompt:
  - If you see the direction arrows pointing outward as shown, click on the object ❶ to change the direction of the arrows.

click on object to change arrow direction ❶

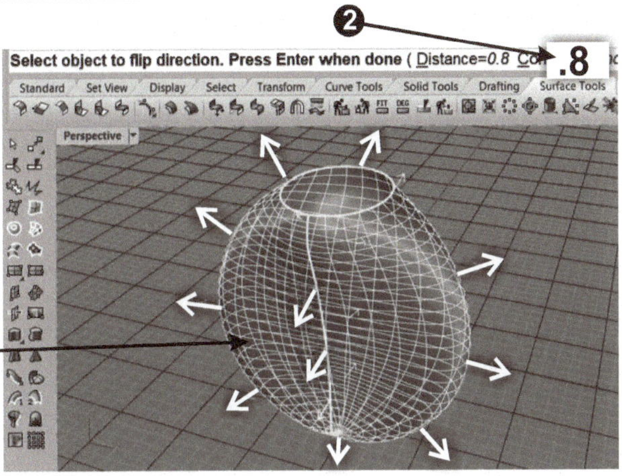

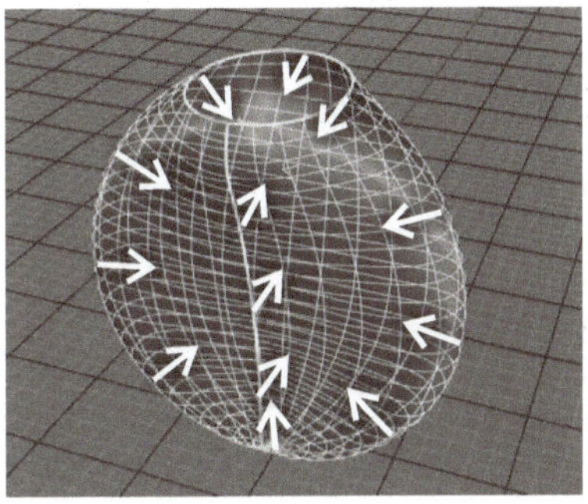

- The direction arrows are now all pointing inward which will be the direction of the surface offset.
- Type "**.8**" ❷ and press **Enter** for the offset distance which will designate metal thickness of the hollowed out signet ring.

- Press **Enter** to end the command.

Fig. 11

- You can select to view the new cutter on the inside of the outer surface.

- Select and **Delete** the outer surface which is not longer needed.

select and delete
outer surface

Fig. 12

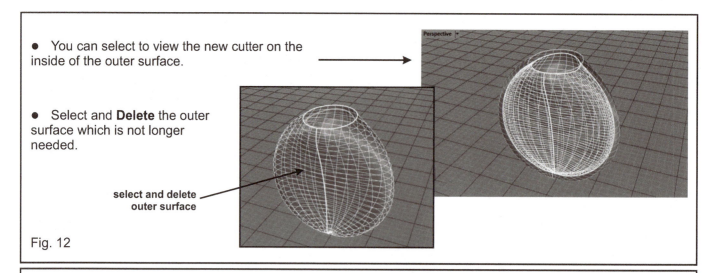

- **Rebuild** the new cutter:
  - **U direction: 75 control points**
  - **V direction: 75 control points**

Fig. 13

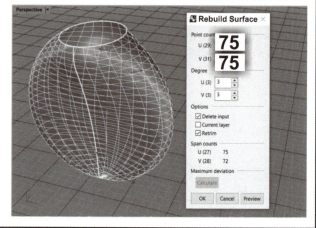

- Select the cutter and click on the **Show Edges** command.

LEFT-CLICK for
Show Edges
command

- This surface may show 2 naked edges.

- The Naked edge at the top **1** is OK and will be capped later in the exercise.

- The Naked edge in front **2** needs to be fixed.

Fig. 14

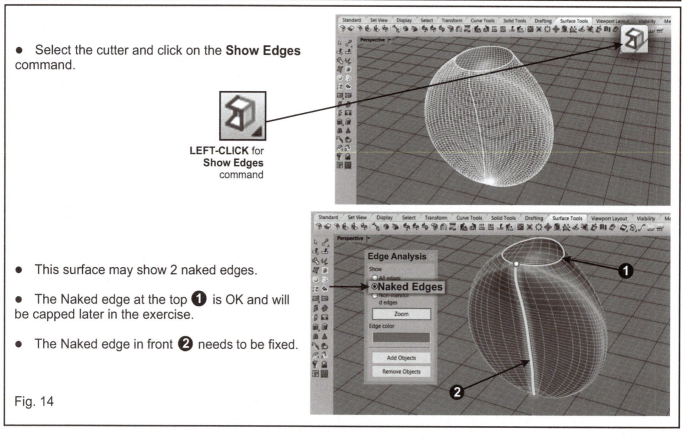

469

- Turn on the **ring splitting ref** layer.

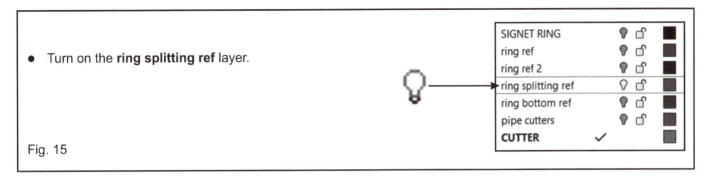

Fig. 15

- **Top Viewport.**   Top ▼

- Select the cutter **1** and click on the **Split** command.
  - **Select cutting objects. Press Enter when done** prompt:
    - Select the **ring splitting ref** line **2** and press **Enter.**

Split command

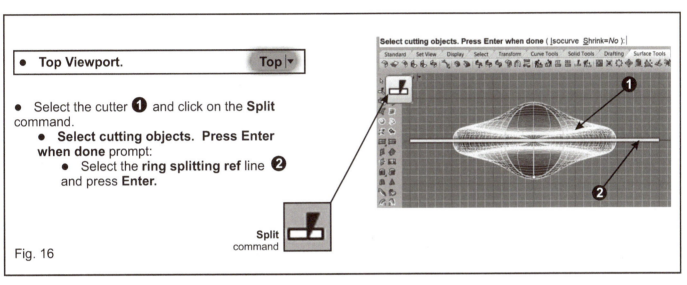

Fig. 16

- Turn off the **ring splitting ref** layer.

Fig. 17

- Select and **Delete** the two surface segments that have been split off from the rest of the cutter.

- The back half remains after the front of the cutter with the faulty geometry has been deleted.

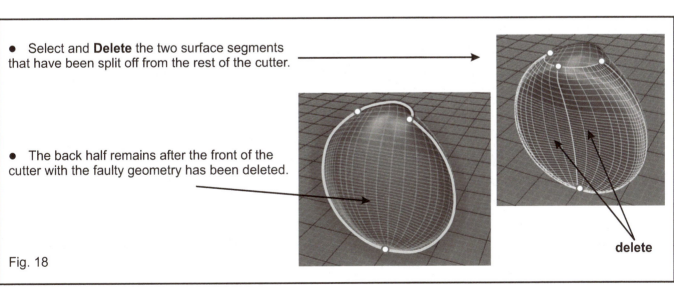

delete

Fig. 18

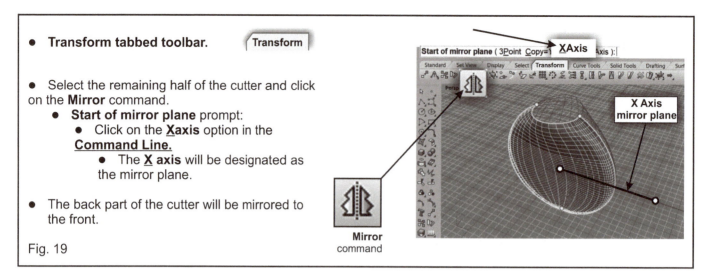

- **Transform tabbed toolbar.**　[Transform]

- Select the remaining half of the cutter and click on the **Mirror** command.
  - **Start of mirror plane** prompt:
    - Click on the **Xaxis** option in the **Command Line.**
      - The **X axis** will be designated as the mirror plane.

- The back part of the cutter will be mirrored to the front.

Fig. 19

Mirror command

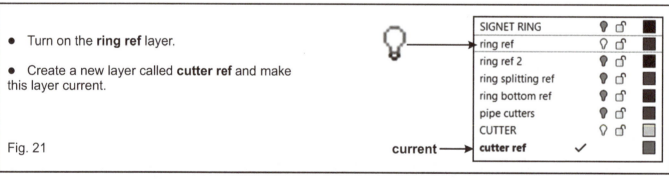

- **Join** the front and back pieces together.

Join command

Fig. 20

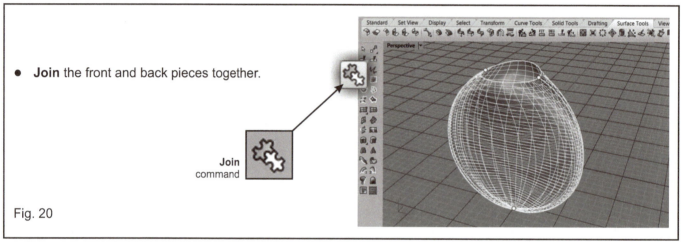

- Turn on the **ring ref** layer.

- Create a new layer called **cutter ref** and make this layer current.

Fig. 21

SIGNET RING		
ring ref		
ring ref 2		
ring splitting ref		
ring bottom ref		
pipe cutters		
CUTTER		
cutter ref	✓	

current ➝ **cutter ref**

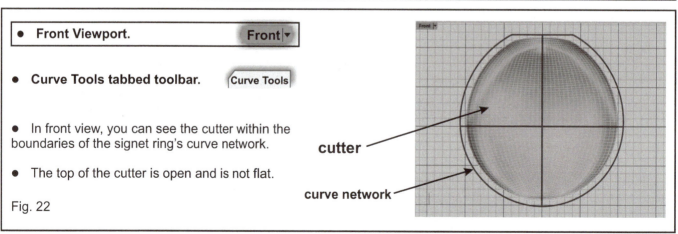

- **Front Viewport.**　[Front ▾]

- **Curve Tools tabbed toolbar.**　[Curve Tools]

- In front view, you can see the cutter within the boundaries of the signet ring's curve network.

- The top of the cutter is open and is not flat.

Fig. 22

cutter

curve network

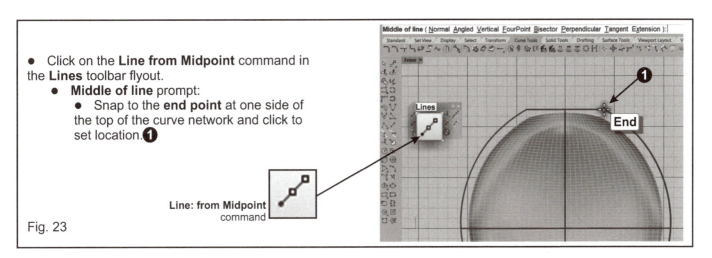

- Click on the **Line from Midpoint** command in the **Lines** toolbar flyout.
  - **Middle of line** prompt:
    - Snap to the **end point** at one side of the top of the curve network and click to set location.❶

Line: from Midpoint command

Fig. 23

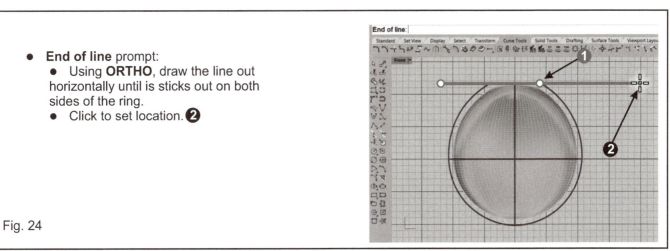

- **End of line** prompt:
  - Using **ORTHO**, draw the line out horizontally until is sticks out on both sides of the ring.
  - Click to set location. ❷

Fig. 24

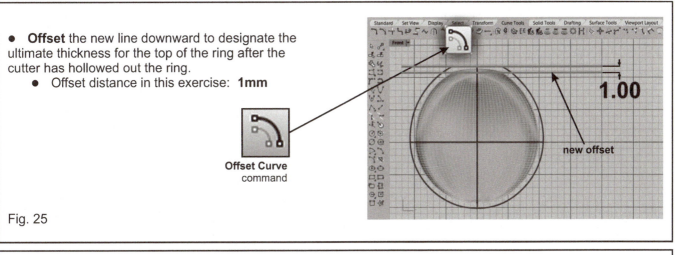

- **Offset** the new line downward to designate the ultimate thickness for the top of the ring after the cutter has hollowed out the ring.
  - Offset distance in this exercise: **1mm**

1.00

new offset

Offset Curve command

Fig. 25

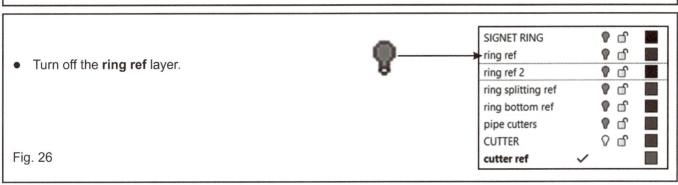

- Turn off the **ring ref** layer.

SIGNET RING			⬛
ring ref			⬛
ring ref 2			⬛
ring splitting ref			⬛
ring bottom ref			⬛
pipe cutters			⬛
CUTTER			⬛
cutter ref	✓		⬛

Fig. 26

- Click on the **Split** command.
  - **Select objects to split. Press Enter when done** prompt:
    - Select the cutter ❶ and press **Enter**.

Split command

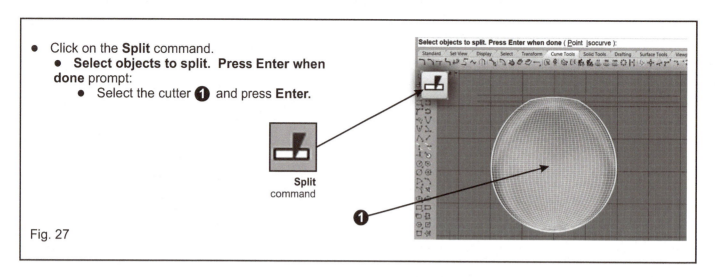

Fig. 27

- **Select cutting objects. Press Enter when done** prompt:
  - Select the curve offset ❷ and press **Enter**.

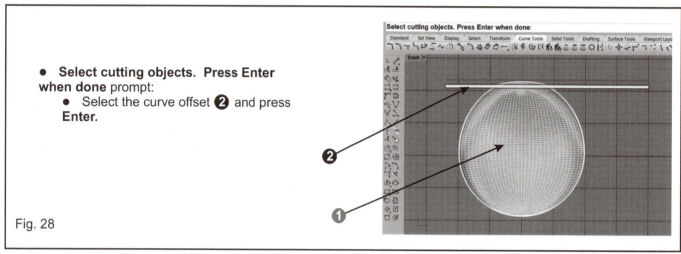

Fig. 28

- Select and **delete** the split-off top of the surface.

- The split-off piece has been deleted. The opening at the top is now planar and can be capped.

delete

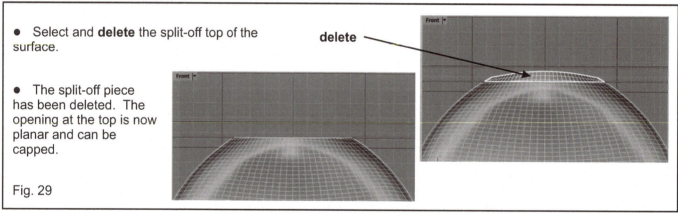

Fig. 29

- Turn off the **cutter ref** layer.

- **CUTTER** layer current.

SIGNET RING			
ring ref			
ring ref 2			
ring splitting ref			
ring bottom ref			
pipe cutters			
current → **CUTTER**	✓		
cutter ref			

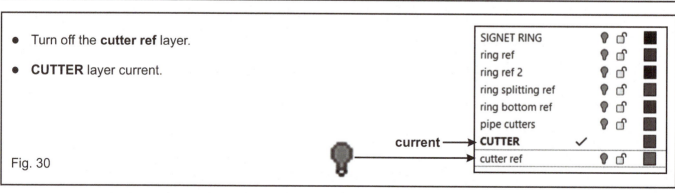

Fig. 30

- • **Top Perspective view.** ➊ ➋

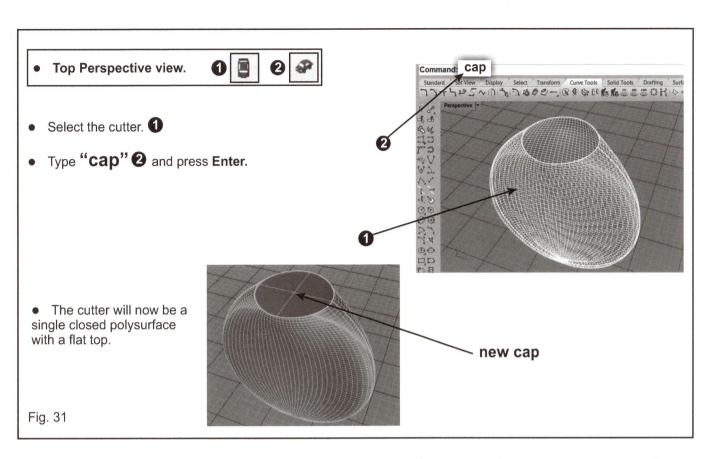

- • Select the cutter. ➊

- • Type **"cap"** ➋ and press **Enter.**

- • The cutter will now be a single closed polysurface with a flat top.

new cap

Fig. 31

- • Create a new layer called **cage.**

- • Make this new layer current.

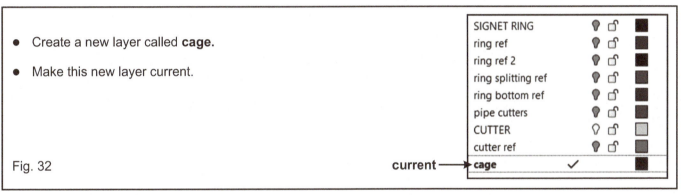

SIGNET RING		
ring ref		
ring ref 2		
ring splitting ref		
ring bottom ref		
pipe cutters		
CUTTER		
cutter ref		
current → **cage**	✓	

Fig. 32

- • **Transform tabbed toolbar.** `Transform`

- • Select the cutter and **LEFT-CLICK** for the **Cage Edit** command.

LEFT-CLICK for **Cage Edit** command

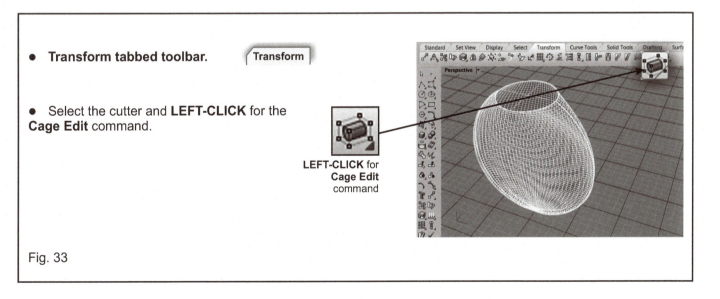

Fig. 33

- **Select control object** prompt:
  - Click the **BoundingBox** option **❶** in the **Command Line.**

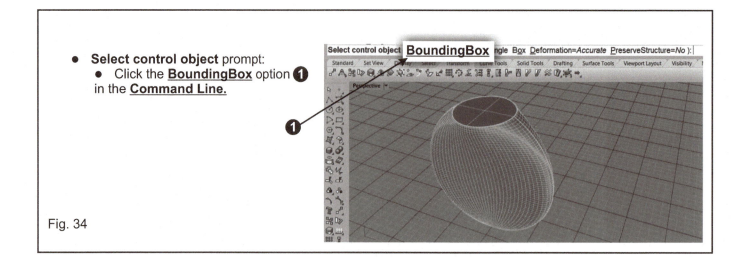

Fig. 34

- **Coordinate System** prompt:
  - Press **Enter** to accept the default **World** setting. **❷**

❷

Coordinate system <World> (CPlane World 3Point):

- **Cage Parameters** prompt: **❸**
  - Press **Enter** to accept the default settings showing control points and degrees for the bounding box that will be created. **❸**

Cage parameters (XPointCount=4 YPointCount=4 ZPointCount=4 XDegree=3 YDegree=3 ZDegree=3):

❹

- **Region to edit** prompt:
  - Press **Enter** to accept the default **Global** setting. **❹**

Region to edit <Global> (Global Local Other):

- A cage object will be created around the cutter.

- Notice the control points in X, Y and Z directions.

- Point editing this bounding box will effect the shape of the surface it surrounds.
  - If you edit the cutter on it's own, you will break the control of the cage over the cutter.

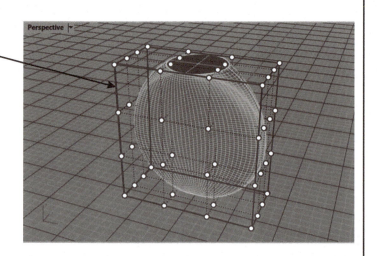

Fig. 35

- Select the bottom rows of the editing cage.

- Notice that what looks like just 4 points selected in the Front viewport, is actually 4 rows of control points selected when viewed in perspective.

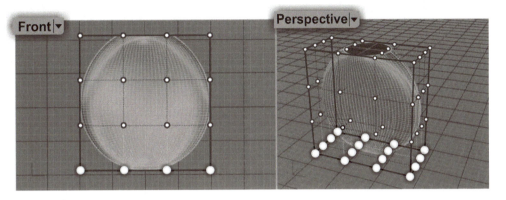

Fig. 36

- Turn the **SIGNET RING** layer back on.

- Make the **SIGNET RING** layer current.

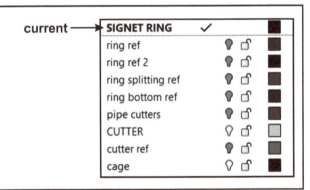

Fig. 37

- Using **ORTHO, Move** or **Drag** the selected control point up about 2mm - or more, depending on how much of the signet ring you want to hollow out.

- Click to set chosen location.

preview

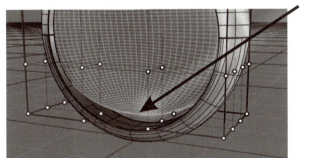

- Notice that the cutter shape has been modified, lifting it's lower part out of the bottom of the ring shank.

Fig. 38

- Turn off the **cage** layer.

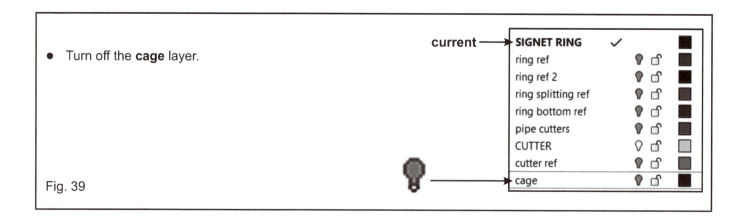

Fig. 39

- **RIGHT-CLICK** on the **SIGNET RING** layer ➊ in the layers panel.
  - Click on the **Select Objects** option ➋ in the context menu that appears.

- All objects on he **SIGNET RING** layer will be selected.

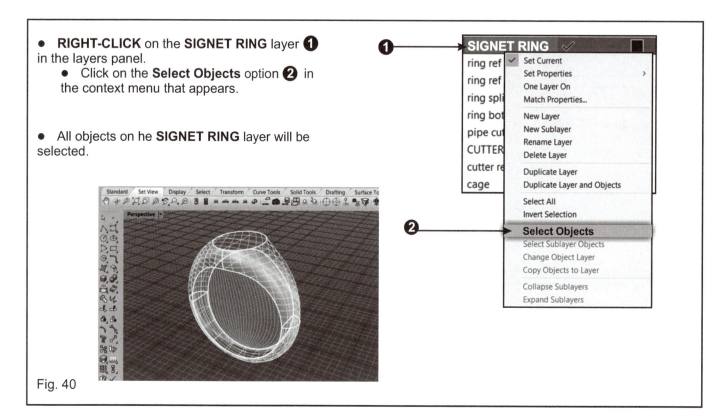

Fig. 40

- Click on the **Join** command.

- The History line will inform you: **"3 surfaces or polysurfaces joined into one closed polysurface."**

Join
command

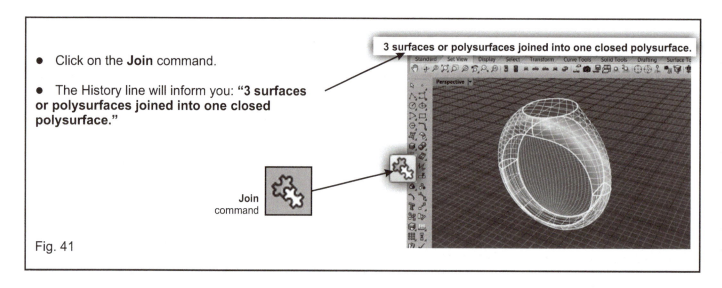

Fig. 41

- **Solid Tools tabbed toolbar.** | Solid Tools |

- Click on the **Boolean Difference** command.
  - **Select surfaces or polysurfaces to subtract from. Press Enter to continue** prompt:
    - Select the signet ring **1** and press **Enter.**

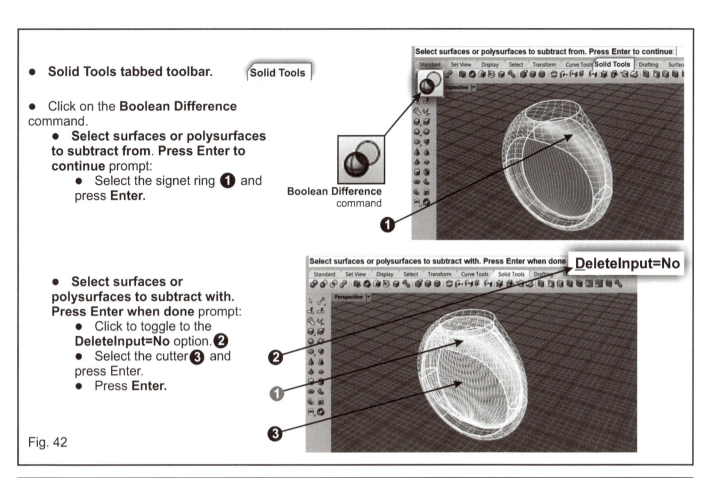

Boolean Difference
command

- **Select surfaces or polysurfaces to subtract with. Press Enter when done** prompt:
  - Click to toggle to the **DeleteInput=No** option.**2**
  - Select the cutter**3** and press Enter.
  - Press **Enter.**

DeleteInput=No

Fig. 42

- Turn off the **cutter** layer.

SIGNET RING	✓		■
ring ref		♀ ⌂	■
ring ref 2		♀ ⌂	■
ring splitting ref		♀ ⌂	■
ring bottom ref		♀ ⌂	■
pipe cutters		♀ ⌂	■
CUTTER		♀ ⌂	☐
cutter ref		♀ ⌂	■
cage		♀ ⌂	■

Fig. 43

- The Signet Ring has been hollowed out.

Fig. 44

478

Signet Rings - Different Shapes

Signet Ring with a Rectangular Top

• **Top Perspective view.** ❶ 📱 ❷ 🎨

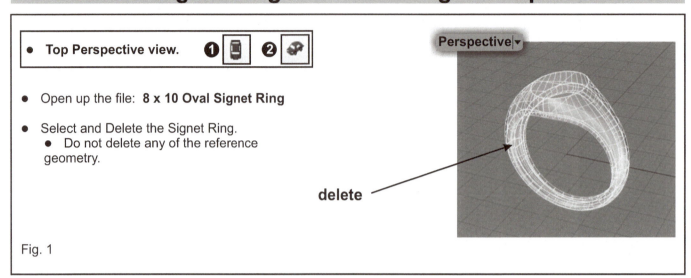

• Open up the file: **8 x 10 Oval Signet Ring**

• Select and Delete the Signet Ring.
   • Do not delete any of the reference geometry.

delete

Fig. 1

• **ring ref** layer current.

current ——→

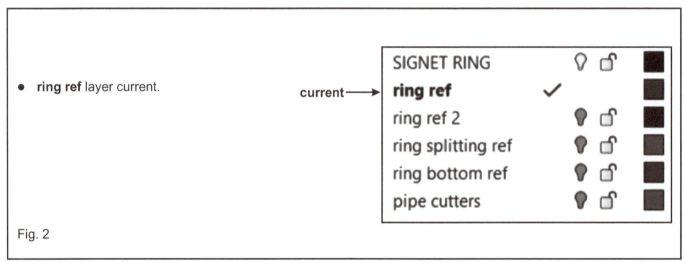

Fig. 2

• **Curve Tools tabbed toolbar.** ⌐Curve Tools⌐

• Using **quad osnap** or **end osnap**, create a line from one side of the top oval to the other.

new line

Line command

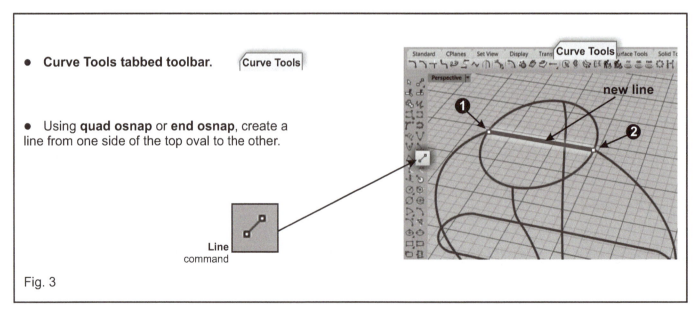

Fig. 3

- Click on the **Rectangle: Corner to corner** command.
  - Click on the **Center** option in the **Command Line.** ❶
  - **Center of rectangle** prompt:
    - Snap to the **mid point** of the new line and click to set location.

Rectangle: Corner to Corner
command

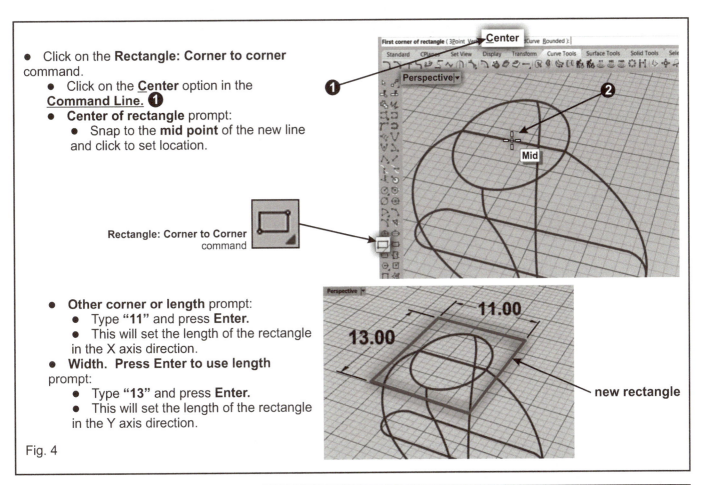

- **Other corner or length** prompt:
  - Type **"11"** and press **Enter.**
  - This will set the length of the rectangle in the X axis direction.
  - **Width. Press Enter to use length** prompt:
    - Type **"13"** and press **Enter.**
    - This will set the length of the rectangle in the Y axis direction.

Fig. 4

- **Select** and **Delete** the oval and the horizontal line on the top of the curve network.

delete

Fig. 5

- Select the two outer curves on the sides and turn on their control points.

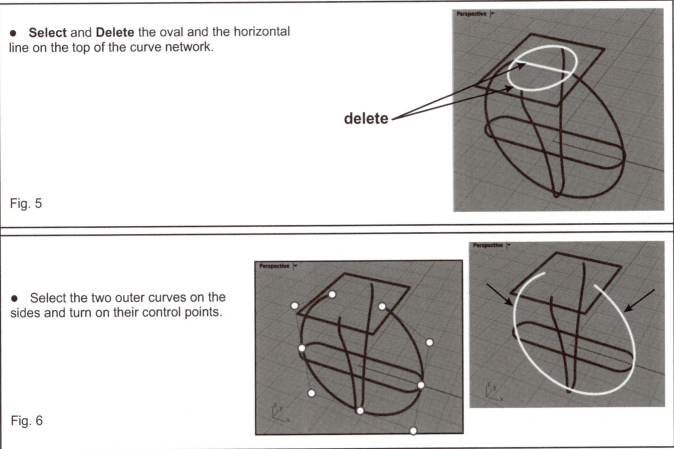

Fig. 6

- On each side, drag the top control point outward to the **midpoint** of the sides of the rectangle.

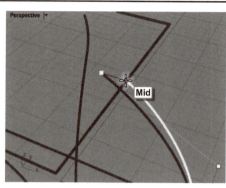

- The two outer curves now end at the sides of the new rectangle.

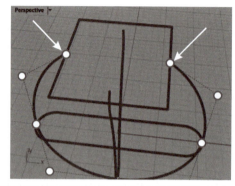

- Press the **Esc key** to turn off control points.

Fig. 7

- Select the other large outer curves and turn on their control points.

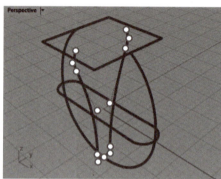 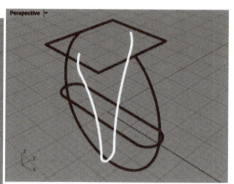

Fig. 8

- **Drag** all 3 control points at the top of the curve over to the **midpoint** of front or back of the rectangle.

- **Drag** the same 3 control points at the other end of the rectangle.

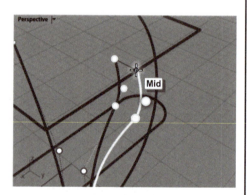

- Both front and back curves have been point edited to come in contact with the **midpoints** of the front and back of the rectangle.

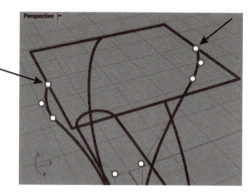

Fig. 9

- The next step will be to soften the corners of the rectangle in order to control how the corners are shaped when the curve network surface is created. Curve Network will only create one surface and will soften angles automatically which results in unpredictable results. More control over the surface will be achieved from an already softened rectangle.

Fillet Corners
command

- Select the new rectangle and click on the **Fillet Corners** command.
  - **Fillet radius** prompt:
    - Type "**.5**" and press **Enter.**

- The corners of the rectangle will be softened to a .5mm radius.

R0.50

Fig. 10

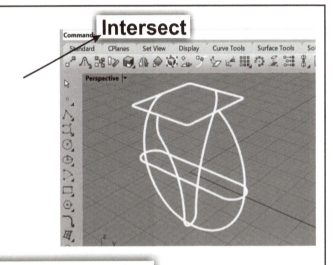

Intersect

- Select all of the network curves, type "**intersect**" and press **Enter.**

- A **point object** will be created at each intersection of the selected curves.
  - Only 12 intersections will be found.

Found 12 intersections

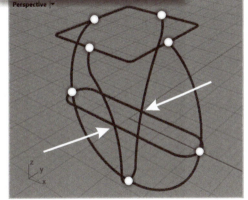

- Notice that the curves at front and back do not intersect with the horizontal curve in the middle of the ring.
  - When the front and back curves were edited for the rectangular shape, their shapes moved away from the horizontal closed curve.

- **Undo** or **Delete** the point objects.

Fig. 11

- **Transform tabbed toolbar.** Transform

  - Select the closed horizontal curve and click on the **Scale 1-D** command in the **Scale toolbar flyout.**
    - **Base point. Press Enter for automatic** prompt:
      - Type **"0"** and press **Enter. ❶**

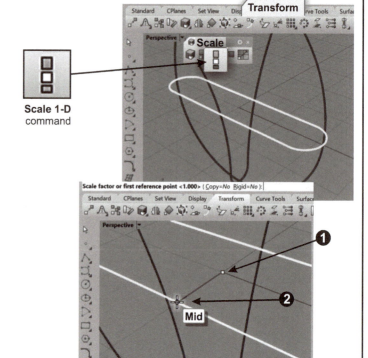

Scale 1-D
command

  - **Scale factor or first reference point** prompt:
    - Draw the cursor over to one side and snap to the **midpoint** of the selected curve.❷
    - Click to set location.

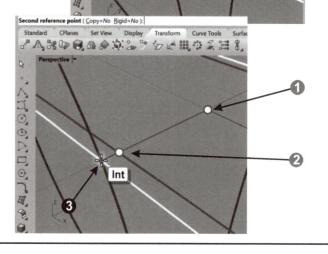

  - Using **ORTHO**, draw the cursor over to the nearby large curve.
    - Snap to the **intersection.**
    - Click to set location. ❸

- The scaled curve will now intersect the 2 large vertical curves.

Fig. 12

Found 14 intersections.

- Select all network curves, type **"intersect"** and press **Enter.**
  - This time all curves will intersect.
  - The history line will say: **Found 14 intersections.**

- **Undo** or **delete** all point objects.

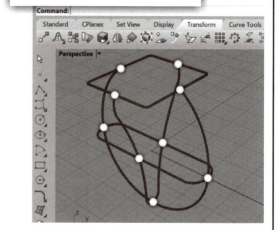

Fig. 13

- **SIGNET RING** layer current.

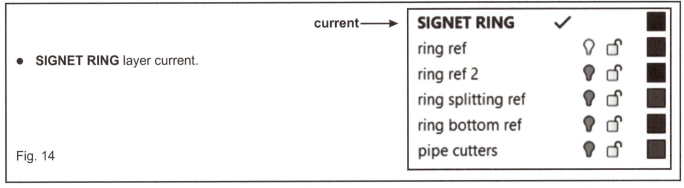

Fig. 14

- **Surface Tools tabbed toolbar.** Surface Tools

- Select all of the network curves and click on the **Surface from Network of Curves** command.
    - A preview of the surface will be visible in the display mode that you are using.
    - Click on the **OK button** to complete the command.

Surface from Network of Curves
command

- The finished curve network.

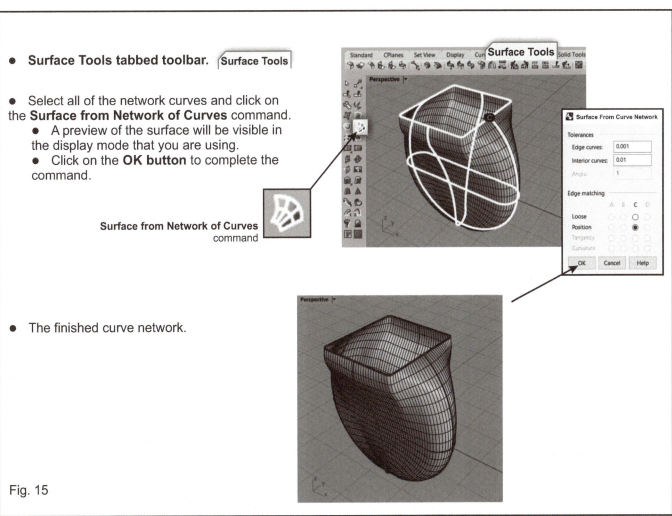

Fig. 15

- Turn off the **ring ref** layer.

Fig. 16

- The seam for this finished network surface is on the side of the ring.
- The next step will be to move this seam to the middle of the ring.

seam ———

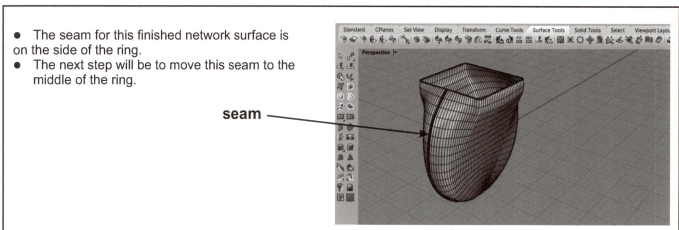

- Select the new surface and click on the **Adjust Closed Surface Seam** command.
  - As you draw the cursor over the surface, notice a preview line of the seam's new location will follow.

preview line ———

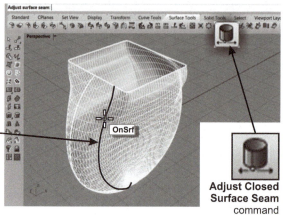

**Adjust Closed
Surface Seam**
command

- Drag the seam around to the front of the ring and snap to the **midpoint** of the rectangle as shown.
  - Turn the **ring ref** layer back on as you work so that you can snap to the **midpoint** of the front edge.

Fig. 17

- The surface seam is now at the middle of the ring.

- **Select** the ring, type **"cap"** and press **Enter.**

- A new planar surface will close off the top of the ring which is now a single **closed polysurface.**

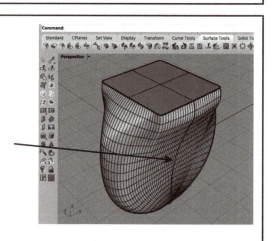

Fig. 18

- Turn the **ring ref 2** layer back on.

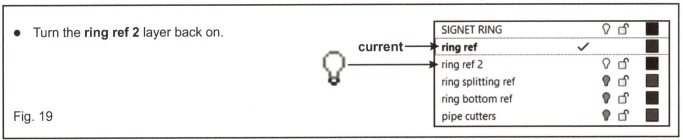

Fig. 19

- **Solid Tools tabbed toolbar.** [Solid Tools]

- Use the previously described **wire cut** command to cut out the finger opening.
- ref: *8 x 10mm Oval Signet Ring* tutorial, Figs. 49-51

Wire Cut command

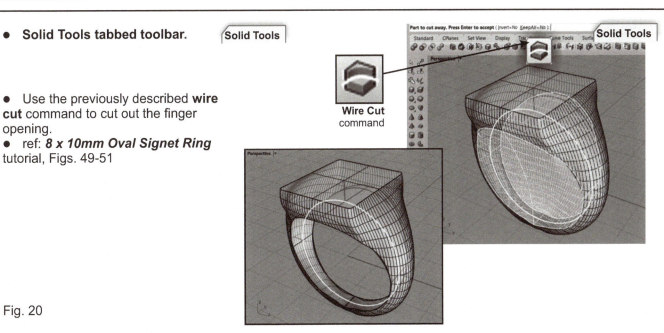

Fig. 20

- Split away and remodel the bottom of the ring as previously described.
  - ref: *8 x 19mm Oval Signet Ring* tutorial, Figs. 55-75

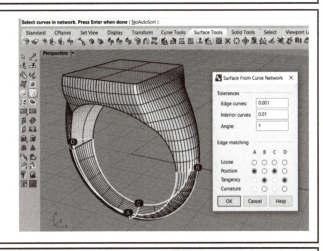

Fig. 21

- Use the previously described strategy to soften the inner edges of the ring.
  - ref: *8 x 10mm Oval Signet Ring* tutorial, Figs. 76-89

Fig. 22

486

- **ring ref** layer current.

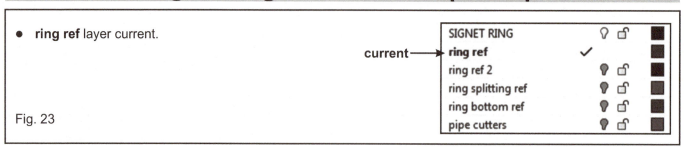

Fig. 23

- Select and **Delete** the polysurface of the rectangular signet ring.

- Save the new file as **star shaped signet ring.3dm.**

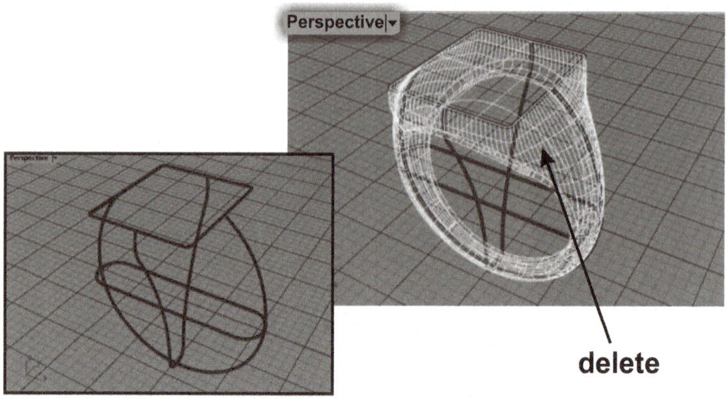

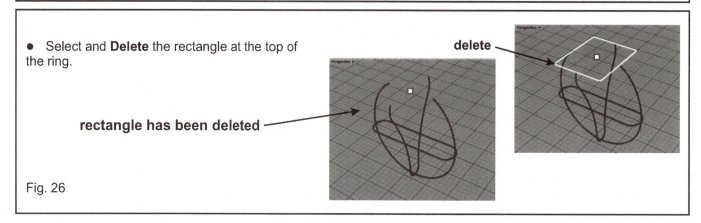

delete

Fig. 24

- Select the rectangle curve **❶**, type **"AreaCentroid"❷** and press **Enter.**

- A **point object ❸** will be created in the exact center of the rectangle.

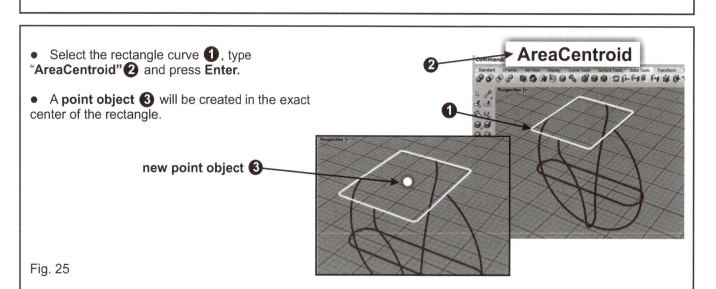

new point object **❸**

Fig. 25

- Select and **Delete** the rectangle at the top of the ring.

delete

rectangle has been deleted

Fig. 26

- **Curve Tools tabbed toolbar.** `Curve Tools`

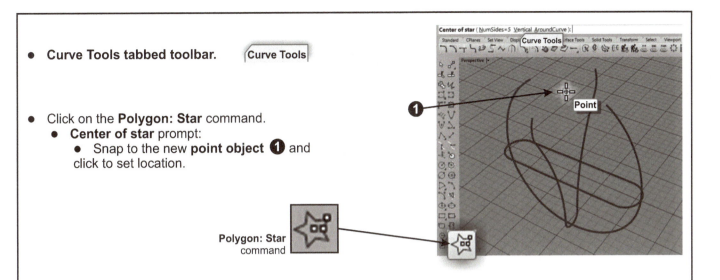

- Click on the **Polygon: Star** command.
  - **Center of star** prompt:
    - Snap to the new **point object** ❶ and click to set location.

Polygon: Star
command

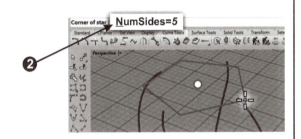

- **Corner of star** prompt:
  - Click on the **NumSides=5** option ❷ in the **Command Line.**

- **Number of sides** prompt:
  - Type **"6"** and press **Enter.**

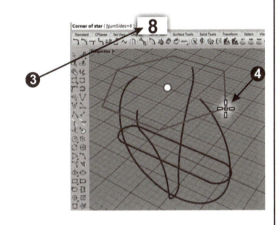

- **Corner of star** prompt:
  - Type **"8"** ❸ and press **Enter.**
    - This will set the radius of the star.
  - Using **ORTHO**, drag the cursor to the right in the **Xaxis direction.**
    - This distance will be constrained to 8mm.
    - Click to set location. ❹

- **Second star radius. Press Enter for automatic** prompt:
  - Press **Enter** to make a default star shape.

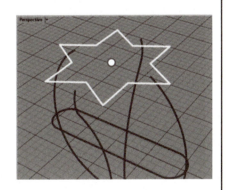

Fig. 27

- Select the new star and click on the **Fillet Corners** command.

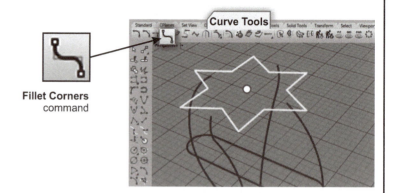

Fillet Corners
command

- **Fillet Radius** prompt:
  - Type "**.5:**" and press **Enter.**

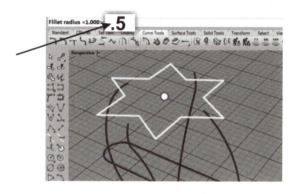

- The angles of the star will all be softened to a .5mm radius.

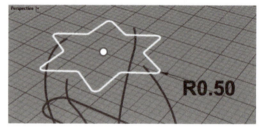

R0.50

Fig. 28

- Turn on control points for the vertical profile curve on the right.

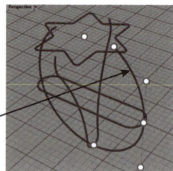

- Click and drag the top control point out to the quad on the side of the star as shown.

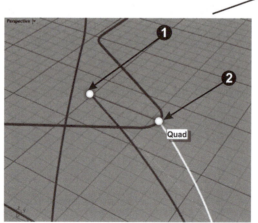

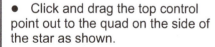

Fig. 29

- Point edit the curve on the other side of the ring in the same way so that both side curves are touching the outer **quads** of the star.

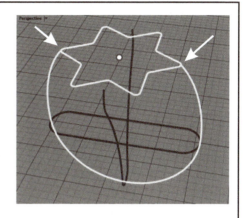

Fig. 30

- Turn on the control points for the front vertical profile curve.

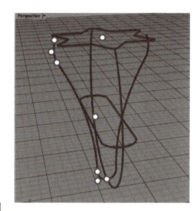

- Select the top 3 control points and drag so that the top control point snaps to the near inner quad of the star.

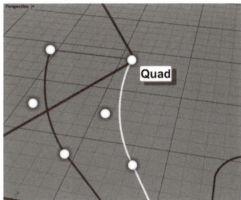

- Point edit the back curve in the same way.

- Now both front and back curves will be in contact with the star.

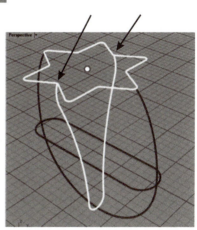

Fig. 31

- Select all network curves, type **"intersect"** and press **Enter.**

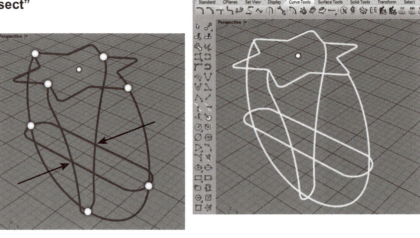

- **Point objects** will be created at all intersections.

- Because of the point editing of the front and back curves, these curves are not intersecting the central closed curve.

- Undo the intersect command.

Fig. 32

- **Transform tabbed toolbar.**   [Transform]

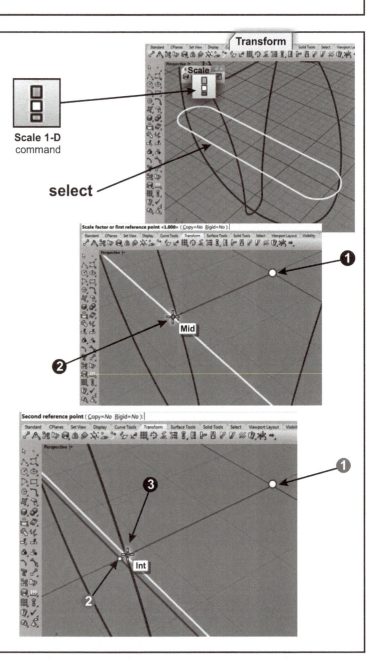

- Select the closed horizontal curve and click on the **Scale 1-D** command in the **Scale toolbar flyout.**
  - **Base point. Press Enter for automatic** prompt:
    - Type **"0"** and press **Enter.** ❶

Scale 1-D command

select

- **Scale factor or first reference point** prompt:
  - Draw the cursor over to one side and snap to the **midpoint** of the selected curve. ❷
  - Click to set location.

- Using **ORTHO**, draw the cursor over to the nearby large curve.
  - Snap to the **intersection.**
  - Snap to set location. ❸

- The scaled curve will now intersect the large vertical curve.

Fig. 33

- Select all network curves, type **"intersect"** and press **Enter.**

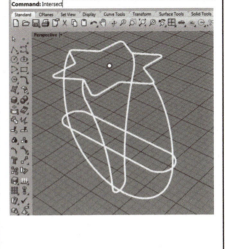

- **Point objects** will be created at all intersections.

- Undo the intersect command.

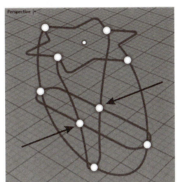

Fig. 34

- **SIGNET RING** layer current.

current ──→
SIGNET RING	✓	■
ring ref	♀ 🔓	■
ring ref 2	♀ 🔓	■
ring splitting ref	♀ 🔓	■
ring bottom ref	♀ 🔓	■
pipe cutters	♀ 🔓	■

Fig. 35

- **Surface Tools tabbed toolbar.** [Surface Tools]

- Select all network curves and click on the **Surface from Network of Curves command.**

Surface from Network of Curves command

- Click on the **OK button** in the **Surface from Curve Network** box to end the command.

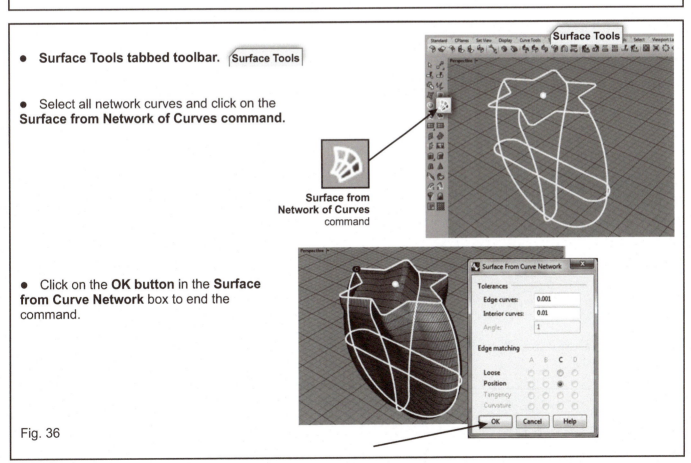

Surface From Curve Network

Tolerances

Edge curves:	0.001
Interior curves:	0.01
Angle:	1

Edge matching

	A	B	C	D
Loose	○	○	◉	○
Position	○	○	●	○
Tangency	○	○	○	○
Curvature	○	○	○	○

OK   Cancel   Help

Fig. 36

- Turn off the **ring ref** layer.

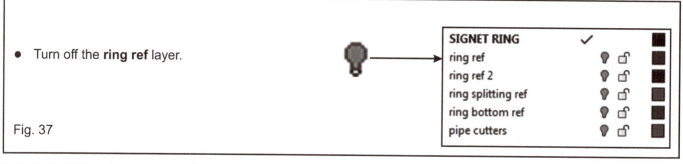

SIGNET RING	✓		■
ring ref		💡 🔓	■
ring ref 2		💡 🔓	■
ring splitting ref		💡 🔓	■
ring bottom ref		💡 🔓	■
pipe cutters		💡 🔓	■

Fig. 37

- Notice the seam on the side of the ring. This seam needs to be moved to the center of the ring.

- Use the technique shown in Fig. 17 to move the seam.

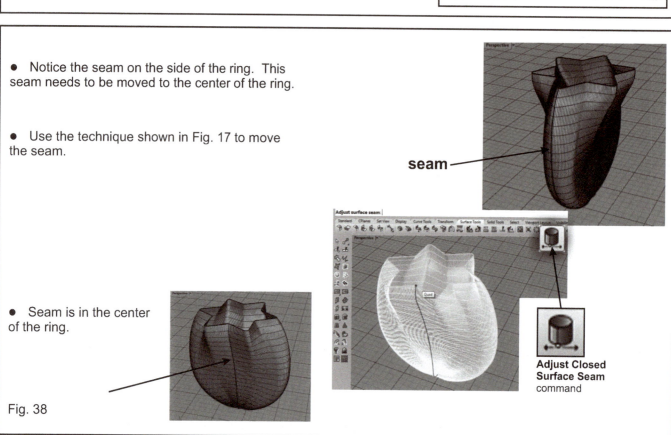

seam

- Seam is in the center of the ring.

Adjust Closed Surface Seam command

Fig. 38

- Select the surface, type **"cap"** and press **Enter.**

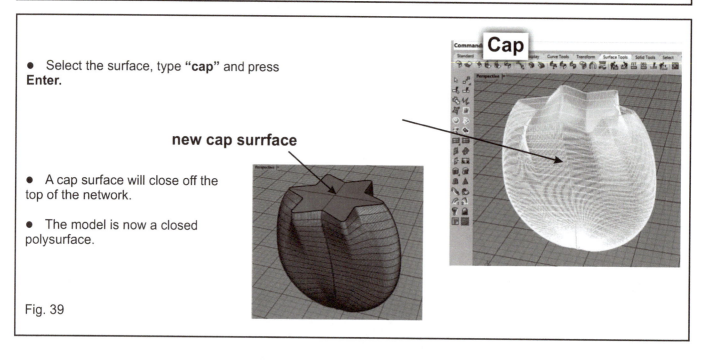

Cap

new cap surrface

- A cap surface will close off the top of the network.

- The model is now a closed polysurface.

Fig. 39

- **Solid Tools tabbed toolbar.**　　Solid Tools

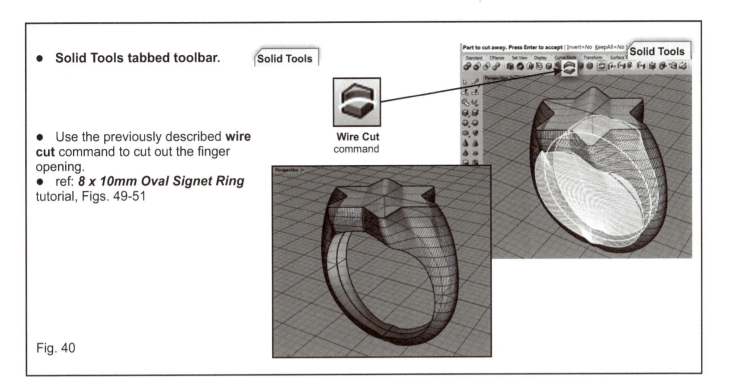

Wire Cut
command

- Use the previously described **wire cut** command to cut out the finger opening.
- ref: *8 x 10mm Oval Signet Ring* tutorial, Figs. 49-51

Fig. 40

- Split away and remodel the bottom of the ring as previously described.
  - ref: *8 x 10mm Oval Signet Ring* tutorial, Figs. 55-75

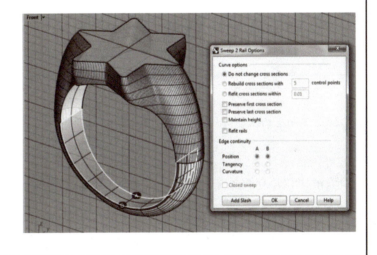

Fig. 41

- Use the previously described strategy to soften the inner edges of the ring.
  - ref: *8 x 10mm Oval Signet Ring* tutorial, Figs. 76-89

Fig. 42

Signet Ring - Rounded Top
Additional Reference Geometry to Add Control to the Shape of the Ring

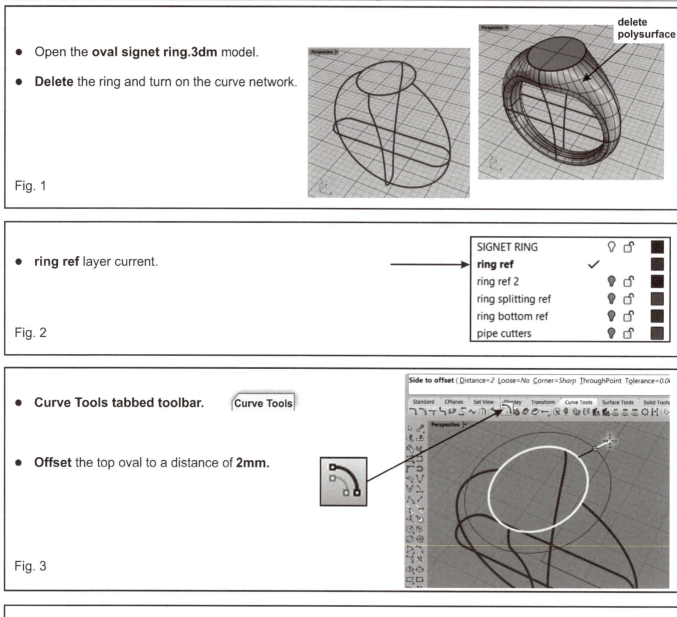

- Open the **oval signet ring.3dm** model.

- **Delete** the ring and turn on the curve network.

delete polysurface

Fig. 1

- **ring ref** layer current.

SIGNET RING		💡 🔓	⬛
ring ref	✓		⬛
ring ref 2		💡 🔓	⬛
ring splitting ref		💡 🔓	⬛
ring bottom ref		💡 🔓	⬛
pipe cutters		💡 🔓	⬛

Fig. 2

- **Curve Tools tabbed toolbar.**   Curve Tools

- **Offset** the top oval to a distance of **2mm**.

Side to offset (Distance=2 Loose=No Corner=Sharp ThroughPoint Tolerance=0.0

Fig. 3

- **Rebuild** the new offset to **16 control points.**

rebuild

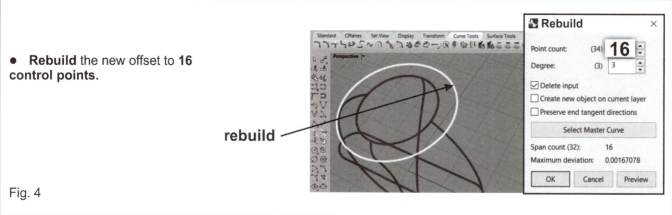

Rebuild ×

Point count: (34) **16**
Degree: (3) 3

☑ Delete input
☐ Create new object on current layer
☐ Preserve end tangent directions

Select Master Curve

Span count (32):   16
Maximum deviation: 0.00167078

OK   Cancel   Preview

Fig. 4

- **Delete** the original inner oval.

- turn on the control points for all 4 curves leading up to the top of the ring.

- **Drag** the top control points of all 4 curves to snap to the **quads** of the new oval.

Fig. 5

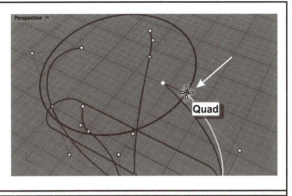

- **Drag** all 4 curves to meet the center oval.

- All 4 curves have been point edited to touch the center oval.

Fig. 6

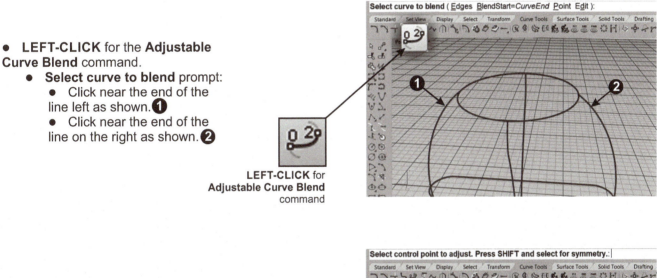

- **LEFT-CLICK** for the **Adjustable Curve Blend** command.
  - **Select curve to blend** prompt:
    - Click near the end of the line left as shown. ❶
    - Click near the end of the line on the right as shown. ❷

LEFT-CLICK for
Adjustable Curve Blend
command

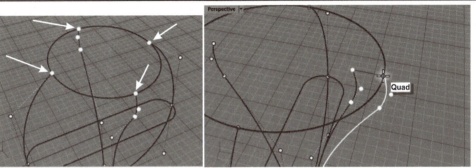

- The **Adjust Curve Blend** box will appear.
  - Select the **Tangency** option in both columns.

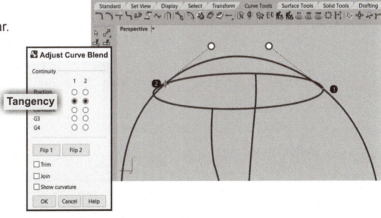

Fig. 7

- Press down the **Shift Key** and drag one of the control points downward.
  - The other control point will move as well because you are pressing down the shift key which gives you the symmetry option.
- **Pick point** prompt:
  - Click when the preview curve is to your liking.
  - Click the **OK button** or press **Enter** to end the command.

Fig. 8

preview curve

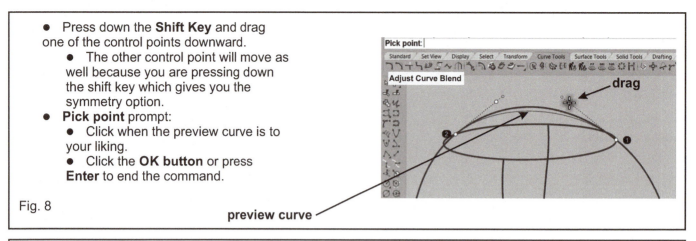

- Use the **Arc: Start, End, Point on Arc** command to create an arc in the other direction as shown.

Arc: Start, End, Point on Arc
command

Fig. 9

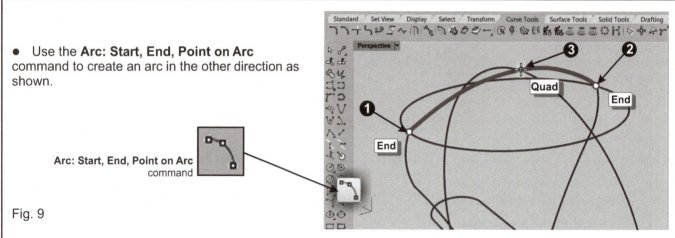

- **Rebuild** the new arc to **7 control points.**

Fig. 10

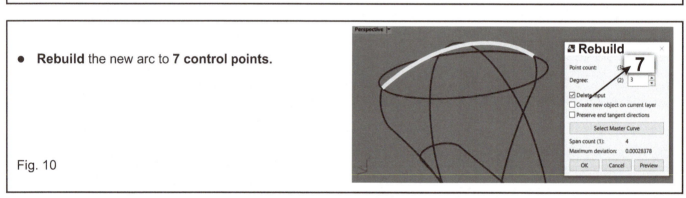

- Click on the **Match Curve** command.
  - **Select open curve to change - pick near end** prompt:
    - Click to select near one end of the new arc. ❶

Match Curve
command

Fig. 11

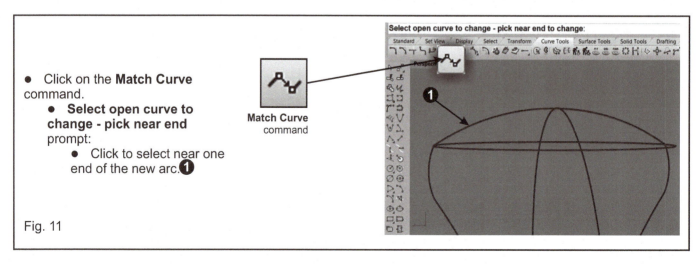

497

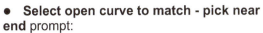
- **Select open curve to match - pick near end** prompt:
  - Click near the end of the nearest large curve as shown. ❷

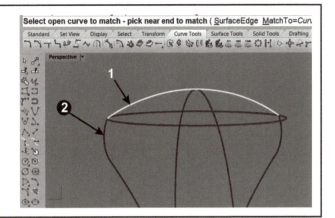

Fig. 12

- Select the settings shown in the **Match Curve** box.
  - Notice that the preview shows the arc being adjusted to be tangent to the second curve chosen.
  - Click on the **OK button.**
    ❶

❷

- The two curves are now tangent.

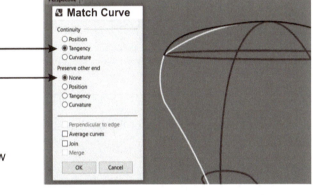

Fig. 13

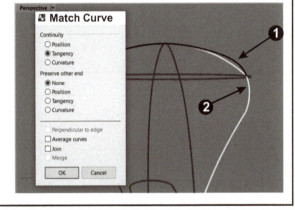

- Use the same command to make the other end of the arc tangent to the curve below it.
  - **Curve to change:** ❶
  - **Curve to match:** ❷

Fig. 14

- **Split** the arcs with each other so that you have 4 separate pieces on top of the ring.

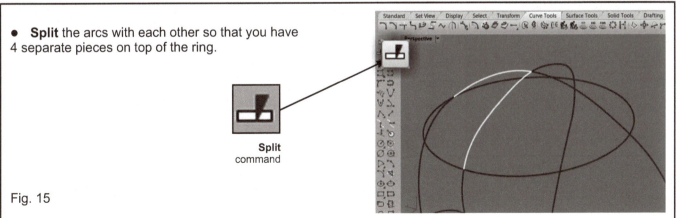

Split
command

Fig. 15

498

- **Join** one of the arc segments to the curve below it.
- Join the other 3 ards to curves below them

- The result will be 4 separate curves as shown.

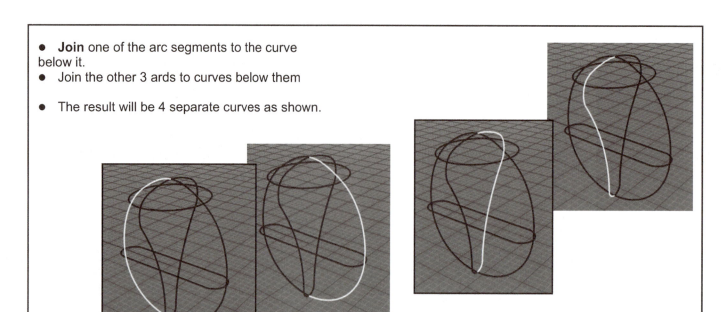

Fig. 16

- Turn on the control points for the oval on top of the ring.

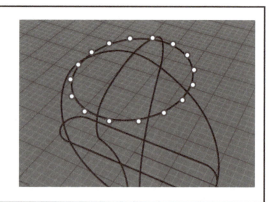

Fig. 17

- **Top Viewport.**   Top ▾

- **Transform tabbed toolbar.**   ⌐Transform⌐

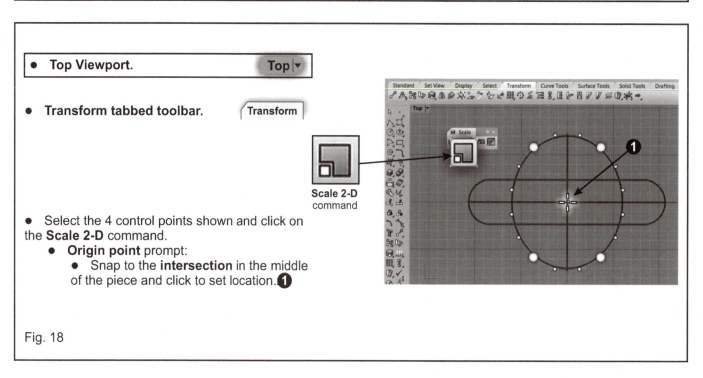

Scale 2-D
command

- Select the 4 control points shown and click on the **Scale 2-D** command.
  - **Origin point** prompt:
    - Snap to the **intersection** in the middle of the piece and click to set location. ❶

Fig. 18

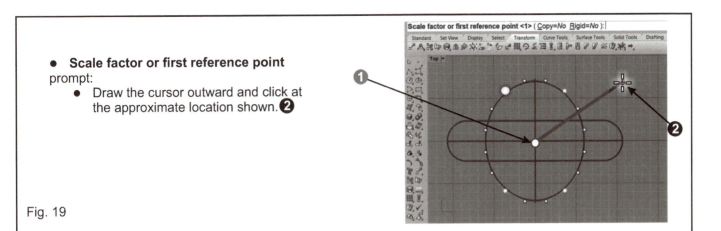

- **Scale factor or first reference point**
  prompt:
    - Draw the cursor outward and click at
      the approximate location shown.❷

Fig. 19

- **Second reference point** prompt:
    - Draw the cursor back inward until the
      preview looks like the one shown.
    - Click to set location. ❸

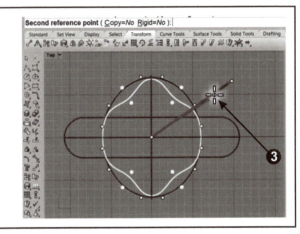

Fig. 20

- **SIGNET RING** layer current.

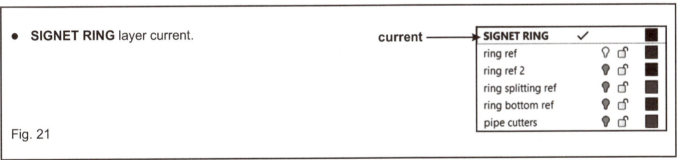

Fig. 21

- **Top Perspective view.** ❶ ❷

- **Surface Tools tabbed toolbar.** Surface Tools

- Select all 6 curves and click on
  the **Surface from Network of
  Curves** command.
    - Click the **OK button.**

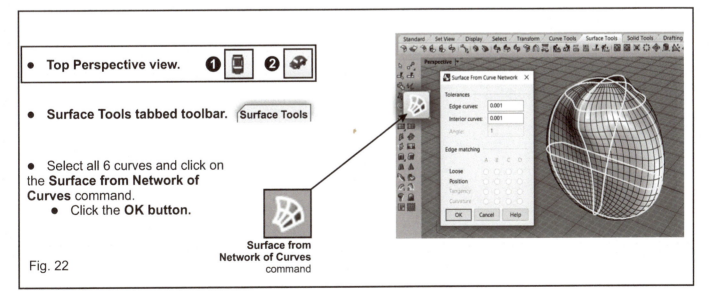

**Surface from
Network of Curves**
command

Fig. 22

- The resulting surface.

- Note: Even though the editing of the top oval caused it to be not in contact with the front and back vertical curves, a surface will still be created.

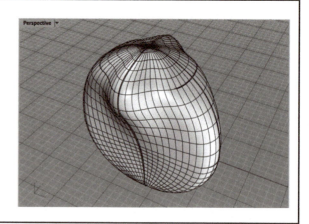

Fig. 23

- Cut the finger hole and finish the ring, referencing previous strategies.
    - ref: 8 x 10 Oval Signet Ring, Figs. 47-89.

Fig. 24

- The finished ring.

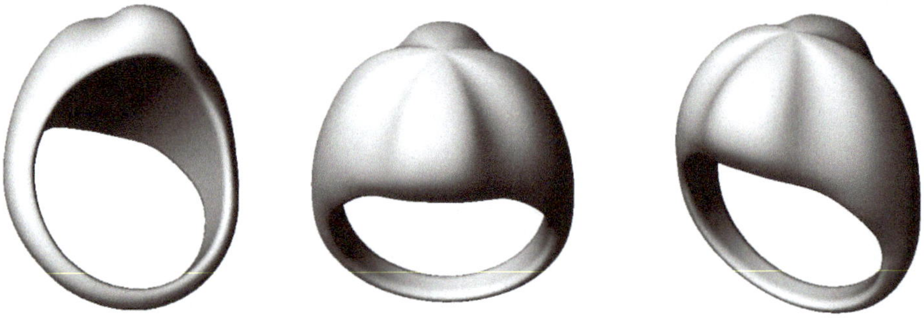

Fig. 25

Twisted Wire Look - Band Ring
Band ring using Flow Along Curve command.

- Create the layers shown.

- **target curve** layer current.

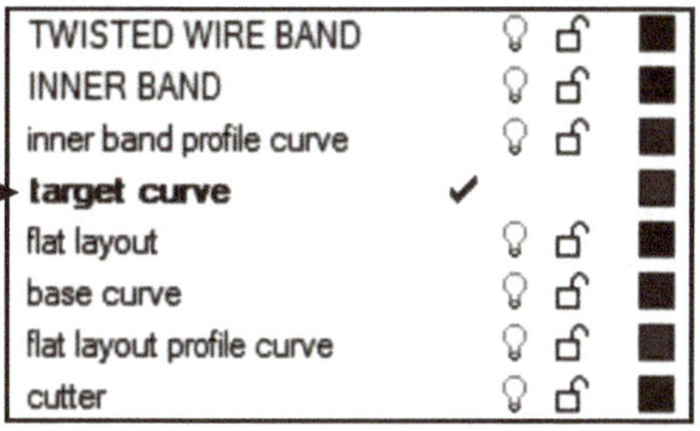

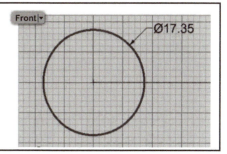

TWISTED WIRE BAND   ♀ 🔓 ■
INNER BAND   ♀ 🔓 ■
inner band profile curve   ♀ 🔓 ■
➤ **target curve**   ✓ ■
flat layout   ♀ 🔓 ■
base curve   ♀ 🔓 ■
flat layout profile curve   ♀ 🔓 ■
cutter   ♀ 🔓 ■

Fig. 1

Creating the Flat Layout

- **Front Viewport.**   **Front ▾**

- Create a **17.35mm diameter circle** around **"0"**.

Fig. 2

Front ▾   Ø17.35

- **Top Perspective viewport.**   ❶ 🚗   ❷ 🚙

- Select the circle, type **"length"** and press **Enter.**
  - The **History Line** will inform you that the length of the circle's curve is **54.507mm long.**

Fig. 3

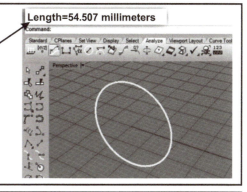

Length=54.507 millimeters

- **base curve** layer current.

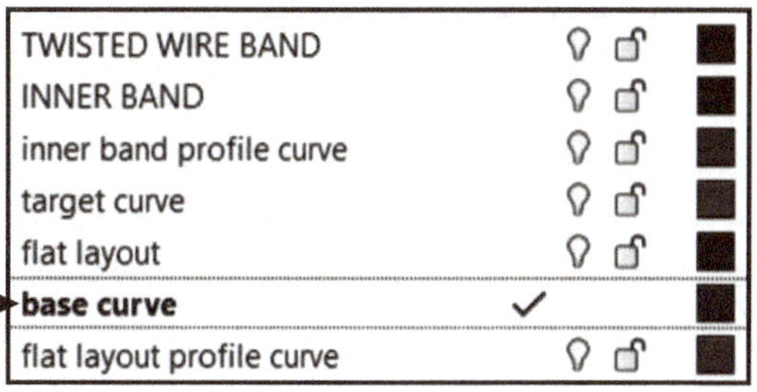

current ➤

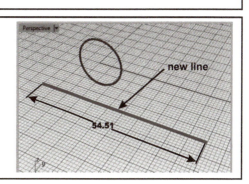

TWISTED WIRE BAND   ♀ 🔓 ■
INNER BAND   ♀ 🔓 ■
inner band profile curve   ♀ 🔓 ■
target curve   ♀ 🔓 ■
flat layout   ♀ 🔓 ■
base curve   ✓ ■
flat layout profile curve   ♀ 🔓 ■

Fig. 4

- Using **ORTHO**, create a **54.507mm line** on the construction plane.

  - Note that the dimension created for this line reads 54.51. This is because in the Rhino Options settings for this dimension style, the precision is set at .01.

Fig. 5

new line

54.51

- Type **"point"** (**Point** command) and press **Enter.**

  - **Location of point object** prompt:
    - Use **End osnap** to create a point at the left end of the line as shown.

Fig. 6

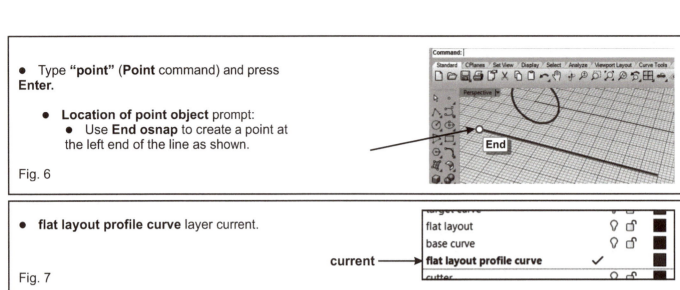

- **flat layout profile curve** layer current.

Fig. 7

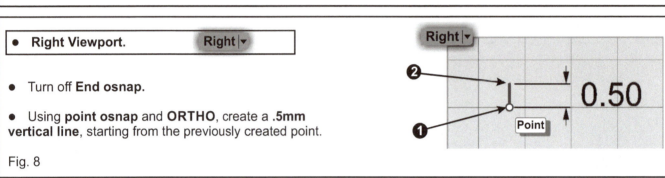

- **Right Viewport.**   Right ▼

- Turn off **End osnap.**

- Using **point osnap** and **ORTHO**, create a **.5mm vertical line**, starting from the previously created point.

Fig. 8

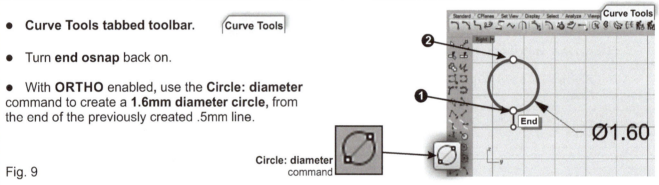

- **Curve Tools tabbed toolbar.**   Curve Tools

- Turn **end osnap** back on.

- With **ORTHO** enabled, use the **Circle: diameter** command to create a **1.6mm diameter circle,** from the end of the previously created .5mm line.

Circle: diameter
command

Fig. 9

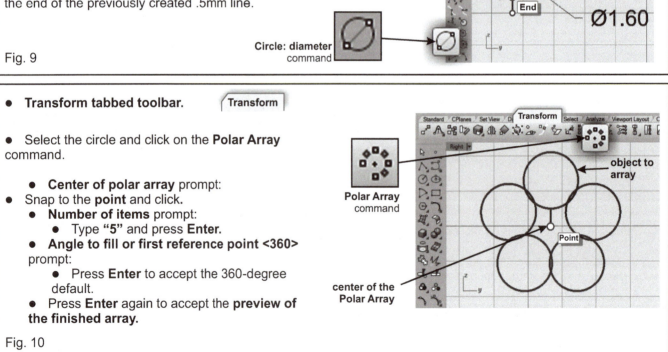

- **Transform tabbed toolbar.**   Transform

- Select the circle and click on the **Polar Array** command.

  - **Center of polar array** prompt:
- Snap to the **point** and click.
  - **Number of items** prompt:
    - Type **"5"** and press **Enter.**
  - **Angle to fill or first reference point <360>** prompt:
    - Press **Enter** to accept the 360-degree default.
  - Press **Enter** again to accept the **preview of the finished array.**

Polar Array
command

object to array

center of the
Polar Array

Fig. 10

503

- Select all of the circles and use the **Trim** command ❶ to trim them out as shown. Press **Enter** to end the command.

- When the trim is completed and the circles are still selected, click on the **Join** command ❷ to join them into a closed curve.

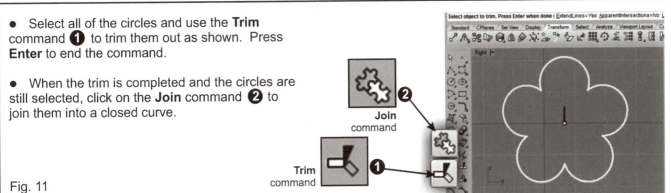

Join command

Trim command

Fig. 11

- **Curve Tools tabbed toolbar.**   Curve Tools

- Select the new closed curve and click on the **Fillet Corners** command.
  - **Fillet radius** prompt:
    - Type "**.15**" and press **Enter**.

Fillet Corners command

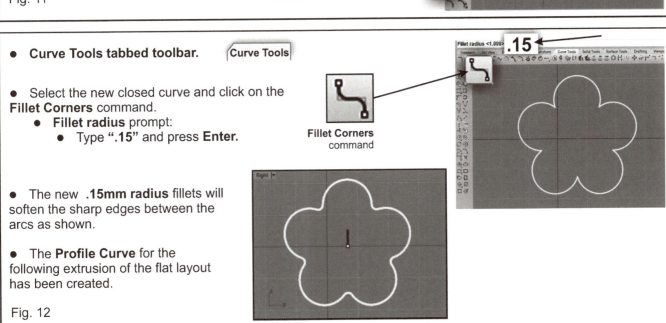

- The new **.15mm radius** fillets will soften the sharp edges between the arcs as shown.

- The **Profile Curve** for the following extrusion of the flat layout has been created.

Fig. 12

- **flat layout** layer current.

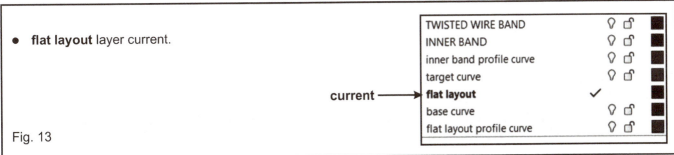

TWISTED WIRE BAND		♀ ⌒	■
INNER BAND		♀ ⌒	■
inner band profile curve		♀ ⌒	■
target curve		♀ ⌒	■
flat layout	current →	✓	■
base curve		♀ ⌒	■
flat layout profile curve		♀ ⌒	■

Fig. 13

- Type "**UseExtrusions**" and press **Enter.**

- **Planar extrusion output object type** prompt:
  - Click on the **Polysurface** option in the **Command Line.**
  - Press **Enter.**

- The extrusion in the next step will now be a surface, not an extrusion, and will have geometry for this exercise.

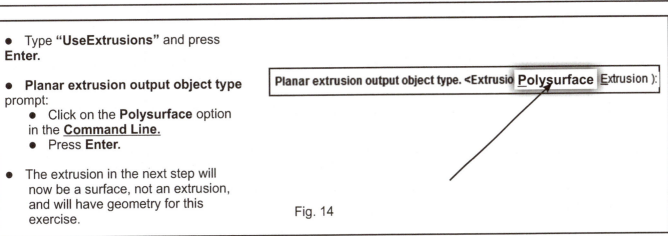

Planar extrusion output object type. <Extrusio **Polysurface** Extrusion):

Fig. 14

- **Top Perspective view.** ❶ [icon] ❷ [icon]

- **Surface Tools tabbed toolbar.** [Surface Tools]

- Select the new **flat layout profile curve** ❶ and click on the **Extrude Straight** command.

Extrude straight

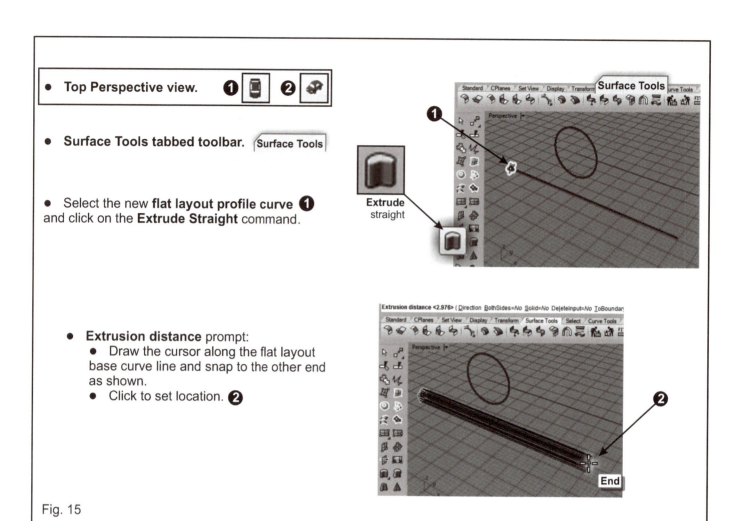

- **Extrusion distance** prompt:
  - Draw the cursor along the flat layout base curve line and snap to the other end as shown.
  - Click to set location. ❷

Fig. 15

- The new extrusion will be a single surface.

- Select the new surface and type **"Rebuild"**.

  - **Rebuild** to the values shown, 60 control points in both the U and V directions. ❶

  - Check to make sure that the Degree is **3** in both directions. ❷

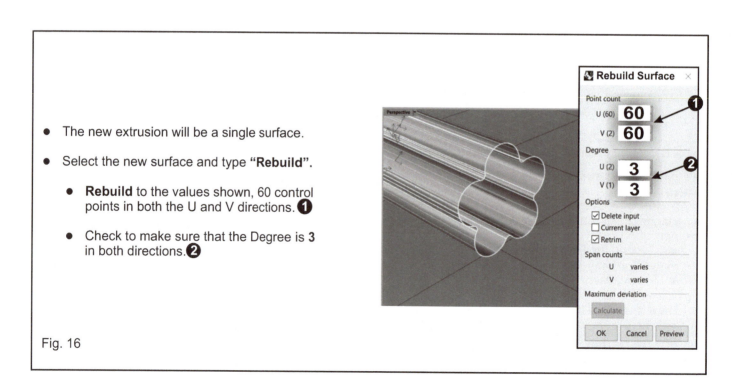

Fig. 16

- **Transform tabbed toolbar.**

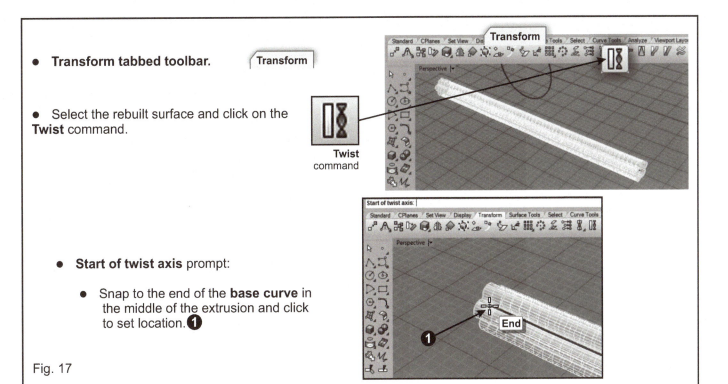

- Select the rebuilt surface and click on the **Twist** command.

- **Start of twist axis** prompt:

  - Snap to the end of the **base curve** in the middle of the extrusion and click to set location. ❶

Fig. 17

- **End of twist axis** prompt:

  - Snap to the other end of the **base curve** and click to set location. ❷

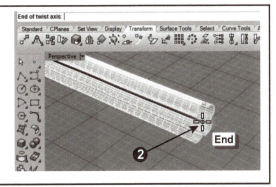

Fig. 18

- **Angle or first reference point** prompt:

  - Type **"1800"** and press **Enter.**
    - *This number was chosen because it is divisible by 360 which means that when this twisted element is flowed to create a twisted wire ring band, the surface edges of the two ends will be in exact alignment.*

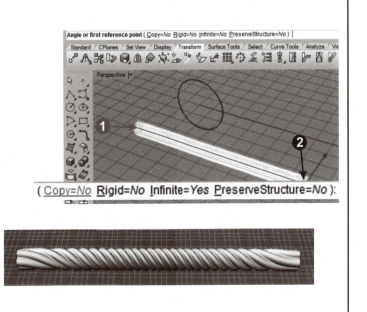

- But the default twist configuration has not twisted the extrusion evenly along it's entire length.

- **Undo** or **Delete** this twist.

Fig. 19

506

- Press **Enter** to repeat the **Twist** command.

- When you get to the **Angle or first reference point** prompt:
  - Click to toggle the **Infinite=No** option in the command line to **Infinite=Yes**.
  - Complete the command with the same angle as before.

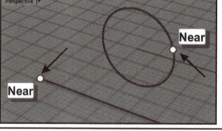

- The twist will be even along the whole length of the piece.

Fig. 20

Flowing the Flat Layout Along the Ring Curve

- Temporarily hide the **flat layout** layer to view the base and target curves.

- Make another layer current for the time being.

Fig. 21

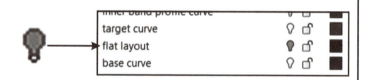

- Select the **target curve** and the **base curve**, type **"dir"** (**Analyze Direction** command), and press **Enter**.

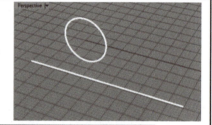

- **Arrows** showing the **directions** of both of the selected curves will appear.
- **Points** show the start and end points of the curves.

- Press **Enter** to end the command.

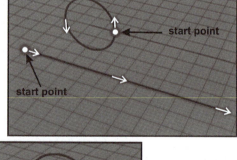

- Type **"point"** and place point objects near the start points on both of the curves, using **near osnap.**

- These will mark the locations of the **matching ends** for these two curves.

Fig. 22

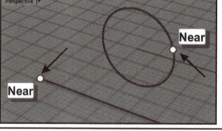

- Turn the **flat layout** layer back on.

Fig. 23

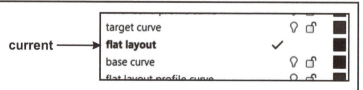

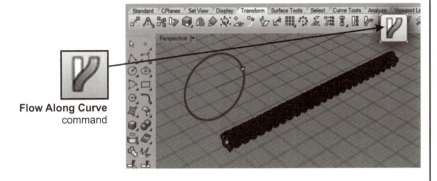

- Click on the **Flow Along Curve** command.

Flow Along Curve command

- **Select objects to flow along a curve. Press Enter when done** prompt:
  - Select the twisted surface and press **Enter**.
    - ***Do not** select the base curve that runs inside the twisted surface.*

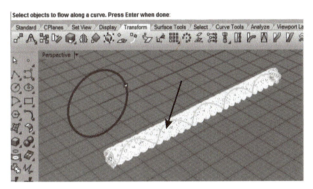

Fig. 24

- **Base curve. Select near one end** prompt:
  - Select the **base curve** that runs through the twisted surface. ❶
    - *Select near the starting end where you placed the point object.*

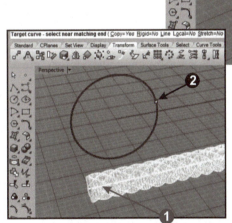

- **Target curve. Select near matching end** prompt:
  - Select the target curve near the matching end where you placed the control point.

- A copy of the flat twisted wire layout will be **"flowed"** along the round target curve.

- Change the new twisted wire ring shape to the **TWISTED WIRE BAND** layer.

Fig. 25

Using Split and Join to make the Twisted Wire Band a Closed Polysurface

- Turn off the following layers;
  - **flat layout**
  - **base curve**
  - **flat layout ref**

- **cutter** layer current.

Fig. 26

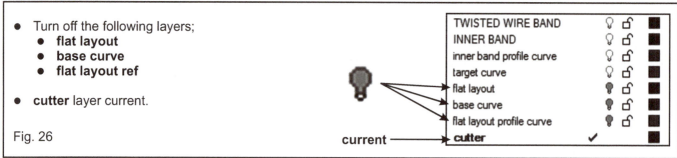

TWISTED WIRE BAND		
INNER BAND		
inner band profile curve		
target curve		
flat layout		
base curve		
flat layout profile curve		
cutter	✓	

current ⟶

- **Select tabbed toolbar.** `Select`

- Click on the **Select Closed Surfaces** command in the **Select Surfaces toolbar flyout**.

- The twisted wire band will not select because, according to Rhino, it is not a closed surface.

Fig. 27

accesses the **Select Surfaces** toolbar flyout

Select Closed Surfaces command

No objects added to selection

- Select the twisted wire band, type **"ShowEdges"**, and press **Enter**.

- When the **Edge Analysis** box appears, make sure that the **Naked Edges** setting is selected.

Edge Analysis
Show
- All Edges
- **Naked Edges**
- Non-Manifold Edges

Zoom

Edge color

Add Objects
Remove Objects

- Where the two ends of the flat layout met, Rhino shows Naked Edges.

- *Even though the end seams of the flat layout have met perfectly, Rhino does not consider this a closed surface.*

Fig. 28

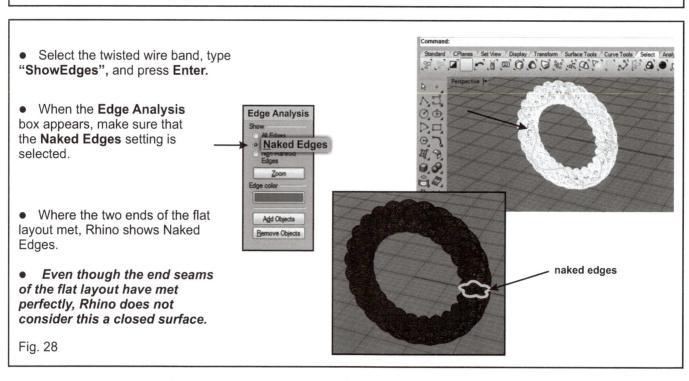

naked edges

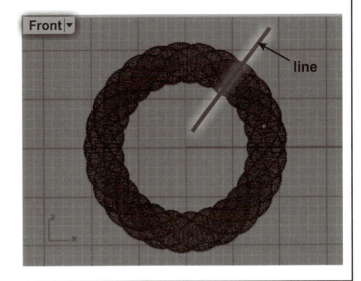

- **Front Viewport.**   Front ▾

- Create a **Line** that starts somewhere inside the finger opening and which extends to the outside.

Fig. 29

- Select the twisted wire band **❶** and **LEFT-CLICK** for the **Split** command.

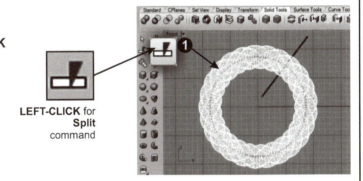

LEFT-CLICK for
Split
command

- **Select cutting objects. Press Enter when done** prompt:
  - Select the new line **❷** and press **Enter.**

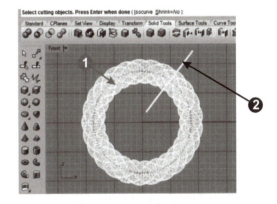

- The twisted wire band has now been split into two pieces.

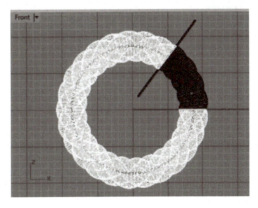

Fig. 30

- Select both pieces of the twisted wire band and click on the **Join** command.

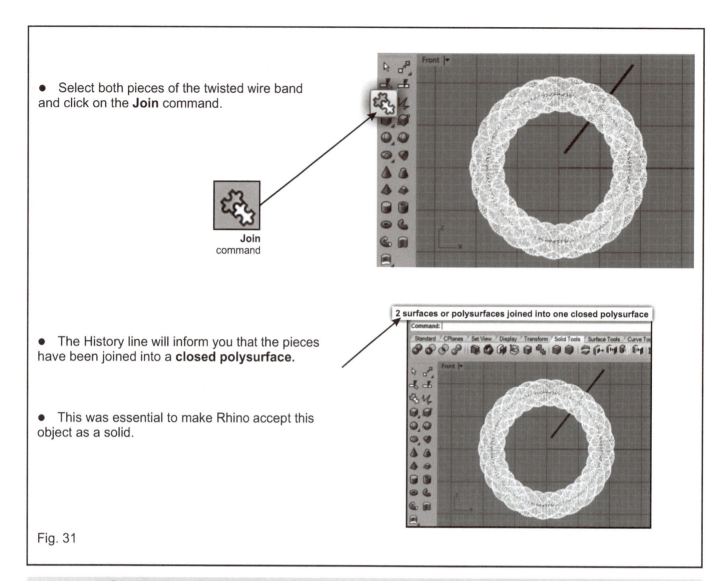

Join
command

- The History line will inform you that the pieces have been joined into a **closed polysurface.**

- This was essential to make Rhino accept this object as a solid.

2 surfaces or polysurfaces joined into one closed polysurface

Fig. 31

Cutting out the inside of the Twisted Wire Band

- **Curve Tools tabbed toolbar.**　Curve Tools

- Select the twisted wire band, type **"lock"** and press **Enter** to **Lock** the twisted wire band.
  - You can also click on the **Lock Command** in the **Standard Tabbed Toolbar.**

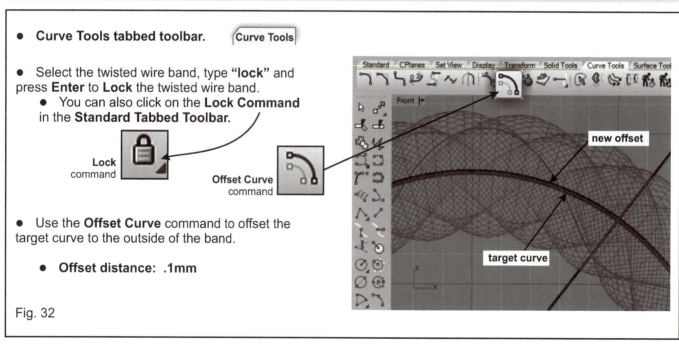

Lock
command

Offset Curve
command

new offset

target curve

- Use the **Offset Curve** command to offset the target curve to the outside of the band.

  - **Offset distance: .1mm**

Fig. 32

- **Solid Tools tabbed toolbar.**   ⌐ **Solid Tools** ⌐

- Select the new **cutter curve** and click on the **Extrude closed planar curve** command.
  - Make sure that you toggle on the **BothSides=Yes** in the **Command Line.**

  Extrude closed planar curve command

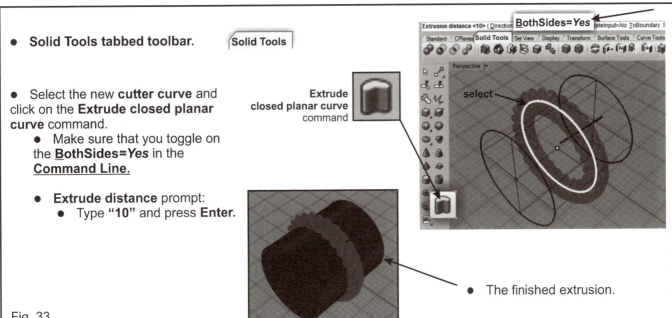

- **Extrude distance** prompt:
  - Type **"10"** and press **Enter.**

- The finished extrusion.

Fig. 33

- Type **"unlock"** to **Unlock** the twisted wire band ring.

- Click on the **Boolean Difference** command.

  Boolean Difference command

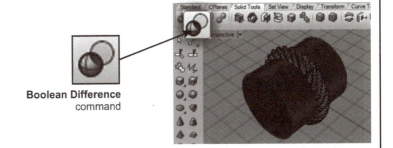

- **Select surfaces or polysurfaces to subtract from. Press Enter when done** prompt:

  - Select the twisted wire band and press **Enter.**

  select twisted wire band

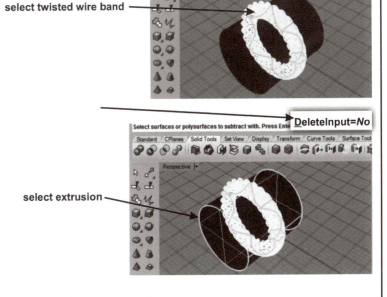

- **Select surfaces or polysurface to subtract with** prompt:

  - Make sure that you click to toggle to the **DeleteInput=No** option in the **Command Line** to **save the cutting object** after the boolean difference command is completed.

  - Select the extrusion and press **Enter.**

  select extrusion

Fig. 34

- Turn off the **cutter** layer and you will see that the inside of the band has been cut out.

Fig. 35

- **inner band profile curve** layer current.

- The **cutter** layer has been turned off.

Fig. 36

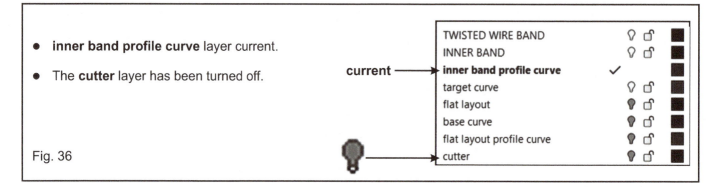

current →

TWISTED WIRE BAND
INNER BAND
inner band profile curve ✓
target curve
flat layout
base curve
flat layout profile curve
cutter

Revolved Inner Band with History

- **Right viewport**   Right ▾

- **Curve Tools tabbed toolbar.**   Curve Tools

- Use the **Line: from midpoint** command to create a **6mm line** that starts at the top quad of the target curve on the inside of the ring.

Fig. 37

accesses **Lines** toolbar flyout

Line: from midpoint command

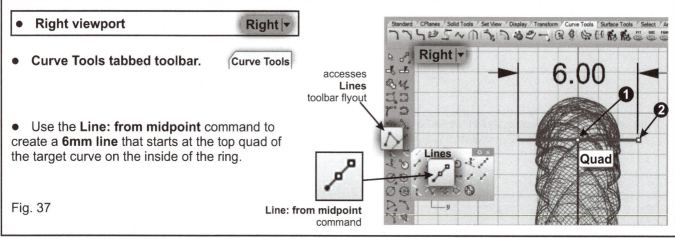

- Use the **Rectangle: 3 points** command to create a rectangle that snaps to both ends ❶ ❷ of the line created in the previous step

  - **Width** prompt: Type ".8" and press **Enter.**

- Draw the cursor upward and click to set location. ❸

Fig. 38

Rectangle: 3 Points command

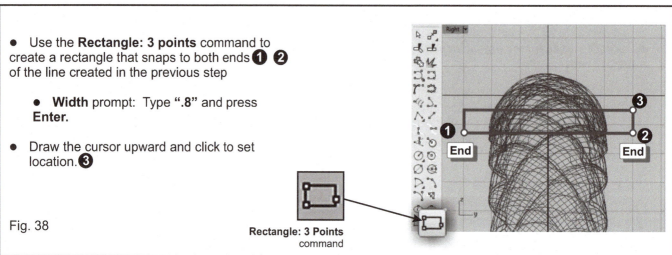

- Use the **Arc: Start, End, Direction at Start** command to create the arc shown.

  - **Start of arc** prompt:
    - Snap to the end point of the top left corner of the rectangle and click to set location. ❶
  - **End of arc** prompt:
    - Type **"1"** and press **Enter** to set the diameter of the arc.
    - Draw the cursor to the right and, using **ORTHO**, click to set location. ❷
  - **Direction at start** prompt:
    - Using **ORTHO**, draw the cursor straight up and click to set location. ❸

Fig. 39

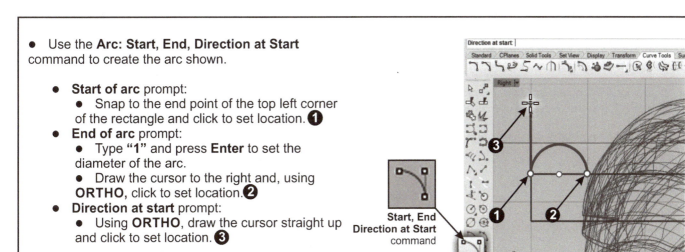

Start, End
Direction at Start
command

- Use the **Arc: Start, End, Direction at Start** command again to create an additional arc on the end of the rectangle.
  - Use **ORTHO** when setting the direction at start. ❸

Fig. 40

- **Mirror** the arcs to the other side of the ring.

Fig. 41

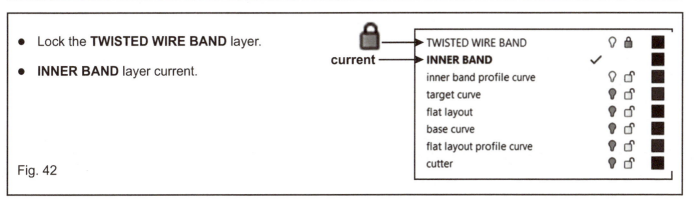

new
mirrored
copies

Editing the Inner Band

- Lock the **TWISTED WIRE BAND** layer.

- **INNER BAND** layer current.

Fig. 42

current

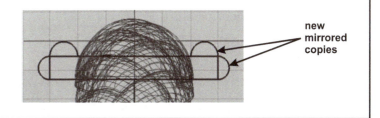

TWISTED WIRE BAND	♀ 🔒 ■
INNER BAND	✓ ■
inner band profile curve	♀ 🔓 ■
target curve	♀ 🔓 ■
flat layout	♀ 🔓 ■
base curve	♀ 🔓 ■
flat layout profile curve	♀ 🔓 ■
cutter	♀ 🔓 ■

514

- Use the **Trim** or **Curve Boolean** command to trim out the design.

- If you used **Trim,** use the **Join command** to join all elements together to create a closed curve.

- *Delete the original 6mm straight line.*

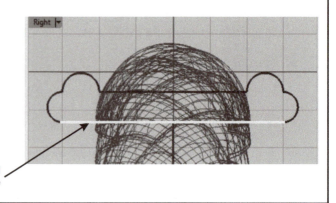

delete the original 6mm line

Fig. 43

- Turn off the **TWISTED WIRE BAND** layer.

TWISTED WIRE BAND		💡 🔒	■
INNER BAND		✓	■
inner band profile curve		💡 🔓	■
target curve		💡 🔓	■
flat layout		💡 🔓	■
base curve		💡 🔓	■
flat layout profile curve		💡 🔓	■
cutter		💡 🔓	■

Fig. 44

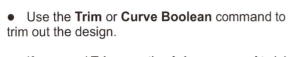

- **Top Perspective view.** ❶ 🖥 ❷ 🚗

- Click to turn on **Record History.** | Record History |

- Select the inner band profile curve and **left-click** on the **Revolve** command.

  - **Start of revolve axis** prompt:
    - Type **"0"** and press **Enter. ❶**
  - **End of revolve axis** prompt:
    - Using **ORTHO,** draw the cursor up or down along the **Y axis** and click to set direction. ❷

  - **Start angle** prompt:
    - Click to select the **FullCircle** option in the **Command Line.**

left-click for **Revolve** command

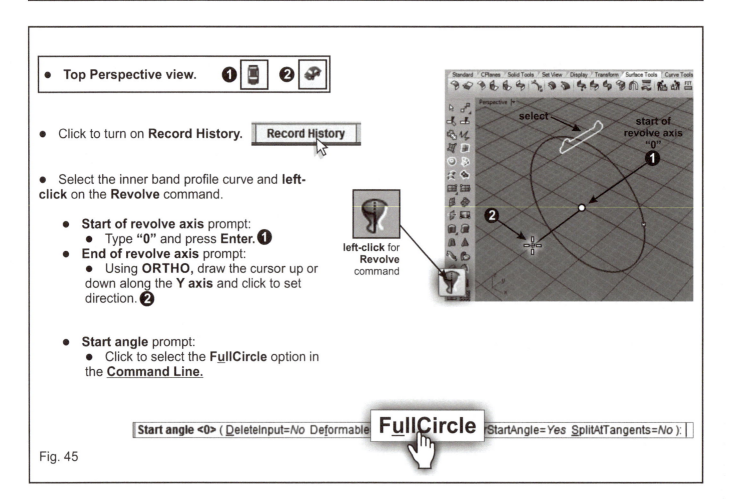

| Start angle <0> (DeleteInput=No Deformable **FullCircle** StartAngle=Yes SplitAtTangents=No): |

Fig. 45

- The **inner band** has been created.

- Turn on the **TWISTED WIRE BAND** layer to view both elements of the ring.

- Displayed here in Rendered Viewport mode.

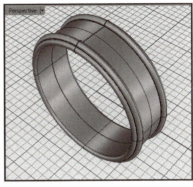

Fig. 46

- Turn on the control points on the **inner band profile curve**.

- Select the top 6 control points shown and **Move** them up **.3mm.**

- **History** will update the inner ring band to show higher sides.

- Control point editing of this curve will further edit the inner ring band.

Fig. 47

- **Front Viewport.**   Front ▾

- **Curve Tools tabbed toolbar.**   Curve Tools

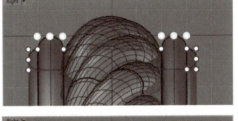

- Select the **inner band profile curve** and click on the **Adjust closed curve seam command.**

    - Note the point and the white arrow that appear at the location of the closed curve seam. ❶

Adjust closed curve seam
command

Fig. 48

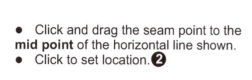

- Click and drag the seam point to the **mid point** of the horizontal line shown.
- Click to set location. ❷

- *This will ensure a symmetrical rebuild of this profile curve.*

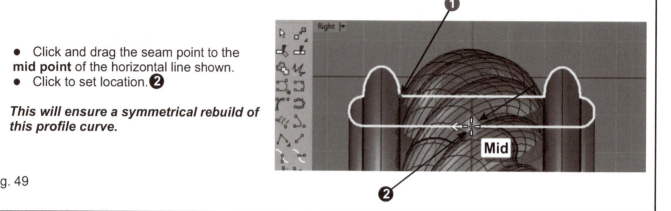

Fig. 49

- **Rebuild** the profile curve to **35 control points.**

- The shape of the inner ring band will be updated to reflect the new smoothness of the rebuilt profile curve.

- In this illustration, two of the control points have been deleted for a different look.

Fig. 50

1mm Stone Maquette
Simple Stone, Faceted Stone, Stone Hole & Seat cutters
Modeling the stone maquette

- Create layers shown.

- **1mm RD stone curves** current.

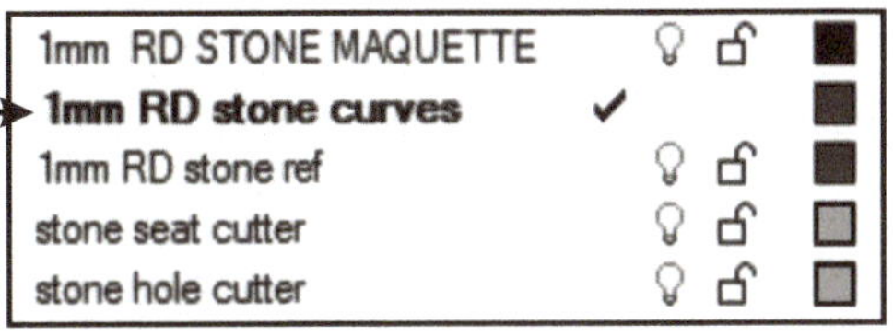

Fig. 1

1mm RD STONE MAQUETTE	♀ 🔓 ■
1mm RD stone curves ✓	■
1mm RD stone ref	♀ 🔓 ■
stone seat cutter	♀ 🔓 ☐
stone hole cutter	♀ 🔓 ☐

- **Curve Tools tabbed toolbar.** [Curve Tools]

- Create 2 circles around "0",
  - **1mm diameter** - stone girdle diameter ❶
  - **.53mm diameter** - stone table diameter ❷

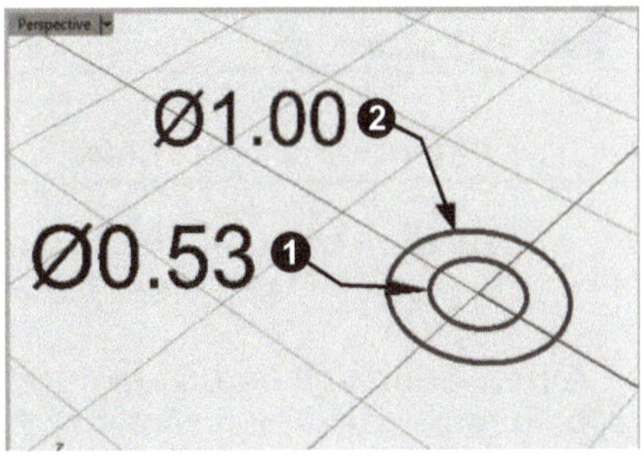

Fig. 2

Ø1.00 ❷
Ø0.53 ❶

- **Front Perspective view.** ❶ 🚗 ❷ 🚙

- Using **ORTHO**, move the **.53mm circle** upwards to a distance of **.18mm**.

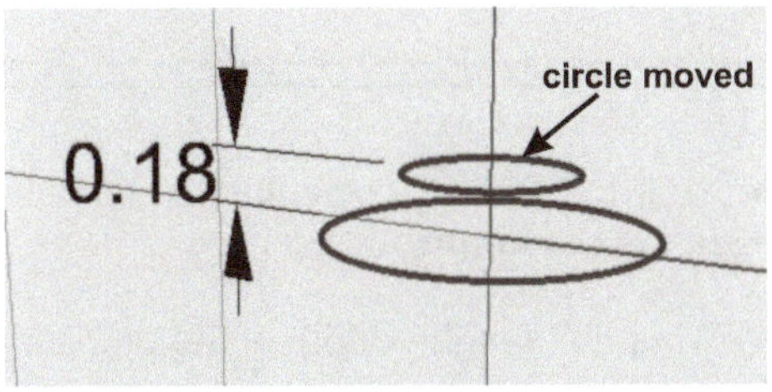

Fig. 3

0.18

circle moved

- Click on the **Offset Curve** command.

  - Type **".01"** in the **Command Line** and press **Enter**.
  - Click to toggle on the **BothSides** option.❶
  - Click to toggle the InCPlane=No option to **InCplane=Yes**.❷

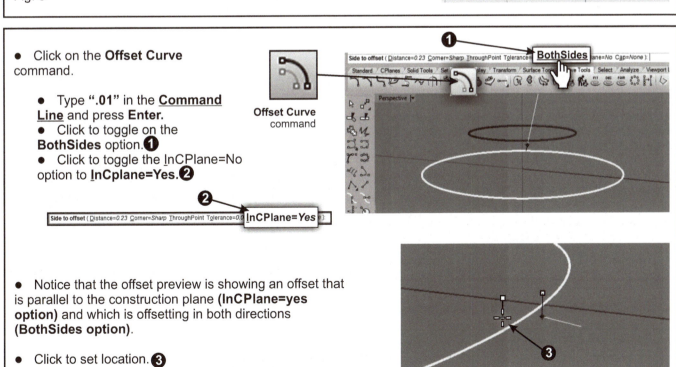

❶
Side to offset (Distance=0.23 Corner=Sharp ThroughPoint Tolerance= | **BothSides** |ane=No Cap=None).

Standard / CPlanes / Solid Tools / Set ...

Offset Curve command

❷
Side to offset (Distance=0.23 Corner=Sharp ThroughPoint Tolerance=0.0 | **InCPlane=Yes** |).

- Notice that the offset preview is showing an offset that is parallel to the construction plane (**InCPlane=yes option**) and which is offsetting in both directions (**BothSides option**).

- Click to set location. ❸

Fig. 4

- The two new offsets define the thickness of the girdle of the stone (.02mm).

- The original curve will be a reference that will define the center of the girdle.

Fig. 5

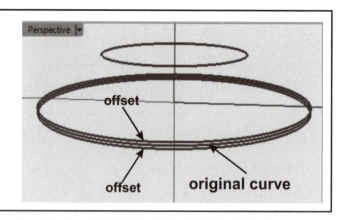
offset

original curve

offset

1mm RD stone ref ✓ ■

- Type **"point"** and press **Enter.**

  - **Location of point object** prompt:
    - Type **"0"** and press **Enter.**

- **A new point will be created on "0"** which will be a reference for the center of the girdle of the stone.

Fig. 6

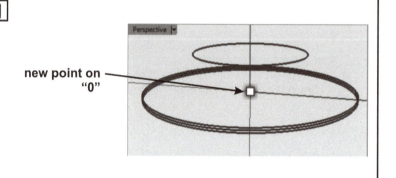
new point on "0"

- Using **ORTHO, copy** the point downward to a distance of **.43mm.**

- This defines the depth of the stone's pavilion.

Fig. 7

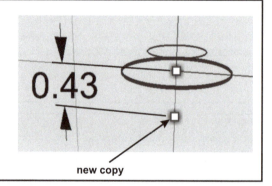
0.43

new copy

- Make sure that the circle that runs through the center of the girdle and the point that rests on **"0"** are both on the **1mm RD stone ref layer.**

- The other objects should be on the **1mm RD stone curves** layer.

- *When the stone is finished, the 1mm RD stone curves layer will be turned off or deleted.*

Fig. 8

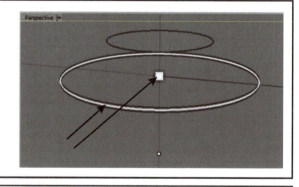

- **1mm RD STONE MAQUETTE** layer current.

- Turn off the **1mm RD stone ref** layer.

Fig. 9

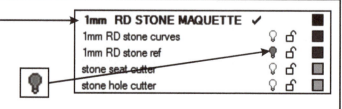
1mm RD STONE MAQUETTE ✓
1mm RD stone curves
1mm RD stone ref
stone seat cutter
stone hole cutter

- **Surface Tools tabbed toolbar.** Surface Tools

- Click on the **Loft** command.

  - **Select curves to loft. Press Enter when done** prompt:
    - Select the 3 curves and the single point in the **1mm RD stone curves layer** and press **Enter.**

  - **Drag seam point to adjust. Press Enter when done.**
    - Make sure the seam is straight and press **Enter.**

Fig. 10

- The default **Normal** loft shape will give you the rounded shape shown.

- Change the **Style** drop-down setting to **Straight Sections.**

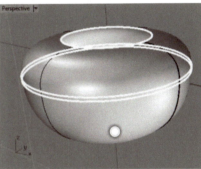

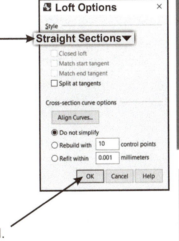

- Click the **OK** button the finish the command.

Fig. 11

- Select the stone, type **"cap",** and press **Enter** to close the top of the stone.

- The stone is now a closed polysurface.

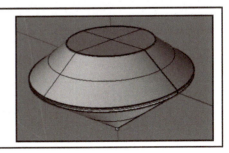

Fig. 12

Modeling the Stone Seat Cutter

- Turn off both the stone curves and stone ref layers.

- **stone seat cutter** current.

Fig. 13

1mm RD STONE MAQUETTE		♀ 🔓	■
1mm RD stone-curves		♀ 🔓	■
1mm RD stone ref		♀ 🔓	■
stone seat cutter		✓	☐
stone hole cutter		♀ 🔓	☐

- Type **"polyline"** and press **Enter.**
  - **Start of Polyline**: the end point at the bottom of the stone. **1**
  - **Next Point of Polyline**: snap to the end or quad point at the lower edge of the girdle **2**
  - Use **ORTHO** when making the **2nd segment** which should be about **.6mm long**. **3**
  - Press **Enter** to end the command.

Fig. 14

3rd segment .6mm long **3**

- **LEFT-CLICK** on the **Revolve** command.

  - **Select curves to revolve. Press Enter when done** prompt.
    - Select the new polyline and press **Enter.**

LEFT-CLICK for
Revolve command

- **Start of revolve axis** prompt:
  - Snap on the end point at the bottom of the stone and click to set location. **1**

- **End of revolve axis** prompt:
  - Using **ORTHO**, draw the cursor down and click to set the end of the revolve axis. **2**

- **Start angle** prompt:
  - Click on the **FullCircle** option.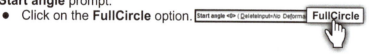

- The completed revolve.

Fig. 15

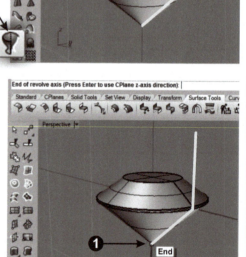

- Select the new stone seat cutter, type **"cap"**, and press **Enter**.

- The top has been closed and the cutter is now a closed polysurface.

- *Delete the reference geometry that you used to revolve the cutter.*

Fig. 16

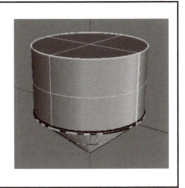

Modeling the Stone Hole Cutter

- **Lock** the **1mm RD STONE MAQUETTE** layer.

- **stone hole cutter** current.

Fig. 17

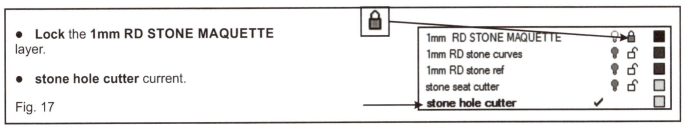

1mm RD STONE MAQUETTE	🔒	■
1mm RD stone curves	🔓	■
1mm RD stone ref	🔓	■
stone seat cutter	🔓	☐
stone hole cutter	✓	☐

- **Top Perspective view.** ❶ ❷

- Create a **.6mm diameter circle** around **"0"**.

.6mm diameter circle around "0"

- Select the new **.6mm** diameter circle and click on the **Extrude Straight** command.

- Make sure that the **BothSides=Yes** option is toggled on.

- **Extrude distance** prompt:
  - Type **"2"** and press **Enter**.

- If necessary, "cap" the new extrusion.

Extrude Straight command

- The stone with its seat and hole cutters are finished.

- *Delete the reference geometry circle.*

Fig. 18

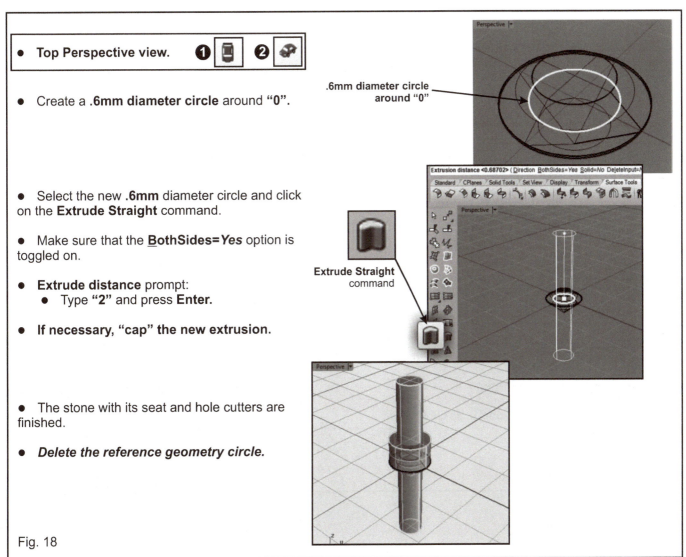

Importing and Scaling the Round Faceted Stone

- A faceted stone model will be added so that after the model is finished, rendering can look better.

  - Go to the **www.rhinoforjewelry.com** website.
    - Click on the navigation button, **support files for textbook.**
      - Click on the link, **files for textbook**
        - Click on the file called **3mm Round Faceted stone.**
  - When the Rhino file opens, save it to you computer.

- Make the **1mm RD stone ref** layer current.

- Turn off all other layers.

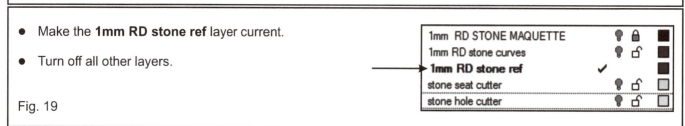

Fig. 19

- Click on **File** in the **Menu Bar.** ❶

- Click to select **Import.** ❷

- Navigate to your designated file to select **3mm ROUND FACETED STONE** ❸

- Click the **Open** button.

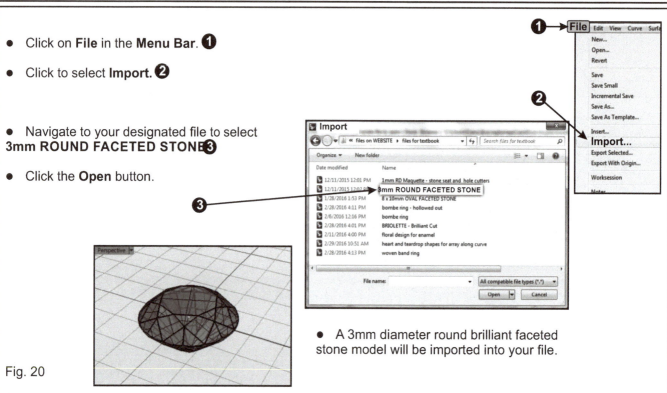

- A 3mm diameter round brilliant faceted stone model will be imported into your file.

Fig. 20

- Select the round brilliant stone and it's reference geometry.
  - ***Do not select the smaller stone ref circle in the center.***

- Type **"group"** and press **Enter.**
  - The stone and its reference geometry will be grouped.
  - Turn off the **3mm FACETED STONE layer.**

- The reference geometry for the maquette and the round brilliant will remain visible.

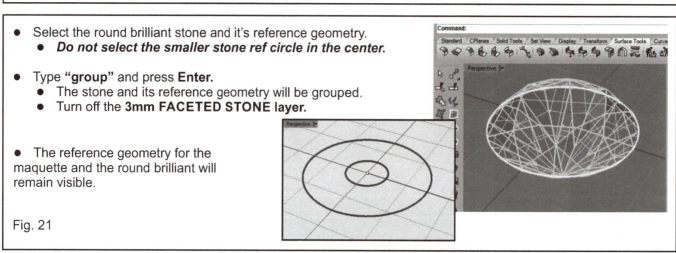

Fig. 21

- **Transform tabbed toolbar.**   `Transform`

- Select the larger outer circle and **LEFT-CLICK** on the **Scale 3-D** command.

  - **Origin point** prompt:
    - Type **"0"** and press **Enter.** ❶

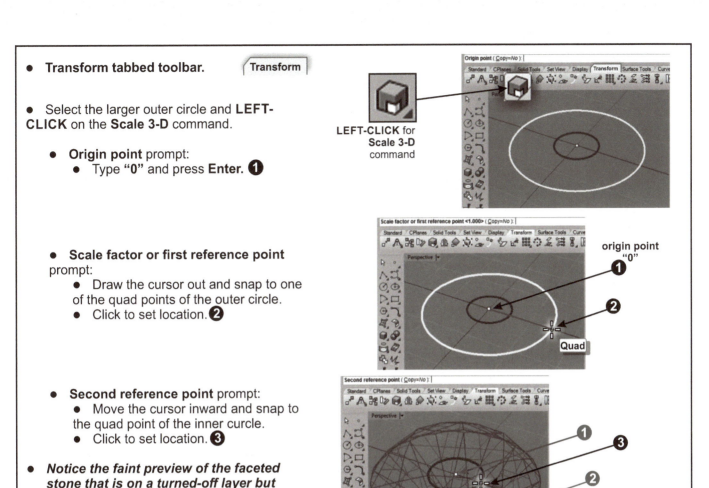

LEFT-CLICK for
Scale 3-D
command

  - **Scale factor or first reference point** prompt:
    - Draw the cursor out and snap to one of the quad points of the outer circle.
    - Click to set location. ❷

origin point "0"

  - **Second reference point** prompt:
    - Move the cursor inward and snap to the quad point of the inner curcle.
    - Click to set location. ❸

- *Notice the faint preview of the faceted stone that is on a turned-off layer but which is grouped to the outer circle being scaled.*

Fig. 22

- The larger circle has been scaled to the same size as the smaller circle.

- Turn on the layer for the **3mm RD FACETED STONE** and notice that the stone has been scaled down as well, because it was grouped with the circle that was scaled down.

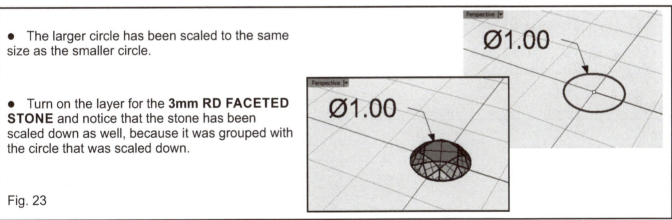

Fig. 23

- Delete the **1mm RD stone curves** layer and the **1mm rd faceted stone ref** as they will not be needed.

- Change the name of the layer for the round faceted stone to reflect the fact that it is now 1mm in diameter, not 3mm.

1mm RD STONE MAQUETTE		♀ ⌂	■
1mm rd stone ref	✓		■
stone seat cutter		♀ ⌂	□
stone hole cutter		♀ ⌂	□
1mm ROUND FACETED STONE		♀ ⌂	■

- **Save** this file as **1mm RD Maquette - stone seat and hole cutters.**

Fig. 24

Eternity Band
Prong Set Wirework 1ct Band

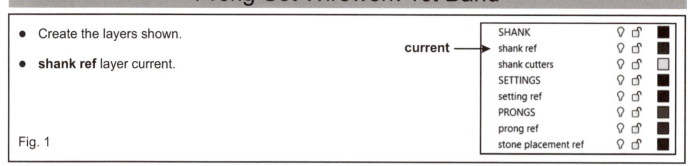

- Create the layers shown.

- **shank ref** layer current.

current ⟶

SHANK	♀	🔓	■
shank ref	♀	🔓	■
shank cutters	♀	🔓	☐
SETTINGS	♀	🔓	■
setting ref	♀	🔓	■
PRONGS	♀	🔓	■
prong ref	♀	🔓	■
stone placement ref	♀	🔓	■

Fig. 1

Importing and Scaling the Stone

- **Front Viewport.**   Front ▼

- Create a circle around **"0"** with a diameter of **17.35mm.**

Ø17.35

Fig. 2

- Click on **File** in the **Menu Bar.** ❶

- Click to select **Import** in the drop-down context menu.
    - Navigate to your designated folder to select **1mm Stone Maquette with Stone Seat and Stone Hole Cutters.** ❸
        - *This Rhino file was modeled and saved in the previous chapter of this book.*
    - Click the **Open** button.

        - *Also available for download on the* ***www.rhinoforjewelry.com*** *website on the* ***files for textbook*** *page.*

Fig. 3

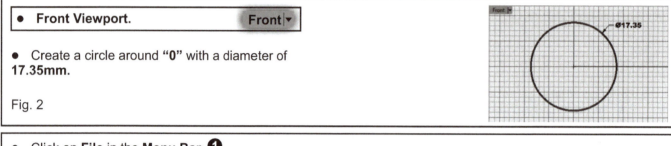

- **Top Perspective view.** ❶ 🔲 ❷ 🚗

- The stone and its layers will be imported into the Rhino file.

- **Delete** the 2 cutter layers as they will not be needed for this project.

delete these
2 layers

SHANK	♀	🔓	■
shank ref	♀	🔓	■
shank cutters	♀	🔓	☐
SETTINGS	♀	🔓	■
setting ref	♀	🔓	■
PRONGS	♀	🔓	■
prong ref	♀	🔓	■
stone placement ref	♀	🔓	■
1mm RD STONE MAQUETTE	♀	🔓	■
1mm rd stone ref	♀	🔓	■
stone hole cutter	♀	🔓	☐
stone seat cutter	♀	🔓	☐
1mm ROUND FACETED STONE	♀	🔓	■

Fig. 4

- Holding down the **Shift key,** multi select all 3 stone layers:**①**
  - **1mm RD STONE MAQUETTE**
  - **1mm rd stone ref**
  - **1mm ROUND BRILLIANT CUT**

- **Right-click** on one of the selected layers.

  - Click to select the **Select Objects** option in the drop-down menu.

- All of the stone layers will be selected.

- Type **"group"** and press **Enter.**

- *All of the objects will be grouped together.*

Fig. 5

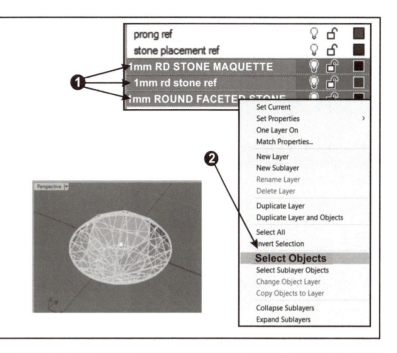

- Turn off the 2 stone layers:
  - **1mm RD STONE MAQUETTE**
  - **1mm ROUND FACETED STONE**

Fig. 6

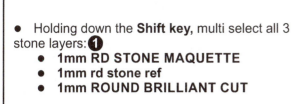

- **Transform tabbed toolbar.** `Transform`

- **LEFT-CLICK** on the **Scale 3-D** command.

  - **Select objects to scale** prompt:
    - Select the objects on the **!mm rd stone ref** layer.
      - These two objects will actually select together as they are grouped together.
    - Press **Enter.**

  - **Origin point** prompt:
    - Type **"0"** and press **Enter.**
  - **Scale factor or first reference point** prompt:
    - Type **"3.8"** and press **Enter.**

Fig. 7

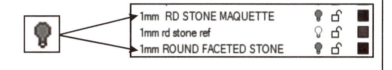

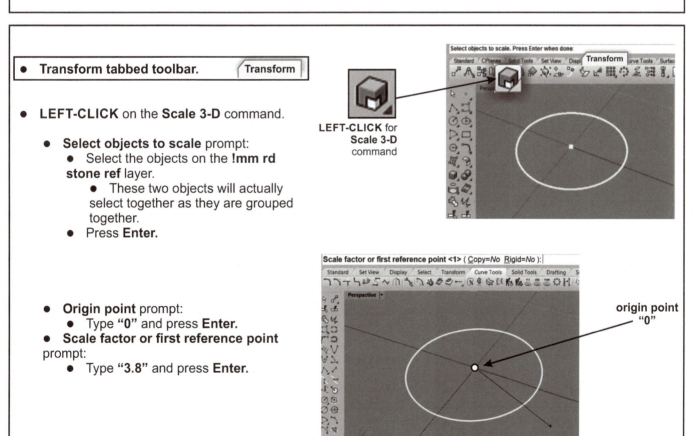

LEFT-CLICK for **Scale 3-D** command

origin point "0"

- The new diameter of the stone is **3.8mm** which is a **.2ct stone**.

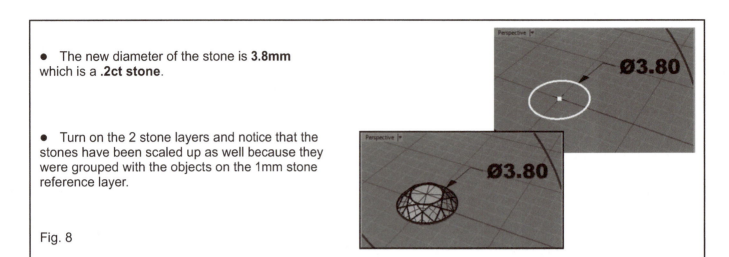

- Turn on the 2 stone layers and notice that the stones have been scaled up as well because they were grouped with the objects on the 1mm stone reference layer.

Fig. 8

Arraying and Spacing Out of the Stones

- **Curve Tools tabbed toolbar.**   Curve Tools

- Turn off the two stone layers.

stone placement ref   ✓   ■

- Select the stone ref circle (point will select too) and type **"offset"**.

- **Offset the circle outward to a distance of .05mm.**

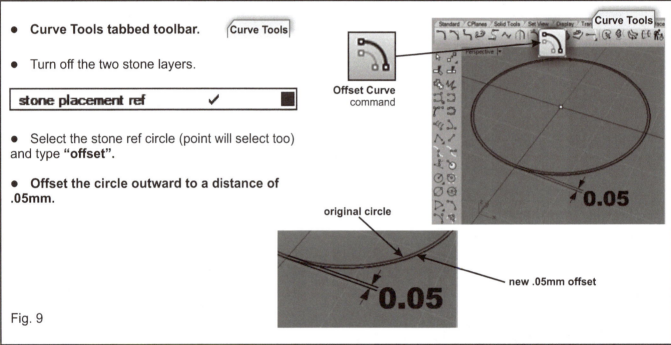

Offset Curve command

original circle

new .05mm offset

0.05

Fig. 9

- Type **"point"** and carefully place a point at the left and right **quad points** of the **new offset circle**.

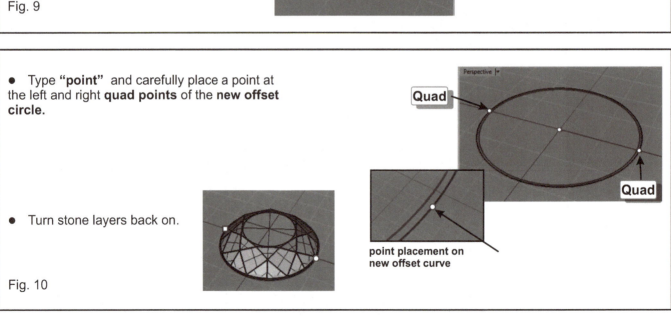

Quad

Quad

- Turn stone layers back on.

point placement on new offset curve

Fig. 10

- **Front Viewport.** Front ▼

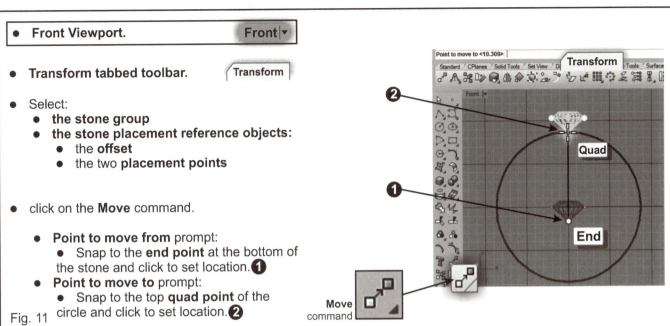

- **Transform tabbed toolbar.** Transform

- Select:
  - **the stone group**
  - **the stone placement reference objects:**
    - the **offset**
    - the two **placement points**

- click on the **Move** command.

  - **Point to move from** prompt:
    - Snap to the **end point** at the bottom of the stone and click to set location. ❶
  - **Point to move to** prompt:
    - Snap to the top **quad point** of the circle and click to set location. ❷

Fig. 11

Move command

- Click to toggle on **Record History**.

Record History

- Select the stone group and the stone placement ref objects and click on the **Polar Array** command.

Polar Array comnand

  - **Center of polar array**: 0
  - **Number of items: 19**
  - **Angle to fill or first reference point: 360°**
  - Press **Enter** to accept the pink preview image of the array.

center of polar array "0"

- The completed array.

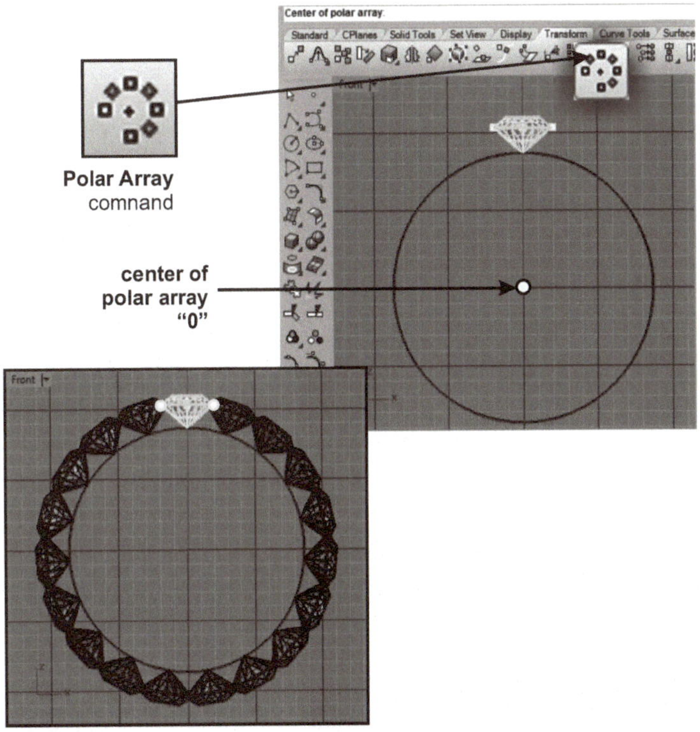

Fig. 12

- Notice that the stones intersect each other.

- The next step will be to move the stones outward so that they will be a gap of .1mm between them.

- Turn off the two stone layers for the next step.

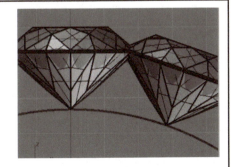

Fig. 13

- **Front Perspective view.**

- Zoom in on the top stone and it's neighbor to the right.

- Using **point osnap**, create a line from one of the placement points to the other as shown.

Fig. 14

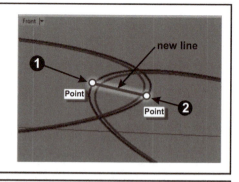

- Click on the **Line: from Midpoint** command in the **Lines** toolbar flyout.

  - **Middle of line** prompt:
    - **Snap** to the **midpoint** of the new line and click to set location. ❶

  - **End of line** prompt:
    - Type **"0"** and press **Enter.** ❷

- The finished line will run through the middle of the new line ❶ and end at **"0".** ❷

Fig. 15

accesses the **Lines** toolbar flyout

Line: from Midpoint command

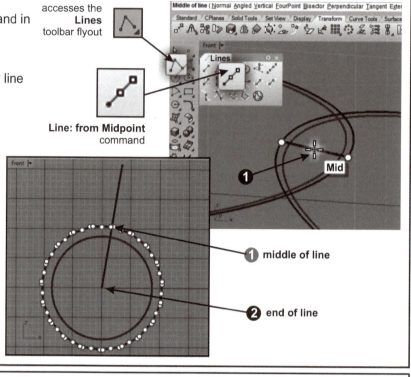

❶ middle of line

❷ end of line

- **Front Viewport.** Front ▾

- Select the curves for the top stone:
  - **1mm RD stone placement ref**
  - **1mm RD stone ref**

- Type **"move"** and press **Enter.**

  - **Point to move from** prompt:
    - Snap to the **placement point** on the right of the stone and click to set location.❶
  - **Point to move to** prompt:
    - Using **ORTHO**, move the cursor straight up and snap to the **intersection** with the new line as shown. Click to set location.❷

Fig. 16

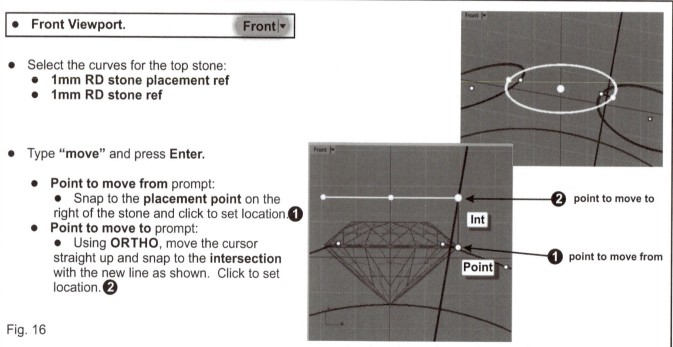

❷ point to move to

❶ point to move from

- History has updated the other curves and points.

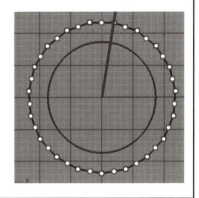

Fig. 17

- **Top Perspective view.**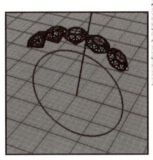

- Turn on the stone layers and notice how the stones have also updated.

- **Delete** all stones and their reference geometry except for the five stones at the top of the ring.

Fig. 18

- **setting ref** layer current ❶

- Turn off the **stone placement ref** layer. ❷

- Turn on the **1mm RD STONE MAQUETTE** layer. ❸

- Turn off the **1mm ROUND FACETED STONE** layer. ❹

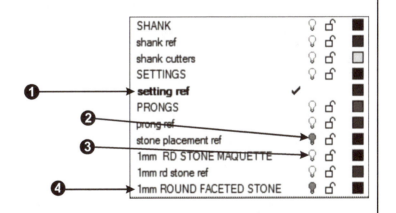

Fig. 19

- With just the stone maquette and stone ref curves showing, notice that, with the move in Figs. 16-17, History adjusted the space between stones to **.1mm**.

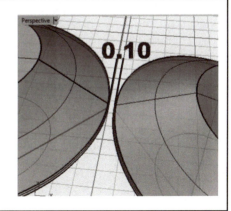

Fig. 20

- Turn off the **1mm STONE MAQUETTE** layer.

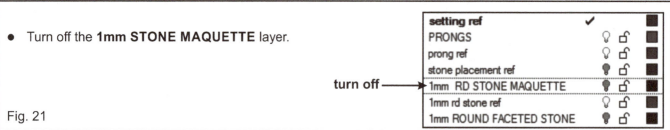

turn off ⟶

Fig. 21

- **Curve Tools tabbed toolbar.**   [Curve Tools]

- Click on the **Line** command.

  - **Start of line** prompt:
    - Snap to the right **quad** point on the top stone curve and click to set location. **1**
  - **End of line** prompt:
    - Type **"0"** and press **Enter.** **2**

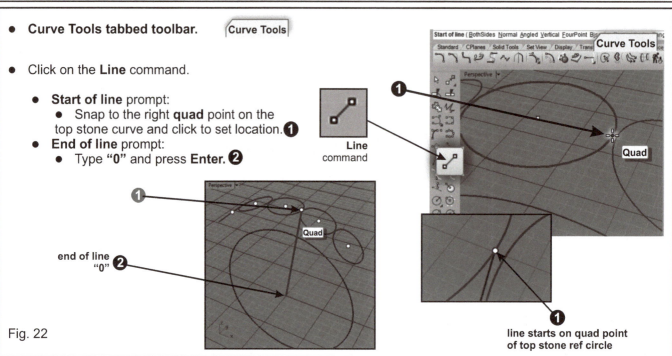

Line command

Quad

end of line "0" **2**

Fig. 22

1 line starts on quad point of top stone ref circle

- **Front Viewport.**   [Front ▾]

- Turn the **1mm STONE MAQUETTE** layer back on.

- Click on the **Circle: tangent, tangent, radius** command.

  - **First tangent curve** prompt:
    - Draw the cursor over the seam of the maquette stone and, when you see the white constraint line, click to set location. **1**
  - **Second tangent curve or radius** prompt:
    - Type **".45"** and press **Enter.**
  - **Second tangent curve or radius** prompt:
    - Draw the cursor over to the setting reference line and, when you see the white constraint line, click to set location. **2**

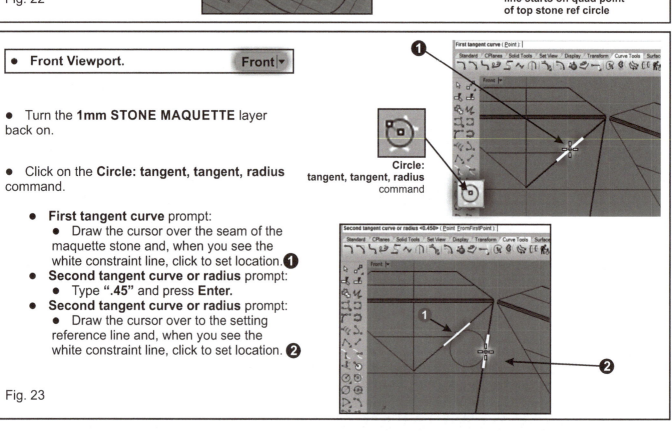

Circle: tangent, tangent, radius command

Fig. 23

● The finished profile curve for the seat of the stone.

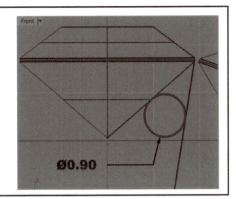

Fig. 24

● Use the same technique to create a second circle of the same **.9mm diameter**, tangent to the placement curve and the ring band ref curve shown.

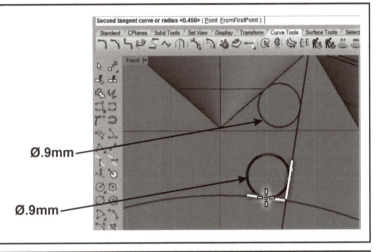

Ø.9mm

Ø.9mm

Fig. 25

● Offset the original circle from Fig. 2 outward to a distance of .45mm.

Offset Curve
command

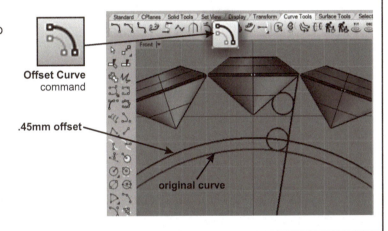

.45mm offset

original curve

Fig. 26

● **Offset** the stone placement line to the left at a distance of **.45mm.**

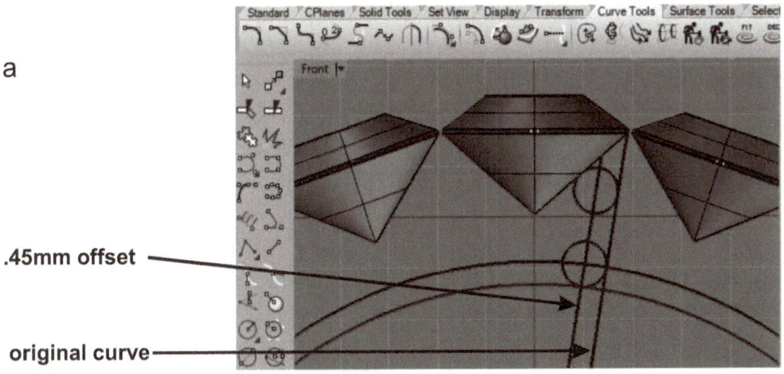

.45mm offset

original curve

Fig. 27

- Select the two offsets, type **"intersect"**, and press **Enter.**

- A **point object** will be created at the intersection of the two selected curves.

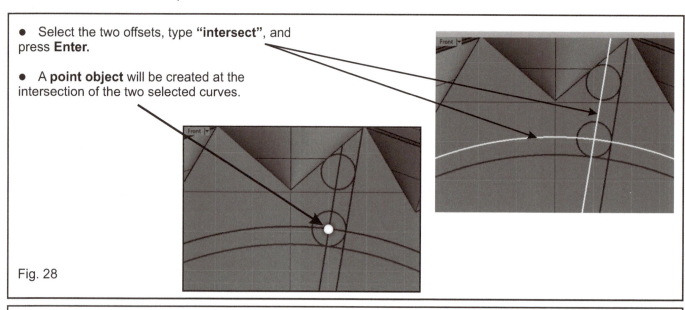

Fig. 28

- Type **"mirror"** and press **Enter.**

- Follow <u>**Command Line**</u> prompts to **Mirror** the point to the other side, using the Y axis as the **mirror plane.**
  - You can click on the **YAxis** option in the <u>**Command Line**</u> to designate the Y Axis as the mirror plane.

Fig. 29

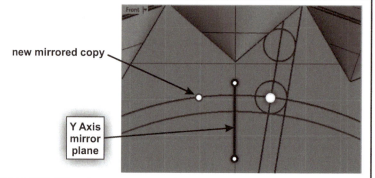

new mirrored copy

Y Axis mirror plane

- **Top Perspective view.** ❶ 🔲 ❷ 🔀

- Using the **Circle: diameter** command, create a circle, snapping to the points just created.

Circle: diameter command

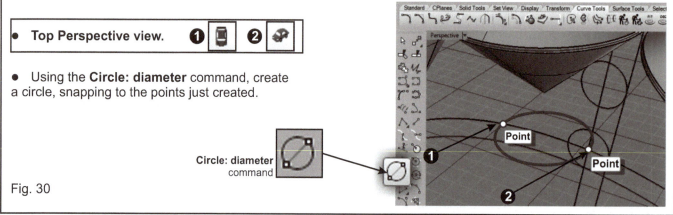

Point

Point

Fig. 30

- Select the new circle and the offset and click on the **Curve from 2 Views** command.

Curve from 2 Views command

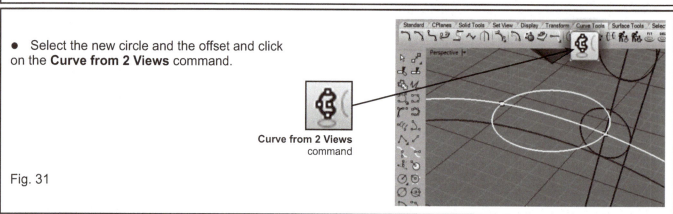

Fig. 31

- A new circle will be created the is bent slightly, following the curve of the ring band shape.

- Lock or Delete the original circle

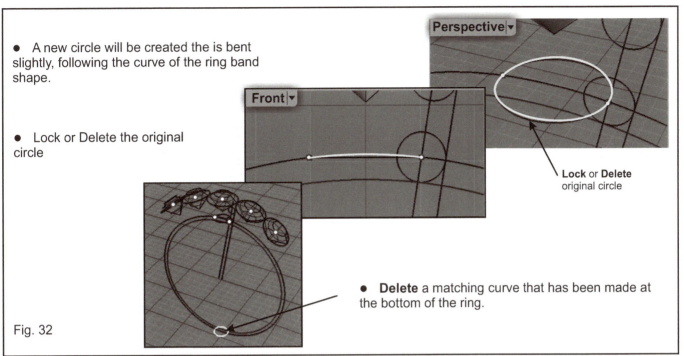

Lock or **Delete**
original circle

- **Delete** a matching curve that has been made at the bottom of the ring.

Fig. 32

- **Solid Tools tabbed toolbar.** Solid Tools

| SETTINGS | ✓ | ■ |

- Select the new circle and click on the **Pipe: flat caps** command.

  - **Radius for closed pipe** prompt:
    - Type "**.45**" and press **Enter.**
  - **Point for next radius. Press Enter for none** prompt:
    - Press **Enter.**

Pipe: flat cape
command

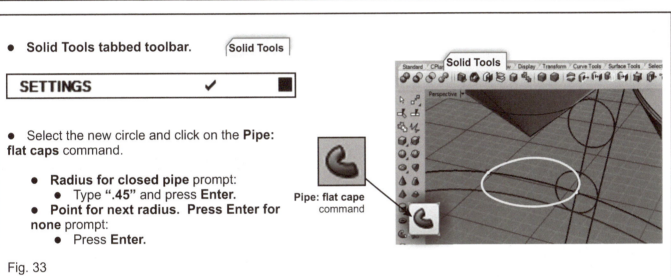

Fig. 33

- A base for the setting has been created.

front view

- The base follows the shape of the ring band.

Fig. 34

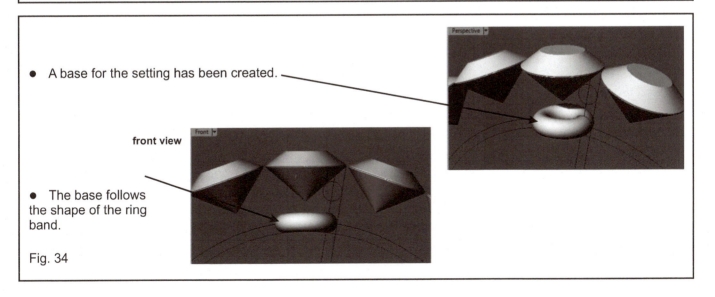

- **Front Perspective Viewport** ❶ ❷

- **Surface Tools tabbed toolbar.** [Surface Tools]

- Select the small circle created in Fig. **23-24** and **LEFT-CLICK** on the **Revolve** command.

  - **Start of revolve axis** prompt:
    - Type **"0"** and press **Enter.** ❶
  - **End of revolve axis** prompt:
    - Using **ORTHO**, draw the cursor along the **Y axis** and click to set location. ❷
  - **Start angle** prompt:
    - Click on the **FullCircle** option in the <u>**Command Line**</u>. ❸
    - Press **Enter.**

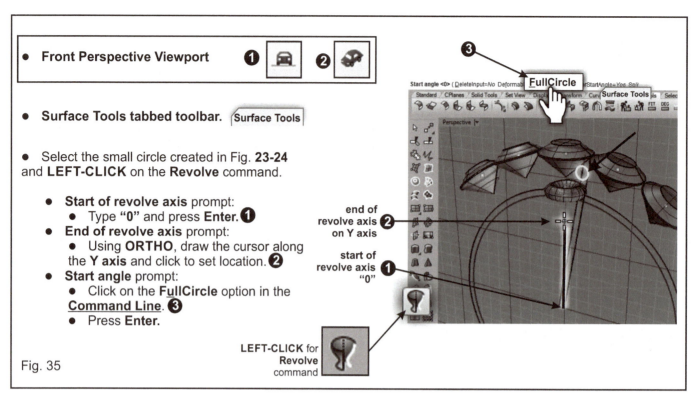

end of revolve axis ❷ on Y axis

start of revolve axis ❶ "0"

LEFT-CLICK for **Revolve** command

Fig. 35

- The stone seat has been created.

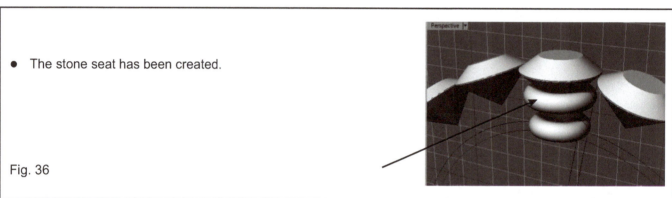

Fig. 36

Stone Setting - Prongs

- Turn off these layers:
  - **SETTINGS**
  - **setting ref**

- **prong ref** layer current

current ──→

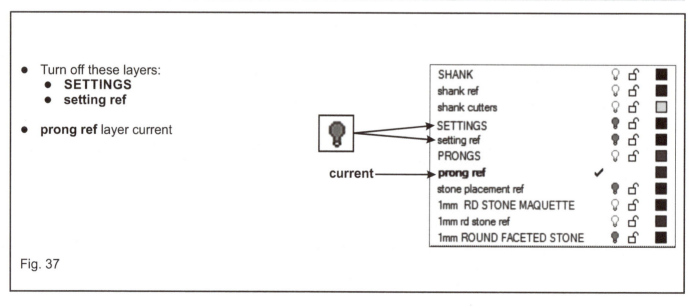

Fig. 37

- **Curve Tools tabbed toolbar.**   [Curve Tools]

- Select the **1mm rd stone ref** circle on the girdle of the top stone and click on the **Offset Curve** command

  - **Side to offset: the inside of the circle.**
  - **Offset distance: .3mm**

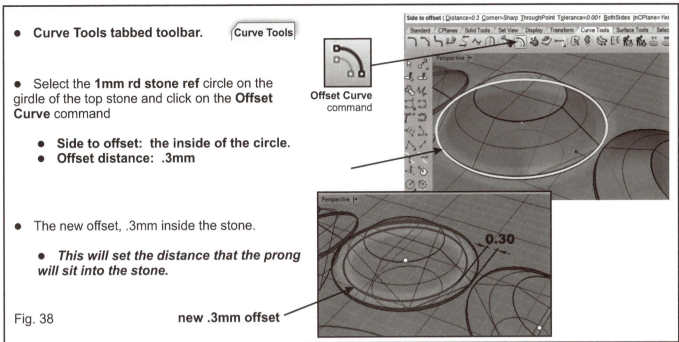

Offset Curve
command

- The new offset, .3mm inside the stone.

  - ***This will set the distance that the prong will sit into the stone.***

Fig. 38   new .3mm offset

1mm RD STONE MAQUETTE   💡 ⌂ ⬛

- Using **ORTHO**, use the **Circle: diameter** command to create a **.9mm circle** from the right **quad** of the new offset **①** over to the right as shown. **②**

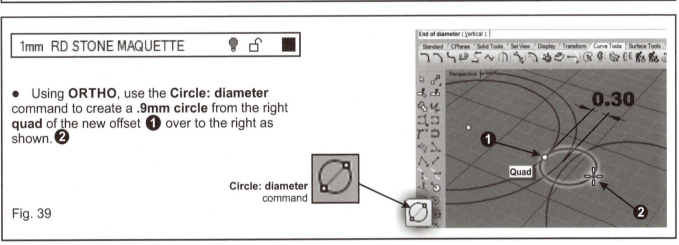

Circle: diameter
command

Fig. 39

- Create a line from the **center** of the new circle down to **"0"**.

  - **Start of line** prompt:
    - Snap to the **center** of the new circle and click to set location. **①**
  - **End of line** prompt:
    - Type **"0"** and press **Enter.②**

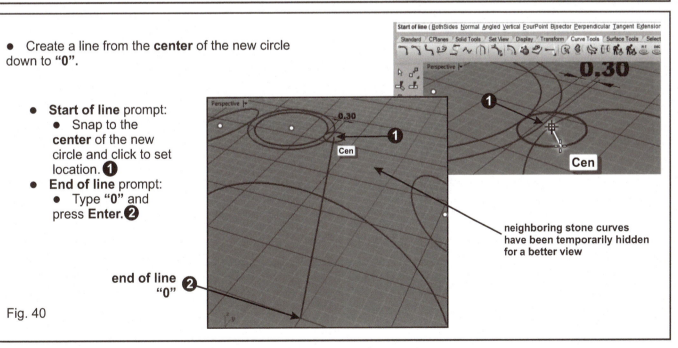

neighboring stone curves have been temporarily hidden for a better view

end of line **②**
"0"

Fig. 40

- **Front Viewport.**   Front ▼

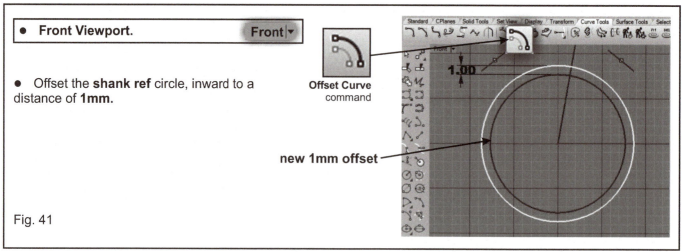

- Offset the **shank ref** circle, inward to a distance of **1mm.**

Offset Curve
command

new 1mm offset

Fig. 41

- Use the new offset to **Trim** away part of the straight line created in **Fig. 40**.

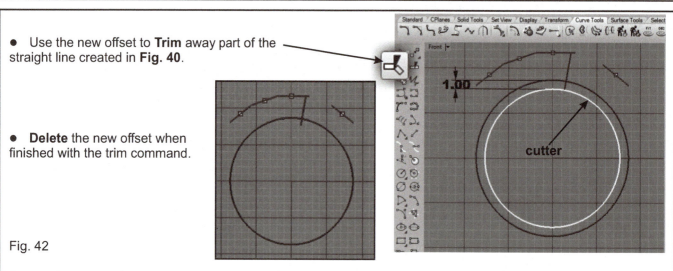

- **Delete** the new offset when finished with the trim command.

cutter

Fig. 42

- Click on the **Extend by Line** command in the **Extend** toolbar flyout.

accesses the **Extend** toolbar flyout

- **Select curve to extend** prompt:
  - Click near the top of the newly trimmed line.**❶**
- **End of extension or enter extension length** prompt;
  - Type **"1"** and press **Enter.❷**

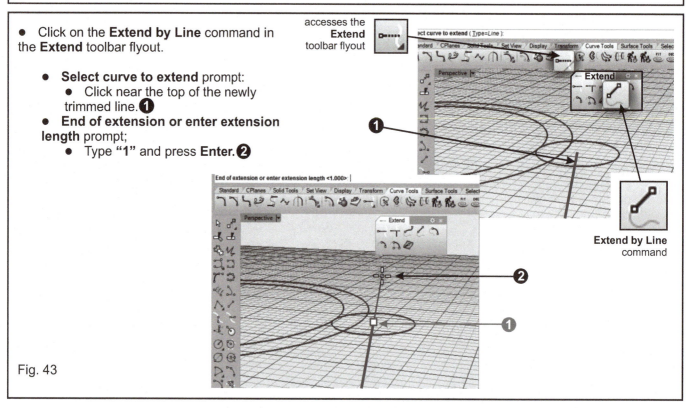

Extend by Line
command

End of extension or enter extension length <1.000>:

Fig. 43

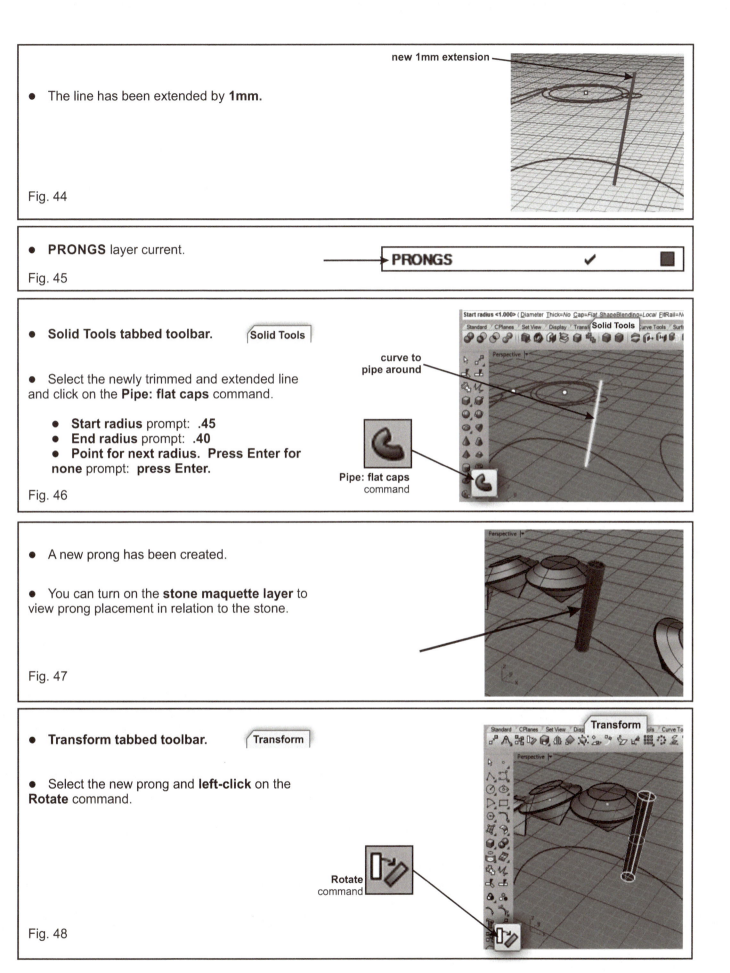

- The line has been extended by **1mm**.

new 1mm extension

Fig. 44

- **PRONGS** layer current.

PRONGS ✓ ■

Fig. 45

- **Solid Tools tabbed toolbar.**   [Solid Tools]

- Select the newly trimmed and extended line and click on the **Pipe: flat caps** command.

  - **Start radius** prompt: **.45**
  - **End radius** prompt: **.40**
  - **Point for next radius. Press Enter for none** prompt: **press Enter.**

Fig. 46

curve to pipe around

Pipe: flat caps
command

- A new prong has been created.

- You can turn on the **stone maquette layer** to view prong placement in relation to the stone.

Fig. 47

- **Transform tabbed toolbar.**   [Transform]

- Select the new prong and **left-click** on the **Rotate** command.

Rotate
command

Fig. 48

- **Center of rotation** prompt:
  - Snap to the **Point** in the center of the stone and click to set location.

- **Angle or first reference point** prompt:
  - Type **"-50"** and press **Enter.**
    - The "minus" sign means that you will rotate in a clockwise direction.

- The newly rotated prong.

- Type **"show"** and press **Enter** to unhide the hidden elements.

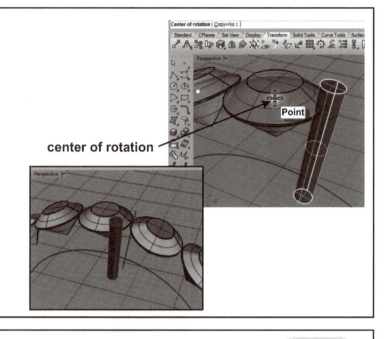

center of rotation

Fig. 49

- **Solid Tools tabbed toolbar.**   Solid Tools

- Select the **shank ref** circle and click on the **Extrude closed planar curve** command.

  - **Extrusion distance** prompt:
    - Click to toggle on the **BothSides=*Yes*** option.
    - Type **"5"** and press **Enter.**

  - The finished **10mm extrusion**.

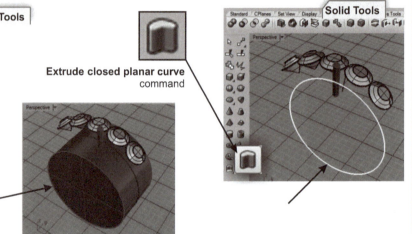

Extrude closed planar curve
command

Fig. 50

- Select the prong and click on the **Boolean Difference** command.

  - **Select surfaces or polysurfaces to subtract with. Press Enter when done** prompt:
    - Select the new cutter extrusion and press **Enter.**

- **Delete** the new cutter extrusion after the command is completed.

- The prong will be cut to fit the inside of the band.

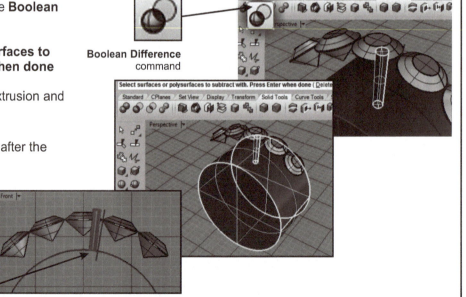

Boolean Difference
command

Fig. 51

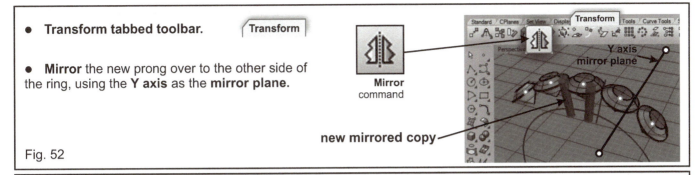

- **Transform tabbed toolbar.** ⌐Transform⌐

- **Mirror** the new prong over to the other side of the ring, using the **Y axis** as the **mirror plane.**

Mirror command

Y axis mirror plane

new mirrored copy

Fig. 52

- *note: You may want to turn off the stone maquette layer for better visibility.*

- Turn on the **SETTINGS** layer.

- Select the two prongs and the two setting elements and type **"group".**

- Press **Enter.**

Fig. 53

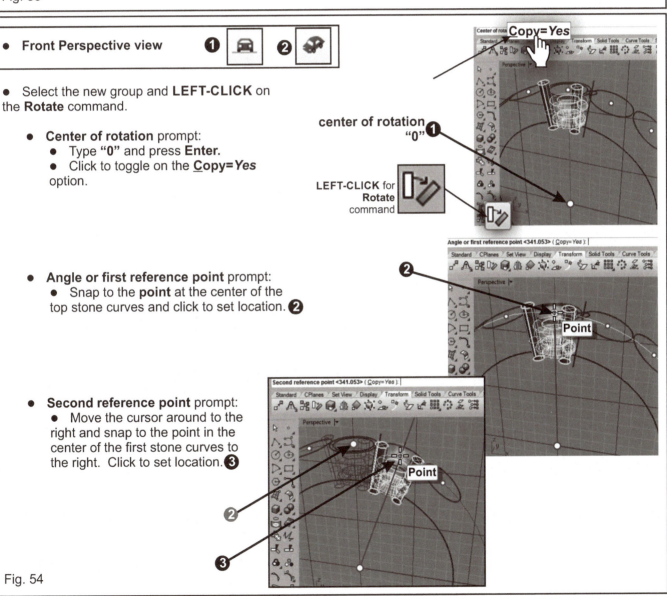

- **Front Perspective view** ❶ 🚗 ❷ 🚗

- Select the new group and **LEFT-CLICK** on the **Rotate** command.

  - **Center of rotation** prompt:
    - Type **"0"** and press **Enter.**
    - Click to toggle on the **Copy=Yes** option.

center of rotation "0" ❶

LEFT-CLICK for **Rotate** command

Copy=Yes

  - **Angle or first reference point** prompt:
    - Snap to the **point** at the center of the top stone curves and click to set location. ❷

Angle or first reference point <341.053> (Copy=Yes):

Point

  - **Second reference point** prompt:
    - Move the cursor around to the right and snap to the point in the center of the first stone curves to the right. Click to set location. ❸

Second reference point <341.053> (Copy=Yes):

Point

❷

❸

Fig. 54

540

- **Second reference point** prompt:
  - Draw the cursor over to the next stone to the right and snap to the **point** in the center of the stone curves. Click to set location. ④

- Press **Enter** to end the command.

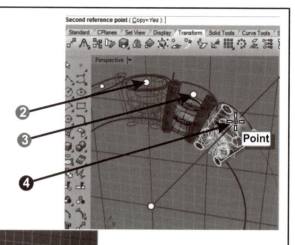

- Two copies have been rotated into position on the right side of the ring.

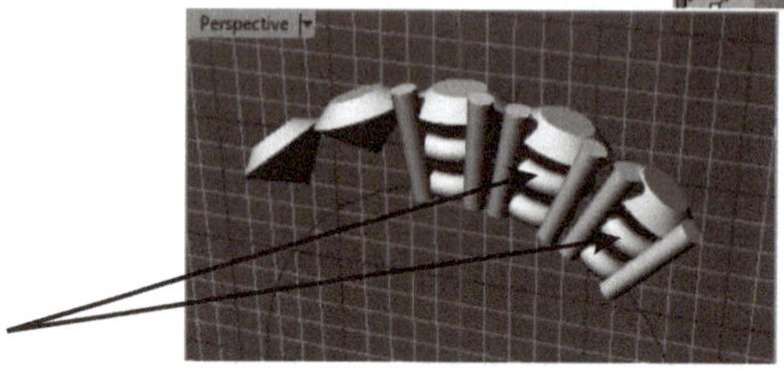

Fig. 55

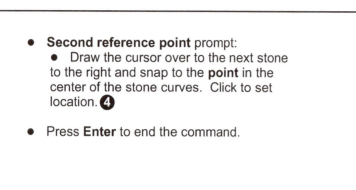

- **Mirror** the two copies over to the left side of the ring, using the **Y axis** as the **mirror plane**.

Mirror command

new mirrored copies

Y axis mirror plane

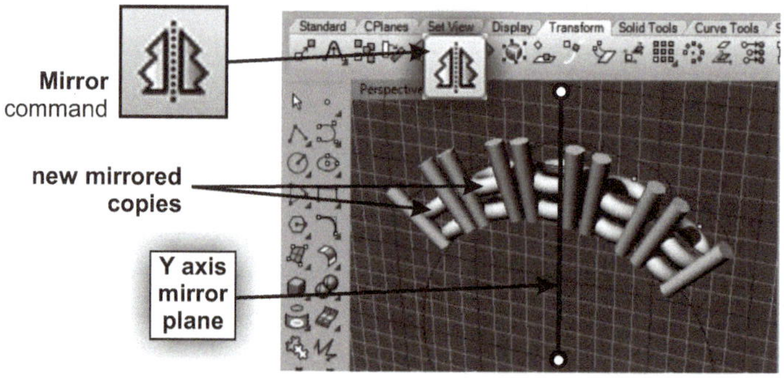

Fig. 56

- Window select all 5 settings and type **"ungroup"**.

- This **ungrouping** is necessary for the next step.

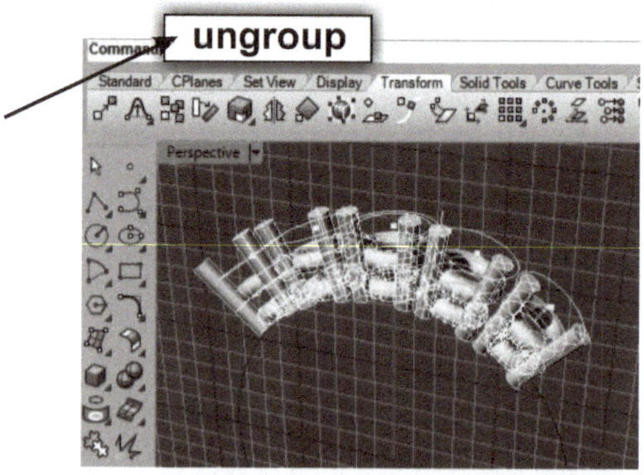

ungroup

Fig. 57

- Select all of the prongs and **Mirror** them to the back of the ring.

- Use the **X axis** as the **mirror plane**.

X axis mirror plane

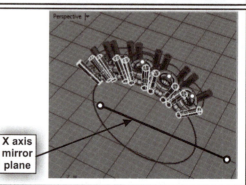

Fig. 58

- You can temporarily turn stone layer(s) on to view them in the completed settings.

Fig. 59

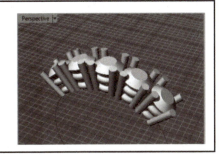

Modeling the Ring Shank

- Turn off all layers, except for the **SHANK** layer and the **shank ref** layer.

- **shank ref** layer current.

Fig. 60

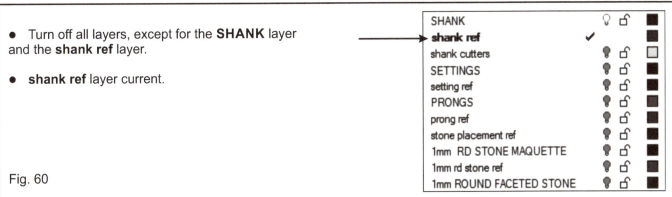

SHANK		💡 🔓 ■
shank ref	✓	■
shank cutters		💡 🔓 ☐
SETTINGS		💡 🔓 ■
setting ref		💡 🔓 ■
PRONGS		💡 🔓 ■
prong ref		💡 🔓 ■
stone placement ref		💡 🔓 ■
1mm RD STONE MAQUETTE		💡 🔓 ■
1mm rd stone ref		💡 🔓 ■
1mm ROUND FACETED STONE		💡 🔓 ■

- **Right Viewport.**   **Right ▼**

- **Curve Tools tabbed toolbar.**   Curve Tools

- Click on the **Ellipse: diameter** command.

    - **Start of first axis** prompt:
        - Click on the quad on top of the **shank ref** circle (seen here from the right view) and click to set location. ❶

Ellipse: diameter command

- **End of first axis** prompt:
    - Draw the cursor upwards.
    - Type **"2.1"** and press **Enter.** ❷

- **End of second axis** prompt:
    - Type **"2.45"** and press **Enter.** ❸

Fig. 61

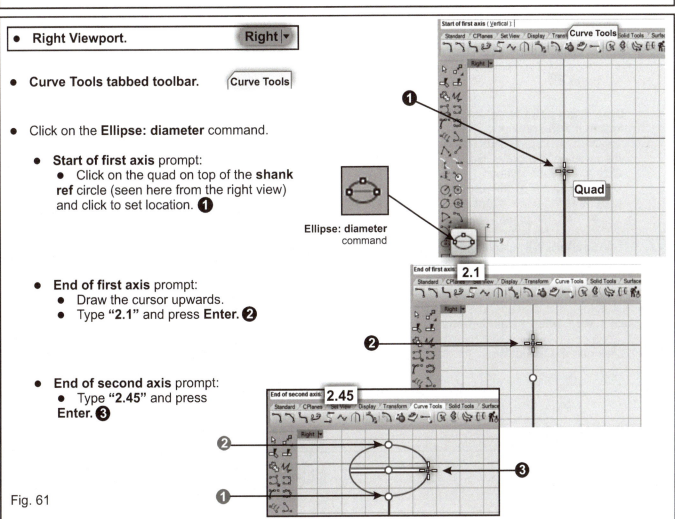

- Using the same technique, create a **2mm x 3mm ellipse** off the quad point at the bottom of the circle.

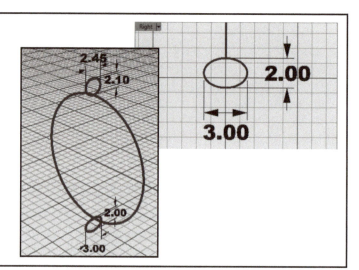

Fig. 62

- **Top Perspective view.** ❶ ❷

- **Surface Tools tabbed toolbar.** [Surface Tools]

- Click on the **Sweep 1 Rail** command.

  - **Select rail** prompt:
    - Select the circle. ❶

  - **Select cross section curves** prompt:
    - Select the two ellipses and press **Enter.** ❷

  - **Drag seam point to adjust. Press Enter when done** prompt:
    - Drag the seam points to snap to the quads of the circle. Be sure to click to set each location.
    - Make sure that both arrows are pointed in the same direction.
      - To change an arrow direction, click on the **Align Cross Sections** ❶ button and click on an arrow point.
  - Press **Enter.**

  - Click to select the **Closed Sweep** ❷ option in the **Sweep 1 Rail Options** box.

  - Click on the **OK button.**

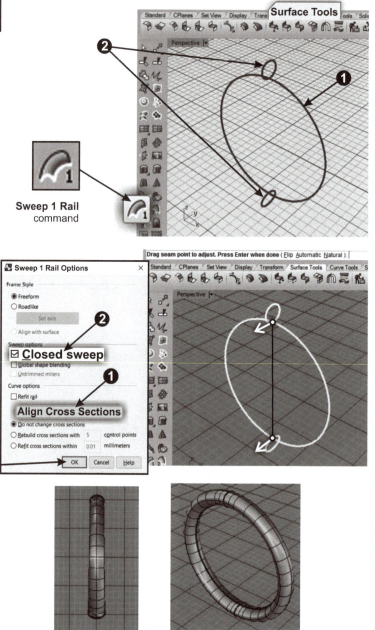

Sweep 1 Rail command

- The finished sweep

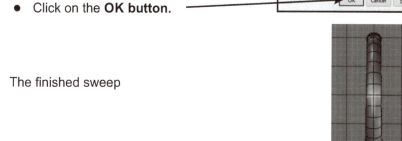

Fig. 63

- Notice that when the setting and prong layers are turned back on, the shank is intersecting the settings.

- The shank will need to be trimmed out.

Fig. 64

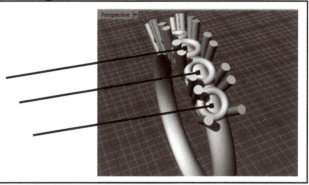

- Turn off all of the layers except for:
  - **shank cutters**
  - **setting ref**
  - **1mm RD stone ref**

- **shank cutters** layer current.

Fig. 65

SHANK			
shank ref			
shank cutters	✓		
SETTINGS			
setting ref			
PRONGS			
prong ref			
stone placement ref			
1mm RD STONE MAQUETTE			
1mm rd stone ref			
1mm ROUND FACETED STONE			

- Select the line that runs through the two circles of the **setting ref** layer. ❶

- **RIGHT-CLICK** on the **shank cutters** layer.❷

- Select the **Copy Objects to Layer** option in the context menu that appears.❸

- Turn off the **setting ref** layer.

Fig. 66

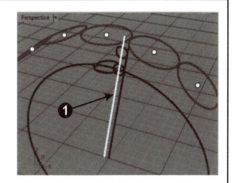

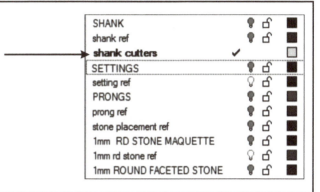

- **Front Viewport.**   Front ▾

- Turn on the **SETTINGS** layer.

- Mirror the cutting line over to the other side of the ring, using the **Y axis** for the **mirror plane.**

- Use the same technique as in **Figs. 54-56** to **Rotate with the copy option** and to **Mirror** these two cutting lines to the other settings.

Fig. 67

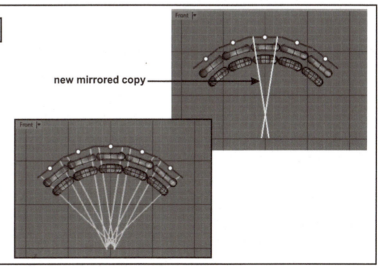

new mirrored copy

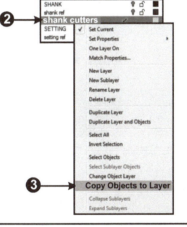

- Turn on the **SHANK** layer and turn off all other layers except for the **shank cutter** layer.

- Select the ring shank ❶ and click on the **Split** command.

  - **Select cutting objects. Press Enter when done** prompt:
    - Select all of the cutter lines and press Enter. ❷

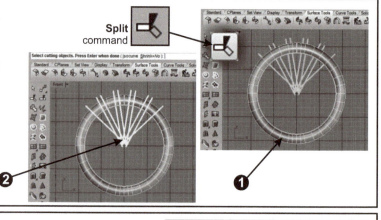

Split command

Fig. 68

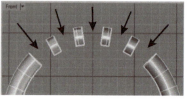
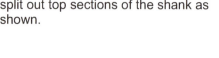

- Select and **Delete** all of the larger split out top sections of the shank as shown.

Fig. 69

sections deleted

sections to be deleted

- Select all of the remaining shank sections and type **"cap"**.

- All of the separate sections will now be closed polysurfaces.

- These remaining sections will fill in the gaps between the settings.

Fig. 70

all sections are now closed polysurfaces

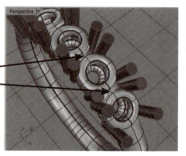

- **Solid Tools tabbed toolbar.**   Solid Tools

- Turn on the layers for the settings and prongs.

- Use the **Boolean Union** command to make the ring one closed polysurface.

- Turn on the faceted stone layer for a better display for rendering.

Fig. 71

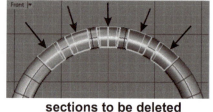

Boolean Union command

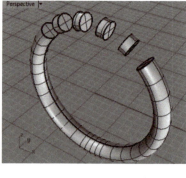

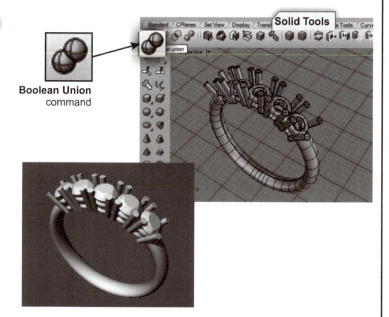

Textures

Color
☐ (empty - click to assign) ... 100%

Transparency
☐ (empty - click to assign) ... 100%

Bump
☐ (empty - click to assign) ... 100%

Environment
☑ **Emap - Rhino arches polished silver** ... 65%

- Rendered Viewport material properties for the **SHANK**, **SETTINGS**, and **PRONGS** layers:
  - **Envionment:**
    - **Emap - Rhino arches polished silver.**
  - **65% strength**

- Rendered Viewport material properties for the **faceted stone** layer:
  - Gloss finish: **approx. 11%**
  - Textures:
    - Color: **DIAMOND 3 at 100% strength**
    - Environment: **Diamond 3** at 35% strength.

Basic Settings

Color: ⬛

Gloss finish: 0 **11%** 100

Reflectivity: 0% 100

Transparency: 0% 100 IOR: 1.00

Textures

Color
☑ DIAMOND 3 ... **100%**

Transparency
☐ (empty - click to assign) ... 100%

Bump
☐ (empty - click to assign) ... 100%

Environment
☑ DIAMOND 3 ... **35%**

Fig. 72

Modeling the Ring

- Create the layers shown.

- **ring ref** layer current.

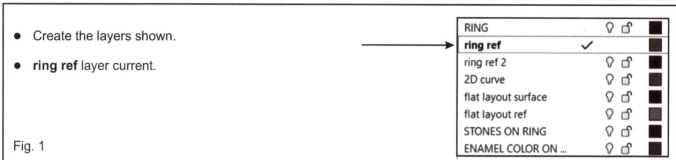

Fig. 1

- **Front Viewport.**   Front ▾

- **Curve Tools tabbed toolbar.**   Curve Tools

- Create a **17.35 diameter circle** around **"0"**.

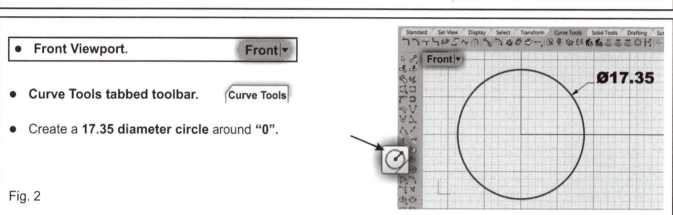

Ø17.35

Fig. 2

- **Offset** the circle to the outside.
  - **Offset distance: 2mm**

Offset Curve
Command

circle to be offset

new
offset

2.00

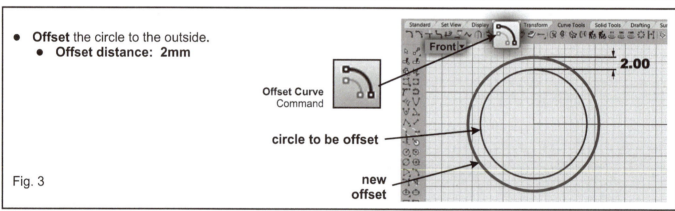

Fig. 3

- **Top Perspective view.**   ❶ 🗔   ❷ 🚗

- With **ORTHO** engaged, use the **Line: from Midpoint** command in the **Lines** toolbar flyout to create two lines at the top and bottom **quads** of the inner circle.
  - **middle of line: ❶**
  - **end of line: ❷**

  - **line at top: 10mm long**
  - **line at bottom: 4mm long**

Line: from Midpoint
command

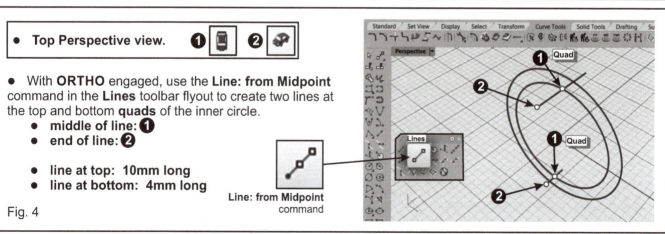

Fig. 4

- **2D curve** layer current.

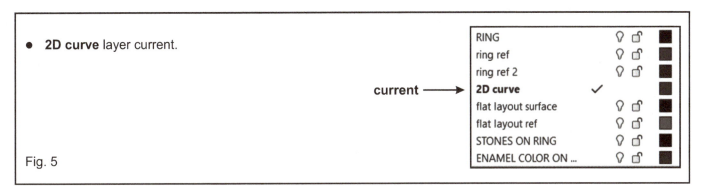

Fig. 5

- Using **end osnap**, create a new **Line** between the ends of the two lines just created.

  - **start of line**: ❶
  - **end of line**: ❷

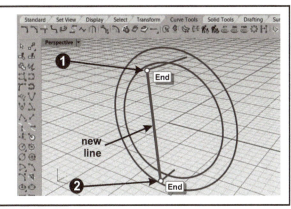

new line

Fig. 6

- **LEFT-CLICK** for the **Extend Curve** command.
  - **Select curve to extend** prompt:
    - Click near the top on the new line. ❶

LEFT-CLICK for
Extend Curve
command

- **End of extension or enter extension length** prompt:
  - Draw th cursor upward and note the preview line that follows it.
  - Type **"4"** and press **Enter.** ❷

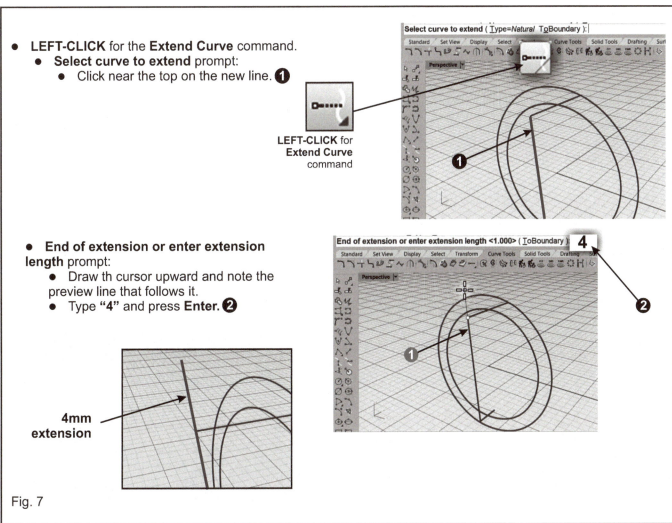

4mm extension

Fig. 7

- The command will continue to prompt you to **Select curve to extend. Press Enter when done.**
  - Click near the bottom end of the line. ❸

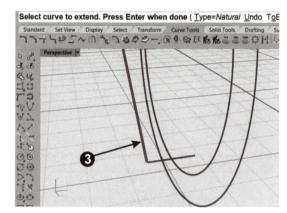

- **End of extension or enter extension length** prompt:
  - Draw the cursor downward and note the preview line. ❹
  - Press **Enter** to opt for the new default **4mm** length.
    - The bottom end of the line will be extended at a length of 4mm.❺
  - Press **Enter** to end the command.

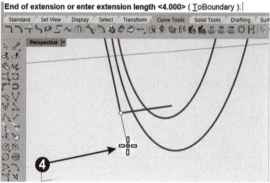

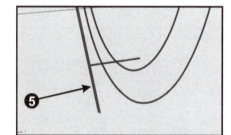

Fig. 8

- **ring ref** layer current.

current ⟶

RING	♀ ⌂	■
ring ref	✓	■
ring ref 2	♀ ⌂	■
2D curve	♀ ⌂	■
flat layout surface	♀ ⌂	■
flat layout ref	♀ ⌂	■
STONES ON RING	♀ ⌂	■
ENAMEL COLOR ON ...	♀ ⌂	■

Fig. 9

- Click on the **Curve from 2 Views** command.
  - **Select first curve** prompt:
    - Select the original circle.❶

Curve from 2 Views
command

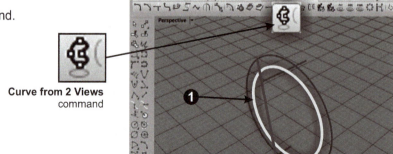

Fig. 10

- **Select second curve** prompt:
  - Select the new line. ❷

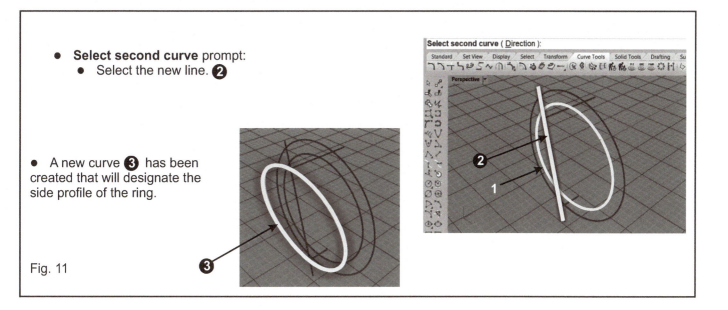

- A new curve ❸ has been created that will designate the side profile of the ring.

Fig. 11

- Select the outer offset curve ❶ and the 2D curves line ❷ and click on **Curve from 2 Views** again.

Curve from 2 Views
command

- Another new curve ❸ has been created that is a combination of the two selected curves.

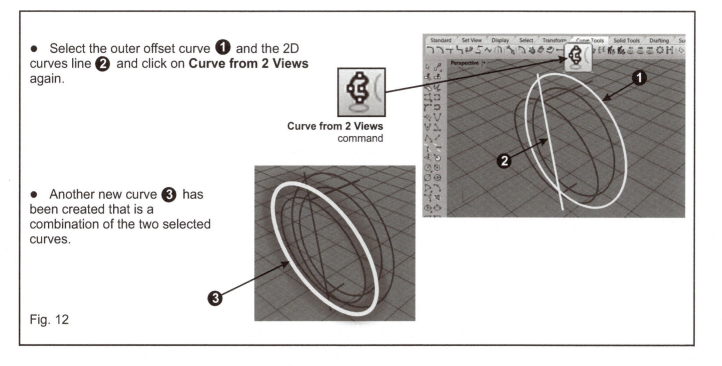

Fig. 12

- The 2 new curves are created by the selection of two curves that are each planar in their different construction planes.

- This is what they will look like in their original construction planes.

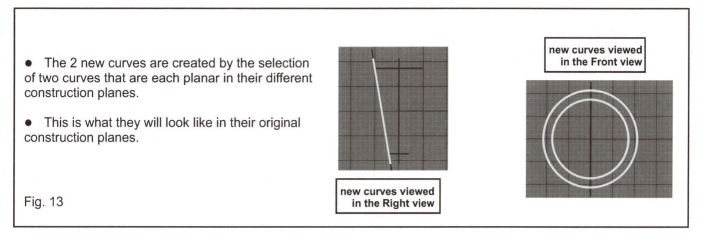

new curves viewed in the Front view

new curves viewed in the Right view

Fig. 13

- Select the two new curves and Rebuild to 11 control points.
  - Each individual selected curve will rebuild to 11 control points.

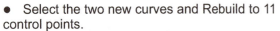

Rebuild
command

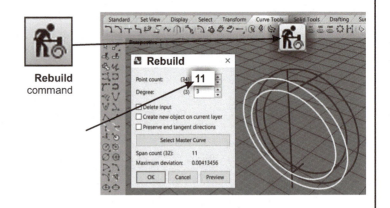

Fig. 14

- **Transform tabbed toolbar.**

Transform

- Select the two new rebuilt curves and click on the **Mirror** command.
  - Click on the **XAxis** option ❶ in the **Command Line** which will designate the Xaxis as the mirror plane.

Mirror
command

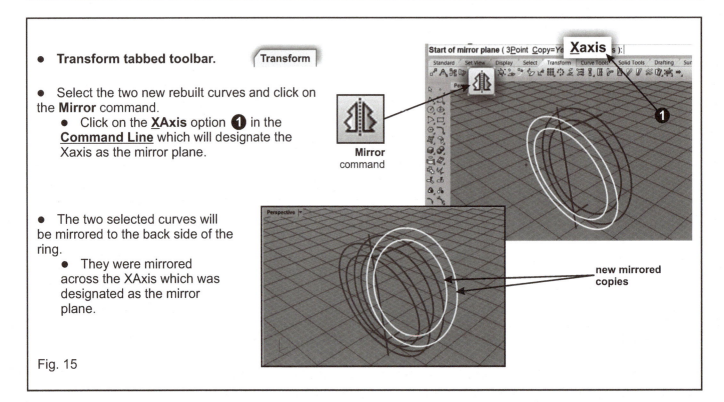

- The two selected curves will be mirrored to the back side of the ring.
  - They were mirrored across the XAxis which was designated as the mirror plane.

new mirrored copies

Fig. 15

- Select the two original circles, type **"hide"** and press **Enter.**

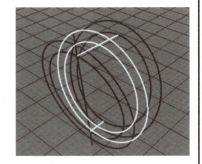

- The two new sets of outer curves will remain visible.

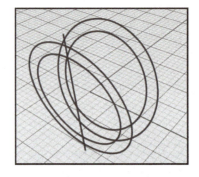

Fig. 16

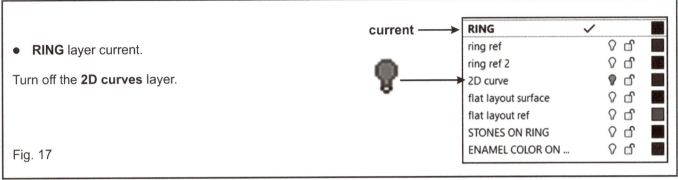

- **RING** layer current.

Turn off the **2D curves** layer.

Fig. 17

- **Surface Tools tabbed toolbar.** Surface Tools

- Click on the **Loft** command.
  - **Select curves to loft. Press Enter when done** prompt:
    - Select the curves in the order shown.
    - Press **Enter.**

Loft
command

- **Drag seam point to adjust. Press Enter when done** prompt:
  - Using **quad osnap**, drag all control points to the bottom quads of the selected curves.
  - Press **Enter.**

Quad

- A preview of the loft will appear, along with the **Loft Options** dialog box.
  - Click to turn on the **Closed Loft** option.
  - Click on the **OK button** to complete the command.

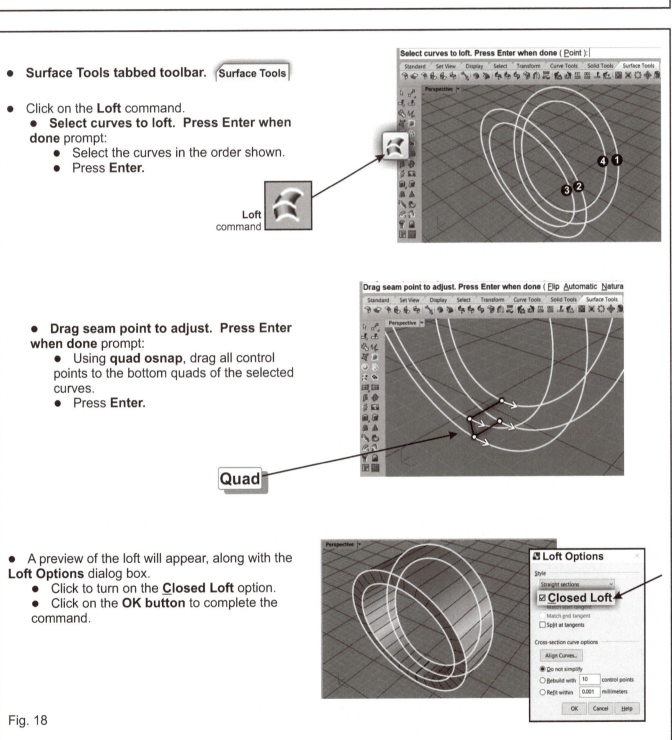

Fig. 18

- The closed polysurface of the ring has been created.

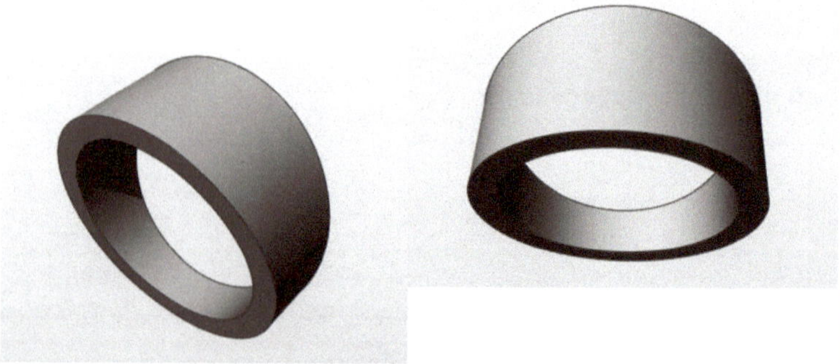

Fig. 19

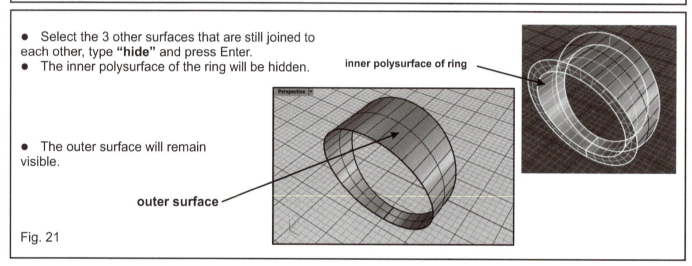

- **RIGHT-CLICK** for the **Extract Surface** command.
    - **Select surface to extract. Press Enter when done** prompt:
        - Extract the outer surface of the ring and press **Enter.**

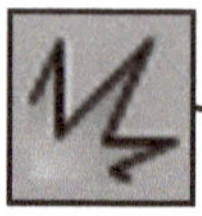

RIGHT-CLICK for **Extract Surface** command

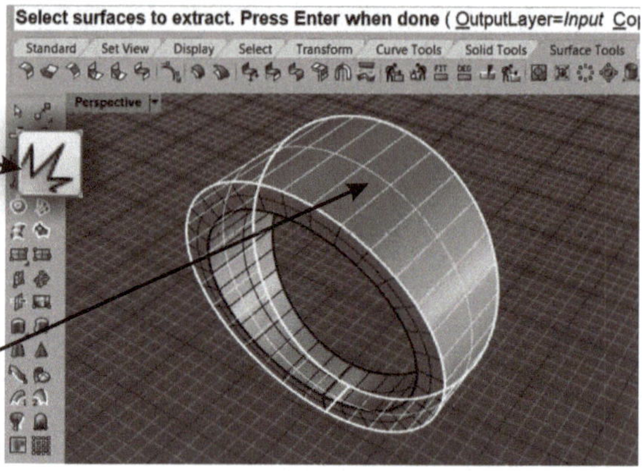

Select surfaces to extract. Press Enter when done (OutputLayer=Input Co
Standard
Set View
Display
Select
Transform
Curve Tools
Solid Tools
Surface Tools
Perspective

surface to extract

Fig. 20

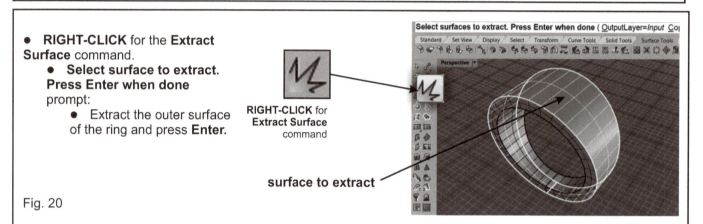

- Select the 3 other surfaces that are still joined to each other, type **"hide"** and press Enter.
- The inner polysurface of the ring will be hidden.

inner polysurface of ring

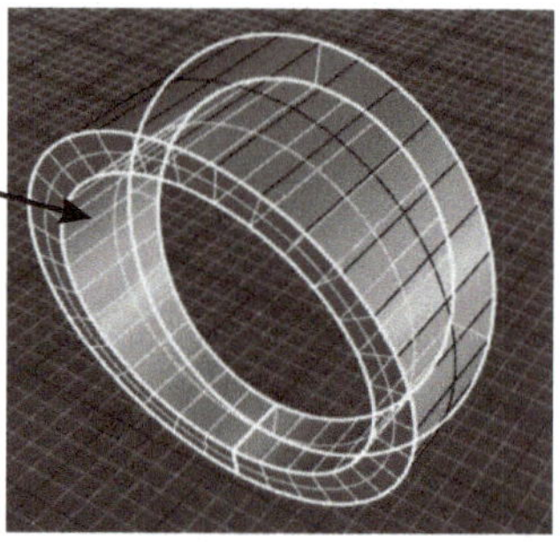

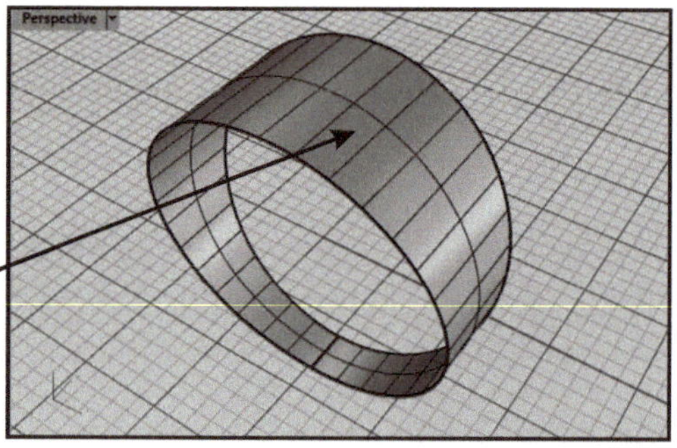

Perspective

- The outer surface will remain visible.

outer surface

Fig. 21

Creating the Enamel Cavities

- **ring ref 2** layer current.

current

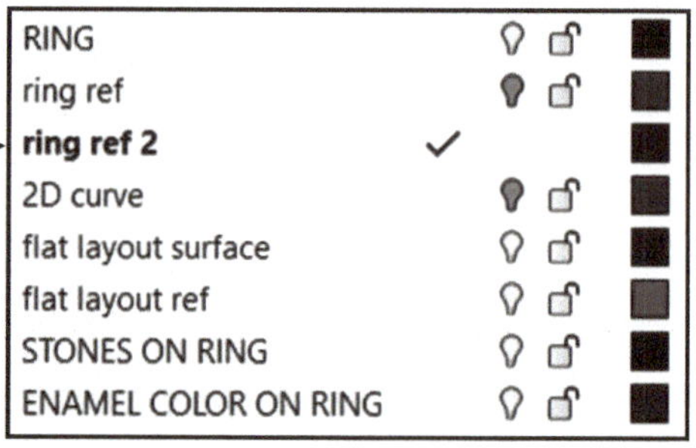

RING
ring ref
ring ref 2
2D curve
flat layout surface
flat layout ref
STONES ON RING
ENAMEL COLOR ON RING

Fig. 22

- **Standard tabbed toolbar.** **Standard**

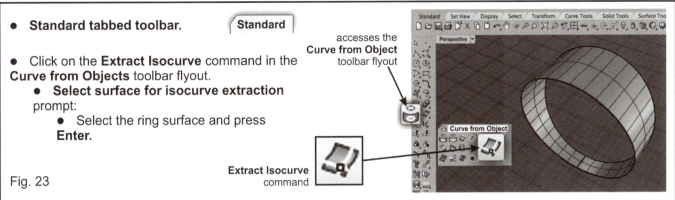

- Click on the **Extract Isocurve** command in the **Curve from Objects** toolbar flyout.
  - **Select surface for isocurve extraction** prompt:
    - Select the ring surface and press **Enter.**

accesses the
Curve from Object
toolbar flyout

Extract Isocurve command

Fig. 23

- **Select isocurve to extract** prompt:
  - Run the cursor over the surface and notice how a preview curve follows it.
  - Snap to the **mid point** of the seam at the bottom of the ring and click to set location. ❶
  - A curve has been created on the ring's surface in the direction of the isocurves.

- To change isocurve line direction, click on the **Toggle** option in the **Command Line.** ❷

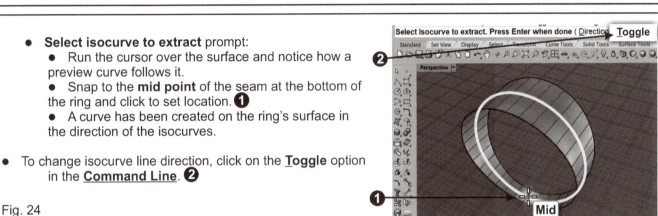

Fig. 24

- The direction of the preview line has been changed.
- Draw the cursor up and snap to the **mid point** of the previously created line.
- Click to set location. ❸

- Click to create another line ❹ about 3mm above the side of the ring.
- Press **Enter** to end the command.

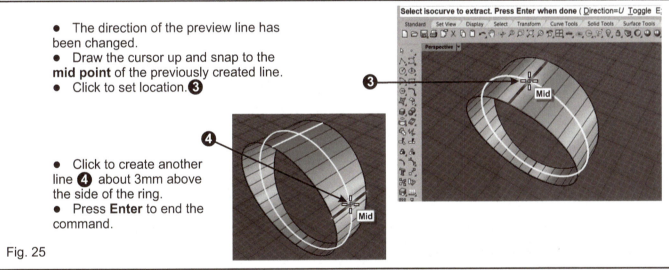

Fig. 25

- **Mirror** the line on the side over to the other side of the ring.

- Use the **Y axis** as the **mirror plane.**

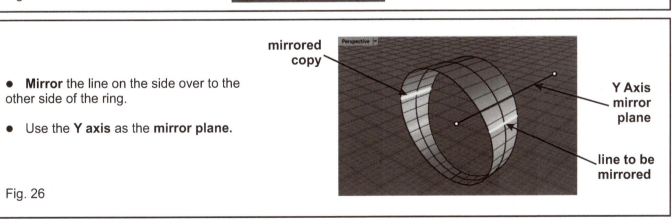

mirrored copy

Y Axis mirror plane

line to be mirrored

Fig. 26

- **flat layout surface** layer current.

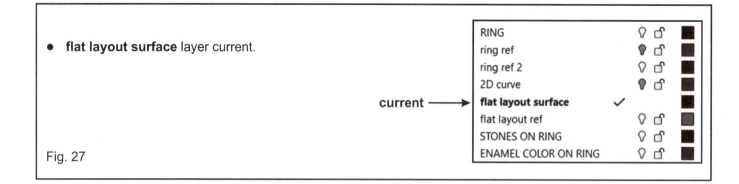

current ──────▶

RING	♀ ᗡ	■
ring ref	♀ ᗡ	■
ring ref 2	♀ ᗡ	■
2D curve	♀ ᗡ	■
flat layout surface	✓	■
flat layout ref	♀ ᗡ	■
STONES ON RING	♀ ᗡ	■
ENAMEL COLOR ON RING	♀ ᗡ	■

Fig. 27

- **Surface Tools tabbed toolbar.** [Surface Tools]

- Click on the **Unroll developable surface** command.
  - *This surface is **"developable"** because it is curved in just one direction. You could not use this command on a bombe shape because that surface is curved in more than one direction.*

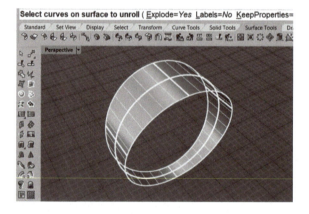

Unroll Developable Surface command

- **Select surface or polysurface to unroll** prompt:
  - Select the ring surface.
- **Select curves on surface to unroll** prompt:
  - Select all of the curves on the surface that were just created.
  - Press **Enter.**

Fig. 28

- A new **"unrolled"** surface, of the same dimensions, will appear on the construction plane along the Y Axis.

- The selected curves on the surface will also appear on the unrolled surface.

- The design of the enamel cavities will be worked out on this surface and then the design elements will be **"flowed"** back on to the surface of the ring.

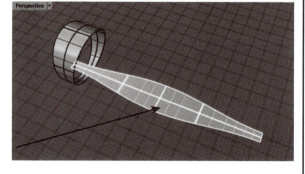

new unrolled surface

Fig. 29

555

- Drag and Rotate the new surface and reference geometry so that they lie in the X Axis direction to make the design work easier visually.

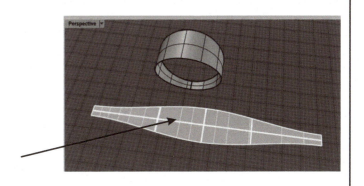

Fig. 30

- Select the curves that were unrolled along with the surface and **right-click** on the **flat layout ref** layer. ❶

- Click to select the **Change Object Layer** option ❷ in the drop-down menu.

- The curves will changed to the **flat layout ref** layer.

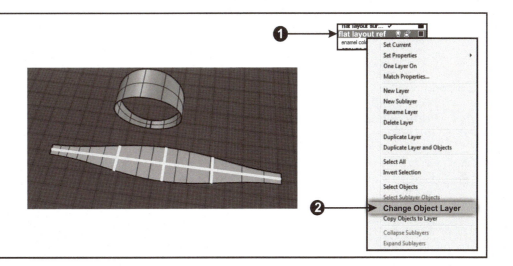

Fig. 31

- Turn off the **ring ref 2** layer.

RING		♀ ⌂	■
ring ref		♀ ⌂	■
ring ref 2		♀ ⌂	■
2D curve		♀ ⌂	■
flat layout surface	✓		■
flat layout ref		♀ ⌂	■
STONES ON RING		♀ ⌂	■
ENAMEL COLOR ON RING		♀ ⌂	■

Fig. 32

- Click on **File** in the **Menu Bar**. ❶

- Click to select **Import** in the drop-down context menu. ❷

    - Navigate to your designated folder to select **floral design for enamel.3dm** ❸
    - Access this in the **tutorial files** folder you downloaded from the website, www.rhinoforjewelry.
        - ***Support files for textbook<files for textbook***
    - Click the **Open** button.

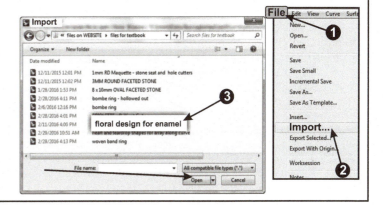

Fig. 33

- The floral design, with its single layer called **floral design for enamel**, will be imported onto the construction plane, centered on **"0"**.

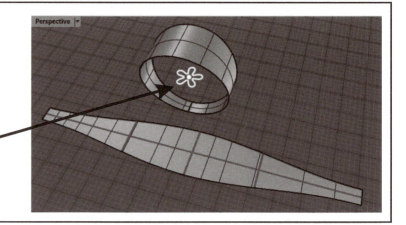

Fig. 34

- Select the motif and click on the **Copy** command.
    - **Point to copy from:** ❶
    - **Point to copy to:** ❷

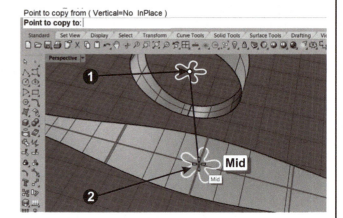

- **Point to copy to** prompt:
    - Use **near osnap** to create another copy on the side as shown. ❸
    - Press **Enter** to end the command.

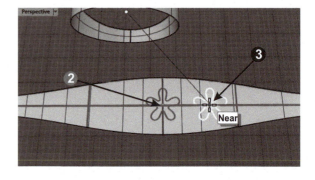

Fig. 35

- To refine the design, select the floral design on the right, type **"rotate**, and press **Enter**.
    - **Center of rotation:** ❶
    - **Angle or first reference point:** ❷
    - **Second reference point:** ❸

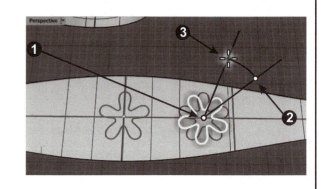

Fig. 36

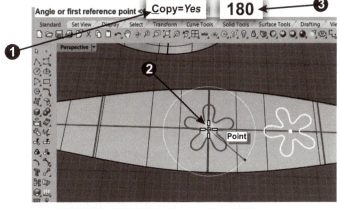

- **Center of rotation** prompt:
  - Click to toggle to the **Copy=Yes** ❶ option in the **Command Line.**
  - Snap to the point ❷ in the middle of the floral motif and click to set location.
- **Angle or first reference point** prompt:
  - Type **"180"** ❸ to set the angle of rotation and press **Enter.**

- The finished rotation creates a copy on the other side of the layout.

Fig. 37

Adding Flush Set Stones for Design Accents

- Drag the motif away from the center of the workspace. This will make space for the import of the stone in the next step.

Fig. 38

- Click on **File** in the **Menu Bar.**❶

- Click to select **Import** in the drop-down context menu.❷

  - Navigate to your designated folder to select **1mm RD Maquette - stone seat and hole cutters.3dm** ❸
  - Click the **Open** button.

    - Access this in the **files for tuto**rials folder you downloaded from the website, www.rhinoforjewelry.
    - **Support files for textbook<files for textbook.**
  - Click the **Open** button.

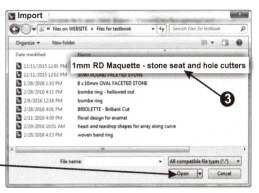

Fig. 39

- The stone and it's layers will be imported.

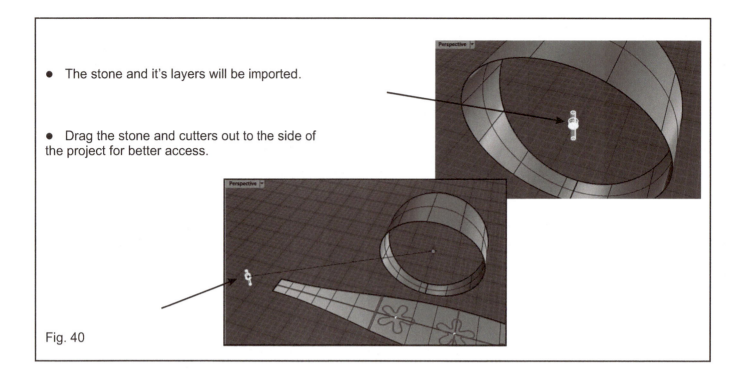

- Drag the stone and cutters out to the side of the project for better access.

Fig. 40

- **Front Viewport.**   Front ▾

- Select the point in the middle of the stone, type **"copy"**, and press **Enter.**
    - **Point to copy from:** ❶
    - **Point to copy to:** ❷

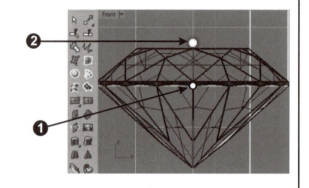

- The point has been copied to a location slightly above the top of the stone as this will be the point of reference when orienting the stone to the surface of the layout and the ring.

Fig. 41

- **Top Perspective view.**   ❶ 🚗 ❷ 🐢

- **Standard tabbed toolbar.**   ⌐ Standard

- Window select the stone and all of it's related objects and click on the **Group** command.

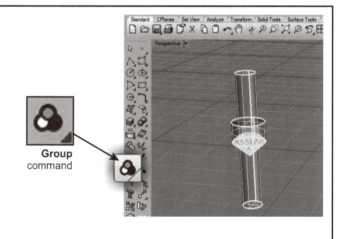

Group command

- When one element of this group is selected all will select.
- When one element of this group is edited or copied, the other elements in the group will update *even if their layers are turned off.*

Fig. 42

- Select the flat layout surface, type **"dir"** (for the **Direction** command), and press **Enter**.
  - *The direction arrows ("surface normals") must point upward as shown so that the stones that will be oriented to the surface in the next step will not be upside down.*
  - If necessary, click on the surface to change the arrow direction so that the arrows point up.
  - Press **Enter** to end the command.

Fig. 43

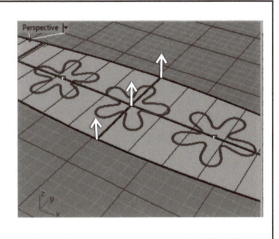

- Turn off the **stone seat cutter, stone hole cutter,** and **1mm ROUND BRILLIANT CUT** layers.

Fig. 44

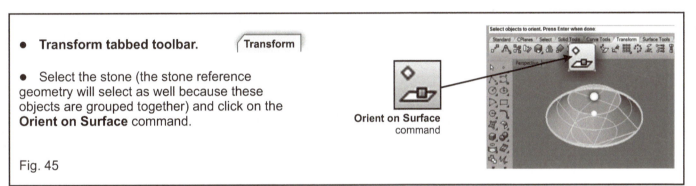

1MM ROUND STONE MAQUETTE	♀ ☁	■
stone reference geometry	♀ ☁	■
round brilliant	♀ ☁	■
STONE SEAT CUTTER	♀ ☁	□
STONE HOLE CUTTER	♀ ☁	□

- **Transform tabbed toolbar.**   〔**Transform**〕

- Select the stone (the stone reference geometry will select as well because these objects are grouped together) and click on the **Orient on Surface** command.

Orient on Surface
command

Fig. 45

- **Base point** prompt:
  - Snap on the point at the top of the stone and click to set location. **①**

- **Reference point for scaling and rotation** prompt:
  - Using **ORTHO**, draw the cursor straight up and click to set direction. **②**

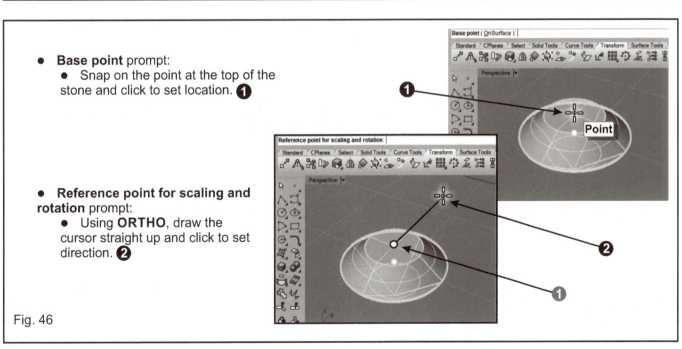

Fig. 46

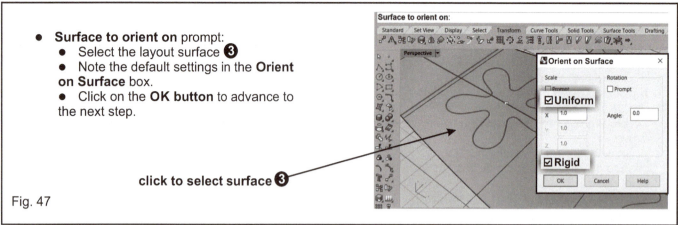

- **Surface to orient on** prompt:
  - Select the layout surface ❸
  - Note the default settings in the **Orient on Surface** box.
  - Click on the **OK button** to advance to the next step.

click to select surface ❸

Fig. 47

- **Point on surface to orient to** prompt:
  - In the **Command Line,** click to toggle the Copy=*No* option to **Copy=*Yes*.** ❹
  - As you draw the cursor over the surface, a preview of the stone will follow it.
  - Click on the approximate location shown. ❺
  - Press **Enter** to end the command.

Fig. 48

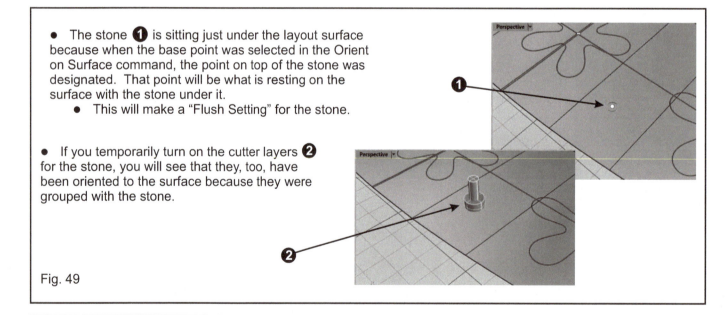

- The stone ❶ is sitting just under the layout surface because when the base point was selected in the Orient on Surface command, the point on top of the stone was designated. That point will be what is resting on the surface with the stone under it.
  - This will make a "Flush Setting" for the stone.

- If you temporarily turn on the cutter layers ❷ for the stone, you will see that they, too, have been oriented to the surface because they were grouped with the stone.

Fig. 49

- The next step will be to orient more stones on to the flat layout surface but for this step, each stone will be scaled at a specific designated diameter.

- Click on the **Orient on Surface** command again and follow previous steps.

Fig. 50

- **Surface to orient on** prompt:
  - Change the **Scale** setting in the **Orient on Surface** box from Uniform to **Prompt.** ❶
  - Press the **OK button** to proceed to the next step.

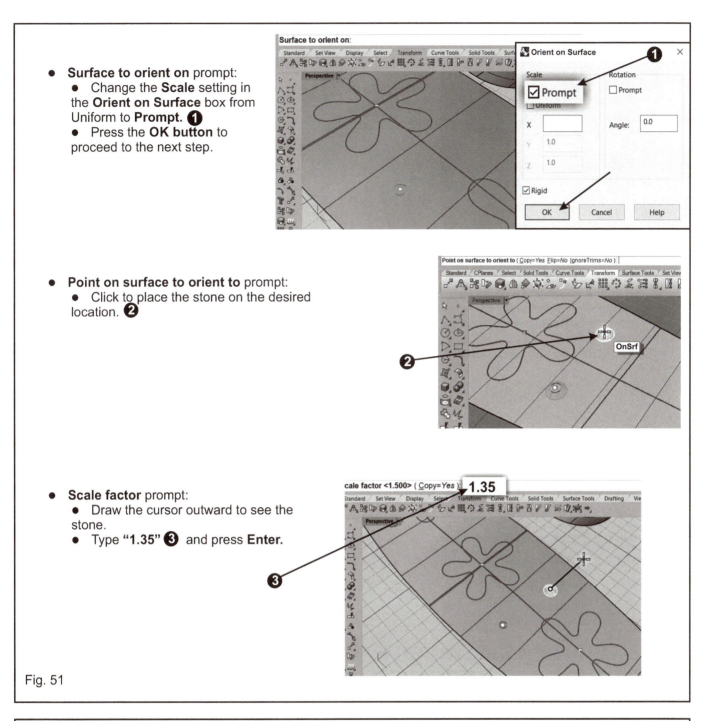

- **Point on surface to orient to** prompt:
  - Click to place the stone on the desired location. ❷

- **Scale factor** prompt:
  - Draw the cursor outward to see the stone.
  - Type **"1.35"** ❸ and press **Enter.**

Fig. 51

- A new **Ø1.35mm diameter** stone has been created.

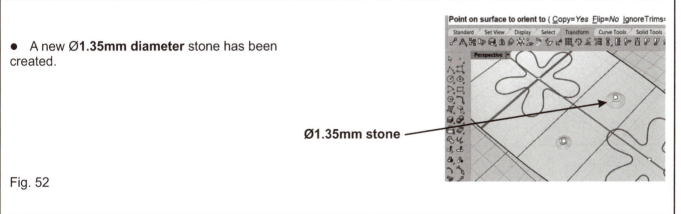

Ø1.35mm stone

Fig. 52

- Move the cursor and click on the approximate location shown. ❶
- Draw the cursor outward to see the stone.
- **Scale factor** prompt:
  - Type "**1.45**" and press **Enter**.

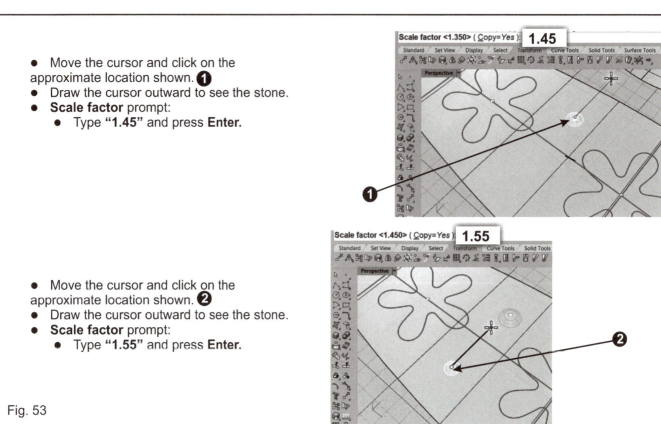

- Move the cursor and click on the approximate location shown. ❷
- Draw the cursor outward to see the stone.
- **Scale factor** prompt:
  - Type "**1.55**" and press **Enter**.

Fig. 53

- If you turn on the other layers associated with the stone, you will see that they have been oriented and scaled along with the visible element you used in the **Orient on Surface** command.

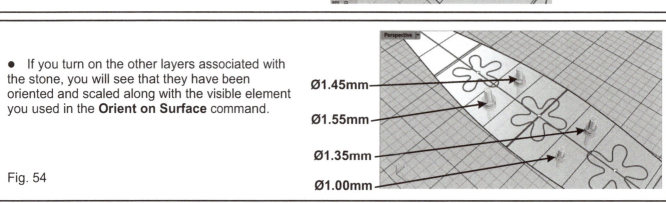

Ø1.45mm
Ø1.55mm
Ø1.35mm
Ø1.00mm

Fig. 54

Flowing the Design to the Surface of the Ring

- Notice all of the layers that are now turned off.

- **flat layout surface** layer current.

current ⟶ flat layout surface

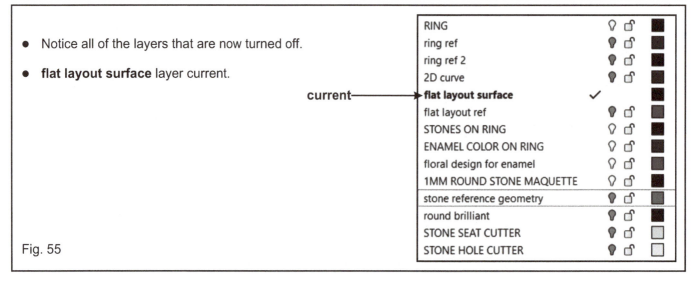

RING			
ring ref			
ring ref 2			
2D curve			
flat layout surface	✓		
flat layout ref			
STONES ON RING			
ENAMEL COLOR ON RING			
floral design for enamel			
1MM ROUND STONE MAQUETTE			
stone reference geometry			
round brilliant			
STONE SEAT CUTTER			
STONE HOLE CUTTER			

Fig. 55

- Select the original stone and floral design motif that are sitting on the construction plane.
  - Type **"lock"** and press **Enter** to lock these objects.

Fig. 56

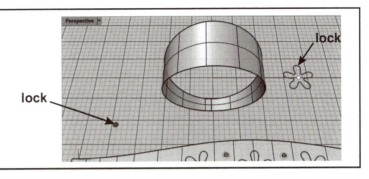

- Select both layout and ring surfaces, type **"dir"**, and press **Enter.**

- Make sure that the normal arrows on the ring are pointing outward.

- Make sure that the normal arrows on the flat layout are pointing upward.

- Press **Enter** or **Esc** to exit the command.

Fig. 57

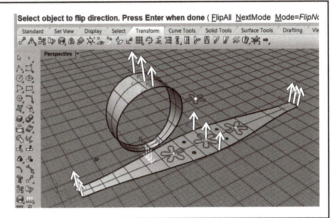

- In the next step, stones and floral design curves will be flowed on to the surface of the ring.
- Before using this command, it is necessary to designate **"matching corners"** for the flat layout surface and the ring surface.

Fig. 58

- **Zoom** in on the left end of the flat layout.

- Select the flat layout surface, type **"dir"** (for the **Direction** command), and press **Enter.**
  - The white surface normal arrows will appear and, when you run the cursor over the surface, it will display the **U** and **V** directions of the surface.
  - **U direction arrows: red**
  - **V direction arrows: green**

- **This is a good direction for both arrows so you can press Esc to cancel the command.**
  - Use **Command Line** options to adjust arrow directions.

Fig. 59

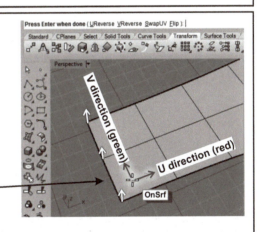

- Type **"point"** and press **Enter.**

- Use **near osnap** to place a point on the surface edge shown.
- This will be a mark to show where to click to designate the corner of this surface in the **Flow Along Surface** command coming up.

Fig. 60

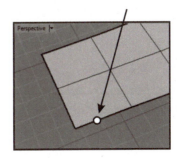

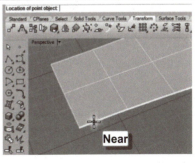

- Select the ring surface, type **"dir"**, and press **Enter**.

- Navigate to the bottom of the ring.

- Draw the cursor over the top left corner as shown and note that the **U** direction arrow needs to be re-directed so that it will be pointed to the left.
  - Click on the **Ureverse** option to change the direction of the **U arrow**.

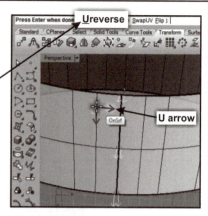

- The **U arrow** has been reversed and now this corner (although it looks upside down) now matches the designated corner on the flat layout.
- Press **Enter** to complete the command.

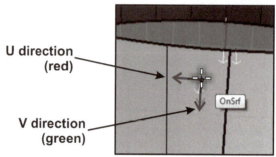

- note: The arrows on your piece may not be pointing in the directions shown. Use the other editing options in the **Command Line** to adjust directions.

Fig. 61

- Note the location of the two points indicating the locations of the two matching corners of layout and ring surfaces.

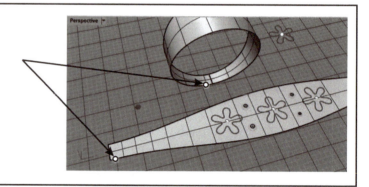

Fig. 62

- **Transform tabbed toolbar.**

- Click to turn on **Record History.**

- Select the floral designs and click on the **Flow Along Surface** command.

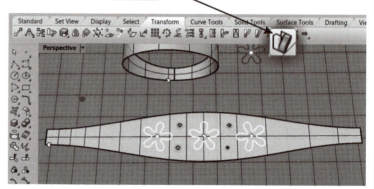

Fig. 63

565

- **Base surface - select near a corner** prompt:
  - Make sure that you are toggled to the **R̲igid=*No*** option. **❶**
  - Click on the edge **❷** near the point that you placed in the lower left corner of the layout surface.

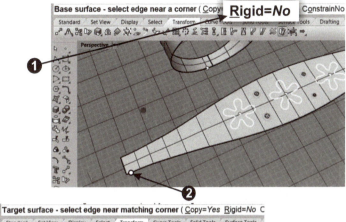

- **Target surface - select near matching corner** prompt:
  - Click on the edge where the point was placed to designate this as the matching corner.

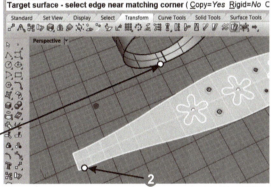

Fig. 64

- The floral design curves have been **"flowed"** to the ring surface.

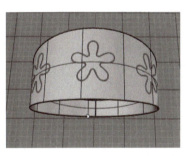

Fig. 65

- Click on **Record History** again.

- Select all of the stones on the layout surface and click on the **Flow Along Surface** again (or just press **Enter** to repeat the command).

Flow Along Surface command

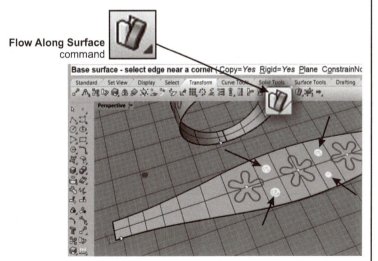

Fig. 66

- **Base surface - select edge near a corner** prompt:
    - **Important**: Make sure to toggle the Rigid=No option to Rigid=Yes **1**
        - ***When the stones flow to the surface, you don't want them to mold themselves to the surface the way the floral design curves did because stones are, by their nature, rigid.***
    - Click to select the flat layout surface on the edge **2** near the designated corner as before.

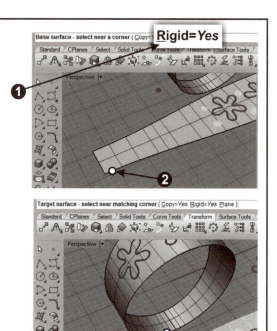

- **Target surface - select edge near matching corner** prompt:
    - Click to select the ring surface on the edge **3** of the designated matching corner.

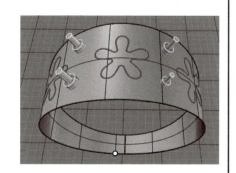

Fig. 67

- If you turn on the layers of the objects that were grouped with the stones, you will see, even though their layers were turned off, that they, too, were flowed to the surface.

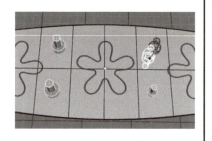

Fig. 68

- If you want, you can further edit the design on the flat surface on the right side of the design.

- History will update the *changes **on the surface of the ring*** because History was used for the Flow Along Surface command.

Fig. 69

- Make sure that all of the stone layers are turned off.

Fig. 70

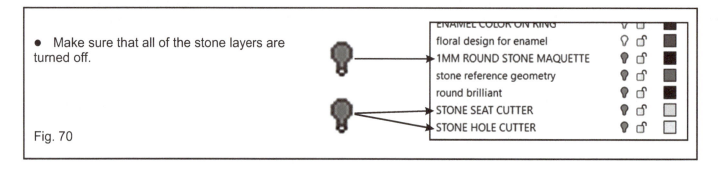

ENAMEL COLOR ON RING			■
floral design for enamel	♀	⚿	■
1MM ROUND STONE MAQUETTE	♀	⚿	■
stone reference geometry	♀	⚿	■
round brilliant	♀	⚿	■
STONE SEAT CUTTER	♀	⚿	□
STONE HOLE CUTTER	♀	⚿	□

- Select the surface of the ring. **1**

- Click on the **Split** command.

Split
command

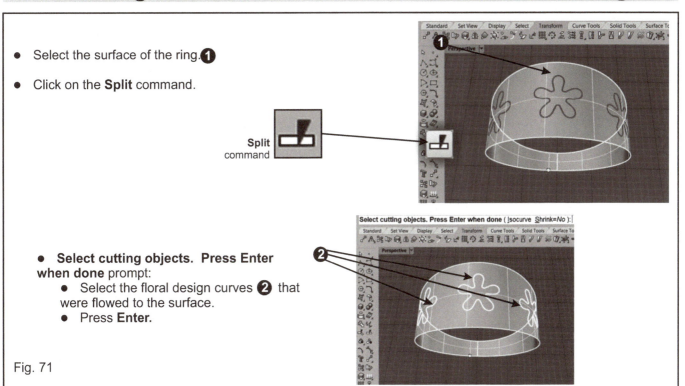

- **Select cutting objects. Press Enter when done** prompt:
  - Select the floral design curves **2** that were flowed to the surface.
  - Press **Enter.**

Fig. 71

- **RING** layer current.

- Turn off the following layers:
  - **flat layout surface**
  - **flat layout ref**
  - **floral design on enamel**

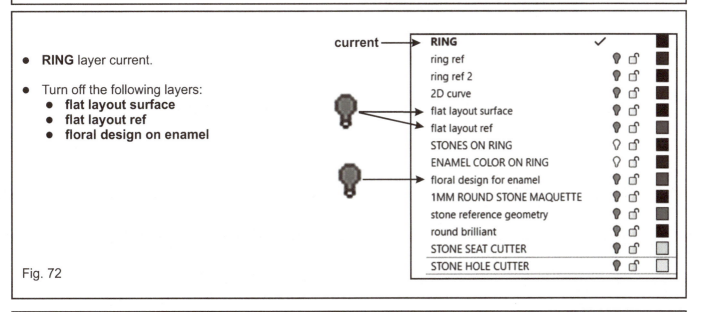

Fig. 72

- The black outlines of the floral shapes are actually surface edges where the ring surface was split by the floral design curves.

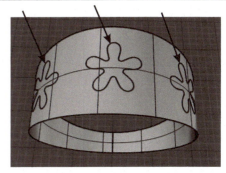

Fig. 73

- **Surface Tools tabbed toolbar.** `Surface Tools`

- Select the little split out floral surfaces **1** and click on the **Offset Surface** command.

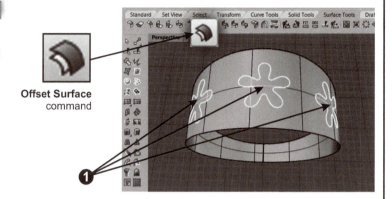

Offset Surface
command

- **Select object to flip direction. Press Enter when done** prompt:
  - Notice that the surface direction arrows are pointed outward.
  - Click on the **FlipAll** option **2** in the **Command Line.**

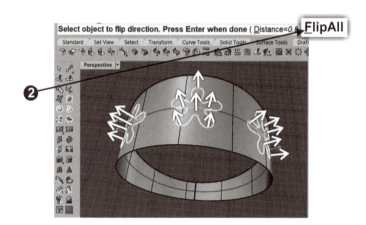

- The surface direction arrows are now all pointed toward the inside of the ring. **3**
- Make sure that the **Solid=Yes** option is displayed in the **Command Line** options.
- Type **".8"** and press **Enter** to set the depth of the offset.
- Press **Enter** to complete the solid offset.

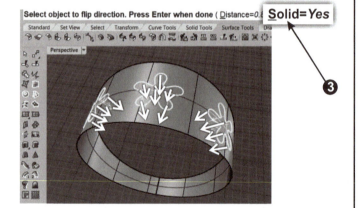

- All three little surface have been offset to the inside of the ring to a depth of .9mm. All 3 offsets are **closed polysurfaces**.

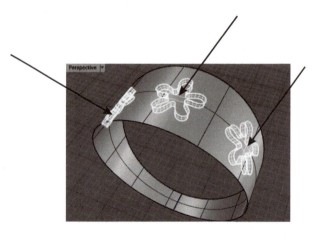

Fig. 74

- **Hide** the main ring surface for visual clarity in the next step.

- **RIGHT-CLICK** on the Explode button for the **Extract Surface** command.

RIGHT-CLICK for **Extract Surface** command

- Click to extract the ***top surfaces only*** from all three solid offsets as shown.
- Press **Enter** to finish the command.

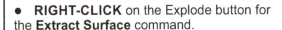

Select surfaces to extract. Press Enter when done (_OutputLayer=Input_

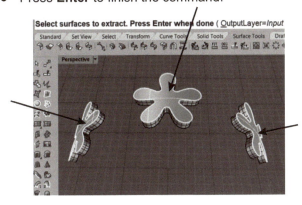

click to extract the top surface only from each solid offset

Fig. 75

- With the extracted surfaces still selected, **RIGHT-CLICK** on the **ENAMEL COLOR ON RING** layer. ❶

- Click on the **Change Object Layer** option ❷ in the drop-down menu to change the layer of the selected objects.

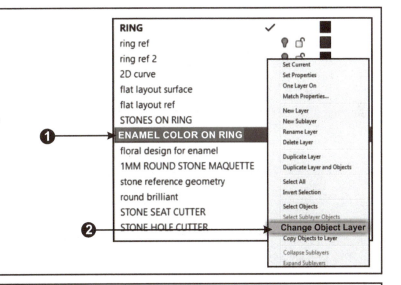

RING	✓	■
ring ref	💡 🔓	■
ring ref 2		■
2D curve	
flat layout surface	
flat layout ref	
STONES ON RING	
ENAMEL COLOR ON RING	
floral design for enamel	
1MM ROUND STONE MAQUETTE	
stone reference geometry	
round brilliant	
STONE SEAT CUTTER	
STONE HOLE CUTTER	

Set Current
Set Properties
One Layer On
Match Properties...
New Layer
New Sublayer
Rename Layer
Delete Layer
Duplicate Layer
Duplicate Layer and Objects
Select All
Invert Selection
Select Objects
Select Sublayer Objects
Change Object Layer
Copy Objects to Layer
Collapse Sublayers
Expand Sublayers

Fig. 76

- Type **"Show"** and press **Enter.**

- The surface and inner polysurface of the ring band will be visible again.

- Notice that the extracted enamel surfaces are now displayed in the color of the ENAMEL COLOR ON RING layer.

surface

inner polysurface

Fig. 77

- Turn off the **ENAMEL COLOR ON RING** layer.

Fig. 78

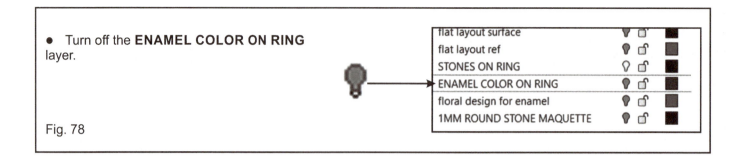

- With the **ENAMEL COLOR ON RING** layer turned off, the enamel cavities are visible.

Fig. 79

- Select all elements of the ring:
  - Outer surface.
  - Inner polysurface that is now visible.
  - Open polysurfaces that are the enamel cavities.

- Click on the **Join** command.

Join
command

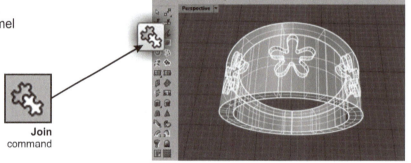

- The ring will now be a single closed polysurface.

- The **History Line** should say: **5 surfaces or polysurfaces joined into one closed polysurface.**
  - This number may vary, depending on how many enamel cavities have been developed in your design.

Fig. 80

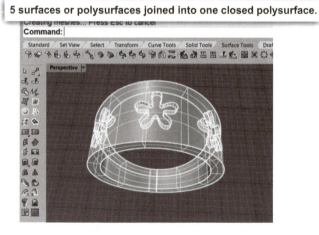

5 surfaces or polysurfaces joined into one closed polysurface.

- **Solid Tools** tabbed toolbar. `Solid Tools`

- **LEFT-CLICK** for the **Fillet Edges** command.
  - **Select edges to fillet** prompt:
    - Type **".8"** and press **Enter** to designate the radius of the fillet. **❶**

LEFT-CLICK for **Fillet Edges** command

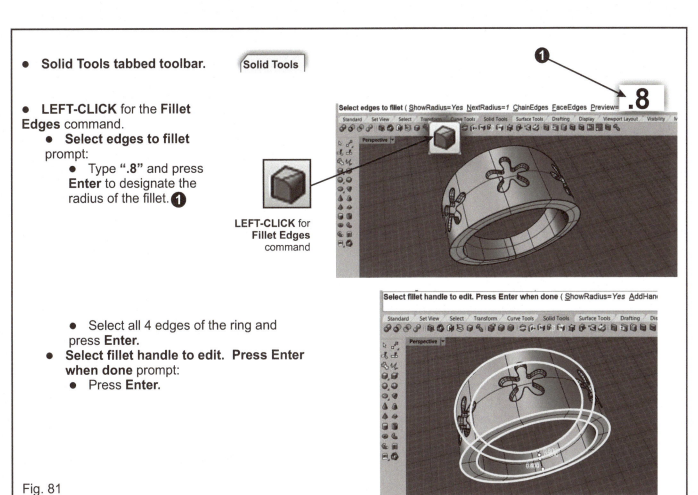

  - Select all 4 edges of the ring and press **Enter.**
  - **Select fillet handle to edit. Press Enter when done** prompt:
    - Press **Enter.**

Fig. 81

- The edges of the ring will be rounded.

- If the fillets do not work, try a smaller fillet radius.

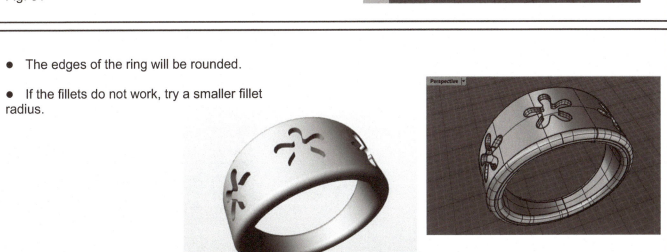

Fig. 82

- Turn on the **stone seat cutter** and the **stone hole cutter** layers.

- All other layers associated with stones are turned off.

Fig. 83

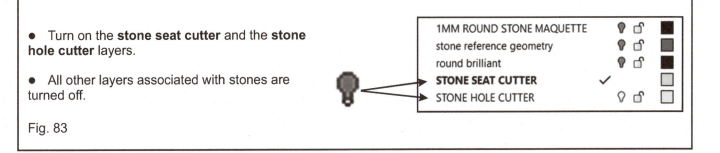

- **Standard tabbed toolbar.** `Standard`

- Select all of the **stone seat cutters** and **stone hole cutters** and click on the **Ungroup** command.
  - You must ungroup all of these objects or the upcoming Boolean Difference command will not work.

Fig. 84

Ungroup command

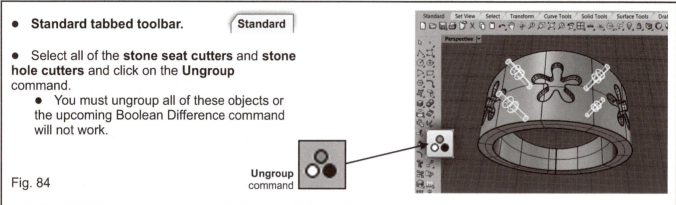

- **Solid Tools tabbed toolbar.** `Solid Tools`

- With the stone cutters still selected, click on the **Boolean Union** command.
  - Because both seat and hole cutters will be used, it is useful to boolean these two cutters together so that the Boolean Difference command needs to be employed only once.
  - ***This will break History but that is OK because you will have finished the editing of the design.***

Fig. 85

Boolean Union Command

- Click on the **Boolean Difference** command.
  - **Select surfaces or polysurfaces to subtract from** prompt:
    - Select the ring ❶ and press **Enter.**

Boolean Difference command

- **Select surfaces or polysurfaces to subtract with** prompt:
  - Make sure to toggle to the **Deleteinput=*No*** option.❷
  - Select the cutters ❸ and press **Enter.**

Fig. 86

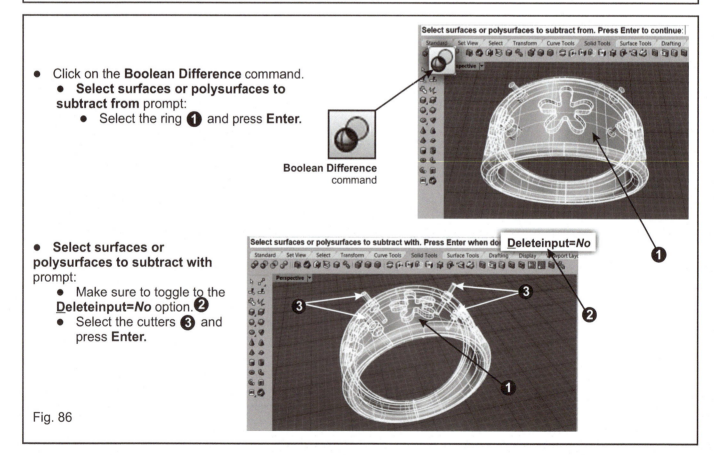

- Turn off the following layers:
  - **STONE SEAT CUTTER**
  - **STONE HOLE CUTTER**

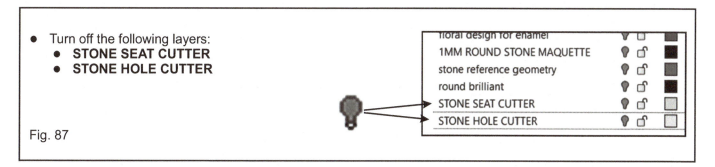

Fig. 87

- Notice that the stone seats and stone holes have been cut out.

Fig. 88

- Turn on the following layers:
  - **ENAMEL COLOR ON RING**
  - **ROUND BRILLIANT**

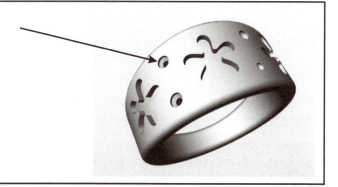

Fig. 89

- Select all of the **round brilliant** stones ❶ on the ring.

- **RIGHT-CLICK** on the **STONES ON RING** layer.❷
  - Click on the **Change Object Layer** option ❸ in the drop-down context menu.

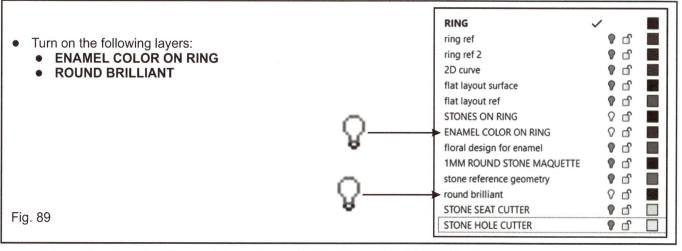

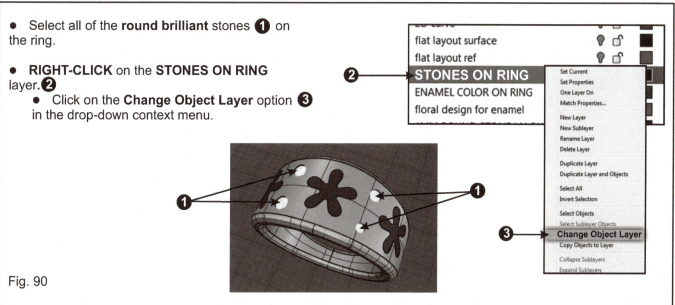

Fig. 90

● Now you can turn off the original **round brilliant** layer.

Fig. 91

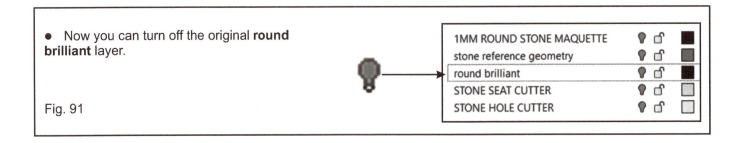

1MM ROUND STONE MAQUETTE	🔆 ⛬ ⬛
stone reference geometry	🔆 ⛬ ⬛
round brilliant	🔆 ⛬ ⬛
STONE SEAT CUTTER	🔆 ⛬ ⬜
STONE HOLE CUTTER	🔆 ⛬ ⬜

● You can apply **solid fillets** to the stone holes on the inside of the ring for a smoother, more finished look.

● In this example, a fillet radius of .5mm was used.

● Note: If you have stones close to the edge, the fillets may not cut through the previous fillet surfaces on the sides of the ring.

Fig. 92

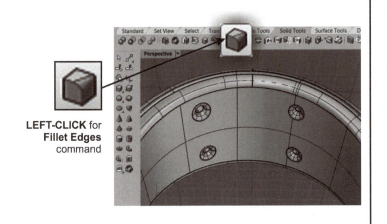

LEFT-CLICK for **Fillet Edges** command

● Displayed with Rhino Render properties in **Raytraced** display mode.

Fig. 93

Additional Enamel Strategies

Interpolate on Surface

- **pendant ref** layer current.

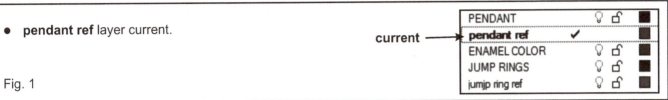

current →

PENDANT	♀ 🔒	■
pendant ref	✓	■
ENAMEL COLOR	♀ 🔒	■
JUMP RINGS	♀ 🔒	■
jumjp ring ref	♀ 🔒	■

Fig. 1

- **Top Viewport.** Top ▼

- **Curve Tools tabbed toolbar.** Curve Tools

- Use the **Ellipse: from Center** command to create a 20mm x 30mm ellipse around **"0"**.

Ellipse: from Center command

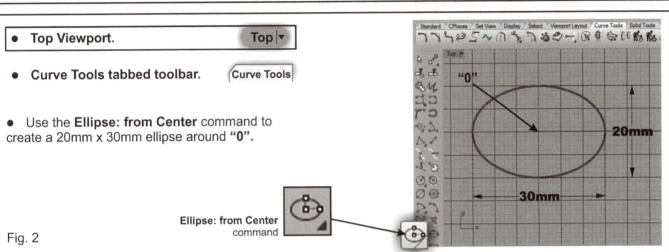

Fig. 2

- **Top Perspective view.** ❶ 📱 ❷ 🚗

- **Solid Tools tabbed toolbar.** Solid Tools

- Click on the **Ellipsoid: from Center** command.
  - **Ellipsoid center** prompt:
    - Type **"0"** and press **Enter.**
  - **End of first axis** prompt:
    - Snap to the quad point on the right of the ellipse and click to set location.❶
  - **End of second axis** prompt:
    - Snap to the quad point on the bottom of the ellipse and click to set location. ❷
  - **End of third axis** prompt:
    - Type **"4"** and press Enter.

- The resulting solid ellipse will measure **30mm x 20mm x 8mm**

Ellipsoid: from Center command

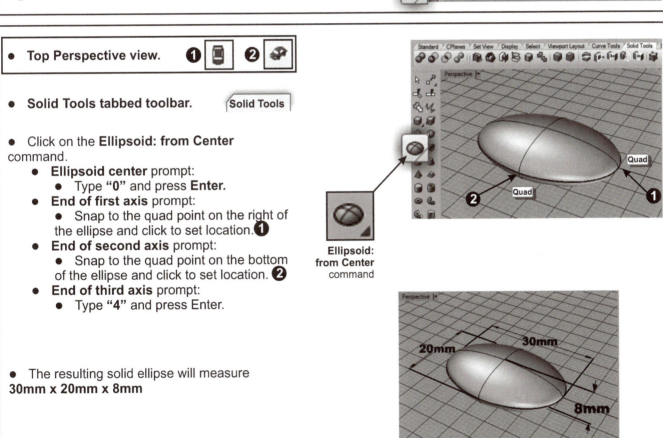

Fig. 3

- Click on the **Split** command.
  - **Select objects to split. Press Enter when done** prompt:
    - Select the solid ellipsoid and press **Enter. ❶**

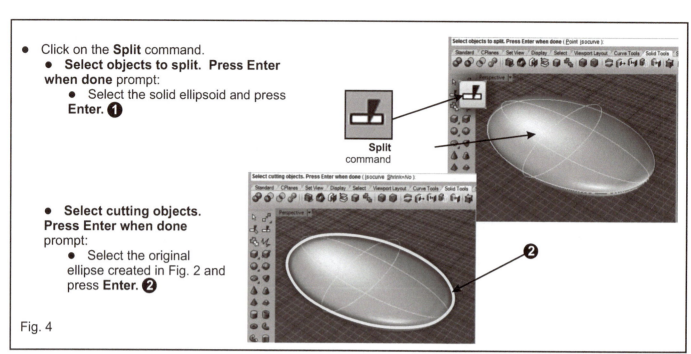

  - **Select cutting objects. Press Enter when done** prompt:
    - Select the original ellipse created in Fig. 2 and press **Enter. ❷**

Fig. 4

- Select the bottom split-off section of the ellipsoid, type **"hide"** and press **Enter.**

- The selected bottom split off segment of the ellipsoid will be hidden.

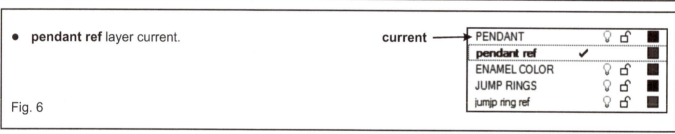

Fig. 5

- **pendant ref** layer current.

current ⟶

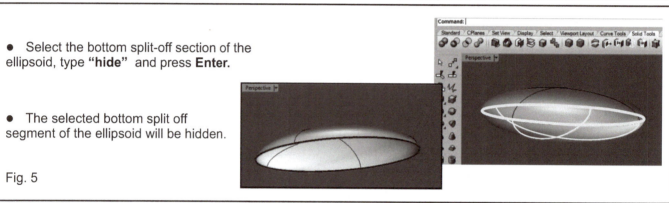

PENDANT	♀	🔒	■
pendant ref	✓		■
ENAMEL COLOR	♀	🔒	■
JUMP RINGS	♀	🔒	■
jumjp ring ref	♀	🔒	■

Fig. 6

- **Top Viewport.**   Top ▾

- **Curve Tools tabbed toolbar.**   Curve Tools

- Click on the **Interpolate on Surface** command in the **Curve** toolbar flyout.
  - **Select surface to draw curve on** prompt:
    - Select the ellipsoid surface.

accesses the **Curve** toolbar flyout

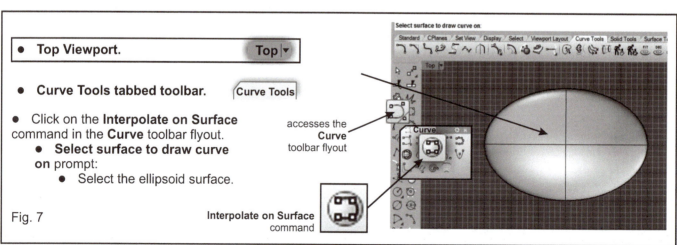

Fig. 7

Interpolate on Surface command

- **Start of curve** prompt:
  - Click where you want to start the interpolate points curve.

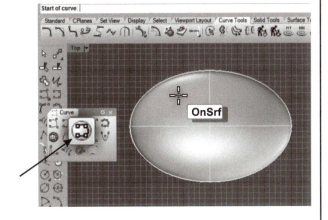

- **Next point. Press Enter when done** prompt:
  - Continue to click to create the interpolate points curve.

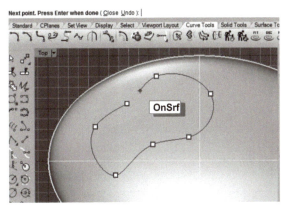

- To make sure that this is a closed curve, snap to the first point or click on the **Close** option in the **Command Line.**

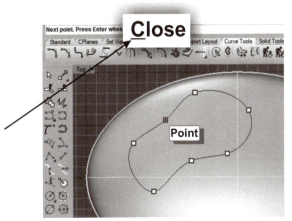

- You can continue to create freeform curves on the domed surface.

- All these curves need to closed curves.

- After you have finished with the curves, you can proceed to create enamel cavities.

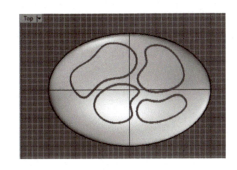

Fig. 8

- The enamel cavities have been completed and the bottom part of the ellipse has been made visible again. (see strategy used in the *Domed Pendant* with **Enamel** tutorial)
- All elements have been joined together to create a closed polysurface.

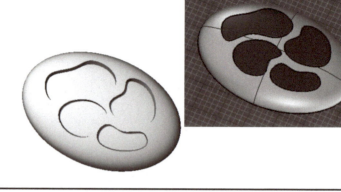

Fig. 9

Creating Jump Rings

- **jump ring ref** layer current.

Fig. 10

current ⟶ **jumjp ring ref** ✓

- **Top Viewport.** **Top** ▼

- **Curve Tools tabbed toolbar.** Curve Tools

- Click on the **Circle: Center, Radius** command.
  - **Center of circle** prompt:
    - Use **near osnap** to snap on the rim of the ellipsoid as shown.

Circle: Center, Radius
command

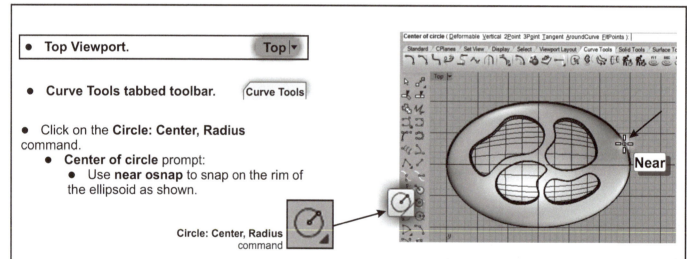

- **Diameter** prompt:
  - Type **"3"** (or the diameter you choose) and press **Enter.**
    - This will set the inner diameter of the jump ring.

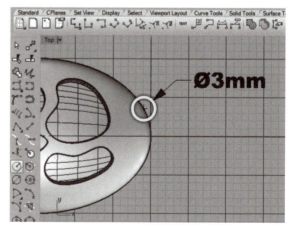

Fig. 11

- Offset the circle to a distance of **.5mm**.

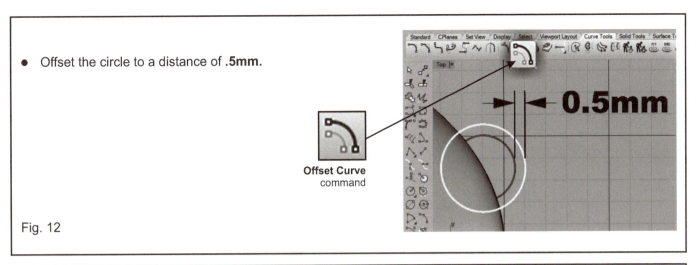

Offset Curve
command

Fig. 12

- **JUMP RINGS** layer current.

current ⟶

PENDANT	💡 🔓 ⬛
pendant ref	💡 🔓 ⬛
ENAMEL COLOR	💡 🔓 ⬛
JUMP RINGS	✓ ⬛
jumjp ring ref	💡 🔓 ⬛

Fig. 13

- **Solid Tools tabbed toolbar.**　　**Solid Tools**

- Select the new offset and click on the **Pipe** command.
  - **Radius for closed pipe** prompt:
    - Type **".5"** and press **Enter**.
  - **Point for next radius. Press Enter for none** prompt:
    - Press **Enter.**

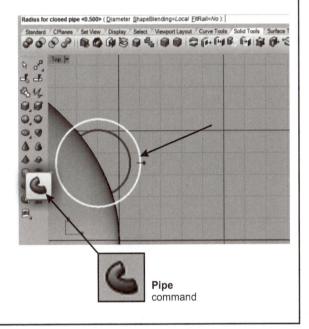

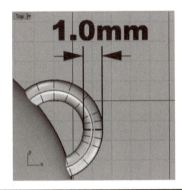

1.0mm

- The finished jump ring
has a **1mm wire thickness**.

Pipe
command

Fig. 14

- **Mirror** the new jump ring to the other side of
the pendant/necklace.

- Save this file as **Enamel Pendant-Necklace 1**

Fig. 15

Sketch on Surface and Pipe Commands

- Select and explode the pendant.

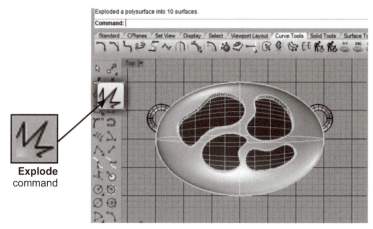

Explode
command

- Window select and **Delete** all enamel cavities and enamel color surfaces.

Fig. 16

- **Surface Tools tabbed toolbar.** Surface Tools

- **LEFT-CLICK** for the **Untrim** command.
  - **Select edge to untrim** prompt:
    - Click on the edge of one of the empty holes as shown.
    - The selected opening will be **"untrimmed"**.

- **Select edge to untrim** prompt:
  - Continue to "untrim" the rest of the openings.

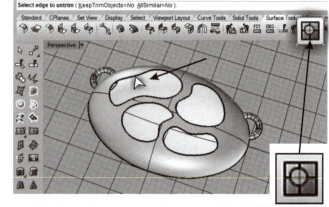

LEFT-CLICK for
Untrim
command

- After "untrimmming" all of the holes, the model will be a single closed surface again.

Fig. 17

- Select and **Hide** the bottom surface again.

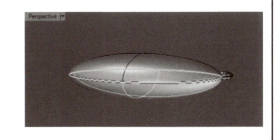

Fig. 18

- **PENDANT** layer current.

- **Lock** the **JUMP RINGS** layer.

Fig. 19

- **RIGHT-CLICK** for the **Sketch on Surface** command.
  - **Select surface to sketch on** prompt:
    - Select the surface.
  - **Click and drag** to sketch on surface.
  Press **Enter when done** prompt:

RIGHT-CLICK for
Sketch on Surface
command

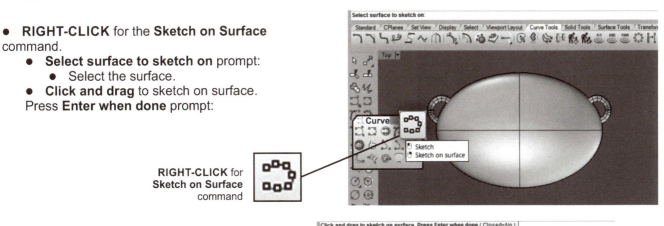

- Sketch on the surface to create your design and press **Enter** when done.

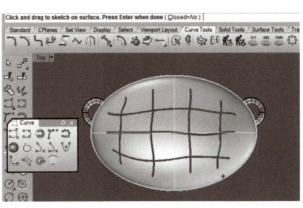

Fig. 20

- You can **Drag** or **Control Point Edit** to update your design.

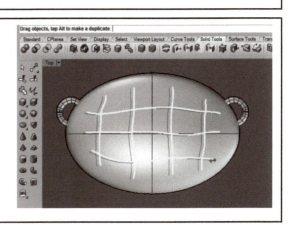

Fig. 21

- After editing, the edited curves will no longer be in contact with the surface.

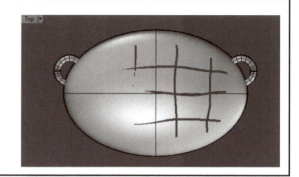

Fig. 22

- Select the curves, type **"pull"** (button for **Pull Curve** command is in the **Curve from Object** toolbar) and press **Enter.**

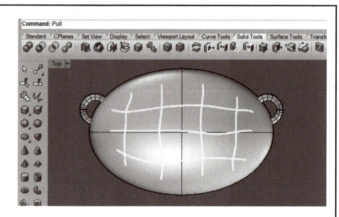

DeleteInput=*Yes*

- **Select surfaces and meshes that pull. Press Enter when done** prompt:
  - Make sure that the **DeleteInput=***Yes* option is enabled in the **Command Line.**
  - Select the surface and press **Enter.**

select surface

- The curves have now been "pulled" to the surface which means that they are once again in total contact with the surface.

Fig. 23

- Create a new layer named **cutters** and make that new layer current.

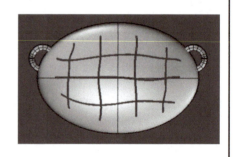

Fig. 24

PENDANT		♀	⌂	■
pendant ref		♀	⌂	■
ENAMEL COLOR		♀	⌂	■
JUMP RINGS		♀	🔒	■
jumjp ring ref		♀	⌂	■
current ⟶	**cutters**	✓		■

- **Solid Tools tabbed toolbar.**　Solid Tools

- Select all of the sketched curves and click on the **Pipe: Flat Caps** command.
  - **Pipe radius** prompt:
    - Press **Enter** to accept the default pipe radius of **1mm.**

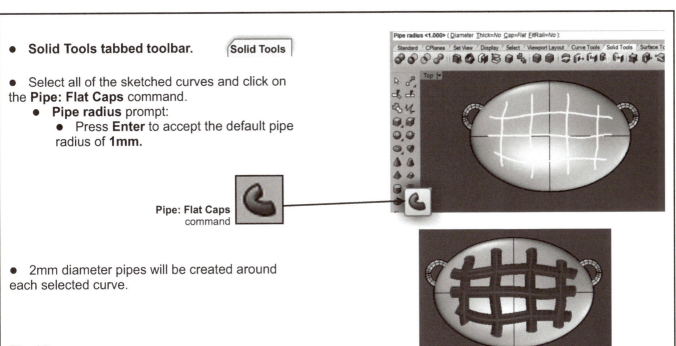

Pipe: Flat Caps
command

- 2mm diameter pipes will be created around each selected curve.

Fig. 25

- If pipes cross each other, as in this design, select all of the pipes and click on the **Boolean Union** command.

- The pipes will now be one single closed polysurface.

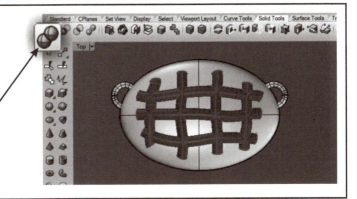

Fig. 26

Boolean Union
command

- Turn off the **pendant ref** layer.

- **PENDANT** layer current.

Fig. 27

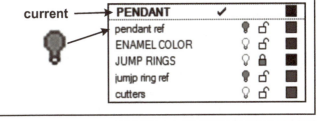

current

PENDANT	✓	■
pendant ref	💡 🔓	■
ENAMEL COLOR	💡 🔓	■
JUMP RINGS	💡 🔒	■
jump ring ref	💡 🔓	■
cutters	💡 🔓	■

- Click on the **Split** command.
  - **Select objects to split. Press Enter when done** prompt:
    - Select the surface of the pendant and press **Enter. ❶**

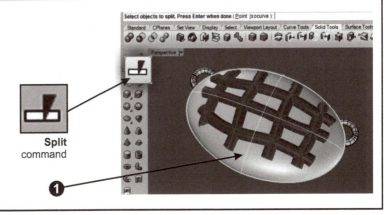

Split
command

Fig. 28

❶

584

- **Select cutting objects** prompt:
  - Select the cutter ❷ and press **Enter**.

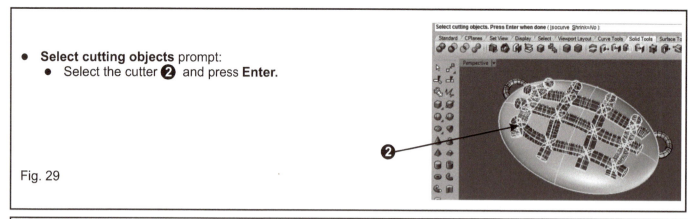

Fig. 29

- Turn off the **cutters** layer.

Fig. 30

- Black lines on the surface will show where it has been split to make the design for the enamel.

Fig. 31

- **Surface Tools tabbed toolbar.** [Surface Tools]

- Select the split off surface shown and click on the **Offset Surface** command.❶

  Offset Surface
  command

- **Select object to flip direction. Press Enter when done** prompt:
  - Click on the **FlipAll** option in the **Command Line.** ❷

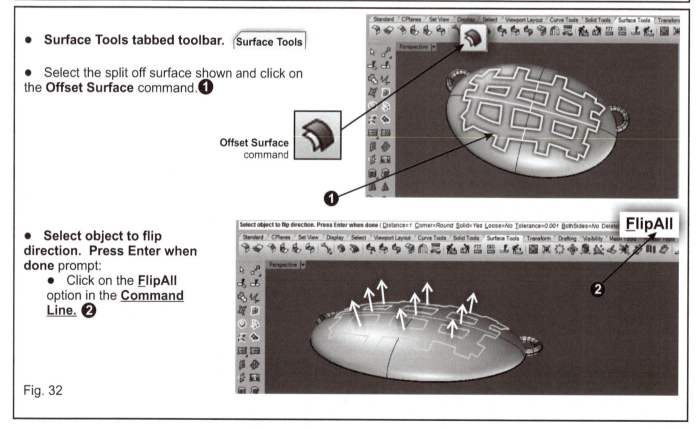

Fig. 32

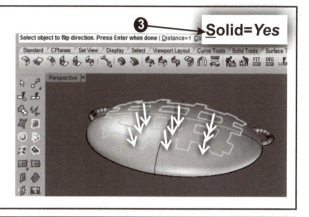

- Normal arrows will now be pointing down, setting the direction of the surface offset.
  - Make sure that the **Solid=*Yes*** option ❸ is enabled in the **Command Line.**
- Press **Enter** to accept the default **1mm offset distance** and complete the command.

Fig. 33

- Look on the reverse side of the surface and you will see the solid extrusion that was just created.

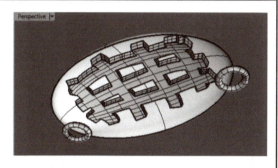

Fig. 34

- **RIGHT-CLICK** for the **Extract Surface** command.
  - **Select surfaces to extract. Press Enter when done** prompt:
    - Select the top surface of the new surface solid offset and press **Enter.**

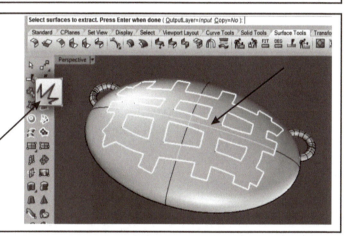

RIGHT-CLICK for
Extract Surface
command

Fig. 35

- The newly extracted top surface has been changed to the **ENAMEL COLOR** layer.

- Turning off the enamel color layer will reveal the shape of the model.

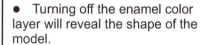

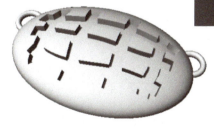

Fig. 36

- Type **"show"** and press **Enter** to bring the bottom of the ellipsoid back to visibility.

Fig. 37

- Window select the pieces of the ellipsoid and enamel cavity and click on the **Join** command.

- The ellipsoid and its enamel will now be a single closed polysurface.

Join
command

Fig. 38

- Now you can unlock the **JUMP RINGS** layer and select it along with the rest of the model to use the **Boolean Union** command to create a single closed polysurface.

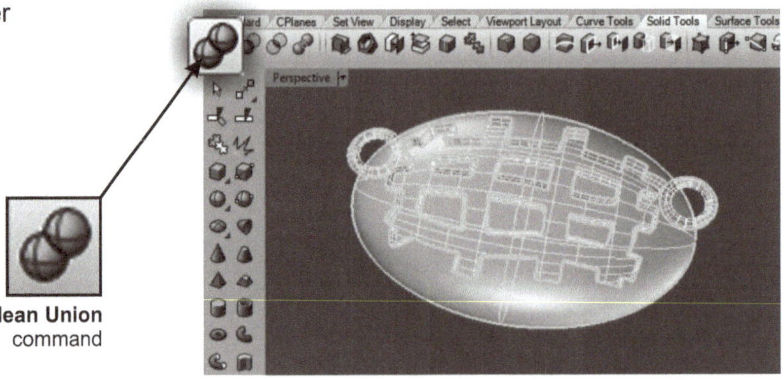

Boolean Union
command

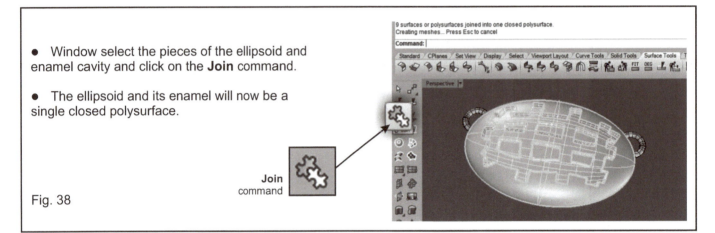

Fig. 39

Model of a Flower
Cage Edit command for Editing Polysurfaces

Modeling the Basic Flower Shape

- Change the names of the two top layers to:
  - **PETALS**
  - **petal ref**
  - **CAGE**

- **petal ref** layer current.   Fig. 1

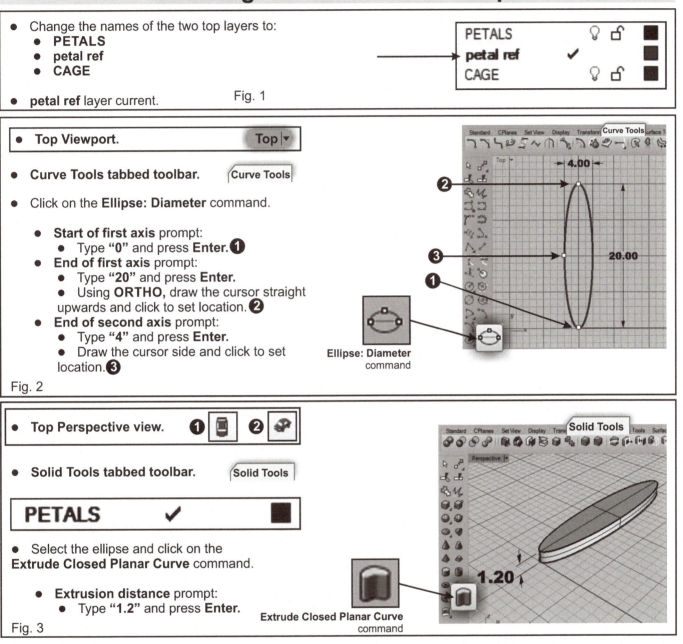

- **Top Viewport.**   `Top ▼`

- **Curve Tools tabbed toolbar.**   `Curve Tools`

- Click on the **Ellipse: Diameter** command.

  - **Start of first axis** prompt:
    - Type **"0"** and press **Enter.** ❶
  - **End of first axis** prompt:
    - Type **"20"** and press **Enter.**
    - Using **ORTHO**, draw the cursor straight upwards and click to set location. ❷
  - **End of second axis** prompt:
    - Type **"4"** and press **Enter.**
    - Draw the cursor side and click to set location. ❸

Ellipse: Diameter command

Fig. 2

- **Top Perspective view.** ❶ ❷

- **Solid Tools tabbed toolbar.**   `Solid Tools`

PETALS ✓ ■

- Select the ellipse and click on the **Extrude Closed Planar Curve** command.

  - **Extrusion distance** prompt:
    - Type **"1.2"** and press **Enter.**

Extrude Closed Planar Curve command

Fig. 3

- Select the new extrusion and **LEFT-CLICK** on the **Explode** command.

LEFT-CLICK for **Explode** command

Fig. 4

- **Delete** the vertical surface.

- Two surfaces remain.

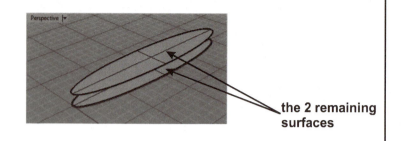

the 2 remaining surfaces

Fig. 5

- **Surface Tools tabbed toolbar.** Surface Tools

  - Click on the **Blend Surface** command.

    - **Select segment for first edge** prompt:
    - Click on the edge of one of the surfaces.❶
    - **Select next segment for first edge. Press Enter when done** prompt:
    - Press **Enter.**
    - **Select segment for second edge** prompt:
    - Select the edge of the other surface.❷

Blend Surface command

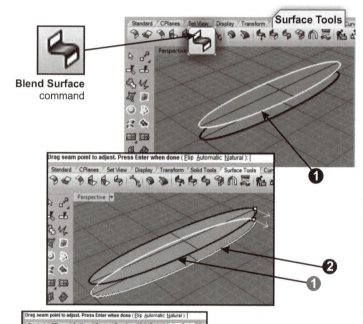

  - **Drag seam point to adjust. Press Enter when done** prompt:
    - Make sure that the seam is straight.
    - Press **Enter.**

  - Select the **Tangency** option in the **Adjust Surface Blend** dialog box.
  - Click the **OK button** to complete the command.

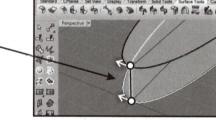

- The completed blend surface will create a smooth transition between the top and bottom surfaces.

- Displayed here in **Rendered viewport mode.**

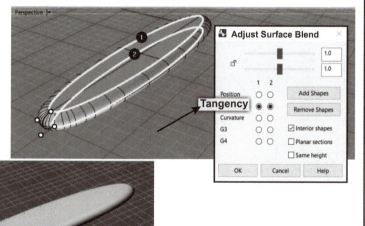

Fig. 6

- Window select all 3 surfaces and click on the **Join** command.

- The **History Line** will tell you: *3 surfaces or polysurfaces joined into one closed polysurface.*

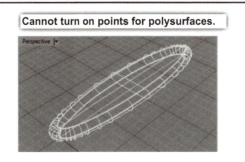

3 surfaces or polysurfaces joined into one closed polysurface.

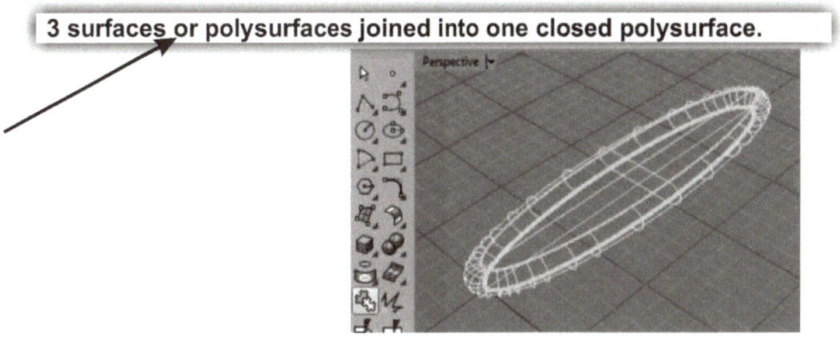

Fig. 7

- The next step will be to edit the polysurface into a graceful petal shape.

- Select the new closed polysurface, type **"PointsOn"**, and press **Enter.**

  - The **History Line** will inform you that you **Cannot turn on points for polysurfaces.**

Cannot turn on points for polysurfaces.

Fig. 8

- Select the polysurface and click on the **Turn On Solid Control Points** command in the **Solid Tools** toolbar flyout.

- Only two solid control points will appear along the seam.

- This will be too limited for the editing of this shape.

Fig. 9

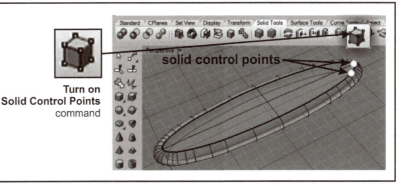

Turn on Solid Control Points command

solid control points

Cage Edit Command

- Turn off **petal ref** layer.

- **CAGE** layer current.

Fig. 10

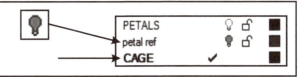

PETALS		
petal ref		
CAGE	✔	

- **Transform tabbed toolbar.** [Transform]

  - **LEFT-CLICK** on the **Cage Edit** command.

    - **Select captive objects. Press Enter when done** prompt:
      - Select the petal polysurface and press **Enter.**
    - **Select control object** prompt:
      - Click on the **BoundingBox** option in the **Command Line.**
    - **Coordinate system <World>** prompt:
      - Press **Enter** to accept the default **World** option - the default viewports are all in the "World" coordinate system.

Fig. 11

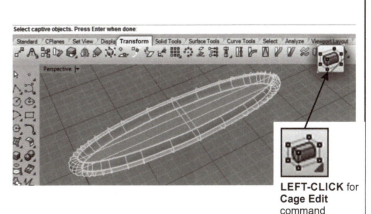

Select captive objects. Press Enter when done:

LEFT-CLICK for **Cage Edit** command

- **Cage points** prompt:
  - Select the **XPointCount=4** option in the <u>**Command Line.**</u>
    - **XPointCount <4>** prompt: type **"7"** and press **Enter.**

  - The <u>**Command Line**</u> will now reflect the adjustment of the amount of points in the **X** direction.

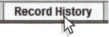

Cage points (XPointCount=7 YPointCount=4 ZPointCount=4 XDegree=3 YDegree=3 ZDegree=3):

Fig. 12

- **Region to edit <Global>** prompt:
  - Press **Enter** to accept the default **Global** option - the editing cage will control the whole object.
  - A preview of the Editing Cage will become visible.
  - Press **Enter** to end the command.

- The completed editing cage will feature control points in the X, Y, and Z directions.

- Note that in the X direction, there are 7 rows of control points as specified.

  - note: A cage is also referred to as a **control object.**

- Press the **Esc** key to turn off control points.

Fig. 13

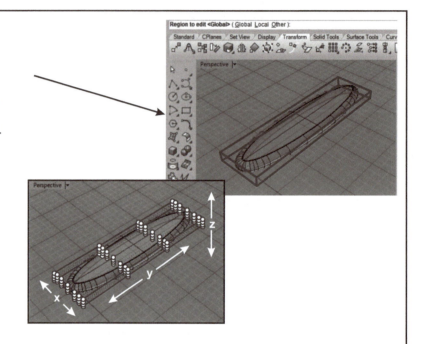

- Click to turn on **Record History.**

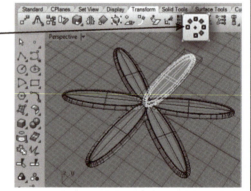

Polar Array command

- Select the **petal -** but **NOT THE CAGE** - and click on the **Polar Array** command.

  - **Center of polar array: "0"**
  - **Number of items: "6"**
  - **Angle to fill or first reference point:** press **Enter** to accept the **360° default.**
  - Press **Enter** again to accept the preview shown of the finished polar array.

Fig. 14

- Select all of the petals, type **"lock"**, and press **Enter.**

Fig. 15

Cage Editing the Flower

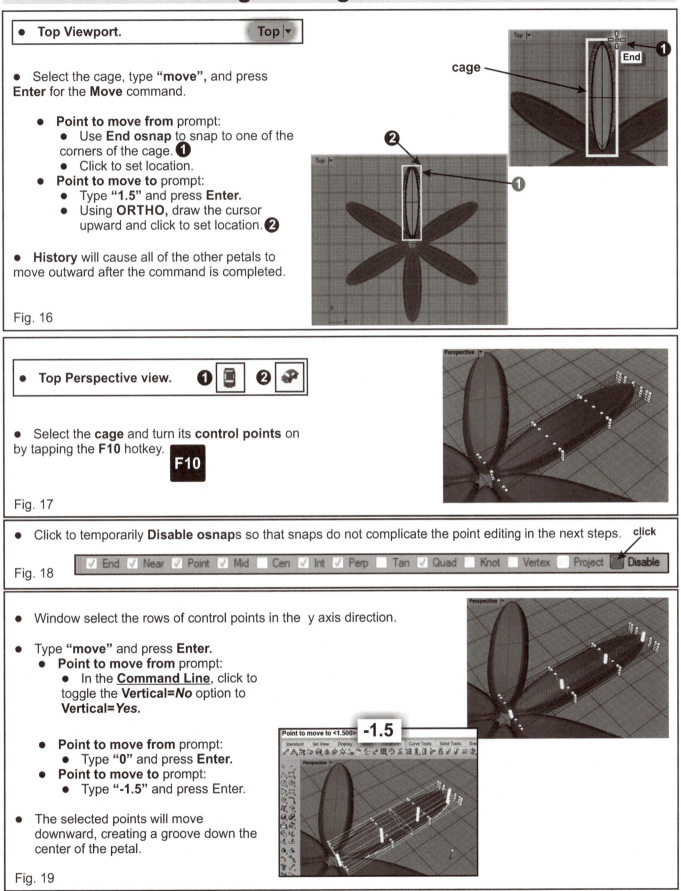

- **Top Viewport.**   Top ▼

- Select the cage, type **"move"**, and press **Enter** for the **Move** command.

  - **Point to move from** prompt:
    - Use **End osnap** to snap to one of the corners of the cage. ❶
    - Click to set location.
  - **Point to move to** prompt:
    - Type **"1.5"** and press **Enter.**
    - Using **ORTHO,** draw the cursor upward and click to set location. ❷

- **History** will cause all of the other petals to move outward after the command is completed.

Fig. 16

cage

- **Top Perspective view.**   ❶ 🖥   ❷ 🔄

- Select the **cage** and turn its **control points** on by tapping the **F10** hotkey.   **F10**

Fig. 17

- Click to temporarily **Disable osnap**s so that snaps do not complicate the point editing in the next steps.   click

Fig. 18
☑ End ☑ Near ☑ Point ☑ Mid ☐ Cen ☑ Int ☑ Perp ☐ Tan ☑ Quad ☐ Knot ☐ Vertex ☐ Project ☐ Disable

---

- Window select the rows of control points in the y axis direction.

- Type **"move"** and press **Enter.**
  - **Point to move from** prompt:
    - In the **Command Line**, click to toggle the **Vertical=No** option to **Vertical=Yes.**

  - **Point to move from** prompt:
    - Type **"0"** and press **Enter.**
  - **Point to move to** prompt:
    - Type **"-1.5"** and press Enter.

- The selected points will move downward, creating a groove down the center of the petal.

Point to move to <1.500>   **-1.5**

Fig. 19

- **History** will again update the child objects.

Fig. 20

- Select the middle two rows of control points, type **"move",** and press **Enter** for the **Move** command.

    - **Point to move from** prompt:
        - Make sure that the **Vertical=Yes** option is toggled on.
    - **Point to move from** prompt:
        - Type **"0"** and press **Enter.** ❶
    - **Point to move to** prompt:
        - Type **"3"** and press **Enter.** ❷

    - If necessary draw the cursor upward and click to set location.

- The rest of the petals will update.

- *Note: you can also click and drag these points in a vertical direction if you hold down the Ctrl key while dragging.*

Fig. 21

- Click to enable the object snaps once again. You can disable them again after this next step.   Fig. 22

- Select the two outer rows of control points shown.

- The next step will be a 3-D Rotation in which you will set the desired rotation axis.

- **RIGHT-CLICK** for the **Rotate 3-D** command.

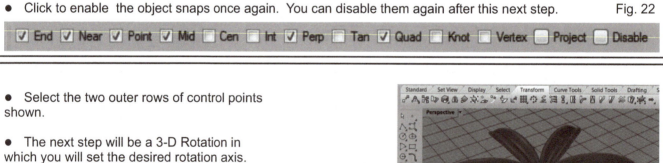

RIGHT-CLICK for **Rotate 3-D** command

Fig. 23

- **Start of rotation axis** prompt:
  - Snap to one of the control points in the middle of the outer row.
  - Click to set location. **❶**

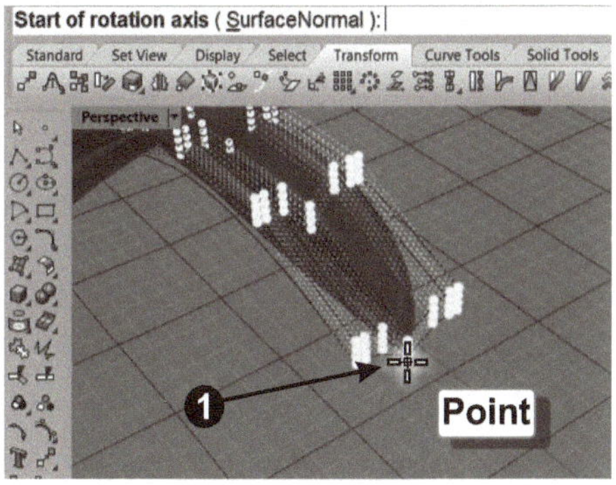

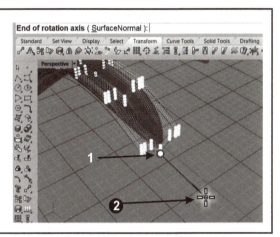

Fig. 24

- **End of rotation axis** prompt:
  - Draw the cursor upward in the general direction of the Y Axis as shown for a comfortable distance of about 8mm and click to set location. **❷**

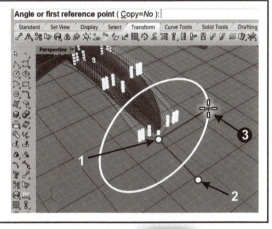

Fig. 25

- **Angle or first reference point** prompt:
  - When the white preview circle appears, click on a location like the one shown to set the first reference point. **❸**

Fig. 26

- **Second reference point** prompt:
  - Draw the cursor around to rotate the selected control points around the designated axis.
  - Click to set a location similar to the one shown. **❹**

- note: you also can type an exact angle, in this case about **"50"** and press **Enter** to get the same result.

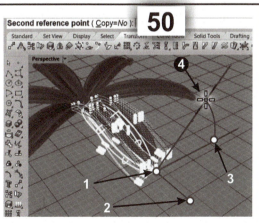

Fig. 27

- When the rotate 3-D command is completed, the rest of the petals will update.

- The petals now have a twisted look created by the use of the Rotate 3-D command.

Fig. 28

- The next two steps will widen the petals at their inner ends and then to create an overlapping of the petals.

- Select the row of control points at the inner end of the cage and click on the **Scale 1-D** command in the **Scale toolbar flyout.**

accesses the
Scale
toolbar flyout

Scale 1-D
command

Base point. Press Enter for automatic. (Copy=*No* Rigid=*No*):

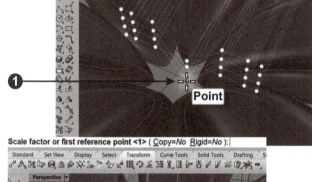

- **Origin point** prompt:
  - Snap to one of the points in the center group and click to set location.❶

Scale factor or first reference point <1> (Copy=*No* Rigid=*No*):

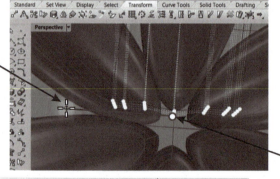

- **First reference point** prompt:
  - Using **ORTHO**, draw the cursor out to the side as shown and click to set location.❷

Second reference point (Copy=*No* Rigid=*No*):

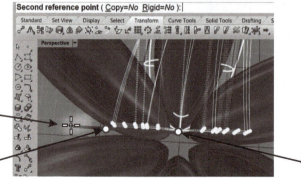

- **Second reference point** prompt:
  - Draw the cursor further out about 2mm and click to set location. ❸

Fig. 29

- The petals are now intersecting each other at the center of the flower.

- The next editing will cause a subtle overlapping effect of the petals in this location.

Fig. 30

- Select 3 rows of control points at the left side if the cage as shown.

- Activate the **Move** command again, making sure that the **Vertical** option is turned on.

  - **Point to move from** prompt:
    - Type "0" and press **Enter.**
  - **Point to move to** prompt:
    - Type "1" and press **Enter.**

Move
command

- The petals will now overlap at the center of the flower.

Fig. 31

- You can select the next row of control points and use the **Scale 1-D** command again to widen the petal at that point.
  - **Base point:** ❶
  - **First reference point:** ❷
  - **Second reference point:** ❸

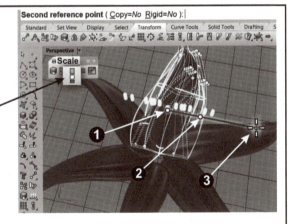

Scale 1-D
command

Fig. 32

Importing a Round Faceted Stone

- Click on **File** in the **Menu Bar**. ❶

- Click to select **Import** in the drop-down context menu. ❷

  - Navigate to your designated folder to ❸ select **3mm ROUND FACETED STONE**.
    - *This Rhino file was modeled and saved in a previous chapter of this book.*
  - Click the **Open** button.

    - *Also available for download on the www.rhinoforjewelry.com website on the files for textbook page.*

Fig. 37

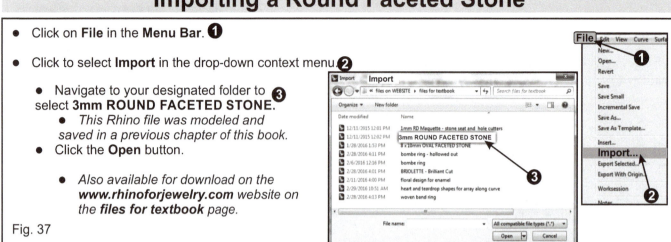

- The stone will appear centered on **"0"**.

- The next step will be to raise the stone a little so that it does not intersect the petal objects and also allows for some room for future setting.

Fig. 38

- **Front Viewport.**   Front▼

- Select the stone and it's reference geometry, type **"move"**, and press **Enter.**

  - **Point to move from** prompt:
    - Type **"0"** and press **Enter.** ❶
  - **Point to move to** prompt:
    - Type **"1"** and press **Enter.**
    - Using **ORTHO**, draw the cursor upward and click to set location. ❷

- The stone should now be slightly above the center of the flower and not intersecting with it.

Fig. 39

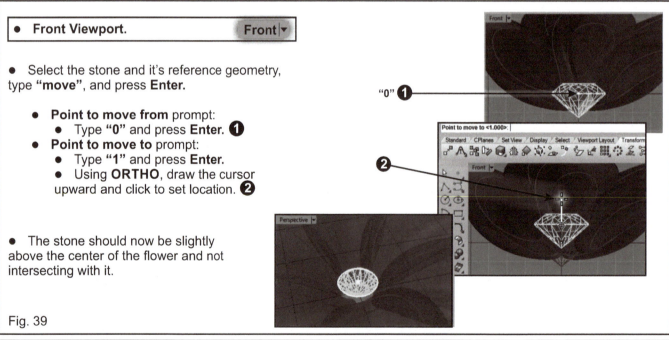

- Turn off the **PETALS** layer.

- Create two 2 layers:
  - **BEZEL**
  - **bezel ref - current**

Fig. 40

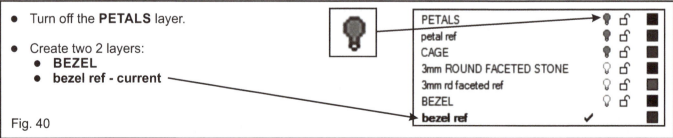

PETALS		
petal ref		
CAGE		
3mm ROUND FACETED STONE		
3mm rd faceted ref		
BEZEL		
bezel ref	✓	

- Click on the **Polyline** command.

    - **Start of polyline** prompt:
        - Snap to the **End point** at the bottom of the girdle as shown and click to set location. **1**

    - **Next point of polyline** prompt:
        - Type "**.7**" and press **Enter.**
        - Move the cursor over to the side of the stone and use **Near** or **Intersection** osnap to snap to the side of the stone - you actually will be snapping to one of the many facet seams.
        - Click to set location. **2**

- Continue to draw the profile curve for the bezel using **ORTHO** for all angles after the second location.

- Note that the drawing has already been started with locations **1** and **2**

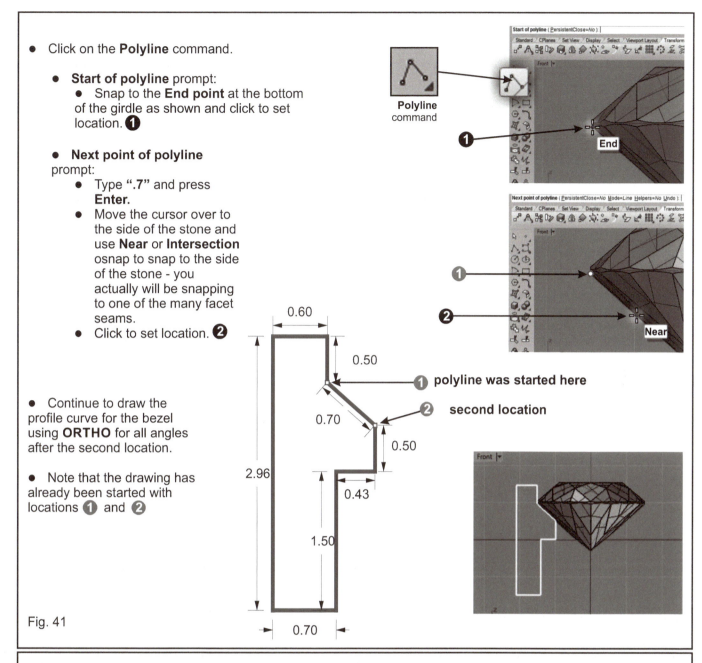

1 polyline was started here

2 second location

Fig. 41

- To ensure that the profile curve for the bezel is perfectly planar (lying flat on the construction plane), select the new polyline and click on the **Project to Cplane** command.

    - **Delete input objects** prompt:
        - Click on the **Yes** option in the **Command Line** and press **Enter.**

- The polyline will lie flat on the construction plane.

Fig. 42

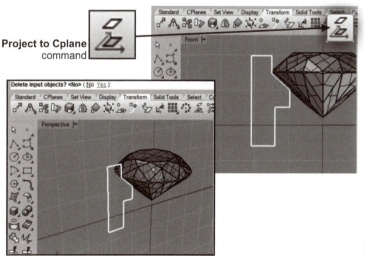

- Front Perspective view. **1** 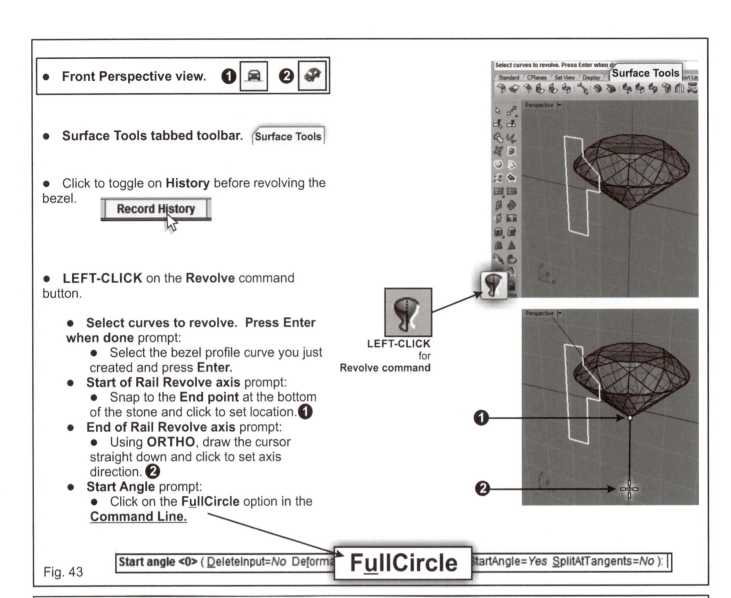 **2**

- **Surface Tools tabbed toolbar.** ⌐Surface Tools⌐

- Click to toggle on **History** before revolving the bezel.

  | Record History |

- **LEFT-CLICK** on the **Revolve** command button.

  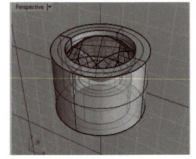

  LEFT-CLICK
  for
  Revolve command

  - **Select curves to revolve. Press Enter when done** prompt:
    - Select the bezel profile curve you just created and press **Enter**.
  - **Start of Rail Revolve axis** prompt:
    - Snap to the **End point** at the bottom of the stone and click to set location.**1**
  - **End of Rail Revolve axis** prompt:
    - Using **ORTHO**, draw the cursor straight down and click to set axis direction. **2**
  - **Start Angle** prompt:
    - Click on the **FullCircle** option in the **Command Line.**

Fig. 43

| Start angle <0> (DeleteInput=No Deforma **FullCircle** StartAngle=Yes SplitAtTangents=No): |

- The completed bezel which is History enabled.

- Turn on the **PETALS** layer and note that it will be necessary to slightly raise both stone and bezel to allow more bezel material for setting the stone.

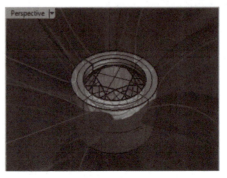

Fig. 44

● Select the bezel profile curve, the stone, and the stone's reference geometry and type **"move"** once again.

  - **Point to move from** prompt:
    - Type **"0"** and press **Enter.**
  - **Point to move to** prompt:
    - Type **".5"** and press **Enter.**
    - Draw the cursor upward as before and click to set location.

● History will update the bezel's location.

● The bezel will now have more clearance to facilitate the future setting process.

Fig. 45

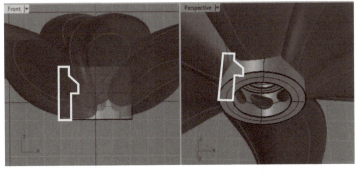

● Notice that from the Front and Perspective views, you can see that the bottom of the bezel needs to be raised up so that it does not extend below the level of the outer tips of the petals.

Fig. 46

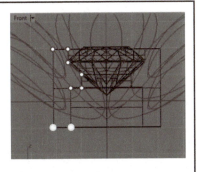

● Select the bottom 2 control points of the bezel profile curve, type **"move"**, and press **Enter.**

● Use the **Move** command to move these points directly upward at a distance of .4mm.

Fig. 47

● History has updated the bezel and the bottom of the bezel has been raised to a better height under the flower.

Fig. 48

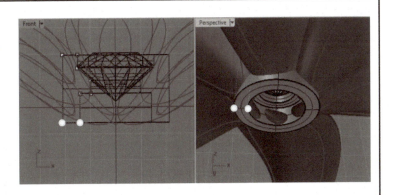

Wire Cutting out the Petals Inside the Bezel

- Notice that the inner tips of the petals intersect the inner part of the bezel.

- Cage Editing could solve this but for this exercise, these tips will be trimmed out using the **Wire Cut** command, a trimming command that leaves a closed polysurface, similar to the Boolean Difference command.

Fig. 49

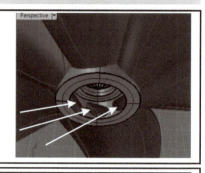

- Create a new layer called **cutters** and make this layer current.

- Notice that all layers are turned off except:
  - **PETALS**
  - **BEZEL**
  - **cutters** (current)

Fig. 50

PETALS		
petal ref		
CAGE		
3mm ROUND FACETED STONE		
3mm rd faceted ref		
BEZEL		
bezel ref		
dim		

current ⟶ **cutters** ✓

- **Top Perspective view.**

- Type **"offset"** and press **Enter.**

  - **Select curve to offset** prompt:
    - Select the outer seam of the bezel as shown.
  - **Side to offset** prompt:
    - Type **".2"** and press **Enter.**
  - **Side to offset** prompt:
    - Draw the cursor inward toward the center of the bezel and click to set location.

- A **.2mm offset** has been created.

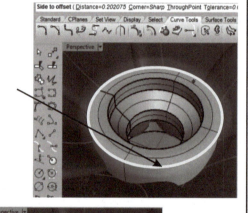

new offset

Fig. 51

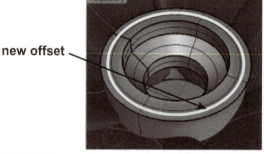

- Select the new offset and repeat the offset curve, creating **another .2mm offset** toward the center of the bezel.

previous offset

new offset

Fig. 52

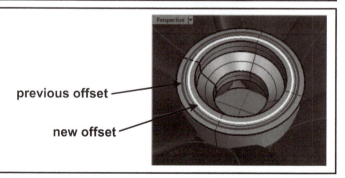

- Type **"unlock"** and press **Enter** to unlock the petals.

- Turn off the **BEZEL** layer for a better view of the petals and their cutters.

- The reason for creating 2 cutters is so that you can stagger the cutting of the petals to make the future Boolean Union command go more smoothly as the trimmed seam will not be touching each other.

Fig. 53

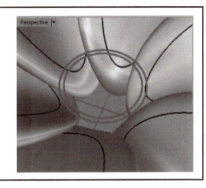

- **Solid Tools tabbed toolbar.** ⌜Solid Tools⌝

- note: isocurves have been made visible again for more clarity in these illustrations.

Wire Cut command

- Click on the **Wire Cut** command.

  - **Select cutting curve** prompt:
    - Click to select one of the offset curves just created.
  - **Select objects to cut**. **Press Enter when done** prompt:
    - Select three petals, alternating the choices so you don't select two neighboring petals.
    - Press **Enter**.

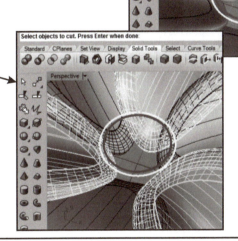

Fig. 54

- **Cut depth points. Press Enter to cut through object** prompt:
  - Press **Enter** to cut *completely* through the 3 selected petals.

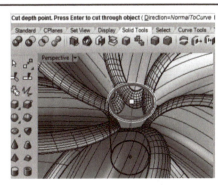

Fig. 55

- **Part to cut away. Press Enter to accept** prompt:
  - You will see the pieces that will be cut away previewed as highlighted objects.
  - If the part of the petals that you want to cut away not highlighted, click on the **Invert=*No*** option to toggle it to **Invert=*Yes***.
  - Press **Enter**.

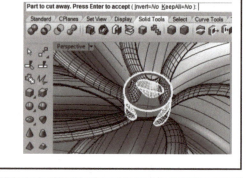

Fig. 56

- The inner tips of the designated petals have been cut away, leaving only the tips of the other 3 petals.
- Unlike the Split or Trim commands, these petals are still solid closed polysurfaces. This command is more like the Boolean Difference command.

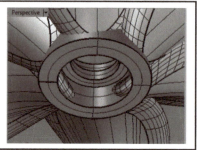

Fig. 57

- Repeat the **Wire Cut** command, using the other offset curve that you did not use before to cut away the tops of the other 3 petals.

- *Important: When using this command, note that the cutter will by default cut vertically to the construction plane unless directed otherwise which is more complicated. This is why top perspective was used for this step.*

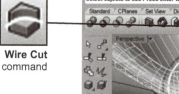

Wire Cut
command

Fig. 58

- If you turn the **BEZEL** layer back on and view the model from the top, you can see the way the tips of the petals have been trimmed so that they are now hidden inside the bezel.

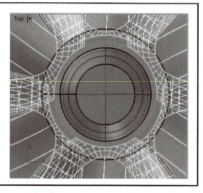

Fig. 59

- Use the Boolean Union command to finish the model when ready for printing.

Fig. 60

- Starting from different petal shapes can be a good way to design different flower shapes.

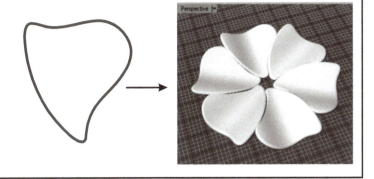

Fig. 61

ClearAllMeshes - Reducing the Size of Your File when Saving

- Files that use CageEdit can become very large, may be difficult to send via email, and will take up space on your hard drive.

- Type **"ClearAllMeshes"** and press **Enter.**

- All Render and Analysis "meshes" will be cleared and the file will save much smaller.

- The file will revert Wireframe mode.

- Shade and other meshes can be re-created for any display mode that you specify.

- Render settings will a remain as part of the file and can be used again whenever you need.

Fig. 62

604

Ring Band with Wavy Pave Design
Flow Along Surface, Array Along Curve on Surface,

Creating the Ring Band

- Create the layers shown.

- **ring ref** layer current.

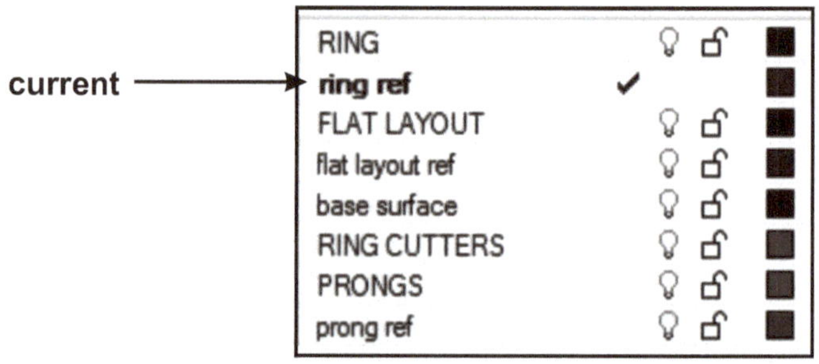

current ⟶

RING		♀	🔓	■
ring ref	✓			■
FLAT LAYOUT		♀	🔓	■
flat layout ref		♀	🔓	■
base surface		♀	🔓	■
RING CUTTERS		♀	🔓	■
PRONGS		♀	🔓	■
prong ref		♀	🔓	■

Fig. 1

- **Front Viewport.**   Front ▼

- **Curve Tools tabbed toolbar.**   Curve Tools

- Create a circle around **"0"**.
    - **Diameter: 17.35mm**

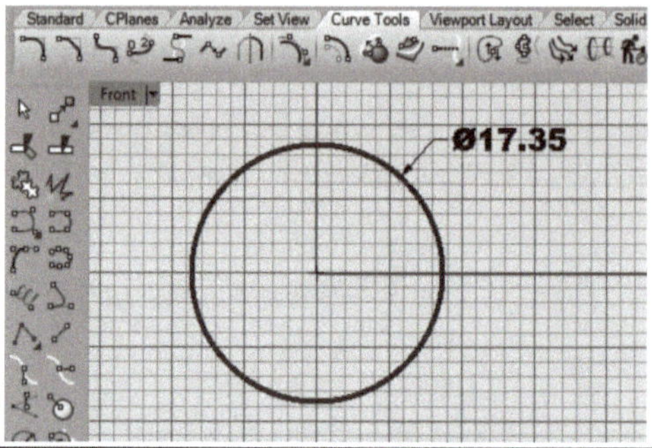

Ø17.35

Fig. 2

- **Right Perspective view.** ❶ 🚗 ❷ 🚙

- Click on the **Line: from Midpoint** command in the **Lines** toolbar flyout.
    - **Middle of line:**
        - Snap to the upper **Quad** of the circle.
        - Click to set location ❶
    - **End of line:**
        - Type **"4"** and press **Enter.**
        - Using **ORTHO**, draw the cursor outward and click to set location. ❷

- An 8mm line will be created.

accesses the **Lines** toolbar flyout

8.00 ❷

Quad

❶

Line: from Midpoint command

Fig. 3

- Using **ORTHO**, create a 2mm line straight up from the **midpoint** of the line just created.
    - **Start of line:** ❶
    - **End of line:** ❷

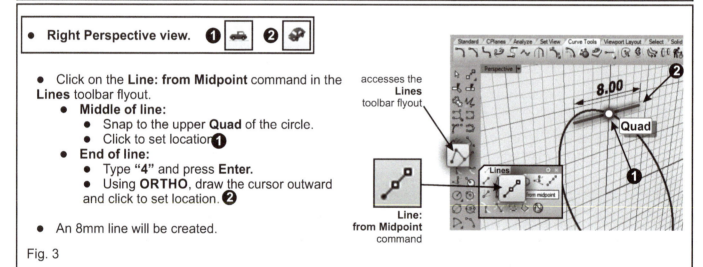

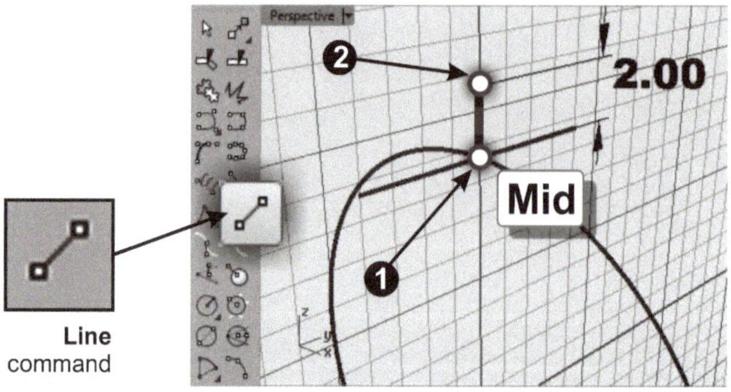

Line command

2.00

❷

Mid

❶

Fig. 4

- Click on the **Arc: start, end, point on arc** command.
  - **Start of arc:** ❶
  - **End of arc.** ❷
  - **Point on arc.** ❸

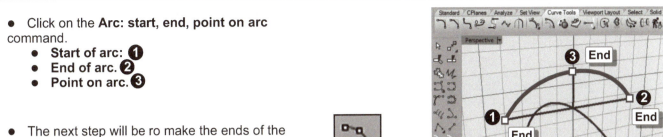

- The next step will be ro make the ends of the arc less sharp, adding more fullness to the sides of the ring profile.

Fig. 5

Arc: Start, End, Point on Arc command

- **Right Viewport.**   Right ▾

- Select the new arc and turn on its control points.

- Select the two points shown, type **"Scale1D"** and press **Enter.**
  - **Origin point:**
    - Snap to the middle control point ❶ and click to set location.
  - **Scale factor or first reference point** prompt:
    - Draw the cursor out, snap to one of the selected control points and click to set location. ❷
  - **Second reference point** prompt:
    - Draw the cursor down and snap to the **Intersection** of the arc and the straight line. ❸

- The direction constraint of the **Scale-1D** command has created a wider distance between the two selected points. This causes them to end up perfectly aligned vertically with the ends of the arc.
- The arc is now fuller on the sides.

Fig. 6

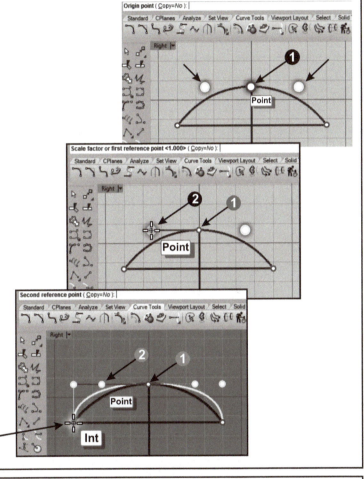

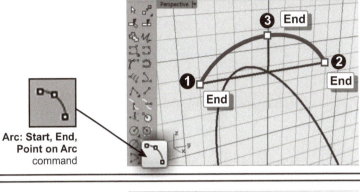

- Click on the **Fillet Curves** command.
  - Click to toggle to the **Join=No** option. ❶
  - Type **".5"** ❷ and press **Enter** to set the radius of the fillets.
    - **Select first curve to fillet** prompt:
      - Click near the end of one of the curves. ❸

Fillet Curves command

Fig. 7

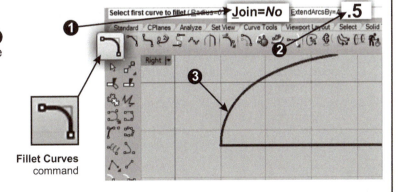

606

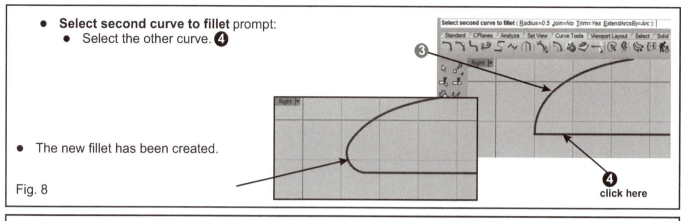

- **Select second curve to fillet** prompt:
  - Select the other curve. ❹

- The new fillet has been created.

Fig. 8

click here

- Fillet the curves on the other side of the ring profile that is being created.

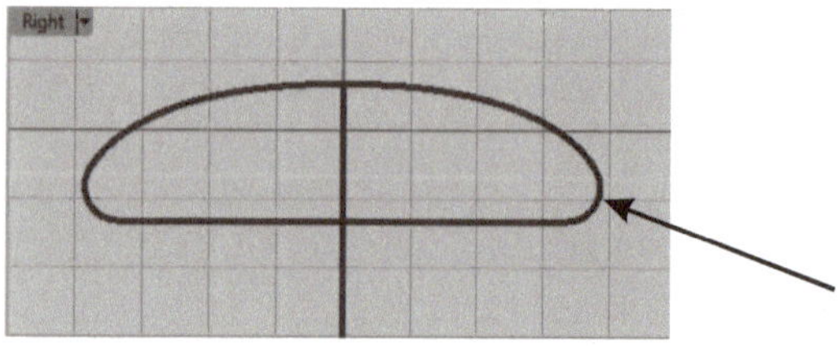

Fig. 9

- Select the two fillets and the bottom line and click on the **Join** command.

- **DO NOT join the top arc to the other curves.**

- The 2mm straight vertical line from Fig. 4 can be deleted.

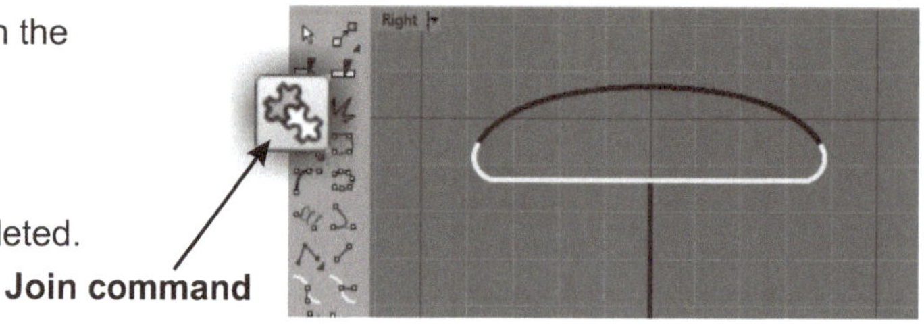

Fig. 10

Join command

- **RING** layer current.

current ⟶ **RING** ✓

ring ref

FLAT LAYOUT

Fig. 11

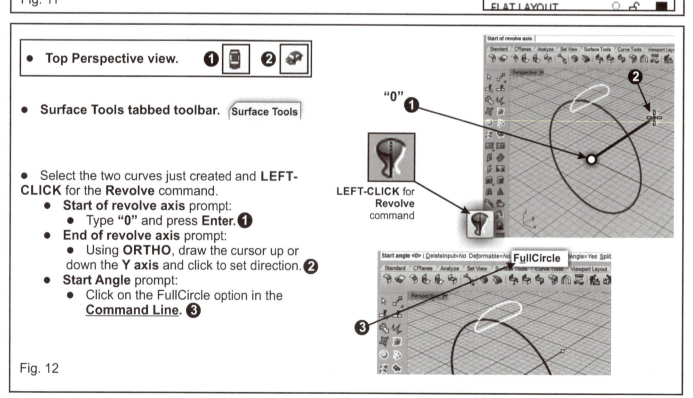

- **Top Perspective view.** ❶ ❷

- **Surface Tools tabbed toolbar.** Surface Tools

- Select the two curves just created and **LEFT-CLICK** for the **Revolve** command.
  - **Start of revolve axis** prompt:
    - Type **"0"** and press **Enter.** ❶
  - **End of revolve axis** prompt:
    - Using **ORTHO**, draw the cursor up or down the **Y axis** and click to set direction. ❷
  - **Start Angle** prompt:
    - Click on the FullCircle option in the **Command Line.** ❸

"0" ❶

❷

LEFT-CLICK for **Revolve** command

FullCircle

❸

Fig. 12

607

- After you click on the **FullCircle** option, the revolve will be completed.

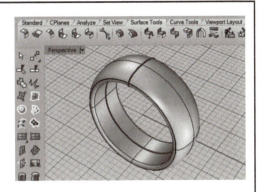

Fig. 13

- Select the inside surface of the ring, type **"hide"**, and press **Enter.**

- The inside surface of the ring band will be hidden.

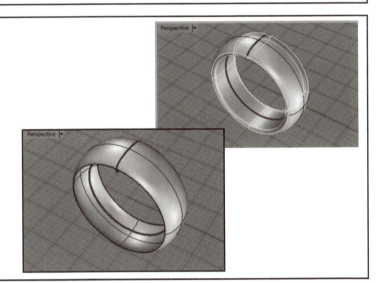

Fig. 14

- Turn off the **ring ref** layer.

- **flat layout ref** layer current.

current —→

RING	♀	🔓	⬛
ring ref	💡	🔓	⬛
FLAT LAYOUT	♀	🔓	⬛
flat layout ref	✔		⬛
base surface	♀	🔓	⬛
RING CUTTERS	♀	🔓	⬛
PRONGS	♀	🔓	⬛
prong ref	♀	🔓	⬛

Fig. 15

Flat Layout:Creating the Wavy Pave Pattern for the Ring

- **Standard tabbed toolbar.**   Standard

- **LEFT-CLICK** on the **Create UV Curves** command in the **Curve from Object** toolbar flyout.

accesses the
Curve from Object toolbar flyout

Create UV curves command

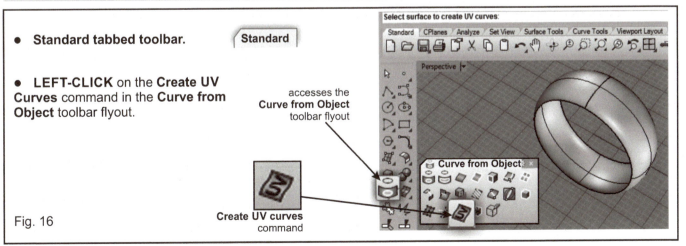

Fig. 16

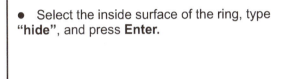
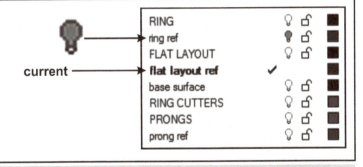

- **Select surface to create UV curves** prompt:
    - Select the ring surface.
- **Select curves on surface to create UV curves** prompt:
    - Press **Enter** as there are no curves on the surface.

Fig. 17

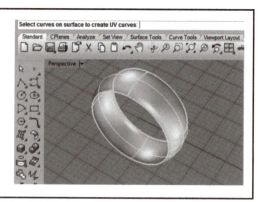

- A rectangle will appear on the construction plane which is the exact area of the ring surface.

Fig. 18

- Drag the new rectangle in front of the ring for better access

- Select the rectangle and **Explode** it into 4 separate lines..

Fig. 19

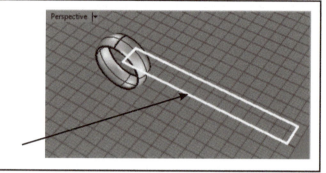

LEFT-CLICK for **Explode** commad

- **Top Viewport.** Top |▼

- **Curve Tools tabbed toolbar.** Curve Tools

- **Offset** the top and bottom lines of the rectangle.
    - **Offset distance: 3mm**

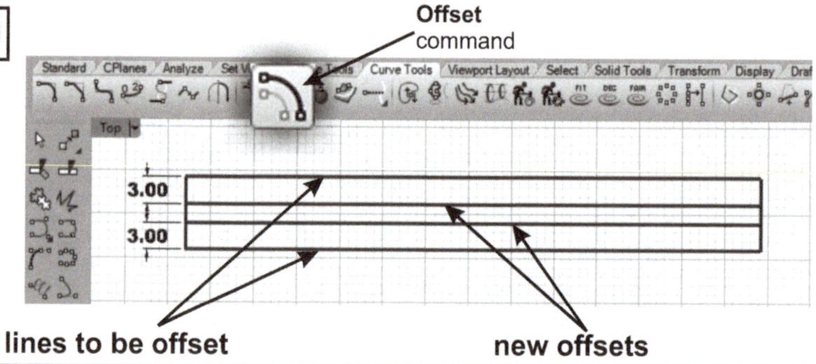

Fig. 20

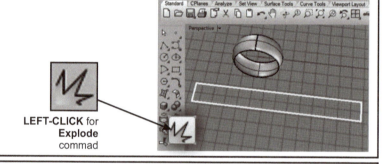

Offset command

3.00

3.00

lines to be offset   **new offsets**

- **Standard tabbed toolbar.** Standard

- Select the 2 new offsets and **RIGHT-CLICK** for the **Divide Curve by Number of Segments** command in the **Point** toolbar flyout.
    - **Number of segments** prompt:
        - Type **"8"** and press **Enter.**

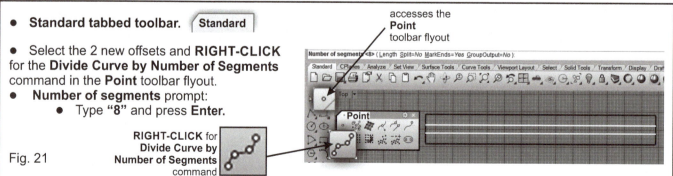

accesses the **Point** toolbar flyout

Number of segments <8> (Length Split=No MarkEnds=Yes GroupOutput=No):

Point

RIGHT-CLICK for **Divide Curve by Number of Segments** command

Fig. 21

- The two offsets have each been divided into 8 equal "segments" by the placement of **point objects.**

Fig. 22

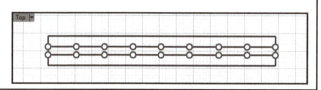

- Select two sets of points as shown, type **"copy"**, and press **Enter.**
    - **Point to copy from** prompt:
        - Snap to the **Point** shown.
        - Click to set location. ❶

    - **Point to copy to** prompt:
        - Snap to the point shown.
        - Click to set location. ❷
        - Press **Enter** to end the command.

Fig. 23

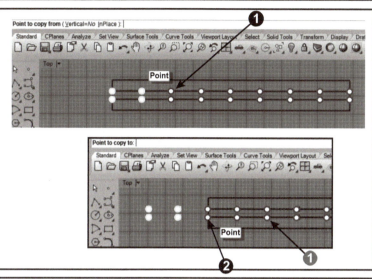

- Select the two new copies, type **"mirror"**, and press **Enter.**
    - **Start of mirror plane** prompt:
        - Snap to the **mid point** of one of the long horizontal lines. ❶
    - **End of mirror plane** prompt:
        - Using **ORTHO**, draw the cursor down and click to set the direction of the **mirror plane.** ❷

Fig. 24

objects to be mirrored   **new mirrored copies**

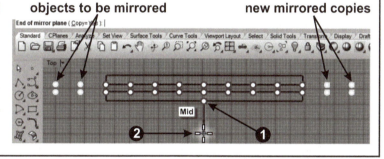

- **FLAT LAYOUT** layer current.

Fig. 25

RING	○	⌂	◼
ring ref	○	⌂	◼
FLAT LAYOUT	✓		◼
flat layout ref	○	⌂	◼
base surface	○	⌂	◼
RING CUTTERS	○	⌂	◼

- Using the **Curve: Interpolate Points** command, create the wavy curve shown, using **point osnap** for accurate placement.

LEFT-CLICK for
Curve: Interpolate Points
command

- The finished wavy curve.

Fig. 26

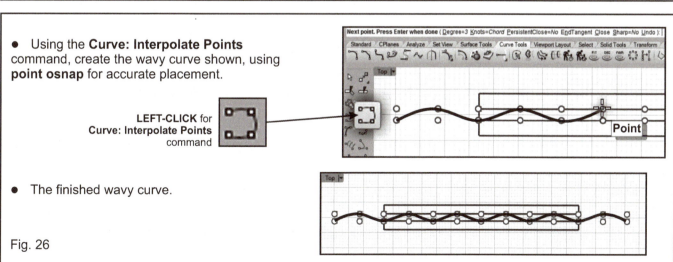

610

- Click on the **Trim** command.
  - **Cutting objects** prompt:
    - Select the two perpendicular line segments on the ends of the rectangle.
    - Press **Enter**.
  - **Select objects to trim** prompt:
    - Click on the ends of the wavy line that extend out past the original rectangle.
    - Press **Enter** when both ends are trimmed away.

Fig. 27

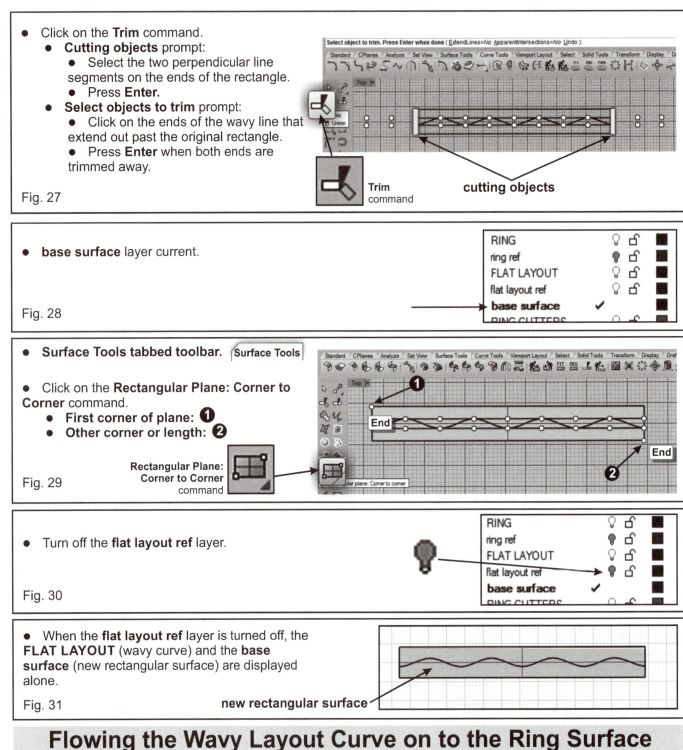

Trim command

cutting objects

- **base surface** layer current.

Fig. 28

RING		
ring ref		
FLAT LAYOUT		
flat layout ref		
base surface	✓	
RING CUTTERS		

- **Surface Tools** tabbed toolbar. Surface Tools

- Click on the **Rectangular Plane: Corner to Corner** command.
  - **First corner of plane:** ❶
  - **Other corner or length:** ❷

Rectangular Plane: Corner to Corner command

Fig. 29

End

End

- Turn off the **flat layout ref** layer.

Fig. 30

RING		
ring ref		
FLAT LAYOUT		
flat layout ref		
base surface	✓	
RING CUTTERS		

- When the **flat layout ref** layer is turned off, the **FLAT LAYOUT** (wavy curve) and the **base surface** (new rectangular surface) are displayed alone.

Fig. 31

new rectangular surface

Flowing the Wavy Layout Curve on to the Ring Surface

- **Top Perspective view.** ❶ ❷

- Select the base surface, type **"dir"** (the script for **"direction"**), and press **Enter**.

Fig. 32

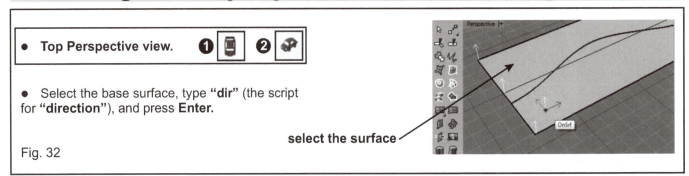

select the surface

OnSrf

- Note the direction of the **U** and **V** arrows attached to the cursor.
  - If the U and V arrows are not in the orientation shown, use the options in the **Command Line** to bring them into the alignment shown.

- The white arrows (surface normals) need to be pointing up, indicating the this is the top side of the surface, or it's "Normal Direction".
  - If necessary, click on the surface to "flip" these arrows so that they point up.
  - Press **Enter** when done.

Fig. 33

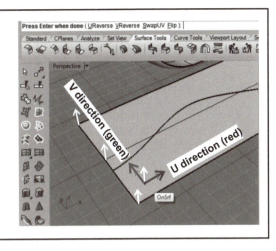

- Type **"point"** and press **Enter.**

- Use **near osnap** to place a point on the edge shown, close to the corner but not on it.
  - This will serve to make this as a designated corner for the *Flow Along Surface* command coming up.

Fig. 34

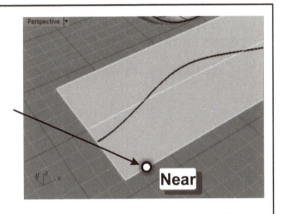

- Select the ring surface, type **"dir"**, and press **Enter.**

- The white "normal" arrows need to be pointing outward.

- U and V directions should be as shown, matching the directions of these arrows on the base surface.
  - Adjust if necessary, using the options in the **Command Line.**
  - This is now the "matching corner" to the designated corner on the base surface just set in Fig. 34.

Fig. 35

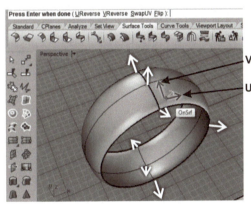

- Type **"point"** and press **Enter.**

- Using **near osnap** as before, place a point on the edge shown to mark this "matching corner" that you will need for the Flow Along Surface command in the next step.

Fig. 36

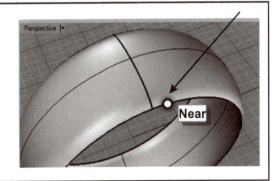

- **Transform tabbed toolbar.** Transform

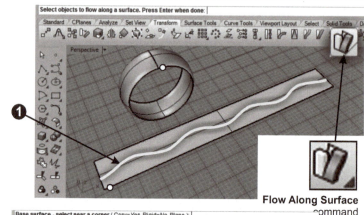

- Click on the **Flow Along Surface** command.
  - **Select objects to flow along a surface. Press Enter when done** prompt:
    - Select the wavy curve on the base surface and press **Enter.** ❶

Flow Along Surface
command

- **Base surface - select near a corner** prompt:
  - Click on the base surface edge near the point that you placed earlier. ❷

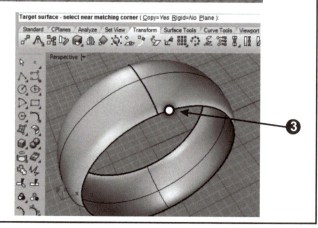

- **Target surface - select near matching corner** prompt:
  - Click on the edge near where you placed the point earlier.

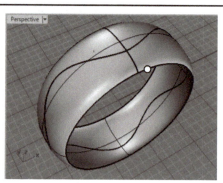

Fig. 37

- The wavy curve will be flowed on to the surface of the ring.

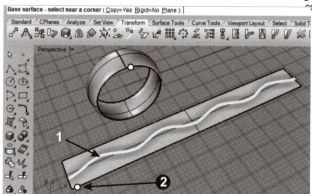

- Select the flowed curve and change it to the **RING CUTTERS** layer.

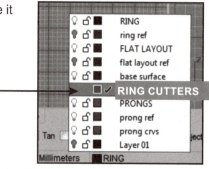

Fig. 38

613

- Make sure the following layers are turned off:
  - **ring ref, FLAT LAYOUT, flat layout ref,** and **base surface**

- **RING CUTTERS** layer current.

Fig. 39

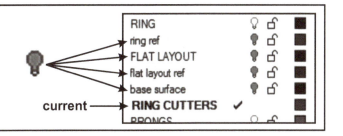

- Select the flowed wavy curve, type **"rebuild"**, and press **Enter**.

- **Rebuild** the curve to **40 control points**.

- Because this curve was flowed onto a surface, it has many control points and more complex geometry. Rebuilding gives this curve simpler geometry for the pipe command in the next step.

Fig. 40

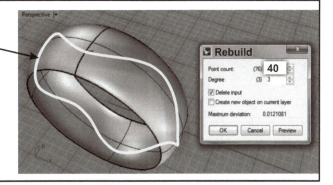

Creating the Path for the Wavy Pave Design Element

- 2mm stones will be used. The wavy design path will be cut to allow space on each side of the stones and a narrower base upon which the stones will be seated.

- **Solid Tools tabbed toolbar.**   Solid Tools

- Select the rebuilt wavy line **❶** and click on the **Pipe: Flat Caps** command.
  - **Radius for closed pipe** prompt:
    - Click on the **Diameter** option **❷** in the **Command Line.**
    - Type **"2.9"** and press **Enter** to set the **diameter** for the pipe.**❸**
  - **Point for next diameter. Press Enter for none** prompt:
    - Press **Enter** for none.

- A **2.9mm** diameter closed pipe has been created.

Fig. 41

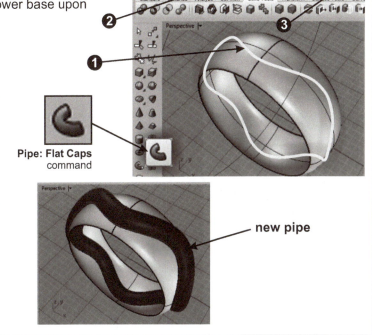

Pipe: Flat Caps
command

new pipe

- Click on the **Split** command.
  - **Select objects to split. Press Enter when done** prompt:
    - Select the ring surface and press **Enter.**

Fig. 42

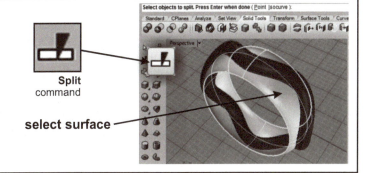

Split
command

select surface

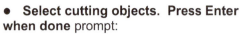

- **Select cutting objects. Press Enter when done** prompt:
  - Select the **pipe** and press **Enter.**

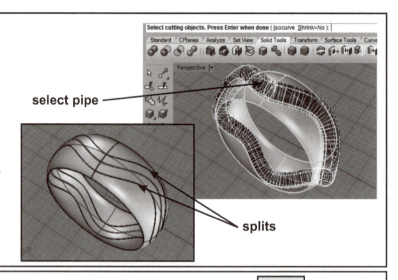

select pipe

splits

- **Delete** the pipe.

- The two heavy lines on each side of the wavy line indicate where the surface of the ring has been split by the pipe.

Fig. 43

- If the split does not work, you might need to move the location of the pipe's surface seam.

- Click on the **Adjust closed surface seam** in the **Surface Tools tabbed toolbar.**
  - Toggle to the direction shown and move the new seam slightly away from the ring's seam on top of the ring.
  - Then try the split again.
  - Remember that rebuilding the wavy line (Fig. 40) was important for the creation of the pipe.

Fig. 44

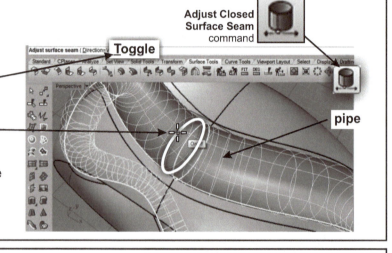

Adjust Closed
Surface Seam
command

Toggle

pipe

- Create another **Pipe** with a diameter of **2.25mm** around the same wavy curve.

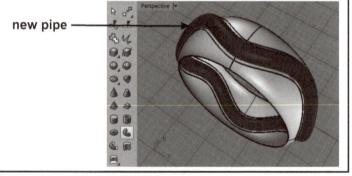

new pipe

Fig. 45

- Click on the **Split** command again.
  - **Select objects to split. Press Enter when done** prompt:
    - Select the small split-off surface just under the pipe.

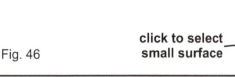

Split
command

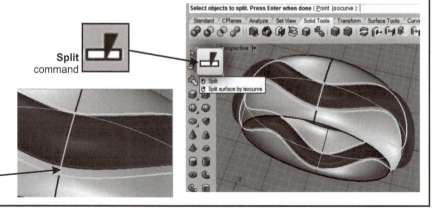

click to select
small surface

Fig. 46

- **Select cutting objects. Press Enter when done** prompt:
  - Select the **pipe** and press **Enter**.

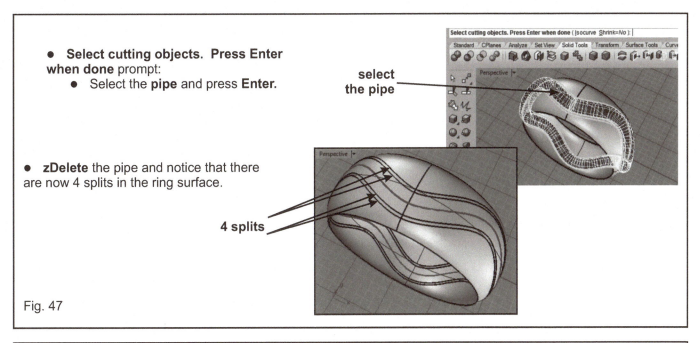

- **zDelete** the pipe and notice that there are now 4 splits in the ring surface.

4 splits

select
the pipe

Fig. 47

- **RING** layer current.

- Turn off the **RING CUTTERS** layer.

Fig. 48

- Carefully select and **Delete** the two skinny surfaces on each side of the wider center surface.

2 skinny surfaces deleted

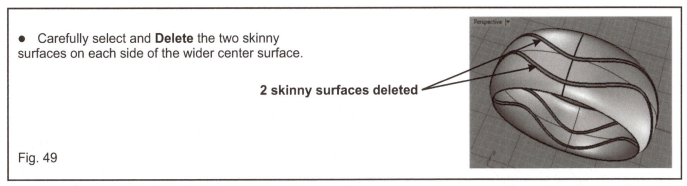

Fig. 49

- **Surface Tools tabbed toolbar.** [Surface Tools]

- Select the wavy surface in the middle of the ring and click on the **Offset Surface** command.
  - **Select object to flip direction. Press Enter when done** prompt:
    - Click on the surface, if necessary, to make the white normal arrows point inward as shown as this sets the direction of the offset.
    - Toggle to the **Solid=No** option because you only want a surface offset, not a solid.

Offset Surface
command

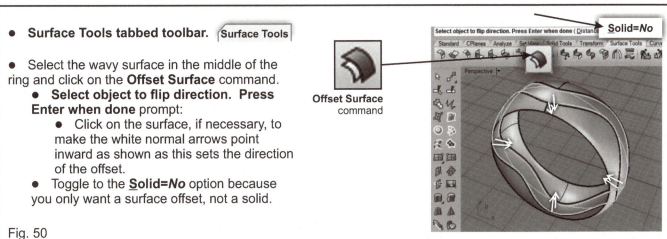

Fig. 50

- Type **".35"** and press **Enter**.
  - This is the approximate distance between the table and the girdle for the 2mm round stones that will be used.
- **Select object to flip direction.**
  Press Enter when done prompt:
  - Press **Enter** again to finish the command.

- **Delete** the original outer surface that was offset to see the new offset sitting on the inside.

Fig. 51

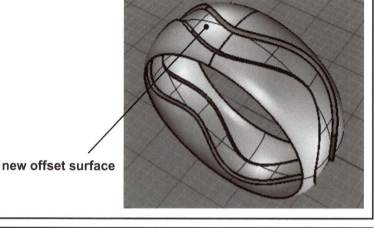

new offset surface

- Select the **ring ref** layer. ❶

- Click on the **New Layer button.** ❷
  - A new layer line ❸ will appear just below the selected **ring ref** layer line.

New Layer
button

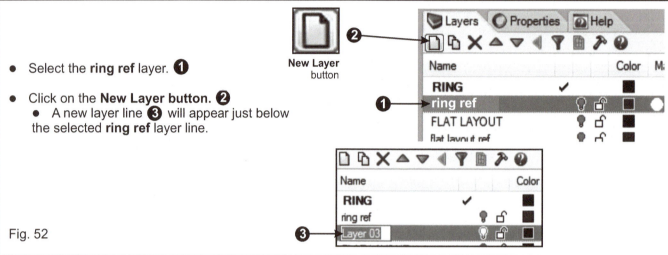

Fig. 52

- Name the new layer **ring ref 2** and make this layer current.

Fig. 53

current

- Zoom in to the top of the ring.

- Type **"line"** and press **Enter**.
  - **Start of line** prompt:
    - Snap to the **end point** of the seam at the top of the ring as shown.
    - Click to set location. ❶
  - **End of line** prompt:
    - Snap to the **end point** of the seam on the other side of the small gap.
    - Click to set location. ❷

- Navigate to the other side of the top of the ring and create another, snapping to the **end points** of the seams as before.
  - **Start of line:** ❸
  - **End of line:** ❹

Fig. 54

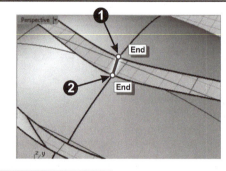

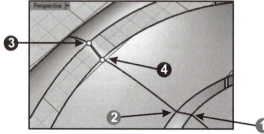

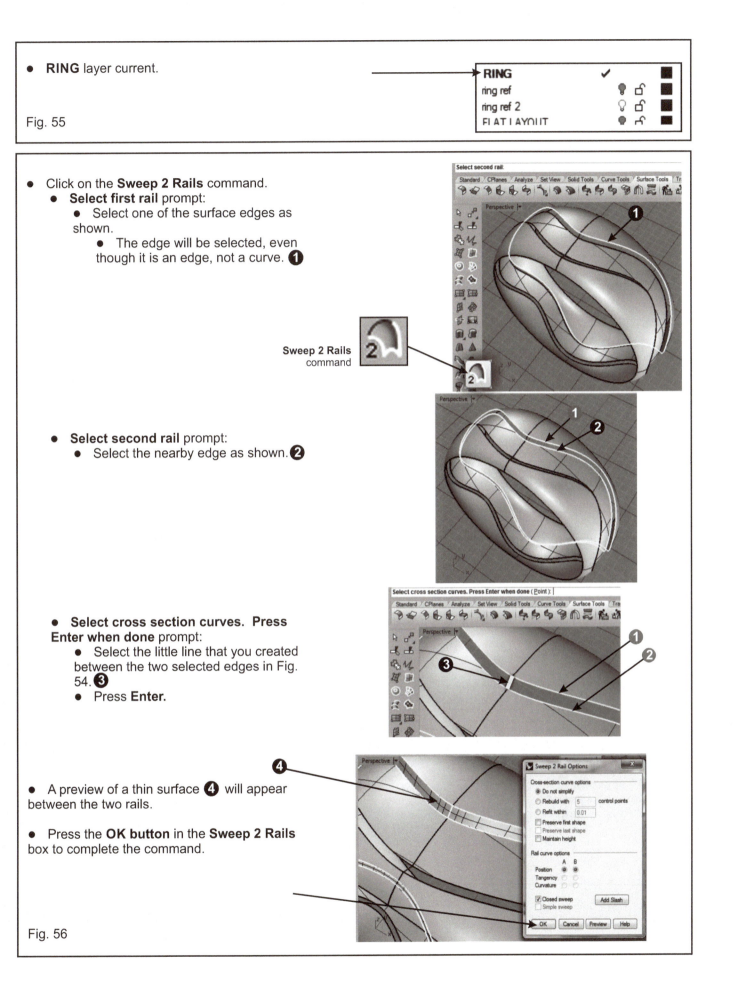

- **RING** layer current.

Fig. 55

RING ✓
ring ref
ring ref 2
FLAT LAYOUT

- Click on the **Sweep 2 Rails** command.
  - **Select first rail** prompt:
    - Select one of the surface edges as shown.
      - The edge will be selected, even though it is an edge, not a curve. ❶

Sweep 2 Rails
command

- **Select second rail** prompt:
  - Select the nearby edge as shown. ❷

- **Select cross section curves. Press Enter when done** prompt:
  - Select the little line that you created between the two selected edges in Fig. 54. ❸
  - Press **Enter.**

- A preview of a thin surface ❹ will appear between the two rails.

- Press the **OK button** in the **Sweep 2 Rails** box to complete the command.

Fig. 56

- Use the same technique to create a narrow surface on the other side of the ring.
  - **First rail:❶**
  - **Second rail:❷**
  - **Cross section curve:❸**

  - Press the **OK button** in the **Sweep 2 Rails** box to complete the command.

Fig. 57

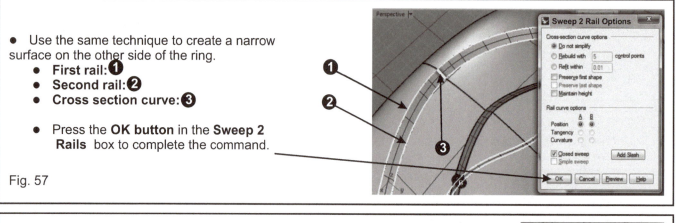

- Select and **Delete** the inner offset surface.

select and delete

inner surface is deleted

Fig. 58

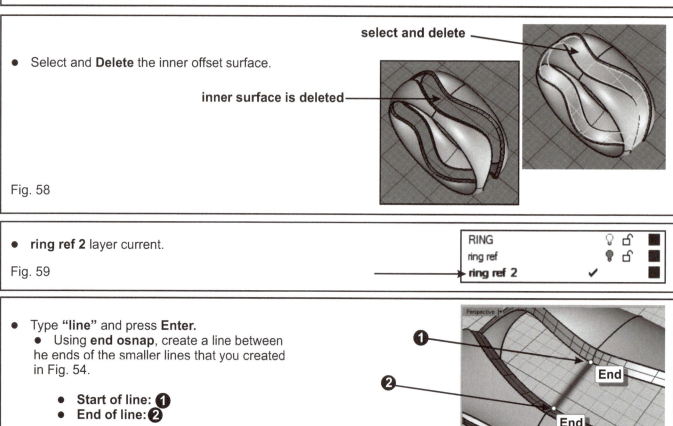

- **ring ref 2** layer current.

Fig. 59

RING	♀ 🔓 ■
ring ref	♀ 🔓 ■
ring ref 2	✓ ■

- Type **"line"** and press **Enter.**
  - Using **end osnap**, create a line between he ends of the smaller lines that you created in Fig. 54.

    - **Start of line: ❶**
    - **End of line:❷**

Fig. 60

- Use the **Sweep 2 Rails** command again to create a surface in the center of the ring.
  - **First curve: ❶**
  - **Second curve:❷**
  - **Cross section curve:❸**

Fig. 61

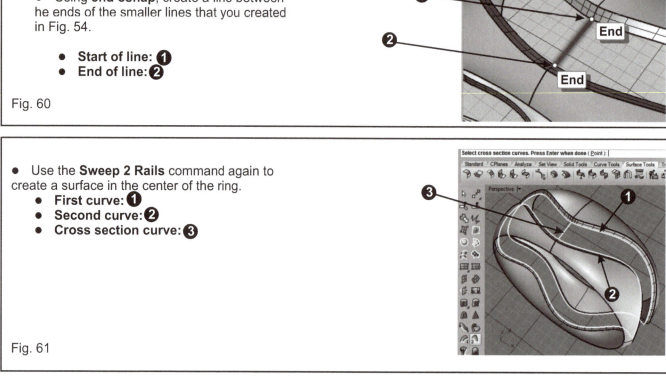

- Press the **OK button** to complete the command.

Fig. 62

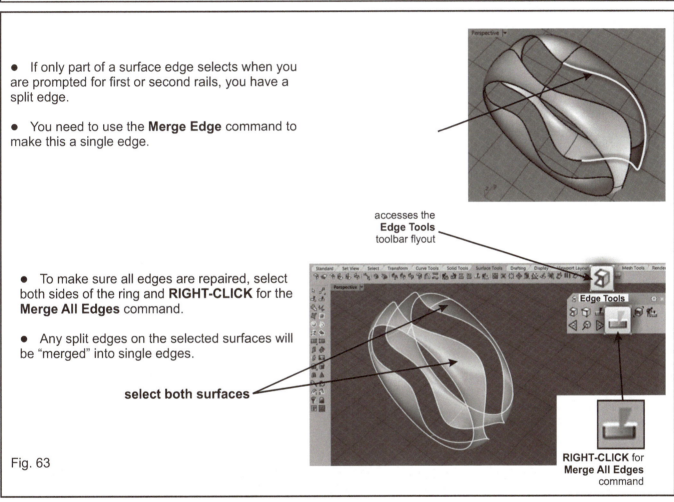

- If only part of a surface edge selects when you are prompted for first or second rails, you have a split edge.

- You need to use the **Merge Edge** command to make this a single edge.

accesses the
Edge Tools
toolbar flyout

- To make sure all edges are repaired, select both sides of the ring and **RIGHT-CLICK** for the **Merge All Edges** command.

- Any split edges on the selected surfaces will be "merged" into single edges.

select both surfaces

Fig. 63

RIGHT-CLICK for
Merge All Edges
command

- Select all 5 surfaces and click on the **Join** command.

Join
command

Fig. 64

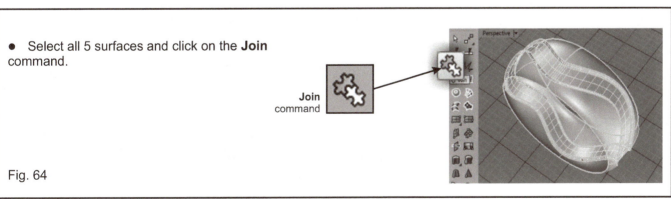

- After joining the surfaces together, **LEFT-CLICK** on the **Show Edges** command to check for **Naked Edges.**

LEFT-CLICK on the **Show Edges** command.

Fig. 65

- The **Edge Analysis** box will open.
  - Make sure that you select the **Naked Edges** option.
- The two outer edges of the ring will show a pink color. They should be the only Naked Edges on the piece as all 5 of the surfaces were Joined together.

- Click to **"X"** out of the **Edge Analysis** box or **RIGHT-CLICK** on the **Show Edges** command button to end the command.

Naked Edges option

Naked Edges

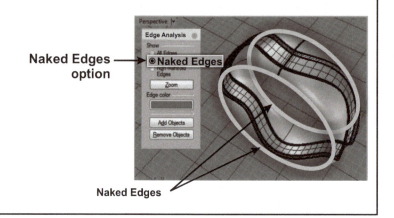

Fig. 66

Flowing Stones on to the Ring

- Click on **File** in the **Menu Bar**. ❶

- Click to select **Import** in the drop-down context menu. ❷

  - Navigate to your designated folder of downloads from the www.rhinoforjewelry.com website to select **1mm RD Maquette - stone seat and hole cutters.**
  - Click the **Open** button. ❸

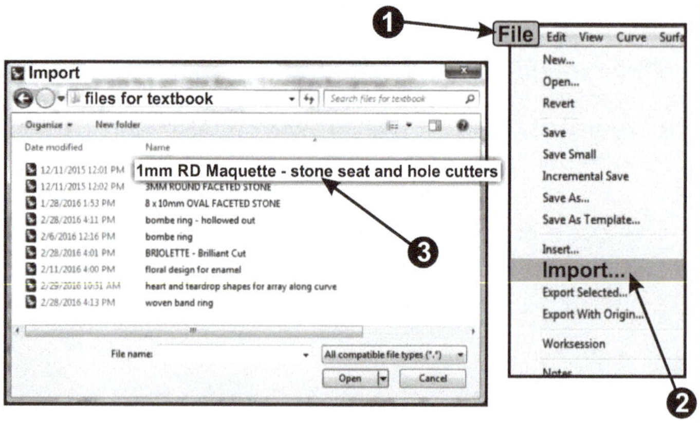

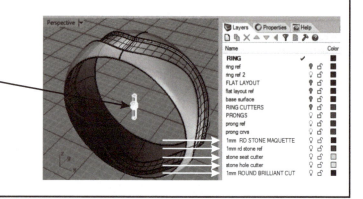

Fig. 67

- The 1mm RD Maquette stone and it's cutters will be imported into the file, along with it's layers.

- Note that a faceted stone has also been imported along with the other objects.
  - This will be good for rendering.

Fig. 68

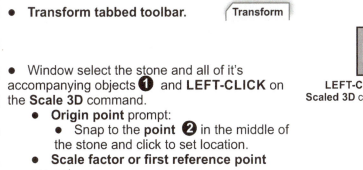

- **Transform tabbed toolbar.** `Transform`

- Window select the stone and all of it's accompanying objects **❶** and **LEFT-CLICK** on the **Scale 3D** command.
  - **Origin point** prompt:
    - Snap to the **point ❷** in the middle of the stone and click to set location.
  - **Scale factor or first reference point** prompt:
    - Type **"2"** to set the **scale factor ❸** and press **Enter.**

- The 1mm stone has been scaled up 200% and is now a **2mm diameter stone.**

Fig. 69

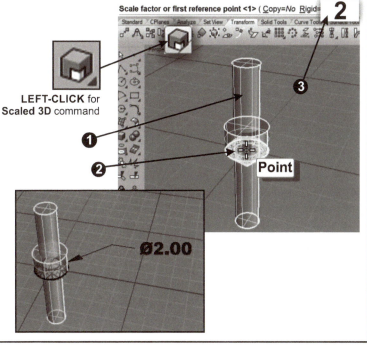

LEFT-CLICK for
Scaled 3D command

Scale factor or first reference point <1> (_C_opy=No _R_igid=

Point

Ø2.00

- **ring ref 2** layer current.

Fig. 70

RING		♀ ⌂	■
ring ref		♀ ⌂	■
ring ref 2	✓		■
FLAT LAYOUT		♀ ⌂	■
flat layout ref		♀ ⌂	■
base surface		♀ ⌂	■
RING CUTTERS		♀ ⌂	■

- **Standard tabbed toolbar.** `Standard`

- The next step will be to create a curve on the middle surface that will act as a guide for the array of the pave stones.

- Click on the **Extract Isocurve** command in the **Curve from Object** toolbar flyout.
  - **Select surface for isocurve extraction** prompt:
    - Click on the center surface.
  - **Select isocurve to extract** prompt:
    - As you run the cursor over the surface, make sure that the direction of the preview curve runs along the length of the surface.
      - Click on the Direction option to toggle to the desired direction of the preview curve, if necessary.

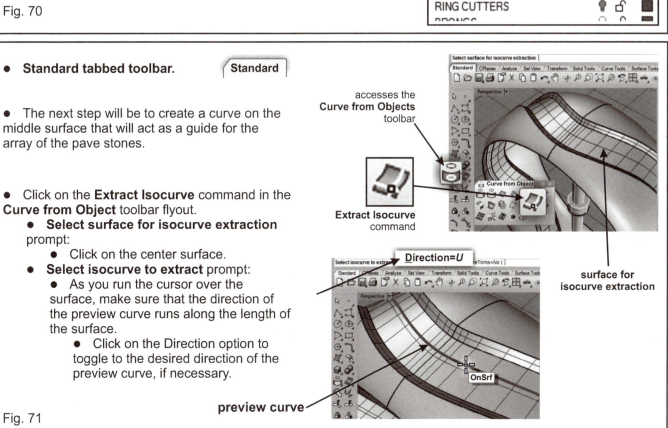

accesses the
Curve from Objects
toolbar

Extract Isocurve
command

Direction=U

surface for
isocurve extraction

preview curve

Fig. 71

- Snap to the **Mid point** of the seam at the top of the ring and click to set location.
- Press **Enter** to end the command.

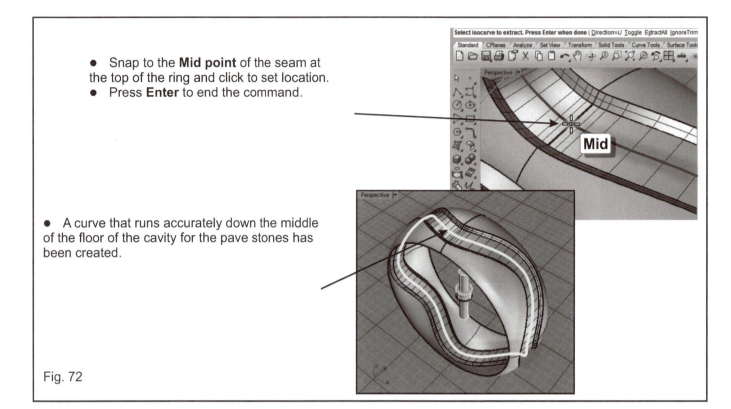

- A curve that runs accurately down the middle of the floor of the cavity for the pave stones has been created.

Fig. 72

- Before Arraying stones to the ring's surface, it is good to check the direction of the ring's surface so that the stones will be sitting upright, not upside down.

- Select the ring, type **"dir"**, and press **Enter.**

- What you need to see is the white normal arrows pointing outward.
    - If necessary, click on the ring to "flip" the direction of the arrows so that they point outward as shown in this illustration.

- Press the **Esc** key to exit the command.

Fig. 73

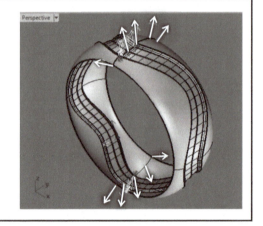

- Select the stone and it's accompanying objects and click on the **Group** command.

- All of these elements are now grouped together.

Group
command

- Drag the stone group out from inside the ring for better accessability.

drag

Fig. 74

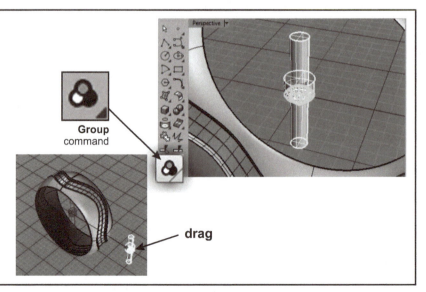

- **Transform tabbed toolbar.** ⌐Transform⌐

- Click on the **Array Along Curve on Surface** command.
    - **Select objects to array. Press Enter when done** prompt:
        - Select the stone group ❶ and press **Enter.**

Array Along Curve on Surface command

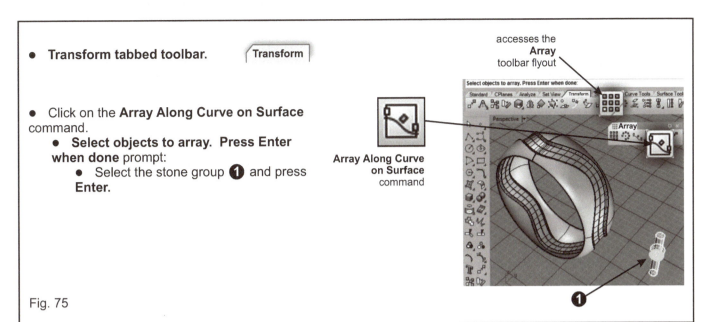

Fig. 75

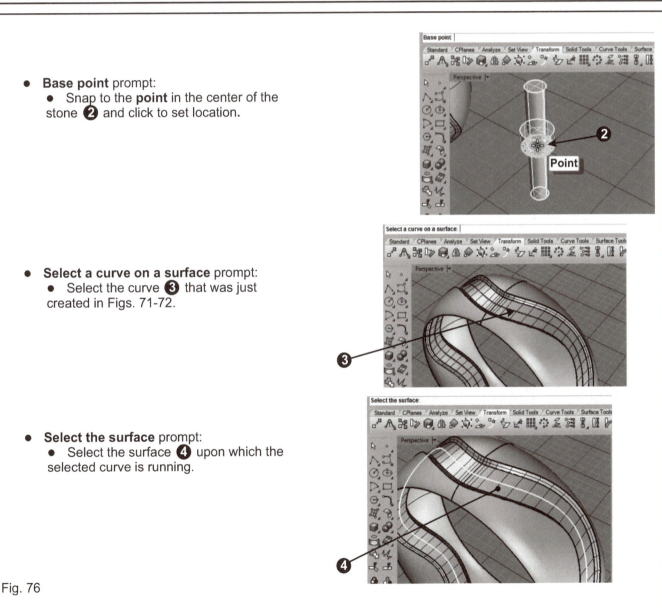

- **Base point** prompt:
    - Snap to the **point** in the center of the stone ❷ and click to set location.

- **Select a curve on a surface** prompt:
    - Select the curve ❸ that was just created in Figs. 71-72.

- **Select the surface** prompt:
    - Select the surface ❹ upon which the selected curve is running.

Fig. 76

- **Position objects or distance from last** prompt:
  - Click to select the **Divide** option. ❺
- **Number of objects** prompt:
  - Type **"32"** and press **Enter.**❻
  - Press **Enter** a second time to complete the command.

- The stone group will be arrayed along the surface, following the path of the designated curve.

Fig. 77

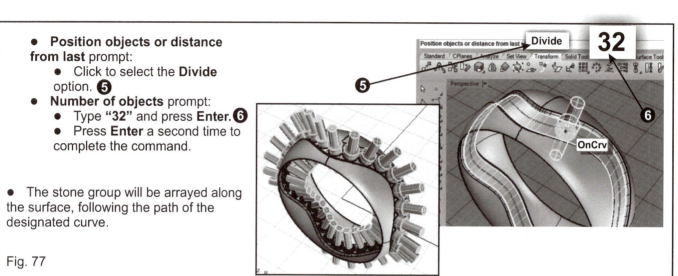

- Turn off the **ring ref 2** layer.

- You can rename the **1mm RD stone maquette**, the **1mm rd stone ref** and the **1mm ROUND BRILLIANT CUT** To reflect the fact that the stones are now 2mm not 1mm.

- Turn off the **stone seat cutter, stone hole cutter,** and the **2mm ROUND BRILLIANT CUT**

Fig. 78

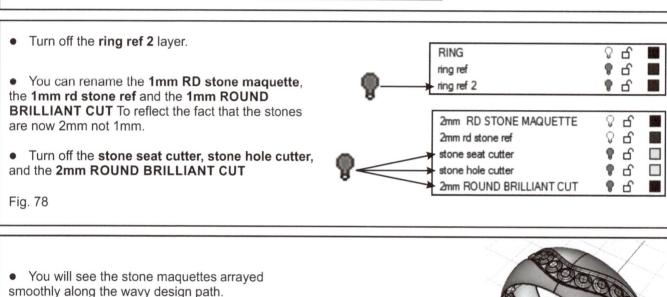

- You will see the stone maquettes arrayed smoothly along the wavy design path.

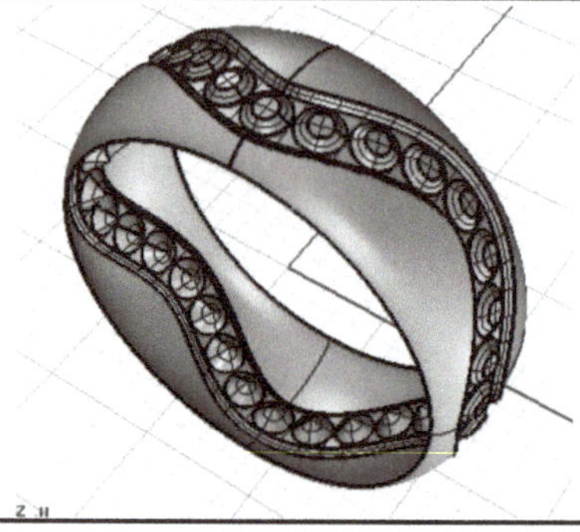

Fig. 79

- Now, turn off the **2mm RD STONE MAQUETTE** to view the 2mm rd stone ref geometry along the ring band.

- **prong ref** layer current.

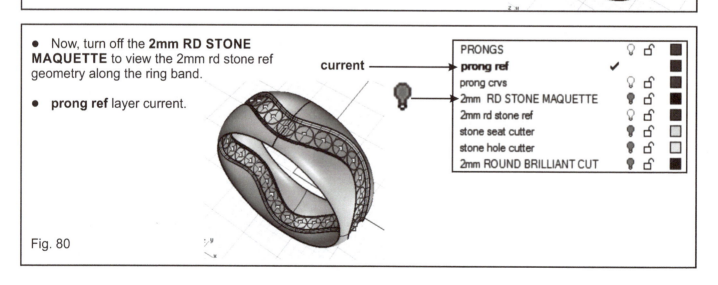

Fig. 80

Creating the Small Prongs ("Beads")

- **Curve Tools tabbed toolbar.** | Curve Tools |

- Click on the **Circle: Tangent to 3 Curves** command in the **Circle** toolbar flyout.
  - Draw the cursor over to one of the circles until you see a white constraint line, telling you that you can click to set the first tangent curve. Do this for the other circle and for the side seam in turn.
    - **First tangent curve: ❶**
    - **Second tangent curve or radius: ❷**
    - **Third tangent curve: ❸**

Fig. 81

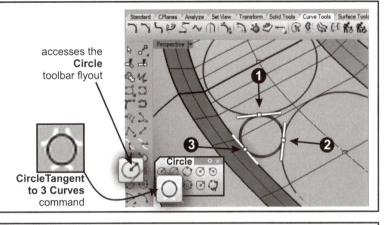

accesses the **Circle** toolbar flyout

CircleTangent to 3 Curves command

- Continue to use the **Circle: Tangent to 3 Curves** command to create more circles in the 4 rows shown.

- You do not have to create circles for all of the stones on the ring because the bead prongs will be created from these circles and will be then be Mirrored and Polar Arrayed around the rest of the ring.

Fig. 82

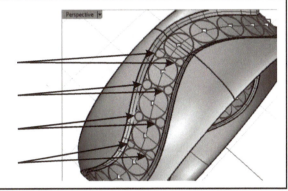

- **Front Viewport.** Front ▾

- Click on the **Line from Midpoint** command in the **Lines** toolbar flyout.
  - **Middle of line** prompt:
    - Type **"0"** and press **Enter. ❶**
  - **End of line** prompt:
    - Type **".25"** and press **Enter.**
    - Using **ORTHO**, draw the cursor straight up or down and click to set location. ❷

Fig. 83

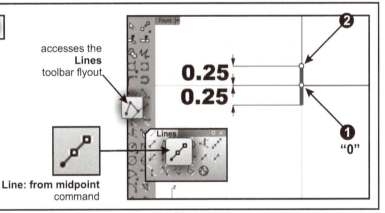

accesses the **Lines** toolbar flyout

Line: from midpoint command

0.25
0.25

"0"

- **Top Perspective view.** ❶  ❷

- **Transform tabbed toolbar.** | Transform |

- Click on the **Orient on Surface** command.
  - **Select objects to orient. Press Enter when done** prompt:
    - Select the little line you just created and press **Enter.**
  - **Base point** prompt:
    - Snap to the **mid point ❶** of the line and click to set location.

Fig. 84

Orient On Surface command

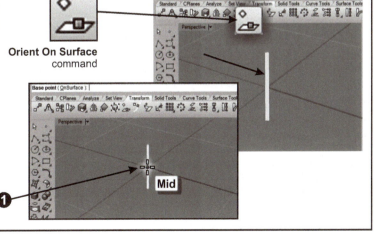

Mid

- **Reference point for scaling and rotation** prompt:
    - Using **ORTHO**, draw the cursor back and click to set direction location.❷

Fig. 85

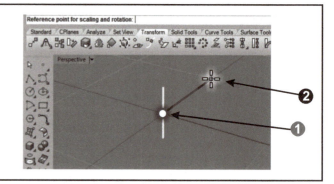

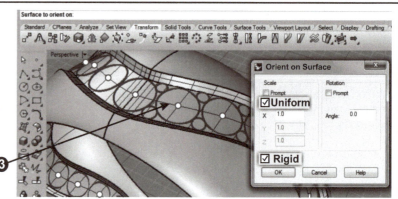

- **Surface to orient on** prompt:
    - Click on the surface on which you flowed the stones.❸
    - Click the **OK button** in the **Orient on Surface** box to accept the settings shown.

- **Point on surface to orient to** prompt:
    - Make sure to toggle to **Copy=Yes** ❹ in the **Command Line.**
    - Draw the cursor over to one of the little prong circles and snap to the center of that circle. ❺
        - Remember that the cursor needs to be touching the boundary of the circle for **center osnap** to work.

- Notice that half of the little line is sticking out of the surface while half is on the other side. It is centered in the prong circle.

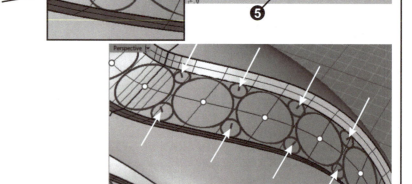

- Continue to orient the little line in the center of the rest of the prong circles.
    - Press **Enter** to end the command.

Fig. 86

- Turn off the **2mm rd stone ref** layer.

- **PRONGS** layer current.

Fig. 87

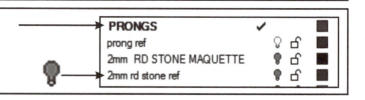

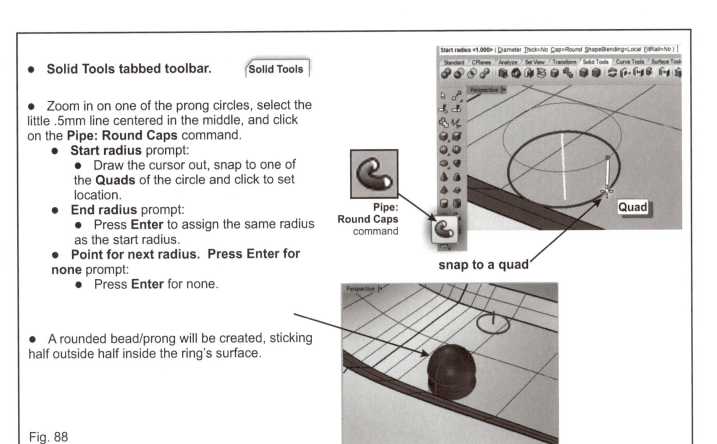

- **Solid Tools tabbed toolbar.** `Solid Tools`

- Zoom in on one of the prong circles, select the little .5mm line centered in the middle, and click on the **Pipe: Round Caps** command.
  - **Start radius** prompt:
    - Draw the cursor out, snap to one of the **Quads** of the circle and click to set location.
  - **End radius** prompt:
    - Press **Enter** to assign the same radius as the start radius.
  - **Point for next radius. Press Enter for none** prompt:
    - Press **Enter** for none.

Pipe:
Round Caps
command

snap to a quad

- A rounded bead/prong will be created, sticking half outside half inside the ring's surface.

Fig. 88

- Use the same procedure to create the rest of the prongs.

- Because you specified the radius of each prong by snapping to the quad of it's circle, each prong is exactly the same diameter as the prong circle in which it sits.

Fig. 89

- Turn off the **prong ref** layer.

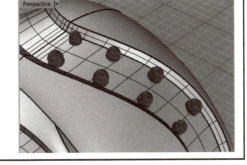

Fig. 90

- Select all of the prongs, type **"mirror"**, and press **Enter.**

- **Mirror** the prongs to the other side of the ring, using the **Y axis** as the **mirror plane.**

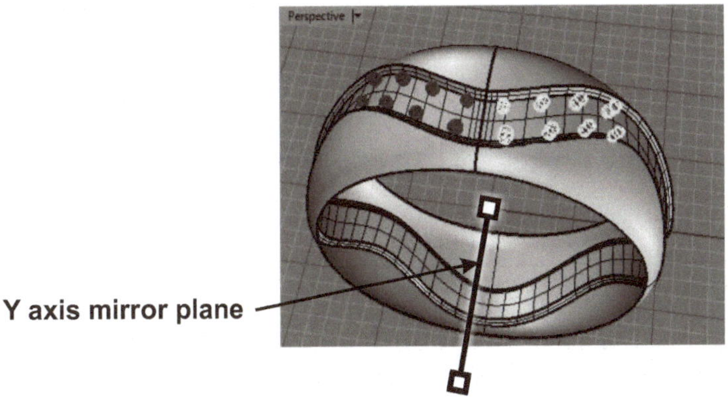

Y axis mirror plane

Fig. 91

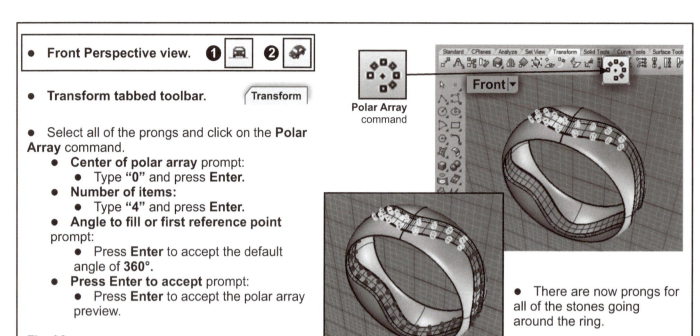

- **Front Perspective view.** ❶ [car icon] ❷ [car icon]

- **Transform tabbed toolbar.** `Transform`

- Select all of the prongs and click on the **Polar Array** command.
  - **Center of polar array** prompt:
    - Type **"0"** and press **Enter.**
  - **Number of items:**
    - Type **"4"** and press **Enter.**
  - **Angle to fill or first reference point** prompt:
    - Press **Enter** to accept the default angle of **360°.**
  - **Press Enter to accept** prompt:
    - Press **Enter** to accept the polar array preview.

Fig. 92

Polar Array command

- There are now prongs for all of the stones going around the ring.

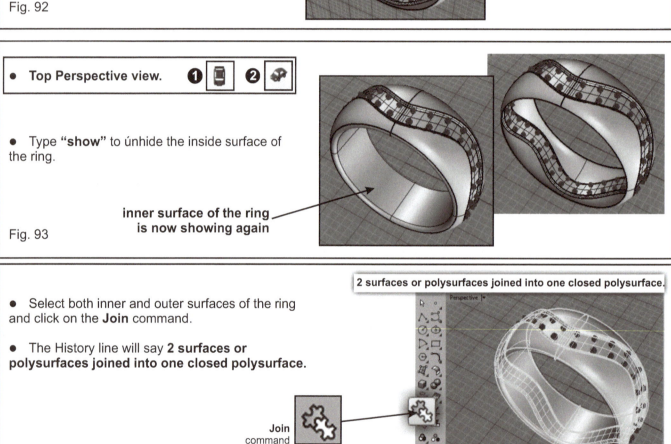

- **Top Perspective view.** ❶ [icon] ❷ [car icon]

- Type **"show"** to únhide the inside surface of the ring.

inner surface of the ring is now showing again

Fig. 93

- Select both inner and outer surfaces of the ring and click on the **Join** command.

- The History line will say **2 surfaces or polysurfaces joined into one closed polysurface.**

2 surfaces or polysurfaces joined into one closed polysurface.

Join command

Fig. 94

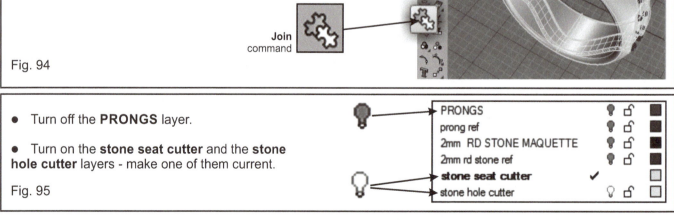

- Turn off the **PRONGS** layer.

- Turn on the **stone seat cutter** and the **stone hole cutter** layers - make one of them current.

Fig. 95

PRONGS		♀ ⌂ ■
prong ref		♀ ⌂ ■
2mm RD STONE MAQUETTE		♀ ⌂ ■
2mm rd stone ref		♀ ⌂ ■
stone seat cutter	✓	□
stone hole cutter		♀ ⌂ □

- Select all of the seat and hole cutters and click on the **Ungroup** command.
  - Click several times to make sure that all grouped objects are ungrouped.

- *All of the cutters will be separate now. This step is essential for the Boolean commands to work in the next steps.*

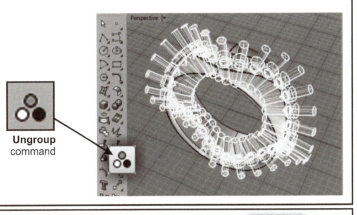

Ungroup
command

Fig. 96 ▼

- **Solid Tools tabbed toolbar.**   Solid Tools

- Select all of the cutters and click on the **Boolean Union** command.

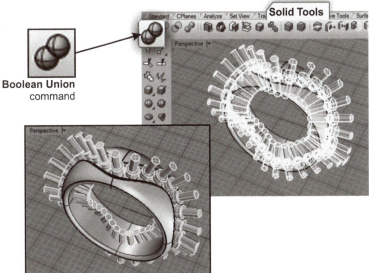

Boolean Union
command

- Stone seat cutters and stone hole cutters will be Booleaned together so that they are now all single cutters that will cut stone seats and stone holes at the same time.

Fig. 97

- Click on the **Boolean Difference** command.
  - **Select surfaces or polysurfaces to subtract from** prompt:
    - Select the ring **1** and press **Enter.**
  - **Select surfaces or polysurfaces to subtract with** prompt:
    - Toggle the DeleteInput=*Yes* option to **DeleteInput=*No* 2** so that you do not lose the cutters after this command.
    - Select all of the cutters **3** and press **Enter.**

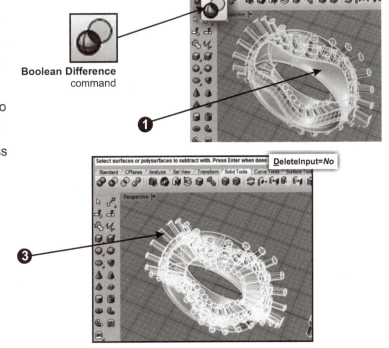

Boolean Difference
command

Fig. 98

- **RING** layer current.

- Turn on the **PRONGS** layer.

- Turn off both cutter layers.

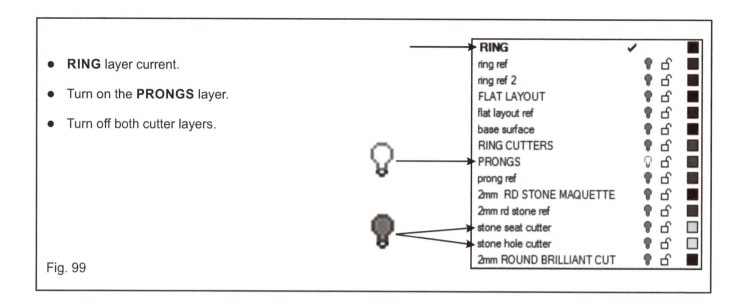

Fig. 99

- Stone seats and holes have been cut.

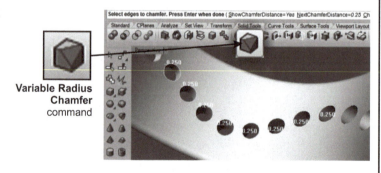

Fig. 100

- To finish off the stone holes on the inside, click on the **Variable Radius Chamfer** command.
  - **Select edges to chamfer** prompt:
    - Type **".25"** to set the **Chamfer Distance** and press **Enter.**
    - Select inner edges of the holes - you can select more than one.
  - **Select chamfer handle to edit. Press Enter when done** prompt:
    - Press **Enter.**

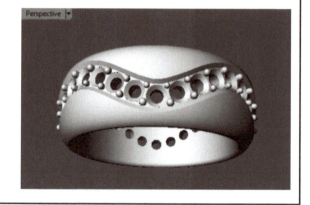

Variable Radius Chamfer command

- The completed chamfers.

Fig. 101

- Finished and rendered ring. Custom materials used. (see Render chapter)
  - Metal material properties:
    - Color: **gold**
    - Gloss finish: **yellow at 26% strength**
    - Environment: **Emap - gold 3 at 65-75% strength**
      - Use environment map from downloaded course materials.

  - Diamond material properties:
    - Color: White
    - Gloss finish: **white at 5% strength**
    - Transparency: 44%
    - Texture category:
      - Color: **Diamond 3 at 65% strength.**
      - Environment: **Diamond 3 for Color and Environment at 100% strength.**
        - Use Texture and Environment map from downloaded course materials.

Fig. 102

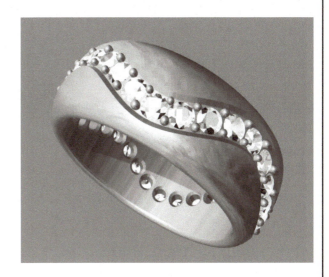

- Rendered Viewport mode.

632

Aliases

- Click on the **Tools** heading in the **Menu Bar.** ❶

- Click on **Options** at the bottom of the **Tools Drop-down.** ❷

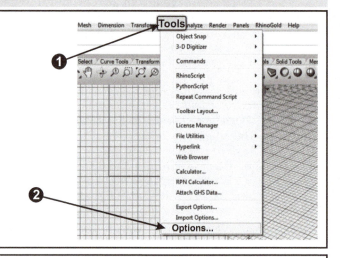

Fig. 1

- Click to select the **Aliases** category. ❶

- The Aliases page on the right will show the default list of Aliases.
    - **Alias** column: shows the text of each alias to be typed in the **Command Line** as you are working on a project.
    - **Command Macro** column: Shows the script of the command that will be activated.

- Select one of the lines in the list shown. ❷
- Click on the **Delete Key.** ❸

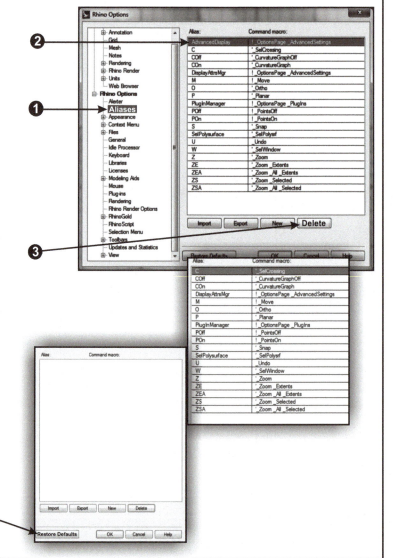

- The formerly highlighted Alias has been deleted from the list.

- Continue clicking on the Delete button until all of the Aliases but the last remaining one have been deleted.
- Select the one remaining alias and click on the Delete button one last time.

- The list has been completely deleted.

- You can always click on the **Restore Defaults** button to get the default list back.

Fig. 2

- Click on the **New** button to start a new list of useful Aliases.❶

- A new line appears in the Alias list page, prompting you for an **Alias** and a **Command Macro.** ❷

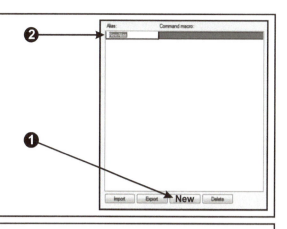

Fig. 3

- Type a new Alias in the Alias column.
- Type the new command macro in the Command Macro column.

- Make the list shown.

- Before each **Command Macro**, in the right column, type an **explanation point** and then an **underscore: !_**

  - **explanation point:** cancels any command you were in before typing the alias and pressing **Enter.**
  - **underscore:** means that the command will be run in English.
  - **spaces:** make sure to include all spaces as they are meant as prompts and can not be omitted.

Fig. 4

Alias:	Command Macro:
C	!_Copy
E	!_Explode
H	!_Hide
HH	!_Show
J	!_Join
L	!_Lock
LL	!_Unlock
M	!_Move
MH	!_Mirror pause 0 0,1,0
MV	!_Mirror pause 0 1,0,0
R	!_Rotate
RE	!_Rebuild
S	!_Split
T	!_Trim
Z	Zoom

- **MH (Mirror horizontal) and MV (Mirror vertical) aliases in detail:**
- Make sure to include all **punctuation** and **spaces**. Note the **commas** in the scripts at the far right.

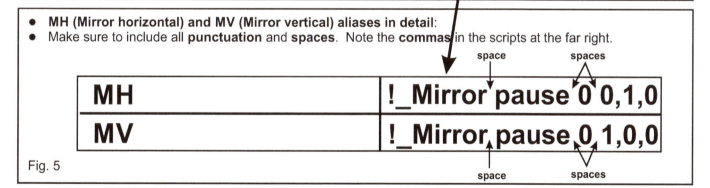

Fig. 5

- Click on the **Export** button to export this list of Aliases. ❶

- Save your aliases as a text file in the Save Text File box that opens. ❷

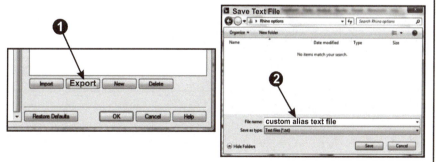

Fig. 6

- For practice, **Delete** all of the aliases in the list and then click on the **Import** button.

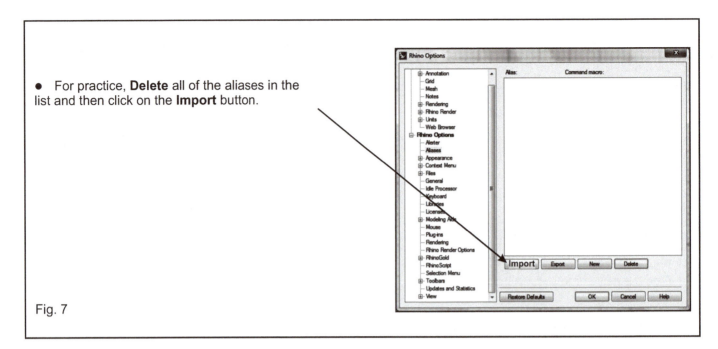

Fig. 7

- When the **Open Text File** box opens, navigate to the folder that contains the options that you exported and saved.

- Select the text file that contains the options and click on the **OK button.**

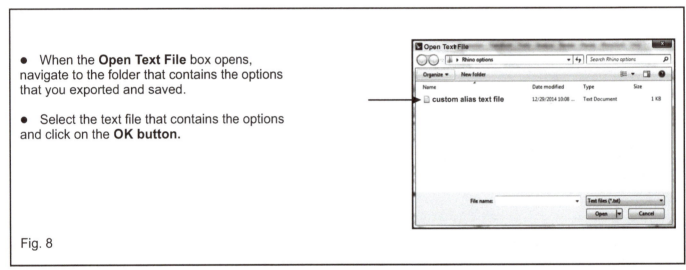

Fig. 8

- The list will be imported into the Aliases window and you will be notified via a little box that the aliases have been found and imported.

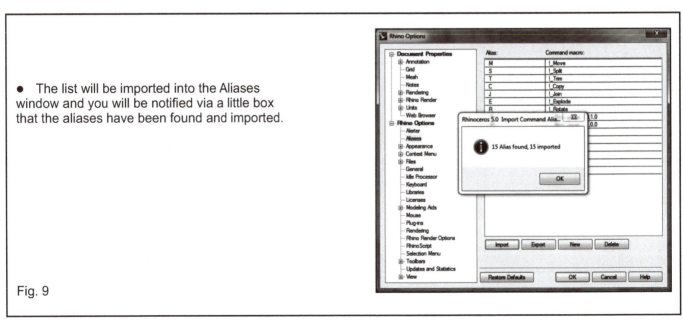

Fig. 9

Hotkeys

- Click on the **keyboard** category.

- On the keyboard page you will see:
  - a **Key** column showing the hotkeys. If you scroll down, you will see options that include hotkeys in combination with other keyboard keys that can offer additional hotkey assignments.
  - a **Command Macro** column that shows the commands/mode changes assigned to the various hotkeys and hotkey combinations.

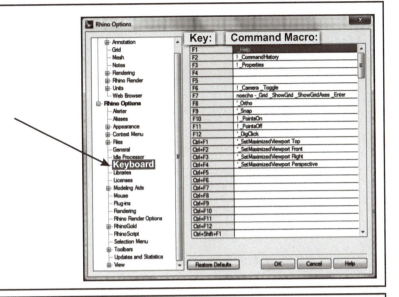

Fig. 10

- Type commands in the **Command Macro** column as shown, leaving the ones that are not indicated by arrows. Some of these new commands will replace some of the default commands.

  - Type over existing Macros by highlighting them which will prompt you to type a new command.
  - The **exclamation point** cancels any previous command that may be running.
  - The **underscore** runs the command in English.
  - The **apostrophe** will make the command a **"nested command"**. This means that you can toggle it on and off while another command is running.
    - For example, **Snap** (Grid Snap) and **Ortho** need to be nested so that you can toggle them off and on while you are working.

Key:	Command macro:
F1	' _Help
F2	! _CommandHistory
F3	! _Properties
F4	0,0
F5	Undo
F6	Redo
F7	noecho - _Grid _ShowGrid _ShowGridAxes _Enter
F8	' _Snap
F9	' _Ortho
F10	! _PointsOn
F11	' _GradientView
F12	' _RenderedViewport
Ctrl+F1	' _SetMaximizedViewport Top
Ctrl+F2	' _SetMaximizedViewport Front
Ctrl+F3	' _SetMaximizedViewport Right
Ctrl+F4	' _SetMaximizedViewport Perspective

Fig. 11

- Be sure to click the **OK button** to set these settings.

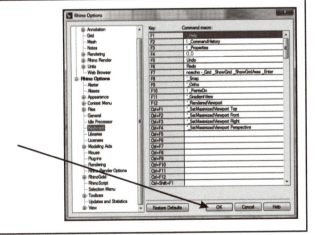

Fig. 12

Aliases

MH (mirror horizontal) & MV (mirror vertical)

- Create a circle above the **X axis** and to the right of the **Y axis**.

- **Select the circle.**

- Type **MH** in the **Command Line.** ❶
- Press **Enter.**

Fig. 1

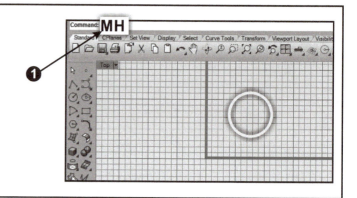

- The selected circle will be **mirrored horizontally over the Y axis** to the other side. ❷
- The **Y axis** was the designated Mirror Plane, as scripted in the Command Macro for this command alias.

- With the original circle still selected, type **MV** in the **Command Line**. ❸
- Press **Enter.**

Fig. 2

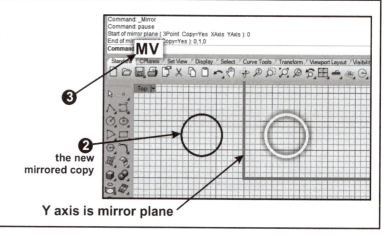

the new mirrored copy ❷

Y axis is mirror plane

- The selected circle will be mirrored vertically across the **X axis.** ❹
- The **X Axis** was the designated mirror plane as scripted in the command Macro for this command alias.

- **MH** stands for **"mirror horizontal"**
- **MV** stands for **"mirror vertical"**

Fig. 3

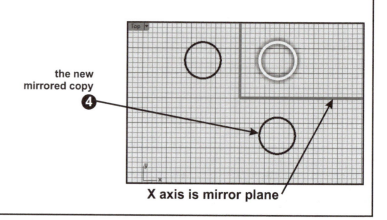

the new mirrored copy

X axis is mirror plane

Hide Objects (H) & Show Objects (HH)

- Type **"H"** in the **Command Line**. ❶
- Press **Enter.**

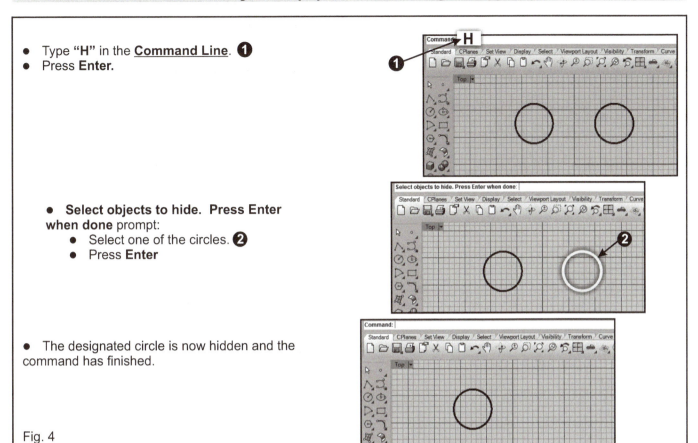

- **Select objects to hide. Press Enter when done** prompt:
  - Select one of the circles. ❷
  - Press **Enter**

- The designated circle is now hidden and the command has finished.

Fig. 4

- Type **"HH"** in the **Command Line**. ❶
- Press **Enter.**

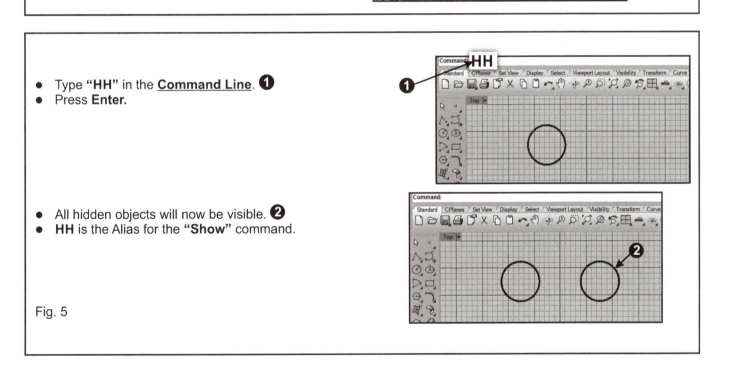

- All hidden objects will now be visible. ❷
- **HH** is the Alias for the **"Show"** command.

Fig. 5

Lock Objects (L) & Unlock Objects (LL)

- Pre-select one of the circles. **❶**

- Type **"L"** in the **Command Line.** **❷**
- Press **Enter.**

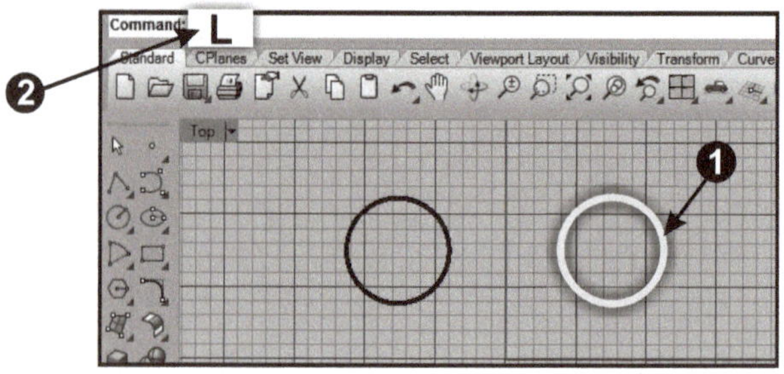

Fig. 6

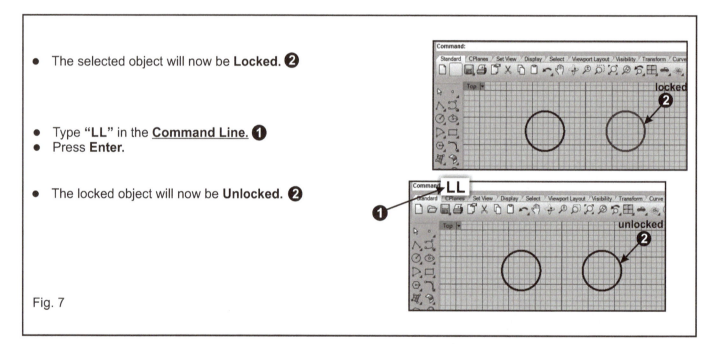

- The selected object will now be **Locked.** **❷**

- Type **"LL"** in the **Command Line.** **❶**
- Press **Enter.**

- The locked object will now be **Unlocked.** **❷**

Fig. 7

Other Single Letter Aliases

- Type the single letter of the alias
- Press **Enter**
- Follow **Command Line** prompts.

Hotkeys

F1	'_Help	• Press the F1 key to open a Rhino Help window. • Press the F1 key when you are in a command and Rhino Help will open to explain the actual command you are using.
F2	!_Command History	• Press the F2 button to get a box that shows all of the commands you have used in the session that is now open. • The text can be saved to a .txt file or copied to be pasted elsewhere.
F3	!_Properties	• Press the F3 key to see the **Properties** window or Panel.
F4	'_WireframeViewport	• Press the F4 key to return to basic WireframeViewport display mode. Useful in 3D modeling.
F5	Undo	• Press the F5 key for the **Undo** command. Hold it down for multiple undos.
F6	Redo	• Press the F6 key for the **Redo** command. Hold it down for multiple redos.
F7	Grid visibility toggle	• Press the F7 key to toggle the grid off and on.
F8	'_Ortho	• Press the F8 key to toggle ortho mode on and off.
F9	'_Snap	• Press the F9 key to toggle grid snap on and off.
F10	!_PointsOn	• Press the F10 key to turn on the control points of selected objects.
F11	'_GradientView	• Press the F11 key to toggle a gradient view on and off..
F12	('_RenderedViewport)	• Press the F12 key to toggle Rendered View display mode on and off. (used in 3D modeling)

INDEX

Make 2D Drawing (2D Draw) command, 308-310
    Adjusting Hidden Line type/color on Layer, 309-310
Adjust Closed Curve Seam, *From* a Polyline to a Butterfly 77; *1D and 2D Scaling* 197; *Rail Revolve Command - Puffed Heart 391; Bombe Ring 418; Twisted Wire Look - Band Ring 516*
Adjust Closed Surface Seam, *Bombe Ring 424; 8 x 10 Oval Signet Ring 450; Signet Rings - Different Shapes 485, 493*
Adjustable Curve Blend, *Signet Ring - Rounded Top 496*
Aliases, *see Workspace*
Analysis
    Angle, 47-48
    Diameter, 48
    Distance, 47
    Length, 46
    Radius, 48
Angle Constraints, 36-37
Area Centroid, 487
Arc
    Arc: Center, Start, Angle, 199-200; *Revolved Ring Band 372-373*
    Arc: Start, End, Point on Arc, 200-201; *Revolve Command 381*
    Arc: Start, End, Direction at Start, *Technical Drawing - Necklace Layout 201-202, 208-209; Bombe Ring 416*
Array
    Array Along Curve, *Arraying Around a Square 217-218; Cluster Around an Oval Center Stone 220-222; Arraying Around a Freeform Curve 231-234*
    Array Along Curve on Surface, *Ring Band w Wavy Pave 624*
    Polar Array, 207; 209-211; 218; *in different viewports 281-282; ring from solid objects 285*
    Polar Array with History, *Creating Designs w the Leaf Tracing 180-181*
Blend Surface, *Signet Ring 464-465; 589*
Boolean Commands
    Boolean Difference, 288; 434; 478; 539
    Boolean Union, 285; 296; 301; 545
Cage Edit, *Hollowing Out Bombe Ring 430-432; Hollowing out Signet Ring 474-476; Model of a Flower 590-596*
Cap (Cap Planar Holes), 382; 398; 451
Check, *checking selected objects 269*
Circle
    Circle: Center, Radius, 38-39; 83; 176
    Circle: Diameter, 40; 83; 86; 87; 88; 211; 219
    Circle: Tangent, Tangent, Radius, 85-86; *ThroughPoint option 227-228; 357; 531*
    Circle: Tangent to 3 Curves, 89-90; 222-223; 626
Circumscribed Polygon: Center, Radius – see Polygon
Clearing Render Meshes "ClearAllMeshes", 245
Command History Window – see Workspace
Command Line – see Workspace

Control Points,
    Control Point (or Edit Point)Editing; *From a Polyline to a Butterfly 78-81; Tracing the Picture Plane Image 163*
    For Surfaces and Polysurfaces; 270; *single surface 273;*
    Solid Control Points; 271-272
Copy, *Move & Copy* Commands 66-67; *Trim Command* 68-70; *Technical Drawing* - Simple Ring 134-136
    Click & Drag w Alt Key, 67
    Copy - Specified Locations, 66
Copy Objects to Layer – see Layers
Create UV Curves, Ring Band w Wavy Pave Design 608
Curve Boolean, *Revolve Command 383*
Curve from 2 Views, *Bombe Ring* 8 x 10 Oval Signet Ring 421-422,441; *Eternity Band 533-534; Flat Tapered Ring w Enamel & Flush Set Stones 549, 550*
Curve from Object
    Duplicate Edge, *8 x 10 Oval Signet Ring 461*
    Extract Isocurve, *Creating Curves on the Surface of an Object 305; Flat Tapered Ring w Enamel & Flush Set Stones 554*
    Object Intersection (Intersect), *8 x 10 Oval Signet Ring 458; Signet Rings - Different Shapes 483*
    Section, *8 x 10 Oval Signet Ring 442-443*
De-Selecting Objects, *Selecting & De-Selecting Objects 29*
Dimensions
    Applying dimensions, 49-52
    For 3D objects, 303-307
    Control Point Editing a Dimension, 61
    Dimension Settings, 53-55
    Dimension Styles, 55-59
    Editing a Dimension Text, 61
    Control Point Editing Dimensions, 59-61
Aligned Dimension, 304; 306
    Angle Dimension,
Diameter Dimension, 304
    Linear Dimension, 303; 306
Direction (Analyze Direction), *Bombe Ring - Hollowing Out 433; Flat Tapered Ring with Enamel and Flush Set Stones 564-565*
Direction Constraint ("Tap the Tab Key"), *Rail Revolve Command - Puffed Heart 393*
Display Modes,
    Artistic Viewport, 245
    Changing Display Modes; *quickest way 246*
    Ghosted Viewport, 243
    Pen Viewport, 244
    Raytraced Viewport, 312-313;
    Raytraced with Neon Viewport, 313
    Render Mesh Settings, 245
    Rendered Viewport, 243; *rendering 311-327*
        Rendering Settings Panel, *backdrop 311-313; ground plane 317-319*
        Materials Library
            Gold, 313-314
            Silver, 315-316
            Gemstones, 320-322
        Custom Metal Materials, 323
        Custom Gemstones, *diamonds 324; colored faceted stones 326; cabochons 327*
        Assign to Layers, 325

Shade, 243
Shaded Viewport, 242
Toggle Flat Shade Mode, 246
Toggle Shade Selected Mode; 246
Wireframe Viewport, 242
Technical Viewport, 244
X Ray Viewport, 244
Divide Curve by Number of Points – see Point
Divide Curve by Number of Segments, see Point
Document Properties – see Workspace
Downloading Supporting Files, 21-22
Downloading Rhino Training Files, 23-24
Draw Order, 137-138
Duplicate Edge – see Curve from Object
Edit Points, *Tracing the Picture Plane Image* 164
Ellipse
    Ellipse: from Center, *Intro to Some More Basic Shapes* 105; *Cluster* Around an Oval Center Stone 219
    Ellipse: Diameter, *Intro to Some More Basic Shapes* 106; *Technical Drawing - Simple Pearl ring* 130; *Eternity Band* 542-543
Environment Map, *Rhino Rendering* 323, 325
Explode, *Freeform Curves* 156; *Arraying Around a Stone* 216; *Extrusions*, Polysurfaces and Surfaces 269
Exporting & Importing Rhino Options – see Workspace
Extend
    Extend by Line, *Bombe Ring* 417
    Extend Curve, *Technical Drawing - Necklace Layout* 205; *Flat Tapered Ring w Enamel & Flush Set Stones* 548
    Extend by Arc to Point, *Rail Revolve Command - Puffed Heart* 390; 437, 439-440
Extend Surface command, *Bombe Ring - Hollowing Out* 429-430
Extract Isocurve – see Curve from Object
Extract Sub Curve, *Bombe Ring - Hollowing Out* 409
Extract Surface, *Extrusions*, Polysurfaces and Sufaces 267; *Rail Revolve* Command - Puffed Heart 399
Extrude
    Extrude Closed Planar Curve, *Extrusions, Polysurfaces and Surfaces* 267; *Ring from Basic Solid Objects* 287-288; *Extruded Jewelry Shapes* 353, 358; *Twisted Wire Look - Band Ring* 512
    Extrude Straight, *Twisted Wire Look - Band Ring* 505; *1mm Stone Maquette* 522
    Extrude Surface, *Extruded Jewelry Shapes* 362
    "Use Extrusions" option, *T*wisted Wire Look - Band Ring 504
Fillet Corners, *Extruded Jewelry Shapes* 358; *Signet Rings - Different Shapes* 482
Fillet Curves, *Revolved Ring Band* 375-376; *Rail Revolve Command - Puffed Heart*391
Fillet Edges, *Ring from Basic Solid Objects* 286; *Flat Tapered Ring w Enamel and Flush Set Stones* 572
Floating Toolbars, see Workspace
Flow Along Curve, 508
Flow Along Surface, *Flat Tapered Ring w Enamel and Flush Set Stones* 563-567; *Ring w Wavy Pave* 611-613
Freeform Curves, 149-156
    Adding a Kink, 152-153
    Control Point Curves, 149-150
    Interpolate Point Curves, 151
    Open Freeform Curves, 153-154

Group
    Group, *Flat Tapered Ring w Enamel & Flush Set Stones* 559; *Band Ring w Wavy Pave Design* 623
    Ungroup, *Flat Tapered Ring w Enamel & Flush Set Stones* 573; *Band Ring w Wavy Pave Design* 630
Help, *Rhino Help* – see Workspace
Hide (and Show), *Creating Designs w the Leaf Tracing* 170; *Bombe Ring - Hollowing Out* 427
History, *Creating Designs w the Leaf Tracing* 171-183; *Sweep 1 Rail with History* 401-404
History Warning, *Creating Designs w the Leaf Tracing*175
Hotkeys – see Workspace
Import, *1mm Stone Maquette* 523; *Eternity Band* 525; *Flat Tapered Ring w Enamel & Flush Set Stones* 558, 558; *Model of a Flower* 597; *Ring Band w Wavy Pave Design* 621
Interpolate on Surface, *Additional Enamel Strategies* 577-578
Interpolate Point Curve – see Freeform Curves
Intersect command - *See Curve from Object*
Join Command, 31-32; 132; 155
Layer Material – see Material Properties for Rendered Viewport Mode
Layers, 93-104
    Adding & Deleting Layers, 101
    Changing Object Layers, 98-100
    Copy Objects to Layer, 467
    Layer Display Colors, 97-98
    Layers Tabbed Panel Location, 93
    Layers Panel, 93-95
    Locking layer, 102
    Moving Layers in Layers Panel, 102
    Naming Layers, 96
    New Layer Button, 101; 617
    Select Objects option, 103; 477
    Turning Off Layers, 104; 132; 207; 208
Layout, 328-349
    Additional Layout Pages, 345-
    Appearance, *color* 331
    Curves & Text on Layout, 343-345
    Detail Windows,
    Creating Detail Windows, 331-332; *new detail window* 336-
        Copying Detail Windows, 334-335; 347-348;
Hide in Detail, 341
        Point Editing Detail Windows, 335-336
Scaling Detail Windows, 333-334
        Managing Layers for Detail Windows, 340-342
    New Layout, 329-330
    Printing Layout Sheet, 349
    Unit Settings, 328
Length Constraints, *Anatomy of a Line and a Polyline* 36-37
Line, *Anatomy of a Line and a Polyline* 36-37 33-34
    Line: from Midpoint, *Technical Drawing - Simple Pearl Ring*125; *Extruded Jewelry Shapes* 360; *8 x 10 Oval Signet Ring* 436
    Line: Vertical to Cplane, *Revolve Command* 380; *Rail Revolve & Sweep 1 Rail Commands* 385; *Rail Revolve Command - Puffed Heart* 392
Linetypes - *see Printing*

Lock, *Twisted Wire Look - Band Ring* 511
Lock toolbar, *Sculpting Simple Rings* 300
Lock Swap, *Sculpting Simple Rings* 300
Loft, *Sweep 2 Rails Command* 411-412, 413; *Bombe Ring* 425-426; *1mm Stone Maquette* 520; *Flat Tapered Ring w Enamel* & Flush Set Stones 552
Match Curve, *Signet Ring - Rounded Top* 497-498
Merge All Edges, *Bombe Ring* 425; *Ring Band w Wavy Pave Design* 620
Mirror, *Stone & Prong Layout* 90-93; *Technical Drawing* - Simple Pearl Ring 126, 131; Creating Designs w the Leaf Tracing 171, 173, 178-179; *Technical Drawing - Necklace Layout* 206; 226; *277-279;* Cluster Around an *Oval Center Stone 296*
Move, *Move & Copy Commands* 62-67
    Click & Drag, 62
    Move Command, 63; 169-170
    Move - Specified Distance, 64
    Move - Specified Location, 65
    Moving Control Points, 295; 297
Moving the view, see Panning the View
Multi-Selecting Objects, *Selecting & De-Selecting Objects* 29
Naked Edges, 414-415
    Show Edges command, 414; 469
New Layer button – see Layers
Object Snap, 43-45
Object Intersection (Intersect) – see Curve from Object
Offset Curve, 84-85; 87; 122; 204; 220; *ThroughPoint option* 221; *ThroughPoint option* 228-229; *In Cplane option 518*
Offset Surface, *Bombe Ring - Hollowing Out* 428; *Hollowing Out the Signet Ring* 468-469; *Flat Tapered Ring w Enamel & Flush Set Stones* 569
Opening Rhino, 1-2
Orient on Surface, Enameled Band *560-563; Ring Band w Wavy Pave 626-627*
Ortho Mode, 41
Pipe – see Solids
Panels – see Workspace
Panning the view,
Picture Plane
    Placing Picture Frame in Workspace, 157-158
    Missing Picture Frame,
    Transparency adjustment, 159-160
    Tracing Picture Plane Image, 161-164

Point
    Divide Curve by Number of Segments, *Technical Drawing - Necklace Layout 203-204; Rail Revolve - Puffed Heart 392; Ring Band w Wavy Pave Design 609-610*
Point Editing, 79-81
    Continue Control Point Curve, 74
    Control Point Editing a Torus; 289-301
    Point Edit with History, 173; 177-178
    Insert Knot, 80
    Point Edit Toolbar Flyout, 80
    Using Scale,
    Turning Ctrl/Edit Points On and Off, 78; 164,
Polar Array – see Array

Polygon
    Circumscribed Polygon: Center Radius, *Intro to Some More Basic Shapes* 112
    Polygon: Center, Radius, *Intro to Some More* Basic Shapes 111; *Briolette - Step* Cut 365
    Polygon: Edge, *Intro to Some More* Basic Shapes 113
    Polygon: Star, *Signet Rings - Different Shapes* 488
Polyline, *Anatomy of* a Line and a Polyline 35-36, 37; *From a Polyline to a Butterfly* 73-75; *Stone & Prong Layout* 89
Printing, 139-142
    Custom Linetypes, 146-147
    Centerline Linetype, 145
    Dotted Linetype, 144
    Linetypes explained, 143-144
    Print Color, 148
    Print Width, 148
Project to Cplane, *Model of a Flower* 598
Properties Panel, *Applying dimensions 58-59; Creating Designs w the Leaf Tracing 181*
Rebuild
    Rebuilding 2D Lines/Curves, *From a Polyline to a Butterfly* 76-78
    Rebuilding a Surface, *Sculpting Simple Rings 290, 294, 297; Rail Revolve Puffed Heart* 392
Record History – see **History**
Rectangle, *Intro to Some More Basic 2D Shapes* 107-110
    Rectangle: 3 Points, *Sweep 2* Rails Command 408; *Twisted Wire Look - Band Ring* 513
    Rectangle: Center, Corner, 108
    Rectangle: Corner to Corner, 107; *Technical Drawing* - Simple Pearl Ring 129; *Revolve Command* 382
    Rectangle: Rounded Arc Corners, 109
    Rectangle: Rounded Conic Corners, 110
Rectangular Plane: Corner to Corner – See Surface
Revolve
    Rail Revolve, *Rail Revolve & Sweep 1 Rail Commands* 386; *Rail Revolve Command - Puffed Heart* 399
    Revolve, *Revolved Ring Band* 374; *Revolve* Command 381, 384; *Twisted Wire Look - Band Ring* 515
Rhino Options, 16-18
    Basic settings 16-18
Document properties 14-15
    Exporting and Importing Rhino Options, 19-20
Rhino Templates, *opening Rhino 1-2*
Rotate 2D,
    Rotate 2D Command, 117-121
        Freehand 117-118
        Using Osnap 119-120
        Specified rotation angles 120-121
    Rotate 2D, *Arraying Along a Freeform Curve 234, 236*
    rotate w copy, *Technical Drawing - Simple Pearl Ring* 133, *Eternity Band* 540-541
    rotate with History, Creating Designs with the Leaf Drawing 172, 174

Rotate 3D, *Model of a Flower 594*
Scale, *1D and 2D Scaling 184-198*
    Point Editing Using Scale, *circle* 190-195; butterfly design 195-198
    Scale 1D, 184-186; *Technical Drawing - Necklace Layout 211-213, 215; Sculpting Simple Rings 290-291, 293-294; Revolved Ring Band 377; Signet Rings - Different Shapes 483*
    Scale 2D, 187-189; *Sculpting Simple Rings 293, 298-299, 300-301*
    Scale 3D, *Sculpting Simple Rings 302;* 524
    Scale Factor, 189-190; 526' 622
Select
    Select Lightweight Extrusion Objects, *Extrusions, Polysurfaces & Surfaces 266*
    Select Points, *8 x 10 Oval Signet Ring 444*
    Select Polysurfaces toolbar, 266
        Select Polysurfaces, *Extrusions, Polysurfaces & Surfaces 268; Briolette - Step Cut 368; Briolette - Brilliant Cut 371*
        Select Closed Polysurfaces, *Extrusions, Polysurfaces & Surfaces 266, 268*
        Select Open Polysurfaces, *Extrusions, Polysurfaces & Surfaces 268*
    Select Surfaces toolbar, *Extrusions, Polysurfaces & Surfaces 266, 269*
        Select Closed Surfaces, *Extrusions, Polysurfaces & Surfaces 269; Twisted Wire Look - Band Ring 509*
        Select Open Surfaces, *Extrusions, Polysurfaces & Surfaces 269*
        Select Surfaces, *Briolette - Step Cut 367; Briolette - Brilliant Cut 371*
Selecting/De-Selecting Objects, 29-30
Selection Menu, 30
Set View toolbar, 250
Set View Toolbar, *getting back to default top view 28; returning to default perspective viewport 251-253*
Show Edges – see Naked Edges
Sidebar – see Workspace
Sketch on Surface, *Additional Enamel Strategies 582*
Solid Control Points (Turn on Solid Control Points), *Model of a Flower 590*
Solid Fillet (Variable Radius Solid Fillet),
Solids, *Introduction to Simple Solid Objects 254-265*
    Box, 254-255; *Extrusions, Polysurfaces & Surfaces 267-268; Point Editing Basic Solid Objects 276*
    Cone, 257-258
    Cylinder, 263
    Ellipsoid: from Center, 256-257; *Ring from Basic Solid Objects 284-285; Extruded Jewelry Shapes 359*
    Pipe: Flat Caps, *Ring from Basic Solid Objects 283-284; 8 x 10 Oval Signet Ring 462; Eternity Band 534, 538*
    Pipe: Round Caps, *Ring Band w Wavy Pave 628*
    Pyramid, 259
    Sphere, 255-256; *Mirror & Polar Array Commands in 3D Space 276-277, 280-281*
    Star Pyramid, 261
    Torus, 240-241; 265; 279-280; *sculpting simple rings 289*
    Truncated Cone, 258
    Truncated Pyramid, 260
    Truncated Star Pyramid, 262
    Tube, 264
Splash Screen, *Rhino Splash* – See Workspace
Split, *Technical Drawing - Necklace Layout 206; Extruded Jewelry Shapes 360 361*
Square, *Arraying Around a Square 216*
Star,
    Star – Default Star Shape, *Intro to Some More Basic Shapes 114-115; Signet Rings - Different Shapes 488*
    Star with Specified Radii, *Intro to Some More Basic Shapes* 115-116
Status Bar – see Workspace
Surface
    Rectangular Plane: Corner to Corner, *Ring Band w Wavy Pave Design 611*
    Surface from 3 or 4 Corner Points, *Briolette - Step Cut 366-367; Briolette - Brilliant Cut 370*
    Surface from Network of Curves, *Bombe Ring 423; 8 x 10mm Oval Signet Ring 449; Signet Rings - Different Shapes 484, 492; Signet Ring - Rounded Top 500*
    Surface from Planar Curves,
Sweep 1 Rail, *Rail Revolve & Sweep 1 Rail Commands 387-388; Sweep 1 Rail Command 401-403; Eternity Band 543*
Sweep 2 Rails, *Sweep 2 Rails Command 410-411, 413; 8 x 10 Oval Signet Ring 460; Ring Band w Wavy Pave 618-619*
"Tap the Tab Key" – see Direction Constraint
Templates
    Opening Rhino, 1-2
    Saving your Document Properties as a Template 15
Text command, 248
Tabbed Toolbars,Toolbar Flyouts – see Workspace
Toolbar Groups – see Workspace
Toolbars – see Workspace
Tooltips – see Workspace
Tools toolbar; 245
Tracing a Picture Frame Image,
Trim, 68-72; 102-104; 132; with History 183; 207; 224
Twist, *Twisted Wire Look - Band Ring 506*
Ungroup – see Group
Unlock,
Untrim, *Hollowing Out the Signet Ring 467; Additional Enamel Strategies 581*
Unroll Developable Surface, 555
"Use Extrusions" option – see Extrusions
Using Command Shortcuts – see Workspace
Utilities toolbar: 245
Variable Radius Chamfer (Chamfer Edge), 630
Variable Radius Fillet – see Fillet Edge
Viewports
    Construction Planes, 237
    Default Configuration, 3-4; 237
Navigation for 2D drawings, 25-28
    Navigation for 3D Perspective view, 239-241
Viewport Properties, 3-4; 237-239
    Viewport Tab Controls, 329; 331
Working in Different Viewports; 247-249

What, checking *for details about a selected object 270*
Wire Cut, *Signet Ring* 451-453; 486; 494; 602; 603
Workspace
        Aliases, *Rhino Options 633-635, 637-639*
        Command History Window, 3, 5
        Command Line, 3, 5
        Document Properties, 14-15
        Exporting & Importing Rhino Options, 19-20
        Floating Toolbar, 9
        Help, *Rhino Help*, 3, 13
        Hotkeys, *Rhino Options 636, 640*
        Menu Bar, 3
        Panels, 3, 10-12
        Rhino Help, 3, 13
        Rhino Screen, 3-4
        Rhino Window, 3
        Sidebars, 3, 7-8
        Splash Screen, 1-2
        Status Bar, 3, 12
        Tabbed Toolbars, 3, 9
        Toolbar Flyouts, 6
        Toolbar Groups, 7-8
        Toolbars, 6
        Tooltips, 6
        Using Command Shortcuts,
Zebra Surface Analysis, 350-351
Zoom, *for 2D 25-27*
        Getting Back into Top View, 28
        Zoom Extents, 26; 203
        Zoom Selected, 26
        Zoom Window, 27

Dana Buscaglia has had many years of experience as a designer and a CAD model maker for the jewelry industry.

The author of the textbooks, **Rhino for Jewelry** and **Rhino 5.0 for Jewelry,** Dana has been teaching CAD for Jewelry at the Fashion Institute of Technology since 2004.